Resolutions 3

RESOLUTIONS 3

Global Networks of Video

Ming-Yuen S. Ma and Erika Suderburg, Editors

University of Minnesota Press

Minneapolis

London

An earlier version of chapter 17 appeared as "Video Art from Central and Eastern Europe in the Transitland Archive," in *Transitland: Video Art from Central and Eastern Europe 1989–2009,* ed. Edit András, 229–44 (Budapest: Ludwig Museum of Contemporary Art, 2009). An earlier version of chapter 22 appeared as "Screen Eroticisms: Exploring Female Desire in the Work of Carolee Schneemann and Pipilotti Rist," in *Screen/Space: The Projected Image in Contemporary Art,* ed. Tamara Trodd (Manchester: Manchester University Press, 2011).

Published by the University of Minnesota Press
111 Third Avenue South, Suite 290
Minneapolis, MN 55401-2520
http://www.upress.umn.edu

ISBN 978-0-8166-7082-6 (hc)
ISBN 978-0-8166-7083-3 (pb)

A Cataloguing-in-Publication record for this book is available from the Library of Congress.
Printed in the United States of America on acid-free paper

The University of Minnesota is an equal-opportunity educator and employer.

20 19 18 17 16 15 14 13 12   10 9 8 7 6 5 4 3 2 1

Contents

Acknowledgments

We offer our deep thanks to the many editorial and contributing voices who worked on this project. We thank our editors at the University of Minnesota Press, Jason Weidemann, Danielle Kasprzak, and Richard Morrison. Doryun Chong's astute translation work and informed opinions on Korean contemporary media art are much appreciated. We thank the contributors for making the project possible and for expanding its scope to a global scale. In addition, we thank Anne Bray, Marcel Odenbach, Viet Le, Richard Fung, Yong Soon Min, Coco Fusco, Tran T. Kim-Trang, Laura U. Marks, Beverly O'Neill, Precious Lovell, Andrea Liss, Bill Anthes, and Goddy Leye, who lent their expertise and knowledge at this project's inception by suggesting possible contributors and organizations and other avenues that broadened the book's scope. We thank the scholars, artists, activists, and other invested parties who participated in the Resolution 3 symposium and the *Narrowcast* exhibition and contributed both directly and indirectly to the shaping of this book.

We thank Carol Stakenas, executive director of LACE (Los Angeles Contemporary Exhibitions), who initiated the Resolution 3 project and saw it to its end three years later, contributing staff, resources, personal support, and good humor along the way. She generously allowed access to LACE's archive during the early stages of our research. David James, Michael Renov, Joy Silverman, Patti Podesta, and Bruce Yonemoto were similarly generous in offering their personal recollections and anecdotes from the first and second Resolutions. We thank Glenn R. Phillips and Catherine Taft at the Getty Research Institute for making available invaluable resources. The Resolution 3 project would not have been possible without the institutional collaboration between LACE and Pitzer College, nor without the guidance from our advisory committee and the efforts of our steering committee. For their tireless work and invaluable contributions to the project, we thank Pitzer and LACE staff members Ciara Ennis, Franco Castilla, Tracy Biga MacLean, Jim Stricks, Stephanie Hutin, Eduardo Gonzalez, Andrew C. Jordan, Anna Mendoza, Laurie Babcock, and Stephanie Guerra, as well as our interns, Erin Garrovillas and Olivia Sajjadieh.

The project Resolution 3: Video Praxis in Global Spaces, of which this book is a part, is funded through the generous support of the Andy Warhol Foundation for the Visual Arts, the City of Los Angeles's Department of Cultural Affairs, the Getty Foundation, Intercollegiate Media Studies at the Claremont Colleges, the James Irvine Foundation, Metabolic Studio (a direct charitable activity of the Annenberg Foundation led by artist and trustee Lauren Bon), Pitzer College (through the Pitzer Art Galleries, the Endowed Fund for Media Studies, the Frederick J. Salathé Fund, and the Pitzer Summer Research Assistantship), the Scripps Humanities Institute, and the members of LACE. LACE and its programs are supported by the Hollywood Chamber of Commerce Community Foundation, the Jockey Hollow Foundation, the Los Angeles County Arts Commission, the Morris Family Foundation, the Pasadena Art Alliance, Side Street Projects, and Stone Brewing Company. Parts of this book are funded by a Pitzer College faculty research grant.

Another Resolution

ON GLOBAL VIDEO

Ming-Yuen S. Ma and Erika Suderburg

> We have approached the matter of video "resolution" in another
> way, not after the technologically based habit of providing hard
> edges that define the object, but by offering to view a range of
> critical perspectives—multiple, even disjunctive conceptual and
> ideological matrices through which to *know* video as a contem-
> porary cultural phenomenon. As we have noted throughout this
> introduction, the plurality of this enterprise is necessitated by an
> explosion of forms, function, uses, and effects of electronic media
> in the 1990s. Rather than serving to "resolve" the matter at hand,
> our hope for these essays is that they will engender argument,
> debate, contestation, and, in the end, new thinking on video in
> all its manifestations.
>
> » Michael Renov and Erika Suderburg, "Resolving Video," in
> *Resolutions: Contemporary Video Practices*

The introduction to *Resolutions: Contemporary Video Practices* ends with a challenge to engage with a medium that was beginning to explode virally, decisively
expanding instantly recordable and quickly disseminated audiovisual content's
infiltration into and impact upon cultural sites and quotidian situations. In the
more than fifteen years since its publication, this intricate, rhizomatic plurality
has proliferated to the point of ubiquity—video and video technology permeate and restructure contemporary culture on a daily basis and are vital to the
formation and maintenance of global communities and spaces. Video is thoroughly integrated into our contemporary mediascape in instances as diverse as
YouTube, Vimeo, blogging, surveillance, amateur porn, gaming, online media
festivals, video on demand, Internet reportage of the so-called war on terror,
anticorporate and antiglobalization activism, recent global political and social
unrest, various natural or man-made disasters, and increasingly hi-tech and elaborate media installations housed at elite art institutions; the list exponentially
multiplies second by second.

In 2003, for example, filmmaker Jim Hubbard and writer Sarah Schulman began an oral history project in which they videotaped interviews with surviving members of the AIDS Coalition to Unleash Power/New York (ACT UP/New York), an AIDS activist organization founded in 1987. With its stated aims of presenting "comprehensive, complex, human, collective, and individual pictures of the people who have made up ACT UP/New York" and documenting the motivations and experiences of the women and men whose actions have "transformed entrenched cultural ideas about homosexuality, sexuality, illness, health care, civil rights, art, media, and the rights of patients," the ACT UP Oral History Project now is a raw database of over 130 interviews in video and text formats that can be accessed for free online or at the San Francisco Main Library and the New York Public Library.[1]

Quest for Saddam, a first-person shooter video game, was released by Petrilla Entertainment in 2003. Sold for $14.95, the game follows the format of creator Jesse Petrilla's previous game *Quest for Al-Qa'eda: The Hunt for Bin Laden,* which he characterizes as "an outlet to express emotions of the September 11 attacks. . . . It's a way to work out the anger left over from America's most disastrous terrorist attack." Petrilla is also a founder of the United American Committee (UAC), a political action group focused on "promoting awareness of Islamist extremist threats in America." On September 10, 2006, the group hung Osama bin Laden in effigy in front of a mosque in Culver City, California. Also in 2006, Global Islamic Media Front (GIMF), a Europe-based radical Islamic organization with ties to al-Qaeda, released *Quest for Bush: The Night of Bush Capturing* for free on the Internet. A hacked version of *Quest for Saddam, Quest for Bush* replaces Saddam Hussein with George W. Bush as the objective of the hunt and American soldiers with jihadists as avatars for the player. In 2008, Iraqi American artist Wafaa Bilal created *The Night of Bush Capturing: Virtual Jihadi,* which features further modifications from *Quest for Bush*'s hacking of *Quest for Saddam.* Casting himself as a suicide bomber, Bilal proposes a fictional response to the real-life death of his brother, who was killed by a U.S. missile strike at a checkpoint in Najaf, Iraq. According to Bilal, the work draws attention to Iraqi civilians' vulnerability to violence and manipulation from both the occupying forces and extremist groups like al-Qaeda. Since it was completed *The Night of Bush Capturing: Virtual Jihadi* has been routinely censored, and its exhibition has been shut down at multiple venues, most notably at the Rensselaer Polytechnic Institute in 2008.[2]

The Prada Transformer was a building designed by architect Rem Koolhaas and located in Seoul, South Korea. Commissioned by the Italian fashion company, the building was designed as a tetrahedron and could be rotated to serve different functions. Each side of the tetrahedron, in the shape of a hexagon, rectangle, cross, and circle, corresponded to a function: fashion show, cinema, art gallery, and public event, respectively. Opening in April 2009, the Prada Transformer hosted an exhibition of skirts designed by Miuccia Prada, a film festival programmed by Alejandro González Iñárritu and Elvis Mitchell, an art installation of sculptural objects and video projection by Nathalie Djurberg, and a takeover event comprising 130 architecture, fashion, film, fine art, and graphics students from ten Korean universities. The building was dismantled at the end of 2009, upon the completion of the student takeover event.[3]

Prada commissioned Chinese media artist Yang Fudong to create *First Spring* (a nine-minute video and its accompanying still images), which was used as a part of the advertising campaign for Prada's spring/summer 2010 menswear collection.[4]

In 2009 five high school boys in Thailand lip-synched and danced to the song "Nobody" by the South Korean girl pop group the Wonder Girls, with each member taking on the persona and dance choreography of one of the Wonder Girls. The boys' performance, held at school while in their school uniforms, was videotaped and uploaded to YouTube. The video went viral. It was, at the time, the most popular YouTube video from Thailand to date, with over 1,300,000 views. The boys were dubbed the Wonder Gays and became celebrities both in Thailand and abroad, with offers for television appearances and recording contracts. Though the initial response to the Wonder Gays phenomenon in the Thai media and online was congratulatory—the introduction to their TV interview claimed that their video was more popular than Susan Boyle's, herself a YouTube phenomenon—the celebration of their popularity soon shifted into debates on whether these boys, who were flamboyantly effeminate in their performance, were appropriate representatives of Thai national identity and masculinity on a global forum such as YouTube.[5]

The current Arab Spring uprisings have been fueled and multiplied by social networking, the impact of the audiovisual, and the cell phone/Web matrix's ability to portably and instantaneously broadcast the evolving revolution. Ironically, the passing of Gil Scott-Heron, composer of "The Revolution Will Not Be Televised," also marks this period.[6] Scott-Heron brilliantly targeted the total corporate control of broadcast access, which continues to run unabated and is now emboldened by the U.S. Supreme Court's recent ruling that corporations are human beings with civil rights. Scott-Heron's oft-quoted prescience aside, in Tunisia and Egypt the revolution was televised through a barrage of one-person networks that continue to serve as templates for the ongoing struggles in Libya, Syria, Yemen, Jordan, Israel, and Palestine. After the self-immolation of Tunisian Mohamed Bouazizi, a street vendor unable to make a living on the streets of Sidi Bouzid (one of a string of such acts that received little notice), a video of his mother leading a peaceful protest outside the mayor's office was posted on the Web. These images were then culled and uploaded by Al-Jazeera's Mubasher channel, a new media team that trawls the Internet looking for video from across the Arab world. Local activists in Tunisia were unable to widely post themselves owing to censorship, electrical blackouts, cell tower sabotage, phishing deluges, and other direct attacks mounted by an increasingly desperate government. With the police still refusing to meet with Bouazizi's family, social networking and Web video postings instigated what many participants and journalists termed a "spontaneous uprising" that spread across the country and directly led to the Tunisian revolution and the rapid departure of President Ben Ali. As Rochdi Horchani, a relative of Bouazizi's, succinctly locates the power of the images he helped disseminate, "We could protest for two years here, but without videos no one would take any notice of us." The media blackout was broken because of "a rock in one hand, a cell phone in the other."[7]

Despite their wild discrepancies, spanning the global and local, the corporate and grassroots, the public and private, the high and low, and the East, West, and middle, video is at the center of all of these case studies (of which we could have cited many more). As a media platform, digital document, and viral communication and organizing tool, video and its accompanying technological iterations have reached an unprecedented global ubiquity, traversing national borders, languages, cultures, and communities. Although intellectual discourse on video is similarly ubiquitous, studies devoted to the documentation, historicization, and theorization of video culture itself remain few and far between. This book is the third volume in a series comprising *Resolution: A Critique of Video Art* (1986), edited by Patti Podesta, and the aforementioned *Resolutions: Contemporary Video Practices* (1996), edited by Michael Renov and Erika Suderburg.[8] *Resolution: A Critique of Video Art,* one of the first critical texts on video art published in the United States, called for the development of a "resonant critical language" with which the video art produced in the United States and Europe, starting in the late 1960s, could be discussed.[9] The first books on video in the United States, including Michael Shamberg's *Guerrilla Television* (1971) and *Video Art: An Anthology* (1976), edited by Ira Schneider and Berl Korot, were produced by and for the then-nascent community of video artists, critics, curators, and exhibition spaces. Their countercultural tone and collective format reflected the spirit of the era. *Video Art* was a continuation of Schneider and Korot's involvement with the video magazine *Radical Software,* which itself emerged from the activities of the Raindance Corporation—one of the early video collectives. Michael Shamberg was also a Raindance member and was listed as publisher in the first issue of *Radical Software,* in 1970.[10] Other books on video from the 1970s, including *The New Television: A Public Private Art* (1977), edited by Douglas Davis and Allison Simmons, and *New Artists Video: A Critical Anthology* (1978), edited by Gregory Battcock, also followed the Raindance publications in emphasizing the collective voice of video that defined this era.

Following the paradigm set by the earlier publications on video, *Resolution* situated video discourse between "critical writing in experimental film and the current flowering of critical language about broadcast television" and included contributions by writers from the fields of film and art criticism, media studies, and critical theory.[11] In addition, it also brought together scholars, critics, artists, and curators in a conversation that emerged from a myriad of perspectives, approaches, trainings, and methodologies. In this way, *Resolution* emphasized interdisciplinarity and plurality as two of the fundamental characteristics of discourse on video culture, which has been reaffirmed in the scholarship on the subject since published.[12] In addition to the publication, the first Resolution project included an exhibition of twenty-seven single-channel videos produced by U.S. artists that took place at LACE (Los Angeles Contemporary Exhibitions), one of the longest-running alternative art spaces in Los Angeles, as well as a one-day symposium that brought together the artists, writers, and critics involved in the project.[13] While reflecting the interdisciplinary and plural discourses in the book, the exhibition and symposium components also emphasized the process-oriented approaches in the early development of video culture in the United States, as well as its organic integration of production, exhibition, and criticism.[14]

During the 1980s and into the 1990s, video as a genre, a practice, and/or a medium yielded a finite number of texts that originated in sociology, television studies (a nascent, prodigious renegade child of film studies), art history, documentary studies within anthropology, applied activist actions, and the fertile plains of the freshly minted media studies, currently nested under the anamorphic disciplines of new media studies and visual culture. Video as a rubric presented dicey, medium-specific detours and elaborate extrapolations of what it was not (i.e., television or film), and in defining what it was not, definitions abounded—from Martha Rosler's "Video: Shedding the Utopian Moment," a reintroduction of Alan Kaprow's assertion that no art can hold a candle to images of the moon landing, to David Antin's infamous buzz-kill that video was "old wine in new bottle," a sober trumping of the breathless flush of technological possibility and the vast, uncharted promises with which video injected itself into art practice.[15] Undergirding the roller coaster ride from Nam June Paik's Portapaked cab ride to the Café A Go Go to today's personalized SUV and cell phone video screens, the surveyor of video's situation in the 1980s and 1990s hurtled from one deliciously contradictory maze to another.[16] With origin stories situated within a late-1960s utopian conjuring of the unseen margins' infiltration of the monolith medium (as a people's broadcast/sentinel), textual preoccupations with how to mark a medium—and recollect its passing and its rising—produced some intriguing improvisational parameters.

This inherent eclecticism rendered the anthology format organic for a contemporary discussion of video. In the mid-1980s into the 1990s, video appeared as a subject heading or organizing principle in a handful of volumes that tackled access, politics, DIY (do-it-yourself), exhibition, impact, and context using video as a cultural and medium-specific marker. Integral to the shift away from locating video as either bad handmade television or ossified gallery/museum artifact were specific interventions into the literature that bespoke a widening consideration of a medium or a set of technological contexts whose possibilities could enfold varying discourses, activisms, and theories and potential paradigms shifts. Central to this period were texts that straddled fine lines among searching for a theorization of a medium, denying such a possibility, and constructing an alternate media landscape. Theresa Hak Kyung Cha's *Apparatus* (1981), Peter D'Agostino's *Transmission: Theory and Practice for a New Television Aesthetics* (1985), John Handhardt's *Video Culture: A Critical Investigation* (1986), Rob Perre's *Into Video Art: The Characteristics of a Medium* (1988), and *Illuminating Video: An Essential Guide to Video Art* (1991), edited by Doug Hall and Sally Jo Fifer, all constructed an open field of hybrid practices where maker, critic, historian, and theorist could foment. This set forth a range of possibilities in which more-focused texts, like Sean Cubitt's *Videography: Video Media as Art and Culture* (1994) and his earlier *Timeshift: On Video Cultures* (1991), could fashion a sharpened discourse around the possibilities inherent in a rapidly morphing set of practices loosely gathered under the rubric of *video,* predating gaming culture and Web streaming but informed by activist, documentary, performance, television fan, experimental film, and art object narratives.

The early part of the 1990s was a period of decisive attention to video's impact on contemporary culture, with interventions designed to infiltrate and explode monocultural narratives through decisive and political deployments of video in alternative, feminist, queer, and radical cultural sites that shifted academic and popular cultural views. Works such as *How Do I Look? Queer Film and Video* (1991), edited by the collective Bad Object Choices, Alexandra Juhasz's *AIDS TV: Identity, Community, and Alternative Video* (1995), Rosa-Linda Fregoso's *The Bronze Screen: Chicana & Chicano Film Culture* (1993), Deirdre Boyle's *Subject to Change: Guerrilla Television Revisited* (1997), and José Esteban Muñoz's *Disidentifications: Queers of Color and the Performance of Politics* (1999)—alongside the pioneering articles of Doug Davis, Chris Straayer, Wulf Herzongenrath, Martha Gever, Holly Willis, Ken Kirby, Peter Weibel, Dorine Mignot, Michael Nash, Kathy High (editor of the ongoing journal FELIX), Barbara Osborne, John Greyson, and Kate Horsfield—decisively challenged how video was examined and practiced and remain foundational to a larger corpus of video literature. Within this textual flux, film studies and print journalism integrated and grappled with video's impact in ongoing bylines by Raymond Bellour, DeeDee Halleck, Lisa Steele, Amy Taubin, Peggy Gale, Michael Renov, Anne-Marie Duguet, Marita Sturken, and David James, effectively rendering video a holographic seat at the table straddling television and film studies and helping to articulate media studies as a discipline. During this period many of these authors were practitioners and curators, as well as writers and contributors to Canadian, German, Australian, U.S., and French journals, papers, and magazines, laying stepping-stones for today's media interdisciplinarity.

Squarely a product of this burgeoning milieu, 1996's *Resolutions: Contemporary Video Practices* provided a textual commons for such inquiries and was specifically designed to serve as a bridge between linear histories of video reception and production and video's cultural currency. The volume was conceptualized as a forum for investigating alternative deployments of and the current possibilities of video's definition and that definition's fascinating and ongoing unraveling and reconstitution. *Resolutions* strove for a global playing field beyond art world limitations, North American politics, and auteur theory aggrandizement and embraced the disintegrating boundaries between film, television, media, and art disciplines. *Resolutions* grew from the editorial marriage of cutting-edge film studies, situated in the University of Southern California's School of Cinematic Arts in the form of Michael Renov, a seminal theorist of the film and video documentary, and the video programming collective at LACE, in the form of one of its volunteer members, Erika Suderburg, and under the capable, impassioned, and eclectic leadership of Anne Bray and, later, Adriene Jenik.[17] This promiscuous meeting of the ways resulted in one of the first books to tackle video as a medium across disciplines from a theoretical, activist, practical, hybrid, and transnational perspective, collecting texts from scholars, practitioners, and engaged observers. This was not exactly a shotgun wedding of the academy, activists, documentarians, and other malcontents but an editorial convergence dead set on a mash-up of agendas that helped not only to examine and perhaps create new areas of study and production but also to shift the discussion to multiple facets that define the text currently in your hand (or on your screen) in terms of foci, reach, impact, and the future forum configuration for the next set of questions.

The boundaries between medium specificity's collapse and new media studies assimilate television, gaming, film, and video studies, whereas visual studies continues to embattle the edifice of art history as a discipline. The location of video as projected moving image occupies a landscape of streaming, posting, gaming, cloud locations, home editing, and live phone broadcasts and begs the question of where video situates itself in relation to its many practitioners—amateur, professional, and unaligned. Singular studies of what it means to use the medium in the twenty-first century include the fascinating hybrid work undertaken by Anne Friedberg, who situates screen space and reception within a historical and theoretical trajectory in *The Virtual Window: From Alberti to Microsoft* (2006), and Peter Lunenfeld's deft ongoing interrogation of the digital domain and its repercussions *The Secret War between Downloading and Uploading: Tales of the Computer as Culture Machine* (2011), as well as his earlier works *Snap to Grid: A User's Guide to Digital Arts, Media, and Cultures* (2001) and *User: InfoTechnoDemo* (2005). Lunenfeld in consort with Lev Manovich, whose seminal work is *The Language of New Media* (2002), established new parameters and limitations alongside a profound backstory unearthed and prodded by the nascent workers within media archaeology and Variantology. These progeny texts, which explode disciplinary strictures and propose a deep back and future history of media artifacts, include Errki Huhtamo's *Media Archaeology: Approaches, Applications, and Implications* and Friederich Kittler's recent *Optical Media* (2011), as well as his foundational earlier works *Discourse Networks 1800/1900* (1992) and *Gramophone, Film, Typewriter* (1999), in tandem with patriarch of the variantological quest Siegfried Zielinski's *Deep Time of the Media: Toward an Archaeology of Hearing and Seeing by Technical Means* (2008).

Alongside these visionary, disciplinary-busting activities springs a series of works bent on shaping a narrow canon, a proliferating series of totalizing histories both considered and hagiographic. They do so while exploding anew as ubiquitous witness and revolutionary (e.g., the ongoing Arab Spring uprisings) and vexing and picking away at various corporate masters who produce and control the means of production, while dreaming of going viral. Literature that currently investigates video as a singular subject includes the canonizing, commemorative, and much-needed historical overviews of Michael Rush's *Video Art* (2003), *Video Art* (2006), coedited by Sylvia Martin and Uta Grosenick, Catherine Elwes's *Video Art: A Guided Tour* (2005), and *Feedback: The Video Data Bank Catalog of Video Art and Artist Interviews* (2006), coedited by Kate Horsfield and Lucas Hilderbrand. These overviews coexist apart from and comingled within elaborate theoretical structures not quite so chronologically bound, like Janine Marchessault's *Fluid Screens, Expanded Cinema* (2008), Laura U. Marks's *Enfoldment and Infinity: An Islamic Genealogy of New Media Art* (2010), and Yvonne Spielmann's *Video: The Reflexive Medium* (2010), texts that interrogate a wide variety of cultures' ubiquitous moving image production and the receptacles and products that continually rewrite our global image bank in a nanosecond.

Given the global ubiquity of video and the still-limited number of studies devoted to the topic since the publication of *Resolutions: Contemporary Video Practices* (many of the early publications mentioned are out of print and difficult to find), we assert that now is the time to reinstigate vigorous and wide-ranging debate on video praxis. Following the mandate of the series' preceding volumes and assessing the current debates, *Resolutions 3: Global Networks of Video* examines the theoretical, historical, and current implications of video art and video-based production in contemporary media culture. The contributors to this volume extrapolate and improvise upon this mandate and embark on analyses of what now is a forth decade of video practices as marked within and outside the margins of art production, networked interventions, festival codification, projected spectacle, museum entombment, and 24/7 streaming. Intending to broaden, contest, and amplify the mediated space that was defined, problematized, and interrogated by its two predecessors and many of the titles mentioned, this volume examines the ever-morphing state of video's deployment as examiner, tool, journal, reportage, improvisation, witness, riff, leverage, and document. In a cultural landscape that refers to artists, designers, architects, chefs, game authors, moving image makers, and educators as content providers and students, patients, viewers, and political constituents as receptive, paying clients, we feel it is paramount to locate and imagine the spaces, architectures, and platforms (virtual and otherwise) where oppositional, twisted, sincere, perverse, angry, poetic, interrogative, activist, and ambient video resides. *Resolutions 3* is designed as an investigation into what currently constitutes video culture as a global medium and how that medium manages to continue to resist classification while morphing into a larger continuum, and it reinvents the parameters of deployment and engagement. This collection seeks to continue the forum provided by its predecessors in order to further augment the possible spectrums of image making within and without institutions, boundaries, and codification.

This book is part of a larger project, Resolution 3: Video Praxis in Global Spaces, that reinvents the exhibition/symposium/publication format of the first Resolution project. Conceived on the occasion of LACE's thirtieth anniversary, the Resolution 3 project, like the Resolution project, includes a traveling exhibition and a three-day symposium. Our aim is to revisit LACE's history as one of the key presenters of video art in Los Angeles while assessing the global presence of video in our contemporary lives. The Resolution 3 project began with the exhibition *Narrowcast: Reframing Global Video 1986/2000,* which opened at the Pitzer Art Galleries in September 2008.[18] This exhibition engaged directly with LACE's video history in that it re-presented five single-channel works selected from Resolution's 1986 video exhibition and paired them with five contemporary works, ranging from video installations to performances to works that engaged with networked video platforms such as YouTube, framing the medium's brief history both formally and thematically.[19]

The Resolution 3 symposium then took place over three days, October 24–26, 2008, in Los Angeles and Claremont, California. It began at the Claremont Colleges, where media scholars, artists, and activists, many of whom were involved in this book and the *Narrowcast* exhibition, came together for a series of peer-to-peer exchanges and conversations on notable aspects of contemporary video culled from the works in *Narrowcast* and abstracts for this book. Several of the contributors here have further developed their ideas based on their experiences at the symposium. In addition to roundtable discussions that took place during the first day, the subsequent days of the symposium, which took place at LACE, included video screenings, workshops, panels, and artist dialogues exploring the issues of catastrophe, duration, the politics of transcultural production, body, and performance. The symposium's program was organized by Irina Contreras, Lucas Hilderbrand, Micol Hebron, Ashley Hunt, and Jessica Lawless—Los Angeles–based media artists, activists, and scholars—with participation from the staff of LACE, the Scripps Humanities Institute, and Pitzer's Media Studies Program. Collective input from the artists, audiences, and other participants were also incorporated into the programs as much as possible. Indeed, from the institutional to the individual level, the principle of collectivity guided our conception and realization of the Resolution 3 project.

Examining the work of the Raindance Corporation and Videofreex, Deirdre Boyle points out the importance of collectives in the development of early video documentaries in the United States, which she describes as a period of "radical plurality."[20] This book explores the role of video collectives in the development of video art in the United States in essays by Lucas Hilderbrand, Kenneth Rogers, Alexandra Juhasz, Nancy Buchanan and Catherine Taft, and others. In fact, this book itself is the result of collaboration at many, if not all, points of its conception and realization. From our coeditorship to the plethora of viewpoints and methodologies in our contributors' approaches to studying and writing about video to the expertise and efforts of our steering and advisory committees to the different moments when a larger public of interest—such as the participants at the symposium and the viewers at *Narrowcast*—contributed to its focus and structure, the spirit of collectivity deeply and extensively informs this book.[21] In choosing to work collaboratively, we both assert the continual importance of collectives in contemporary video and media art and reinvent its praxis to better examine our present-day cultural, social, and political milieu.

The discussion groups at the Resolution 3 symposium were organized around overarching ideas and common concerns culled from the submitted abstracts for this book. Some of these, including debates around medium specificity, issues of gender and sexual politics, antiracist struggles and decolonization, and the relationship between video and new media, are ongoing areas of investigation in video discourse that were introduced in the previous Resolution(s) volumes and continue to be debated here in their contemporary iterations, whereas others, including the discussion around video and its role in globalization, its spatial praxis in urban environments, and what Rogers calls an "embedded video practice"—video as a part of mobile, socially networked media—are relatively new topics in video and media scholarship. Despite the usefulness of these ideas and issues when structuring the discussion at the symposium, we decided against using them as subject headings in the present volume. As was the case in *Resolutions: Contemporary Video Practices,* these categories are limiting, and they ultimately lead to a compartmentalization that does not allow for the dialogue across topics, disciplines, and methodologies we believe the subject requires. Subject headings seem doomed to be constricting, immediately outdated, and artificial. Instead, we propose a series of rubrics developed out of the discussions at the symposium and further theorized through our reading of the essays in this book:

MEDIUM SPECIFICITY. There is a decay and collapse of medium specificity in video discourse. Increasingly, video is no longer articulated as the poor cousin of film—there is a merging of video and film technologies, and video's status vis-à-vis film has been redrawn theoretically and materially.

INTERDISCIPLINARITY. Sites of video's interrogation now include film and television studies, art history, performance studies, literary criticism, cultural studies, new media theory, sound studies, architecture, design, and many others. Video discourse fluidly moves among these disciplines in a wide variety of combinations on an ever-shifting ground.

INSTITUTIONALIZATION. Previously, alternative practices in video— including appropriation, performative and self-reflexive strategies, collective production, and guerilla tactics—have been institutionalized in the museum/gallery industry and in mass media. They can no longer be purely discussed in terms of institutional critique and resistance.

RECEPTION AND DISTRIBUTION. The exhibition, circulation, collection, and archiving of video have undergone massive shifts since the 1960s and 1970s. These shifts have also reconstituted the reception and distribution of content.

GLOBALIZATION. From its emergence as an omnipresent feature in the international art market to its central role in facilitating exchanges among cultures, video is now practiced and theorized in global spaces. It is a part of the global flow of capital, labor, and media.

Though these rubrics have certainly informed the order of this book's essays, ours is only one of many ways by which readers can navigate these intersecting and overlapping criteria. And even though we highlight specific essays within the following descriptions, most fit into several, if not all, of these rubrics. As a reflection of how video has been disparately institutionalized across disciplines, these groupings overlap and reinforce each other. As editors, we seek to expand, reconfigure, and disintegrate categories, in turn creating new gaps and fissures that open sites of inquiry and, perhaps, anticipate future volumes compiled under new sets of circumstances. Readers are encouraged to follow the path we have chosen, but in the spirit of video's unruly origins and ever-morphing application, we also challenge them to find their own paths, read against the grain, and discover their own rubrics.

Medium Specificity

With the merging of multiple media production processes (video, film, photography, sound, interactive media, games) onto a single digital platform, some of the material differences that distinguished film and video—film being an essentially chemical and photographic medium and video, an electronic medium—are becoming less and less relevant to the study of contemporary media. The digital platform allows, in the form of moving image editing software (such as Final Cut Pro and AfterEffects) and sound editing software (such as ProTools), for the mixing of video and film footage in the postproduction process—a tendency within experimental media since the 1980s—to be done with increasing ease and facilitates output of the completed work in a wide range of media, both digital and analog, as well as for myriad delivery systems, both broadcast and narrowcast.

These developments in media technology parallel a development within media scholarship that considers works from a variety of media platforms and across disciplines in the same study. Amelia Jones's essay examines feminist art practice, specifically the articulation of female eroticism, through her discussion of the commonalities and differences between a film and a video work produced almost thirty years apart (*Fuses,* 1964–67, and *Pickleporno,* 1994), both by a key feminist artist of her generation (Carolee Schneemann and Pipilotti Rist, respectively). Jones's analysis of feminist screen-based cultures is echoed in Michael Rush's study of contemporary installations using video projection. In his discussion of works by David Claerbout, Julian Rosefeldt, Eija-Liisa Ahtila, Bill Viola, and others, Rush deploys the notion of the cinematic to contextualize these large-scale, immersive, and often narratively driven works. The blurring of film and video takes a haunting turn in Akira Mizuta Lippit's essay, in which he examines the representation of dead, analog video technology in the *Ringu* series of Japanese supernatural horror films—itself adapted from Suzuki Koji's novel of the same title—and their Hollywood copies. In his discussion the obsolete VHS videotape returns as a lost object and ghost to replicate itself in both the filmic narratives and our contemporary mediascape, virally contaminating both with its video ether.

Sean Cubitt's essay, which addresses the relationship between the changing nature and use of vectors and the changing nature and use of video in the globalizing structure of Internet delivery, expands upon the discussion of medium specificity from the perspective of digital new media. Indeed, new media theory and culture suggest many ways in which a traditional, medium-specific video discourse is outdated. Derrick Burrill, for example, looks at how tweaking—the practice of remaking and using preexisting materials—has replaced the old models of pure production, copying, and sharing. His essay focuses on a particular kind of tweaking, known as mods or modifications, practiced among video gamers, which presents an interesting tweak itself on discussions around authorship and textuality—issues long debated within cinema studies, as well as under the auspices of the humanities. Other essays in this volume that investigate new media forms, including those by Holly Willis, Kathy High, Alexandra Juhasz, and Kenneth Rogers, address topics as diverse as video art on YouTube and site-specific video projections in public spaces. Collectively, they deliver video out of its most-oft-discussed, single-channel, and screening-based context and relocate it within newer, more distributed and spatialized practices.

Other approaches to addressing the issue of medium specificity can be found in essays by Ming-Yuen Ma, Hea Jeong Lee, Jennifer Doyle, Jesse Lerner, Yvonne Spielmann, Laurence Rickels, Erika Suderburg, and Lucas Hilderbrand. In these studies the authors apply theories and methodologies from other media (film, sports, advertising, ethnography, literature, visual art, sound) to video and show how they both conform to and challenge the boundaries of these discourses.

Interdisciplinarity

Video discourse was interdisciplinary from its inception. The first generation of independent video makers came to this then-new medium from diverse backgrounds, including the visual arts, dance, performance and body art, conceptual art, avant-garde music, the counterculture, writing, political activism, and a plethora of other practices. Likewise, the first generation of critical writing on video drew from film theory, art criticism, poststructural theories, and other disciplines. Both of the preceding Resolution(s) volumes exemplified this interdisciplinary approach to the study and critique of video. This interdisciplinarity is now firmly established as one of the defining characteristics of the field. Not surprisingly, the majority of the essays in this book take an interdisciplinary approach to the study and analysis of video, drawing from some of these disciplines and others, including feminism, critical race theory, psychoanalysis, political theory, sound culture, performance studies, architecture, design, and scientific discourses, as well as first-person autobiographical narratives.

Some of these exchanges among disciplines are highlighted, as they are in the conversation between art historian David Joselit and Faisal Devji, a historian and an expert on global jihad, whereas some are implicit, as in the essays by Kathy Rae Huffman, Rush, Jones, Willis, and a number of others whose works cross between art history and media studies. New media theory is an interdisciplinary thread that runs through the work of Burrill, Rogers, Juhasz, Cubitt, High, Willis, Suderburg, and Spielmann. Jennifer Doyle's investigation of how gender and sexuality is performed within the iconography of sports draws from video, filmic, and photographic representations of soccer in the art context and critiques them through feminism and queer theory. Laurence Rickels's discussion of Diana Thater's video installation *Electric Mind* (1996) similarly ties together theoretical locations as diverse as the psychoanalytic theories of Sigmund Freud and Melanie Klein, Henri Bergson on the meaning of the comic, and Gilles Deleuze and Félix Guattari on "becoming animal" and relates them to the writings of Edgar Rice Burroughs, the author of the Tarzan series.

As they were in *Resolutions,* the issues of gender, sexuality, race, identity, and subjectivity continue to be paramount for many of the contributors to this book, including Jones, Ma, High, Burrill, Jennifer Friedlander, Jessica Lawless, Kathleen Ash-Milby, Lionel Manga, Myriam-Odile Blin, and others. Nguyen Tan Hoang looks at the representation of race and sexuality in his study of queer Asian experimental documentaries and problematizes what he calls the "reeducation of desire" for their intended gay Asian male audience. Drawing from feminist and queer theories and transnational studies, as well as the ongoing debate on representations of masculinity in gay porn, Nguyen proposes no less than a complete retooling of Asian masculinity via a queer dyke/trans subjectivity.

Freya Schiwy takes Jacques Rancière's concept of the political—a process that "makes visible what had no business being seen"—and reads it against Mexican and Bolivian community media that are linked to Indigenous movements. Also from an Indigenous studies perspective, Beverly Singer makes connections between her home space in New Mexico and the Il Ngwesi Maasai territory in north-central Kenya, linking American and African indigenity through her first-person account of a collaborative exchange sponsored by UNESCO and designed to enhance the communication capacities of Indigenous peoples globally. The other first-person narrative in the book, by Lionel Manga, also approaches the discussion of video production from a wide array of disciplinary perspectives, including history, politics, journalistic account, postcolonial critique, and personal diary.

Institutionalization

The use of video in institutional critique—another theme from the previous Resolution(s) volumes—is continued in essays by Doyle, Manga, Blin, Schiwy, Hilderbrand, Rogers, Spielmann, and others. An emerging tendency in current discourse moves away from discussing video as unmediated documentation and visual evidence. Ming-Yuen Ma's essay explores the use of sound in Tran T. Kim-Trang's experimental video *The Blindness Series* and argues for moving beyond the "visual hegemony" within the institution of human sciences and, in particular, visual art and media studies via new audiovisual relationships constructed in experimental media such as Tran's. Aliza Shvarts's controversial senior art project at Yale University provides Jennifer Friedlander with a case study in which video's function as documentation is called into question through the project's relationship to simulation and indeterminacy. Setting aside the polarizing debates on the content of Shvarts's project, in which she repeatedly inseminated herself while taking herbs to induce a miscarriage during a nine-month cycle and documented the process on video, Friedlander instead focuses on how the artist (then an undergraduate student) interacted with Yale the institution and how the Yale administration handled the controversy in the ensuing media frenzy, ultimately problematizing the role of video in documenting the artist's double deception.

Whereas some essays expand upon or interrogate the discourse of video as institutional critique, others examine video as an institutionalized practice—more specifically, strategies used in the first and second generations of video art such as appropriation, *détournement,* deconstruction, parody, and multiple and nonlinear narratives, as well as a host of others now regularly seen in works shown in elite art institutions and in mass media. Indeed, the exhibition of video within established museums, galleries, and international venues such as the Venice Biennale is now par for the course. Nancy Buchanan and Catherine Taft's study of the new clout of video art within the international art market shows precisely how a medium previously considered "a communicative, easily distributed, people's cheap media form" is now a limited-edition or unique art object bid on by wealthy art collectors at auction houses and a fashionable accessory that can lend a bit of cultural capital to Parisian couture houses like Chanel.[22]

Hea Jeong Lee explores another kind of video art institutionalization. In her analysis of contemporary Korean video art, she finds that Nam June Paik, who left Korea in the 1950s and became known as one of the founders of video art in the United States and Europe, now manifests as an institutionalized return of the repressed in the work of younger Korean artists. Paik's work, introduced to South Korea via satellite transmission in 1984, represented both the politically repressed (Paik was a part of the Cold War generation that witnessed the division of Korea, considered by the majority of Koreans to be a national trauma) and technologically unavailable (the color television was just being introduced to South Korea in the 1980s). The recent opening of the Nam June Paik Art Center in South Korea represents both an uneasy posthumous homecoming for Paik and brings to the surface his previously repressed influence on contemporary Korean art and media production.

Alexandra Juhasz's unconventional essay—itself a critique of the inadequacies of institutionalized discourse in the study of new media forms and a dysfunctional cousin of her pioneering video book *Learning from YouTube*—looks at how the institutionalized genre of art video fares in the networked Web 2.0 environment of YouTube.[23] Haunted by dead links and frozen screen grabs, Juhasz's text documents her search for art video on YouTube, which yielded some expected (most of what is called art on YouTube exists outside of the critical and scholarly definition of art) and some unexpected (YouTube's value for media artists may lie in its seemingly limitless archive of every imaginable genre of video) findings, and in the process she critically reads the institutional discourse of video art history against this new media platform. Jessica Lawless also discusses YouTube in her essay (as do a number of the other authors), but instead of looking for art, she focuses on moments of everyday resistance and emergence, in this case a transgression against the institution of socially acceptable gender roles by two young people who are "simply being themselves." Set against YouTube's marketplace of images, these young people's transituated performance opens up a space for the (mis)recognition of gender, which Lawless also finds and analyzes in a promotional poster for *California Video*—a major survey of video art held recently at the J. Paul Getty Museum.

Reception and Distribution

As mentioned, one of the effects of video's institutionalization is its entry into the space of museums, galleries, and high-profile international survey exhibitions. These new venues for showing video raise issues and spark debates that are markedly different from those that arose out of the primarily festival, screening-based, and largely grassroots contexts that defined the exhibition and reception of video from the 1970s to the early 1990s. The surge of interest in video at art institutions and by art collectors has also changed the parameters of its distribution and preservation. Recent advancements in digital media technology offer new solutions to the preservation of video—a timely development, since the first generation of video art from the late 1960s and 1970s is rapidly deteriorating due to the life span of analog videotapes. This also brings up, however, a number of issues concerning access, historicization, curation, and medium specificity—both new and ongoing debates within video discourse that are highlighted by these recent changes.[24]

Kathy Rae Huffman's essay is a narrative of the process involved in selecting the ninety-five videos in Transitland, an archive of works made in ex–Eastern Bloc countries since the fall of the Berlin Wall. Huffman outlines the history of video production and exhibition within Central and Eastern Europe while highlighting contemporary issues brought up by the diverse works selected for Transitland. Video and digital media projections in public spaces—an exhibition strategy that takes video outside of the traditional exhibition venue of museums and galleries—are discussed in Holly Willis's and Kathy High's essays. High focuses her survey on six projects in which artists "take video to the streets, using video projectors, wireless devices, and cameras to open up public dialogue on issues including the plight of immigrants, recovering abolitionist histories, the failing economy, antiwar protests, and public opinions." Buchanan and Taft, Rush, and Juhasz write about the politics of exhibiting video, whereas Joselit and Devji, Jones, Lippit, Lee, Friedlander, and Lawless focus on different aspects of reception and spectatorship in their work.

Jesse Lerner's discussion of *Día dos,* a recent documentary by P'urépecha maker Dante Cerano, situates this work within the history of Mexican Indigenous media production while showing how Cerano evokes the genres of ethnographic film, wedding video, beer commercial, and hip-hop music video while confounding and complicating the genre expectations of his viewers, highlighting the insider/outsider perspectives and the hybridity within Mexico's Indigenous communities.

Writing from three distinct perspectives, Cubitt, Suderburg, and Manga present studies relating to the issues of access and production in media today. Lucas Hilderbrand and Kenneth Rogers also discuss these issues. Hilderbrand's study, on one hand, outlines and historicizes the different models for distributing and marketing video art, as well as the material conditions and economic realities within which they produce and operate—issues that have undergone little public or scholarly examination till now. Rogers's, on the other hand, focuses on embedded video practice, which situates the medium within a complex of social practices and media technologies. Realizing that the strategic interventions and nonstandard genres of the early decades of video practice have been institutionalized and incorporated into the culture at large, Rogers turns to the video hosting sites of Web 2.0 and examines, through both utopian and dystopian lenses, their potential for democratized, equitable access to video distribution.

Globalization

Web 2.0 is a global network, and the discussions of access, distribution, exhibition, and marketing of video are very much a part of how we understand the global flow of media and capital. As the subtitle of this book suggests, the theorizing and practice of contemporary video now take place in a globalized context. Virtually all of the contributors in this volume recognize this fact and address it in different ways.

Some of them, including Rogers, Lippit, Juhasz, Hilderbrand, Rush, Spielmann, Doyle, Jones, and Buchanan and Taft, implicitly acknowledge this development by drawing the works they discuss from an international arena. Their studies assume that any scholar writing about contemporary video practice should engage with a global context. Holly Willis, writing about "media artists using video and interactivity in public space to reflect on issues of power, infrastructure, and the body as it becomes networked," draws her examples from works presented in the United States, Italy, Mexico, Germany, and other urban spaces across the globe. Similarly, Yvonne Spielmann looks at how artists in Europe and Japan, as well as the Japanese and European collaborative group doubleNegatives Architecture, understand media tools as instruments of intervention in a global media environment. Erika Suderburg, also thinking about how new media tools can be used as instruments of intervention as well as participation and reinvention discusses Perry Bard's *Man with a Movie Camera: The Global Remake* (2008–present). Bard's collaborative project is an international collective remake of Dziga Vertov's *Man with a Movie Camera* (1929) that redeploys Vertov's *kinoks* (roving camerapersons / reporters / witnesses dedicated to the making of moving images as "a living evolutionary process" that depicts "life-as-it-is"). They upload their own remade sequences and link them to Vertov's original frames, which then can be viewed as a part of a database of overlapping uploads that merge into multiple versions of the remade film and / or projected onto urban spaces.

Differing from these internationalist works, essays with a regional emphasis, including those by Lee, Huffman, and to a certain degree, Nguyen, highlight the effects of globalization and the transnational aspects of their study as sites of interrogation through postcolonial politics. Lionel Manga and Myriam-Odile Blin, both writing about African video, represent this perspective in different ways. In Manga's first-person narrative, he pointedly critiques the privilege of access and entitlement often assumed by first-world scholars and artists and vividly contrasts them with the harsh realities of political repression, poverty, and social unrest in his hometown of Douala in Cameroon. The act of bearing witness, both a necessity and a privilege in Manga's account, is taken up in Blin's discussion of recent video and new media production in Francophone Africa. Looking at works by Goddy Leye, Guy Wouété (whose misadventures during the riots in Douala are chronicled by Manga), and Achille K from Cameroon; Fatou Kandé Senghor, Art Fang Saar, and Mansour Ciss Kanakassy from Senegal; and Michèle Magema from the Democratic Republic of Congo, Blin distinguishes individual aesthetics and connects common themes—hunger, war, political repression and torture; AIDS, cholera, and other diseases; the historical trauma of slavery; African Muslim identity; and rare glimpses of freedom of expression, collective reconciliation, and the power of remembrance—shared by these diverse works.

The dynamic between the regional and the global is offset by the contributors studying Indigenous media. Kathleen Ash-Milby's essay on Native American video art—along with the contributions from Singer, Schiwy, and Lerner—brings up issues of Native sovereignty and the need for cultural protectionism while stressing the importance of embracing both remembrance and hybridity. The question asked collectively by this group of scholars, which also applies to most of the other historical, regional, economic, cultural, and otherwise marginalized groups discussed in this book, is how to productively interact with a hyperlinked, global image culture while maintaining a sense of one's cultural roots and home community. David Joselit and Faisal Devji's dialogue on the global media network of the current jihad provides some insightful yet unsettling answers to this question. The exchange between Joselit and Devji focuses on locally produced jihadist media intended for distribution via the global media network. The two debate and discuss the unlikely correlations between "terrorist" media strategies and video art practice, interrogating the production, circulation, and visibility of such media on a worldwide network and global screens through a theory of the ethics of images.

Conclusion

Since ongoing developments in digital technology have made video production more and more accessible, it is our goal to chart the continuing propagation of video and to offer a renewed engagement that the medium currently demands while facilitating a series of linked conversations on current deployments of this chameleon-like tool, with attributes and affinities that continue to mutate with inventive zeal and surprising reimaginings. This volume is by no means comprehensive of video's geographical and intellectual reach, itself a statement that speaks to the exponential growth of the medium and its fields of study. Instead, we opt for a collection of in-depth, compelling case studies that suggest the overall scope and shape of the field without actually rendering it in hard edges and full resolution.

Contributors to this volume suggest and unpack many possibilities, exploring the incursions of a slippery medium into globalization, sexual politics, intercultural relationships, postcolonial legacies, the museum / gallery industry, capital, historical provenance, locative practice, and spatial occupation in rubrics that raise (and sometimes answer) myriad questions about video discourse and its environs. In short, this volume seeks to contribute to a widening multidisciplinary inquiry into the nature of video production as tool, essay, documentation, and witness. *Resolutions 3* is a forum for articulating the global impact of recording and broadcast media, however those actions are defined and in whatever spaces they reside. We wish to continue the shape-shifting, process-oriented conversation that the previous volumes began and expand those trajectories into examining what constitutes the engaged cultural production of sound and image in the twenty-first century and how these artifacts are dispersed and reenvisioned.

NOTES

1. ACT UP Oral History Project website, accessed August 11, 2011, www.actuporalhistory .org.

2. See "Virtual Jhadi," Wafaa Bilal's website, www.wafaabilal.com/html/virtualJ.html; see also Zach Whalen, "*Quest for Bush/Quest for Saddam*: Content vs. Context," *Gameology,* September 26, 2006, www.gameology.org/node/1269; Jose Antonio Vargas, "Way Radical, Dude," *Washington Post,* October 9, 2006, www.washingtonpost.com/wp-dyn/content/ article/2006/10/08/AR2006100800931.html.

3. See www.prada-transformer.com for more information on the project.

4. See Yang Fudong, *First Spring,* YouTube video, 9:11, uploaded January 18, 2010, originally released on Prada's website, www.youtube.com/watch?v=nhswOlqbPUU.

5. Dredge Byung'chu Käng discusses the Wonder Gays in detail in his essay "Paradise Lost and Found in Translation," *GLQ: A Journal of Lesbian and Gay Studies* 17, no. 1 (2011): 178–81.

6. "The Revolution Will Not Be Televised" appeared on Gil Scott-Heron's 1970 debut album *Small Talk at 125th and Lenox* and remains, along with his "Winter in America," one of the most important twentieth-century protest songs in English. In 2010 he was booked to play in Tel Aviv. Palestinian activists, as reported in the *Telegraph* on May 28, 2011, contacted him and stated that "your performance in Israel would be the equivalent to having performed in Sun City during South Africa's apartheid era. . . . We hope that you will not play apartheid Israel." He cancelled the gig. Heron died in May 2011.

7. Yasmine Ryan, "How Tunisia's Revolution Began," *Al Jazeera English,* January 26, 2011.

8. Patti Podesta, ed., *Resolution: A Critique of Video Art* (Los Angeles: Los Angeles Contemporary Exhibitions, 1986); Michael Renov and Erika Suderburg, eds., *Resolutions: Contemporary Video Practices* (Minneapolis: University of Minnesota Press, 1996).

9. Patti Podesta, introduction to *Resolution,* 3–4.

10. See Davidson Gigliotti, "A Brief History of RainDance," *Radical Software,* accessed August 9, 2011, www.radicalsoftware.org/e/history.html.

11. Other publications on video from the 1970s and 1980s often situated artist-produced videos against broadcast television. See David Antin's frequently referenced essay "Video: The Distinctive Feature of the Medium," in *Video Culture: A Critical Investigation,* ed. John Hanhardt (New York: Peregrine Smith Books, 1986), 147–66; and Beryl Korot and Ira Schneider, eds., introduction to *Video Art: An Anthology* (New York: Harcourt Brace Jovanovich, 1976), 3. Publications from this period on avant-garde cinema and experimental film, such as Gene Youngblood's *Expanded Cinema* (New York: Dutton, 1970), often included discussions of early artist videos.

12. Both *Video Art: An Anthology* and *Video Culture: A Critical Investigation*—published the same year as *Resolution*—took similar approaches in their anthology format and mix of artists, scholars, and curators as contributors, as have later publications, including Renov and Suderburg, *Resolutions*; and Doug Hall and Sally Jo Fifer, eds., *Illuminating Video: An Essential Guide to Video Art* (New York: Aperture in association with the Bay Area Video Coalition, 1990).

13. The exhibition was on view from April 18 to May 10, 1986, and the symposium took place on May 3 of the same year, both at LACE. Historically speaking, the twenty-seven videos in the exhibition were an important survey of U.S. and European artists working in video during the early to mid-1980s—many of whom, including Bill Viola, Tony Oursler, Mike Kelley, Juan Downey Jr., Antonio Muntadas, Bruce and Norman Yonemoto, Max Almy, and Lyn Blumenthal, have become important figures within the history of video art and

have influenced the practice of younger generations of video artists in the United States and internationally. The symposium was an important occasion when critics, scholars, and artists, many of whom contributed to *Resolution,* came together to discuss and debate what later became the tenets of discourse on video art. LACE was founded in downtown Los Angeles in 1978 by a small group of artists. It is a nonprofit organization that provides a local venue for both Los Angeles–based and international artists and advocates and exhibits innovations in art making. LACE has nurtured not only several generations of young artists but also newly emerging art forms such as performance art, video art, digital art, and installation-based work. See LACE's website at www.welcometolace.org.

14. For the process of organizing the Resolution project, see Podesta, introduction to *Resolutions,* 4–6.

15. See David Antin, "Video Art: Old Wine New Bottle," *Artforum,* June 1974, 20; and Martha Rosler, "Video: Shedding the Utopian Moment, " in *Illuminating Video,* eds. Hall and Fifer, 31–50.

16. Video's introduction as an artist/consumer tool was marked by Nam June Paik's acquisition of a Portapak in 1968, shortly after its introduction into the U.S. market by Sony.

17. Anne Bray founded Freewaves, an ongoing international festival of video and new media. Adriene Jenik is a pioneer of Distributed Social Cinema.

18. The exhibition was cocurated by Ma and Ciara Ennis, director/curator of Pitzer Art Galleries. After two months at Pitzer College, it travelled to LACE in December 2008 and closed in March 2009; see the Pitzer Art Galleries' web page archive at http://www.pitzer .edu/offices/galleries/exhibits/07-08/narrowcast.

19. The curatorial choices for *Narrowcast* were made with a number of contemporaneous events in mind. The J. Paul Getty Museum's *California Video* exhibition was a large-scale survey of regional video art from the late 1960s to the present; see Glenn Phillips, ed., *California Video: Artists and Histories* (Los Angeles: Getty Research Institute, 2008). Hollywould: Freewaves 11th Festival of Experimental Media Art featured 160 experimental videos and films and media art from around the world; see Freewaves' web page for past festivals at http:// freewaves.org/past-festivals/2008. Both of these events took place within a year of Resolution 3. Rather than retread the steps of these events and present another survey exhibition, we opted to set up a series of conceptual, formal, and historical frames using a smaller selection of works, one that we hoped would leave more room for linkage and interpretation from our viewers. The ten artists in *Narrowcast*—five from Resolution, Lyn Blumenthal, Juan Downey, Antonio Muntadas in collaboration with Marshall Reese, Michael Smith, and Bill Viola; and five contemporary, Natalie Bookchin, Mark Boulos, Regina José Galindo, Pablo Pijnappel, and Artur Żmijewski—were selected and paired in a way that emphasized resonance and precedence. Separated into five loose categories (embroidered narratives, autobiographical confessionals, restaging histories, documentary and reportage, trance and ritual) the works in *Narrowcast* reframed content and formal strategies that were as relevant in 1986 as they are now, thereby reflecting the range and inventiveness of the nontraditional narrative structures central to these artists' works.

20. Deirdre Boyle, "A Brief History of American Documentary Video," in *Illuminating Video,* eds. Hall and Fifer, 31–50.

21. See http://www.pitzer.edu/academics/ims/resolution3/index.html for a complete list of the individuals and organization that collaborated on Resolution 3.

22. Finn Tybo Andersen and Karena Nomi, eds., "Martha Rosler Talks" (transcription of discussion at Tea for 2000, Copenhagen, Denmark, 2000).

23. Juhasz's video book was published online as an experimental joint venture between MIT Press and USC's *Vectors* electronic journal, with funding from the Andrew W. Mellon

Foundation and the National Endowment for the Humanities; see vectors.usc.edu/projects/learningfromyoutube.

24. The video program and collection at the Long Beach Museum of Art (LBMA) is a good object lesson that illustrates some of these recent developments. Established in 1974 and closed down by the museum in 1995, the LBMA video program and collection was long regarded as one of the most important public video art archives in the world. Cataloging and preservation efforts began at LBMA in the early 1990s, but for ten years the collection languished at the museum's video annex after it had terminated the program (and virtually all of its support and curatorial staff). In 2005 the collection was transferred to the Getty Research Institute, which began restoring and preserving selected works from the collection. Some of these works were shown in the *California Video* exhibition at the J. Paul Getty Museum in 2008. Though the Getty's housing and preservation of the LBMA video collection was an important intervention in restoring a deteriorating archive and making some of it available to the public, debates arose around the selection for the exhibition, particularly its representation of feminist artists and artists of color. The decision to preserve selected works from the collection was also considered controversial by some in the field. For more discussion of the history of the LBMA's video program and collection, see David A. Ross, Peter Kirby, Kathy Rae Huffman, Joe Leonardi, Kira Perov, and Carole Ann Klonarides, "RECOLLECTIONS: A Brief History of the Video Programs at the Long Beach Museum of Art"; and Kathy Rae Huffman, "Art, TV, and the Long Beach Museum of Art: A Short History," both in *California Video,* ed. Phillips, 252–68, 279–84.

Moving Images

ON VIDEO ART MARKETS AND DISTRIBUTION

Lucas Hilderbrand

In his essay "Dispersion," multimedia artist Seth Price searches for answers to the role of art today and its relation to infrastructures of distribution. Although he looks back to Duchamp's readymades and conceptual art as prior models, in describing what he terms "distributed media" he is very much speaking to our own moment: a time of numerous possibilities for making work public through various technologies and platforms. But it is also a moment when the array of delivery media can also seem confounding and when the critical language for articulating artistic practice does not yet communicate everything at stake. He writes, "The task becomes one of packaging, producing, reframing, and distributing; a mode of production analogous not to the creation of material goods, but to the production of social contexts."[1] This artist's essay raises issues that have been essential to it, particularly the ways that distribution continues to matter both to making this work publicly accessible and to making it meaningful.

Since the mid-1990s, video has both exploded as a popular mode of artistic practice and undergone continual technological transformations. In the art scene the rise of the limited-edition projected video installation and the turn toward a cinematic aesthetic have reinvigorated the video art form, while audiences everywhere have adopted the World Wide Web for communications, and DVD, which has surpassed VHS as the dominant home video format, has already been declared obsolete. This essay attempts to examine the shifting terrain that is video art, with attention to the technologies, institutions, and infrastructures that have come to define the form and facilitate its public exhibition.

In the previous Resolution(s) anthology, Michael Nash proclaimed the death of video art. Published in the mid-1990s, he was writing at a moment of transition, as gallery artists largely were transitioning from single-channel work to installation and as the enthusiasm for CD-ROMs and new media art was hitting its fever pitch. Video art has been in transition ever since, though the predicted convergences and distribution models have oftentimes been subject to delays, detours, and sudden shifts. But Nash's claim that "decisions to produce film or video are dictated almost entirely by distribution issues and practical considerations" seems to remain relevant—even if these practical considerations about distribution typically have been marginalized within the history of video art.[2] In this essay I address such gauche topics as the art market, video release prices, and free online sharing because the economics of video matter. These issues are complex, in part, because of the ways the video medium is so ill suited for control or commodification.

Pinning down the medium of video art remains a thorny issue, even though artists have been exploring the form since the 1960s. Video Data Bank director Abina Manning describes the medium as defined by electronic signals and as being technology based, suggesting that there is "some specificity but not *one* specificity" to the variability of contemporary video works.[3] Others concurrently suggest that it makes more sense to speak of media art rather than video art, as the boundaries among video, film, and computer-based forms have blurred in the past decade or so. Although video art as *art* might be conceived as a set of aesthetic concerns, creative practices, or ideologies, it has always also been bound to its underlying technologies of production and exhibition. Those technologies that are most appealing to artists have often been the newest forms, creating a condition whereby media art is based upon ever-changing platforms. This has raised both opportunities and challenges for video distribution.

Video art as a medium has always negotiated a fundamental contradiction: that it is created through technologies of reproduction but must in some way be subject to conditions of control to secure artistic integrity and scarcity to create market value. This is a factor that dates to the origins of video art and that exposes the strangeness of video art sales and distribution. Videotape was, at its base, a technology of recording, and yet videotape-based art was often defined by liveness, ephemerality, three-dimensional spaces, and even limited copies. Each of these ways of conceiving video is arguably in opposition to what the technology is capable of doing: video is essentially recorded, fixed, two-dimensional, and eminently copyable.

Video art has also always had an uneasy relationship to the marketplace. One recurring problem has been sustaining the creation of new video art in a capitalist economy without commercializing the work itself. On the flip side lies the problem of making video, which fundamentally seems to refuse some of the qualities of traditional art forms, commodifiable. In the 1976 anthology *Video Art,* Hermine Freed makes the following claim, which now seems quaint in its utopianism: "Videotape can by-pass all of the problems of marketability, reproduction, availability, and function which no other medium can."[4] With a bit more historical hindsight, in a 1990 anthology Martha Rosler offers the assessment that "museums and granting agencies protect video from the marketplace."[5] Though this is a more measured articulation of the economic realities of video art, those realities themselves have shifted since the 1990s, when video art became newly sellable in galleries. This essay responds to the scene of video distribution since that time, with attempts to historicize how and when current paradigms developed.

This history is only recently passed, and the issues perhaps are obvious to those working in the field. Yet there has been surprisingly little public or scholarly examination of the material conditions that have allowed for the changing category that is video art. Whereas the existing literature on early video has been attuned to institutional issues such as particular technologies, galleries, PBS affiliates, collectives, and public funding opportunities, there seems to be far less documentation of recent activities, making it far more difficult to make cogent sense of the past fifteen or twenty years.[6] Thus, this essay must also acknowledge and negotiate the methodological problems that arise when it is difficult to pin down conceptual and practical turning points to precise dates or influences. I have relied upon conversations and correspondence with professionals in the gallery and video art distribution field, as well as my own personal experiences with video art, to flesh out this account where written work has not provided either the information or even a conceptual map.

Here, I suggest that from the start there have been at least three prominent models for video art's circulation: the gallery-based installation with art market prices; the distribution of single-channel works with institutional pricing for universities, libraries, and museums; and a grassroots model premised on the free circulation of media, whether initiated by a collective spirit in production or by a logic of sharing among audiences. (Obviously, other models have existed, such as efforts toward broadcasting via 1970s PBS affiliates and uses of satellite distribution by Deep Dish TV in the 1980s and 1990s; there have also been occasional efforts at small-scale distribution for individual purchase.) The modes of video circulation I examine here reflect the dominant models in the United States; comparable instances exist internationally, but this is admittedly not a global analysis.

Video Art in the Gallery

Perhaps affirming the "art" in video art, video has existed within the gallery framework since at least the late 1960s. Relatively quickly, video was likewise incorporated into the museum scene with such exhibitions as *The Machine as Seen at the End of the Mechanical Age* (Museum of Modern Art, 1968), *A Special Videotape Show* (Whitney Museum of American Art, 1971), and *Projected Video* (Whitney, 1975). These shows simultaneously gave legitimacy to a burgeoning technology and gave the cachet of relevance to the museums. Even the position of a video curator was invented as early as the 1970s.[7] But it was also during this period that video was first commodified as a kind of work that could be sold through the gallery system—though commodifying video would remain a difficult proposition for decades.[8]

Although many single-channel works were produced through and exhibited in galleries, the video installation was important for making video work in the gallery context. Many early video installations were unlike single-channel works because they relied upon real-time closed-circuit video feeds rather than permanent recordings. The effect in such installations was often about producing cognitive dissonance and phenomenological confusion: seeing oneself live from behind, as in Bruce Nauman's *Live-Taped Video Corridor* (1970), or seeing oneself in the present but slightly delayed, as in Dan Graham's *Present Continuous Past(s)* (1974). Such works negotiated video's two opposing temporal tendencies of instantaneity and delay; simply consider the peculiarity of "live-taped" in Nauman's title. Works premised upon liveness could be installed or performed but were not completed works that could be distributed like films. The hailed turn toward the cinematic in limited-edition videos two decades later suggested a move away from liveness and interactivity toward a fixed text.

A form often defined in dialectical relationship to broadcast television, video nonetheless was almost always seen on a monitor that superficially, at least, resembled the common domestic entertainment form. At the level of the interface, video looked like television, even if its content refused the kinds of narrative familiar to home viewers or, indeed, commercial production values. Video's status as a time-based art that required durational viewing also made it unlike painting or sculpture, so that from the start its installation in galleries has been complicated. There has always been the problem of how to exhibit a single-channel work in gallery spaces, and these questions continue. Should video be shown as a continual loop or with predetermined start times? With amplified sound or with headphones? With multiple works competing for time on a single monitor or with dedicated outposts for each work?

Video installation through the 1980s and, to a diminishing extent, during the 1990s often meant a Sony Trinitron monitor perched on a plinth. Videos, whether single or multichannel, would play in loops, with little or no playback control afforded to the viewer. Often, these monitors would be installed in rooms painted white, with full overhead lighting. Just about every material factor of the installation—narrative indifference to when the viewer walked by, sound either mixing with other videos or confined to germ-ridden headphones that were often broken, smallish images, glare from the lights—discouraged audience engagement. It is little wonder, then, that video remained fairly marginal to contemporary art practice and, in market terms, hard to sell. Certainly, some museum curators, notably Barbara London at MoMA, did champion video art and explorations of new installation models during the 1980s, and some artists, such as Tony Oursler and Bill Viola, were technological innovators.[9] Yet galleries had a difficult time promoting the form.

What changed to allow for the revaluation of video art was the technology and the way it looked. During the 1990s video art shifted from a format almost exclusively exhibited on monitors in bright rooms to a format almost exclusively projected in darkened ones. Correspondingly, by the 1990s broadcast television ceased to be the primary referent for video art; instead, media art started to resemble cinema, though with more flexibility for spectator/screen relations. By the early to mid-1990s, video projection technology allowed for more immersive installations with larger images. By increasing the size and luminance of the image, video art arguably became more divorced from the television monitor. Large-scale projection images also moved from white-walled galleries to black boxes—dark rooms where the focal point was the video image. The problems of duration and disorientation for viewers who entered the installation space during the middle of a piece persisted, but at least there was more incentive to engage if the visuals were monumental and/or compelling enough to capture the viewer's attention. With the move to projection and dedicated spaces, the video artwork was no longer just a videotape. It became a whole immersive world with technological and architectural elements that could not be easily replicated by the home video viewer. The video work was not just the reproducible text but also the more complex specifications for its presentation that would only rarely be fabricated. Suddenly, a limited-edition model made more sense for video art than ever before.

The galleries drove the shift toward limited-edition video in the 1990s, a trend quickly observable at art fairs and in museums. The idea of the limited edition comes from printmaking and photography: those other visual forms for which there is no original, just an artificially restricted number of copies approved and signed by the artist. But the installation element of video also bears the influence of three-dimensional forms such as sculpture and performance: a list of specifications that can be replicated but that must be done so in accordance to the artist's intentions. To further distinguish limited-edition videos from distributed art tapes or mass-market releases or home video recordings, galleries in the 1990s tended to sell works on LaserDisc, an analog disc format that had better resolution than tape formats and that had a small but dedicated following as a collector's format. Noneditioned study copies of works would occasionally be available on VHS. DVD was introduced to the consumer electronics market in 1997 and replaced LaserDisc as the gallery exhibition format sometime after 2000, when computers with DVD burners made their reproduction more affordable. Master and archival-editioned copies are now typically made on a more stable, professional format than DVD. Limited editions typically run three to five authorized copies, with nonsale artists' proofs or preview copies sometimes numbering far more.

The turning point for projection installation appears to be 1992–93, with mainstream recognition by the mid-1990s and widespread emulation by the end of the decade. Gary Hill's *Tall Ships* (1992), installed at Documenta IX and then included in the 1993 Whitney Biennial, was a major breakthrough installation, as it featured a series of life-sized video projections addressing the spectator from opposing sides of a corridor. In the best article to date on video installation, Liz Kotz similarly identifies 1993 as the watershed moment, with references to Stan Douglas's and Diana Thater's large-scale installations.[10] That same year, Douglas Gordon's infamous *24 Hour Psycho* (1993) slowed the eponymous Hitchcock film down to an impossible-to-see-in-full twenty-four hours. Although that work has been discussed as an example of appropriation art or as a test of durational perception, it also was, as is important to note, conceived and executed in relation to the conditions of playback and projection. Rather than altering the source text, Gordon manipulated the machine playing the videos. In each of these cases, video had to be installed in some way that made sense of exhibiting durational audiovisual works within gallery spaces that had historically featured visual works that existed primarily in space rather than through time. The turn toward installation video as a major international trend was institutionally recognized with *Video Spaces* (MoMA, 1995). By the 1999 Venice Biennial, video installation black boxes had reached the point of art world saturation.

The viability of video projection relies, of course, upon the projectors themselves. The earliest video projectors, dating to the 1970s, were barrel-shaped black-and-white projectors that projected grainy images; as a result, few artists engaged them for presenting their work. Video installation and even projection did exist dating back to the early 1970s, notably in works by Keith Sonnier and Peter Campus, but the technology remained unsatisfactory for many. As Peter Frank reflects, "Earlier projectors were not only prohibitively expensive, but also ludicrously unfaithful to the transmitted image. The magnification of the image made the electronic scan lines all too pronounced, and the color registration, where possible, was extremely sour."[11] Later, color cathode ray tube projectors allowed for color video projection via a three-beam system that emitted color-separated images in red, green, and blue; this system increased the prominence of video projection, but the projectors were hulking, and the color and image detail remained lacking compared with traditional monitors. Furthermore, tape technologies developed for playback on monitors often looked far grainier when projected. During the 1990s data projectors became smaller and more affordable, with colors integrated into a single lens, though their mass availability arguably had little to do with what was happening on the art scene. Rather, the boom of personal computers and nonartistic multimedia presentations, most commonly using PowerPoint, drove the popular adoption of video projectors at universities, offices, and conference centers.[12] With lowering costs and gradually improving luminosity, color fidelity, and resolution, more galleries could easily enter the field of video projection. The most common projectors have been liquid crystal display (LCD) projectors, which feature improved color accuracy and energy efficiency—these projectors are essentially what are called data projectors, as they are fine for PowerPoint and legible images in bright venues. More appropriate to art venues and cinema-style screens are digital light processing (DLP) projectors, which offer better contrast, detailed blacks, color intensity, and a higher-resolution image.[13]

As the technology for production and projection improved and became more accessible the production values of video art dramatically increased in many cases. For instance, Matthew Barney's influential five-part Cremaster Cycle (1994–2002) came to aspire toward feature film duration, sets, and costumes, if not exactly classical Hollywood narrative coherence. Barney's gallerist, Barbara Gladstone, essentially became his executive producer. Barney's videos, elaborate productions of fantastical worlds, were costly to produce and too obscure for mainstream release as an indie film yet fascinating as an expansion of gallery-based video art. These video works' ambition required a new kind of commodification in the art market and were among the most influential in pushing the trend toward expensive limited-edition works. Barney also sold sculptural environments related to the videos, as well as photographic prints of characters and settings from his videos. The boundaries of video art began to blur from the moving images to their installation and their peripheral sculptural and photographic tie-ins. Some artists continue, however, to sell their videos only as stand-alone works, without secondary materials in other media.

But how is the value for limited-edition video art established? One principle of the art market is that the value of an artist's work is symbolic: it is established in relation to the artist's cultural capital as someone who sells work and whose work is collected by important individuals or, better yet, museums. It is also relational, so that the value of an artist's work is contingent upon the recent selling price of the same artist's other work, a value that is typically inflated by auctions. Third, the valuation of an artist's work can only go up or stay stable; the art market would collapse if artists' works deflated in value. Therefore, in a bad art economy galleries will not discount the price of an artists' work the way a traditional store might have a sale to encourage business; the galleries must, instead, sell nothing and wait for the market to return to a point of stabilization or inflation. So the valuation of video art installation is related to the symbolic and, therefore, actual market value of an artist's work. The more famous or influential the artist, the higher the going rate.

But there is also something of a formula for how sale prices are established in the first place, a formula that comes out of sculpture. As José Freire, proprietor of Team Gallery in New York, informed me, "The market value for bronze sculptures, I was taught many years ago, was the cost of fabrication times three. Something like this holds true for video. A third of the edition's total selling price is usually the budget; a matching third goes to the artists; and the exhibiting galleries divide the final third."[14] This model allows successful artists to mount increasingly ambitious projects.

Video or media artists have long worked in differing modes: the same artist will create some works as single-channel pieces and others as installations, shifts that may or may not correlate to different periods in his or her career. These different kinds of works necessitate, then, different modes of representation or distribution. A number of early video artists have long had single-channel works in circulation even if they later moved into installation work. For a time in the 1990s, however, some artists who exhibited in galleries were reluctant to also explore distribution for their works as single-channel pieces for the institutional market. That has started to change with artists such as Paul Chan and Cory Arcangel returning to a prior model of working with both a gallery (Greene Naftali in Chan's case and Team in Arcangel's) and a distributor (Video Data Bank and Electronic Arts Intermix, respectively). Just as video art forms are variable, so are the ways they are distributed.

Video Art Distributors

Limited-edition installation became a mode of practice to reconcile the video medium with the space of the gallery and the logic of the art market. But if we rewind video history a bit, we can also see an alternative mode from the very beginning. Significantly, video's adoption by artists was linked to its mobility and its difference from traditional art forms. Much of the originary appeal of video was that it circulated in the world differently from film, photography, and other forms of art. Artists' oft-cited embrace of the Portapak during the 1960s liberated video from the studio and allowed amateurs to go out into the world, record it, and instantly play recordings back. The early ideologies of media access and democratization suggest dispersal and a desire for distribution (of both the technologies of production and the works themselves). But video also appeared at a moment when artists were problematizing the very idea of art and of its related systems for creating value; video art emerged amid movements toward performance and conceptual works, dematerialization, and critiques of commodification. Video distribution became an alternative to the fine art market model. Like galleries, distributors help artists build a creative profile, but they also circulate their work more widely and make the most of video's reproductive potential. These distributors release what might be called "unlimited editions"[15]—unnumbered releases of fixed single-channel works on VHS, DVD, or professional formats such as three-quarter-inch U-matic, Betacam SP, and more recently, Digital Betacam.

Video distribution was, from the start, also the subject of questions. As Allison Simmons reflected during video's first decade, "They immediately encountered a horde of problems—legal as well as ideological—arising from conflict over the nature of a video work: is it public information or a unique (though easily duplicated) art work?"[16] The common practice of collaborative production in many cases also raised concerns of authorship, ownership, and creative control after collectives dissolved. Chris Hill points to one of the problems with video, which is a matter not only of reproducibility but also of unknown longevity: "As unedited documentation of live events, with grainy black and white images of unknown stability, video also had questionable archival, and therefore investment, value within the art market."[17] These questions and issues made video difficult to sell in a gallery context but did not preclude more flexible and immediate modes of distribution.

Video art distribution simultaneously offered an alternative to and actually came out of the New York gallery scene. Leo Castelli, among the most influential gallerists of the 1960s, began providing artists with the material support to explore video production and a distribution outfit for tapes and films; many of the seminal works by Vito Acconci, Lynda Benglis, Bruce Nauman, and others now considered part of the early video canon came out of the Castelli gallery. Video was never a particularly lucrative format for the gallery, however, so Castelli ceased video distribution in 1985. Its collection was divided—and in many cases has been shared—by Electronic Arts Intermix (EAI) and Video Data Bank (VDB).

For the past few decades, EAI and VDB have been the leading distributors for single-channel video art in the United States.[18] EAI, based in Chelsea, one of the prime art gallery neighborhoods of New York, is perhaps seen as more intimately connected with the visual art scene. VDB, located in Chicago and affiliated with an art school, is perhaps more immediately associated with educational markets. Yet both distribute work to museums, galleries, schools, and libraries, and both have international clients. Both distributors acquire work by new artists through open submissions that are reviewed, as well as by scouting at festivals and galleries. One way in which the distributors are perhaps different from the gallery scene is that they are nonexclusive in their distribution agreements with their artists. Both also provide context and resources for video art, past and present, through publications, public programs, and online resources.

EAI itself came out of the gallery scene; it was founded in 1971 by Howard Wise, whose gallery had exhibited the seminal video installation show *TV as a Creative Medium* two years earlier.[19] EAI's distribution collection and philosophy function like a gallery in that EAI represents artists, insofar as it distributes their entire bodies of work. Its roster emphasizes artists whose work explores and experiments with media as an art form, and many simultaneously exhibit work in galleries. Although the works distributed are not unique objects or artificially limited in edition, EAI sees itself as committing to long-term relationships with artists that span future releases, preservation of older works, and educational programs to contextualize the field. EAI also engages in efforts to address best practices for video exhibition and to deal with technological change and its implications when formats become outmoded; one such effort is its online resource guide (www.eai.org/resourceguide).

VDB was founded in 1976 by Kate Horsfield and Lyn Blumenthal while they were students at the School of the Art Institute of Chicago, and it continues to operate through affiliation with the school. In many cases VDB distributes artists' entire bodies of work and helps to build their careers in ways comparable to EAI, but its collection and its activities are somewhat broader. The VDB collection is more eclectic than EAI's, with particular strengths in grassroots media, feminism, documentary, autobiography, historical reenactment, and identity politics. This is not to say that its video makers are not also formalists, just to say that there is a marked orientation toward social critique and political media in its catalog. VDB also specializes in distributing video collections, whether as individual artist compilations or anthologies that offer historical or thematic overviews. Its most important collection, *Surveying the First Decade: Video Art and Alternative Media in the U.S., 1968–1980,* has become the essential resource for college courses covering early video. This collection has also made VDB the de facto canon maker for this early work and how it is taught. In recent years VDB has moved into producing DVD box sets, including a rerelease of *Surveying the First Decade,* as well as newly organized collections by artists such as Yvonne Rainer, George Kuchar, Peggy Ahwesh, and Paul Chan. Finally, VDB also produces and distributes a large collection of artist interviews.

Video art has typically been distributed at institutional rates, which are significantly below limited editions' gallery prices but higher than mass-market prices. With the development of a mainstream home video market for feature films in the late 1970s and early 1980s, a broad catalog of new and classic movies became widely available to audiences as inexpensive rentals, generally between $0.99 and $3.00. Although these mass-produced releases also were available for purchase at higher rates, consumers tended to associate videotape with frugal, temporary entertainment. The affordability of home video movie releases derived from a combination of rental stores driving the rental rates far below what studios would have preferred and the economies of scale that allowed for inexpensive mass-market releases. In part because video artworks have never had the broad releases of feature films, volume has not driven prices down. One of the recurring complaints from educators about distributors such as EAI and VDB (as well as other companies releasing works at institutional rates) is their expense, generally somewhere in the $100 range for a rental and in the $200 to $300 range for a sale to an educational venue. Yet the institutional rates for libraries and universities have not changed significantly since they were set decades ago, so that the rates essentially have not been adjusted for inflation. The fees also vary considerably according to a range of factors, including the type of institution, the duration of use, and the publicness of that use; for instance, the rate for classroom screening would be less than the fee for broadcasting a work or the price for an archival copy acquired by a museum. What is being leased or sold in many cases is a set of rights, such as public performance rights, not just a copy of the work. For individual researchers, both EAI and VDB offer on-site viewing of their collections for little or no cost.

Both distributors are nonprofit organizations, and both rely upon a combination of distribution revenue and public funding. As it is an independent organization, VDB earns approximately 90 percent of its operating income from rentals and sales, with the other 10 percent from public or foundation arts grants. (The nonprofit organization also receives space and some of its salary lines in kind from the School of the Art Institute of Chicago.) Revenues are split fifty-fifty with artists, and VDB pays out royalties twice a year.[20] In the case of EAI, "public funding is critical for the maintenance and development of important initiatives such as [their] preservation projects, online resources, public programs, viewing access, and [their] digitization efforts."[21] Both VDB and EAI distribute works dating back decades, so their artists continue to receive residuals for years on end, as long as the work is in circulation. Both work to keep artists' work available, and this sustained distribution has maintained interest in work that without distribution probably would not have continued to be available or even preserved. These distributors' efforts also help artists and scholars see new works within a medium-specific genealogy.

Distributors have been cautious of new distribution formats because of the enormous costs to change platforms and the potential for new technologies to be short lived. For decades distribution was predominantly via VHS, the most accessible video format, though both distributors have moved into DVD. But the issue of distribution is more complex than just tapes and discs. According to executive director Lori Zippay, EAI distributes in various formats according to the client's needs: "We don't release titles on particular formats, as in the film distribution model; all of our distribution is, in effect, 'customized.' A school orders a DVD, a museum orders a Digital Betacam, a festival a DVCam, an exhibition space a Betacam SP, etc., and we create a copy on that format from a submaster for that particular order. That's part of the complexity (and the beauty) of this distribution model; it's very context- and venue-specific."[22]

Both distributors continue to deal with evolving issues of format specificity, technological obsolescence, and new platforms for distribution. The earliest video work has reached an age when restoration is essential, and even relatively recent work raises questions for how it should be presented. Does it matter, for instance, if a video piece that originated in an analog format is now distributed and shown digitally? Does a work such as Joan Jonas's *Vertical Roll* (1972), conceived in relation to cathode ray tube monitors continue to make sense if seen projected or on a flat LCD screen? Both distributors are working on digital preservation initiatives to anticipate continued technological change and sustain their collections' availability. They now offer works in a range of digital platforms for different uses, such as password-protected streaming previews, high-definition Blu-ray discs for distribution, and MiniDV, DVCAM, Digital Betacam, and/or hard drive screening formats. As of June 2012, both were testing online delivery for educational institutions, with plans for full operation within a few months (for VDB) and in early 2013 (for EAI).

Grassroots Distribution

Whereas galleries and video art distributors have remained relatively constant sites for making video art visible, a third model for video art accessibility has remarkably shifted in ideology and location. For lack of a better umbrella term, I will be calling this third category *grassroots video distribution*. This is the model that remains the most uncertain and probably the one most open to speculation.

Our written histories of video art's first decade suggest a proliferation of collectively produced video projects that strove to decentralize the media industry by giving voice to an idealistic notion of the people, rather than the privileged few with access to the airwaves.[23] These attempts at self-representation and alternative media also typically refused individual authorship, instead operating under the name of the various and shifting collectives that produced them—for example, People's Video Theater, Videofreex, Video Free America, Downtown Community Television, Broadside TV, People's Communication Network, and Top Value Television. In some cases these organizations held rap sessions, called feedback sessions, in which they watched and discussed their just-recorded interviews. Some collectives took to the road, as when Videofreex reconceived themselves as the Media Bus and toured to bring video production and playback to different communities. In other instances tape exchanges by mail took place between different organizations, in the model of creating an alternative media distribution network. In the 1980s this collective-production model most famously became associated with the progressive media critique and activist videos of Paper Tiger Television, though Paper Tiger's self-distribution more resembled the policies of EAI or VDB. These video efforts operated, for the most part, outside the logic of the art market and independent of other distributors. They operated on the principle of collectivity and sharing, of democratization of the media. The producers themselves defined the terms of this grassroots model.

Exploiting the reproducibility of video, there has also long been a parallel bootleg economy for video art that operates outside of the marketplace but that does not necessarily come from intentionality on the part of the artists. I employ the term *bootleg* to suggest the unremunerated copying of personal, research, or teaching copies of video artworks; such practices are different from piracy, as they typically are not cases of black-market profiteering. The circulation and collecting of these copies had been, until the 2000s, a matter of personal analog copying from VCR to VCR and had existed on a fairly small scale as tape trades between artists or as practices of duping tapes rented for screenings (for instance, a professor or curator might make a habit of making personal copies of tapes rented for classroom/festival/museum screenings). These practices of copying tapes existed in particular art, education, and exhibition milieus, and they also functioned as an extension of market practices of making preview or study copies of works available. But the reproductive degeneration of analog personal copies also marked these copies *as* copies, thus in many cases making them insufficient for public exhibition.[24] Such practices assuredly violated rental contracts, but they did serve to make the work better known.

With the digitization of video and the rise of online video streaming and torrent-facilitated file distribution since 2000, the scale of video art sharing—on the part of audiences rather than artists or collectives themselves—obviously has increased dramatically. As of this writing, the most prominent websites for video art sharing—with or without the artists' consent—are YouTube, Vimeo, and UbuWeb. These sites offer a broad if idiosyncratic array of artists' works: on YouTube videos can be randomly titled and even misidentified, which creates problems for searchability, whereas on UbuWeb works are organized by artist's name, with claims to greater curatorial vision. Both claim to deactivate videos if the artists or rights holders alert the site of infringement. These sites have raised concerns about copyright infringement and enforcement and about taking control of the manner of exhibition away from artists. Vimeo, which is more artist friendly, allows users who upload videos to keep them open to all potential viewers or to control access by making videos password protected. The grassroots model has always been informed by a politics—even an ethics—of accessibility, although the current politics of media commons becomes more ethically murky when the audience rather than the artists determine the availability of works.

Video art, as a form that is most accessible in university media libraries or in museums, has long been an art that is difficult for many potential audiences to access. Unlike two-dimensional visual art forms, illustrations in books offer little indication of the work; indeed, even a book with lush color plates can give little sense of the sound, transitions, or pace of video works. The enormous contribution that these sharing sites offer is the vastly expanded accessibility of previously elusive video works.

Yet it seems that very few artists post their own works to such sites. To date, most online video streaming does not financially compensate the artists. Venues such as ReFrame (www.tribecafilminstitute.org/filmmakers/reframe) have emerged with subscription or pay-per-view models that do compensate artists who upload work, though compared with YouTube the exposure and audience they offer is comparatively small. But perhaps more important to most artists, online video sharing rarely presents the work in its ideal conditions: online video, because of compression and its sourcing from bootleg copies, sometimes is available only in low-resolution version. Such videos often also appear in small windows, may stall or freeze during transmission, and are surrounded by interface text, images, and advertisements that may distract from the work. Added to these concerns, people tend to browse the Internet in a multitasking, grazing mode that is not always conducive to the kinds of attention "difficult" or conceptual video works necessitate. Thus, video sharing acts in opposition to the logic of galleries or EAI and VDB, all of which collaborate with artists in determining where work circulates, in which contexts, and on which formats.

The current state of video sharing is perhaps too elusive to rigorously assess and too uncertain to predict. I include this third model in this essay, however briefly, because it would be negligent not to acknowledge its existence and suggest, at the very least, its potential to transform the existing models. As a technology-based art form, video art must evolve with technological changes or else become obsolete. Online video could redefine the shape, space, and circulation of video art, just as the medium's exhibition and sales were reimagined as black box installations in the 1990s. Authorized and illicit video will in all probability continue to circulate outside the art market, and restricted-access subscription and pay-per-view online rental models are envisioned as central to the future of video distributors.

Conclusion

Since its beginnings, video art has circulated in public through different infrastructures: galleries, distributors, and grassroots sharing. Although the institutions are distinct, they are not necessarily mutually exclusive and continue to reflect different modes of work and artist intentions. The conceptual issues for video art have remained remarkably constant, even as the technologies have become variable. I occasionally return to the early history of video art throughout this essay to stress that the issue of distribution has always been a problem for the form, a problem that has been one of the distinctive attributes of the medium but that for the most part has never been claimed as such. The ways that video can be distributed, sold, and exhibited has been very much dependent upon the available technologies and prominent formats at any given time.

Since the mid-1990s, *video art* or *media art* have largely connoted the art market model of rare editions or the imagined convergent future of online data streaming. Yet both EAI and VDB continue to distribute tangible media and remain distinct from the gallery and the video sharing models. As EAI's Zippay situates the current distribution scene:

> It's very interesting that over the past decade two seemingly opposing new models for video art have flourished: the limited edition video art market, and the streaming or downloading of artists' works online. It's also interesting that many artists work with both models, which reach different audiences and operate under different economies. EAI (and other similar distributors) falls somewhere between these two models, incorporating some aspects of both but still representing a different (and we feel necessary) paradigm.[25]

Galleries and distributors continue to help us understand media practices in the contexts of broader art histories and even in relation to the same artists' other works. They exist to make the work public and to help it circulate. At the same time, video sharing arises from a spirit of setting the media free, and new Web video sharing sites help works to circulate farther and faster. All three institutional models of distribution remain essential, even as the form remains ever on the move.

NOTES

My thanks go to Rebecca Cleman, José Freire, Abina Manning, and Lori Zippay for sharing their insights into video art sales and distribution and to Ming-Yuen Ma and Cynthia Chris for further feedback on the text.

1. Seth Price, *Dispersion* (New York: 38th Street Publishers, 2008); originally written for the Ljubljana Biennial of Graphic Art (2001–2).

2. Michael Nash, "Vision after Television: Technocultural Convergence, Hypermedia, and the New Media Arts Field," in *Resolutions: Contemporary Video Practices,* eds. Michael Renov and Erika Suderburg (Minneapolis: University of Minnesota Press, 1996), 382.

3. Abina Manning, interview with author, October 29, 2009.

4. Hermine Freed, "'Where Do We Come From? Where Are We? Where Are We Going?,'" in *Video Art: An Anthology,* eds. Ira Schneider and Beryl Korot (New York: Harcourt Brace Jovanovich, 1976), 211.

5. Martha Rosler, "Video: Shedding the Utopian Moment," in *Illuminating Video: An Essential Guide to Video Art,* eds. Doug Hall and Sally Jo Fifer (New York: Aperture, 1990), 49.

6. For histories of early video art, see Allison Simmons, "Television and Art: A Historical Primer for an Improbable Alliance," in *The New Television: A Public/Private Art,* eds. Douglas Davis and Simmons (Cambridge: MIT Press, 1977); Marita Sturken, "Paradox in the Evolution of an Art Form: Great Expectations and the Making of a History," in *Illuminating Video,* eds. Hall and Fifer, 101–21; Chris Hill, "Attention! Production! Audience!— Performing Video in its First Decade, 1968–1980," Bay Area Video Coalition website, http://

www.experimentaltvcenter.org/sites/default/files/history/pdf/hillattention_1063.pdf; Kate Horsfield, "Busting the Tube: A Brief History of Video Art," in *Feedback: The Video Databank Catalog of Video Art and Artist Interviews,* eds. Horsfield and Lucas Hilderbrand (Philadelphia: Temple University Press, 2006). Glenn Phillips makes an interesting distinction between the East Coast and the West Coast in terms of the kinds of institutions that sustain video art: galleries, arts councils, foundations, and PBS stations in New York and Boston versus art schools in Southern California. See Phillips, introduction to *California Video: Artists and Histories* (Los Angeles: Getty Research Institute, 2008), 4. Early articles specific to video distribution are available through the Video History Project's website at http://www.experimentaltvcenter.org/history/collections/collections_texts.php3.

7. Barbara London, *Video Spaces: Eight Installations* (New York: Museum of Modern Art, 1995), 14.

8. As David Ross recounts, "In 1969, Los Angeles dealer Nicholas Wilder made the first sale of an artist's videotape in the United States—Bruce Nauman's *Video Pieces A-N*—to a European collector." Ross, "The Personal Attitude," in *Video Art,* eds. Schneider and Korot, 246.

9. Oursler has explored the possibilities of video projection in multimedia sculptural installation, most notably by projecting animated video faces onto strangely shaped dolls since *The Waiting* (1992). Viola has long worked with the most advanced technology, from his time at the Sony Atsugi Research Center in the early 1980s to his use of flat-screen monitors for slow-motion videos that evoke paintings, such as *The Quintet of Remembrance* (2000) and the high-definition projection in *The Raft* (2004).

10. Liz Kotz, "Video Projection: The Space between Screens," in *Theory in Contemporary Art Since 1985,* eds. Zoya Kocur and Simon Leung (Malden, Mass: Blackwell, 2004), 101–16. For another important essay on video installation, see Margaret Morse, "Video Installation Art: The Body, the Image, and the Space-in-between," in *Illuminating Video,* eds. Hall and Fifer.

11. Peter Frank, "Video Art Installations: The Telenvironment," in *Video Art,* eds. Schneider and Korot, 204. David Ross observes, "Artists found themselves confined to producing videotapes to be viewed in museums which would be regarded, by most, as sculpture that demanded too much time to view and interfered with a casual stroll through museum galleries. . . . It should be noted that these works, with perhaps the exception of Campus's, were produced by artists whose primary relationship to the medium had developed around the production of videotapes, as entities unto themselves" rather than as three-dimensional sculptural or architectural installations. Ross, "The Personal Attitude," in *Video Art,* eds. Schneider and Korot, 246–48.

12. Keep in mind that PowerPoint would have no reason to exist as software without projectors to make presentation possible. Before data projectors, in some cases transparent LCD screens could be used in conjunction with overhead projectors. Meanwhile, the electronics and film industry began exploring options for digital distribution and projection that would save huge sums of money on striking prints and shipping the heavy reels to theaters. The studios urged adoption, but cinemas were resistant to the cost of installing entirely new equipment.

13. Chris Meigh-Andrew's *A History of Video Art* (New York: Berg, 2006) is the history most attentive to projection technology, but this account remains a bit vague on the dates. LCD projectors were available by the end of the 1980s and were manufactured by the electronics firms Sony, Samsung, and Panasonic and by computer peripheral firm Epson during the 1990s. No one particular model or manufacturer appears to have spurred the technology's adoption in the art world. Alongside the new projection technologies, the mid-1990s marked widespread transitions from analog to digital production technologies, including digital video cameras and computer editing software such as Media 100 and, later, Final Cut Pro.

Suddenly, the elements of video were no longer stored on tapes but on hard drives. Digital production and postproduction technologies were embraced because the original recordings featured more color saturation, more contrast, and crisper lines; there was also no more image degeneration through reproduction or editing. Yet analog formats such as Betacam SP remained for a long time the standard for tape masters.

14. José Freire, e-mail correspondence with author, November 21, 2009.

15. Phrase borrowed from Lori Zippay and Rebecca Cleman, e-mail correspondence with author, November 23, 2009.

16. Simmons, "Television and Art," 13.

17. Hill, "Attention! Audience! Production!," 24.

18. Comparable distributors exist in other countries, such as Lux (Britain), Argos (Belgium), Montevideo (Netherlands), Hamaca (Spain), and V-Tape and numerous other Canadian distributors. Distribution is state funded outside the United States to a far greater extent than it is within.

19. Anna Canepa Video Distribution, The Kitchen, Synapse, and the Stefanotty Gallery (in association with Art/Tapes in Florence, Italy) were other early entrants into New York–based video art distribution.

20. Manning, interview with author, October 29, 2009.

21. Zippay and Cleman, e-mail correspondence with author, November 23, 2009.

22. Zippay, e-mail correspondence with author, November 29, 2009.

23. Seer, among other accounts, Patricia Mellencamp, "Video and the Counterculture," in *Global Television,* eds. Cynthia Schneider and Brian Wallis (Cambridge: MIT Press, 1988), 199–224; Deirdre Boyle, "A Brief History of American Documentary," in *Illuminating Video,* eds. Hall and Fifer, 51–69, and *Subject to Change: Guerrilla Television Revisited* (New York: Oxford University Press, 1997); and Martha Rosler, "Video: Shedding the Utopian Moment," in *Illuminating Video,* eds. Hall and Fife.

24. I examine the politics and aesthetics of bootleg videos beyond video art more fully in my book *Inherent Vice: Bootleg Histories of Videotape and Copyright* (Durham, N.C.: Duke University Press, 2009).

25. Zippay, e-mail correspondence with author, November 23, 2009.

Mobile Indeed

THE MARKETING OF VIDEO ART AND VIDEO ART AS MARKETING

Nancy Buchanan and Catherine Taft

> It is very important to stress that video is a distribution of ideas
> and not an object; the very nature of it being unlimited is a victory
> over speculation in art.
>
> » Maria Gloria Bicocchi, *Art / 22 / Tapes*

Vito Acconci laughed as he described to Liza Bear how artists moved from gallery to street in the 1970s, having abandoned traditional object-making: "We thought that what we were doing was going to completely change the gallery system; probably that it was going to change the *whole* system, not just the gallery system." He ruefully remarked that instead all they did was "allow the system to bulge."[1] Although Acconci and others thought their performances were unsalable, they were not averse to salability and so transformed the gallery only from a store to a supermarket.[2] Indeed, today auction houses are able to sell nearly anything defined as art, including VHS tapes. "When young video artists are now selling their tapes for hundreds of thousands of dollars," Martha Rosler declares, "and it's a limited-edition—unique object—you know that the history of video as a communicative, easily distributed, people's cheap media form is being erased."[3]

Historians generally agree that artists followed three main directions beginning in the late 1960s and early 1970s: community and activist documentary video, which often incorporated narrative elements; conceptual and performance work; and direct experimentation with the tools of electronic media. Reflecting a community-driven spirit, these three areas were seen as equally important components of video practice. Many early video artists working from a community approach produced tapes collectively.[4] Through collaborative attitudes, artists began to participate in and engage with the media, transforming its meaning and scrutinizing its value.

In his early description of distinctive features of the medium, David Antin asserts that video art defined itself in opposition to the forms of network television.[5] Support from the nonprofit television centers in Boston (WGBH), New

York (WNET), and San Francisco (KQED) was crucial, however, to artists' abilities to produce work. Beginning with WGBH's *The Medium Is the Medium* in 1969, public broadcasting offered video equipment and production studios, funded residencies, and created broadcast opportunities for artists.[6] Recipients of this public largesse included Allan Kaprow, Bill Viola, Nam June Paik, poet Joanne Kyger, and Steve Beck, whose video synthesizer was completed with educational television funding. Radical programming continued on PBS until the mid-1990s, thanks to a handful of extraordinary producers like Russell Connor and Fred Barzyk.[7] Although viewers often enthusiastically praised these programs, government and foundation monies eventually ran out, never to be renewed. With the demise of National Endowment Fellowships for individual artists and restrictive guidelines for independent support, funding today has shrunk to relatively few grants from the Independent Television Service (ITVS), the majority of which are awarded to documentary projects.[8]

As more artists began working with media, more-pointed political and cultural critiques emerged. Rage against American business as usual was central to 1970s media-focused publications like *Radical Software*. In the journal's first issue, "A Demand on the Networks"—written in response to media coverage of the killings of unarmed student demonstrators at Kent State—is printed on the same page as an editorial by Gene Youngblood that challenges independents to change the entire business/broadcast world. He writes, "The media must be liberated, must be removed from private ownership and commercial sponsorship, must be placed in the service of all humanity. We must make the media believable. We must assume conscious control over the videosphere."[9] Other theoretical publications echoed this rallying cry.

The Fox was published briefly from 1975 to 1976 by Art & Language Foundation, whose editorial board included conceptualists Mel Ramsden, Sarah Charlesworth, Joseph Kosuth, Preston Heller, Michael Corris, Andrew Menard, and Ian Burn. *The Fox*'s editors focused on ideology, recognizing the danger of artists' co-optation and careerism. Adrian Piper proposes in an essay that artists price their work according to time and materials costs. With artist wages at a "scale of an average blue or white-collar worker," Piper imagines that her scheme could have the following potential outcomes:

> It might happen that since under this program neither the artist nor the dealer nor the buyer stands to make a profit on works of art, producing and acquiring works of art might die out. Art, as well as art-as-speculation and art-as-investment security might disappear. . . . On the other hand . . . it might happen that such a program facilitated producing art as a modest means of self-support for more artists by making it more economically accessible to more people.[10]

But this is an example of that 1970s utopian thinking. Most successful artists do not physically produce their work, only conceptualize it, hiring others to make the product. If named artists spent only a small amount of time thinking, treating studio assistants in a manner commensurate with Piper's formula would be a tricky maneuver. Would the workers earn more than the boss?

Although it was a time of increased commercialism and social tension, the 1970s also cultivated an idealistic culture of art as gift: artists freely mailed videotapes back and forth, brought equipment to neighborhood meetings, established community workshops, visited schools, and shared skills with each other and an interested public. The Los Angeles Woman's Building's Feminist Video Workshop and the Long Beach Museum of Art's Video Program were two important video production centers that thrived in this inclusive climate.[11] Much of this cooperative spirit continued into the early 1980s; public access centers throughout the United States increasingly began operating as hubs for media critiques like those of Paper Tiger Television, which starting in 1981, used Manhattan cable studios to expose mythologies of all media.[12] In the 1980s artists in New York's Lower East Side banded together to create numerous public events and huge group exhibits in empty storefronts, and in 1986 the Monday / Wednesday / Friday Video Club began operations, distributing copies of artists' films and videos, priced from $29.95 to $39.95.[13]

The blue-chip art market boomed throughout the 1980s but was destined to end; on October 19, 1987, also known as Black Monday, global stock markets from Hong Kong to New York collapsed. In the United States stocks fell by nearly 23 percent, leaving the economy and the art market painfully unstable into the early 1990s. As artist Diana Thater describes making video at this time:

When I was in graduate school, the art market crashed and then the first Gulf War started . . . a lot of galleries closed. We never had, as artists do today, ideas about becoming art stars. We thought that if we could make a living and maybe get a little teaching job, then we could die not in the gutter, but we had no aspirations toward being famous. . . . My first few shows were in domestic spaces and the gallerists didn't even have desks, let alone video projectors. . . . The sort of amateur hour we were having in L.A. in 1990, '91, '92 was interesting and exciting because we were all working with very little and people are always more creative when they have almost nothing.[14]

The economy quickly rebounded with the rise of the personal computer, a new commodity that inflated the market into the dot-com bubble. While this also produced the era of digital and Internet art, the gallery and museum system remained relatively conservative in its approaches toward display and support of media arts. By the end of the 1990s, the art world had largely discarded notions of equity, as video quickly became a valuable commodity in the gallery, museum, and art fair circuit.

Post-Reagan greed escalated the dismantling of social programs throughout the country and tore down the last restraints keeping savings and loan banks from engaging in speculative lending (resulting in debt that is still being paid, on top of the most recent bailouts). Several heads of so-called thrifts built art collections with bank money.[15] Auction houses that had been discreetly improving prices for contemporary art, along with those of old masters and antiquities, now stepped into the spotlight. Though painting comprised the bulk of high-end auction offerings, more ephemeral work was added to the mix. Could this change somehow mirror the creation of incomprehensible financial instruments that rocked the financial world? Surely, the ability to aver "worth" is strained when one considers credit default swaps or the life of celluloid VHS videotape. Single-channel video works sold at auction since 2005 have brought in up to $377,600; one VHS tape sold for $10,200.[16]

Artists need to survive, of course; though many have day jobs, the dream is to support oneself solely through art production. Though Los Angeles dealer Nick Wilder sold the first artist's tape in 1969, early marketing efforts in limited-edition video (Anna Canepa, Sonnebend) failed to attract many investors.[17] In 1977 Hermine Freed (herself a video producer) attempted to define how the special characteristics of video art might enhance a collection.[18] Nevertheless, video distribution companies like Electronic Arts Intermix (EAI), established by dealer Howard Wise in 1970, continue to provide academic institutions, galleries, and museums with reasonably priced video rentals and sales.

Does only speculation drive the pricing of nonutilitarian goods? Conservation of artwork aims to prevent the inexorable progress of entropy. But the preservation of video art presents entirely new issues—e.g., obsolescence of equipment and tape formats, the volatility of digital storage, the ethics of reproduction of the original.

Today's market restricts content while demanding superficial innovation. Cultural critic Theodor Adorno insists that art *cannot* be linked to society if it is to sustain its autonomy. Adorno characterizes autonomy as "the will to refrain from the impulse to invest a work of art with a meaning external to the experience of that work."[19] In other words, art can ever be only about art. But Thierry de Duve, examining the transposition of Kant's ideas of taste and judgment within today's art world, describes the freedom enjoyed by artists today rather differently:

> Yes, artists are free: they are free and free to exchange whatever, but
> only there where exchanges take place, in the market. They are also
> free to do whatever, but the violence of this freedom is no longer that

of revolution, it is merely that of economic competition. All the styles, manners, forms, and media are interchangeable.[20]

Though it is understandable that Adorno, having witnessed the Fascist harnessing of media spectacle and the postwar growth of advertising, is wary of didacticism, today's cozy merging of brands and artists surpasses the literalness of political art gestures. Michael Corris points to 1970s conceptual artists' institutional critiques as radical departures that could have relevance today in terms of the sphere of production and distribution, and Julian Stallabrass concludes *Art Incorporated* with the following statement:

> The plausibility and power of art's freedom are on the wane . . .
> the particular freedoms of art . . . may open a utopian window on a
> less instrumental world [but] they also serve as effective pretexts for
> oppression. . . . To break with the supplemental autonomy of free art
> is to remove one of the masks of free trade. Or to put it the other way
> around, if free trade is to be abandoned as a model for global develop-
> ment, so must its ally, free art.[21]

Others have focused on the manner in which today's artists are complicit with the market, some delighting in their own Warholian celebrity.

Chris Burden Promo was broadcast in 1976 on commercial television in twenty-four thirty-second commercial spots in New York and Los Angeles. Simple yellow text zooms large on a bright-blue screen as the artist's voice intones, "Leonardo da Vinci . . . Vincent Van Gogh . . . Pablo Picasso . . . Chris Burden . . . ." Recently seeing this piece on a museum monitor removed most of its original humor; it seems merely a truism.[22] As an update, *Untitled ($29.95)* is RTMark's (an anonymous art collective formed to undermine corporate structure) critique of celebrity video. After a computer-synthesized narrator recites artists' names and prices, it exclaims, "It's only a videotape, for God's sake!," encouraging viewers to smuggle cameras into galleries and appropriate artist-made video for all to enjoy at the reasonable price of $29.95. Many young video artists follow the current trend of offering photos or other ephemera used in the production of a video to enhance gallery sales of an already-editioned video.[23] Thus, if the edition sells out to private investors, then another infinitely reproducible video will be less available for public viewing.

Video in Vogue: A Mixed Bag

At approximately the same time that video's market price escalated, fashion collaborations with the art world picked up speed. But art and fashion have long had relations. As writer Christ Townsend describes, "You can almost hear Cecil Beaton's shutter closing on Jackson Pollack's paintings, backdrops for a 1951 fashion shoot; almost hear Man Ray, in 1920's Paris, apologetically negotiating the complex seam of compromise which allowed his studies of Poiret's dresses, shot on manikins for *Vogue,* to appear in the historically conscious, aesthetically pure pages of that avant-garde organ, *La Révolution Surréaliste.*"[24] At the moment, the most important fashion labels are falling over each other to court the best-known artists (or is it the other way around?), especially to collaborate on designer handbags. Richard Prince, Vanessa Beecroft, and Takashi Murakami recently teamed up with Louis Vuitton to produce these highly coveted, ultimate luxury items.[25] Murakami's 2007–8 retrospective even included an in-museum Louis Vuitton handbag boutique—which was alternately viewed as genius or tasteless. Nevertheless, the artist released two anime videos (in 2002 and 2008) celebrating his collaboration with the fashion house. To take this fusion of art and fashion to another extreme, Bernard Arnault, one of the richest men in France—also listed as one of the world's top-twenty art collectors; a onetime owner of the third-largest auction house, Phillips de Pury & Company; and, to no surprise, a 47.5 percent owner of LVMH (Louis Vuitton Moët Hennessy)—is planning a Louis Vuitton museum in Paris to showcase the art that inspired LVMH designers like Marc Jacobs and Christian Dior.[26] The line between for-profit and nonprofit art undertakings becomes blurrier.

Partnerships between artists and designers have been many and fruitful (and not necessarily blatantly commercial) as their public expressions have become wildly overstated in recent years. The Chanel Mobile Art Pavilion is a dramatic example of how art and, specifically, video have become attractive accessories for the fashion industry. The pavilion, designed by renowned architect Zaha Hadid and championed by designer Karl Lagerfeld, was conceived of as a spaceship-like traveling container in which twenty international artists would exhibit art required to relate to Chanel's 2.55 quilted, chain-strap handbag.

In April 2008, the 7,500-square-foot pavilion opened in Hong Kong, followed by a stop in Tokyo before finishing its tour in New York's Central Park. At each site, entrance to the pavilion was free, but visitors needed one of the limited number of tickets, all 23,000 of which sold out within hours of becoming available; in this respect Chanel was able to feign an egalitarian art-is-for-everyone air while retaining the exclusivity of its brand.

As part commercial and part contemporary art spectacle, Mobile Art's PR machine expertly orchestrated an event that was excessively hyped and hypnotically slick.[27] Before the art pod even landed in New York, the Mobile Art website flaunted a sophisticated use of video, broadcasting time-lapse video of the pavilion's construction, MTV-like clips of opening parties, virtual visits to the Hong Kong and Tokyo locations, and taped press conferences starring Lagerfeld and

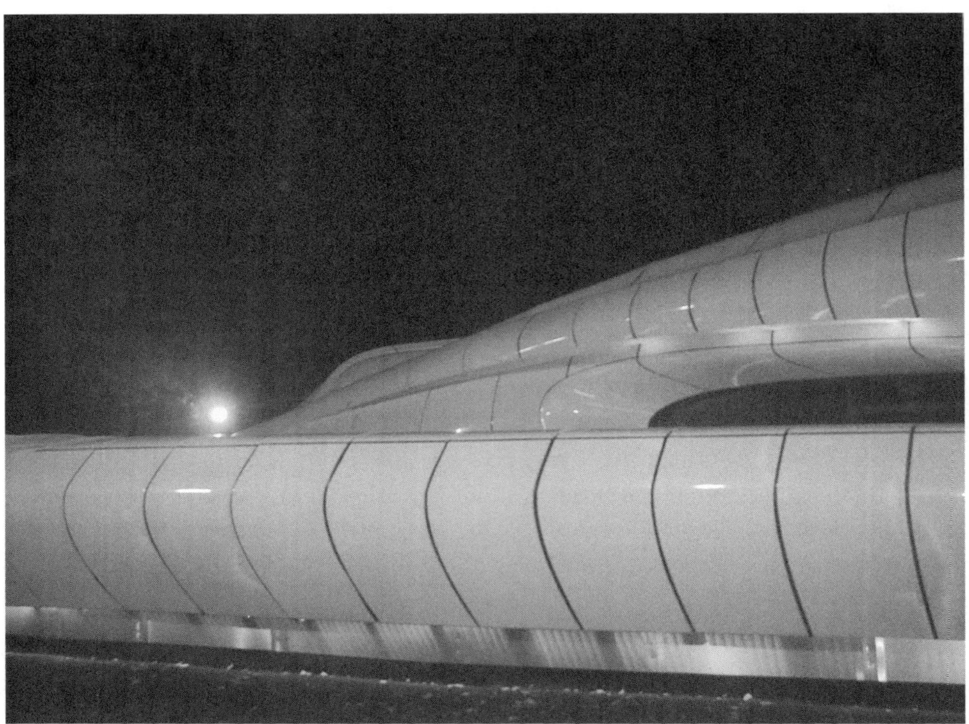

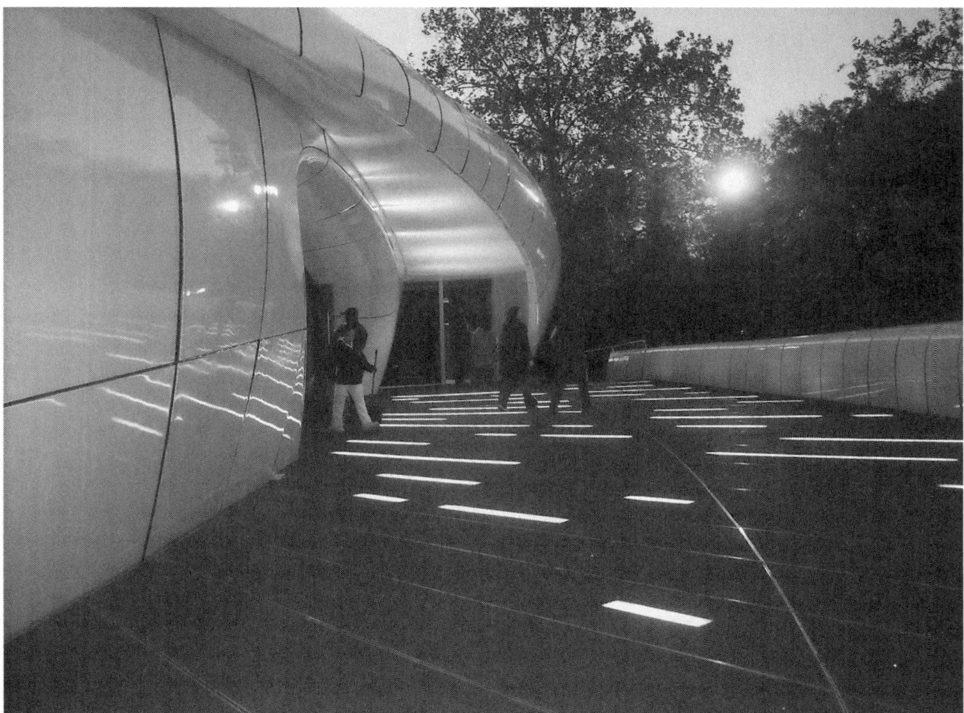

Exterior view of the Zaha Hadid–designed Chanel Mobile Art Pavilion, a 7,500-square-foot temporary art container installed in New York's Central Park from October 20, 2008, to November 9, 2008. Photographs by Catherine Taft.

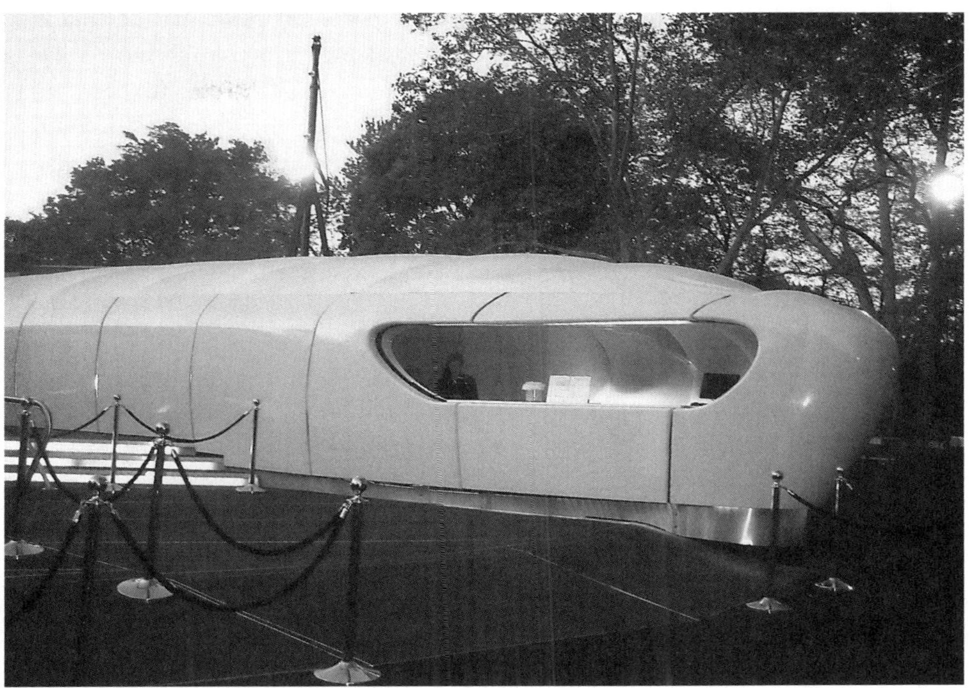

Exterior view of the Zaha Hadid–designed Chanel Mobile Art Pavilion, a 7,500-square-foot temporary art container installed in New York's Central Park from October 20, 2008, to November 9, 2008. Photograph by Catherine Taft.

Hadid. Just as the project's publicity was a typically contrived affair, so too was the physical experience of moving through the Chanel installation itself. From the minute one queued up to enter the capsule, a highly controlled form of spectatorship began; each visitor was escorted into the exhibition and fitted with a personal MP3 player through which the recorded, seductive voice of French actress Jeanne Moreau guided the viewer throughout the space. An audio track called a Soundwalk, by French artist Stephan Crasneanscki, directed the viewer where and when to move and at what to look; described the artwork for the viewer while offering a short narrative for images and objects; and instructed viewers to participate with certain pieces, like Yoko Ono's *Wish Tree.* Curated by Fabrice Bousteau, editor in chief of the French magazine *Beaux Arts,* Chanel Mobile Art included international artists Sophie Calle, Daniel Buren, David Levinthal, Y. Z. Kami, Leandro Erlich, Nobuyoshi Araki, and Stephen Shore. Though the roster of artists was certainly impressive, many of the works on view presented either predictable, advertisement-like imagery or a formulaic, forced edginess, as with Araki's slide show of women bound by purse straps, Levinthal's S/M photos of mannequins hooded and gagged with purse leather, or an oversized teddy bear chained to the padded walls of a shipping container.[28]

Works incorporating video were similarly problematic or just peculiarly placed. One of the first works encountered was Japanese artist Tabimo's *At the Bottom*, a large, well-like projection space that viewers gazed into to view animated images allegedly inspired by the dreams of Chanel customers (chrysalis forms hatching butterflies, ocean waves turning into abstracted soaring birds). Indian artist Subodh Gupta contributed the video installation *All Things Are Inside*, which juxtaposed clips from Bollywood films in which a purse was a major narrative element with images of laborers and street scenes. The Russian collective Blue Noses produced *Fifty Years after Our Common Era or Handbags' Revolt*, a sculptural installation in which video projections on the bottoms of large cardboard boxes depicted nude women in a stop-motion-like frenzy of purse chasing. Sylvie Fleury's *Crystal Custom Commando* presented an oversized Chanel handbag tipped on its side to reveal a larger-than-life Chanel makeup compact; in place of a mirror, a monitor revealed a futuristic scenario of Barbarella-like bombshells riding motorcycles and using various models of Chanel handbags for target practice, all the while looking perfectly coiffed. It is important to note that only one work was intentionally left out of the New York Mobile Art installation, *Jesus and Chanel Bags*, Belgian artist Wim Delvoye's tattooed taxidermy pigs that came with matching purses.[29] While the religious undertones of this work may have been judged as too provocative for (even post-Giuliani) New York audiences, images of sexualized violence, the misogynistic portrayal of women, and incongruous commentary on global labor issues seemed unchecked in the curation of this show.

Although Chanel planned to send the Mobile Art exhibition to London, Moscow, and Paris, it cancelled the tour after the U.S. dates, citing the September 2008 downturn of the U.S. economy and using the official line, "The image that such an event would have conveyed in the next cities would no longer have been in the spirit of the times."[30] Lagerfeld seems to admit the point was marketing, "We had so much press [after Hong Kong and Tokyo] that there was little more to add. . . . I always thought the building was a sculpture. I prefer it empty."[31] Opening October 20, 2008, the poor timing of the New York exhibition began to taint Chanel Mobile Art with the impression of consumerist excess in the face of economic collapse. *New York Times* architecture critic Nicolai Ouroussoff published a derisive review of the project, stating:

> The pavilion sets out to drape an aura of refinement over a cynical marketing gimmick. Surveying its self-important exhibits, you can't help but hope that the era of exploiting the so-called intersection of architecture, art and fashion is finally over. . . . The pavilion's coiled form, in which visitors spiral ever deeper into a black hole of bad art and superficial temptations, straying farther and farther from the real world outside, is

an elaborate mousetrap for consumers. The effortless flow between one space and the next, which in earlier projects suggested a desire to break down unwanted barriers, here suggests a surrender of individual will.[32]

Though one could easily argue that the Chanel Mobile Art Pavilion was a timely experiment in relational aesthetics—a conceptual rethinking of the white cube exhibition space that stresses an experimental, improvised, unfinished, and open-ended relationship between art and its surroundings—such an approach to the artwork (situated in the transparently commercial efforts of Chanel) seems fraught with conceptual and political pitfalls. In his 1998 publication *Relational Aesthetics,* critic and curator Nicolas Bourriaud articulates a new trend in European contemporary art that took "as its theoretical horizon the realm of human interactions and its social context, rather than the assertion of an independent and *private* symbolic space."[33] As Claire Bishop points out, however:

> Such work seems to derive from a creative misreading of poststructuralist theory: rather than the *interpretations* of a work of art being open to continual reassessment, the work of art *itself* is argued to be in perpetual flux. There are many problems with this idea, not least of which is the difficulty of discerning a work whose identity is willfully unstable. Another problem is the ease with which the "laboratory" [exhibition space] becomes marketable as a space of leisure and entertainment. . . . One could argue that in this context, project-based works-in-progress . . . begin to dovetail with an "experience economy," the marketing strategy that seeks to replace goods and services with scripted and staged personal experience.[34]

Perhaps, Chanel's Mobile Art project is best understood through the terms of "experience economy." As the company attempted to manufacture a kind of sophistication for its products it associated its goods (the Chanel handbag) with renowned artists and architects, garnering commercial value (and novelty) from the cultural authority of Art. And after all, what could be more "scripted and staged" than Jeanne Moreau whispering through an MP3 player, "Stay with me. Don't wander off. I *need* you, spectators . . . voyeurs"?[35]

It is not simply the fashion industry that has found new and dubious ways to capitalize on art and, specifically, video's intellectual prestige; even the art world itself—its dealers, critics, collectors, and artists, who have long profited from the salability of art as symbolic capital—is exercising a surprising degree of proprietary control over artistic production and how it exists in the world. Within the past decade, for example, the art world (particularly its emerging artists) has become incredibly fascinated with the mystique of the late Bas Jan Ader, a Dutch conceptual artist who lived and worked in Los Angeles from the mid-1960s to the mid-1970s. Ader's career was tragically cut short in 1975 when he set out to sail alone from Cape Cod to Ireland as part of his opus performance work *In Search of the Miraculous*. Ader was lost at sea with only the wreckage of his small boat recovered, yet he left behind a small, cohesive body of largely non-object-based work comprising photography, film, and other ephemera and documentation. Today, homage to Ader is not uncommon, perhaps because his actions and expressions still resonate with a life meticulously devoted to (or sacrificed for) art. Artists, including Skip Arnold, Lisa Rovner, and Fernando Sanchez, among countless others, have borrowed from his slight body of work, re-creating and referencing his films, quoting his writing, or sketching out his portrait. The official Bas Jan Ader web page even solicits and hosts video homages inspired by Ader's most renowned films, like *I'm Too Sad to Tell You* and *Fall I*.[36] Although the estate seems to be sanctioning and fostering the appropriation of Ader's oeuvre, this move more tellingly exposes how an estate can have jurisdiction over an artist's name, image, and aesthetic and their use in the public at large.

By no coincidence, Ader's resurgence is occurring at a time when many young artists, fresh from their MFA programs, are entering the art world with high expectations for success, the barometer of which is shaped by the monetary value of art. In many ways, Ader has become an icon for the posthumous market resuscitation of an artist's career and for the marketability of ephemeral art.[37] California artist David Horvitz's video-cum-action-film *Rarely Seen Bas Jan Ader Film* is one of the many works that reference Ader's life and career, but Horvitz cleverly sets this work apart by tapping into the fascination surrounding Ader while simultaneously subverting the marketability of his myth. In 2007 Horvitz uploaded a few seconds of film footage onto YouTube with the title *Rarely Seen Bas Jan Ader Film* and a description claiming that the otherwise incomplete or unusable film was found in Ader's locker at the University of California–Irvine (where Ader taught and where Horvitz currently teaches) sometime after he had disappeared. The short black-and-white footage depicts a figure riding a bicycle from the beach into the ocean before it abruptly stops.

Soon after it was posted, YouTube received a complaint from the representative of Ader's estate, Patrick Painter Gallery, and in response the gallery deleted the video from YouTube on the grounds that "this material [was] infringing."[38] Despite heated e-mails exchanged between Horvitz and Patrick Painter Gallery, Horvitz reposted the video to YouTube the very next day.

In 2009 Horvitz exhibited this project at 2nd Cannons Gallery in Los Angeles by displaying the video clip, a flip-book produced from stills of the footage, and a free broadsheet printed with a photograph of the ocean allegedly taken at Ader's intended location of arrival in Ireland.

The video was also available for free as an open edition of burned DVDs and

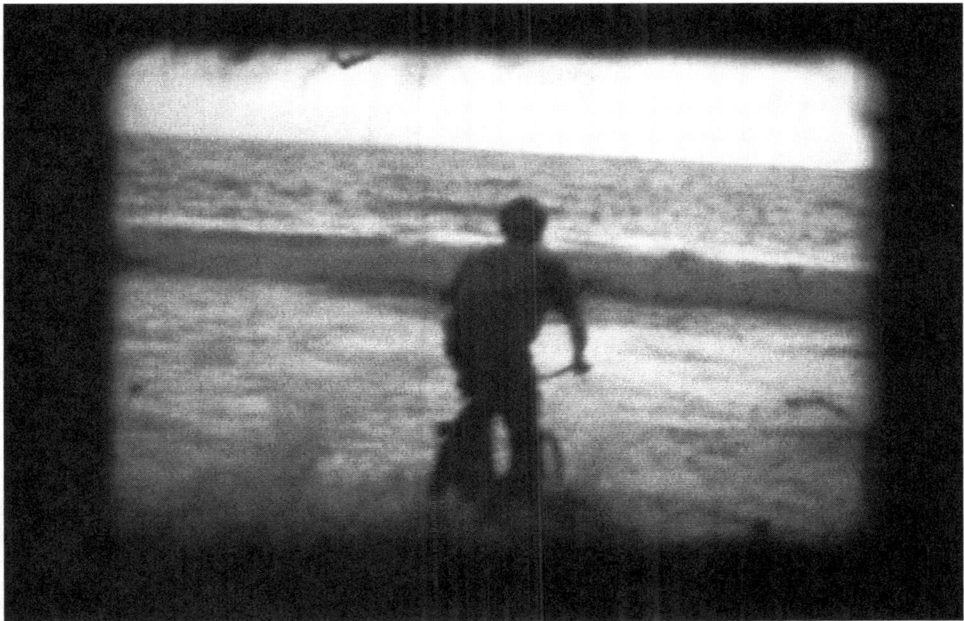

Video still from *Rarely Seen Bas Jan Ader Film* (2007) by David Horvitz. Single-channel video made from film transfer, black-and-white, 7 seconds. Photograph courtesy of David Horvitz and Brian Kennon.

as a free downloadable digital file.[39] In the months leading up to his exhibition, Horvitz posted a series of images of the ocean on his website and asked visitors to help him decide which to use for the newsprint edition. This sort of interactive and inclusive art making is not new to conceptual art, but it nevertheless seems like a surprising and unexpected course for a young artist to take. Given the opportunity for a solo exhibition, Horvitz's interest was not in making objects that would sell out but rather in spinning an elaborate narrative and fabricating intangible traces of an artwork, all the while engaging his viewers in the process.

Horvitz's use of YouTube as an alternative distribution platform marks a growing trend among young video artists to display and promote their work outside of the traditional gallery system. And as YouTube provides the ability for users to create their own channels, such sites also allow the public to take an active role in a type of curating or programming of video content. Although YouTube and similar websites have been used by network television corporations and other companies as a marketing tool, the majority of content is developed by private individuals from twenty-two different countries. In many ways, such social networking sites have empowered a new generation of artists and filmmakers to communicate and connect globally via their artistic production.[40] As with the early media and television experiments—artists broadcasting video

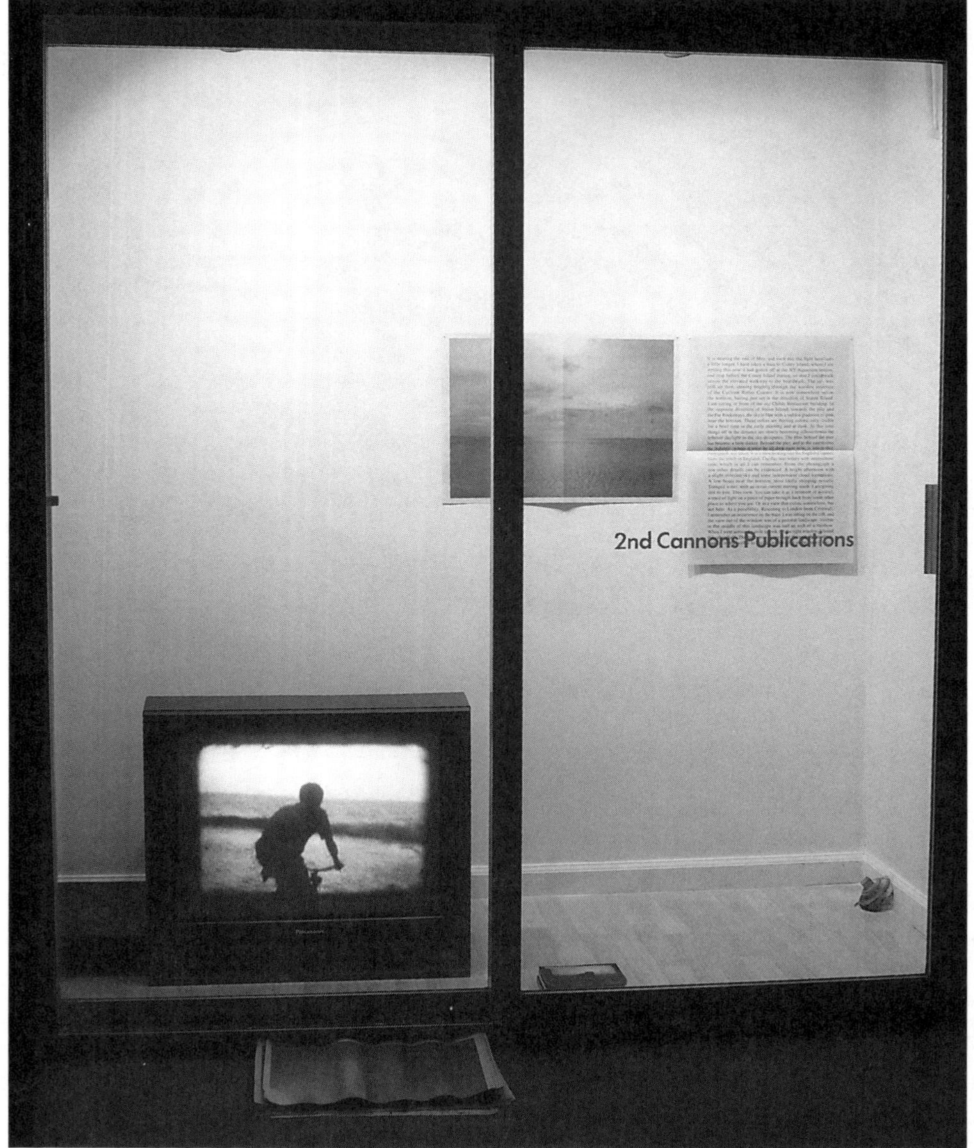

Installation view of *David Horvitz: Rarely Seen Bas Jan Ader Film* at 2nd Cannons Gallery, Los Angeles, June 27, 2009, to August 8, 2009. Photograph courtesy of 2nd Cannons Gallery and David Horvitz and Brian Kennon.

through purchased commercial air time, public access, early forms of cable, or early satellite systems—today's technologies serve as both raw material and practical tool in the endless sharing, streaming, uploading, editing, and repurposing of images and ideas. It is remarkable that in the market-driven economy of the early twenty-first century, media artists have a free and vital means of presenting their artwork and supporting others, regardless of commercial or institutional support, and a way to regain a degree control over what was once an otherwise received (or one-way) media reality.

How we see ourselves within contemporary life has always been prime material for video. In his unusual meditation *Sex, Art and the Dow Jones,* Jean-Charles Massera cites numerous artists' locating, internalized media identity.[41] How deeply are we as subjects created by advertising, television, pornography, and the Internet? Massera urges a return to considering oneself in relation to society:

> Get out of the logic that consists in letting ourselves be absorbed by the object of our obsessions. . . . Stop taking my immediate environment for the horizon. . . . Get away from intimacy and emotions to recreate a bond with the community from which we've retreated. . . . Strive to grasp the historical dimension of our experience—a dimension from which we have been separated. . . . If the subject has been cut off from History: Produce forms of experiencing this History. Get back in touch with History starting with what we are capable of grasping.[42]

The revelation that a huge percentage of the global economy is based on precarious financial instruments (boiling down to wagers on success or failure—remember the options on terrorist attacks?) acknowledges the elephant in the room.[43] No longer is it necessary to pretend that the so-called free market is invincible, nor that competition is fair and open to all.

Jon Ippolito promotes the use of open licensing as developed for Internet software and "copyleft" permissions for reproduction. Ippolito sees a danger that the art business might absorb online projects, prompting his argument that "property, intellectual or personal, is the enemy of art."[44] As he characterizes the lottery mentality (artists wary of criticizing art marketing for fear they might jeopardize their own, just-around-the-corner stardom), "To say the art market helps the starving artist is tantamount to saying the lottery helps the poor; it profits a tiny percentage, and distracts the rest from their impoverished social position with dreams of sudden affluence."[45] David Joselit also sounds a call to arms: "Imagine modes of art and art history that function as political science. Stop pretending to subvert commodification by demonstrating what everyone knows—that capital is everywhere. SEIZE THE WORLD AS A READYMADE and BREAK OPEN ITS CIRCUITS."[46] And Adrian Piper reminds us that artists are doomed in a game they cannot win: "In a free market if art does not sell it will not achieve the visibility required . . . but if it does sell, and thereby achieves such visibility, whatever positive ethos it might once have promoted will be subordinated in advance to the need to maximize profits."[47]

Art—and, in particular, video art—can choose to reevaluate itself and its worth to society as a whole. As Massera proposes, "If spectacular and mediatized forms speak on our behalf, if they are constantly addressing us as a generic, synthetic subjectivity founded on statistics and the market economy, then think-up forms that escape the control of instrumental reasoning while enabling us to reverse the communication trajectory that fixes us in the position of passive recipients."[48] The fantasy of art stardom need not be today's only goal. Jesse Drew inquires, "Is video art concerned only with new forms or the self-conscious use of the medium? Or can it work to reintegrate media practice with daily life, challenge complacency and cultural passivity, and confront the public's expectations and prejudices?"[49] Either artists will find some way to address these issues, or the most visible art—including video—will exist merely as window dressing for fancy shops and trophies in the vaults of private collectors.

NOTES

1. Liza Bear, *Video Pioneers,* color video, 30:00, 1977.

2. In 1988 Vito Acconci founded Acconci Studios, a collaborative team designing public architecture and space projects. He remarks that rather than viewers, he wishes to have "users, and inhabitants and participants." Bryant Rousseau, "The ArchRecord Interview," *Architectural Record,* http://archrecord.construction.com/features/interviews/0718Acconci/0718Acconci-1.asp.

3. Finn Tybo Andersen and Karena Nomi, eds., "Martha Rosler Talks" (transcription of discussion at Tea for 2000, Copenhagen, Denmark, 2000).

4. Jesse Drew, "The Collective Camcorder in Art and Activism," in *Collectivism after Modernism,* eds. Blake Stimson and Gregory Sholette (Minneapolis: University of Minnesota Press, 2007), 95–113.

5. David Antin, "Television: The Distinctive Features of the Medium," in *Video Art,* exhibition catalog (Philadelphia: Institute of Contemporary Art, 1975); republished with revisions as "Television: Video's Frightful Parent," *Artforum* 14, no. 4 (December 1975), 36–45.

6. See Chris Hill, "Attention! Production! Audience!—Performing Video in its First Decade, 1968–1980," Bay Area Video Coalition website, http://www.experimentaltvcenter.org/sites/default/files/history/pdf/hillattention_1063.pdf

7. Haggerty Museum of Art, *Fred Barzyk: The Search for a Personal Vision in Broadcast Television,* with contributions by Nam June Paik, Curtis L. Carter, Brian O'Doherty, Charles Johnson, Barbara London, George Fifield, Fred Barzyk, and Mary Ide (Milwaukee, Wis.: Haggerty Museum of Art, Marquette University, 2001).

8. Funded by the Corporation for Public Broadcasting, ITVS was established by a congressional mandate in 1991 to foster plurality and diversity in public television (http://itvs.org). Of the few remaining video funders, the Rockefeller Foundation notably awarded $35,000 fellowships to media artists working in all forms from 1988 to 2008. This program was since ended.

9. Gene Youngblood, *Radical Software* 1, no. 1 (Spring 1970): 16.

10. Adrian Piper, "A Proposal for Pricing Works of Art," *The Fox* 2 (1975): 48–49.

11. The Woman's Building was founded in 1973 and closed in 1991, and the Long Beach Museum of Art's Video Program operated from 1974 through 1999.

12. Paper Tiger Television's current projects include an examination of gentrification in Brooklyn and the right to the city movement for urban justice.

13. Alan Moore, "A Brief History of the MWF Video Club," in *Captured: A Film/Video History of the Lower East Side,* ed. Clayton Patterson (New York: Seven Stories Press, 2005). The MWF Club has ceased distribution, concentrating on an attempt to archive all its materials.

14. Glenn Phillips, ed. *California Video: Artists and Histories* (Los Angeles: Getty Research Institute, 2008), 231.

15. Stephen Pizzo, Mary Fricker, and Paul Muolo, authors of *Inside Job: The Looting of America's Savings and Loans* (New York: McGraw Hill, 1989), list figures and cite numerous examples, such as that of Don Dixon, who took his wife, Dana, to a special audience with His Holiness the Pope where they presented the pontiff with an Olaf Weghorst painting of an American Indian. The ironies here are almost too much to bear: valued at $40,000, the painting was actually owned by Vernon Savings and Loan.

16. See auction results for Bruce Nauman at the VideoArtWorld website, accessed June 28, 2012, http://www.videoartworld.com/srch_results.php?keyword=Nauman§ion=Auctions.

17. David Ross, "A Provisional Overview of Artists' Television in the US," in *New Artists Video,* ed. Gregory Battcock (New York: Penguin, 1978), 142. Ross also remarks in the same essay that "since video, like much conceptual performance work, is essentially uncollectible, its patrons must focus on the sponsorship of inquisitive rather than acquisitive activity" (146).

18. Hermine Freed, "Collecting Video," *Print Collector's Newsletter* 8, no. 4 (1977): 109–12.

19. "After Modernism's Nervous Breakdown, What Do Artists Want?" in *Wounds: Between Democracy and Redemption in Contemporary Art,* ed. David Elliot (Stockholm: Moderna Museet, 1998), 27–34.

20. Thierry de Duve, *Kant after Duchamp* (Cambridge: MIT Press, 1996), 350.

21. Julian Stallabrass, *Art, Incorporated: The Story of Contemporary Art* (New York: Oxford University Press, 2004), 200–201.

22. This work recently was on view in *Moving Image: Scan to Screen, Pixel to Projection,* organized by Karen Moss for the Orange County Museum of Art, Newport Beach, California, April 12 to September 27, 2009. A similar example of a video artist achieving master-like acclaim is evident in the recent exhibition of Bill Viola alongside Leonardo da Vinci at the Italian Cultural Institute of Los Angeles from December 2 to 12, 2009; see "Leonardo da Vinci and Bill Viola," Italian Cultural Institute of Los Angeles website, http://www.iiclosangeles.esteri.it/IIC_LosAngeles/webform/SchedaEvento.aspx?id=333&citta=LosAngeles.

23. In an e-mail exchange between Buchanan and an artist enrolled in a studio doctorate program, the student earnestly stated that as a rule an edition of videos should consist of no more than five.

24. Chris Townsend, *Rapture: Art's Seduction by Fashion* (New York: Thames and Hudson, 2002), 12.

25. As an example of the importance of handbags in the current culture, in June 2009 Reuters broke the news that the French luxury goods brand Hermès had established its own crocodile farms in Australia in order to meet the high demand for exotic leather handbags, some of which cost over $50,000. Such leather goods account for 40 percent of the company's business, perhaps explaining why Hermès would resort to animal cruelty for profit.

26. Don Thompson, *The $12 Million Stuffed Shark: The Curious Economics of Contemporary Art* (New York: Palgrave Macmillan, 2008). 98, 220.

27. On October 30, 2008, we visited the Chanel Mobile Art pavilion in New York. We were able to secure two tickets (after much difficulty) through the generous assistance of a friend whose relative worked in senior-level marketing for a major national department store.

Though we remained critical and questioning of the project at large, the entire experience of traveling to and moving through the exhibition was thrilling and delightful—the kind of fantasy one would expect from a multimillion-dollar commercial undertaking.

28. Could this have been a sly reference to Lagerfeld's limited-edition teddy bear, wearing dark glasses and black leather? See Amy Odell, "Get Your Karl Lagerfeld Teddy Bear for Just $1,500!," *New York,* August 22, 2008, http://nymag.com/daily/fashion/2008/08/get_your_karl_lagerfeld_teddy.html.

29. Images of the artwork can be found at http://ifitshipitshere.wordpress.com/2008/03/10/the-mobile-chanel-art-exhibit-2.

30. See www.chanel-mobileart.com.

31. "Chanel Puts the Brakes on Mobile Exhibition," *Blouin Artinfo,* December 24, 2008, http://www.artinfo.com/news/story/29882/chanel-puts-brakes-on-mobile-exhibition.

32. Nicolai Ouroussoff, "Art and Commerce Canoodling in Central Park," *New York Times,* October 20, 2008, http://www.nytimes.com/2008/10/21/arts/design/21zaha.html?_r=1&ref=arts.

33. Emphasis is in original. Nicolas Bourriaud, *Relational Aesthetics* (Paris: Presses du Reel, 1998), 14.

34. Emphases are in original. Claire Bishop, "Antagonism and Relational Aesthetics," *October* 110 (Fall 2004): 51–79.

35. Excerpt transcribed from Stephan Crasneanscki's Chanel Mobile Art audio guide. The Chanel Mobile Art website describes Crasneanscki's practice as creating "cutting-edge audio guides in which the listener is able to step into the life of a narrator as they guide you through their neighborhood streets and local hang-outs. Soundwalk mixes fiction and reality in a cinematic experience giving the listener the impression of being in a film." See "Soundwalk" under "The Exhibition" and "The Artists" at www.chanel-mobileart.com. For Chanel Mobile Art it appears that Crasneanscki wanted to give the listener the impression of being in a Chanel commercial.

36. See www.basjanader.com.

37. A similar posthumous revival is now happening with the career of Guy de Cointet, another Los Angeles–based European artist from the 1970s who died tragically young and left behind a cryptic and ephemeral body of work. In such instances, estates and dealers are likely to create editioned series of reproducible works—photographs and videos—as saleable items.

38. In conversation with 2nd Cannons Gallery's Brian Kennon, July 2009; quote taken from a press release for David Horvitz's *Rarely Seen Bas Jan Ader Film* exhibition at 2nd Cannons Gallery, June 27–August 8, 2009. When YouTube users upload a video, a warning message is always displayed by the host site, stating, "Do not upload any TV shows, music videos, music concerts or commercials without permission unless they consist entirely of content you created yourself. The Copyright Tips page and the Community Guidelines can help you determine whether your video infringes someone else's copyright."

39. The download was previously available at http://www.davidhorvitz.com/index4.html. On January 6, 2012, Horvitz posted on his website, "A few days before the New Year I decided to remove all the content off my web-site, and start this blog from scratch" (http://davidhorvitz.com/wordpress/?tag=video). The download is no longer available, yet this also reflects the fluid and transient relationship Horvitz has to his artistic production.

40. Artists that have presented their video work on YouTube include Brian Bress, Ryan Trecartin, Kalup Linzy, and Jennifer Sullivan, among countless others. Although some of these artists have gained commercial recognition and have begun showing in galleries, much of their work is still available for free online.

41. Jean-Charles Massera, *Sex, Art and the Dow Jones* (New York: Lukas and Sternberg, 2003).

42. Ibid., 78.

43. Noah Shachtman, "The Case for Terrorism Futures," *Wired,* July 30, 2003, http://www.wired.com/politics/law/news/2003/07/59818.

44. John Ipplito, "Why Art Should Be Free," three.org, http://three.org/ippolito/writing/why_art_should_be_free. Jon Ippolito's "Why Art Should Be Free" was originally published in August 2002 on the Listservs rhizome.org and nettime.org. A version entitled "The Digital Sanctuary" was subsequently printed in Lucy Kimbell, ed., *New Media Art: Practice and Context in the UK 1994–2004* (London: Arts Council England/Cornerhouse, 2004).

45. Ipplito, "Why Art Should Be Free."

46. David Joselit, *Feedback: Television against Democracy* (Cambridge: MIT Press, 2007), 175.

47. Diarmuid Costello and Dominic Willsdon, introduction to *The Life and Death of Images,* ed. Diarmuid Costello and Dominic Willsdon (Ithaca, N.Y.: Cornell University Press, 2008), 25.

48. Massera, *Sex, Art and the Dow Jones,* 109.

49. Drew, *Collectivism after Modernism,* 97.

New Media States

WEB 2.0 AND EMBEDDED VIDEO PRACTICE

Kenneth Rogers

> The NEW MEDIA STATE is predicated on media control. The NEW
> MEDIA STATE is dependent on television for its existence.
>
> » Richard Serra, *Television Delivers People*

In Richard Serra's famous 1973 polemic against television, a series of strident theses on TV scroll upwards on a blank, blue screen, accompanied by a sound track of cheery Muzak noxiously chirping in the background. His point of attack is the mainstream commercial broadcast paradigm, which he describes in all caps as the NEW MEDIA STATE, in which the carefully managed collusion between the corporate oligarchy and state power has served to keep the ownership and control of the means of television production and distribution out of the public realm. One of the piece's more provocative implications is the notion that television spectators are not consumers of products but products consumed, converted into demographic blocs that can be quantified, aggregated, and sold to advertisers.

When Serra produced *Television Delivers People,* he was likely unaware how prescient his assessment of the television spectator truly was. Today, video products of all kinds are embedded within online architectures that have refined, with increasing statistical accuracy and specificity, techniques for extracting information and data from spectators to sell to advertisers. Paradoxically, a more thoroughgoing monetization of the television spectator—now more appropriately termed the *user*—has been achieved through a system in which strict hegemonic control of broadcast content has appreciably decreased. In its day the audience for *Television Delivers People* was a generation of alternative video practitioners working in the shadow of that system, but the generation confronting today's dominant media paradigm finds it comprised of a more distributed array of technologies and cultures that lacks the centralized verticality critiqued by Serra.

One of the more urgent questions faced by video practice today is how to act against this new distributed system—how to use new media technologies to continue to exert pressure upon systems of privilege and power, as well as to critique and provide constructive alternatives to dominant assemblages of technology, society, and politics.[1] It progressively becomes more apparent that the strategic interventions advanced during the early decades of video practice have diminished in their forcefulness. Virtually all of the early nonstandard genres of video have been incorporated into the culture at large. The use of site-specific video installation can be encountered in almost any airport, office lobby, or shopping mall; the struggle for horizontal networks of video distribution has been superficially allayed by platforms like YouTube, Vimeo, and Google Video; the destandardized, retooled apparatus found in everything from television *décollage* and raster art to large-scale video projection loses its impact as video sprouts like a weed from every crevice and at every scale, from the minuscule screens on tablets and smartphones to gargantuan video projections and flat-screen TVs. The availability of affordable production and postproduction tools has spawned—among other things—video genres of appropriation, reediting, and redistribution. Reappropriations of commercial TV are now commonplace in Web video mashups; guerrilla video culture is echoed in the ambush tactics of the legions of TMZ video paparazzi and reality television programs; and the politics of identity, personal narratives, and the aesthetics of amateurism have been incorporated into a massive, sprawling subgenre of countless uploaded video confessionals. Grassroots video culture often consumes much of its resources not by organizing around a cause but by creating pings of viral chic that hope to capture clickactivist market share of the global attention economy. The formerly disruptive insertion of video into the international museum and gallery system has given way to its commodification and seamless integration into that system as simply one among many media comprising the artist's palette.

Perhaps, video practice was victimized by its own success, and it was inevitable that the strategies once intent on producing vibrant and creative responses to the layered anatomies of power would inevitably be outflanked, rendered ineffective by the very power they once critiqued. Because many early video practices have been unwittingly conscripted by hegemonic power, the anxiety over the potential subsumption of video practice into the dominant logic of free-market capitalism generally tends to shape the next wave of that practice around the narrative of the unrelenting forces of co-optation. This has encouraged the impetus toward tactical avant-gardism, reinforced by the presumed effectiveness of a video practice that acts quickly to forestall co-optation's front wave. Although useful in certain cases or at certain instances, when overemphasized this line of action plays a one-dimensional politics of fashion that binds the idea of politically efficacious media to that which must remain forever in advance of the mainstream. The drawback of a purely tactical tendency is that it can lead to careless technological fetishism—a gratuitous use of the most recent material advances of video and media technology without thinking through their embedded relations. Video practice based on emphasizing a shallow love affair with smartphone apps, geomapping technology, video chat, or social media often results in artists and activists inadvertently providing an independent wing of early-adopter market research for such technologies and platforms. For example, since both the 2009 Iranian election protests (widely portrayed as having been ignited by viral video) and the 2011 Arab Spring used cellular-based SMS and social media technologies as organizational tools, they were coined "Twitter revolutions" by the American mainstream media, illustrating how the popular misconception of revolutionary technological determinism can result in delivering measurable cachet to the social media industry. Despite such misrepresentations, the advantages of the tactical media approach are that it moves beyond the binary distinction between mainstream and alternative media and the tired notion that power unfailingly adapts to resistance. It has provided a flexible way to mobilize against the deterritorialized power of capital through direct action using a DIY sensibility and drawing from the latest available *détourned* tools. Yet in too often privileging the rhetoric of the tool itself over the larger strategy of social organization around it and in preferring the quick strike to the long engagement, it often foregoes the possibility of building forms of sustainable media practice: networks, groups, systems, and projects that can remain in place, adapt, and regenerate over longer periods of time—a long and slow approach that takes time to develop and patience to execute.[2]

There are other approaches to understanding the changing role of video practice that branch out of the tactical media and sidestep the co-optation narrative. The aforementioned examples become merely a single aspect of a more extensive and systemic transformation in video within a changing context of social, political, and technological relations. This article is an attempt to understand one of these developments: the logic of embedded video practice, a practice that no longer qualifies the medium as stand-alone but as always already inextricable from a complex of other social practices and media technologies. Although *embedded* is a technical term borrowed from Web API (Application Protocol Interface), which permits cross-communication between platforms, applications, programs, and objects, I am not interpreting the term in a strictly technological sense. Rather, I am specifically referring to how technological conditions are indistinguishable from social and political ones—or more precisely, how the technological order has become embedded in the social and political order and, conversely, the social and political in the technological. Seeking to uncover this larger principle of overlap in technosociality and technopolitics in the constrained proportions of embedded video practice is a way of pursuing a more general strategy in an emergent logic of media organization that is characterized no longer by a system of vertical institutional power but by one of open and flexible power, a power immanent to the things it governs.[3] This dispersed, flexible model of immanent power does not depose the older model of hegemonic and vertical media organization but coexists alongside it, reorganizing those older structures of power common to the general political-economic imperatives of neoliberal globalization. Embedded video practice is indicative of the operations of that power, but it also refers to the use of techniques of insinuation and virality that can invent sustainable alternative systems based on transcoding and adjacency—i.e., simultaneously relevant to multiple spheres of practice, forms of technology, and cultural spaces.

If we return to 1973, when Serra launched his attack against the new media state, his theses targeted what was then the reigning hegemony of vertically integrated television networks that maintained control through centralized monopolies on content driven by a profit model based on consumer advertising. Although the forms of monopolistic competition that emerged as the dominant paradigm of U.S. television appeared to be shaped by the euphoric postwar consumer boom, the precedent in national policy for the three network media monopolies had already been set by the Radio Act of 1927, which solidified a collusive relationship between the state and the privatized, for-profit commercial networks, thus signaling the death knell for decentralized, independent, nonprofit, and local radio production.[4] Television emerged with the commercial broadcast paradigm ready at hand, and the visual medium immediately found itself operating in perfect symbiosis with the centralized, corporate market economy based on promoting an ethos of freedom through consumer choice. In other words, early television bypassed a more self-determining, bottom-up phase of social and technological development and arrived with its economic and structural model already in place from the radio days.

For Serra and his contemporaries, as well as the generation of video practitioners that followed, the struggle against the centralized communication paradigm was paramount. The diverse strategies that have come to characterize the first three decades of video practice were often situated in opposition to the hegemonic forces of mainstream television. During the 1960s and 1970s, organizations like Videofreex, the Raindance Corporation, Global Village, TVTV, and the People's Video Theater established alternative video practices based on forms of revolutionary collectivism and direct democracy. Utopian and countercultural, they based these alternative practices around a response to centralized media institutions through the promotion of democratized access to video production technology. *Radical Software,* a journal founded in 1970 by the Raindance Corporation and edited by Paul Ryan, Ira Schneider, and Beryl Korot, was influential in creating a video counterpublic sphere by opening up a discursive space in which strategies of direct response in video aesthetics, politics, and technology could be discussed collectively. Guerilla video tactics, such as those advocated by Michael Shamberg, outlined ways for the portable videographer to mount run-and-gun strikes that would capture events that could provide an on-the-ground perspective that was not filtered through network monopolies, while feminist video makers mounted a formidable critique against gender inequity. Throughout the 1980s artists like Dara Birnbaum initiated a transition from social and political organizational strategies to the tactic of talking back to the mainstream media in its own idiom. Rather than attempt to create a sustainable outside, these strategies of appropriation reedited the dominant language of television to bring to the surface hidden and naturalized ideological subtexts.[5] Paper Tiger Television sought democratized, equitable access to free speech via television and the right to express dissenting points of view. The proliferation of media channels during the 1990s' tech boom witnessed the widening of cable bandwidth, the growth of direct-broadcast satellites, the expansion of the HTML Internet browser, and the rise of digital video, yet nearly all of these narrowcast alternatives were still fixed in the realm of individual consumer choice. As a result, the important rise of identity-based work about race, class, gender, sexuality, politics, Indigenous and postcolonial experience, nationalism, and globalization, all tendencies that provided video practice with a polyvocal identitarian diversity, was often caught between polarized ideologies, whether the hard censorship pressure coming from the reactionary Right (the ongoing legacy of the culture wars) or the soft manufacture of consent from the corporate shills of the establishment Left (the depoliticized, humanist inclusiveness of a Benetton ad). Concurrent with all of this, video played an important role in the changing face of studio art practice by placing institutional pressure on the maintenance of Bourdieuian class distinction through the judgment of taste in high art.

Clearly, the layered history of video practice cannot be characterized as a unified front but a plurality of genres, schools, and tactics. Likewise, mainstream television itself comprises its own internal heterogeneity resulting from its numerous layered transitions between technological platforms, as well as the diversification of audiences and programming in the effort to expand and capture new and emerging markets. The heterogeneous strategies that characterized video practice from the mid-1960s to the early 2000s shared, however, a common concern: they were bound together by the fact that they either explicitly or implicitly applied oppositional pressure to the dominant technopolitical paradigm of the commercial broadcast system that had been in place since the early 1950s. Although the concerns and tactics of video practices have been diverse, from the creation of countercultural networks and publics to the unearthing of subjugated knowledges and histories, video practice is always and invariably situated in opposition to the mainstream media, which remains the leviathan against which these alternative traditions are defined.

What has remained constant throughout this paradigm has been its primary orientation around the capture and manipulation of market share through the monopoly and ownership of and the control over content. The television industry's cultural forms and genres, strategies, demographic models, platforms of production and distribution, and market capital have been constantly undergoing revision and modification, but what has endured through these modifications is the fundamental idea of content monopoly. Simply put, the source of television's power and capital is located in its capacity to monopolize control over content at every level of production and to force this content to travel through the bottleneck of its vertical distribution apparatus. In equal measure, the overwhelming tendency of alternative video practice has been content based, albeit in a counterhegemonic way. The efficacy of critique and of countermeasures against the corporate monopoly on content has been based on the production of alternative content that subverts this system and speaks from that system's inassimilable margins. In many ways this was an effective and empowering strategy of response to the dominant assemblage of media power at the time of video's arrival, but the approach also carries with it an enduring legacy that may be less suitable for the situation we confront today. This situation derives from the fact that video practice has long overemphasized the power of the text-based approach, a notion widely reinforced in critical theory that art, media, and cultural productions are essentially autonomous textual objects that contain meaning or content to be received and interpreted by a viewer. Grant Kester terms this notion the "textual paradigm," and it still holds a kind of rhetorical primacy within critical art discourse.[6] There is nothing inherently wrong with or meaningless or ineffective about content-centric approaches to video practice. In fact, when facing the particular assemblage I outline, one could argue that it was a historically appropriate response to the reigning logic of technopolitical organization. The problem is that this logic has undergone significant alteration during the past decade so as to diminish the effectiveness of content-centric video practice. The content-centric/text-based approach within video practice should be reevaluated against the logic of embedded video in Web 2.0.

This essay fleshes out a few ideas of what this crucial alteration might constitute and how it might affect the future of video practice. As noted, the mainstream media paradigm has been undergoing modifications and expansions since the arrival of broadcast television in the early 1950s, yet only recently has it adopted a model of video-based production and distribution that runs counter to content monopolization not from the subversive margins of free-market capitalism but rather from its center. This model is coextensive with the widely discussed transition to Web 2.0, the next layer of Web tools and applications that emphasize user-oriented and social networking services and applications rather than treat the Web as a platform for decentralized content delivery. Generally speaking, the interfaces and systems of Web 2.0 allow users to upload and produce their own content by offering services that facilitate interaction with other users in the system and permit access to the content and information those users upload. Blogs; wikis; social networking sites; online text, photo, and video editing services; open-source CMS systems; social bookmarking; and playlist management systems are just some of the online applications that have risen in recent years and begun to significantly reshape the flow of Internet traffic. A combination of technological, political, and social factors have converged to make the conditions for Web 2.0 possible. The general increase in bandwidth, advances in search functions, and the dramatic drop in the cost of cloud data storage have lead to a shift in the attitude and culture of Web users, who have become more oriented around free resources, sociality, community, and networking, while policies that precariously support net neutrality have so far prevented the seizure of higher-bandwidth traffic for select groups. The new way of understanding the Web has moved away from viewing it as a portal for accessing externally generated and managed content and toward envisioning it as a conglomeration of software and applications that permit users to create and share their own content. The recent undoing of the disastrous merger between Time Warner and AOL symbolizes the end of an old regime. The decoupling of the Internet service provider from the content provider is a telling indicator that the era of a broadcast network/content-based Web has receded while the profiles of corporations like Google, Netflix, and Facebook, who have no direct ownership of or governance over the infrastructure that delivers their various products, have become dominant. The power to influence network organization has moved into the hands of firms who organize and manage content rather than those who produce and distribute it.

In regards to its effect on the public sphere, the prognosis of Web 2.0 within network theory has reached both the utopian and the dystopian ends of the spectrum. Critics like Yochai Benkler suggest that Web 2.0 is indicative of a powerfully progressive move toward a "networked information economy" that permits a greater potential for democratized social discourse in the public sphere through individual communication liberated from the industrial information economy. Broadcast television is, for example, part of the industrial information economy in that it is a model of mass production applied to information and thus delimits users' participation, as they have agency only at the site of reception, much in the same way that users can choose whether or not to consume a product.[7] Ben Roberts cautions that Benkler's unbridled optimism that the networked space can not only facilitate rational debate among communities but actually bring about effective political change is actually a misreading of Habermas, who maintains that the public sphere should remain a solely discursive space and never engage in direct political action. Benkler somewhat naïvely presumes that political empowerment can be achieved through the concepts already essential to the tenets of liberal democracy. Roberts also critiques Benkler's explanation of how the Web creates systems of "nonmarket production" like file sharing or the uploading of user-produced content for exchange in Web-based gift economies by examining whether these might be nothing more than the exploitation of user labor through the extraction of surplus value.[8]

Indeed, it is hard not to see both faces of this debate in many of the tools and tactics within Web 2.0. As much as Web 2.0 undoubtedly offers new arrangements of possibility, a healthy suspicion of the reigning economic base that drives the participatory user-oriented systems of the networked information economy is absolutely critical. The fine line between the two sides of the Web 2.0 debate becomes even less distinct when one considers how the new media arrangement between a Web host or platform and the end user involves a whole complex of interdependent economic incentives. The incentive of the user is usually viewed as the potential for various types of cultural empowerment through open exchange—e.g., the sharing around common interests, identities, communities, or political orientations—whereas the economic incentive of the host is to hook the end user by offering a system that enables these exchanges. This crowdsourcing profit model offers free services that enable users to create profiles and produce and distribute content that appears on a given site, which will effectively draw in more users, increasing the site's profitability. Social networking sites like Facebook, YouTube, Pinterest, and Instagram accumulate their capital from a cytoarchitectonic organization of prosumers—end users who are both the producers and consumers of content. Such sites profit little from original content but simply organize cellular affordances that delimit the shape in which these cellular content exchanges can occur. The real profit is then made by monetizing the users' digital footprints as they navigate the site, share information, upload documents, make posts, and interact with other users.

Although there may be grounds for identifying the progressive potential of the networked information economy seen by Benkler, one should do so with caution. When a site like Amazon's Mechanical Turk uses crowdsourcing to pool user labor for online employers who assign tasks that resemble addictive play at wages far below the minimum in a more or less unregulated space, it is quite evident that Web 2.0 is not simply a benign upgrade of an outdated model of the Internet. Web 2.0 is a new technopolitical assemblage that extends global economic inequities into the realm of network society and creates concentrations of capital in zones Manuel Castels describes as "the space of flows."[9] A soft and flexible model of power effectively operates within this advancing system in a variety of ways: the capture, codification, and monetization of user attention; the capitalization of user-generated content without compensation; the exploitation of user labor in ways that are not coded as labor but as self-interested DIY projects; and the channeling of content around hubs of exchange. These are all indications that Web 2.0 is part of a widespread economic strategy that collapses concepts of political freedom with market freedom and diminishes the potential for collectivity, civic awareness, and the ability to place pressure upon the sphere of the public authority. Curiously, socially networked Web 2.0 platforms create the semblance of a free space of exchange by maintaining the window dressing of the older broadcast paradigm. The YouTube case is exemplary. It embraces the Web 2.0 model, and yet the visual brand of the site wraps that utility in a skeuomorph of the video tube, and its motto commands, "Broadcast Yourself," as if to assert that users are finally freely empowered to enter the fray of the dominant broadcast paradigm as individuals who had formerly been denied access to the mode of mass distribution. But such a liberation can be boasted only after the power behind it has already been neutralized and the driving monetization apparatus of YouTube has been divested from its control over content.

Video hosting sites emerge as an essential aspect of Web 2.0, and as a consequence, much of video practice has been thoroughly restructured around this divestment from a content-centered/text-based paradigm. The broadcast paradigm commands market share through a content monopoly that delineates the mainstream from other alternative/minor forms of content in order to maintain and maximize a viewership that remains attentive to that programming. Web 2.0 video hosting sites function by organizing an open space that encourages users to produce and distribute their video content to a (potentially) mass audience (but, more likely, to a very narrow and culturally specific one), and this user-generated content freely comingles with commercial content. Broadcast television produces an audience of spectators that can then be sold to an advertiser; Web 2.0 channels seek a critical mass of users who offer up their free labor in voluntarily accumulating a diversity of readily available content for the site. Broadcast is vertical in its organization; it maintains control at every level of production and distribution. Web 2.0 is not so much horizontal as molecular in that it strictly determines the protocols of exchange between each node in the system. Broadcast is decisively text centered in its systemic organization—it adheres to a sender/receiver transmission schematic from the point of broadcast to the point of reception (what Web 1.0 would term an *end user*). Web 2.0 involves a distributed schematic, collapsing the distinction between sender and receiver and creating an open-ended system where objects in circulation never reach an end destination but produce the experience of ongoing redistribution, or "successive dispersals"[10] without "terminal destination."[11] Of course, the broadcast paradigm still coexists with Web 2.0, but with a greatly diminished capacity to determine the governing strategic organization of the system. The new *dispositif* of Web 2.0 does not supplant the old but redistributes its interior lines of force into a new technopolitical layer.[12]

What does this mean for a video practice that seeks to put pressure upon the structural conditions of the new system? How can one act to provide constructive alternatives to the dominant assemblages? Embedded video is a uniquely situated development that comprises the complete expression of the system of flexible power but that also might enable this system's undoing. One of the peculiar contradictions of Web 2.0 is that each site's desire to command attention and market share is dependent upon the degree and facility with which it makes content on competing Web 2.0 sites available. The capacity to receive and present content from other sites with ease and to make one's own content available to those sites is an essential condition of its survival within this new mode of functionality. Video-based social bookmarking sites like MyVidster, Videosift, or the now defunct Vodpod, for example, provide no video hosting capacity of their own but simply use embedded technology to facilitate the user's ability to amass and manage video content from all corners of the Web. The organization of video data within a particular context now is primary, and its production, distribution, and storage, secondary. Video practice is dominated by the medium's situation within and alongside other objects and frameworks. Video is meaningful only as content that is embedded in technological frameworks that interact with other media forms and data sets, which themselves circulate within variegated social and cultural economies. The content-based mode of understanding video practice is secondary to its placement within these adjacent milieus.

But the technological assemblages of Web 2.0, though often operated through commercial centers, are not constructed as top-down architectures that determine new social relations but are also shaped by the communities and forms of social organization they contain. This shaping occurs in two ways, one internal and the other external to the system. The internal form derives from data that is collected by the system, channeled through collaborative filtering algorithms that process data sets of great complexity, and then returned to the online community in the form of an "enhanced" user experience. The design of the system is carefully orchestrated to manage the data that serves the interests of the firm while catering to the end user by fashioning the appearance of open and free user interaction that is direct, spontaneous, and unmediated. The external form of social organization characteristic of Web 2.0 is less technologically bound and more of a bottom-up activation of social media by groups of people who are not exclusively online communities but for whom the online experience is simply another lateral extension of an already-existing social network It is from this external relation that we can develop a way of understanding embedded video practice as something that resists the flexible power of the new technopolitical assemblage by approaching it from below and using it as a transactional space to effect social and political change. This external relation involves looking for forms of video practice that are in fact embedded, but embedded in such a way that they (1) disarm top-down notions of media technology and the fetishization of digital tools, (2) establish a lateral interchange with an external social field, and (3) define its practice in relation to alternative cultural circuits and forms of market production.

The cultural work of the Bulbo collective exemplifies this external and alternative understanding of embedded video practice in that almost all of the collective's media projects are realized through their circulation within already-existing social networks and organizations. Bulbo (www.bulbotv.com) is a group of Tijuana-based media artists and cultural workers who work in multiplatform media production. One of their ongoing video-based projects, Bulbo TV, was launched in 2002 amid a thriving public practice and alternative arts and music movement that included groups like Radio Global, Nortec Collective, and the Transborder Collective, as well as new alternative spaces such as La Casa de Túnel and Lui Velazquez. From 2002 to 2004, Bulbo TV applied their own brand of community-based collectivity to a weekly half-hour documentary-style TV magazine that was broadcast over the local Canal 22, which not only reached greater Tijuana and Rosarito but whose signal also crossed the border to reach parts of Chula Vista, California, in the South Bay of San Diego. Later, Bulbo's programming was broadcast nationally via Canal 52 MVS, which exposed their local practice to a wider Mexican audience. Throughout this period Bulbo did not so much produce video as approach video content production as a means of exchange by opening a space for a kind of cultural transaction between communities or subcultures that were adjacent to the video production itself. In much of this work, the video piece was not the end goal of the transaction but simply provided a platform for collaborative exchange and open dialogue within the communities in which they were working.

By the time Bulbo's broadcast period came to a close, the collective had produced over fifty programs. Bulbo TV had helped them to develop a way of approaching embedded video practice not bound to technological understanding of the medium but based on the process of sharing labor and resources among the collaborative partners around media production in order to open informal networks of transaction and exchange that could flow both ways. A recent video project produced in Mexico City typifies this process. *Monumento a Tenochitlán 40: Voces de tepito* (Monument to Tenochitlan: Voices of the people, 2008) seems a fairly straightforward social documentary about the 2007 expropriation of a large residential building by the Mexican government in a district in Mexico City known as Tepito, an area notorious for a thriving black market that lies directly adjacent to one of the dominant commercial centers of the city, El Zócalo. Known as an epicenter of the production and distribution of pirated materials and counterfeit commodities, from DVDs to clothes to soccer balls, Tepito also boasts a rich history of independently produced artisanal goods that extends back to the pre-Columbian Aztecs. One of the crucial aspects of Tepiteño culture is its existence as a self-organized, informal economy that has adamantly

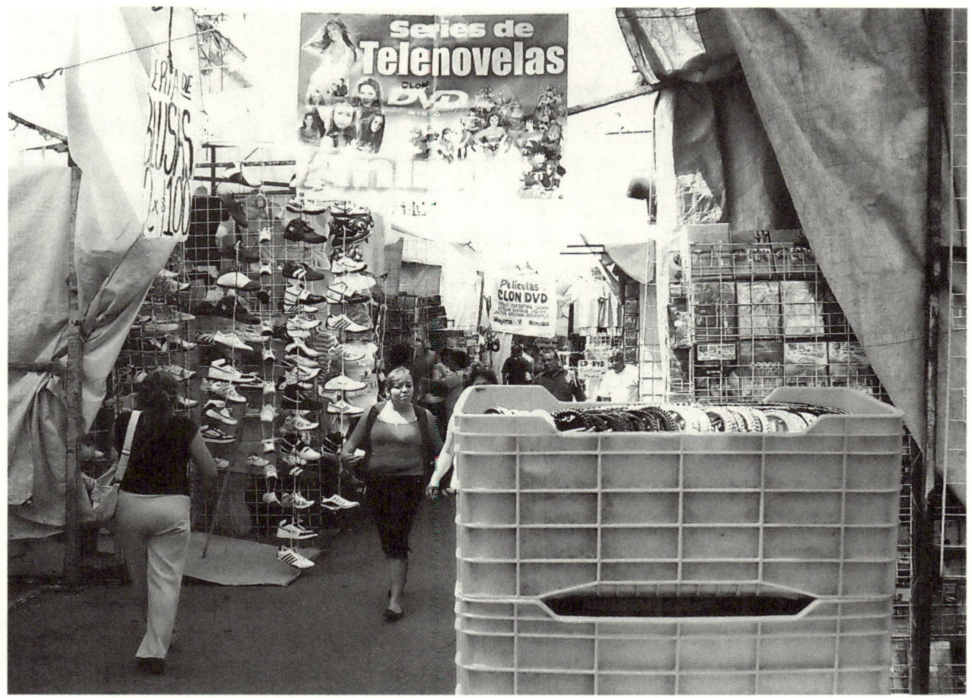

The Tepito market on Aztecas Street, 2008. Courtesy Galatea Audio/Visual.

maintained its autonomy from the reaches of both the Mexican state and officially sanctioned commercial interests. On weekends sections of the local streets are covered in nylon tarps and subdivided into a series of *puestos*—small stalls or booths where independent vendors sell their goods.

Each street is managed by its own organizer, who contracts the vendors into informal profit-sharing agreements. *Monumento a Tenochitlán 40* tells the history of Tepito through interwoven interviews of local Tepiteños specifically detailing how the expropriation of a building at the address of Tenochitlán 40 was justified by the specious rationale that it was a haven for a large narcotics operation, which was widely regarded as a thinly veiled land grab driven by the encroaching forces of privatization and gentrification on an area in proximity to the more affluent El Zócalo, much of which had, by 2007, already been acquired by telecom billionaire Carlos Slim Helú.[13]

Emphasized as a content-based / text-based project, *Monumento a Tenochitlán 40* might stand for nothing more than an indistinct documentary statement about a local struggle—a conventional social documentary at best, a problematic ethnography at worst. But Bulbo has quite carefully and deliberately deemphasized the video as a stand-alone piece and reemphasized the medium's value as something derived from how it is carefully embedded in a particular social network and a local economy of exchange. The video was made in collaboration with a loose alliance of art and community organizations working in and around Tepito, including Obstinado Tepito, El Centro de Estuidos Tepiteños, Asociación de Comerciantes Establecidos, Semifijos y Ambulantes del Barrio de Tepito, A.C., and the Galería José María Velasco. Even more significant is the fact that the documentary's initial circulation was intended for the residents and the merchants of that local community for the purpose of distributing information and creating political awareness around a specific local crisis involving the community's relationship to the Mexican state. The project of *Monumento a Tenochitlán 40* deployed video as one device within an arrangement of many others in order to produce dialog and exchange around a specific local social issue. More significant than the content of the video was the way in which it was situated within an economic circuit endemic to the problem it addressed. The video was not only produced in collaboration with the local residents and merchants of Tepito as a way for that community to address itself but also distributed and sold on DVD within the very same *puestos* that were vending pirated media, from Hollywood movies to classic Mexican cinema to pornography. The video object was introduced into Tepito's informal economy and sought to coexist alongside and bolster local Tepiteño consciousness in both its content and in the participatory way it flowed through the community, thus becoming both a social and an economic object of exchange within the very system it was bringing to light. The money earned from the video's sale went back to the community, and the resonance of the piece became valued not as a discrete text but as a transactional hub within a preexisting social and economic network. *Monumento a Tenochitlán 40* sought not to represent but to connect to and to facilitate a specific conversation that Tepiteños were already having among themselves.[14]

Following a lengthy discussion about issues of new media and Web 2.0, it might seem peculiar to conclude with a relatively low-tech case study, but I think this is precisely the appropriate point, one that moves the discourse about video and Web 2.0 away from a model of technological determinism. Extrapolating from the Deleuzian adage that technology is always social before it is technical, one can urge that embedded video should first condition an emergent social practice before it is used to define a technological one.[15] Tepito is a networked community that is not formed at the cutting edge of materially defined technological innovation, and yet it affects and is affected by the same underlying assemblage of power that has shaped a comparatively high-tech media organization like Bulbo. Just as surely as the global neoliberal condition influences the culture and structure of Web 2.0 interfaces, that condition also has a powerful effect on the local politics and informal economy of Tepito. An expanded understanding of embedded video might help to circumvent the term's technological overemphasis and create new affiliations across lines of disparity in power

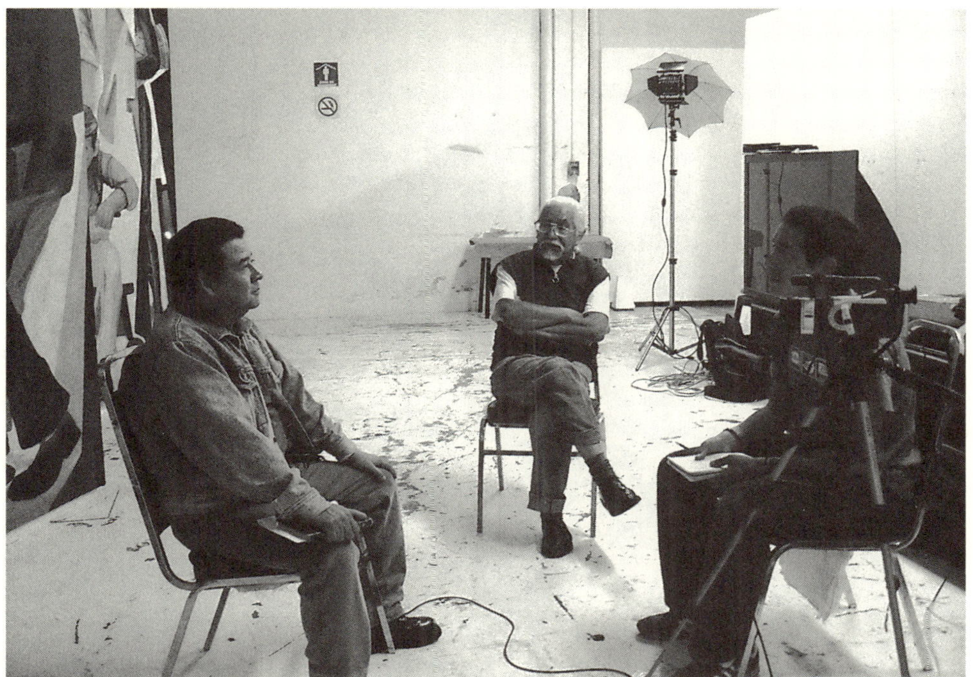

Bulbo member Juan Eduardo Navarrete Pajarito *(right)* in conversation in 2008 with local activists Filepe Hernandez Moreno *(center)*, coordinator for Tepito's Cultural Peña Morelos, and Diego Cornejo *(left)*, member of Comité Martes de Arte en Tepito. Courtesy Galatea Audio/Visual.

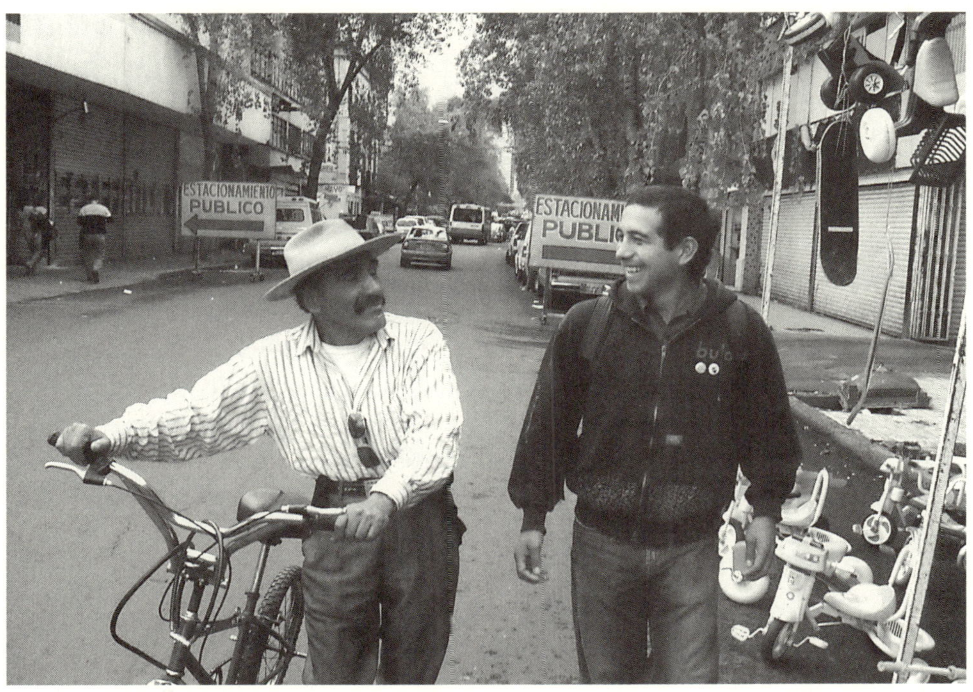

Arturo Ayala "Tirantes" of Tepito with Juan Navarrete Pajarito, 2008. Courtesy Galatea Audio/ Visual.

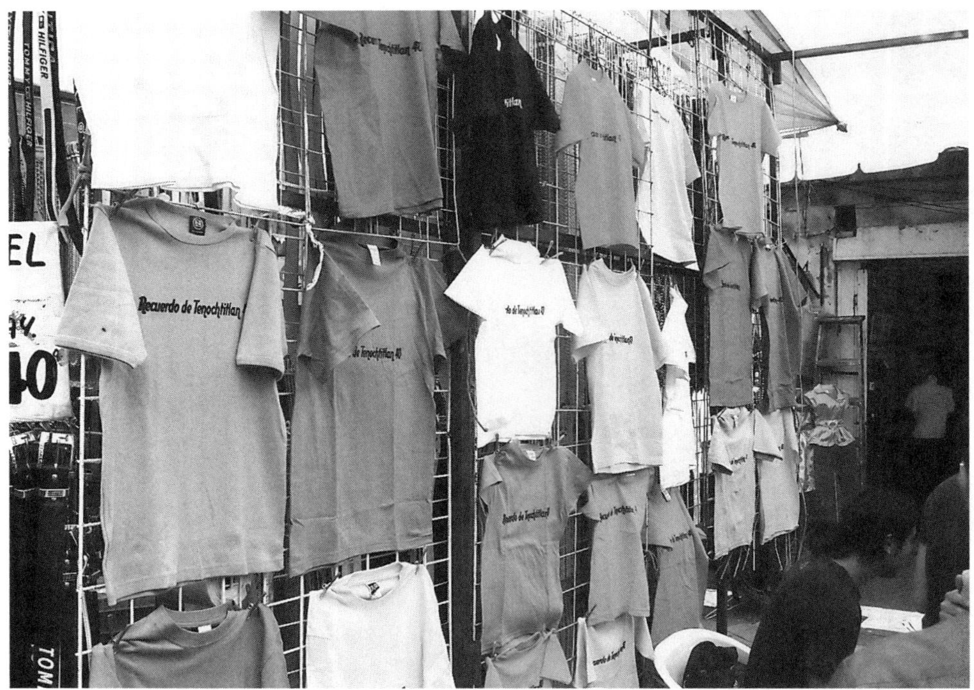

Booth in the Tepito market where Bulbo screened and distributed *Monumento a Tenochtitlán 40,* 2008. Courtesy Galatea Audio/Visual.

exacerbated by cultural factors of class and race or structural and material factors such as access to media technology, education, or capital. What *Monumento a Tenochitlán 40* demonstrates is that the culture of Web 2.0 is a symptom of a new form of political and economic power that is partially realized in media technology and more broadly extends into areas adjacent to that technology across the material surfaces of society. There are certain procedures within these technological and social structures that if pursued carefully and rigorously, might avail themselves for new possibilities of direct action. Video practitioners may very possibly be operating under this elusive system of soft power for some time to come, but the capacity to flexibly embed video in new social environments for different needs and purposes reveals an approach to media production and direct action politics that can help video practice support tactics of empowerment without seeking them in opposition to content.[16]

NOTES

1. I use the term *video practice* to reference all forms of nonmainstream video praxis, including all categories of video art, alternative video, experimental video, activist video, amateur video, subcultural video, and subaltern/postcolonial video.

2. Wallace Heim, "Slow Activism: Homelands, Love and the Lightbulb," in *Nature Performed: Environment Culture and Performance,* eds. Bronislaw Szerszynski, Wallace Heim, and Claire Waterton (Oxford: Blackwell Publishing, 2003), 183–202.

3. *Technopolitics* is a term that I borrow from a collective, open-source, Web-based research collective called the Next Layer; see www.thenextlayer.org. The group uses the term to describe the complex interaction of market regulation, world systems analysis, and autonomous Marxism to go beyond the limitations of paradigm shifts and epistemic space while still seeking a way to understand general historical periods and transitions. In the interest of clarity, however, I retain the use of the term *paradigm* but understand it not as the expression of a given episteme but as a governing topology of power relations operating within a defined social space. I retain the term with aid from the less structural and unifying way it is understood by Giorgio Agamben as an analogical relationship between historical particularities. Giorgio Agamben, *The Signature of All Things: On Method,* trans. Luca D'Isanto and Kevin Attell (New York: Zone Books, 2009), 31.

4. Robert McChesney details how the simultaneous rise of the three major networks, NBC, CBS, and ABC, and the Radio Act of 1927 (followed by the Communications Act of 1934) together effectively quashed independent, nonprofit radio culture through a coordination between the state (the Federal Radio Commission) and commercial interests. Robert W. McChesney, *The Political Economy of Media: Enduring Issues, Emerging Dilemmas* (New York: Monthly Review Press, 2008), 157–80.

5. Dara Birnbaum, "Talking Back to the Media," in *Resolution: A Critique of Video Art,* ed. Patti Podesta (Los Angeles: Los Angeles Contemporary Exhibitions, 1986), 51–56.

6. "Existing art theory is oriented primarily towards the analysis of individual objects and images understood as the product of a single creative intelligence. This approach privileges what I've described as a 'textual' paradigm in which the work of art is conceived as an object or event produced by the artist beforehand and subsequently presented to the viewer. The artist never relinquishes a position of semantic mastery, and the viewer's involvement is primarily hermeneutic. While there is significant latitude in the viewer's potential response to the work (clinical detachment, self–reflection, shock, etc.), they can exercise no real or substantive effect on the form and structure of the work, which remains the singular expression of the artist's authoring conscious." Grant Kester, "Collaboration Art and Subculture," *Caderno videobrasil* 2 (2007): 10. See also Grant H. Kester, "Aesthetic Enactment: Loraine Leeson's Reparative Practice," *Art for Change: Loraine Leeson, 1975–2005* (Berlin: Neueun Gesellschaft für Bildende Kunst, 2005).

7. Yochai Benkler, *The Wealth of Networks: How Social Production Transforms Markets and Freedom* (New Haven, Conn.: Yale University Press, 2006).

8. Ben Roberts, "Beyond the 'Networked Public Sphere': Politics, Participation and Technics in Web 2.0," *Fibreculture Journal* 14 (2009), http://fourteen.fibreculturejournal.org.

9. Manuel Castells, *The Rise of the Network Society,* vol. 1 of *The Information Age: Economy, Society and Culture,* 2nd ed. (New York: Wiley-Blackwell, 2000).

10. Anna Munster and Geert Lovink, "Theses on Distributed Aesthetics: Or, What a Network Is Not," *Fibreculture Journal* 7 (2005), http://seven.fibreculturejournal.org.

11. On the contrast between what Igor Kopytoff refers to as a "terminal destination" and what Nitin Govil calls a "transversal commodity," see Igor Kopytoff, "The Cultural Biography of Things: Commoditization as Process," in *The Social Life of Things: Commodities in Cultural Perspective,* ed. Arjun Appadurai (Cambridge: Cambridge University Press, 1986), 64–91. Nitin Govil, "War in the Age of Pirate Reproduction," *Sarai Reader* 4 (2004): 379–83.

12. One will obviously detect the Foucauldian emphasis in my language here. The immanent power of Web 2.0 operates through a comprehensive *dispositif* of diverse and heterogeneous elements that are strategically arranged for the expression of a particular political

utility directed at the effective government of populations. On relevant discussions of the *dispositif,* see Nikolas Rose and Paul Rabinow, "Foucault Today," in *The Essential Foucault: Selections from the Essential Works of Foucault, 1954–1984,* eds. Nikolas Rose and Paul Rainbow (New York: New Press, 2003).

13. The revitalization project of El Distrito Centro Histórico has been so heavily invested in by Carlos Slim that the district has been locally dubbed Slimcentro. Since 2000, Slim has acquired enormous swaths of historic real estate under the contested premise that this is a gesture of altruistic and patriotic philanthropy. Many critics sharply dispute this claim, however, offering the convincing alternative that preservation and revitalization are simply public relations spin for an aggressive land grab of undervalued real estate. Virginia Cabrera Becerra, "Política de renovación en centros históricos de México," *Centro-h: Revista de la organización latinoamericana y del caribe de centros históricos* 1 (August 2008): 26-39, http://www.revistacentro-h.org/pdf/5.pdf.

14. Earlier, I discuss how Bulbo's idea of collaborative exchange includes the notion that all parties who interact leave with a direct investment in the transaction. In addition to circulating on the Tepito streets, *Monumento a Tenochitlán 40* also circulated widely online. For viewers and participants not part of the Tepito conversation but part of the Bulbo network, the Tenochitlán project also embedded the video on its own website (www.bulbo.tv) and as part of the Obstinado Tepito project (obstinadotepito.com). In each case, the piece spoke to a different audience, addressed a different set of questions, and circulated in a different cultural economy.

15. Gilles Deleuze, *Foucault,* trans. Sean Hand (Minneapolis: University of Minnesota Press, 1988).

16. I thank artist/activist Yutsil Cruz, who has worked tirelessly with Obstinado Tepito using a slow activist approach, for her hospitality and generosity in introducing me to the Tepito community.

Public Stances

Kathy High

The first decade of the millennium brought about the immanent collapse of the empire as we knew it. It was a decade filled with disillusions, dreams gone bad, and disappointments. The divisiveness of governments' actions, creating bad wars and even worse economic deals, isolated their populations and segregated our societies. Public space remains a kind of commons, however, a place of shared experience, a place to bring people back together. As we can see from recent global uprisings, public space is a place of collective celebration and of protest, resistance, prayer, and negotiation. The video and new media work that has enduring effect for me is work performed in a public space, stirring a public imagination. And because this work somewhat escapes the confines of the art world, it, to borrow from Nato Thompson, "emphasizes social relationships" and "constitutes a sort of political action."[1]

This essay surveys six different projects by artists who use video as an integral part of their art projects: they take a camera, a wireless device, or a video projector to the streets. It is not about documentation of performances or street actions—although these projects may become documentation. It is about how these artists use video as a strategy to open up a public dialogue and encourage cross-talk, understanding, and public provocation. Themes touched on include the plight of immigrants, recovering abolitionist histories, the failing economy, antiwar protests, and public opinions. This essay is written with the same urgency with which the projects were made—coming from a need to act as a trigger for future action.[2]

Projections

There are projects that use bodies and video projections to break down and deterritorialize public spaces, to inject a monkey wrench into the neat social fabric of our cultures and, thus, allow for an anomaly, a discovery. *Culture jamming* is a term that now has a long history of being used to describe this kind of cultural interference, rehistoricized haunting, and resourceful fracture in our civilized worlds. Here are some examples of public projects using projections that have opened up new readings of old themes.[3]

A person dressed in a bright-blue head-to-toe hooded outfit walked the streets. She looked like a monk or, certainly, a strange, foreign being. She carried a small video camera in front of her and a small monitor behind. She was also tethered to a black-clothed, ominous, military-esque person—a helmeted guard of sorts—who stalked behind her with another video camera.

This mysterious couple was part of the project *Negotiations* (2006), by Daniela Kostova in collaboration with Olivia Robinson. It was a site-specific performance that explored the (in)visibility of immigrants, or "Aliens." The artists' description of the performance "system" is as follows:

> The *Negotiations* system uses readily available computer and surveillance technology to create the real-time video. Two characters embody the system, an Alien (in blue) and an Authority (in black). Each has a video camera which is linked to a computer embedded in the Authority's costume. Custom software composites the two video streams to create a negotiated final video. The resulting imagery is solely from the Authority's point of view wherein the Alien has been replaced with her or his own point of view. The Alien carries a small monitor where s/he and passers-by can view the final video as it is being created. The Authority rarely takes her camera off of the Alien, the surveyed subject.[4]

These costumed characters appeared highly visible in public and brought lots of attention to their presence. But in the live composite video seen on the small monitor carried by the Alien performer, the chroma-key-blue costume was keyed out of the picture—erased and blended with the surroundings, making the performer dissolve and become invisible. The Alien's handheld camera image was keyed into the blue of the costume and filled the body of the Alien in this mixed-video image. It was this immigrant narrative of crossing back and forth from being easy to spot to flamboyantly visible to faded and disappeared that the artists were affecting with their public performance.

In an earlier iteration of the project, *Invisible Suits* (2005), blue-suited Kostova walked the streets of Sophia, Bulgaria. A Bulgarian by birth, Kostova returned to Bulgaria after spending a few years in the United States. Her return to Sophia in 2004 made her realize the state of being in between cultures, misplaced, a nomad, a gypsy—a feeling as if she did not belong anywhere. This feeling resulted in the creation of this visible/invisible costume and project. Kostova brought to the public her heightened presence as a foreigner and her sense of erasure as she was finally keyed out, cut out, and blurred with the landscape. This blurring is the dual reality of one who exists in a super-self-conscious way in public (afraid to be so exposed) but also is unseen, overlooked, and dismissed by society. It is an inside/outside view. As Kostova states:

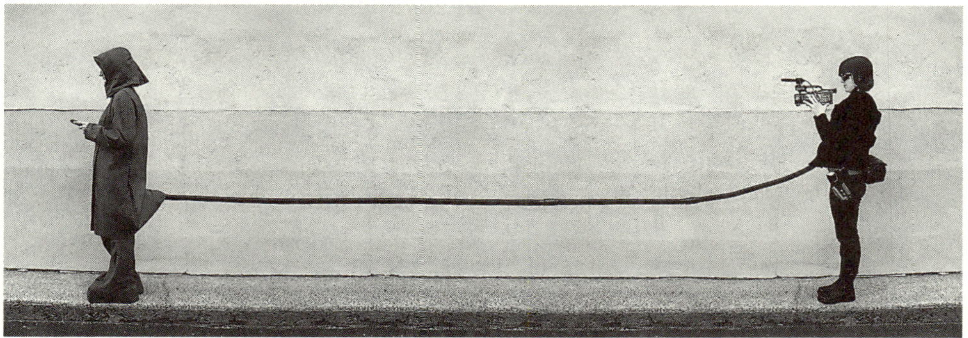

Negotiations (2006) by Daniela Kostova and Olivia Robinson, live performance, photograph courtesy of the artists.

These suits allow me to explore issues of silence and absence, integration and estrangement in different political and cultural environments.
While drawing from theoretical concepts like the "invisible immigrant"
and the double consciousness, through this work I am also exploring the
space between the objective and subjective points of view.[5]

Negotiations was the next iteration of the *Invisible Suits* project. Here, the
articulation of the figure of the immigrant and the figure of the state became
apparent. Whereas in *Invisible Suits* a cameraperson always trailed behind the costumed characters, following and documenting their activities, in *Negotiations* this
documenter was brought into the dialogue of the project—not just as an extra but
as an equal contender. As Kostova and Robinson write about the work:

As both a conspicuous costume and virtual assimilation act, each performance has fostered the development of a site-specific story. Recurring
themes that emerged from the performances include: estrangement and
integration; cultural economics of "authority"; placidity of legality; territory and ownership; and mediation of experience.[6]

Negotiations appeared sometimes playful, sometimes strange, and sometimes
oppressive. The public was alternately entertained by, confused by, or empa-
thetic with the street performance in *Negotiations,* identifying their own stories
with this performance of otherness. These states of engagement pushed the
ideas of presence and disassociation enacted by the performers, leaving the public with a perhaps more complex understanding of the reality and the negotiations of alienation.

Recovering ghosts, forgotten voices, and vanished places were impulses behind
the project *Spectres of Liberty/The Ghost of Liberty Street,* a temporary projection

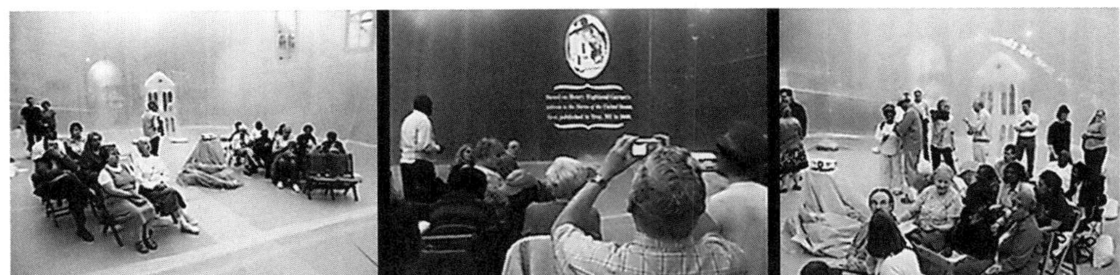

Spectres of Liberty (2008) by Dara Greenwald, Josh MacPhee, and Olivia Robinson. *The Ghost of Liberty Street Church* installation, Troy, N.Y., interior shots, photograph courtesy of the artists.

and marker that held public attention because of its ethereal aesthetic. This site-specific project was designed to relocate a disappeared abolitionist local history and literally was a building propped up by air. At the same time, the fierce messages of the people behind *Spectres of Liberty* were anything but fragile and made evident the need for certain histories of resistance to be revisited and remembered.

The project *The Ghost of Liberty Street* (2008), by Dara Greenwald, Olivia Robinson, and Josh MacPhee, was an inflatable life-size re-creation of the Liberty Street Presbyterian Church in Troy, New York—an important meeting place for the Underground Railroad in the 1840s.[7] Projected onto the inflated building were digital animated images and text of the church's Reverend Henry Highland Garnet, known for his public support of the fight against slavery. In the artists' words:

> We animated this ghost church through video projections, sound, and
> digital animations representing Henry Highland Garnet and his words.
> The church provided a theatre in which to hold a cultural event that
> brought community members to think more deeply about the space, its
> history, and its relevancy for today.[8]

The origins of the project came out of the artists' community involvement. Living in Troy, Robinson, MacPhee, and Greenwald had participated in various projects retelling histories. One project included the politicizing of Troy's Victorian Stroll—a traditional Christmas costume street fair meant to encourage shoppers. During the Victorian Stroll an activist group dressed as Victorian laborers and conducted a street protest recalling the actual labor battles that occurred in Troy and Upstate New York in the late 1800s. MacPhee and Greenwald were also involved in the anarchist ad hoc group b.l.o.c., which designed projects about the history of the fight against slavery. Robinson had previously created large, inflatable projects with different community groups in Baltimore. She suggested producing inflatable structures of Troy's historic buildings that the mayor's office was at that time destroying (Troy's mayor, Harry Tutunjian, was nicknamed Demolition Harry). From this suggestion and their prior projects around radical histories of Troy, these artists combined skills to come up with the premise for the *Spectres* project. The name *Spectres of Liberty* came later when they "thought it was relevant that it was on Liberty Street and the project was about the history of liberation."⁹

The Ghost of Liberty Street was held on the corner of Liberty Street, between Third and Fourth streets in downtown Troy, on the evening of May 30, 2008 (in conjunction with Troy Night Out, a local event that opens galleries and stores to the public). The inflatable church was blown up with one large electronic fan. It rose over a few hours like a ghost from the dead—at once elegant and haunting. Video projections animated the inside and outside spaces with Henry Highland Garnet's words from the 1840s: "Let your motto be resistance! resistance! resistance! No oppressed people have ever secured their liberty without resistance."¹⁰ These words were meant to inspire and provoke the public to consider how they could be applied to current political situations.

Hundreds of local residents attended, including one woman who had attended the original church. The public, while delighted with the piece, felt that the artists should have made the project last longer than its one-night existence (in fact, this project was produced again in Syracuse in the summer of 2010). This public endorsement was appreciated but led the artists to also wonder if *Spectres* was as provocative as it needed to be. As MacPhee writes about the public response:

> [One] comment was that the event was really great, and the church really beautiful, but is it possible to translate these representations of the past into the present? Do people seeing this church, which basically represents resistance to slavery and injustice, transition that acknowledgment of revolt into a call of action for today, against the war, or present day slavery, or other injustice? A very good question.¹¹

A very good question, indeed. Can public works such as these trigger action? And how effective is public art in motivating activism? These questions have been asked before this, but at least this project relocated the historic motivation for resistance by re-creating a literal space for dialogue, inspiration, and (possible) action. *Spectres of Liberty/The Ghost of Liberty Street* acted as a reminder of our lack of such public spaces and the need for continued communal struggle for human rights.

OUT: Operation Urban Terrain (2003/2004), a live-action wireless-gaming urban intervention by Anne-Marie Schleiner, was a street action that made visible the violence for which American culture is known.¹² In *OUT* the streets of New York City were painted with projected gaming images to remind U.S. citizens of their continuous involvement in international militarized actions. *OUT* was not a reminder of 9/11 but rather evoked how much Americans strike out against others in the world. Much like *Spectres of Liberty*, this project also was a call to action.

OUT was performed in the streets of New York City just prior to the 2004 Republican National Convention. The convention, held August 30 to September 2, 2004, at Madison Square Garden, triggered street protests and interventions by progressive factions all over the city. President George W. Bush and Vice President Dick Cheney were up for reelection, and many in the public were furious that they might continue to push their conservative agenda. Activists were demonstrating across the country, especially rallying in New York. The police force mounted and deployed increasingly restrictive measures, including armed forces and technology to contain the protesters (such as the Long Range Acoustic Device, which is capable of firing off signals of up to 150 decibels into crowds).[13]

Anne-Marie Schleiner, who is known for VELVET-STRIKE (2002–4), an insertion project retagging shoot-'em-up war games with countermilitary graffiti, describes *OUT* as follows:

> OUT takes its name from MOUT a military term for Military Operations in Urban Terrain. Many military simulation computer games implement MOUT. For example, the US Army developed game Full Spectrum Warrior trains gamers in MOUT combat. OUT is a criticism of the increasing militarization of civilian life, which has been implemented in the US and elsewhere since 911. The Patriot Act, surveillance of public libraries, and the increased powers of government to hold citizens in military custody without trial are instances of these increased powers of government instigated by the Bush administration.[14]

OUT, a public protest performed as an urban artistic intervention, took place on August 28, 2004, during the setup for the convention. Late-night performances were held in various locations around New York in Midtown, Harlem, and Brooklyn. Two women dressed in stealth outfits and high-tech gear negotiated the streets, one carrying a laptop and the other a projector pointed at various buildings along their route. The projections revealed the rest of the team working in collaboration with the street-walking women. The women were "connected through a mobile wireless bicycle to an online team of five game players located around the world. They intervene[d] on servers in a popular online military simulation game with performance actions carried out by the whole team."[15]

The New York *OUT* performance was witnessed by probably just a few. Perhaps, the online community was more aware of *OUT*'s invasion. The intention and message were made clear to the passersby with flashing texts that read:

> Republicans OUT of New York. The United States OUT of Iraq and the Middle East. Escalating worldwide Militarism and Violence, from whatever source, (right wing oil hungry U.S. capitalists or wealthy Islamic

fundamentalists), OUT of Civilian Life. The U.S. Army and Pentagon computer game developers OUT of the minds of prepubescent gamers.[16]

The women performers acted as sexy secret agents, infiltrators on the streets with their projected hacked gaming messages. Their performance was also a disruption of the usual military game flow, a raid online to challenge the norm of first-person-shooter environments, a call to action, a provocation for other street skirmishes, and a kind of anarchistic clash with the incoming conservative crowds for the Republican National Convention. *OUT* was a subtle public dance of resistance.

Networks

Often projects that involve a network of public participants to complete them, to activate them and to make them a reality, also break down authority, disperse ownership, and thus allow the public to define the parameters. Networking in these particular cases involves using the Internet and television broadcast networks and also simply "networking"—or, talking with people in the streets.

Produced on the heels of the Argentina economic crisis, GARLIC=RICH AIR (2002) was a project by Shu Lea Cheang about trade, sharing airwaves, and sustainability.[17] In GARLIC=RICH AIR organic garlic was traded on the streets in a new artist-initiated economy. The artist Shu Lea Cheang is best known for her activist, transgressive, and queer works, such as the *Brandon* project (1998–99), for which she held an online public trial in tandem with the real trials of the men accused of killing Teena Brandon.[18] But Cheang also has a long-standing commitment to creating sustainable ecologies. She recently started a long-term project about farming, to "engage artists in eco-bio-media issues," on her twenty-one-acre farm in Upstate New York called the Andes Sprouts Society.[19] These projects bring together Cheang's interest in emergent media forms, radical technologies, and networked exchanges, creating collective opportunities, as well as the potential for revolutionary change through sustainable cultures.

Phase one of GARLIC=RICH AIR was to harvest the fields of organic garlic in Upstate New York. In the next phase an online live-trading center was developed using garlic as the main commodity, its worth determined by the traders themselves. Cheang set up the Garlic Credito Trueque Club—modeled after the trading clubs in Buenos Aires—with an online digital commons. During the late 1990s' economic crisis in Argentina, when the economy collapsed from huge inflation, El Club de Truque (The Club of Exchange) did not involve exchanging money for goods or services but instead developed an extensive barter system allowing people to create their own self-sufficient, alternative participatory economies. In GARLIC=RICH AIR Cheang developed a sophisticated online trading site and public market where people could register and then trade anything digital for garlic credits. Ten years in advance, Cheang anticipated our current economic recession:

> In a fictional "after the crash" scenario, organic garlic has been recently ordained as new social currency, serving as "credito" for a global shared network. In the first phase of this project, Cheang organized the harvesting of 10,000 garlic plants, cultivated by organic farmer Tovey Halleck in upstate New York, by generations of old and new media artists this summer. These organic cloves, which took 10 years to cultivate, constitute the garlic standard in this artist-initiated economy.[20]

In a final phase Cheang also explored the use of public airwaves—finding open Wi-Fi spots, "network nodes," around New York City. This notion of opening up the city for Web users came at the very beginning of our current Wi-Fi culture, so Cheang's concept of riding around to find and expose the "commons" was radical for the time. Cheang set up mobile urban farm stands, using a traveling painted truck that traveled around New York with garlic to trade.

Once the valuation of the garlic credit had been established, the third phase of the project focused on enacting a virtual to physical commodities exchange through New York's Wi-Fi network. On September 27, 28, and 29, 2002, a designer truck equipped with loads of garlic and wireless technology served as a mobile urban farm stand. The truck utilized selected New York wireless network nodes for online and on-site street trading activities. Members of the online Credito Trueque Club could exchange virtual garlic with edible organic garlic at the designated truck posts. Passersby also were welcome to participate in garlic trading with their own offers.

At the various street-side public trading posts, excited urban participants offered buttons, pens, drawings, food, and other assorted items in trade for the organic garlic. All was videotaped and uploaded to the Web. Cheang's GARLIC=RICH AIR was a prefigurative project, imagining organic food as the prized item of the future, and in our current moment of global recession, the trading club idea could excite alternative possibilities for exchanges and the creation of radical, new global markets.

Another trickster extraordinaire, Ximena Cuevas, also uses media for political aims. In 2001 Ximena Cuevas produced a video performance piece from her on-air appearance on a popular Mexican television show called *La tombola* (The raffle). There, she gave the public back the TV airwaves.

On *La tombola* the participants flamboyantly performed their parts, discussing recent love affairs, divorces, and marriages, slinging sexual innuendos at each other, flirting with each other, and insulting each other—the usual reality TV talk show antics. In contrast, Cuevas, once welcomed by the show's host, proceeded to act as an extremely bored contestant and refused to contribute to the banal discussions.

Cuevas was at that time no stranger to being in the public eye. As a very public figure—being a successful video artist and also the daughter of the well-known sculptor José Luis Cuevas—Ximena Cuevas used the public media to speak about her own causes. Shortly before her public appearance on *La tombola,* Cuevas was approached by journalists from the popular weekly magazine / celebrity gossip rag *TV notas.* They wanted to write a story about the daughter of the famous José Luis Cuevas. Ximena Cuevas presented the journalist with a couple options: rather than focus on her as the daughter of José Luis, they could write about her either as an internationally recognized video artist or as a lesbian. The headline of the *TV notas* article about Ximena that week read, "Daughter of Famous Sculptor is a Lesbian."

The next week, the *TV notas* journalists hounded Ximena for a glimpse of her girlfriend. Ximena's girlfriend would have nothing to do with her pranksterish behavior and refused to partake in any interviews. At the time, I was visiting Mexico City, producing a Mexican–U.S. issue of FELIX, a journal on media arts, with Ximena and others.[21] Ximena phoned me early one morning and asked me to help her: Ximena and I posed as lovers in three different *TV notas* issues. Her very public celebrity relationship as an out lesbian was a progressive act performed before the Mexican pop culture.

The *TV notas* ruse was done around the same time as Ximena's *La tombola* TV appearance and probably prompted her being invited onto the show. But with this TV public, Ximena took a further step than she had in the *TV notas* articles. Toward the end of *La tombola,* Ximena exclaimed to the show's host that she was bored with this so-called entertainment. He became flustered and tried to placate Ximena, asking her to speak her mind. Cuevas pulled out a small Sony camcorder from the suitcase she had brought with her and started speaking directly to the TV public. Looking straight into the TV camera lens, she pointed her small video camera directly at the broadcast audience, thus confronting the public. Then she asked or, rather, pleaded with the public that they not take interest in her life but rather in their own. In a shaky but determined voice, Ximena said, "The only thing I hope is that at least there's one person out there . . . who has a life of their own, who is interested in their own life, their own life, their own life . . . ."

This dare to the viewers presented a break from typical one-way broadcasting. This break with the mystique of the corporate dominant culture was a challenge to resist capitalism and consumption habits and to participate more fully in life. Much like Ernie Kovacs in his famous 1950s TV broadcasts, in which he often broke down the fourth wall and spoke directly to the TV audience, Ximena's acting out both highlighted an alternative, personal approach to broadcast production and encouraged and challenged the public to act with more individual courage.

The compelling feature-length documentary video *in complete world* (2008), by Shelly Silver, also furthers the notion of individualism and real democracy.[22] *In complete world* is a collection of street interviews and public opinions broadly about the state of our existence. Whereas the other projects used the artistic work as the central trigger for public engagement, in *in complete world* Silver uses her camera somewhat neutrally—in a way that is open and searching for, in her own words, a "cumulative" public voice. And perhaps *in complete world* is an answer to the challenge set out by Ximena Cuevas to be interested in one's own life.

This vox pop project was started in 2007, prior to the heated 2008 presidential elections. Sensing an urgency in that moment, Silver asked the New York street public questions about their sense of well-being, as well as their individual versus collective responsibilities. The project echoes an earlier video by Silver, *Former East Former West* (1994), in which she interviews hundreds of German citizens in Berlin just two years after the fall of the Berlin Wall, asking them what it means to be German at that particular historical moment.[23] In *in complete world,* Silver interviews 130 New Yorkers. In Silver's words, "It is a testament to the people of NYC in this new millennium, who freely offer up thoughtful, provocative and at times tender revelations to a complete stranger, just because she asked."[24]

Silver refers to this piece as a "user's manual for citizenship in the 21st century." The questions vary from those about self-satisfaction ("What would you define as being happy?") to those concerned with citizen responsibilities ("Are we responsible for the government we get?" and "Do you think global warming exists? Do you feel responsible for global warming?") to questions recognizing a general cultural malaise ("Do you feel you have control over your life?" and "What are you most scared of?"). These questions introduce a considered dialogue about our collective hopes and fears of the future. Though Silver is perhaps searching to discover some answers for herself through this public inquiry, in *in complete world* she gracefully weaves (i.e., edits) the interviews into a conversation about our shared obligations and accountability for things such as wealth, war, and the protection of civil rights.

In fact, Silver took on the project because of her own feelings of dissatisfaction with her life in New York. As she states:

> I started shooting *in complete world* in 2007, because I was angry and disillusioned with the US, and more importantly, NYC, where I was born and have put in a good deal of quality time. This city, "my" city, was (is) increasingly white, rich and homogenized, and I was feeling alienated and pushed out economically and culturally. In the interest of full disclosure I'll add that I was also frustrated with my own inactivity and powerlessness in the face of the disastrous direction this country has moved in for

the last eight-plus years. Rather than leave New York and the US, or, perhaps, in preparation to do so, I decided to take my camera and find out
who these people were that I was sharing a city with, by asking them
the very same questions I was asking myself.[25]

There are no right or wrong answers in *in complete world*. There are no over-
simplified sound bites. The various opinions expressed are diverse and singular,
although edited skillfully to be in conversation with one another. Each answer
builds on the last and allows us to understand the various personalities and attitudes. We even identify with different characters as they become more well
rounded with each cycle of question and answer, asking the questions to ourselves. Silver removes herself, as documentarians often do. But this removal is
more about giving space to the speakers, allowing for a collective public voice to
rise up and take shape. Silver states:

> I instead chose, strenuously, to remove the central authoritative presence
> from my film. . . . *in complete world's* structure is based on accumula-
> tion. . . . I found this structure of accumulation allowed for and encour-
> aged complexity—having each person interviewed in the position of
> directly answering a question (unmediated by commentator or "expert")
> and putting the viewer (again without commentator or expert) into the
> active position of building/making sense of the film over time.[26]

This act of nonhierarchical intervention by the filmmaker is a strategy to
remember. *In complete world* shows Silver's ability to create a sophisticated but
open-ended public engagement and portray a multifaceted picture of our state
of the state. It also prompts us to ask ourselves how we got where we are today
and what our responsibilities are in all of this mess. Silver, like the other artists
discussed, intervenes in the public voice to invent a new understanding of our
power struggles and, through dialogue, empowers us to create new ways to
remake our world.

NOTES

1. From Nato Thompson's opening remarks for The Creative Time Summit: Revolutions
in Public Practice II (2009).

2. I originally thought to contextualize the works with historical references, such as Dada
antiwar and anticultural projects, Situationist actions, and 1960s to 1970s anarcho-political and
feminist performance works, but rather, I ask the reader to keep in mind these related precursors of absurdist, agit-prop ways of inciting public action and memory.

3. *Culture jamming* is a term used by Mark Dery in his popular article "Culture Jamming:
Hacking, Slashing and Sniping in the Empire of Signs," which originally appeared in 1993 as
pamphlet no. 25 in the Open Magazine Pamphlet Series. In it Dery writes, "Culture jammers

answer to that name. 'Jamming' is CB slang for the illegal practice of interrupting radio broadcasts or conversations between fellow hams with lip farts, obscenities, and other equally jejune hijinks. Culture jamming, by contrast, is directed against an ever more intrusive, instrumental technoculture whose operant mode is the manufacture of consent through the manipulation of symbols." The term *cultural jamming* was first used by the sound collage band Negativland to describe billboard alteration and other forms of media sabotage. On their album *Jamcon '84* (SST, 1985), a mock-serious band member observes, "As awareness of how the media environment we occupy affects and directs our inner life grows, some resist. . . . The skillfully reworked billboard . . . directs the public viewer to a consideration of the original corporate strategy. The studio for the cultural jammer is the world at large." Part artistic terrorists, part vernacular critics, culture jammers, like Eco's "communications guerrillas," introduce noise into the signal as it passes from transmitter to receiver, encouraging idiosyncratic, unintended interpretations.

4. See http://www.iamwhateveryouwantmetobe.com/site/content/negotiations.

5. See http://dani.cult.bg/pages/suits.html.

6. See http://www.iamwhateveryouwantmetobe.com/site/content/negotiations.

7. The church burned down in 1941.

8. See http://spectresofliberty.com/site/about.

9. Dara Greenwald, e-mail correspondence with author, December 18, 2009.

10. From Rev. Henry Highland Garnet's "An Address to the Slaves of the United States of America, Buffalo, N.Y., 1843," originally presented at the 1843 National Negro Convention in Buffalo, New York. It was self-published in New York state in April 1848, along with "David Walker's Appeal," an appeal for ending slavery. Garnet's paper is posted on DigitalCommons@ University of Nebraska–Lincoln, http://digitalcommons.unl.edu/etas/8.

11. Josh MacPhee, e-mail message to Dara Greenwald, December 18, 2009.

12. See http://www.opensorcery.net/OUT. Anne-Marie Schleiner's *OUT* was also funded by the Lyn Blumenthal Memorial Fund's Challenge to the Field Award for 2003/2004; see http://www.vdb.org/lbmf/challenge.html.

13. Ellen Simon, "Technology Playing Roll in GOP Protests: Demonstrators Use Cell Phones, Blogs, More," msnbc.com website, August 30, 2004, http://www.msnbc.msn.com/id/5841974.

14. See http://www.opensorcery.net/OUT/htm/project.htm.

15. Ibid.

16. See http://www.opensorcery.net/OUT/htm/project.htm.

17. See http://garlico2.worldofprojects.info and http://www.dailymotion.com/video/x92ivg_garlicrichairtrade_creation. Shu Lea Cheang's GARLIC=RICH AIR was also funded by the Lyn Blumenthal Memorial Fund's Challenge to the Field Award for 2001/2002; see http://www.vdb.org/lbmf/challenge.html.

18. See http://brandon.guggenheim.org (password required to access).

19. See http://www.andessproutssociety.us.

20. GARLIC=RICH AIR original event invitation, September 2002.

21. See http://www.e-felix.org/aissue6.html.

22. See http://www.shellysilver.com/view.php?id=video&id2=incompletev.

23. See http://www.shellysilver.com/view.php?id=video&id2=east.

24. See http://www.shellysilver.com/view.php?id=video&id2=incompletev.

25. John Menick, "Three Questions for Shelly Silver," John Menick's blog, November 19, 2008, http://blog.johnmenick.com/2008/11/shelly-silver-interview.

26. Shelly Silver's press release for *in complete world,* December 17, 2009.

5 The Voice of Blindness

ON THE SOUND TACTICS OF TRAN T. KIM-TRANG'S
THE BLINDNESS SERIES

Ming-Yuen S. Ma

Using the Negative to Bring out the Positive

I approach Vietnamese American video artist Tran T. Kim-Trang's *The Blindness Series* (1992–2006), a collection of eight experimental single-channel videotapes, in a manner that is markedly different from traditional media scholarship. In this study I do not assume the position of the detached and supposedly objective scholar who has a critical distance from her or his subject. The position I assume in this study is that of the engaged observer.[1] I have known Tran as a longtime friend, colleague, and sometimes collaborator for almost eighteen years. I have participated in the different aspects of *The Blindness Series* and am familiar with the processes through which Tran realized each of the videos.[2] Furthermore, like Tran, I am an artist working in media, familiar with the process of video production, and one who shares some of her concerns and interests. I believe this sustained interaction with and intimate knowledge of the conception, production, distribution, and reception of the videos in *The Blindness Series* provides me with a perspective that is not available to a more traditional media scholar.

In this essay I focus on the audio elements in the eight videotapes. I begin with a general analysis of how sound is used in the series and deduce some overall strategies and tactics that Tran deploys in her use of these audio elements. Although the sound tracks for the videos differ greatly, ranging from polyphonic to minimalist in their makeup, the voice-over narration emerges as one of *The Blindness Series'* central audio devices. I then examine Tran's use of voice through two theoretical frameworks: one, voice as a metaphor for subjectivity and, two, voice in its materiality. I focus my discussion of these frameworks on two of the videos in the series. In the first, I draw from the French feminist vision of a polyvocal and corporeal feminine discourse to discuss the many voices within *Kore* (1994). In the second I use the cinematic sound theories of French writer and composer Michel Chion, primarily drawn from his books *Audio-Vision: Sound on*

Screen and *The Voice in Cinema,* and U.S. feminist film scholar Kaja Silverman's work on the female voice and subjectivity in film in *The Acoustic Mirror: The Female Voice in Psychoanalysis and Cinema* to discuss the phenomenon of vocal embodiment in *Ekleipsis* (1998).

My focus on sound in a video series very much concerned with vision may seem off target to some. I argue, however, that Tran herself adopts a similar strategy in her videos. Her use of blindness—commonly understood as the lack of vision—as both metaphor and phenomena in the series is a strategy of using the negative to accentuate the positive.[3] In her exploration of topics ranging from hysterical blindness to video surveillance to cosmetic eyelid surgery, Tran consistently shows that the lack of vision speaks volume about visuality itself and that those without the ability to see are sometimes able to elucidate and comment on visual culture in ways that the sighted cannot. In my exploration of the sound tactics in the series, I adopt a strategy parallel to Tran's. In the introduction to his book on the history of sound reproduction, *The Audible Past: Cultural Origins of Sound Reproduction,* Jonathan Sterne points out that although much attention has been paid to the theorization of visual culture within the humanities in disciplines such as art, art history, and film and media studies, as well as cultural studies, comparatively scarce efforts have been made to theorize a sound culture. He refers to it as "visual hegemony."[4] Within the field of film and media studies, a particular manifestation of this hegemony can be seen in a lack of studies focused on sound in or as media, in comparison with the plethora of visually centered studies, debates, and schools of thought.[5] In most cases audio components in a film or video are overlooked in favor of visually centered analyses and only addressed as an afterthought, if at all.[6] Michel Chion went as far as declaring that "there is no soundtrack," arguing that "the sounds of a film, taken separately from the image, do not form an internally coherent entity on equal footing with the image track."[7] Chion also points out that in the vast majority of sync-sound films, "each audio element enters into *simultaneous vertical relationship* with narrative elements contained in the image (characters, actions) and visual elements of texture and setting."[8] That is to say, the meaning of an audio element in these films has more to do with the visual image it interacts with than with the other sounds around it.

It is significant to point out that most media scholars of sound have focused their studies on feature-length narrative films. Chion bases his observations primarily on Hollywood cinema and European and Japanese art films. Silverman, like Chion, also bases her discussion primarily on narrative films. Although she cites examples of feminist avant-garde films in her discussion, they are ones that are concerned with expanding upon dominant cinema's feature narrative form.[9] As I hope to demonstrate, Tran's experimental videos, though they share some of the concerns of narrative films, utilize tactics and strategies that are radically different. More important, in her use of sound, the instances in which the audio becomes the primary conveyor of meaning far exceed those I have found in narrative feature films. Of course, Tran's oeuvre represents only a case study, and there is a wide variety of experimental media, each with their different usage and deployment of sound. In a preliminary way, however, I believe the use of sound as the primary conveyor of meaning in Tran's work gestures toward an argument that sound as the primary conveyor is more likely in experimental media—as opposed to narrative feature films—since more of an equilibrium can be struck between the visual and the audio. It follows that in the study of such media, visual hegemony can be challenged and destabilized. By drawing attention to sound in *The Blindness Series,* an element often overlooked in the visually hegemonic field of media studies, I am focusing my discussion of Tran's work on elements outside visual representation and ones that speak to its limitations, thus enacting my own strategy of using the negative to accentuate the positive.

The Uses of Sound in *The Blindness Series*

Tran utilizes a wide variety of audio elements in *The Blindness Series,* including voice-over, interviews, dialogue appropriated from Hollywood films, and recorded conversations and readings, as well as music ranging from Beethoven to the Stereo MCs.[10] Her sound tactics also vary from video to video. The multi-track polyphony of *Aletheia* (1992) and *Kore,* in which the layering and cross-cutting between different audio tracks reflect a channel-surfing aesthetic, are in marked contrast to the stark minimalism of *Operculum* (1993), *Ocularis* (1997), and *Ekleipsis,* in which the voice-over is the primary sound track. Tran herself remarks that as the series progressed she used fewer and fewer appropriated sounds. Instead, in the later videos she shifted her focus to using narration written by herself and others.[11] Whereas the first four videos in the series, *Aletheia, Operculum, Kore,* and *Ocularis,* seem to alternate between polyphonic and minimalist sound tactics, the three videos produced since 1998, *Ekleipsis, Alexia,* and *Amaurosis* (2002), feature minimal sound tracks that privilege the human voice-over music and other found sound. *Amaurosis,* in which Beethoven's "Moonlight Sonata" emerges as the principal audio text, is the exception here.

In his books *Audio-Vision* and *The Voice in Cinema,* Michel Chion identifies the human voice as the sound that is almost always privileged in the cinema. He describes this primacy of speech as "vococentrism," where the human voice "is isolated in the sound mix like a solo instrument—for which the other sounds (music and noise) are merely the accompaniment."[12] The human voice also is a central audio element in *The Blindness Series,* but unlike in the narrative films that inform Chion's writings, Tran's use of the voice is almost exclusively focused on voice-over narration. It is the primary vocal element in all but one of the videos in the series. *Amaurosis* (2002) is a video portrait of blind musician Nguyen Duc Dat organized around a series of interviews with Nguyen. The talking heads interview format is also used in *Kore,* in which Peou Lakhana, an AIDS worker and participant in the video, discusses the relationship between women, AIDS/HIV, and blindness. Although this sequence employs a documentary format, it is in fact staged, and Peou's statements are scripted.[13] *Aletheia, Kore,* and *Alexia* all include voice-over narration, whereas in *Operculum* the plastic surgeons unwittingly narrate most of the video.[14] The sound tracks of *Ocularis* and *Ekleipsis* are entirely composed from voice-overs.

In *Kore, Ocularis, Ekleipsis,* and *Alexia,* voices are frequently altered through the use of analog technology and different vocal accents.[15] The alteration of voices through technology and performance in *The Blindness Series* begins with *Aletheia,* but its usage becomes more prominent in the later works. In *Ocularis* this tactic is used to partly mask the vocal identities of participants who responded to an ad that Tran placed nationally to solicit fears and fantasies about video surveillance. Participants called a 1-800 toll-free phone number and recorded their fantasies on its voicemail. The video includes some of these messages as a part of its sound track, but the pitch of the participants' voices is altered to mask their identities. In other videos from the series, voices are altered to lend different meanings to the narration. *Kore* includes a passage from Georges Bataille's *Story of the Eye* narrated in a male voice with a raunchy southern accent, which destabilizes the national origin of the text with a sexual twist.[16] Its counterpart in the video is an erotic female whisper that describes female masturbatory fantasies involving the eye. This voice is miked close to the body with no reverb, whereas reverb is added to the male voice in order to make the speaker sound like he is speaking from inside a tunnel or through a tube. In *Ocularis* a fictional account of a paranoid woman obsessed with surveillance is narrated by a high-pitched female voice that also sports a southern accent. In this case, however, her accent serves to locate her geographically and also to hint at her racial and class background.[17] In his 1977 essay "The Grain of the Voice," Roland Barthes borrows from Julia Kristeva's use of *pheno-text* and *geno-text* in his effort to distinguish between the phenomena of a song and its materiality.[18] In Barthes's formulation the pheno-song "covers all the phenomena, all the features which belong to the structure of the language being sung, the rules of the genre, the coded form of the melisma, the composer's idiolect, the style of the interpretation," whereas the geno-song "is the volume of the singing and speaking voice, the space where significations germinate 'from within language and in its very materiality.'"[19] He further theorizes the latter's mode of signification as in "not what it says, but the voluptuousness of its sound-signifiers, of its letters—where melody explores how the language works and identifies with that work. It is, in a very simple word but which must be taken seriously, the *diction* of the language." Barthes calls this signifier the "grain" of the voice.[20] Through changing the pitch, reverb, and accents of the voice in her videos, Tran uses its grain to alter the meaning of these passages. In *Ocularis* the diction of the voice-over, as well as its content, contributes equally to the meaning of the narration. In the two narrations from *Kore,* however, the audio processing and accents are emphasized to such a degree that a significant portion of the words in the voice-over becomes difficult to comprehend. So to transpose Barthes's transposition of Kristeva, unlike traditional voice-over narrations, where the pheno-voice-over is usually the conveyor of meaning, the geno-voice-over in these two narrations overwhelms the pheno-voice-over and becomes the primary sound-signifier. Here, the diction of the language has overpowered its words.

Kore: Multivocality as Metaphor

In addition to working with the materiality of a voice, Tran's juxtaposition of many voices within videos such as *Aletheia, Kore,* and *Alexia* engages with recent debates on subjectivity and authorship. The notion of a singular authorial voice has been complicated by theoretical practices such as poststructuralism and deconstruction, where subjectivity is attributed to the act of reading and looking as much as to the act of writing and creating, thereby constructing the meaning of a work through the intermingling of multiple subjects.[21] Feminist critical theory, in particular that which draws from Freudian and Lacanian psychoanalysis, has also contributed to this complex notion of subjectivity, fragmenting the singular voice of the author into many voices speaking within a complex system of repressions and drives, a multitude that challenges the singularity of phallocentric domination in language and in visual culture.[22] Tran's multitrack sensibility and her inclusion of diverse source material in *The Blindness Series* certainly reflect an affinity toward a multivocal model of subjectivity. There also exists within the videos, however, an antithetical privileging of selected voices. These are voices that speak about the experiences of women (*Aletheia, Operculum, Kore, Ocularis,* and *Ekleipsis*), people of color (*Aletheia, Operculum, Kore, Ocularis, Ekleipsis,* and *Amaurosis*), and queers (*Aletheia* and *Kore*), as well as similarly marginalized voices that are under- or misrepresented in dominant media.[23] In this sense *The Blindness Series* shares with other works drawing from marginalized experiences a commitment to create visibility for these groups and to challenge their misrepresentation in the dominant media. These struggles in representation are often described as "finding a voice" or "claiming a voice," in which previously suppressed voices are affirmed and celebrated.[24]

Kore is a good example of how these seemingly contradictory sensibilities can coexist within a singular work. *Kore* incorporates many different voices—in the form of voice-over, text, music, interview, and found sound. In this video that investigates "the conjunction of sexuality with: the eye as purveyor of desire; the sexual fear and fantasy of blindness, with a focus on the blindfold; and women and AIDS,"[25] Tran has drawn from texts by Bataille and Luce Irigaray, as well as *Sexual Behavior in the Human Female, Eros Denied,* and *AIDS and Vision Loss,* music by Loop Guru and A Thousand Points of Light, and film clips from *Zombie, Flesh Gordon, The Dark Half, Gothic, Swelter in Vogue, One Eye Leads, Damage,* and *Tokyo Decadence.* Tran weaves these many and different voices together into a flow of images, sound, and text, often juxtaposing different voices in a single sequence. The opening sequence of the video pairs the techno song "Read My Lips" by A Thousand Points of Light with rescanned images of a woman masturbating. The irony of this juxtaposition recalls the Situationist's method of *detournèment,* where "the reuse of preexisting artistic elements in a new ensemble" can be deployed as a critique of the source material.[26] In this sequence the source material is former U.S. president George H. W. Bush's catchphrase "read my lips"— already decontextualized by the musicians of A Thousand Points of Light, who sampled it in an electronic techno beat. Tran further destabilizes its meaning by pairing the song with a close-up image of a vagina, shot in a circular pan off a video monitor lying flat on the floor. The camera, acting as a surrogate for the viewer's eye, circles the image while zooming in. What is initially perceived to be an abstract, strobing light is revealed to be an image of female masturbation sped up to match the frenetic beat of the song. Though this sequence can certainly be seen as an ironic feminist rebuttal to Bush's conservative politics, it can also be read as a direct reference to Luce Irigaray's essay "When Our Lips Speak Together" in *This Sex Which Is Not One.*[27] The "lips" in the title of this essay refer to both the lips on a woman's mouth as well as her vulval lips.[28] Indeed, Irigaray's vision of female sexuality is an important reference for Tran in this video, and Irigaray's theories of a multivocal, nonhierarchical, and corporeal feminine discourse also correspond to the polyphonic, channel-surfing sensibility in *Kore.*

> Between our lips, yours and mine, several voices, several ways of speaking resound endlessly, back and forth. One is never separable from the other. You/I: we are always several at once. And how could one dominate the other? Impose her voice, her tone, her meaning? One cannot be distinguished from the other; which does not mean that they are indistinct. You don't understand a thing? No more than they understand you.
>
> Speak, all the same. It's our good fortune that your language isn't formed of a single thread, a single strand or pattern. It comes from everywhere at once. You touch me all over at the same time. In all senses.[29]

Feminine discourse (*écriture féminine*) is a practice of writing and speaking proposed by a group of French feminists as a discourse that "will always exceed the discourse governing the phallocentric system; it takes place and will take place somewhere other than in the territories subordinated to philosophical-theoretical domination."[30] Hélène Cixous further describes feminine discourse as "a text that divides itself, pulls itself to pieces, dismembers itself, regroups, [and] remembers itself."[31] Although Tran is working in video, *Kore*'s nonlinear structure and its blending of heterogeneous elements work surprisingly well with Cixous's description of a text-based practice.[32] And Tran's juxtaposition of source material, ranging from horror films to AIDS activist literature to techno music, certainly befits Cixous's pronouncement of letting "the other tongue of a thousand tongues speak."[33] The emphasis on the close relationship between voice, language, and desire in feminine discourse is also evident in *Kore,* where the narration is often modulated with whispers, groans, and other nonverbal sounds of the body. Furthermore, Tran's use of analog audio effects and performance to create particular articulations in the voice-over, such as in the passage from Bataille's *Story of the Eye* performed by the male voice with a southern accent, is very much a realization of Cixous's vision of interweaving writing and voice so that meaning is engendered through the process of writing *and* speaking the text.[34]

Kore operates, however, only up to a point within the paradigm of feminine discourse. Though Tran's efforts to reclaim the blindfold and her exploration into a touch-based eroticism in the video echo Irigaray's notion of a fluid, all-over female sexuality, her inclusion of male voices in *Kore,* as well as her fore-grounding of race, challenges Irigaray's utopian fantasy of "constantly touching herself" and "speaking resound endlessly."[35] Besides quotations from Bataille, *Kore* also includes video segments from two male collaborators. One, by artist Tyler Stallings, features a model spaceship crash landing into a flaccid penis, and the other, contributed by myself, is an excerpt from my video *Slanted Vision* (1995), which was created in collaboration with writer Han Ong. In this segment Super 8 footage of Asian men shot in the streets of Hong Kong and San Francisco is projected onto my face and body and reshot on video. The film and video footage are then edited together with a voice-over, written and performed by Ong, who speaks about reclaiming our subjectivity as queer Asian men through the act of looking.[36] Though feminine discourse is certainly not theorized as being restricted to female practitioners only,[37] and Irigaray repeatedly speaks of being "several at once,"[38] it is undeniable that the multivocality within feminine discourse is very much theorized through the sexual plurality attributed to an essentialized female body.

In her book *The Acoustic Mirror,* Kaja Silverman critiques Irigaray's heavy reliance on the binary opposition of male and female, and she cites Ann Rosalind Jones's enumeration of the psychic, physical, social, economic, and political differences among women, which Irigaray tends to ignore in her utopian discourse.[39] Though Tran seems to depart from the essentialist paradigm of feminine discourse through her inclusion of male voices in *Kore,* it is also significant to note that the men in *Kore* can hardly be considered as normative within the phallocentric system. Bataille's vision of sexuality is perverse, excessive, and equally transgressive across all genders. Tyler Stallings's image of the penis, a symbol of phallic power, is flaccid and crash landed upon. The narrator in my projection sequence articulates his desire for other Asian men. It is also significant to note that the most joyous and pleasurable sequence in *Kore* is one that shows two blindfolded Asian women making love to the Loop Guru's "Hymn," a song that pairs electronic drum beats with South Asian instrumentation and the ecstatic ululation of a female vocalist. In this sequence, at the culmination of the video, the images of the Asian women explode in saturated reds and oranges. The swooning camera is placed very close to the women, giving the viewers a sense of being in the middle of the lovemaking. The footage conveys a sense of haptic tactility through its strobes and blurs—a result from being shot at a low shutter speed. With its imagery of women loving women and its celebration of touch-based pleasure, this climactic sequence in *Kore* can again be read within the paradigm of feminine discourse. Another passage from Cixous seems an apt description here:

> The Voice sings from a time before law, before the Symbolic took one's breath away and reappropriated it into language under its authority of separation. The deepest, the oldest, the loveliest Visitation. Within each woman the first, nameless love is singing.[40]

The key signifiers in this sequence—the blindfold, the Asian features and bodies of the women, the South Asian instrumentation and female vocalist—locate this sequence, however, outside European and American cultural contexts. The pleasure represented here, blinded, nonverbal, and touch based, is apart from European and American paradigms of vision and language. Thus, this sequence and what it represents are also situated outside the discourse of the Lacanian Symbolic. In addition, since one of the Asian women here is Peou Lakhana, whom we have seen speaking as an AIDS worker in other parts of the video, the presumed primitivism of non-Western bodies and the preverbal pleasure of the sequence are disrupted by Peou's other representation as articulate, knowledgeable, rational, and very much within the Western context of an AIDS activist. When the credits roll at the end of the video, we hear Peou's voice reflecting upon her experience performing in this scene. Her self-reflexive voice further complicates any essentialist readings of the lovemaking sequence while it also situates it among the many other voices in the video.

Trauma and Vocal Embodiment in *Ekleipsis*

While Tran's *Kore* incorporates many voices and different modes of articulation, the sound track of another video in *The Blindness Series, Ekleipsis,* is by contrast starkly minimal. In *Ekleipsis* the sound track is composed entirely from voice-over narration. All of the voices in the video are women's voices, which parallel the video's focus on a group of Cambodian women refugees living in Long Beach, California. They are known as the largest group of hysterically blind people in the world.[41] All of the voices in the video have been altered, resulting in different degrees of audibility. These voices fill up most of the sound track and are interrupted only twice in the video by text quotes that are silent.[42] The images from the video are similarly restrained, consisting of shots of the textual history of Cambodia in close-up pans, newsreel photographs of Cambodians during the reign of the Khmer Rouge, and a series of images, separated by black space, that repeats throughout the video, with the clips becoming longer as the video progresses. These sequences are composed from media images of Cambodia appropriated from TV news, documentaries, and fictional film sources, as well as symbolic images that include close-up shots of jewelry, glasses, a pineapple, and rice.[43] The video opens and closes with a low-pitch and distorted voice that speaks in the first person. This is the fictionalized voice of the Cambodian women and the most difficult to comprehend in the video.[44] Other voices in the video include what I call the academic/psychoanalyst voice and the journalistic voice. There are several variations of the academic/psychoanalyst voice. All are high pitched and performed with a haughty accent. The journalistic voice sounds the least altered and is the most clearly audible in the video. While the voice of the Cambodian women frames the video, most of its body consists of exchanges between the two other voices in which the journalistic voice, speaking in the second person, recounts the horrific experiences of the Cambodian women under the Khmer Rouge. The academic/psychoanalyst voice, speaking in the third person, discusses the history of hysteria, trauma, and psychoanalysis in a European and American context. This voice is the most theoretically dense and emotionally detached in the work. There is, about halfway through the video, a brief interlude from these two voices when a young girl recounts, in first person, her experience in the Khmer Rouge labor camps. Tran's sister, Namolisa Slemmons, performs this narration, and Tran performs the other voices.[45]

The French term for voice-over is *voix-off.* According to Michel Chion, voix-off designates any bodiless voice in a film that tells stories, provides commentary, or evokes the past.[46] Chion's book *The Voice in Cinema* is very much concerned with disembodied voices in cinema. In the book he focuses on the concept of the *acousmêtre*—the magical, all-knowing, and all-powerful voice that is not attached to a body and one whose power is lost when its source becomes visible.[47] Chion traces the origins of the acousmêtre to the voice of the *montreur d'images,* the picture presenter who narrated the lantern slide shows that toured through the French countryside in the eighteenth and nineteenth centuries. These shows were one of the precursors to modern cinema, and the voice of the montreur d'images, who read from texts designed to accompany these shows, sometimes called "talking journals," became integrated into the cinematic device of the voice-over.[48] Although Chion bases his observations primarily on narrative cinema, his concept of the acousmêtre is very similar to the voice-of-god narrator used in documentaries. Like the acousmêtre, the voice-of-god narrator is all knowing and often disembodied. Like the montreur d'images, the disembodied narrator in documentaries often dictates meaning to the images that the viewers are watching.[49] Though none of the voices in *Ekleipsis* are synchronized to a body (or "nailed," to use Marguerite Duras's term), the journalistic voice and the academic/psychoanalyst voice both exhibit characteristics of an acousmatic voice.[50] The journalistic voice provides the viewers with information about the experiences of the Cambodian women. It is not quite a voice-of-god narration in that it does not directly comment on the images seen. It connects to the images in video by virtue of its subject matter and at specific moments when objects it mentions appear on the screen.[51] Even though it is often narrating horrific experiences, it remains objective, neutral, and emotionless, very much within the realm of rationality by virtue of its audibility and inflection. The academic/ psychoanalyst voice is denser in that it speaks in a theoretical language, and its accent serves to add to this sense of detachment. It provides metacommentary on the predicament of the women but never connects to their experiences. It intellectualizes their suffering in the abstract language of theories and symptoms.

The third voice in the video, the one that represents the Cambodian women, is the most difficult to hear and to understand. Its pitch is lowered so much that it hardly sounds like a woman's voice. The reverb is distorted to the degree that it sounds like the narrator is swallowing her words or that the words are struggling to burst out of her throat. These effects, along with an exaggerated intonation, make her words virtually incomprehensible. In *The Voice in Cinema,* Chion traces a particular kind of acousmatic voice that he calls the "I-voice." He writes:

> The cinematic I-voice is not just the voice that says "I," as in a novel. To solicit the spectator's identification, that is, for the spectator to appropriate it to any degree, it must be framed and recorded in a certain manner. Only then can it function as a pivot of identification, resonating in us as if it were our own voice, like a voice in first person.[52]

For Chion the I-voice is characterized by two qualities: close miking and dryness, or an absence of reverb. These qualities create in us, the viewers, "an intimacy with the voice, such that we sense no distance between it and our ear," and a lack of "concrete and identifiable space" with which to situate and distance the voice from ourselves.[53] The voice representing the Cambodian women in *Ekleipsis* shares some of the characteristics of Chion's I-voice. It is closely miked and situated very close to our bodies. In fact, I would venture that its sonorous qualities place it inside our bodies. When we hear it, this voice becomes lodged deep inside our throats, struggling to get out, to be formed into comprehensible words. This effect is similar to a concept Chion calls "corporeal implication," "when the voice makes us feel in our body the vibration of the body of the other." Chion also notes that extreme cases of corporeal implication occur "when there is no dialogue or words, but only closely present breathing or groans or sighs."[54] It is significant to note that although the Cambodian women's voice is speaking a comprehensible and powerful text, its articulation of this text renders the meaning of its words virtually incomprehensible, resembling the bodily sounds mentioned.[55] Therefore, the meaning of these passages is conferred not so much in the text of the voice-over but in its sonority. More so than in the two narrations from *Kore,* here the geno-voice-over takes precedence over the pheno-voice-over as the conveyor of meaning. Tran is able to create a voice in which its grain, corporeally implicated deep inside our bodies, can both give us a sense of the horrors these women experienced and impinge upon us the impossible struggle of articulating their experiences in rational speech and language.

Chion also discusses the relationship between vocal embodiment and horror in *The Voice in Cinema,* in which he cites the correlation between the French terms for embodiment (*mise-en-corps*), entombment (*mise-en-bière*), and interment (*mise-en-terre*), closely linking vocal embodiment to death and burial.[56] In his book he uses the example of Alfred Hitchcock's *Psycho* (1960) to elucidate his point. The three speeches delivered by the mother's voice in the film progressively reveal Norman's psychosis by bringing her voice closer and closer to his body. This is accomplished through the progressive elimination of reverb in her voice on the film's sound track, so that by the time Norman is revealed as the murderer, captured, and put in a holding cell at the police station, the mother's voice is completely nailed to his body. We see Norman's face in a close-up, his mouth unmoving, yet we hear the mother's last monologue as if she is speaking from within his body. His gestures and facial expression correspond to her speech. Her voice is dry, and there is no reverb, creating an effect that Chion describes as "to suggest possession by spirits, or ventriloquism."[57] In this impossible embodiment, the dead mother has completely possessed Norman through her voice. For Chion the embodiment of another's voice is almost always a horrific experience. He traces this association between horror and vocal embodiment back to the uterus, where he envisions a child being completely engulfed by the "sonorous envelope" of the mother's voice.[58] Kaja Silverman has critiqued Chion's fantasy as a symptom of male paranoia and castration, and she argues that disembodying the female voice can be a challenge to "every conception by means of which we have previously known women within Hollywood film, since it is precisely *as body* that she is constructed there."[59] In Tran's *Ekleipsis* the horror that is conveyed through impossible embodiment is not the horror of the phallic mother but the horrors of war and atrocities. The voice of the Cambodian women is not the voice of a dead woman. It is a fictionalized voice that draws from the collective witnessing by these women survivors of the horrific acts committed by the Khmer Rouge—acts horrifying enough to disable their vision, rendering them hysterically blind. Yet this voice, like the voice of Norman's dead mother, is out to possess bodies. It lodges itself in our throats, struggling to burst out. We feel its vibrations buried deep within us. We experience the women's trauma through its grain. We are corporeally implicated by how we often distance ourselves, very much in the manner of the other voices in the video, from atrocities that happen in other countries and other cultures. Instead of being engendered within the sound design of the filmic text, the embodiment facilitated by *Ekleipsis* happens outside the video's textual body and inside the bodies of its viewers.

Whether an incomprehensible voice that speaks of the horrors of hunger, torture, and execution or a scene of touch-based pleasure represented in audiovisual imagery, there is a consistent endeavor within Tran's *The Blindness Series* to speak the unspeakable and to show that which cannot be seen. To understand these seeming paradoxes, we return to the beginning of this essay and to the strategy of using the negative to emphasize the positive. Just as the empty spaces in a Chinese landscape painting by thirteenth-century painter Mu-ch'I define its pictorial elements, blindness—the lack of vision—structures our perception of what is visible in this video series. In a similar way, the many voices within *The Blindness Series,* both metaphorical and material, speak to the limitations of visuality. Speaking in many tongues and sometimes in the nonverbal diction of whispers, groans, and cries, these voices speak about what is outside visual representation. What they collectively say is that both pleasure and horror maybe unrepresentable or that our current visually hegemonic system of representation is inadequate to portray these experiences. In her videos Tran presents us with glimpses of possible alternatives: voice, music, touch, multisensory experiences, and multiple subjectivities. In a project that is so concerned with visuality, it is these nonvisual elements that make full what we do see in the videos.

NOTES

1. I draw this position in part from a history of media practitioners who have engaged as actively in theoretical debates as they have in the actual production of media, ranging from Sergei Eisenstein to Glauber Rocha to Trinh T. Minh-ha. Kobena Mercer and Isaac Julien also articulate a similar position of speaking from, as opposed to speaking for, a community in the production of art and media that articulate marginalized experiences. See Kobena Mercer, "Skin Head Sex Thing: Racial Difference and the Homoerotic Imaginary," in *How Do I Look?*

Queer Film and Video, ed. Bad Object Choices (Seattle: Bay Press, 1991), 204; see also Kobena Mercer and Isaac Julien, "De margin and de centre," *Screen* 29, no. 4 (Autumn 1988): 2–10.

2. I first met Tran in 1991 when we were both graduate art students at the California Institute of the Arts. We are now both media studies professors at the Claremont Colleges, Tran at Scripps College and myself at Pitzer College. I am a collaborator in *Aletheia* and *Kore*—contributing segments in both videos—and I shot footage for both *Kore* and *Operculum.* I have screened almost all of the videos in the series as rough cuts and gave Tran feedback before she finalized them.

3. Here, I am paraphrasing Jo, the main character in Wayne Wang's film *Chan Is Missing* (1981). Jo is referring to the fact that the missing Chan was never found in the film, but in the process of looking for him, a vibrant portrait of San Francisco's Chinatown and its colorful residents emerges. One could argue that it is not so much the absent Chan but the community into which he has disappeared that becomes the focus of the film. Besides the reference to Wang's film, the strategy of using negative space in a composition to accentuate positively rendered elements is a central device in Chinese landscape painting and garden design and an aesthetic feature in many East and Southeast Asian cultures.

4. The term is from a quote by Alan Burdick in Jonathan Sterne, *The Audible Past: Cultural Origins of Sound Reproduction* (Durham, N.C.: Duke University Press, 2003), 2–3. For discussions of sound culture in relationship to visual culture, see also James Lastra, *Sound Technology and the American Cinema: Perception, Representation, Modernity* (New York: Columbia University Press, 2000); Douglas Kahn, *Noise, Water, Meat: A History of Sound in the Arts* (Cambridge: MIT Press, 2001); Charles Hirschkind, *The Ethical Soundscape: Cassette Sermons and Islamic Counterpublics* (New York: Columbia University Press, 2006); Emily Thompson, *The Soundscape of Modernity: Architectural Acoustics and the Culture of Listening in America (1900–1933)* (Cambridge: MIT Press, 2004); Mark M. Smith, *Hearing History: A Reader* (Athens: Georgia University Press, 2004); Karin Bijsterveld, *Mechanical Sound: Technology, Culture, and Public Problems of Noise in the Twentieth Century* (Cambridge: MIT Press, 2008); Michael Bull and Les Back, eds., *The Auditory Culture Reader* (Oxford, U.K.: Berg Publishers, 2004).

5. Semiotics, psychoanalysis, and the ongoing debates on representations of race, gender, and sexuality are some obvious examples. There are some media scholars who are moving away from this visually centered approach and are choosing to focus on how other senses affect the production and reception of media. See, for example, Laura U. Marks's work on touch-based cinema, discussed in her books *The Skin of the Film: Intercultural Cinema, Embodiment, and the Senses* (Durham, N.C.: Duke University Press, 1999); and *Touch: Sensuous Theory and Multisensory Media* (Minneapolis: University of Minnesota Press, 2002).

6. Other than a body of historical scholarship focused on the transition from silent to sound film and one on musical film scores, media studies scholarship on sound is few and far between. Michel Chion and Kaja Silverman's work, already mentioned, are notable exceptions, as are Lastra, *Sound Technology and the American Cinema*; and Amy Lawrence, *Echo and Narcissus: Women's Voices in Classical Hollywood Cinema* (Berkeley: University of California Press, 1991). Rick Altman has done groundbreaking work on sound and early cinema, as well as the musical, in *Silent Film Sound* (New York: Columbia University Press, 2007); *The American Film Musical* (Indianapolis: Indiana University Press, 1989); *Sound Theory, Sound Practice* (New York: Routledge, 1992); and *The Sounds of Early Cinema,* eds. Richard Abel and Rick Altman (Indianapolis: Indiana University Press, 2001). Elisabeth Weis and John Belton coedited one of the earlier anthologies on the subject, *Film Sound: Theory and Practice* (New York.: Columbia University Press, 1985).

7. Michel Chion, *Audio-Vision: Sound on Screen,* trans. Claudia Gorbman (New York: Columbia University Press, 1994), 39–40.

8. Ibid., 40.

9. Silverman discusses Laura Mulvey and Peter Wollen's *Riddles of the Sphinx* (1976), Yvonne Rainer's *Film about a Woman Who . . .* (1974), Bette Gordon's *Empty Suitcases* (1980), Patricia Gruben's *Sifted Evidence* (1981), and Sally Potter's *The Gold Diggers* (1984) in *The Acoustic Mirror: The Female in Psychoanalysis and Cinema* (Indianapolis: Indiana University Press, 1988).

10. I cataloged the following musical sources from Tran's seven videos: the Angry Samoans, Ludwig van Beethoven, the Eagles, the Kronos Quartet, Loop Guru, Roy Orbison, Santana, Andrés Segovia, the Stereo MCs, and A Thousand Points of Light, as well as traditional Vietnamese music performed by Luu Thuy and Kim Tien, Xuan Que Huong, and Hanh Van.

11. Tran T. Kim-Trang, e-mail interview with author, June 6, 2004.

12. Chion, *Audio-Vision*, 6.

13. The constructed nature of this sequence is apparent to me because I was the cameraperson who shot it, but I think other viewers are given hints to its fictitiousness through the mannered quality of her speech and the use of preplanned close-up shots.

14. For *Operculum* Tran posed as a women considering cosmetic eyelid surgery to obtain video and audio recordings of the consultations. She told the doctors that her parents in Hong Kong would view the videotapes, recorded by her cousin (played by myself, doubling as camera operator), and decide which doctor to hire. The plastic surgeons were unaware that their recorded voices would be included in an experimental video.

15. Tran explained that she used analog devices such as pitch changes on audio cassette decks, guitar pedals, and the delivery choices of the performer (often herself) to alter the voices. E-mail interview with author, June 6, 2004.

16. *The Story of the Eye* by Georges Bataille was written in French, and the story takes place in France and Spain. Narrating the story in a male voice with a southern accent adds to the text both class and national associations not present in the text itself, which then further alters its sexualized content.

17. Although the identity of the speaker is never revealed in the video, she reads as white and lower middle class, in a similar way to the male narrator for the Bataille text. The content and construction (phrases, word choice, inflection) of her narration provide some clues, which are visually reinforced by surveillance footage of Latino youth questioned by the police in the video, shot from the point of view of the speaker/camera.

18. Roland Barthes, "The Grain of the Voice," in *On Record: Rock, Pop, and the Written Word*, eds. Simon Frith and Andrew Goodwin (London: Routledge, 2000), 294.

19. Ibid., 295.

20. Ibid., 294–95.

21. For examples of literary deconstruction, see the works of Jacques Derrida and Gayatri Spivak. Roland Barthes eloquently wrote about the importance of subjectivity and the act of reading and looking in his many books and essays. See *Camera Lucida: Reflections on Photography* (New York: Noonday Press, 1981).

22. See the work of French feminists, including Hélène Cixous, Catherine Clément, Luce Irigaray, and Monique Wittig. The work of two of these writers, Cixous and Irigaray, are discussed in this essay.

23. Examples include the voices of refugees in *Ekleipsis*, people with AIDS/HIV in *Kore*, and the differently abled in *Amaurosis*.

24. The voice frequently appears in the context of struggles for representation by women, people of color, and queers, as well as other marginalized groups. There are numerous anthologies within the fields of cultural studies and ethnic studies that incorporate "voice" in their titles, as in "the voice of the marginalized" or "voices from the margins." This practice extends into exhibitions, performances, testimonials, oral histories, etc. For example, a docu-

mentary by Arthur Dong on the oldest Asian American media arts center, Visual Communications, is titled *Claiming a Voice* (1990).

25. From the synopsis on the video box of *Kore*.

26. Guy Debord, "Detournement as Negation and Prelude," in *Situationist International Anthology*, ed. and trans. Ken Knabb (Berkeley, Calif.: Bureau of Public Secrets, 1995), 55.

27. The use of *detournèment* in this sequence can be read as commentary on Bush's atrocious record on reproductive rights and AIDS/HIV policies during his term in office, not to mention his role in the 1991 Gulf War.

28. The multiple meaning of the "lips" in this essay can be read into the phrase "two lips kissing two lips," as well as from other parts of the essay of the same title; see Luce Irigaray, *This Sex Which Is Not One*, trans. Catherine Porter (Ithaca, N.Y.: Cornell University Press, 1985), 210. See also Irigaray, *This Sex Which Is Not One*, 24, for discussion of female autoeroticism.

29. Irigaray, *This Sex Which Is Not One*, 209.

30. Hélène Cixous and Catherine Clément, *The Newly Born Woman*, trans. Betsy Wong (Minneapolis: University of Minnesota Press, 1986), 92.

31. Ibid., 84.

32. The French word *ecriture* in *l'ecriture feminine* has been translated variously as "text," "discourse," and other English words to expand its meaning beyond simply writing and into acts of production.

33. Cixous and Clement, *The Newly Born Woman*, 88.

34. Cixous writes, "First I sense femininity in writing by: a privilege of *voice*: *writing* and *voice* are entwined and interwoven and writing's continuity/voice's rhythm take each other's breath away through interchanging, making the text gasp or form it out of suspenses and silences, make it lose its voice or rend it with cries." Cixous and Clement, *The Newly Born Woman*, 92.

35. Irigaray, *This Sex Which Is Not One*, 29, 209.

36. The full text of the voice-over is included here without indications of breaks in Ong's phrasing: "The sea / of likeness. / A Sea of likeness. / The eye, much like a camera, betrays its owner's conscience / seeking out its own reflecting in a crowd / seeking affirmation of self despite Mass Media's instruction to do otherwise / despite Mass Media's recurrent catechism to obliterate the 'I' / and the me / and their various counterparts / If the 'I' and the me / happen to be non-white / That is to say if the 'I' and the me / happen to be me. / Looking, judging, adjusting, affirming . . . / The soul's tongue is the eye / and everyday, by looking, judging, adjusting, / and affirming its mirror image anywhere, everywhere / It reclaims its 'I'ness back from those who attempt to render it / invisible."

37. Cixous cites French writer Jean Genet, a gay man, as an example of writing in a feminine discourse. Cixous and Clement, *The Newly Born Woman*, 84.

38. Irigaray, *This Sex Which Is Not One*, 209.

39. Silverman, *The Acoustic Mirror*, 146–48.

40. Cixous and Clement, *The Newly Born Woman*, 93

41. From the synopsis on the video box of *Ekleipsis*.

42. One of the two quotes recounts an old Buddhist prophecy in which an era of misfortune in Cambodia is foretold. The other is by Sigmund Freud. Two other text quotes appear in the video: one, by David Sanders, is silent and precedes the first voice-over, and the other, by Juan-David Nasio, is located at the end of the video. The last voice-over is spoken over this quote and runs into the end credits.

43. Image sources listed in the end credits of *Ekleipsis* are *ABC 20/20*, *EyeWitness*, *The Killing Fields*, and *Raise the Bamboo Curtain*.

44. Tran, who wrote the narration, identifies this voice as that of the women's and that it is intentionally difficult to hear. E-mail interview with author, June 6, 2004.

45. From the end credits of *Ekleipsis*.

46. Michel Chion, *The Voice in Cinema,* trans. Claudia Gorbman (New York: Columbia University Press, 1999), 49.

47. Ibid., 17–29.

48. Ibid., 49.

49. This is especially evident in more traditional documentaries, such as ethnographic films, and does not apply as much to newer genres, such as cinema verité, which sometimes forego narration altogether.

50. Chion, *The Voice in Cinema,* 130.

51. Some of the objects mentioned in the journalistic narration also appear in the cycle of images. For example, the narration mentions that the Khmer Rouge would single out and kill individuals wearing glasses because it was thought that only intellectuals wore glasses and that women refugees often hid jewelry and other precious objects in their vaginas. The close-up images of a pineapple in the cycle of images also correspond to the explanation in the narration that the pineapple is a visual metaphor for the "all-seeing eyes" of the Khmer Rouge.

52. Chion, *The Voice in Cinema,* 50–51.

53. Ibid., 51.

54. Ibid., 53.

55. The scripts of the Cambodian women's voice-overs is as follows: "I believe in the sacredness of the head. It's considered the seat of the soul and provides exits from one's life essence. This is a commonly held belief amongst Southeast Asians, and maybe that's why I and the other women like myself am experiencing such troubles with our eyes. Touching the head is considered highly personal and is not allowed except by close intimates. The head is the part of the body most frequently abused during our life under the Khmer Rouge. In addition, touching of an older person by a younger person is unacceptable behavior in Cambodian culture, thus the beatings we suffered at the hands of the young boys of 'Angka' were especially traumatic. We believe that the beatings and wartime trauma that we suffered caused much more damage to our vision than reasons due to our age or accidents.

"We are not especially 'suggestible,' an explanation that has been used by some psychiatrists to explain functional visual loss. The fact that we are alive and in the U.S. attests to our will to survive. All but one of us had normal pre-war levels of psychological and social functioning, and all of us would like to be so again. The suggestibility theory seems to ignore our desperate and very real attempts to escape from Cambodia by implying the usefulness and ease of 'escape' through observing and mimicking visual loss. It insults our strengths, and underestimates the extent of the trauma and the horrors of our situation. Any person who underwent the kind of horror we had been subjected to might well be disabled by it.

"It is strength of the inner will, the innermost essence of the self, which distinguishes ascendant personalities. As both a conscious exercise or more unconscious reaction, ascendant personalities engage in a consistent effort to build the strength of will to survive. In contrast to the body of thought which suggests that traumatic experiences must always be indelibly etched on the human soul in a way which leaves scars on life, ascendant personalities provide ample evidence that there is the equal potential for using the experience to reflect on our lives in a more positive way." Tran T. Kim-Trang, script of *Ekleipsis*.

56. Chion, *The Voice in Cinema,* 140.

57. Ibid., 149.

58. Ibid., 61.

59. Silverman, *The Acoustic Mirror,* 73, 164.

6 Making Visible What Had No Business Being Seen

COMMUNITY MEDIA AND THE QUESTION OF THE POLITICAL

Freya Schiwy

For Jacques Rancière, contrary to commonly held ideas, the political does not occur through participation in the established venues of liberal representative democracy. Rather, the administration and negotiation of different claims on the state is what he calls "the police." "Politics is generally seen as the set of procedures whereby the aggregation and consent of collectivities is achieved, the organization of powers, the distribution of places and roles, and the systems for legitimizing this distribution. I propose to call it *the police.*"[1] The political, in contrast, is constituted at the moment when those "who have no part" make themselves present. In Rancière's words, "Political activity is whatever shifts a body from the place assigned to it or changes a place's destination. It makes visible what had no business being seen, and makes heard a discourse where once there was only place for noise; it makes understood as discourse what was once only heard as noise."[2] Consensus here constitutes the return of the police. Mexico and Bolivia have both seen the emergence of community media linked to Indigenous movements, which, however, hold up the idea of consensus as fundamental to a process of wide-ranging political change. This essay explores Indigenous notions of governance and the idea of consensus put forth in Indigenous community videos like *Caracoles: New Paths of Resistance* (Mexico, 2003) and *Overcoming Fear* (Bolivia, 2005). Placing these videos—one a documentary, the other a fiction drama—in dialogue with Rancière means asking if community media can themselves act politically in Rancière's sense. We might also ask if community media can challenge Rancière's concepts.

Jacques Rancière's notion of the political, arising initially from his work on nineteenth-century French workers, encompasses at least three dimensions. First, it seeks to understand the way social actors may change a given political order. Second, "the political" points to the social impact forms of representation such as art or cinema or video may be able to effect. Third, the notion refers to thought itself. How is a regime of knowledge and power, or "visibility," that limits how and what can be represented and thought challenged? Community media in Chiapas and Bolivia similarly speak to these three dimensions.

The Political as Disruption: Offscreen

Caracoles: New Paths of Resistance is a video produced by the Chiapas Media Project (CMP) and intended for distribution in the United States.[3] This media initiative was born in the context of the EZLN's (Ejército Zapatista de Liberación Nacional [National Zapatista Liberation Army]) armed uprising in southern Mexico. The revolt began on January 1, 1994, when poorly armed Mayan Indians, joined with former Marxist revolutionaries, briefly occupied the town halls of several urban centers in Chiapas. The movement initially articulated a critique of NAFTA, neoliberalism, and the Mexican state and has evolved into a long-lasting effort to transform Mexican democracy from below. In 1996, in response to requests from individuals in the Zapatista-controlled territory to gain access to audiovisual technology, the U.S. documentary filmmaker Alexandra Halkin founded the Chiapas Media Project (called Promedios in Mexico), which provides Indigenous communities in Chiapas with access to and training in audiovisual technology, including editing and postproduction centers, as well as computer skills and satellite Internet access.[4]

The Zapatista struggle includes the production and distribution of Indigenous media in Zapatista communities as well as internationally. CMP documentaries have been shown in Mexico, at international Indigenous film and video festivals, and in North American universities. These video shorts are part of a vast production of Indigenous media that span documentaries, docudramas, and fiction films produced by Indigenous activists and their collaborators in Brazil, Bolivia, Canada, Australia, and elsewhere. Indigenous media include video, community television, radio, CDs, and so forth. In Latin America they are primarily distributed and aired in rural Indigenous communities. Research on Indigenous media and reports by media activists often highlight their potential as linked to sovereignty.[5] As Pamela Wilson and Michelle Stewart argue in their introduction to the recently published volume *Global Indigenous Media*:

> Contemporary Indigenous media demonstrate the extent to which the hallmarks of an earlier regime of empire—colonization, forced assimilation, genocide, and diaspora—are being challenged and displaced by new constellations of global power. Indigenous media often directly address the politics of identity and representation by engaging and challenging the dominant political forms at both the national and international level. In this landscape, control of media representation and of cultural self-definition asserts and signifies cultural and political sovereignty itself.[6]

It is commonplace to assume that the global concentration of media ownership represents a challenge to democracy. For Rancière, however, the democratic plurality of the media reduces political potential. Vehemently disagreeing with Baudrillard, Rancière writes that "the world of total visibility carves out a real where appearance has no place to occur or to produce its divisive, fragmenting effects. . . . This is indeed what is set up by the conjunction of media proliferation of whatever is visible and the endless count of opinions polled and votes simulated."[7] From this perspective some might argue that community media produce precisely the appearance of democratic plurality. Or they might be considered a place of catharsis, where the Left is able to articulate its critique but not effect actual change. I maintain, however, that the site of community media indeed constitutes a place where the political meets the police.

The long-standing patriarchal media duopoly in Mexico is increasingly integrated into global media networks of media ownership.[8] The majority of these media are owned by six corporations that have horizontally and vertically integrated multiple facets of production and cross-promotion. They position production, content, and distribution in function of the profit principle. This includes the marketing of diversity. The media sustain the economic interests of the corporate owners of media. In this context the Chiapas Media Project, like CEFREC-CAIB in Bolivia, rearticulates the voices that used to be the objects of ethnographic film and that are—in both national and international perspectives—still more readily associated with a disappearing world. Indigenous media activists appropriate the very technology that has framed their subjectivity in terms of their subordination and marginalization in a globalized world of shining technological innovation, stock market profits, and jet-set academics. Their films maintain, however, a marginal position in relation to commercial mass media. Screening at festivals and in universities, the distribution creates other communication flows that extend the primary site of Indigenous community media: rural networks of video exchange and terrestrial television that constitute a parallel media world. As a social and material practice, community media disrupt; they act politically by creating the means to assume and disseminate a position of equality with the educated and wealthy upper class that dominates discourse in the media and elsewhere.

The Political as Clash: On-screen

On-screen and like recent solidarity documentaries,[9] many community-media productions—such as *Images of the Repression in Oaxaca, You're Saying that We Can't Pass, Achacachi,* and ADOC's documentaries of the Argentine protests in 2001—represent the processes of political disruption in the street.[10] Clashes between protestors and the police are combined with a demand for a new, radical form of democracy. As a social and material practice, community media constitute a political moment of intervention while on-screen viewers are presented with the political event that does not merely demand recognition but itself constitutes an act of transformation, an appropriation of political competency. These videos put forth a discourse about the political, articulated by subjects that have commonly been denied voice and relevance in the national political discourse. Thus, they "subjectivize," to use Rancière's terminology, those who were previously unseen. Community media thus do not merely intervene in the space of mass media but alter the content of this space, as well as the dominant state and for-profit media's networks of ownership and dissemination.

The political discourse assumed in community media may best be understood by taking a closer look at *Caracoles* and *Overcoming Fear.* Released nine years after the EZLN uprising in 1994, *Caracoles* documents the ceremonial inauguration of the *caracoles* and the *juntas de buen gobierno,* the entities of civil self-governance in Zapatista territory that supplanted the administrative units called *aguascalientes,* which had been more directly subject to the EZLN's military control.[11] The forty-two-minute video celebrates the presence of different Indigenous peoples, community authorities, and diverse participants from Europe and North America during the historical gathering. *Caracoles* weaves together footage of uneven quality credited to eighteen Indigenous video makers from four different *caracoles.* It refers to an emerging political form but holds no formal surprises. Nevertheless, this video opens up a new subject position; it acts politically, in Rancière's sense.

Rancière's work on cinema primarily invokes the innovative classics of filmmaking (e.g., Eisenstein, Lang, Rossellini, Godard). His understanding of film's political potential does not, however, reduce the political to the artistic avant-garde. For Rancière, regardless of political intent, film can act politically by producing a "disturbing element," an uncanny experience that affects both "meaning and the withdrawal of meaning."[12] This uncanny element points to a moment of surprise, the creation of a new visibility.[13] Despite its conventional format and dominating narration, *Caracoles* indeed produces an uncomfortable, somewhat frustrating effect that is not provoked by formal experimentation. For those not among the hundreds of Mexican and international participants present during the ceremony and, hence, not finding their reflection on-screen, the video produces in that sense a surprise. *Caracoles* withholds a contextual historical narrative beyond general references to the Zapatista uprising in 1994. It mentions the Zapatista communities' persistence despite the "war of attrition" that Mexican governments—before and after the PRI (Partido Revolucionario Institucional)—have waged since then, yet the video refuses to give an idea of how the *caracoles* operate and what kind of political thinking underlies their organization.[14] It declines, if you like, interpellation into the documentary genre either as formalistically innovative artwork or as educational—that is, as obliged to the expectations of factual information or what Nichols calls the "discourse of sobriety."[15] Perhaps, we could call this an uncanny effect that thwarts expectations and, like Rigoberta Menchú's famous secrets, instead refers to a decolonial knowledge politics where the native informant refuses her traditional role.

The Political as Discourse: Decolonization

The documentary, however, indirectly invites viewers to learn from the Zapatistas. The *caracoles* point to a process of profound sociopolitical transformation in Chiapas that finds parallels in other southern Mexico states. Indeed, Indigenous autonomy and self-governance have long been contested fields, torn between state co-optation and diverse Indigenous efforts to reconstitute traditions of self-governance and thus generate a new model of democracy. *Mandar obedeciendo* has become a key phrase for these wide-ranging experiments with consensus governance.[16] The process resonates with the EZLN's refusal to partake in electoral democracy. The EZLN's Other Campaign advocated abstaining from the Mexican electoral process in 2006 and instead opted to forge a web of relations among diverse groups and actors across Mexican society. As Alicia Swords argues, "As lessons from the Zapatistas are adapted, political learning is diffused through civil-society networks."[17]

Gareth Williams argues that Rancière allows us to advance in understanding the political potential of the Zapatista National Liberation Army. He suggests that the Zapatistas directly challenge the neoliberal state form and that "the EZLN is calling for a deterritorializing shift in the dimension and plane of consistency of what is to be understood by the term *democracy* in Mexico" (emphasis in original).[18] As he succinctly puts it, "Noise makes itself heard and shakes up the structure."[19] Perhaps, given the populist dimensions of the Other Campaign— its reaching out far beyond Indigenous communities within Mexico—Williams's discussion glosses over the relevance of Indigenous concepts of democracy and the issue of decolonization. The complex movement for autonomy and self-governance based on customary law (*usos y costumbres*) in Chiapas, Oaxaca, Tlaxcala, Hidalgo, and Guerrero disappears from view. In other words, what Hernández Castillo calls "silent zapatismo" is not heard here.[20] The Zapatista's notion of intercultural contact and their debates over and experiments with forms of governance are motivated by the translation of Marxist class analysis into the frameworks of anticolonial struggle rather than an integration of Indigenous communities into a Marxist revolutionary struggle.[21] Given this decolonial framework, however, how far can Rancière's concepts really take us in understanding the nature of the political as it is articulated here?

The question of decolonization and its epistemic dimension has rarely entered the debates over how we might think sociopolitical transformations, or political acts in Rancière's sense.[22] The colonial experience grounds a lasting colonial difference in thinking, which is "not just a case of incommensurable cosmologies or worldviews but a difference articulated by the coloniality of power."[23] This difference has resulted in an unevenness in the value of languages and the politics of translation and, most important, in the silencing of ideas by those subalternized in the colonial process. As Enrique Dussel might put it, a different starting point manifests the colonial difference by a subalternized perspective arising from the Indigenous and African experience and lasting consequences of colonial oppression.[24] This includes recuperating and developing means of transmitting ideas in, at least for the academy, unconventional forms. Indigenous media—the production and distribution of radio, video, film, and television by and for Indigenous communities—is one such site.

Consensus, Dissensus

The key terms characterizing the decolonization of democracy in southern Mexico are *mandar obedeciendo* and *consenso,* yet for Rancière consensus clearly reinstantiates a wrong:

> Before becoming a preference for peace over war, consensus is a certain regime of the perceptible: the regime in which the parties are presupposed as already given, their community established and the count of their speech identical to their linguistic performance. What consensus thus presupposes is the disappearance of any gap between a party to a dispute and a part of society . . . it is, in a word, the disappearance of politics.[25]

Thinking from the context of Indigenous media, however, consensus entails two dimensions: one, a given arrangement and, the other, a process of dissent. As is characteristic of Aymara and Mayan languages, the same term often refers to opposites. Consensus and dissensus appear as two sides of the same coin.

The fiction video *Overcoming Fear* (*Venciendo el Miedo*), produced by a Bolivian Indigenous media collective known by its acronym, CEFREC-CAIB, directly addresses the issue of consensus governance.[26] Despite the tremendous impact of colonial violence and exploitation, Indigenous peoples have survived throughout Bolivia, and they assert the memory of alternative forms of society and state not only in the countryside but also in the cities. Alternatives are enacted in the microcosm of Indigenous communities and neighborhoods and increasingly in intercultural relations among diverse communities and Indigenous ethnicities. The Indigenous form of participatory democracy is grounded in interaction between authorities and families in rural highland communities and between rotating community representatives at regional assemblies, particularly in those areas where traditional *ayllu* structures have been revived. This revival is the outcome of the sociocultural "movement to reconstitute the *ayllu* / (*movimiento para la reconstitución del ayllu*)."[27]

The fifty-minute short tells the story of a family that migrates from the highlands to the subtropical Yungas (coincidentally an area known for its coca leaf production). The key scene stages a community assembly that seeks consensus over whether to allow women to hold land titles and whether to create a farming collective that can directly sell their produce in urban markets, thus bypassing the middleman. In the scene all members of the community are present. Both men and women are speaking. Yet the process enacted for the camera refers not to a community established but to a fundamental dispute in which women act politically, in Rancière's sense, by articulating a discourse and performing equality to the men in the community. The women's intervention constitutes women as subjects. At the same time, the scene alludes to two crucial notions of Indigenous governance. One is an assumption of territorial autonomy or sovereignty, which includes a local juridical system that claims its validity over and against any national legislation. The other is the production of consensus. The first dimension—the creation of a local, autonomous rule—can be seen as a form of exodus from the hegemony of the state. It is a political act becoming legible to the state and challenging its very claim on national rule.[28] The second dimension seems, however, to constitute an instance of policing, the reinstantiation of a "wrong," a renewed silencing. The community accepts the women's propositions, which change *usos y costumbres* by transforming community law (women in the video now hold rights to land) and by depicting a process of subjectivization, with one exception: one of the men insists that women's land tenure is incompatible with cultural tradition and unacceptable. The law is passed regardless.

In the film we see the orderly alternation of different positions articulated in a community assembly. The process represented here contrasts sharply with an analysis offered by the late Mixe scholar Floriberto Díaz Gómez. Díaz Gómez maintained that the constitution of consensus in his community in Oaxaca, Mexico, emerged from *cuchicheo,* a massive and disorderly whispering where individuals in the assembly talk at once in order to compare their ideas. *Cuchicheo* attests to the invested participation and attendance of the community that in his Mixe village was destroyed once state-educated members of the community introduced more formal democratic decision making in the 1970s.[29] In CEFREC-CAIB's video *Overcoming Fear,* informal consultation is held only among the women, and it is previous to the assembly.

The scene's importance lies, however, in the enactment of dissent, which I would argue, calls attention to persistent disagreement. Rather than bringing this voice into the community fold, it denotes a space for dispute. Williams explains that "in consensus-regimes, wrong is just not recognized as such (cannot have a language of its own) because it disrupts and possibly suspends the foundations of the consensual."[30] The representation of the dissenting perspective within the video gives, however, this voice a presence; it recognizes wrong as such. In other words, dissent registers. At the same time, *Overcoming Fear* invokes democratic rule by majority. It fuses union and Aymara traditions of governance. Rule is not based, though, on adding up individuals. The women's arguments are not made in the name of individual rights but rather hold up community interests. The video thus intervenes in the very foundations of Western democracy as based in individual rights. The issue is not to allow and contain visibility for all established parties within a community but to indicate a regime of visibility that renders a process of dissent, nevertheless subjected to collective interest.

Unlike CEFREC-CAIB, the CMP/Promedios video celebrating the *caracoles* makes no space for the contentious act of determining community interest. Primarily intended for an international audience, the videos partake in an ethnic politics that seeks to avoid showing internal conflict. *Overcoming Fear* may celebrate, in turn, a more orderly process than the one *cuchicheo* Díaz Gómez describes, but it highlights the way consensus leaves a visible trace of disagreement. In both the Andean and the Mexican context, Indigenous forms of governance make themselves heard and put forth a collective interest, which perhaps only from a liberal, individualist perspective silences or wrongs. In Bolivia and in Mexico, these concepts of governance have begun to spread far beyond the level of small, homogenous communities.

Gareth Williams's discussion of the Other Campaign in light of Rancière misses both the challenge to coloniality that motivates considering the Other Campaign as "potentially political" and the Indigenous philosophical framework underlying radical democracy. For Williams "the EZLN's Sixth Declaration [which announces the Other Campaign] is an appeal 'for [and now Williams is quoting Rancière] a democratic political practice that does not yet exist or, more precisely, has not yet been recognized—and cannot yet be 'named.'"[31] It seems, however, that the model in Mexico has been named; the Zapatistas would call it *mandar obedeciendo* or governance by *usos y costumbres*. Williams is right in that this political practice—like in Bolivia—has not yet solidified and thus maintains an act of political intervention. The video *Overcoming Fear* similarly conceptualizes consensus as a process, a movement, rather than as an existing order of things.

A colleague recently critically remarked that my argument calls for reading ethnography rather than political theory. Part of the effect of coloniality is, however, that there is little written in the idiom of Western philosophy that discusses Indigenous notions of politics. Even less has been translated into English. The intellectual capital attributed to *theory* itself requires provincializing, to recall

Chakrabarty's felicitous term. In light of these considerations, I propose that Indigenous media is not democratic, but it is political. What is political is, from this angle, the discourse and practice of those who have been formerly heard as "noise," transforming the very logic of coloniality that has denied them voice. Politics at once creates new places that only partially overlap with hegemonic ones. This is no entry into an existing place, not merely the desire to be heard. It is the validation through autonomous networks of what formerly circulated as rumor—a process that remains in flux. It helps us understand that political acts theorized from the historical experience of the Americas cannot be separated from the colonial difference. Subjectivization here does not necessarily give way to the police. Rather, the practices discussed here open up ways of thinking consent as maintaining movement—consent as constant change that keeps dissent visible and in tension, only momentarily integrated through the perhaps equally malleable notion of community interest.

NOTES

1. Jacques Rancière, *Dis-agreement: Politics and Philosophy,* trans. Julie Rose (Minneapolis: University of Minnesota Press, 1999), 28.

2. Ibid., 30.

3. Chiapas Media productions are available for sale on their website at www .chiapasmediaproject.org.

4. For a detailed history of the Chiapas Media Project/Promedios, see Alexandra Halkin, "Outside the Indigenous Lens: Zapatistas and Autonomous Videomaking," in *Global Indigenous Media: Cultures, Poetics, and Politics,* eds. Pamela Wilson and Michelle Stewart (Durham, N.C.: Duke University Press, 2008), 160–80.

5. For a discussion of the concept of visual sovereignty, see Michelle Raheja, "Reading Nanook's Smile: Visual Sovereignty, Indigenous Revisions of Ethnography, and *Atanarjuat (The Fast Runner),*" *American Quarterly* 59, no. 4 (2007): 1159–85.

6. Pamela Wilson and Michelle Stewart, introduction to *Global Indigenous Media: Cultures, Poetics, and Politics,* eds. Pamela Wilson and Michelle Stewart (Durham, N.C.: Duke University Press, 2008), 5.

7. Rancière, *Dis-agreement,* 104.

8. See John Sinclair, "The Globalization of Latin American Media," *NACLA: Report on the Americas* 37, no. 4 (2004): 15–19.

9. See *The Revolution Will Not Be Televised* (2002); *A Little Bit of So Much Truth* (2007); *The Take* (2006).

10. See *Images of the Repression in Oaxaca* (produced by Mal de Ojo TV; distributed by Ojo de Agua Comunicación, Mexico, 2007); *You're Saying that We Can't Pass* (produced by Promedios; distributed by Chiapas Media Projec Mexico, 2007); *Achacachi: La insurgencia Aymara* (directed by Daniel Cazés and Magdalena Cajías de la Vega; published by UMSA, Bolivia, 2002).

11. See *Caracoles: New Paths of Resistance* (a production of the *caracoles* with the support of Chiapas Media Project/Promedios; distributed by Chiapas Media Project, Mexico, 2003). For a succinct characterization of the shortcomings of the *aguascalientes* and the need to transform them into *caracoles,* see Justin Podur, "From Aguascalientes to Caracoles," Organic Consumers Association website, October 12, 2003, http://www.organicconsumers.org/chiapas/aguascalientes.cfm.

See also John Ross, "'Los Caracoles': Dramatic Changes in Zapatista Structure Bolster Rebels' Regional Autonomy," Global Exchange website, August 8, 2003, http://www.globalexchange.org/news/los-caracoles-dramatic-changes-zapatista-structure-bolster-rebels-regional-autonomy.

12. Sudeep Dasgupta, "Art Is Going Elsewhere and Politics Has to Catch It: An Interview with Jacques Rancière," *Krisis: Journal for Contemporary Philosophy* 1 (2008): 75.

13. Jacques Rancière, *Politics of Aesthetics,* trans. Gabriel Rockhill (London: Continuum, 2004), 31–32, 45.

14. As Alicia Swords explains, human rights activists prefer the term *war of attrition* over *low-intensity war fare,* since "the war's intensity is not 'low' for its victims." Alicia Swords, "Neo-Zapatista Network Politics," *Latin American Perspectives* 34, no. 2 (2007): 91n12.

15. Bill Nichols, *Representing Reality* (Indianapolis: Indiana University Press, 1991), 3–5, 30.

16. Jonathan Fox discusses the recent history and structure of municipal and submunicipal governance in southern Mexico, some predating national regime change in 2000 and some crystalizing more recently. He concludes that in the case of democratic village governance, local governance bodies are effecting a "long-term transition" that can "provide micro-institutional foundations for broader resistance." Indeed, the institution building at the local level in states like Guerrero, Oaxaca, and Chiapas "have managed to scale up to regional levels." Jonathan Fox, "Rural Democratization and Decentralization at the State/Society Interface: What Counts as 'Local' Government in the Mexican Countryside?," *Journal of Peasant Studies* 34, nos. 3–4 (2007): 549, 550.

17. Swords, "Neo-Zapatista Network Politics," 79.

18. Gareth Williams, "The Mexican Exception and the 'Other Campaign,'" *South Atlantic Quarterly* 106, no. 1 (Winter 2007): 146.

19. Ibid., 142.

20. Rosalva Aída Hernández Castillo, "The Indigenous Movement in Mexico: Between Electoral Politics and Local Resistance," *Latin American Perspectives* 33, no. 2 (2006): 127.

21. Walter Mignolo and Freya Schiwy, "Double Translation: Transculturation and the Colonial Difference," in *Translation and Ethnography: The Anthropological Challenge of Intercultural Understanding,* eds. Bernhard Streck and Tulio Maranhão (Tucson: University of Arizona Press, 2003).

22. In an interview with Sudeep Dasgupta, Rancière himself states that living in France, he has not felt compelled to engage with postcolonial theories of the subject. Dasgupta, "Art Is Going Elsewhere," 75.

23. Walter Mignolo, "The Geopolitics of Knowledge and the Colonial Difference," in *Coloniality at Large: Latin America and the Postcolonial Debate,* eds. Mabel Moraña, Enrique Dussel, and Carlos Jáuregui (Durham, N.C.: Duke University Press, 2008), 236.

24. Ibid., 233–34.

25. Rancière, *Dis-agreement,* 102.

26. For a detailed history and analysis of CEFREC-CAIB video productions, see Freya Schiwy, *Indianizing Film: Decolonization, the Andes, and the Question of Technology* (New Brunswick, N.J.: Rutgers University Press, 2009).

27. María Eugenia Choque Quispe and Carlos Mamani Condori, "Reconstitución del ayllu y derechos de los pueblos indígenas: El movimiento indígena en los Andes de Bolivia," in *Los Andes desde los Andes: Aymaranakana, Qhichwanakana, Yatxatawipa, Lup'iwipa,* ed. Esteban Ticona Alejo (La Paz, Bolivia: Yachaywasi, 2003), 158–59. For an analysis of this movement and its links to the urban Andean Oral History Workshop (THOA), which was founded in the early 1980s by young Aymara university graduates, see Marcia Stephenson, "Forging an Indigenous Counterpublic Sphere: The Taller de Historia Oral Andina in Bolivia," *Latin American Research Review* 37, no. 2 (2002): 99–118. Esteban Ticona Alejo describes the ideal and

the reality of governance in Quechua and Aymara communities and at regional levels in "El Thakhi entre los Aimara y los Quechua o la democracia en los gobiernos comunales," *Los Andes desde los Andes,* 125–46, esp. 137–44.

28. The act is made explicit once one of the estranged members of the community returns and in vain invokes national law as he seeks to recuperate his land.

29. Floriberto Díaz Gómez, "Comunidad y comunalidad," Investigadores Descalzos website, September 18, 2009, http://idescalzos.blogspot.com/2008/09/comunidad-y-comunalidad.html.

30. Williams, "The Mexican Exception," 142.

31. Ibid., 148.

Database, *Anarchéologie*, the Commons, Kino-eye, and Mash

HOW BARD, KAUFMAN, SVILOVA, AND VERTOV CONTINUE THE REVOLUTION

Erika Suderburg

> We blow up cinema, For CINEMA to be seen.
> » Dziga Vertov, *The Laboratory of Hearing,* 1917

> There's never one final answer for any of this, it's always a remix.
> » DJ Spooky

> Is it necessarily to found, always in the ruins of the archive,
> a shadow archive? Another archive that replaces the archive
> that takes place in its own ruin as an afterthought and effect of
> destruction?
> » Akiru Mizuta Lippit, *Atomic Light (Shadow Optics)*

"There in the pyroprosthesis of the archive, are cinders. Nothing will have taken place but the place. How will we think of there?"[1] This is *the* question for video-based projects that play with the parameters of the epic and propose a reconfiguring of how the moving image is fabricated and displayed. How we think of *there* is the question for much of the artifactual debris that constitutes a re-imagining of the modernist European avant-garde's promise of montage-driven revolution. The *there* of these diverse video practices is located on a meandering collision course with Siegfried Zielinski's *Deep Time of the Media,* Alexander Kluge and Oskar Negt's contested and shifted public sphere, and Dziga Vertov's anticanonical *Kinopravda.* This fertile trajectory of theory, moving images, audio remixes, and makers proposes a disintegrated alchemical framework that re-envisions media history and puts forward an *anarchéologie*-excavated legacy in its place.[2] Place is constructed here as a vibrant social reactivation of monumental debris and domestic meanderings and the requisition of street and domestic screens for rationales both political and purposeless.

The monumental artifactual fragments of empire, revolution, resistance, and surveillance are contained and often distilled via video debris. These materials can be articulate tracings that are buried in official archives, objectified as searing memorials, recorded as trace souvenirs, or existent in domestic disregard on laptops haphazardly shoved under unmade bedclothes. They function as witness, artifact, or elegiac ephemera and often invite and require the touch of remembering to activate and transform into organized pictures and sounds. Trace recordings and public and/or discrete dispersions have always driven the experience of recording and reordering. To share is to retrieve and compile and, perhaps, broadcast. Multiple cultural activities rely on debris both found and discarded and then rediscovered and recycled. The personal archive produced by the prosthesis camcorder or phantom-limb cell phone insists that the tourist, fan, repeat viewer, and visitor are interlaced, interpolated, and annotated daily within the "official" memory bank. Reinventions of this vault have been articulated through forms and access systems that are designed to interrogate spatial histories, whether the manifestation is the modernist 1920s city symphony of the European avant-garde, current open-source repositories like the U.S. National Archives Digital Vault and the Prelinger Archives, or the fertile, cannibal fields of YouTube and the *nouveaux auteurs* of Vimeo.

Our desire-fueled, sometimes collectively authored epics, remakes, and sequels are often facilitated by the both utopian and dystopian potential of perpetual documentation and preservation. Our propensity to record audio and visual material alters flotsam and jetsam such that it will now take longer than the remaining life spans of its producers, audience, and collectors to archive, view, and catalog it all. The origin story of our current situation holds some clues and templates and more than a few incendiary admonishments. Dziga Vertov's barely postrevolutionary *kinoks* sought to destroy the artifice of unquestioned documentary witness. The solicited reportage of multiple cameramen was shaped into the possibility of a projected new society formed by the *new (hu)man* with freshly retrained eyes. Kinoks would have come from anywhere, been trained in the field, and become contributors who in turn would train the succeeding generations until a new visual order was established in the fabric of everyday life. "Vertov and his *kinoks* dreamt of a newsreel that would not merely present 'Life-as-it-is' but also stimulate viewers to participate in the 'associative construction' of the projected images."[3] Kinoks would make the film-thing together and, in making it together, fabricate a moving image—a living evolutionary process built on an armature, a series of modular "bloks" that ultimately could be reused indefinitely without removing them from either their efficacy or their morphing truths: truths made truer than truth. Never one to claim veracity in documentary ethics as foundational, Vertov and company strove, as true Constructivist workers, to manufacture a composite closer to experience and ethically devoted to the future Communist society.[4] He and his work fell into oppressed and enforced silence after Stalin's Socialist realist lockdown ended the brief Russian Constructivist experiment. That his body of work, excavated several decades later simultaneously by experimental filmmakers and documentarians in the 1960s, reemerged just as the moving image was subject to multiple revolutionary programs seems a just and lasting reinvention.[5] Article 18 of Vertov's "Artistic Calling Card (1917–1947)," in which he refers to himself in the third person, lays out the kinok challenge:

> *Humanity of Kinoks* (*Čelove čestvo kinokov*) one of Vertov's earliest ideas was to create an army of film scouts (*kino nabljudateli*) and Kinoks in order to abandon single authorship and proceed to mass authorship, to organize an "I-see" montage, "not a coincidental but rather a necessary and all-encompassing global review of the world every few hours." (Knifot Nr. 2).[6]

Man with a Movie Camera (1929), alongside Bruce Conner's *A Movie* (1958) and Peter Kubleka's *Unsere Afrikareise* (Our trip to Africa) (1965), has served multiple generations of post–World War II image makers as an iconographic model for investigational strategies in the moving image and aural ether, inspiring varied activities of recombinatory archival-based work that in turn have triggered myriad reinventions of appropriative remontage well into the twenty-first century. These diverse offspring, productively rustling around in various open archives, range from the Situationist International to DJ Spooky—or Abigail Child and Santiago Álvarez rumbling around Girl Talk with some detour grazing on De La Soul.[7] This module of makers using solicited, unedited, or found images and sounds fabricates works that teeter among ethnography, media genealogy, archival restoration, documentary, art product, and the archaeology of the found, the spent, and the reexamined. Siegfried Zielinski has spearheaded a new multidisciplinary rubric, christened Variantology, that proposes a *deep time* of mediums and their origins. This composite refuses material constraints, finite academic definitions, and stable boundaries and builds a critical force beyond discipline specificity and accepted historical narratives. Variantology is another project of reorientation and forced paradigm shift—if you will, a remix of the telling of media(mystic)mistic origins.[8] Image recovery haunts many of these pursuits, whereas reimaginings of time-based archival, remix, and remake-based projects explore the promise of avant-garde film, video art, found sound and image, database access structures, and disturbed archival repose. Recombination, replacement, reenactment, screen-face annotation, compositing, subtitling, sampling, MU (mash-ups), and the DJ remix are just some of the strategies currently applied to the reconfiguring of witnessed, received, or remade media material.[9]

There are multiple origin points. One such node that examines and performs the appropriation and states the implications of such tactics in contemporary work is Perry Bard's *Man with a Movie Camera: The Global Remake,* an unending, frame-by-frame international collective remake of Vertov's *Man with a Movie Camera* that went online in 2008 and is designed to infinite layers, perpetually morphing as people overlap sequences and overlay their reinterpretative images on an ongoing and infinite basis.[10] The upload interface has metered every shot, categorized each section, and laid out a fastidious template online that documents each shot and gives instructions for uploading a remake side by side with the original frames.[11] One can enter a shot into the database, indexically attached to a specific sequence, and watch the overlapping uploads that merge into multiple versions of the remade film. Which version of the rebooted film is seen at any one time depends on how the algorithm cycles through the material available for each current annotation. If no one has uploaded material, then the original will play alone in the left frame with a black void to its right. This space serves as an invitation to the viewer to remake herself as maker.[12] No screening can ever be identical; its linearity is upended by the possibility of the space of the moving image that is not just three-dimensional but hyperdimensional (hypertextual), with layers cascading unseen behind every shot, potentially accessed at the next screening and the next. The work becomes a site that can be revisited and reworked alongside the steady invitation of the original work, which continues to unspool in the left-hand frame as its database restlessly reconfigures.

Man with a Movie Camera: The Global Remake exists on the Web, at media festivals, and in the gallery and museum but also travels and is launched on outdoor public commons screens. Perry Bard states, "My research is walking the streets," a contemporary *flâneur* with electronic tendrils.[13] Her quandary is getting people up on the screen by making the screen itself permeable. The public open-source archive feeds the machine that simultaneously reimagines, preserves, and subverts the archive. Her project is an ephemeral replicant of Russian Constructivist cinema. These Soviet culture and literacy trains presaged contemporary linkage structures that can be accessed remotely and reconfigured intimately for multiple purposes; the lines of connectivity are not carved out of landscape and hard-won steel but rather etched in networks of fiber-optic cables, transmissions, and hotspot nodes. From the Prelinger Archives to more discrete, personalized activities such as Moby's open-source sound tracks, DJ Spooky's recombinations for Adbusters, and Danger Mouse's *Grey Album* (2004) and its offspring to larger epic and globally projected challenges to corporate and individual copyright like Creative Commons, the potentially radical promise of open-source material communities, these image collators, and their stratagem(s) inform foundational questions about the reconfiguring of collective authorship or reauthorship, video's promise, experimental documentary, and the ability to reexamine representation and power itself using rubrics many centuries old that morph into ever-more-complicated, iridescent, unexpected, promising, and uncontainable tangents.

Bard's collective remake is contingent on redeputizing kinoks. Vertov and cadres moved toward a profound realignment of the Communist struggle, reinventing montage along the way, battling with Eisenstein, and single-handedly attempting to combat narrative "play" films: "I put it to you once more: Revolutionary cinema's path of development has been found. It leads past the heads of film actors and beyond the studio roof, into life, into genuine reality, full of its own drama and detective plots."[14] The new film was constructed of composite intervals, of "life caught unawares" (often very much aware), that posited a utopian future of broadcast images and sounds made collectively and scattered far afield to be gathered and scattered again in a repetition of energetic and transient remakes. It was an investigation, a challenge to see like a kinok, process like a kinok, and make like a kinok. The camera prosthesis of the new twentieth-century (hu)man was to be firmly welded to the low-powered organic nineteenth-century eye and to affect a sea change from which no one would want to or could recover.

In an attempt to write what should be and could not materially be made to happen (just yet), Vertov hypothesizes the connectedness we now take for granted: "Given the swiftness of communication between nations, given the lightening-fast turnover of footage, *Kinogazeta* should be a survey of the world every few hours."[15] Vertov's sacred quest to sever the new audiovisual continuum from a poisonous dependency on literature, narcotic fairytales, and bourgeois melodrama was, as Yuri Tsivian outlines, "complemented by no less manifest intentions to wed them to science—social as much as natural, which in Vertov's frame of reference was the same as saying that cinema must become Marxist."[16] This required a specifically materialistic moving image that would literally enact a dialectic of upheaval triggered by newly born eyes that would transform the film-object by constructing images of *life as witnessed* in order to train the next audience of potential makers. Materialist cinema was constructed and was invested in the demolition of destructive illusion by the new-eye weapon, the kino-eye of an enacted, living Marxist ideology. Vertov's desire to implant his ideological mission into the very fabric of the reimagined moving image template was tied to a specific locational Marxist intervention. Anne Friedberg outlines the very scenography that Vertov implemented and enacted as the basis for his oppositional understanding and discharge of the moving image as a tool against illusion: "If in all ideology men and their circumstances appear upside down as in a camera obscura, this phenomenon arises just as much from their historical life-processes as the inversion of objects on the retina does from their physical life-processes."[17] Friedberg reimagines Marx and Engel's primal site / sight thusly:

> The inversion of "men and their circumstances" in the camera obscura
> implies that there might be a positivist alternative to illusions of ideology.

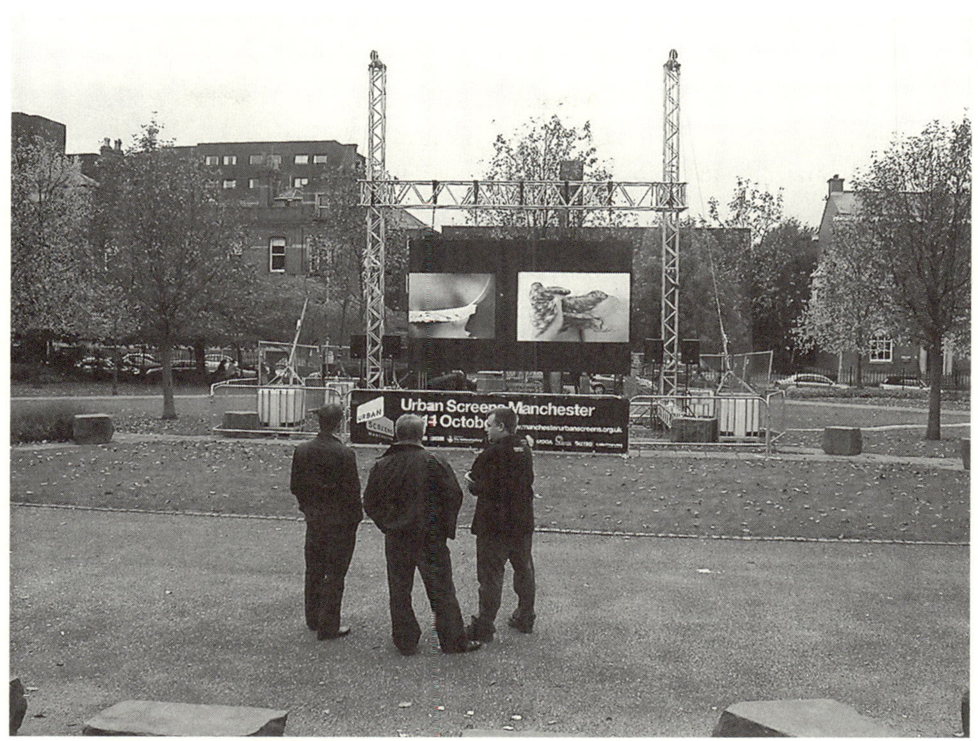

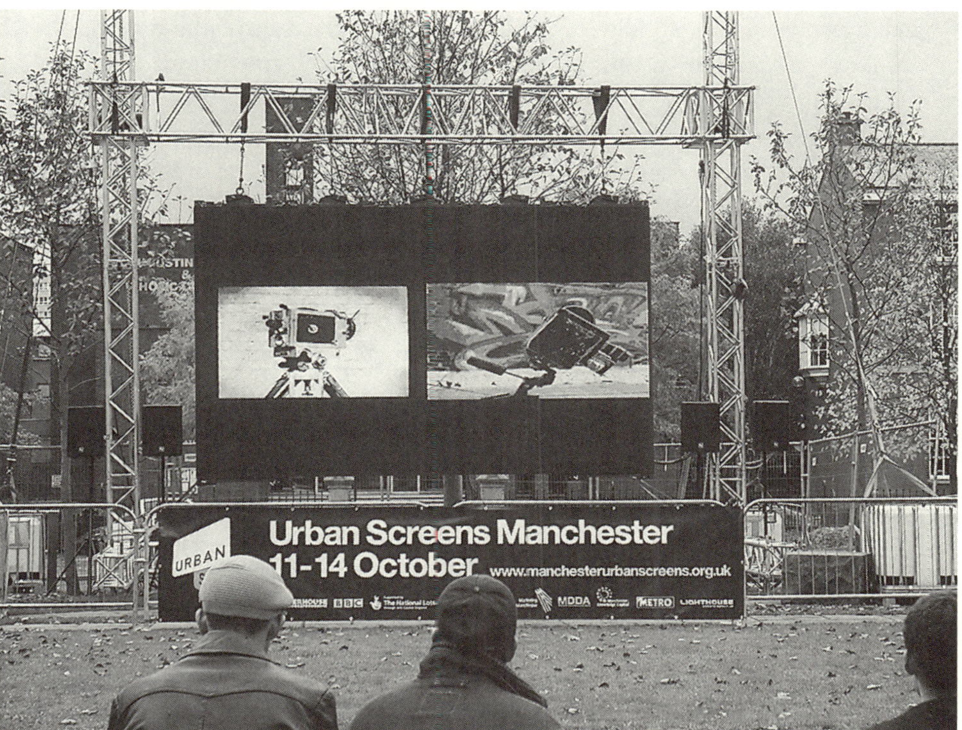

Perry Bard, *Man with a Movie Camera: The Global Remake,* Manchester, England, 2008. Courtesy Tamara Drakulic, Belgrade.

Many commentators have remarked on the timing of Marx and Engel's metaphor. Marx ridicules the camera obscura at the very moment that its apparatical—the photographic camera—was seen as veridical. In 1845 and 1846, the years that *The German Ideology* was written, William Henry Fox Talbot had just produced *The Pencil of Nature* (1844–1846). A few sentences before this passage of *The German Ideology,* Marx and Engels assert that the production of ideas is "directly interwoven with the material activity and material intercourse of man, the language of real life." Marx finds the dual nature of the camera obscura—as scientific instrument and device for illusion—to be a perfect visual analogue for the invisible workings of ideology. While 1845 was the year that marked photography's introduction as an instrument for exact drawing of the natural world (the "pencil of nature") and hence it would seem odd to question the mediating effects of the camera obscura, that year was also the height of the magic lantern's popularity as a projective technique for illusion.[18]

Vertov's hopeful Marxist supraorthodoxy and dogged belief in haptic and optic reeducation required the demise of such an illusion in order to build a Soviet ground zero, a field in which the potential of the moving image could be realized by constructing an ideological key to the very matter of the moving and aural image, a materialist montage made manifest with the building blocks of the true quotidian.[19]

Contemporaneous attacks on *Man with a Movie Camera* as a purely formalist, tricked-out rollercoaster ride decidedly missed the point of Vertov's conception of a materialist cinema. This was a cinema open to sequences of infinite intervals, reimaginings, and self-reflexive wonders designed to reconstitute an anti-illusion of the new man, woman, and child. The reimaging of this project within Bard's remake suggests, consciously or unconsciously, a universalist moving image language made of atomistic, possibly off-handed images designed to be replaced and effectively erased *in perpetuum.* The project devises a screen on which anyone can riff on his interval matrix or dice it into MU morsels with his or her corresponding newly fabricated twenty-first-century interval, abutting the anachronistic but still promising twentieth-century frame by frame, the interstitial space created in between abutted frames being implicitly and invitingly porous.

This is a leap of faith, an investment in the ideological construction of the aural and visual container within which Bard has redeputized the kinok.[20] Echoing Vertov's protoprogrammer vision of the endless archive—where the recombinatory promise of recordings are tied not to merely indexical representation or notions of documentary verisimilitude but to the orchestration of moment, movement, emotional impact, catharsis, and impact rhythm response—Bard essentially reintroduces the possibility of repurposing and reinvention (while presently adrift in the overkill of mediascapes) through a 1929 template that means to unabashedly upend the world order. Bard is explicit about the importance of range, inclusion, and potential, echoing a certain humble Vertovian zeal in proposing that her project is well situated for continuing the journey while pinpointing the absences that demand redress:

> The work explores the capabilities of the Internet to achieve global collaboration by encouraging (organizing) culturally diverse participation and by developing software, which accepts input from many sources (e.g. mobile phone, digital still camera, video, screen-grab) allowing for the greatest range of participation. To ensure that uploads would not be from the usual places the commission (biggerpictureuk.net) was used to commission 12 foreign correspondents (Brazil, Lebanon, Israel, Columbia, Pakistan, Russia, Serbia, Japan, China, Korea, Mexico, and Thailand) whose role it is to spread the word through their mailing lists and to organize the upload of scenes or shots that add up to a minimum of one minute in length. In the beginning of the project I *YouTubed* soldiers who had gone to Iraq—I found footage and invited them to upload their footage, even suggesting where it would fit in the film. The answer I got was it's free to use you have my permission. From my perspective now, if you look at Ruttman vs. Vertov, class is the first thing that comes to mind. Those hierarchies in relation to the remake, to the internet, have to do with the digital divide that manifests itself in my project through absences.[21]

By uploading according to Vertov, Svilova, and Kaufman's template, a participant in *Man with a Movie Camera: A Global Remake* unwittingly or consciously becomes a reenactor of revolutionary montage predicated on the belief that the moving image can reorganize society and sight, reform vision, and liberate maker and viewer alike. Vertov demanded new eyes, and he hoped to help train them. By deploying his template and reinvigorating its rubric, the audience and contributor examine the stretch of movement in time between a 1929 Moscow / St. Petersburg hybrid and a world composite that posits a FIN that might never arrive.

These are atomic and cellular shifts. There is a reason Gilles Deleuze spends a slice of hyperfueled time in *Cinema 1: The Movement-Image* tangoing with *Man with a Movie Camera*. He identifies Vertov's work as a moment of the moving image's complete recognition of itself and of our entry into its field of play. Deleuze is clear in his outline of Vertov in opposition to Eisenstein, an oft-quoted battle that had no rest among Soviet montage debaters. A material evocation of Communism's promise is the very undergirding of *Man with a Movie Camera*. Our present question simply is, What is triggered by this now anachronistic *undocumentary*? Deleuze posits that part of the answer is a complete redefinition

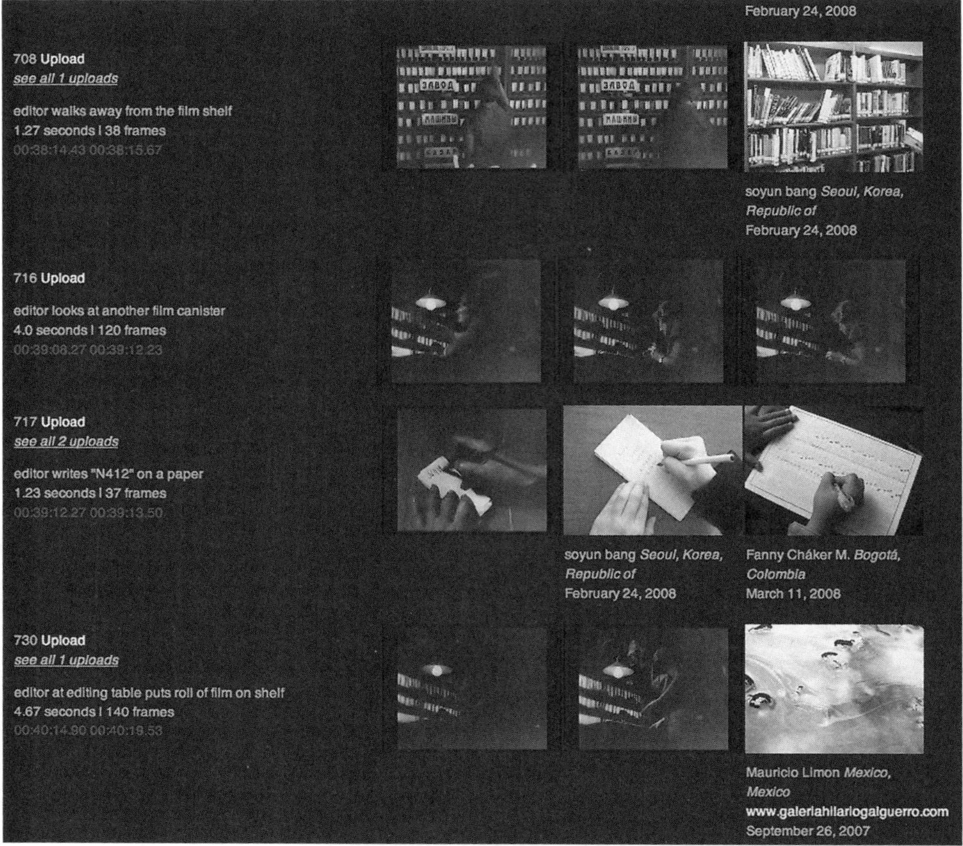

Elizaveta Svilova cataloging shots from original film. Perry Bard, *Man with a Movie Camera: The Global Remake,* upload interface, 2010.

of what makes the moving image function, what frictions and tangents make it sing, sting, and continue to hold relevance.

> Whether there were machines, landscapes, buildings or men was of little consequence: each—even the most charming peasant woman or the most touching child—was presented as a material system in perpetual inter-action. They were catalysts, converters, transformers, which received and re-emitted movements, whose speed, direction, order they changed, making matter evolve towards less "probable" states, bringing about changes out of all proportion to their own dimensions. It is not that Vertov considered beings to be machines, but rather machines which have a "heart" and which "revolved, trembled, jolted about and threw out flashes of lightening," as man could also do, using other movements and under other conditions, but always in interaction with each other.

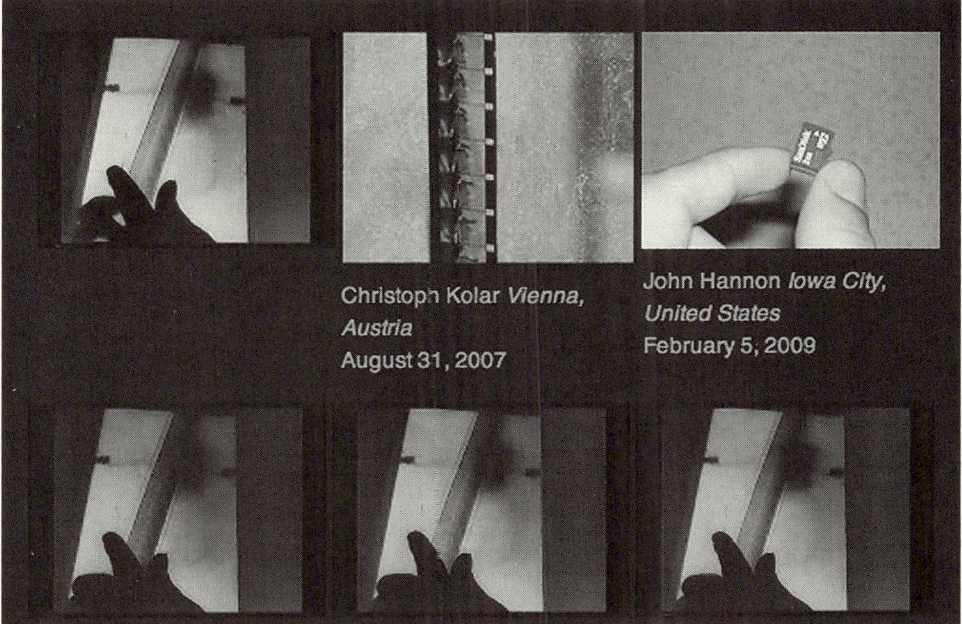

Elizaveta Svilova at editing table from original film. Perry Bard, *Man with a Movie Camera: The Global Remake,* upload interface, 2010.

What Vertov discovered in contemporary life was the molecular child, the molecular woman, the materialist woman and child, as much as systems, which are called mechanisms of machines. Most important were all the (communist) transitions from an order, which is being undone to an order, which is being constructed.[22]

Perhaps, Bard's programmer role is to reconnect the synapses of regard, the potential of this molecular child to a network already imagined by Vertov and cadres as broadcasting a recombined everyday archive that will be constantly drawn down and refilled by the kinoks who will in turn shepherd fresh kinoks. The new eye involves an uploading, a matching, and an annotation of a reseen text. It is always in training, as it is integral to participation, deconstruction, interrogation, and enjoyment of human society. Integral to this reimagining is the understanding of what needs to be broken down, how one reconfigures a moving image, how one choreographs and then rechoreographs a tenuous time sample.

But between two systems or two orders, between two movements, there is necessarily the variable interval. In Vertov the interval of movement is perception, the glance, the eye. But the eye is not the too-immobile eye; it is the eye of the camera, that is an eye in matter, a perception such as it is in matter, as it extends from a point where an action begins to the limit of the reaction, as it fills the interval between the two, crossing the universe and beating in time to its intervals. The correlation between a non-human matter and a superhuman eye is the dialectic itself, because it is also the identity of a community of matter and a communism of man.[23]

As we upload according to template and incise a present image in juxtapositioning to the artifact of 1929 we create an interstitial space that vibrates with possibility. It is a place of ricochet; Vertov's left side of the frame and our own right side form a tertiary montage—a tension of intention and interpretation, a shimmering border begging to be infiltrated. This is a place of possibility, of becoming (again to channel Deleuze). Bard's editorial matrix is sometimes synchronic, annotative, or discordant and in this gumbo, but it also is a space for talk back, the remark, the aside, and the deferred conclusion. It is a site of conjecture born of contribution, an insertion into a fixture that will periodically hold its shape but invites the wavering and wandering pair. To understand the project, simply collect, upload, and then stand back and see how you are echoed, bounced, and partnered. Contribute to the ether-based infinity vault, and you might just be amazed.

NOTES

I fondly dedicate this essay to Lynne Kirby, Michel de Certeau, and Tom DeBiaso, who always knew which train to take and kindly took me along for the ride.

1. Jacques Derrida, *Archive Fever: A Freudian Impression,* trans. Eric Prenowitz (Chicago: University of Chicago Press, 1996), 34, quoted in Akira Mizuta Lippit, *Atomic Light (Shadow Optics)* (Minneapolis: University of Minnesota Press, 2005), 27.

2. This is Rudi Visker's term as redeployed in Siegfried Zielinski, *Deep Time of the Media: Towards an Archaeology of Hearing and Seeing by Technical Means,* trans. Gloria Custance (Cambridge: MIT Press, 2006), 27.

3. Vlada Petric, *Constructivism in Film: The Man with a Movie Camera: A Cinematic Analysis* (Cambridge: Cambridge University Press, 1987), 70.

4. This was a Communist society that never actually existed in the USSR, of course, but Russian Constructivism enjoyed a brief moment of hopeful postrevolutionary, pre-Stalin experimentation.

5. Never a modest man, Vertov wrote a remarkable magnum opus in which he painstakingly lists all his contributions. The essay is prescient for all that he did presee/presage, from the "theory of relativity on screen" to a "mobile projection unit" that took twelve minutes to erect to the "application of montage during shooting." Dziga Vertov, "Artistic Calling Card (1917–1947)," in *The Vertov Collection at the Austrian Film Museum,* eds. Thomas Tode and Barbara Wurm (Vienna: Gesellschaft für Film und Medien, 2006), 72.

6. Ibid., 86.

7. Remarkably, it was Peter Kubelka starting in the early 1960s, along with Peter

Konlechner, who was responsible for proposing the collection and nurturing and maintaining Vertov's archives under the auspices of the Austrian Film Museum. An integral story of intrigue, censorship, and loving restoration is related in the aforementioned volume. Kubelka holds a pivotal position in the education or reeducation / reformation of the Euro-American avant-garde.

8. Zielinski, *Deep Time of the Media,* 27. Zielinski's Variantology indeed takes on the structure of the upended or infiltrated open-source archive in its own self-definition: "Our work on deep time relations between arts, sciences, and technologies does not seek to reinvent the concepts of the media or the arts. The aim is to open up both media and the arts via their interactions with scientific and technological processes. It is our hope that media experts will see their research areas in a broader light than before, and that disciplines which have so far not participated in these discourses (such as theology, classical studies, many areas of the history of science and technology) will develop openness for media questions. Right from the beginning *Variantology / Archaeology of the Media* was conceived as an international research and exchange project. A central part of it is the development of an open and temporal network of outstanding scientists, artists and scholars who engage with the deep time relations of arts, sciences and technologies." "Variantology: On Deep Time Relations of the Arts, Sciences and Technologies," variantology.com.

9. For a wonderful unpacking of MU, or mash-ups, see Paul Miller (aka DJ Spooky), ed., *Sound Unbound: Sampling Digital Music and Culture* (Cambridge: MIT Press, 2008); *Rhythm Science* (Cambridge: MIT Press, 2004); see also Douglas Kahn, *Noise, Water, Meat: A History of Sound in the Arts* (Cambridge: MIT Press, 2001).

10. Collective authorship is extrapolated upon in Petric's *Constructivism in Film,* although Dziga Vertov is used as the legal and facile signatory to the author function in my own text. It is clear that *Man with a Movie Camera,* correctly translated as *(Hu)man with a Movie Camera,* was collaboratively authored on multiple intricate levels by Vertov's brother, Mikhail Kaufman; a cadre of now anonymous kinoks; and Vertov's partner, Elizaveta Svilova. When Vertov is mentioned in conjunction with this film, authorship should be attributed to this collective. This remarkable and fraught topography of early Soviet silent cinema is outlined beautifully in multiple scholarly and fanciful texts. See Yuri Tsivian, ed., *Lines of Resistance: Dziga Vertov and the Twenties* (Indianapolis: Indiana University Press, 2005); Alexander Kluge, "The Filming of 'Added Value': A Plan of Eisenstein and of Dziga Vertov's Brother," in *Cinema Stories,* trans. Martin Broday and Helen Hughes (New York: New Directions, 2007); Dziga Vertov, "About Love for the Living Person," in *Kino-Eye: The Writings of Dziga Vertov,* ed. Annette Michelson, trans. Kevin O'Brien (Berkeley: University of California Press, 1984); and Petric, *Constructivism in Film.*

11. See dziga.perrybard.net.

12. For a beautiful teasing out of the erased female maker, gendered labor, voyeurism, and the figurative power of women in relation to Vertov's author function, see Lynne Kirby, "Vertov and the Cinematic Woman-Machine: The Railroad in the City," in *Parallel Tracks: The Railroad and Silent Cinema* (Durham, N.C.: Duke University Press, 1997), 178–88.

13. Perry Bard, e-mail message to author, December 22, 2009.

14. Vertov, *The Writings of Dziga Vertov,* 32.

15. Ibid., 33

16. Tsivian, *Lines of Resistance,* 9.

17. Karl Marx and Friedrich Engels, *The German Ideology,* ed. C. J. Arthur (New York: International Publishers, 1970), 47, quoted in Anne Friedberg, *The Virtual Window: From Alberti to Microsoft* (Cambridge: MIT Press, 2006), 71.

18. Ibid., 71.

19. Even though *Man with a Movie Camera* was a silent film, Vertov actually began much of his theoretical writing by proposing a radio laboratory. His concept of visual media and audio media were in fact quite similar in intent, and with the advent of sync sound, he began to treat sound and image as equal layers, each subject to reconstitution outside veracity.

20. It follows in the footsteps of the Berlin film academy students who renamed their film school the Dsiga-Wertow-Akademie and Jean Luc Godard and Jean Pierre Gorin's Groupe Dziga Vertov, which was established around the same time, in a 1968 of hopeful radicalities. There are several contemporary examples of redeputized kinoks from Austria to Mexico. See Tode and Wurm, eds., *The Vertov Collection,* 29–42.

21. Perry Bard, e-mail to author, December 22, 2009, sent in response to questions about the project and her intersection with Vertov in terms of ideology and intent.

22. Gilles Deleuze, *Cinema 1: The Movement-Image* (Minneapolis: University of Minnesota Press, 1986), 39.

23. Ibid., 40.

8
City as Screen

Holly Willis

The city is growing ever more sentient, snapping photos of our misbehavior at intersections and videotaping our movement past banks and federal buildings.[1] Our smartphones let us connect with that sensing data, pointing us to the nearest Thai restaurant and illuminating freeways in rivers of red, yellow, or on occasion, green. As we move through the streets we participate within spaces of information, becoming subjects of surveillance, for example, as well as users of the layered streams of data around us. We view the increasingly prevalent video displays, and our interest, gauged by the length of time we might stand in front of a particular display, in turn becomes information compiled in yet another database as material is gathered from the street.[2] In this seemingly casual movement through urban spaces, then, we move from networked subject to object and from viewer to viewed. We connect with networks, often unknowingly, while knowingly interacting with others. In short, we negotiate innumerable interfaces almost continually, being hailed as subjects and enacting subjectivity in a continual media flux. Urban screens are just one part of a larger set of screens that build a network around us. As such, screens are no longer simply dedicated to display; instead, they become components of a larger networked system that unites data, video, and images as digital information.

The November 2009 issue of *Wired UK* grapples with these "digital cities," querying the intersections of media and urban space. Adam Greenfield's contribution to the issue, "Digital Cities: Words on the Street," comments specifically on our embrace of the "digital mediation of everyday life" and notes that we have cheerfully—or in many cases blithely—adopted a host of technologies that we use in our cars, clothing, and phones that connect with global networks in real time, transmitting data back and forth. He goes on to highlight some of the benefits of the real-time, data-enabled city but then turns to the glitch: "The technologies that the networked city relies upon remain opaque, even to those exposed to them daily."[3] According to Greenfield, we need translators, specialists able to understand and explain this complex intersection of technology and culture. Greenfield dubs these specialists "urbanists" and explains that their mandate is to help the rest of us understand the city as process, as networked landscape, and as a queryable surface.

I argue that these translators already exist: they are the media artists who use video and interactivity in public space to reflect on issues of power, infrastructure, and the body as it becomes networked. This work is often overtly political; it is international, appearing in cities around the world; and it has a lengthy history that predates digital technologies that have more recently contributed to its current prevalence. This work often makes visible the invisible and resists the instrumental deployment of media and data within urban spaces, and it functions within a contemporary context to underscore the notion and significance of the interface. Indeed, as video by artists travels outside the traditional spaces of theaters, museums, and galleries we shift away from a culture based on representation and constituted primarily through narrative, discourse, and the image, all of which are encountered by readers or viewers, toward a technological culture, one in which cultural objects *are* technologies and the reader or viewer becomes a user or player. In this view the space of the city becomes an interface, and images become gateways rather than flat surfaces.

Perhaps best known among artists working with video in public space is Krzysztof Wodiczko, who has been projecting controversial images onto public buildings and official monuments for more than twenty-five years. Wodiczko's tactics include the use of scale to make that which is normally small or weak suddenly very large and therefore powerful, as with *The Tijuana Projection,* in which female workers describe abuse in conjunction with large-scale projections of their faces and loudspeakers amplifying their voices; making the invisible visible, as with his 2009 contribution to the Venice Art Biennial titled *Guests,* a video installation showing blurred images of immigrant workers to underscore their combined absence and presence; disruptive metonymy, in which ideas or things that generally remain separate and distinct are united, sparking controversy; and enactment, in which public space becomes very much the product of situated participants who craft that space through their engagement with ideas at a particular time and place. Wodiczko cites the work of Claude Lefort and his advocacy of public space as a site for contention and debate and Chantal Mouffe and Ernesto Laclau's notion of antagonism, which allows for conflict and confrontation in understanding the fundamental construction of democracy, as ideas fundamental to his work. "Public space is an enactment," he says in an interview with critic Patricia C. Phillips, and his projections are attempts to make the building exteriors embody the living, breathing inhabitants of urban spaces.[4]

Many other artists deploy similar tactics. Marie Sester, a New York–based multimedia artist who for the past decade has focused on creating interactive artworks designed for public space, highlights modes of power and control in those spaces. Sester began her career as an architect, but her interest was less in how to build viable structures and more in how architecture affects our understanding of the world. She eventually shifted away from architecture to art and then specifically to the practices of creating installations that address ideas around transparency, visibility, and access.

All three of these interests are fundamental to Sester's project *Access,* which was completed in 2003 but continues to be exhibited internationally and is now a permanent installation at ZKM: Center for Art and Media in Karlsruhe, Germany. The installation combines surveillance technology, a website, a robotic spotlight, and an acoustic beam system and allows Web-based viewers to track unsuspecting pedestrians with a large spotlight. The system can also function autonomously, using motion-detecting software. As people move through either a gallery space or, in some installations, a public space one of them is selected by the spotlight, and he or she is tracked. The beam follows that person despite attempts to evade it; eventually, the light stops. The piece illuminates both our fascination with voyeurism and technologies for spying on others. As Sester points out, however, it also sparks fears of being watched, of being controlled by an increasingly panoptic culture that coerces and controls its subjects through invisible forms of technology.

Rafael Lozano-Hemmer has made a series of public art projects that interrogate the role of people in public. In *Body Movies,* from 2001, Lozano-Hemmer incorporates photographs of people taken on the city's streets and then projected, but the images are visible only in the shadows of people standing in the light. These shadows of visitors can be very large, over seventy-five feet high, and as each portrait is revealed it is replaced by a new one.

Similarly, in his project *Under Scan* (2005), Lozano-Hemmer projected a series of video portraits on the ground of the public squares in several towns in England. The portraits were invisible, however, until people walked into the light of the projection, at which point their shadows revealed the portraits. An exchange took place between the viewer and the video portrait, and one result was a sense of composited and performed social identity that was at once connected to and more than the single, individual body.

Lozano-Hammer also used the bodies of visitors in his 2003 project *Frequency and Volume,* in which shadows cutting into a projection beam tuned into a radio frequency. By moving around in the beam of light, visitors were able to scan the frequency spectrum, with the size of their bodies determining the volume of the sound. Lozano-Hemmer notes that the system could tune in a variety of signals, including air traffic control, cell phones, police dispatches, and so on. "The piece investigates the contested radio space in the context of the increased surveillance of the body as an antenna," writes Lozano-Hemmer.

In an interview in 2005 with José Luis Barrios, Lozano-Hemmer quotes Cicero, saying, "We make buildings and buildings make us." He continues, "Our situation in the globalized city says the opposite: the urban environment no longer represents the citizens, it represents capital."[5] Lozano-Hemmer says that his response is to encourage an "eccentric reading of the environment," as well as "alien memories," namely those that do not come from or belong to the site itself. "I don't want to develop site-specific installations but rather focus on the new temporal relationships that emerge from the artificial situation, what I call 'relationship-specific' art."[6]

With respect to this relationship-specific art, Lozano-Hemmer uses the term *relational architecture,* and though *relational* has since been used by Nicolas Bourriaud to describe a group of specific art practices known as *relational aesthetics,* Lozano-Hemmer's use of the term is more specific. He explains that for him the term has two meanings: first, it refers to the "technological actualizations of urban environments with alien memory," and second, it refers to what he calls "anti-monuments for public dissimulation."[7] In this sense relational architecture is an apparatus for helping produce moments of disjuncture that unsettle comfort zones as bodies become screens or instruments of reception.

Whereas Wodiczko, Sester, and Lozano-Hemmer overtly grapple with the politics of space and attempt to reveal hidden aspects of power, other artists' projects more closely align with institutional agendas. For example, Los Angeles–based media artist Doug Aitken has also created numerous large-scale projection projects, including *sleepwalkers,* which was projected onto the exterior walls of New York's Museum of Modern Art in and around the Abby Aldrich Rockefeller Sculpture Garden between West Fifty-Third and Fifty-Fourth streets in January and February 2007.[8] The project, described as a "broken screen" narrative by Aitken, chronicled the lives of five characters as they moved through the city at night.[9] Visitors to the project strolled around the silent film to see all eight thirteen-minute segments, and the large images, many of them close-ups of characters played by Chan Marshall (Cat Power), Donald Sutherland, and Tilda Swinton, were visible from blocks away.

This project was rich with metaphors: the city as body, as screen, as spectacle; subjects as sleepwalkers and viewers as pedestrians; the screen as window, the city in fragments.[10] The project also invoked "the public." Museum director Glenn Lowry explained, for example, that "a project like this creates a very different dialogue with the public, who we hope will be inspired to think about art in relation to the city itself and to the larger urban experience."[11] The project also sparked fantasies of profit. New York's mayor Michael Bloomberg praised *sleepwalkers* for being "fun, fascinating and, best of all, free" but, more important, extolled its potential role in drawing tourist dollars during a normally slow time after the holidays.[12] "Last year, a record 44 million tourists visited New York City," he said, "with nearly 50% of them visiting our cultural offerings, and through the help of exceptional art events such as *sleepwalkers,* we expect to surpass that total this year."[13]

The financial subtext underlying *sleepwalkers* was even larger. In the weeks prior to its installation, MoMA announced plans to sell an empty parcel of land for $125 million—earning the museum a sizable profit—as part of a larger and continuing redevelopment effort that included the major museum renovation begun in 2004. There were also revelations regarding questionable payments to the museum director that included real estate investments and profits, all of which suggested invisible consolidations of power and finance, which were in turn solidified symbolically in the projection of *sleepwalkers,* as the museum turned itself inside out, ostensibly to open itself to the public while in fact very much in the process of screening information from that public.

Rosalyn Deutsche notes that "the term public frequently serves as an alibi under whose protection authoritarian agendas are pursued and justified."[14] And indeed, though the museum's celebration of *sleepwalkers* touted its attention to the public and Lowry expressed his hopes for "a very different kind of dialogue" with that public, we must acknowledge the strategic mobilization of that somewhat amorphous category as another kind of screening, one intended to conceal rather than reveal, expand, or connect. With its dazzling and immense close-ups, as well as its spare yet fashionable aesthetic and the presence of carefully chosen iconic figures, *sleepwalkers* therefore functioned in service to a bigger-than-life spectacle and very graphically aligned with the museum on which its multiple frames were inscribed; stardom, design, fashion, and immensity combined seamlessly both to embody power and to brand the museum. MoMA's buildings did not represent or even engage the public. Instead, they represented capital, and Aitken's imagery underscored the tension between the material and the digital forms of that capital.

Media artists who project images in public space may therefore function as the translators called for by Adam Greenfield to help the rest of us understand the politics of public space, or they may end up working in alignment with institutions to obscure the functioning of power. We might also question, however, visibility and invisibility in this context and our own responsibilities regarding the ability to see. Lisa Parks has written on the odd amalgam of nature and culture embodied by the cell phone antenna tree, noting that the practice of making these towers resemble trees is not only aesthetic but political. Hiding various infrastructures of the city, such as plumbing and electricity, is common, and "one of its effects is to keep citizen/users naive about the systems that surround them and that they subsidize and use," she asserts. She goes on to note that although we think of ourselves as a networked society, "most members of the public know very little about the infrastructures that support such a designation." She encourages us toward "infrastructure literacy," which suggests a sharing of practices and knowledge broadly rather than the creation of professionals who will explain it to us.

As we grow accustomed to the data-driven, real-time city, then, we should work to understand its infrastructural ramifications and resist instrumental uses of this technology. That resistance forms the foundation for Julian Bleecker and Nicholas Nova's intriguing essay "A Synchronicity: Design Fictions for Asynchronous Urban Computing," a Situated Technologies Pamphlet published in October 2009 by the Architectural League of New York. The essay asserts a provocation, namely to rethink the fetishization of the real-time data-enabled city in order to "stretch out the space of possibility and the space of possible imaginings."[15] What does this mean? In short, Bleecker and Nova are less interested in how data delivered immediately and orchestrated bureaucratically in a top-down approach may "help" city dwellers and, instead, ponder the potential for more speculative and poetic layers of information and for a notion of the city that is not static and fixed but rather in process. In the later part of the conversation that constitutes the text of the pamphlet, Bleecker describes a series of objects that were designed to provoke different ways of interacting with the city, moving beyond the expected and the screen based. "We're in the realm of epistemological monkey-wrenching broadly conceived," he explains.[16] "Creating objects that shift meanings and provide new, unexpected points of view. Or, they may just show you the obvious, but do so in a more legible way."[17]

Video, which has been defined and redefined with regard to its status as a medium from its inception, is becoming part of a larger swirl of data; that said, it remains obstinately present, reflecting what Saskia Sassen dubs the "global city." Sassen describes the contemporary city as an "amalgamation of multiple global circuits that loop through it."[18] What remains physical in the city, she writes, "has been transformed by the fact that it is represented by highly liquid instruments" in a dense, digital infrastructure.[19] If much of the activity that occurs in a global city is indeed completely invisible as the flow of electronic information and finance all around us, the screen—or the building wall that acts as a screen— remains obstinately visible, framing and demarcating what threatens, on the one hand, to overwhelm or, on the other hand, to disappear altogether. Contemporary media artists using video in public space activate discussions and literacies dedicated to understanding and interrogating the global information circuits, and in this way play a key role in helping us understand the digital city around us.

NOTES

1. The word *sentient* intentionally echoes the exhibition *Toward the Sentient City*, which was held September 17–November 7, 2009, curated by Mark Shepard, and organized by the Architectural League of New York City.

2. Anna McCarthy dubs this media "ambient television" in her analysis of public screens in *Ambient Television: Visual Culture and Public Space* (Durham, N.C.: Duke University Press, 2001).

3. Adam Greenfield, "Digital Cities: Words on the Street," *Wired UK,* September 30, 2009, http://www.wired.co.uk/magazine/archive/2009/11/features/digital-cities-words-on-the-street.

4. Patricia C. Phillips, "Creating Democracy: A Dialogue with Kryzsztof Wodiczko," *Public Art Journal,* Winter 2003, 35.

5. José Luis Barrios and Rafael Lozano-Hemmer, "Loose Ends: A Conversation between José Luis Barrios and Rafael Lozano-Hemmer," trans. Rebecca MacSeen (transcript of a teleconference, April 20, 2005), 7, http://www.lozano-hemmer.com/texts/downloadable/InterviewBarrios.doc.

6. Barrios and Lozano-Hemmer, "Loose Ends," 9.

7. Ibid.

8. The project documentation is at http://www.moma.org/interactives/exhibitions/2007/aitken/flash.html.

9. The term *broken screen* also is in the title of Aitken's 2006 collection of interviews with artists interested in nonlinear narrative forms; see Doug Aitken, *Broken Screen: 26 Conversations with Doug Aitken, Expanding the Image, Breaking the Screen* (New York: Trilce, 2006).

10. It has also sparked several neologisms. *New York Times* critic Roberta Smith, for example, couldn't decide between *archivideo* and *videotecture,* adding somewhat oddly that "thanks to technology that allows exterior walls to function as video screens, private homes may soon glow with a self-taught variety." Roberta Smith, "The Museum as Outdoor Movie Screen," *New York Times,* January 18, 2007.

11. "A Conversation with Doug Aitken; Glenn D. Lowry, Director of the Museum of Modern Art; and Anne Pasternak, Director of Creative Time," under "The Project" and "Interview," *sleepwalkers* website, http://www.moma.org/interactives/exhibitions/2007/aitken/flash.html.

12. MoMA and Creative Time, "MoMA and Creative Time Present *Doug Aitken: sleepwalkers,*" press release, http://www.creativetime.org/programs/archive/2006/aitken/press/aitken_011607.pdf.

13. Ibid.

14. Rosalyn Deutsche, "The Question of 'Public Space'" (presentation to the American Photography Institute, National Graduate Seminar, June 1998), http://www.thephotographyinstitute.org/journals/1998/rosalyn_deutsche.html.

15. Julian Bleecker and Nicolas Nova, *A Synchronicity: Design Fictions for Asynchronous Urban Computing,* Situated Technologies pamphlet (New York: Architectural League of New York, 2009), 10.

16. Bleecker and Nova, 34.

17. Ibid.

18. Saskia Sassen, "Making Public Interventions in Today's Massive Cities," *Static,* no. 4 (November 2006): 5, http://static.londonconsortium.com/issue04/pdf/sassen_publicintervensions.pdf.

19. Ibid.

9
Installation and the New Cinematics

Michael Rush

David Claerbout's traveling exhibition *The Shape of Time,* organized by Centre Georges Pompidou in 2007–9, was a cinematic event.[1] The darkened, gray-walled gallery space housed seven huge projections measuring thirteen by forty-two feet. Suspended scrims met firm plaster walls in a cacophony of images and sounds, with projector beams blinding the eyes momentarily and overlapping images from separate projections, disorienting the navigation required for taking in the entire event.

Another monumental video presentation was Julian Rosefeldt's *Asylum* (2001–2). The installation, presented as a nine-channel projection, with screens situated at angles to each other, so subverted the expected cinematic viewing posture that it was almost dizzying. In what might be called a fantastical documentary, *Asylum* depicted immigrants in the so-called new Germany (Asians, South Americans, Muslims, Chinese) performing mundane, repetitive tasks, what one critic refers to as the content of "capitalist slavery."[2]

As video art has matured from its earliest, performance-based roots artists have embraced an idea-driven process that although still possessing strong performative components, is today more abstract and poetic. Contemporary media artists, freed by advances in digital editing technology, are creating new viewing experiences that are best described as cinematic or immersive.

The use of the term *cinematic* in this context is perhaps unfair given the voluminous controversies over medium specificity in media criticism. All of this could get unnecessarily convoluted if we were to parse the word *media* itself, which in this context refers to electronic media, as opposed to the fundamental components of all artworks—that is, *media* as the plural of *medium.* For the sake of argument, let's say that *cinematic* embraces what we commonly associate with traditional cinema: lush images, inventive camerawork and lighting (cinematography), large-scale projection, and passive viewing in a darkened theater. It is this last ingredient that is being challenged in video installation. In fact, cinema itself has become an art of video, with celluloid film disappearing at a rapid rate as the preferred medium of filmmaking. Video has claimed the moving image

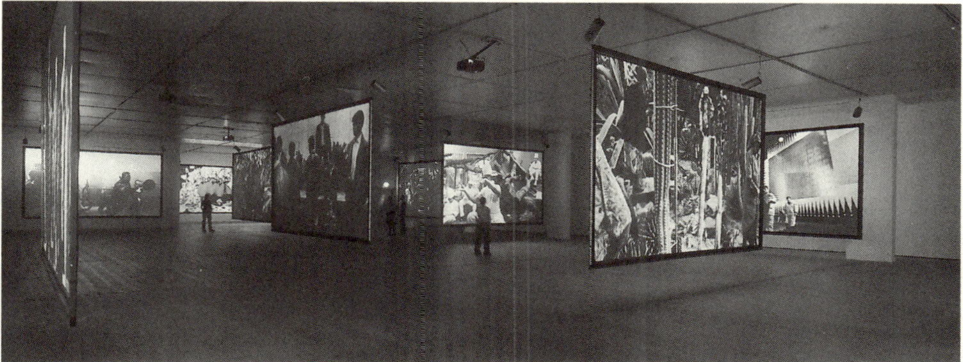

Julian Rosefeldt, *Asylum,* 2002. Courtesy of the artist.

domain. Cinema is now undeniably expanded; installation is prefiguring a new cinematic spectator / image relationship based on interaction.

One of the most common, as well as cogent, forms of this new experience is the multiple-screen projection or installation. Of course, this multisurface presentation has its roots in the earliest days of video art.[3] Frank Gillette and Ira Schneider's *Wipe Cycle* was a nine-monitor installation (though that word was not yet in use) presented in the influential 1969 gallery exhibition *TV as a Creative Medium* at the Howard Wise Gallery in New York. This work, while essentially concerned with live feedback systems and the role of viewers in the televised image, was also prescient in its anticipation of both multiscreen projections and interactive installations. Visitors were taped live as they entered the gallery or as they stood in front of the monitor grid and were able to interact with their own image.

As video art progressed, moving ever closer to immersion, artists such as Bill Viola, Peter Campus, Mary Lucier and a host of others created environments for viewing. Viola's *Room for St. John of the Cross* (1983) was a prime example. The viewer no longer simply related to the binary image / monitor formula but entered a theatrical set where objects and images combined to offer an "experience" of the video narrative, complete with accoutrements of a stage set. In this video the artist re-created the prison cell of the sixteenth-century mystic and placed it in a cubicle within a darkened room (cubicle within cubicle). A large projection of a snowy mountaintop presided over the room(s). Viola's cinematic images were now matched by carefully placed objects that expanded the viewing experience into the realm of the corporally experiential. Subsequent works of his included a large brass bed and spotlight (*Science of the Heart,* 1983) and an enormous fallen tree with electric lanterns on its branches (*The Theater of Memory,* 1985). Such multimedia had existed in the experimental theater for several years (Robert Whitman's *Prune Flat* [1965], for example, featured film and performance interactions), but what was new in the museum context of the video installation was that viewers could wander within the mise-en-scène instead of passively watching it. Furthermore, installations like Viola's were timeless in that they had no narrative arc or denouement and, certainly, no conclusion. There was no beginning, middle, or end. Viewers could pass through the experience at any time, move on, return, and move on again.

In a 2004 essay in *Artforum,* historian David Joselit mourns the loss of the social interactivity of closed-circuit video (a frequently utilized modality in early video) to present-day projections that "tend to hug the architectural envelope rather than produce a second informational circuit within the container of the gallery . . . video is transformed from an apparatus within a space to a new electronic skin that engulfs architectural elements."[4] This utopian notion of sociability when applied to the closed-circuit work of Bruce Nauman, Peter Campus, Joan Jonas, and others grants more to these video structures than they could sustain, or were intended to sustain. They were most often highly individualized experiences of perception altering based on the capacity of live-feed video to disorient the viewer/image relationship. More important, however, is how profoundly more complex multiscreen video installations have become. Interactivity must be seen in the relationship between the viewer and the image(s), as opposed to viewers and each other.

What Joselit describes as viewers becoming actors in the video works of the aforementioned artists (and Dan Graham, as well, who really is the only one who might claim sociability as one of his goals) has now been replaced with viewers as navigators in what can seem like a forest of imagery (Rosefeldt, Masaki Fujihata) that requires not only bodily movement but also a multifaceted mental engagement with image, sound, language, scale, and architectural placement of surfaces. This is interactivity in an expanded understanding of "actor" as one who must physically manage the installation to "see" it.

What Viola and others introduced in the 1980s has significantly evolved in terms of the cinematic sophistication of the image, and this is the core of my concern here. The *new cinematics* refers to a creative process (often indistinguishable from the filming and editing procedures of *movies*) and a viewing experience of larger-than-life color-saturated (or deeply imbued, moody black-and-white) images that transform the everyday into a heightened experience.[5] The video installations of a large contingent of artists are providing this experience, including Douglas Gordon, Eija-Liisa Ahtila, Stan Douglas, Pipilotti Rist, Gabríela Friðriksdóttir, Hiraki Sawa, Isaac Julien, and Aernout Mik, to name but a few. Other cinematic artists, of which there are now many (Mark Lewis and Eve Sussman come to mind), are developing large-form films that retain the single-projection format, as opposed to the immersive, multiscreen format.[6] Here, too, however, when several artists' works are shown in a museum or gallery context, the collective viewing experience of several works approaches a similar sense of immersion, a prime example being Yang Fudong's *Seven Intellectuals in a Bamboo Forest* (2003–7), a sprawling seven-part installation. The entire work is almost two hours long (very atypical in video art terms) and was filmed in 35 mm and then transferred to DVD for projection. Fudong's opus may be the ultimate example of a new cinematic experience in that each part is really a movie unto itself, and viewers move from room to room (and sit on chairs or the floor or lean on walls) to take in all the parts. Clearly, this cannot be done in typical movie houses, but the gallery / museum is perhaps a new model for "movie house." Moreover, the gallery, whose primary function has been to front the economic exchanges that occur in the back room, has evolved into the front line of free, accessible art viewing with elaborate installations made possible by the very backroom economics. For lovers of the moving image, especially the obscure, abstract narratives of Ingmar Bergman or the French New Wave in the late 1950s and 1960s (the films of which were eagerly awaited in cinematheques throughout the Western world), there can be a no more fulfilling experience than immersing themselves in the installations of artists such as Viola, Claerbout, Ahtila, and Kutluğ Ataman.

Viola's *Pneuma* (1994–2009), as presented in 2009 at the James Cohan Gallery in New York, was a meticulously (and expensively) rendered environment with walls and ceiling heights, not to mention carpeting and lighting, all done in strict accord with the artist's wishes. *Pneuma,* titled after a multipurpose Greek word that can refer to an individual soul or the entire life force of the universe, was a three-channel installation begun in 1994. Filmed with both a low-end vintage surveillance camera and an up-to-the-minute high-definition video camera, *Pneuma* was an intensely grainy wave of barely perceptible images that washed over the gallery walls as if they were a seashore at midnight. Projected into three corners, as opposed to directly onto the flat walls, the installation required very close attention in order to decipher anything recognizable. It was particularly important to the artist that the images meet the floor, so that the relationship of the viewer's body to those images would be intimate and immediate. The situation of the projection device, at the point where the walls met, resulted in a very dreamlike diffusion of the recorded content. Projectors were not hidden; visitors could pass in front of their intense light and cast their own shadows onto the wall. Suggestions of a woman's body in repose, a parking lot, a car in the rain, a kitchen countertop, and a child in a field were barely perceivable. Ominous sounds suggested danger or maybe even death, but one was never quite sure.

In this very carefully controlled environment, the cinematic became at once immersive and intensely personal for both the viewer and the artist. There was a mutual seduction here between the creator, Viola, who allowed only the most frugal hints of a narrative, and the viewer, who responded, perforce, with the creation of her own narrative. I assume nothing would have pleased the artist more.

This new cinematic experience has occasionally come from artists who first were identified with traditional cinema (Isaac Julian was a documentary film-maker) and television (Eija-Liisa Ahtila). One of the first split-screen artists was Chantal Ackerman, who actually fragmented her own film *D'est: Au bord de la fiction* (From the east: Bordering on fiction) onto more than three dozen television monitors in her 1993 installation. Viewers were encouraged to wander into this patchwork of TV sets, much like the slow-moving camera in the film as it passed through the bleak, snowy streets of Eastern Europe, where Ackerman's family had come from. The film was spliced in much the same way that the artist's family (and by extension her own psyche) was split and patched together during periods of exile and migration over the years.

Ahtila's transition to the form of installation seems a natural outgrowth of her interest in complex mental states. All of her mature filmic installations revolve around the deep psychological difficulties of a central female character. In her three-screen projection *The Wind* (2002), a young woman, looking at first quite normal, gradually disintegrates into a state of severe paranoia and isolation. Ahtila disrupts the conventional narrative strategy of traditional cinema by dividing her images among three screens. This strategy reflects the multiple layers of reality that real life actually consists of (as opposed to a continuous flow of sequential experiences), as well as the split realities experienced by people who are descending deeper into mental illness. The sculptural divide of the three screens in *The Wind* mirrors the fractured, psychological torments of the central character, Susanna.

Though everything in the film is recognizable (people, objects), Ahtila sustains a sense of mystery and inscrutability throughout. In the opening scenes, a car moves swiftly toward a nondescript apartment building near the highway, but the driver is not revealed. The scene cuts to a cluttered apartment with an open window through which a very strong wind is passing, or so it seems. Susanna, a plain but pleasant-looking woman in a blue sleeveless top, yells to someone, "Shut the door!," but the unidentified male voice responds, "It is shut." When Susanna inquires into the draft's source, the man says it is coming from her imagination. These first words suggest to us that perhaps everything we subsequently see is from Susanna's imagination. As the wind attains tornado force the contents of the apartment fly about and crash to the floor. Then, Susanna begins her disconnected ramblings, which range from her preoccupations with being fat (which she is not) to her inability to shout, as other members of her family do when they are upset. Instead of shouting, she tells us, she bites her fingers to the bone. This action, a familiar symptom in psychiatric descriptions of borderline personality disorder, is an attempt by the patient to feel something, anything, even if it is painful.

Ahtila's swift editing, experienced across three screens simultaneously, keeps

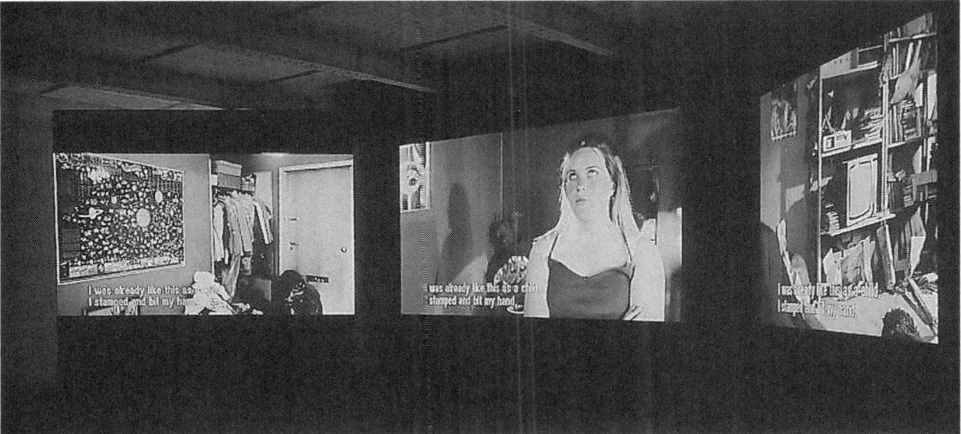

Eija-Liisa Ahtila, *The Wind,* 2002. Courtesy of the artist.

her portrait of Susanna visually arresting. Viewers are never led into the boredom that Susanna's unrelenting verbiage might otherwise induce. One's attention constantly shifts from screen to screen as Ahtila leads us to sympathize with this off-putting character. Susanna's erratic behaviors (e.g., emptying the contents of a box and walking on them, dropping a glass and kicking the pieces under the sink), while unnerving, are never dwelt upon. They happen, and then Ahtila moves on. As the berating voices in her head rage on, a young man appears. He warns her to "keep her hands in her lap," a final rebuff that causes Susanna to sink into catatonia. In a *coup de cinema,* Susanna climbs up the corner of two walls in her living room and squats, facing the camera like a gargoyle on a Gothic cathedral.

Ahtila's cinema, having emerged from the conceptual practices dominant in art in the mid- to late 1980s, has evolved into an elaborate reexamination of cinema itself, re-forming the language of narrative and the space of film presentation. Her installations are as psychologically constructed as the abstract stories of her troubled female protagonists. In her multiscreen presentations, she physicalizes the split mental states of her subjects while inviting viewers to experience a truly expanded, destabilized cinema, one that more accurately reflects the conscious and unconscious states that comprise everyday reality.

Turkish-born artist Kutluğ Ataman very effectively utilizes five screens placed obliquely near each other in *Stefan's Room* (2004) to tell the story of an eccentric resident of Berlin who raises tropical moths in his apartment. Viewers either stand, sit, or walk amid this narrative, their own bodies relating in space to Stefan as he talks about his odd pastime. Here, Ataman exposes a life lived at the edge of normalcy, evoking a highly sympathetic response from viewers whose own feelings of otherness are mirrored in this character.

Belgian artist David Claerbout maximizes digital technology in filmic projections that challenge cinematic traditions, even to the point of making us think we are watching the moving image when in fact we are immersed in a composite of videotaped still photographs (a reflection, obviously, of the twenty-four frames per second in 35 mm film) and moving image. His installations when seen together comprise a cinematic wonder house that wrestles normal time away from the viewer, immersing her in a very disorienting universe that may, at first, seem perfectly normal. *Shadow Piece* (2005) features a photograph of a modernist building with shadows of people at its locked front door. Others begin to approach the door, the shadows conforming to these new arrivals, but viewers begin to feel something mysterious, something amiss. Claerbout injects video footage of people in his studio into the photograph, which remains changeless even as the people come and go. Projected floor to ceiling, the video extends what feels like an invitation to viewers to try to open the doors themselves. *Bordeaux Piece* (2004), clocking in at thirteen hours forty-three minutes, is a looped video consisting of seventy different shots of a ten-minute narrative based on Godard's *Le mepris* (*Contempt,* 1963). Claerbout's central preoccupation in all his work is time; here, he is interested in moving the background (the time of day) forward, filming the same scene every ten minutes from 5:30 A.M. to 10:00 P.M., at which point the actors are in total darkness. Naturally, in common with Douglas Gordon's *Twenty-Four Hour Psycho* (1993), few viewers engage the entire video, but even twenty minutes of it can convey the very elastic nature of time passed. "The story tires itself out," Claerbout has said, "while the background, the décor, does not stop changing . . . the background surpass(es) the narrative."[7] Claerbout, to borrow from T. J. Clark in discussing Poussin, is "so confident of living in several different temporalities at once" that he can offer, in effect, a new cinema not bound by cinematic time.[8] "One of the impacts of digital film," Claerbout says, "is that it takes away the certainty of moving-image time as a forward arrow . . . there are always neighboring moments: before and after. I hope that I have made some works where all three points (before, now and after) occupy the same surface, the same picture."[9] The collective experience of Claerbout's multiscreen exhibition, featuring numerous works projected mostly from floor to ceiling, amounts to nothing short of a cinematic immersion: the exhibition as cinema.

As we contemplate new cinematics, we hope that history will humor us enough to think that any such thing will have some shelf life. In the very near future, these immersive installations will yield to much more heightened cinematic experiences afforded by virtual reality and games. In his essay "The Intelligent Image: Neurocinema or Quantum Cinema?," Peter Weibel writes of a "utopian vision of a totally new, cinematic imaginary with no local restrictions" based on the manipulation of neurons and particles smaller than neurons—in other words, image worlds accessible to anybody, anywhere, anytime, a cinema

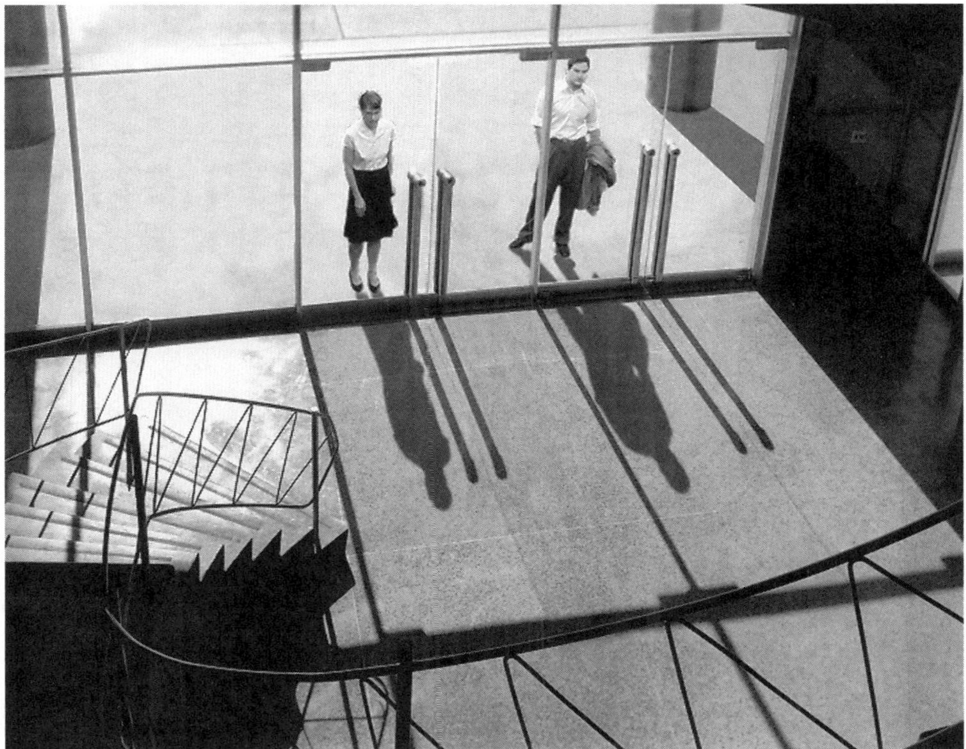

David Claerbout, *Shadow Piece,* 2005. Courtesy of the artist and Yvon Lambert Paris, New York.

without screens based not on receptor technology (cameras) but on effector technology, located in the brain.[10] By this time the cinematic may be only an artifact of a time when the apparatus of projectors, screens, and navigable spaces seemed new indeed.

NOTES

1. The exhibition design was by Tim Lloyd, in cooperation with the artist.

2. Luk Perceval, "Some Words about Asylum," in *Julian Rosefeldt: Asylum* (Ostfildern-Ruit, Germany: Hatje Cantz, 2004), 27.

3. Abel Gance's film *Napoléon* (1927) was also a three-screen projection.

4. David Joselit, "Inside the Light Cube," *Artforum,* March 2004.

5. *Movies* is emphasized here to ground the reader in the common understanding of the components of the cinematic experience common to all movies, not just the artful ones that might be seen in cinema houses.

6. Here, I am talking about visual artists who have not made movies meant for the commercial cinema, including Cindy Sherman, Robert Longo, or Julian Schnabel. Shirin Neshat would also be included in this mix, though she often premieres her films in galleries, where in my opinion, they do not belong.

7. *David Claerbout: The Shape of Time,* exhibition catalog (Zurich, Switzerland: JRP-Ringier in association with Centre Georges Pompidou, Paris, 2007), 14.

8. T. J. Clark, *The Sight of Death: An Experiment in Art Writing* (New Haven, Conn.: Yale University Press, 2006), 125.

9. *David Claerbout,* 13.

10. Peter Weibel, "The Intelligent Image: Neurocinema or Quantum Cinema?," in *Future Cinema: The Cinematic Imaginary after Film,* eds. Jeffrey Shaw and Peter Weibel, exhibition catalog (Cambridge: MIT Press in association with ZKM: Center for Art and Media, Karlsruhe, Germany, 2003), 599.

The Evil Eye of Adolescence

Laurence A. Rickels

Diana Thater's 1996 video installation *Electric Mind* not only refers to earlier incarnations of the story or idea in other media but staggers and fragments them in their ensemble. First, there is the ready-made Pat Murphy short story "Rachel in Love," on which Thater bases her screenplay for *Electric Mind*.[1] The screenplay is a classic adaptation that adheres to the story's happy-ending containment of its volatile premise. But in the video portion or installation, she takes it away.

In conversation with Christiane Schneider, Thater identifies her work as a whole as an attack upon the guilty assumption of a unifying narrative perspective:

> The camera itself was built to make the world monocular—but in my
> work video cameras and projectors serve to multiply, make transparent
> and otherwise undermine the singularity and solidity of animal objects.

In the video installation of *Electric Mind,* legible images of identifiable indexical entries that promise definition pile up as separated segments—for example, "mouse is, a," "cat is, a," "chimp is, a," "girl is, a." Though the links don't add up, they can be incorporated to deliver one sentence: "A mouse is a cat is a chimp is a girl." In her remarks to Schneider, Thater describes the incorporation of narrative through the index as follows: "This sort of indexed narrative removes one from a single point of view and allows for a kind of polyphony—a group of things that seem to exist all at once—because the index is a compressed resequenced version of the book and one is not sure where in the time of the actual text the references will appear. The real time of the text is effaced."[2]

In "Rachel in Love," Aaron, a sort of mad scientist devoted against all odds to his psy-fi notion of transferring identity from brain to brain, loses his wife and daughter in a car accident. By chance or reflex, he had tried his recording techniques on his daughter, and thus, he takes Rachel's mind recording and imprints it on the brain of a chimp, now a hybrid who remains, just the same, his daughter. For the new Rachel, he is "the only person she has ever known. He is her father, her teacher, her friend" (158). Because her chimp body cannot support speech, Aaron trains her in sign language, a prosthesis originally devised for human deaf-mutes. Since the eighteenth century, deaf-mutes have modeled views of language as machinic or structural, upon which programs for alternative communication could be based.

The story begins with Rachel one morning discovering Aaron dead in bed. Rachel is left unprotected for the time it takes death as annihilation to be reclaimed as inheritance and survival by the father's last will and testament. After all the muddle of scientific fact and possibility, it is Aaron's performative declaration in his will that he recognizes the chimp Rachel as his daughter that stabilizes the psychoticizing wake in which Rachel is free game and reinstates her as human subject. Like the mouse folk in Kafka's "Josephine the Singer," animals do not have time to wait around for childhood. After a brief transition of dependency, an animal starts out as a teenager. What comes together in the Rachel hybrid overshoots the plot point that the first Rachel happened to die as a teenager. As in Goethe's *Faust,* reanimation is conceivable in human terms only as rejuvenation back to the starting point of youth. (This is the undertow in myth, group psychology, or video of "becoming animal.")[3]

Though she is identified as having "the mind of a teenage girl, but the innocent heart of a young chimp" (160), Rachel is the hub in which a premature end and a new beginning, a girl and chimp meet but also cross over. When she sees her ape fingers, she remembers her human digits: "memories lie upon memories" (161). "Memories of her girlhood never linger; they land for an instant, then take flight, leaving Rachel feeling abandoned and alone" (162). But which girlhood? She remembers her blonde-haired mother—and her hands—but she also remembers "another mother and another time" (161). She remembers her junior high school dance, and "she also remembers when she was a young chimp: she huddled with five other adolescent chimps in the stuffy freight compartment of a train" (161–62). After she releases all the lab animals and her pets, Rachel is caught and taken to a research lab as a breeder. Her first night at the facility, she has a dream that takes her back to trauma as usual, that of not being the girl that she is or wants to be.

> She looks into her own reflection: a pale oval face, long blonde hair. . . .
> But something is wrong. Superimposed on the reflection is another face
> peering through the glass: a pair of dark brown eyes, a chimp face . . .
> the two images merge and blur. . . . She is a chimp looking in through
> the cold, bright windowpane; she is a girl looking out; she is a girl looking in; she is an ape looking out. (167–68)

But girl and chimp here step into interchangeable places, a move preliminary to the separation and integration of Rachel's combined origins.

All this effort just to become an average European, as the ape protagonist

Rotpeter laments in Kafka's "A Report to an Academy." Humans look at animals only to find a chance or change that recommends their domestication for entertainment. But as Henri Bergson argues in *Laughter,* when the human laughs at the animal thus anthropomorphized, he is laughing only at his own mechanized aspect.[4] The trainable animal studies the humans closely to find in imitation and assimilation a way out. Rachel goes to great lengths to enter a relationship with the local janitor, Jake, a middle-aged deaf man filling the lab's quota for handicapped employees.

She signs to Jake that she is a girl, and he recognizes that she is a very bright chimp. He lets her out during his night shift to help him with the cleaning. Though she promises to go back behind bars after each night out, the plan she in fact harbors, namely to wait and look for a good opportunity to escape, gets disrupted by the idea that she loves Jake (182). This idea of love is the symptom of Rachel's adolescence for which she must find the cure in the acceptance of compromise, identification, and inheritance. Otherwise, she is stuck trying to feel real in the crush of the in-group.

> She loves him, but she does not know how to make him love her back. . . .
> She remembers a high school crush where she mooned after a boy with
> a locker near hers, but that came to nothing. (182)

In the next cage is Johnson, her prearranged match in the breeding department. Johnson enters her dream as the touch of the pre-Oedipal mother. She dreams first of her ape mother, who doesn't understand sign language. Then, her human mother emerges but tells Rachel to stop howling like an ape. When she feels grooming fingers along her back, she assumes the ape mother has returned after the human one vanished. But it's Johnson's magic fingers reaching through the bars (184–85).

Are Johnson and Jake really so different? she wonders now that she's in heat (187). On the night that Jake is too busy staring at his favorite porn pictures to see that Rachel is the willing substitute, "Rachel howls like an infant who has lost its mother, but he does not look up" (188). Afterward, she makes the connection with Johnson. Once they've fled together, she wonders why she thought she loved Jake. In a dream, Aaron authorizes the change of heart: "It doesn't matter what anyone thinks of you. You're my daughter." When she says she wants to be a real girl, the dream father answers, "You *are* real. . . . And you don't need some two-bit drunken janitor to prove it to you!" (191). She does not need the group bond to support her. Her father is back in place—in the place of identification and compromise. It is time for her to be the wife, the guardian of the couple and representative of father. She can now not only mourn her father but also mourn with him while he comforts her. When she awakes, Rachel carves into the wall

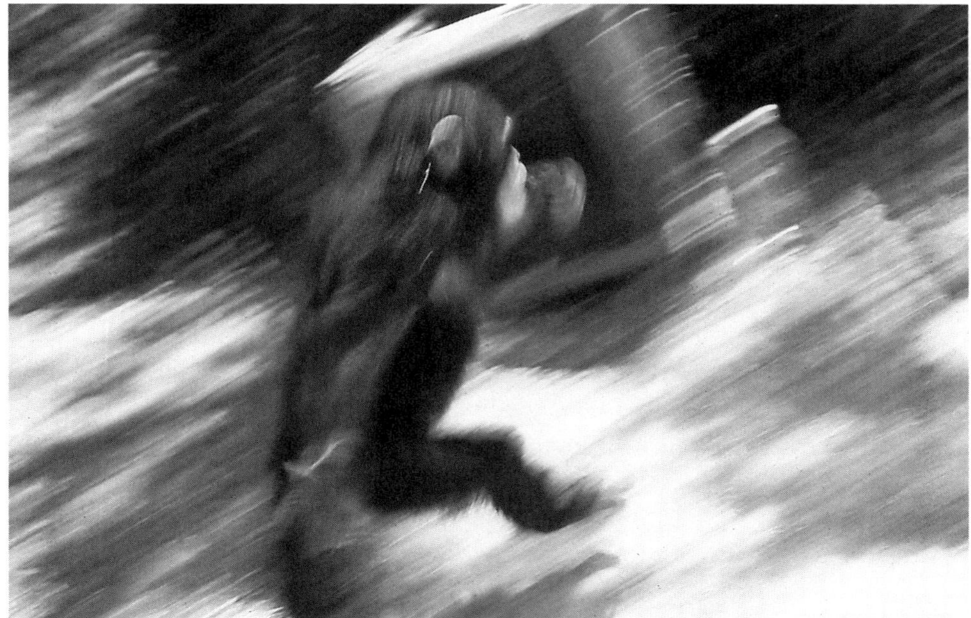

Diana Thater video installation *Electric Mind*, 1996. Courtesy of the artist.

of the cave a heart outlining the exchange of vows her father has assigned and witnessed. It is this fossil that brings mass-media society to her rescue, following in the news prints of *"Lassie, Come Home* with chimps" (189).

Crypt Networks

Rachel is a hybrid who also carries the encrypted Rachel. One crypt always opens onto the encrypted others in the network. In this case the password is Tarzan, both the projected signifier in which Rachel mirrors herself as skewed at the start of the story and the name of the trained chimp Thater uses in the video portion of her installation. The author of the Tarzan series became in 1923 one of the first writers to incorporate, Edgar Rice Burroughs, Inc. (The corporation is still based in Tarzana, the town Burroughs created out of an estate he could not otherwise sustain.) Before Disney, Burroughs embraced the marketing approach of what would come to be known as multimedia (he even compiled an ape to English/English to ape dictionary). Before the Mickey Mouse Club refined the concept, Burroughs adapted the Boy Scouts of America as the Tarzan Clans of America.

Ed was the fifth son; the fourth, Arthur, had lived only twelve days. When Ed was six, a younger brother, Charles Stuart, died at five months. The image of the lifeless infant in his mother's arms can be seen when Tarzan's ape mother, Kala, won't let go of her dead baby—until she finds in baby Tarzan the reanimation she lifts up while dropping the loss into the crib or crypt.

Ed was the shiftless, short-attention-span child: a perennial loser. But it was the loss of siblings that was being protected or pushed back. He was regularly sent away because an epidemic was going the rounds. It's clear that there was overconcern that his early passing not be the third thing that bad fortune brings. As he wrote in his unfinished autobiography of 1929, "Unquestionably my destiny is closely interwoven with pestilences, which may or may not account for my having become a writer."[5]

The ancestry of his mother would be Burroughs's pride and disavowal, which together spells shame. Through his mother he identified with (and idealized) distant relations from Virginia, whereas the more immediate family circle, on both sides, was Union all the way. But the Union his veteran father embodied had to be mediated for Burroughs by the loss of a civil or sibling war.

He wrote a first novel that lifts off into fantasy from the map of his fraternity in Utah, which he kept rejoining, working with his brothers as ranch hand and panhandler when he wasn't working for his father in Chicago. The title, *Minidoka,* also the name of the eponymous hero, was the name of one of the towns on this map. He never showed the manuscript around, even in the family circle. He filed it away with his souvenirs of school, army, and the West, where it remained undiscovered until after his death. It had been time to pack up the mementos: the fraternity was returning to Chicago after all ventures, including a store in Minidoka, had failed. But it was this adventure map of the fraternity that supplied a first foundation for his found and lost ability to sustain a narrative at novel length.

Now commenced for Burroughs a period, between 1905 and 1911, in which the pattern of jobs he pursued, lost, or let go might be considered premeditated. In the course of this long haul of unemployment, he began to suffer nightmares in which, as he confided to the Boston Society of Psychic Research, he "would see figures standing beside" the "bed, usually shrouded."[6] While waiting around on the job, he consumed countless stories in the cheap magazines on the back pages of which he advertised the latest device he was trying to sell. Shifting from background to foreground, a serialized narrative in one of the leading pulp magazines was one more invention he would pitch for sale.

In July 1911 he commenced writing *A Princess of Mars,* the success story that allowed him to be a proper son and father.[7] The protagonist, Carter, who enters a kind of limbo at the loss of the Civil War, is a "Southern gentleman of the highest type" (v). He entrusts to "Burroughs," another Virginian, who is also the author of the foreword, his corpus for safekeeping and scheduling. The manuscript must remain unread for eleven years. The single massive door to Carter's well-ventilated tomb opens only from the inside (vii). Carter opens his narrative with the declaration that he is undead but also fears death. It's because he's so afraid of death (even though he has died twice to date and yet survives) that he is convinced that he is mortal (11). He has always been a man of about thirty, which was about the age of Burroughs (or of his first lost sibling if he could have kept real time) at the time of this breakthrough. Though Carter still appears as he did over forty years ago, he senses that he cannot go on living forever. Some day he will "die the real death from which there is no resurrection" (11). This real death would be the real second death that in a secular setting of denied resurrection ends haunting and undeath.

Into the revolving door of this crypt, Burroughs inserted the new fiction (and series) dedicated to Tarzan. *Tarzan of the Apes,* which first appeared as magazine fare in 1912 and then as a book two years later, spanned the time of publication of Freud's *Totem and Taboo.*[8] There is a rhyme in time between Burroughs's consideration of the superhuman on the terms and turf of primal man and Freud's legend of the primal father.

For around two years, a certain professor at the University of California searched for the roots of Tarzan. In reply to the academic's diplomatic letter of inquiry, Burroughs wrote:

> I have tried to search my memory for some clue to the suggestions that gave me the idea, and as close as I can come to it I believe that it may have originated in my interest in Mythology and the story of Romulus and Remus. I also recall having read many years ago the story of the sailor who was shipwrecked on the Coast of Africa and who was adopted by and consorted with great apes to such an extent that when he was rescued a she-ape followed him into the surf and threw a baby after him.[9]

In *Tarzan of the Apes,* Kala is Tarzan's ape mother not by evolutionary sex but, to the same effect, by dint of mourning (or unmourning): "She had a great capacity for mother love and mother sorrow" (31). It should be clear—it certainly is to Tarzan—that the other conditions of Burroughs's experiment (the novel certainly opens as breeding assignment), like the boy's real pedigree as noble born, are eclipsed by the combo of support Kala gives him. She is the only object he has—to lose—hence her epitaph as inscribed inside Tarzan's inner world: "To lose the only creature in all his world who ever had manifested love and affection for him was the greatest tragedy he had ever known" (75–76).

The Carter vault is replaced by the cabin of Tarzan's birth, which although it houses the dead, serves as a self-storage unit through which Tarzan, beginning in adolescence, comes into his inheritance. It is Tarzan's epistemophilia that the crypt of reason supplies. Before avenging Kala's murder, he pauses to study the

African tribesman who is the culprit. Based on the primer he had found in the cabin, he recognizes him as "Negro," but even more so as "Archer" (77). "Tarzan was an interested spectator. His desire to kill burned fiercely in his wild breast, but the desire to learn was even greater" (78). He learns that the arrow is but the "messenger" delivering the poison that kills. (Burroughs equates the poison at one point with a "virus" [96].)

The ultimate tally of differences between humans and animals leads Tarzan "to hold his own kind in low esteem" (91). Tarzan allows himself the distinction of animal nobility: "When he killed for revenge, or in self-defense, he did that also without hysteria, for it was a very business-like proceeding which admitted of no levity" (83). Tarzan's distinguishing character trait is his delight in playing pranks, often in the setting of his great interest in learning. After studying the interior of a tribal habitation, he piles up a still-life of the family's possessions, placing one of the skulls from their collection on top: "He stood back, surveyed his work, and grinned. Tarzan of the Apes enjoyed a joke" (85). Then he observes the response, "There was much in their demeanor which he could not understand, for of superstition he was ignorant, and of fear of any kind he had but a vague conception" (87).

In *Group Psychology and the Analysis of the Ego,* the work in which Freud revisits the legend of the primal father he had introduced in *Totem and Taboo,* we learn in passing that a joke implements a focusing of attention reminiscent of the indirect method of hypnosis (126), which yields the same result as the direct method.[10] Freud calls hypnosis "a group of two" because it taps into the group dynamic grounded in the primal father as "group ideal, which governs the ego in the place of the ego ideal" (127). Tarzan comes after the death of the primal father as second-generation superhuman. Freud underscores that what Nietzsche seeks in the future belongs in the past: the superman is the primal father, the feared and hated figure of uninhibited self-fulfilment (the only true individual, Freud suggests, thus underscoring that in his science there is no other "individual" to be found) (123). But this superhuman father, once gone, proves to be good and gone. Not only do his adolescent children find that they also have to mourn him, but in time the dead primal father also comes to be installed as the model of mourning (which is successful to the extent that it allows succession). At a time when ideologues (and psychos like Leopold and Loeb) were claiming to see or be the future now of Nietzsche's forecast of the superhuman, Freud rescued the open-ended trajectory of Nietzsche's thought by preserving it in everyone's prehistory as the predestination to mourn.

By reason or by prosthesis, Tarzan succeeds to the kingship of the apes. More interested in pursuing his solitary studies in and around the cabin, however, Tarzan steps down as ruler and enjoins the apes to choose his replacement. He issues one law, that of the group bond, which gives and takes away the fundamental support on which the leader or father depends. Three is both a crowd and the father.

> If you have a chief who is cruel, do not do as the other apes do, and attempt, any one of you, to pit yourself against him alone. But, instead, let two or three or four of you attack him together. Then, if you will do this, no chief will dare to be other than he should be, for four of you can kill any chief who may ever be over you. (170)

After Tarzan comes the law of succession to be carried out by the fraternity. But before this law Tarzan is not alone in his success. Freud identifies critters and insects as the diminished siblings whose bond helps carry the hero, who only appears to proceed solo:

> We often find . . . that the hero who has to carry out some difficult task . . . can carry out his task only by the help of a crowd of small animals, such as bees or ants. These would be the brothers in the primal horde, just as in the same way in dream symbolism insects or vermin signify brothers and sisters (contemptuously, considered as babies). (136)

When Tarzan is learning to read in the parental cabin and crypt, the letters first appear to him as "bugs." The knife Tarzan also discovers in the cabin, which serves him as a single prosthesis putting him over the top of the primary narcissism of bodily conflict, is also the tool for getting to know all about the bugs: "Pieces of bark and flat leaves and even smooth stretches of bare earth provided him with copy books whereon to scratch with the point of his hunting knife the lessons he was learning" (57). He learns to supplement the proper names of the ape language with bug words that introduce a larger frame of difference, one that allows Tarzan a race of his own on the basis of which he can affirm his secondary narcissism. Only the "slow and backward" child (37), from the perspective of animals, has the running start (or the "promise" to be kept in time) that allows him to be hoisted by his prosthesis and group bond. Animals, as instant teens, don't share with us the promise land.

To complete the conditions for his experiment, Burroughs renders Tarzan's apes as a fantasy species related to the gorilla but more intelligent, with Kala at the front of the line: with her round, high forehead, she is the most intelligent. The "Dum-Dum" of these apes is "the first meeting place" from which "has arisen . . . all the forms and ceremonials of modern church and state" (59). These fantasy apes of increased intelligence are, more so than usual with apes, the "awe-inspiring progenitors of man" (31). They embody a missing link. The link with the missing is established when Kala is able to reanimate her dead baby by taking Tarzan to carry the first child forward beyond mourning or substitution. When he begins growing facial hair in adolescence, Tarzan quickly invents shaving with his father's knife to hide the evidence of his ape nature on the inside (109–10).

Sweet Jane

In "The Taboo of Virginity," Freud argues that a husband is still working through his relationship to his father when he's in crisis with his better half, whereas a wife is still going at it with her mother in her struggles with her man.[11] That's why remarriage, Freud allows, so often succeeds where the first marriage fails. Thus, marriage, which for Melanie Klein is always remarriage, succeeds only as mourning, which in this setting means that the internal or ghostly parents achieve integration. Otherwise, as she argues, for example in "A Contribution to the Psychogenesis of Manic-Depressive States," either parent residing in the inner world can advance to the front of the line of evil spirits as, in Klein's words, "a dangerous ghost" (283n1).[12] But the ghost must be appeased, not put to rest. Healthy coupling therefore means generous inclusion of the parental pair you bring together again or re-pair as the individual whole objects separated out in the course of early development from that pathogenic parental combo of the primal scene. For Klein, then, marital sex is shared with these parents, who also get off at your pleasure. It is a bond otherwise supported in grief. In Klein's essay "Mourning and Its Relation to Manic-Depressive States," a certain Mrs. A. (who is Klein's own proxy in this case example of a mother who, like Klein a few years earlier, was bereft of her son) at first felt that "her loss was inflicted on her by revengeful parents." In the course of her mourning work, however, she experienced "in phantasy" "the sympathy of these parents (dead long since)" who "shared her grief as they would have done had they lived." "The tears which she shed were also to some extent the tears which her internal parents shed, and she also wanted to comfort them as they—in her phantasy—comforted her."[13]

When Jane and her party find shelter in the cabin, their first task is to inter the skeletal remains found inside. Tarzan again receives instruction via the cabin, this time in burial and proper mourning. But stay away from Jane—that way civilization lies. The lie of this land is given in Nietzschean shorthand: money, giving only in exchange, and the promise. Jane represents to herself—and represses— her love for Tarzan as primeval. Promises, promises allow her twice in swift succession—the tempo of repression—to block consummation of her love. And yet what she calls primeval is maternal. Her mother died a year ago. Her father addresses his missing wife as ghostly partner with whom he counts on being reunited. The unsettling effects of the loss, rather than senility or lifelong eccentricity, determine his oblivious treatment of Jane and, indeed, of reality (the reality of loss). Father is off to Africa in search of treasure for which he has obtained a loan with his daughter's hand in marriage as security. She's along to protect him. But then she finds herself projecting in her mother's missing place Tarzan's bosom body.

The hybrid Rachel watches one of the Weissmuller Tarzan films on television at the start of Murphy's story (and Thater's screenplay). Weissmuller's incarnation of the superhero, beginning in 1932, enters Tarzan in the contest between American and German interpretations of and identifications with the superhuman. Second-generation animators of heroism (after Leopold and Loeb) counter the interpretation of Nietzsche's superman as master race mascot with the introduction of Superman and Batman, whose superheroism originate in trauma, which divides them from themselves but which ongoing conflict with the evil masterminds doubles and contains. Weissmuller embodies the aesthetic athleticism that Riefenstahl instrumentalizes. Whereas in *Olympia* she cynically intercuts the athletes in action with assorted animals in motion, Tarzan/Weissmuller shares ontology with the beasts of the jungle: the elephant is his neighbor, and a chimp, his adopted child or partner. Here, one might recall that Jane Goodall let it be well known that Tarzan was the inspiration for her life's work.

Tarzan/Weissmuller doesn't say much. But he doesn't need to. These projections are all about Jane. The first film opens with her reunion with her father at his encampment in Africa. Right before she enters, we see the old man gazing longingly at Jane's photograph. (Someone is gone without saying, without commemoration.) She in turn plays coy with the possibilities of his love, which suggests that this isn't the first time she's been overstimulated by his needs. Then, she starts freshening up and getting changed in front of her discomfited father without any show of modesty of her own. She talks about how fascinating Africa is, while he says that he hates Africa, which she can't accept. When he takes her out to witness the natives gathering for market, father and daughter are up against the studio walls. Screen-thin projections of found footage of African tribesmen are on the walls closing in. Jane takes her departure from the close quarters of Oedipal incest and finds her way back to the double-breasted body of noble or pre-Oedipal valuation. Thus, she separates out the double-backed parental body and inaugurates their integration.

In "A Contribution to the Psychogenesis of Manic-Depressive States," Klein underscores a certain mastery of objects under the aegis of omnipotence as the most fundamental manic defense, which allows, however, for endless variation, extending from obsessional separation of the internalized parents to a more fully manic destruction and reanimation of objects. The manic person's omnipotent mastery of objects must "prevent them not only from injuring himself but from being a danger to one another. His mastery is to enable him particularly to prevent dangerous coitus between the parents he has internalized and their death within him" (278).

A good example of this struggle for mastery is the story of Superman, whose original point of departure lies, on Krypton, in the parental underworld of fusion and fission. There are many variations on the origin of one man's manic or super defense. By and large Superman is guided by the obsessional attempt to separate the combination between the maternal commitment to each individual life and the subsuming paternal allegiance to Life in the big picture of the battle of values, imperatives, or the drives. If you want to divert Superman from the big picture (in which the evil masterminds feel at home), just drop one human from the top of a skyscraper. But to neglect the paternal battleground on which the masterminds launch their maneuvers is to risk having left unprotected a greater number of casualties. Or when under catastrophe conditions Superman sets out to save individual lives one by one, he runs out of time to save the one life he does, after all, value most. At which point, as in *Superman: The Movie,* he spins against the linear time of the earth's orbit and, to be kind, rewinds the record of the recent past until the point is reached to save Lois in time.

In the course of making *Electric Mind,* Thater determined that she would never again work with trained wild animals. After this it would be wildlife in its natural, endangered state that she would summon in her work. When animals aren't trainable, as are our pets and the stable and barnyard animals, then dominance alone is exercised nonstop to keep them in check. The trainable animal waits, watches, and always answers. Wild animals do not understand training as communication and community with humans. Thater wanted a shot of the ape running up the mobile camera's tracks. But the animal ran, scared of the camera. What Thater recorded was the alternation in the relation to animals between haunting and hunting.

The individual animal, the animal we spare and keep close, at our disposal, hasn't enough lifetime for overcoming our pet grief. The wildlife of endangered species, which belongs to the big picture of destruction versus preservation, mitigates direct contact with those brief life spans entrusted to our care. Deleuze and Guattari's notion of "becoming animal," which immediately distinguishes the wild animal (like the psychotic from the neurotic) over and against the Oedipal pet, also serves the purpose of diversion from our responsibilities as guardians of trainable animals.[14] Freud argues in *Totem and Taboo* that the introduction of livestock outmoded totemism.[15] But in the everyday lives we share with the animals we spare and keep close, we continue to administer a sacrificial economy of controlled release. The link between food and death must be remade, over and again, from curse into boon. Because the primal father stands behind the relay of substitute sacrifices as the happy meal that yielded survival through the successful mourning it released and contained, we can eat meat and face the otherwise unmournable animal as other.

NOTES

1. To make the adaptation cinematic, Thater expands the media coverage of Rachel's escape (limited in the story to a couple of lines) until she has assembled a crowd of animal rights protesters, scientists, and well-wishers to welcome Rachel home. Although she also fleshes out Jake's porn collection (which is now all about nurses), as well as the soft-core porn Rachel discovers in wastebaskets, Thater does not revise or revalorize the story as a whole. She does, however, make much more of the kittens: Rachel's return home is also her reunion with her pets. Thater's published screenplay includes Murphy's short story "Rachel in Love," in *Electric Mind* (Gent, Belgium: Imschoot, uitgevers, 1996), 155–95. Page references to the story are given in the text.

2. Christiane Schneider, "More Stars than There Are in Heaven: Christiane Schneider in Conversation with Diana Thater," in *Diana Thater: Transcendence Is Expansion and Contraction at the Same Time* (London: Haunch of Venison, 2003), 29, 12.

3. See note 14.

4. Henri Bergson, *Laughter: An Essay on the Meaning of the Comic,* trans. Cloudesley Brereton and Fred Rothwell (Los Angeles: Green Integer, 1999). "Several have defined man as 'an animal which laughs.' They might equally well have defined him as an animal which is laughed at; for if any other animal, or some lifeless object, produces the same effect, it is always because of some resemblance to man, of the stamp he gives it or the use he puts it to" (9).

5. Cited in John Taliaferro, *Tarzan Forever: The Life of Edgar Rice Burroughs, Creator of Tarzan* (New York: Scribner, 1999), 30.

6. Cited in Taliaferro, *Tarzan Forever,* 61.

7. Edgar Rice Burroughs, *A Princess of Mars* (New York: Ballantine Books, 1963). Page references are given in the text.

8. Edgar Rice Burroughs, *Tarzan of the Apes* (New York: Ballantine Books, 1963). Page references are given in the text.

9. Cited in Taliaferro, *Tarzan Forever,* 85.

10. Sigmund Freud, *The Standard Edition of the Complete Psychological Works of Sigmund Freud,* ed. and trans. James Strachey, vol. 18, *Beyond the Pleasure Principle, Group Psychology and Other Works* (London: Hogarth Press, 1955). Page references are to this edition and are given in the text.

11. Sigmund Freud, "The Taboo of Virginity," in *The Standard Edition of the Complete Psychological Works of Sigmund Freud,* ed. and trans. James Strachey, vol. 11, *Five Lectures on Psycho-Analysis, Leonardo da Vinci and Other Works* (London: Hogarth Press, 1957), 193–208.

12. Melanie Klein, "A Contribution to the Psychogenesis of Manic-Depressive States," in *Love, Guilt and Reparation and Other Works (1921–1945)* (New York: Free Press, 1975), 262–89. Page references are given in the text.

13. Melanie Klein, "Mourning and Its Relation to Manic-Depressive States," in *Love, Guilt and Reparation,* 359.

14. In *A Thousand Plateaus,* Deleuze and Guattari consider "becoming animal" as exemplary of "becoming multiple" or "becoming minoritarian." And yet becoming animal is how the overriding investment in multiplicity is first flexed. Only through the animal pack can we become multiple. Thus, the plan of becoming begins with the animal relation. Since becoming multiple means becoming minoritarian, man as majority figure is not an option for

becoming. Man must be divested of his majority share before he can become other. There is inside becoming animal, then, a concise two-point summary of psychoanalytic positions. While the positioning of becoming animal as medium of becoming suggests the totemic relations Freud illuminates in terms of mourning between first and second deaths, the stricture placed on majority man evokes castration, whereby Lacan, for example, in allegiance to one side of Freud's thought, circumvents mourning as secondary to the first death, the initial experience of finitude and lack via castration that renders further contact with loss beside this point.

15. Sigmund Freud, *The Standard Edition of the Complete Psychological Works of Sigmund Freud,* ed. and trans. James Strachey, vol. 13, *Totem and Taboo and Other Works* (London: Hogarth Press, 1955). On the onset of domestication of animals and its impact on totemism, see 136–38.

Media Arts as Intervention

Yvonne Spielmann

When we view the development and establishment of video within the broader context of the emerging electronic media arts, we find that video from the 1990s to the present above all has confronted the integration of computers and the transfer of video processes to the digital computer. Video as a reference and art medium has evolved to include and merge multimedia installation and object art with large-format projections onto larger-than-life screens. One may recall that it was not until the 1990s that video in Euro-American contexts successfully established itself in art exhibitions, whereas its presence at media festivals decreased. Media festivals nowadays rather focus on interactive and network-based works in which video is included solely as an indexical representation tool. The adaptation of video into a multitude of hybridized media realities, however, such as the virtual, the interactive, and the document, is for the most part directed at the problem of representation and movement in a digitally constructed space. But it also shows that video has developed a specific, electronic vocabulary and is acknowledged as a reference medium for a multiplicity of audiovisual experiments in digital media.

A closer look at the contemporary media landscape reveals that the computer (not unlike the variety of applications in video processing) can be used as a multipurpose programmable tool that many artists have modified and applied according to their own needs driven by the intention to interfere with standardized, preformatted media tools and their products in the electronic culture. In the early days of 1970s video exploration, tools were plugged together and built from scratch to create aesthetic expressions that deviated from the industry's standard of the televisual image. Today, artists build on these pioneer experiments and understand these tools as instruments of intervention into the media environment, which has been massively globalized in scale as creative industries have infiltrated many areas of human creativity. My starting point in this essay is to draw attention to some examples in the international media arts that can be identified as aesthetic/cultural interventions, meaning that they demonstrate decisive strategies of creative intervention into the corporate/commercial products of the media cultural environment that surrounds us globally. The importance of creative intervention into "our cultural contemporaneity" has already been deftly highlighted by cultural critic Homi Bhabha in the early 1990s. Bhabha sees the partisan role of the artist's activity in a space of intervention. I return to this position when discussing some strategies of artistic/aesthetic and more widely applicable creative practices that parallel early video interventions and/or regard video as a building block.

To introduce the topic of critical interventions into contemporary media landscapes, let me start by briefly highlighting a few aspects of the present situation—with some reference to the past—and follow with a discussion of aesthetic strategies in the radical or oppositional arts. The examples are intended to demonstrate that radicalized arts practices are important strategies in the present and should be considered as aesthetic interventions anchored in a specific time and place. These arts practices develop tools to transgress and make us aware of media borders in multiple ways and, in doing so, render and make fluid the polarized discourses of East/West and inside/outside that have been established and reinforced over decades. Concurrently, these arts practices act as cultural translations.

First, I consider artists' practices as aesthetic interventions for which the target is to unveil or reveal and to make us think about processes in the media that we usually take for granted and call into question only when there is failure and malfunction. In contrast to these failures, aesthetic interventions can be effective instruments in a critical discourse about dominant media cultures where the arts dissolve, disrupt, and rearrange meaningful contexts of normative media presentations. The aesthetic means can be subtle, ironic, or violent, and they can forcefully dismantle the raw materials of our highly mediated environment. Striking examples within the history of video are represented in particular by Dara Birnbaum's interventions into television programs with video clips that dismantle the banal, redundant, and repetitive structure of television. Other examples are evident in the work of British video pioneer David Hall and Austrian duo Granular Synthesis and their video performances. Second, among contemporary creative practices, I feel two important criteria stand out: one is the crossover of different cultural and media elements in dialogical contexts (for example, in Masaki Fujihata's fieldworks), and the other is the interaction of different views, attitudes, and realities in open-ended processes wherein we experience a variety and diversity of views beyond and across the dominant modes of homogenizing difference (for example, the works by Japanese group doubleNegatives Architecture).

Looking generally at the present situation, it is widely agreed that we have reached a level of mediation that has entered many—maybe too many—areas of our daily life, so much so that it might sound odd or outdated to seek a critical position located in the media arts. Innovation and experimentation in a

Western context is traditionally placed within the history of European avant-garde movements that predicted a technological future, but nowadays, technology is available to almost everyone from childhood onward. We have reached a level of technological application, available to teenagers in their bedrooms, where production, distribution, and consumption seem to fuse. Furthermore, we have developed technical tools for the remediation of all previous media arts, which we can broadcast globally and oftentimes instantaneously with minimal infrastructure. As media critic Marshall McLuhan predicted decades ago, media technologies have become the natural prosthesis of humans and prolong our bodily and sensorial perception, from the real to the virtual.

Today, most of us are happy to employ these novel technologies, devices, and gadgets without much reflection. We do not (usually) refuse to carry all kinds of minicomputers around all day long; we do not protest (much) about the talking machines and all the noisy sounds and images that we encounter in almost every public space and place. They come to us without choice or request: we cannot control or stop them in the same way that we can switch off a television. At the same time, we take advantage of all sorts of new applications that demand our ability to constantly adapt to ever-increasingly complex and interconnected operations while the amount of time and space available to us proportionally decreases. Mobility, flexibility, immediate and permanent accessibility, and contactability around the clock are the main characteristics of a situation that extends across the globe and is greeted by some of us with deep relief, whereas others suffer from exhaustion.

As it stands, even critical debate now seems to have changed profession and to a large extent occupies itself with catching up with the latest technological novelties in a manner that differs sharply from distanced analysis. Because the understanding of the present requires very specific expert knowledge, we are surrounded by a plentitude of expert debates that in different languages and with a growing labyrinth of technical terms and abbreviations, disseminate the order of the new world. For the most part, these voices manifest hierarchies and differences by discussing, for example, almost exclusively Western media as the standard that represents "us," thereby deliberately attributing non-Western media to "them," the "other," without much explanation of the positioning of this discourse. There seems to be an unspoken unwillingness to engage in a real dialogue that would regard it as a matter of course to challenge and rework presumptions of critique. On the contrary, we face an almost jubilant welcoming of the latest consumable tools and the fresh goods of today's cultural industries, which are creating the rules of networked data communication and information, as well as regulation and restriction, on a global scale. It has become difficult to determine any critical discourse and argue aesthetically for interventions into complex and diverse media realities. Perhaps, the whole project of doing so has become obsolete.

But there are other voices that call for investigations into the roots of these issues and for increasing awareness of the contexts of media and cultural specificities. Another goal is to dismantle the supposed neutrality of technological developments. These voices are mostly heard from the past and the earlier days of cultural critique when the digital age and economic globalization were young and embryonic. Prominently in the early nineties, Stuart Hall sharply recognized the simplifying and standardizing mechanisms at work in cultural globalization and the world-system. He observed that "while we live with difference and by the same token enjoy pluralism, we also absorb highly concentrated, corporate, and indeed over-corporate, over-concentrated forms of economic power, power which culturally lives and manifests itself through the same difference and finds pleasure in the incorporation of otherness as the demonstration of its strength."[1]

Unsurprisingly, it almost goes without saying that the other and the outside were largely determined as the non-Western, which means something special and exotic but also lesser and relatively unimportant. One voice in particular can be singled out in providing the answer to the question of where to locate culture between the polarities of self and other, East and West, and inside and outside in the contemporary situation of crossing, mixing, blending, blurring, and other hybridizing combinations. Bhabha points out that critical engagement beyond such polarities keeps cultural dialogue alive and inhabits the in-between zones with dynamic interaction and open-ended processes. In this respect radical artists' practices will manifest themselves as creative interventions. The artists' intervention is seen as the instrument of interrupting the performances of present media cultures and the means of fostering multiperspectival views in a variety of combinations and intercultural voices that express lively dialogue and not dead-end polarities.[2]

To explain this further, I discuss some examples of aesthetic/artistic practices that are situated in the Western and the Eastern, more precisely in the European and Asian contexts, and may serve as effective approaches to readdress such one-sided discourses that look from here to there, inside to outside, West to East. In contrast to these limited perspectives, I suggest cross-directions and regard it as a matter of course to discuss practices that are relevant to the topic of intervention and emerge in different cultural contexts. It is necessary to consider both media and cultural specificities where the parameters of these worlds are relevant to understanding the impact of the practices and their targets. The aesthetic practices under discussion are those that contribute to the overall level of technological media and highlight strategies of intervention. I do not intend to discuss cultural or media specificities and differences as such.

I propose to look in particular at aesthetic practices in media arts in Europe and Japan, where I find cross-relations regarding the innovative and radical use and application of electronic, computational, interactive, and representational modes of presentation. The task is to widen the horizon of discussion and to argue for overcoming some of the still-existing barriers between media and cultural discourses and also between arts and media. It's not about identifying peculiar Japanese and European media arts: the notion of art is also not of interest here. The more interesting question is what are the overriding, effective, and suitable strategies for processes of intervention, dialogue, and violation that can cope with standard media tools and technologies that spread out everywhere. By and large, I also think media debates need to be more culturally informed and cultural debates need to develop their expertise on mediation processes. Both need to be able to cope with complex contexts; both need to become sensitive to the articulation of difference without pushing its operations to the fore.

In 1971, when electronic media were young, British video pioneer David Hall made a series of remarkable TV interruptions that were commissioned by Scottish Television and were meant, unannounced, to interrupt the program flow. Hall provoked dialogue inside television by talking back to the medium with its own means. The idea was that Hall's works would be interruptions to be broadcast without any warning within the regular program. For Hall this insertion of different content within the context of the medium was a way of interacting with the medium as in a dialogue. This became particularly clear when Hall imitated the format of television news and demonstrated the malfunction or even possible destruction of the flow of televisual information.

In a similar way, his self-explanatory videotape *This Is a Television Receiver* (1976) enforces remediation of television through rewinding and rerecording the same videotape three times in a row until the material on-screen becomes a hopelessly jumbled series of ghost images—until it destroys both the meaning and the material of the video while still being projected. The loss of sound and vision from generation to generation of videotape exhausts the capacities of the analog medium of the time. The video work, through demonstrated time shifting, technically deconstructs the essential characteristics of a live medium as it is dismantled at the core of a decaying videotape. This disappearance of understandable sounds and recognizable images finally produces the electronic snow that truly constitutes the raw material of any electronic medium. Hall's installation tape, which needs to be shown on a monitor, merges video and television on the same technical basis, both visually and aurally, and uses video as an intervention into television. As television viewers are forced to see and hear, by exposing the specific properties of the medium, Hall clearly hurts and disrupts the viewers' expectations that are being so powerfully shaped in the 1970s by broadcast television.

Twenty years later, the Austrian artistic duo Granular Synthesis (Kurt Hentschläger and Ulf Langheinrich)—in another approach to using media behavior against the grain—dismantles the raw material from inside. For the live performances of the audiovisual installation *Model 5* (four-channel video projection, Quadrosound, Austria, 1994–96), they allow digitally processed images and sounds from four video output channels and eight audio outputs to interact. This produces a multisensual perceptual experience. The duo's name says it all; granular synthesis separates a videographic recording into units of information and subsequently samples and resynthesizes them.

In *Model 5* the previously recorded image and sound material of the Japanese performer Akemi Takeya is broken down into its smallest processable elements in an analytical process and then, in a process of reconstruction, reassembled in another frequency, so that the image and the sound fragments produced by this recombination deviate from the continuity of the original in a clearly audible and visible way. The synchronicity and stability of the image and the sound are dissolved. The electronic course of the image and sound is no longer synchronized conventionally: image and sound are separated, blurred, and perceived erratically as flickers. Furthermore, the newly produced frequencies are modulated live.

In *Model 5* the audience perceives this intervention into the audiovisual material by means of granular synthesis as violent and painful because the artists dissect the voice and the portrait of Takeya. Her natural rhythm is eliminated and replaced by a mechanical rhythm in the sequence. In effect, a mathematical operation of digital analysis is applied to a video recording of Takeya's performance. Where the base video material stands for continuity in the performance (which in the electronic medium is not mandatory), the digital editing of the live presentation is used to make us aware of the media level. In the work of Granular Synthesis, the audience perceives the presentation as disruptive because synchronicity has been removed.

In a technically different but conceptually related approach, Dutch video installation artist Aernout Mik also causes disorientation and rupture. The work achieves confusion not by violating the material but by presenting violent scenes of group action that never show the violent event. Locations are unclear: all we know is that the events are taking place somewhere in Europe, as the uniforms, vehicles, clothing, and open spaces indicate. Fiction and reality are inseparably blurred. We cannot tell what is real and what is staged. Intense scenes of humiliation, tinged with a flavor of uncertainty, tension, and violence, unfold in front of the camera and us. Opposing sides are not clearly marked or identifiable; the whole situation is unstable. Even the order of events and sides is constantly changing. There is no narrative beginning or end, no inside and outside, no clear borders or rules; everything is somehow merged, confused; everything is possible, and imposed power relations can suddenly reverse. The situation is one of ever-growing alertness, an excess of constant tension. The question arises, Is this real or staged? And does the difference matter?

What kind of reality is Aernout Mik showing in his video installations? There are training camps, police, military, protester demonstrations, groups of displaced people, evacuation and other emergencies, searches, raids and security zones, and warlike scenarios and warfare—in short, a cross-section of daily television news around the world. And yet this uncanny state of emergency and terror somehow gains our contemporary consent when we assume it is real, when we watch the news. What matters in Mik's media world is the presentation format, which renders the materials strange and induces us to interrogate the contexts. The formal strategies are reserved, not competing with the shocking content. He uses dual projections to stress the continuation of such scenes; they are not single events. The editing creates visible blanks and inserts lack—meaningless space that interrupts our viewing for long moments in such a way that we reflect on our interest in viewing such materials. The sound is absent; our full concentration can only be on the visual, and we are kept aware of the artist's position between the presentation and the presented.

In a related series of video works by Mik, the video installation *Training Ground* (two-screen video installation, silent, Netherlands, 2006) a refugee-, war-, or prison camp–like field in the open air is inhabited by different groups, armed and unarmed, who—although there is no direct violence—cannot leave but are exchanging power positions. Another video installation, entitled *Raw Footage* (two-screen video installation with sound, Netherlands, 2006), marks an exception in Aernout Mik's work, in that it is real material with real sound where nothing has been staged. The footage comes from journalists filming the Yugoslavian wars in Serbia, Croatia, and Bosnia. Mik bought the footage from Reuters; it was never broadcast. There is not much difference between this and the enactment in the first video. The effect is disorienting and shocking—especially when we see the teams filming each other in the midst of war. By juxtaposing fiction and reality, we may also get a feeling of how realities converge for those inside the camp. Another uncomfortable result of these works may be that taken together they highlight the necessity of verifying the sources and contexts of materials that are unknowable.

Leaving this cultural context and turning to another, I consider examples of expanded media works by Japanese media artists who incorporate ideas of radical video practices and develop models to revitalize the dialogue between the media and critical perception in ways similar to the examples so far discussed. In the works by the multinational architecture group doubleNegatives Architecture, established by Sota Ichikawa in 1998 (the group participants come from Hungary, Switzerland, and Japan), the aesthetic experiment manifests in video projections that visualize simulations of architectural environments that can be experienced in constant change. These concepts result from using novel technology in processual ways.

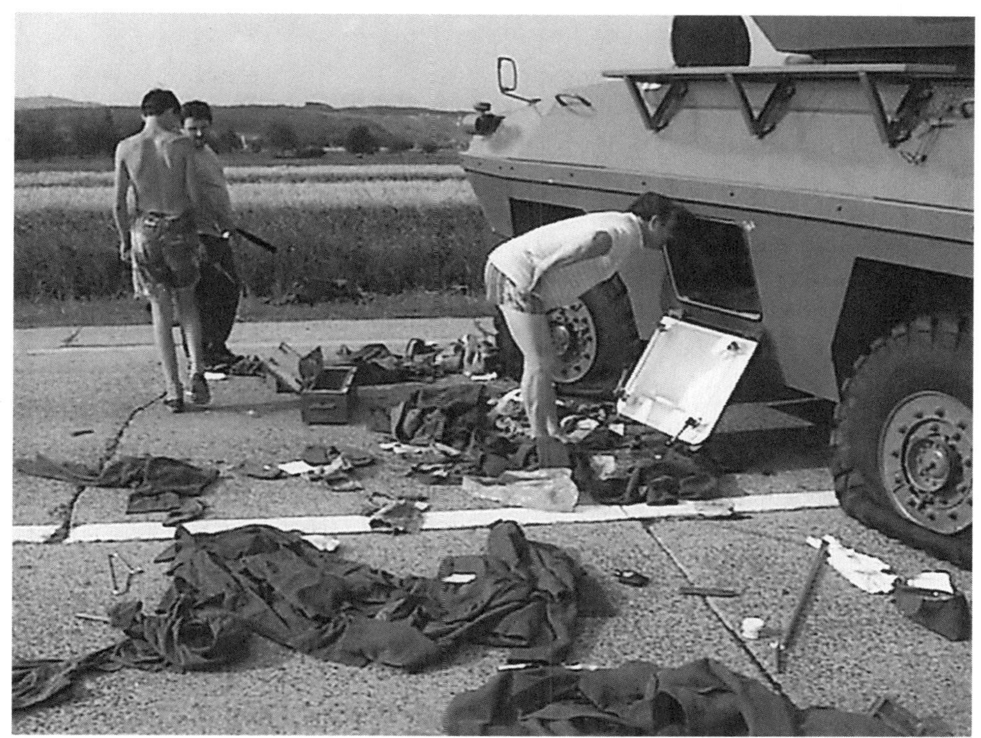

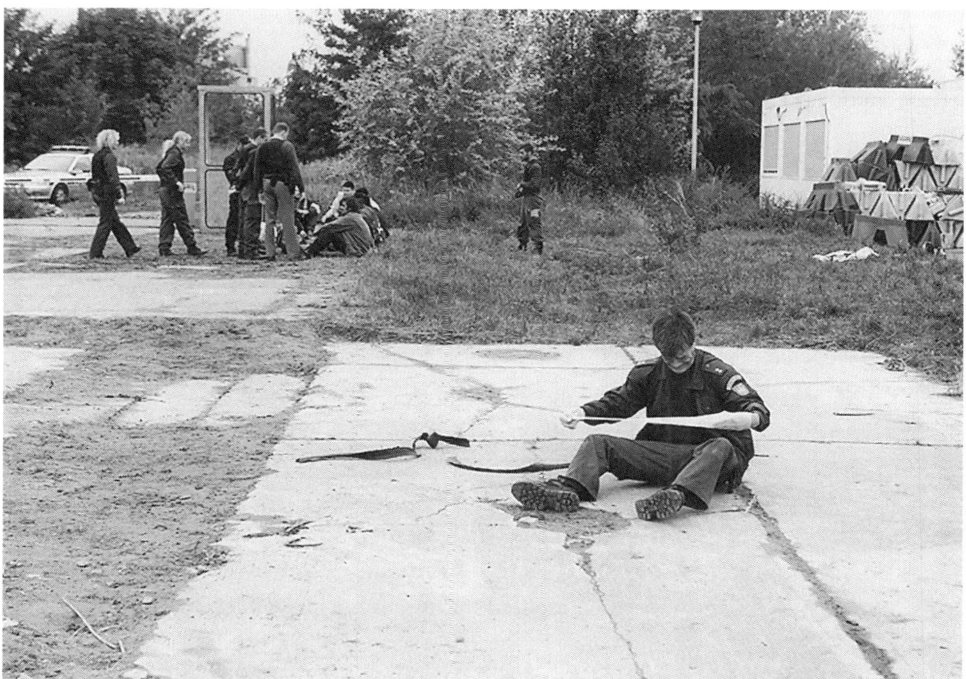

Aernout Mik, *Training Ground,* 2006. Two-screen video installation, Netherlands. Courtesy of the artist.

Part Japanese, part European, the group's philosophy is to use data input from nature/outside (wind, temperature, light) and to employ military technology to build living architecture environments with intelligent sensors. In the architecture project *Corpora in Si(gh)te* (Sota Ichikawa, Max Rheiner, Akos Maróy, Kaoru Kobata, Satoru Higa, Hajime Narakuwa, virtual architecture project, Hungary/Switzerland/Japan, 2007–9), the concept is to decompose the parts and materials of real buildings and reassemble them as an autonomous structure with varying viewpoints called "super-eyes." Superimposed architectural models are built from data measuring light, wind, temperature, and sound. The generated three-dimensional structure in the large-scale projection is constantly changing, demonstrating how the created corpora—which is constructed from the collected and connected data of multiple viewpoints—occupies and dominates the surrounding public space. The super-eyes are self-generating, self-assembling structures that exist in polar coordinates, not in Cartesian parameters. As a result, the project, which was presented at the Yamaguchi Center for Arts and Media, the Venice Architecture Biennale, and Ars Electronica, creates an intelligent structure that dismantles the smart technologies of military surveillance operations, using their sensors and wireless network functions. In a structural parallel to many of the radical video arts discussed, the aim here is to demonstrate how we may change the function of and challenge the ways in which we perceive and behave in relation to disturbing, decentralized, unstable, constantly reassembling media environments that have expanded from video to virtual imagery.

Finally, in the context of artists' interventions, it is important to discuss the fieldwork by Masaki Fujihata that uses mobile technologies and mixes real and virtual spaces for the purpose of interpersonal and intercultural dialogue. In the project *Landing Home in Geneva* (interactive video-computer installation, Japan/Switzerland, 2005), Fujihata gives an example of how to represent transcultural experiences with visual technologies in spatial relations that merge real and virtual data. The intercultural understanding of the concept of home is investigated when Fujihata uses a complex recording system (video camera with parabolic mirror lens, GPS, Personal Data Systems, and positioning data of the camera angle) to interview other foreigners who live and work in and around Geneva as professional interpreters.

In the computer the visual data are transformed into a specific kind of panorama that is interfaced so that each scene has an inside and an outside view. The videographic panoramas are connected in the virtual space in terms of the location and the moving activity of the actual interviews. And the user/viewer of this interactive video-computer installation can maneuver between the different sides of the dialogue during the interviews and experience different views for himself or herself: both distanced viewing and being immersed inside the situation at the same time. Fujihata's participating investigation attempts to employ

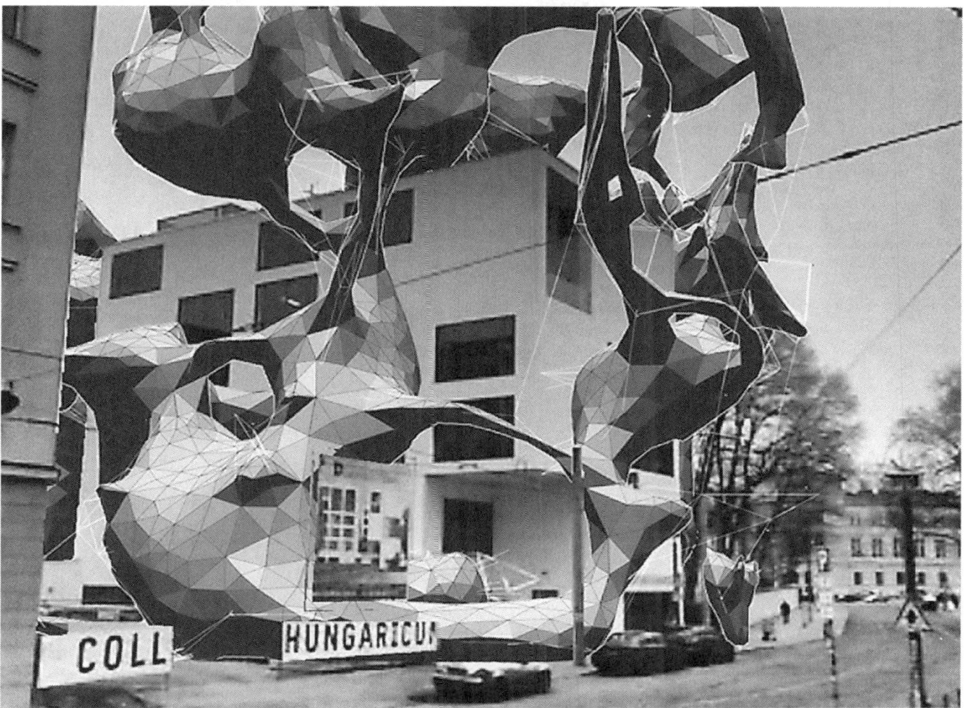

Sota Ichikawa, Max Rheiner, Akos Maróy, Kaoru Kobata, Satoru Higa, Hajime Narakuwa, *Corpora in Si(gh)te,* 2007–9. Virtual architecture project, Hungary/Switzerland/Japan. Courtesy of the artists.

video and the computer to communicate views and attitudes in the translation of cultures across languages and borders.

Extending this observation of borders, differences, and translations from multiple viewpoints, the artist is also the interviewer, and this too is audiovisually integrated within the recorded scene. So this intervention within the processes of field research is further highlighted when we, the viewers and users, see and hear the artist immersed in a real scene as he records it and when we can access the scene through the visible timeline from various arbitrary viewpoints in the virtual. By gaining control of the field and being part of its unfolding vividness, the subject and object positions are shown to be flexible and interchangeable.

To come back full circle to the beginning premise and conclude, what will be the role of media arts in the overall situation once virtual media have become real extensions and communicating partners and we have learned to use media individually as creative tools? In response, one could answer that these days, after almost endless and more tiring than insightful interrogations of modernist and postmodernist conditions of media, arts, and technology, everything has been said before and there is nothing new on the horizon. We face a highly saturated

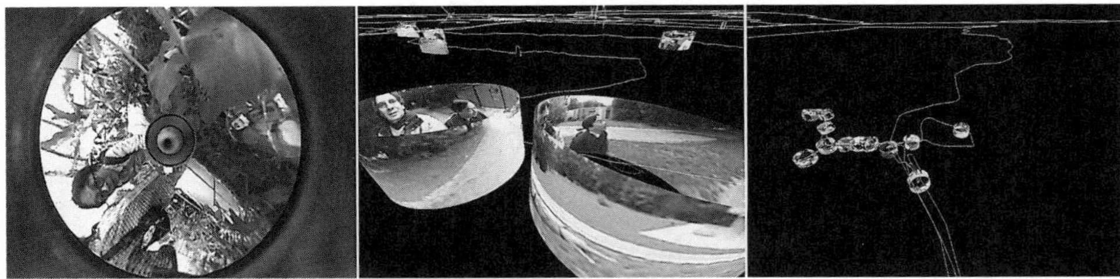

Masaki Fujihata, *Landing Home in Geneva,* 2005. Interactive video-computer installation, Japan/Switzerland. Courtesy of the artist.

tradition of media arts before and after the frenetically debated analog/digital divide in video, which when viewed retrospectively does not really help the discussion of cultural- and media-specific approaches in creative practices.

But there is an alternative point of view wherein we can envision aesthetic practices leading from radical video arts to a larger discourse of dialogue and encounter in the media arts beyond borderlines and differences. They also demonstrate that we do not need to understand and explain all the wonderful new possibilities that emerge in proportion to the growing corporate/commercial global media landscape. They reveal precisely the opposite, that we can regard creative practices that dismantle the structures of audiovisual representations in the media as a fascinating field of production that bypasses all the heated debates on Western/Eastern interactions in the fields of cultural studies and those on the analog/digital divide in the fields of media studies and video discussions. Departing from regular practices in these fields, appreciating technological cultures in new ways is possible when we turn our attention to subversive, ironic, and paradoxical processes in media arts. Artists' practices can be characterized as interventions when they encourage us to reflect our uncertainty while acting and interacting in passages between fixed realities where difference can be enjoyed in the present. And these present interventions have their structural roots in early video practices.

NOTES

1. Stuart Hall, "The Local and the Global: Globalization and Ethnicity," in *Culture, Globalization and the World System,* ed. Anthony D. King (London: MacMillan Press, 1991), 19–39.
2. Homi K. Bhabha, *The Location of Culture* (London: Routledge, 1994).

12

Video Cinema Ether (VCE)

Akira Mizuta Lippit

As analog video technologies receded from the world during the last decade of the twentieth century and electromagnetic tape melted into digital code, video returned to the cinema as a lost object, as the untimely image of a vanishing technology. As the name suggests, analog video signals retain some imprint of the source object, registering fluctuations of intensity in a virtually indexical relation to its referent. Like an electronic photograph, analog video renders the audiovisual world by analogy as its trace. By contrast digital video operates through conversion—data converted into information that is then transmitted and reassembled. Digital video operates more as a plastic art than as a photograph. Analog video retains a relation to its referent, to an original, whereas digital video translates, transposes bodies into code, into simulacra of bodies. One rarely noticed the strong corporeal quality of analog video until it had vanished: analog video generates noise and degenerates over time; its quality weakens with duplication. In the transition from analog to digital formats, digital video illuminated the once-material qualities of analog video. Analog video returned as a new form of materiality lost in the immateriality of the medium that replaced it. In its final moments on earth, video became corporeal by vanishing, revealing the spectral economy that produces video materiality: video becomes material as it disappears.[1] And it does this always in another's body; corporeality achieved always in another's body, the other's body. Video's objecthood, its objectivity, depends on its disappearance from the world through decay, obsolescence, and excessive duplication. As the technology waned its image grew stronger and stranger, becoming in the spaces opened by digital media a true revenant. Video came to be seen as an estranged object infused with nostalgia and anxiety, an object increasingly severed from the present world and defined by a no longer recognizable spatial economy. Almost instantaneously, videotape came to look out of place on-screen, the remnant of a technology until recently familiar, ubiquitous, and in so many ways, natural. In the years leading to and including the turn of the millennium, components of the video apparatus, including TV sets, VCRs, video cameras, editing equipment, and videotapes, came to resemble artifacts from an era no longer imaginable, from an era whose images could no longer be replayed. The image of the video apparatus illuminates not only the media past, the history of technology, but contemporary media practices, as well, especially in relation to the visual spaces defined by video technics. As a technology of vanishing and itself a vanishing technology, the image of the video apparatus engenders a total displacement of space and time and of the bodies that inhabit them. Video reveals an end of the world; in its end video takes the world with it, leaving behind a space filled only with video ether.

"Every society produces a space, its own space," writes Henri Lefebvre.[2] Aside from the abstract spaces instituted and maintained by nations, societies, and cultures—spaces that bear the characteristics of those individual places— Lefebvre suggests that ideologies and even economic systems can also produce spaces, concrete spaces formed from abstractions that establish unique worlds. Objects within such systems generate and animate those proper spaces. On the spaces opened by commodities, Lefebvre writes, "Capitalism and neo-capitalism have produced abstract space, which includes the 'world of commodities,' its 'logic' and its worldwide strategies."[3] The object produces a global "abstract space," according to Lefebvre, a space that is neither actual nor virtual, in some instances imaginary, in yet others unimaginable, and which circulates "worldwide." The world of commodities is a world without people, perhaps, depopulated like the abstract space of ghosts in Kurosawa Kiyoshi's *Pulse* (Kairo, 2001) or of dreams in Cameron Crowe's *Vanilla Sky* (2001), a ghost world in which objects—commodities and things—become subjects of a world without human beings. The world of commodities also forges a passage between isolated individuals, between the very subjects it isolates. The world of commodities fills space with a media ether, a supernatural tissue that Joe Milutis describes as "the nothing that connects everything."[4] This would be the logic of cell phones, Internet sites, and other interactive or communications media. But what if certain commodities, certain objects, certain media objects made possible metaphysical communications, opening a line between incommensurate states of life, between life and death, for example, between the living and the dead? What sort of fantasy or anxiety might be at work in such a device?[5] What sort of world is derived from such anxious fantasies and their symptom commodities?

At another end of the world, at the end of another world, the end of a technology and the archaeology it initiates, appears the VHS videotape in Nakata Hideo's *Ringu* (1998) and its American reproduction, Gore Verbinski's *The Ring* (2002). The short-lived VHS apparatus assumes in these films the role of a commodity and a subject, a thing and a being in ways that might not have been possible until the eve of its disappearance. By 1998 (*Ringu*) and certainly by 2002 (*The Ring*), VHS video technology had become finite, mortal, and nearly invisible. Victor Company of Japan (JVC) developed Video Home System or VHS in 1976 and, after its battle with Sony's Betamax system, dominated much of the video market during the 1980s and into the 1990s, until the advent of Digital Video Disk or Digital Versatile Disc (DVD) technology by Sony, Philips, Toshiba, and Time Warner in 1995. The *Ring* films and their sequels and remakes are as much about the technology they feature, the videotape, as they are a parable about international film circulation and piracy, a phobia about illicit reproduction, and the spread of rumors and diseases. Caetlin Benson-Allott states it bluntly, "This film is about a tape."[6] Benson-Allott continues by envisioning the space inside the videotape, not only the film or footage recorded on it, on the surface of the tape, but the hidden space inside the cassette tape: "While we may effectively think of the videotape as a solid form (like a film reel or a DVD) that just *makes* movies, it is in fact a vessel, a cavity few of us have ever opened, which could harbor any manner of unborn monster."[7] The *Ringu* and *Ring* films are films about monstrous videotapes that circulate throughout the world, defining in their circulation the spaces of the world as such. They are also films about the end of an audiovisual medium. The Japanese originals and American copies (although the distinction is complicated by the fact that Nakata made the American sequel to *The Ring, The Ring Two,* in 2005) are frequently distinguished by the extra *u* appended to the Japanese films, a phonetic rendering of the Japanese pronunciation of the English word *ring.* The floating *u,* or *you,* inscribes a cryptic semantics, a supplementary language that reveals one of the film's critical emphases, the presence of an excess second person. The videotape is addressed to you, who becomes in this address a superfluous second person. The second-person *you* is always in excess. YouTube extends the second-person idiom from broadcast TV (tube) to the Internet: YouTube implicates an unnamed you as the subject of a phantom TV that takes place everywhere, in cyberspace and without origin, and nowhere.[8] You are the subject of an atopic TV that duplicates the space of TV elsewhere. The international *Ring* circle, cycle, or circuit is further disrupted by the Korean version, Kim Dong-bin's *The Ring Virus* (1999), which claims to be original, if not the origin, because it returns more faithfully to the novel on which the films are based, Suzuki Koji's 1991 *Ring.* (In this sense it gestures toward the end of an image, to the end of the circulation of video images and of cinema, by restoring the image to its source in a text, in this case a book.) The international title of the Korean version makes explicit the viral motif that runs throughout each version.

Ringu tells the story of TV reporter Asakawa Reiko (Matsushima Nanako) and her ex-husband, Takayama Ryuji (Sanada Hiroyuki), who race to solve the enigma of an apparently cursed videotape. Anyone who watches this videotape, which consists of an abstract montage of images and words, receives a phone call immediately after the tape ends and then dies within seven days. Asakawa's coverage of the story features the role of urban legends, rumors about a cursed videotape. Both Asakawa and Takayama have watched the videotape and are marked for death; their task has the added urgency of saving their son, Yôichi, who has also viewed the tape. Asakawa's investigative skills are supplemented by Takayama's psychic sensitivities, which give him, like Asakawa, extrasensory perception, although the nature of their ESPs differ. Although Asakawa and Takayama are separated, the family is bound and rebound—reunited—by the viral curse and their search for an antidote to the supernatural death sentence. They are a viral, specular family held together by the shared spectatorship of a videotape.

Asakawa and Takayama trace the videotape to its origins in the Yamamura family and a mother and daughter, Shizuko and Sadako, respectively, who possessed considerable psychic powers. Both are presumed dead, although in Sadako's case the details are unclear, and her death would have been premature. At the family's home Asakawa and Takayama encounter a living relative, Yamamura Takashi (Numata Yoichi), the mother's cousin, who once sought to exploit Sadako's psychic mother, Shizuko, for profit. In spite of the cousin's denials, Takayama discovers the truth about this family when he grasps the relative's arm. An extended flashback begins upon contact between Takayama and Shizuko's cousin, recalling the staged exhibits of Shizuko's psychic power and one fatal incident of Sadako's psychic fury. It is as if the contact between the two men unleashes a flow of historical images, history exposed between their flesh. Yamamura Takashi's body acts as a video archive, a video record of the past, while Takayama's becomes a conduit for this archived past, his body quite literally a VCR. During the playback Asakawa finds herself inserted within the recall; she is there in the past, witness to the origins of the curse. Takayama's embodied, living video effects a virtual reality for the spectator, Asakawa. Toward the end of this hysterical flashback, the monster-daughter Sadako passes through Asakawa, who has entered the diegesis of the past; when Sadako grips Asakawa's wrist inside the flashback, she leaves a bruise on Asakawa's wrist in the present. (In the Hollywood remake Samara grips Rachel's wrist in a dream. Upon awaking, Rachel finds her wrists bruised in the shape of Samara's grip. Samara's touch has passed from dream to reality.) Takayama is broadcasting his psychic visions, serving as an antenna and monitor into which Asakawa is inscribed virtually. She is there, framed within the scene from the past, transported elsewhere into Takayama's biomorphic monitor.

The scene reveals the corporeal economy of *Ringu*: Sadako passes through bodies as easily as she passes through time and space, overcoming and exceeding the limits of time and of life. She moves freely in and out of bodies, in and out of time, passing through screens and borders, her body a videotape that allows her to be virtually anywhere, inside any home with a television and VCR. (She even overpowers the on/off switch, disabling as it were any parental control mechanisms.) She is a product of VHS, of its penetration into the home, a video body that transgresses the surface of the screen and binds disparate worlds by transcending them. Sadako is the source of the video curse, her body a video-cassette. Born with paranormal powers far in excess of her mother's, Sadako possesses the ability to impress her body onto things and into those of others. Murdered by her father, although her actual paternity remains in doubt throughout the *Ringu* cycle, Sadako survives her own death in a well by remaining *live,* animate, moving between media and overcoming physical and temporal boundaries by broadcasting her affect from an underground satellite. (In *The Ring* the infanticide is committed by the girl's mother, who says, "All I ever wanted was you," before placing a plastic bag around Samara's head and then pushing her into the well. Love and death are bound by a logic already inhuman, an inhumanity that too often defines human relations.) Sadako's vehicle is the ubiquitous, mobile videotape that allows her to move freely into anyone's home, into anyone's home video system. She is a virus, a parasite that remains alive, that survives in the bodies of others (she destroys). Sadako demands to live in the visual spectrum she embodies, that embodies others from her perspective. "I see."

Ringu ends twice, if it ends at all (an end that is repeatedly undone by sequels, prequels, and international remakes, synching the series perfectly with the core narrative of *Ringu*); the first, a false ending, appears to bring closure, whereas the second, actual ending leaves the narrative unresolved, irresolvable, and open to further sequels, remakes, circulation, and contagion. In the first ending, Asakawa and Takayama locate Sadako's corpse confined in the well where she was murdered. Having returned her body aboveground once and then re-interred it properly back into the earth, the couple believes, following a certain logic of spectral ontology familiar from *Antigone* to *Hamlet,* that the metaphysical vengeance will end. But Sadako operates according to a different hauntology; hers is a logic of infinite contagion, duplication, and reproduction. She is a video virus, the analog precursor to the computer virus, most notably the one that threatened in 2000 to destroy all digital records of time and history.[9] The second ending, an ending that never ends, which cannot end according to the imperatives of perpetual reproduction and contagion, paradoxically represents a total end of everything, of the world.

In *Ringu* disease and technology fuse and converge with sexuality and reproduction or, more accurately, with reproducibility. Benson-Allott notes the economy that binds technology to a horrific maternity in *The Ring*: "The videotape possesses the ability to reproduce—or to be reproduced, more specifically—at home, by anyone with a spare VCR. *The Ring* employs that fecundity, along with the cassette's unseen inner cavity, to translate technophobia into a fear of reproduction and our fear of reproduction, femininity, and mortality into a fear of the supernatural."[10] Like a series of translations, each iteration of *Ringu* emphasizes different aspects of that fear and the manifestations that they spawn, from sexual aberration to the uncontrollable flow of rumors. At work is a phantom technology that switches from one world to another through various devices: exposure to the videotape is immediately followed by a phone call. The audio-visual spectrum of *Ringu* requires a monstrous form of media convergence, television and telephone, to embody the immaterial Sadako. Suzuki claims that the title *Ring* refers to the sound of the telephone as much as to the image of a circle, solidified as the closing lid of the well in *The Ring*.[11] Sound and image converge in the ring, an onomatopoeic icon of Sadako. Two technologies, VHS video and wired phones, were virtually obsolete by the time Nakata made *Ringu,* replaced by digital video and wireless telephony. Nakata has subtly shifted the historical frame back to the period when the novel was written, from 1998 to 1991, eliminating the presence of mobile phones and restoring the ubiquity of VHS video technology. In this slight rewind the entire world changes. Mobile phones and DVDs are erased in *Ringu* and circumvented in *The Ring,* in which the absence of cell phones and the use of landlines and pay phones are attributed by intimation to poor reception. As a result in both, the image of videos and telephones become otherworldly, extraterrestrial.[12] The videotape *is* the ghost; Sadako and Samara are its media, mediums for the transmission of a phantom technology.

The video, says Takayama, "is not of this world" (kono yo no mono janai). It circulates in another world of commodities, a world outside the world of commodities, an excess or paracommodity that circulates in the outside. In *The Ring* the videotape also originates elsewhere, Benson-Allott writes, if it *originates* at all: "According to Noah, Samara's tape either has no origins (was never recorded, does not exist) or is capable of obscuring its origins."[13] The videotape that comes from outside this world, from another world, is also a nonhuman commodity, an object whose origin is nonhuman. Or else, it is excessively human in a way that exceeds its own humanity. In his reading of *Ringu* and its Japanese sequel, Eric White underscores Sadako's nonhuman dimension and the failed closure it effects. Of the false ending that leads to *Ringu*'s ultimate conclusion, White writes, "The curse could never have been lifted by restoring Sadako symbolically to the human community by means of a proper burial, because she was not herself 'human' to begin with."[14] The ritual burial and peace it brings to the dead only comforts human subjects. Because Sadako "is the supernatural offspring of a human being and a sea monster" (Sadako's hybridity is alluded to vaguely in the film, more forcefully in the novel), the human cycles of life and death never apply fully or properly to Sadako, who is only partially human, quasi human.[15] The metaphysical communications that permeate *Ringu* are thus not only between the living and the dead and the present and the past but also between human and nonhuman beings. The logic and economy of the curse travel through nonhuman worlds and can thus never be resolved according to the protocols of human restitution.

The cursed videotape of *Ringu,* which brings a delayed death to the viewer one week later, can be switched off only by duplicating the tape and exposing it to others, a type of exteriorized suicide circle that turns one's solitude inside out: I transfer my own death to another, addressing my death, as it were, to you. I postpone my death through you. The specific terms of the *Ringu* curse invoke video technology itself, infusing the process of duplication, of electronic reproducibility, with a lethal, viral quality. Technology in *Ringu* is more a metaphysics than a physics, more a passage to nonhuman worlds than a line that connects human beings to each other. *Ringu* imagines video interactively, as a fantastic communications technology, always to the other side, to another world. I address you by transmitting my death to you, our communion marked by a death that we share. What is impossible in life—one body shared by two or more subjects—becomes possible in the intermedial body that video creates and the videotape assumes, a body that serves as intermediary between life and death, between multiple subjects, male and female. The body of our death converges in the videotape, our death shared in one body. The videotape here is both a virus and a host that opens between two bodies, a site and parasite. The videotape is a body that supplements an absent body, a body that no longer exists in the place where it once was. Suzuki's novel draws attention to the viral dimension of the narrative, ascribing Sadako Yamamura's death to smallpox, "the last person in Japan to be infected" with the disease.[16] Suzuki's fictional history of the end of a disease, of the end of smallpox in Japan, is undone by its survival in video transmission: Suzuki imagines the afterlife of viruses in technology, in a technology that transmits lethality as such and whose lethality rests in its transmissibility.

The viral technology of *Ringu* affects the sexes and genders of the subjects it infects. In Suzuki's novel Sadako is a hermaphrodite, born with testicular feminization syndrome, now called androgen insensitivity syndrome. According to the novel, this condition, which produces on Sadako's body the genital organs of both sexes, also renders her unable to bear children. An infertile body marked as an interstice between the sexes makes Sadako neither man nor woman and further in the novel, where Sadako is said to have been fathered by a spirit, not entirely human. This aberration in the anatomical order, Sadako's exceptional biology, opens a new passage into and out of the body, an opening through which video ether flows freely. Sadako's male / female body is already a videotape, in transit, a duplicate body, neither male nor female, human nor nonhuman, irreproducible and completely unable to resist the urge to reproduce illicitly, technologically, telekinetically. Another transgendering occurs in the movement from novel to film. Nakata has changed Asakawa's gender from a man in the novel to a woman in the film. This transition between man and woman is retained in Verbinski's remake of *Ringu*. Sadako's hermaphroditic infertility is similarly transposed in Verbinski's *The Ring* to Richard and Anna Morgan, who adopt Samara when they are unable, despite repeated attempts, to conceive a child of their own.

In Verbinski's remake, which opens with the lines, "I hate television," Rachel (Naomi Watts) picks a fly from within the recorded video while copying it, transporting the fly from a scene inside the tape to the outside world, at which moment Rachel's nose begins to bleed.[17] The passage from one world to another, from one body to another, from video to the outside, is marked in this scene by the displaced menstrual blood (or else the blood from her lost virginity to the specter or blood from a miscarriage) that seeps from Rachel's nasal cavity. The blood represents a rupture in Rachel's body, the passage of another body through hers but also the place of her fertility, a displaced fertility that forces her to reproduce—another body, another videotape. Later in the film, Rachel's ex-husband, Noah (Martin Henderson), experiences a similar nosebleed while searching for Anna Morgan's medical records, and in the final scenes their son, Aidan (David Dorfman), shares in the family hemorrhage. In Suzuki's novel the movement of the parasite specter into the host's body is explicit; the other body passes through the TV screen on its way into the spectator's body. The surface of the TV screen is a phantom hymen torn by Sadako, making possible the movement between material and immaterial worlds. The videotape is its portable, temporary body between bodies. Suzuki describes Asakawa's sensations after the ghost enters his body:

> Once again, Asakawa was filled with nausea. The first time he'd finished watching the video he'd run to the toilet, but this time the evil chill was even worse. He couldn't shake the feeling that something had climbed into his body. This video hadn't been recorded by a machine. A human being's eyes, ears, nose, tongue, skin—all five senses had been used to make this video. These chills, this shivering, were from somebody's shadows sneaking into him through his sense organs. Asakawa had been watching the video from the same perspective as this *thing* within him.[18]

In Suzuki's novel the entry of the parasite into the host's body pushes fluids out of his, her body—vomit, urine, and in the film, blood. "Something had climbed into his body" after watching the video. Visuality defines a portal into and out of the body, opening new orifices and causing the body to leak its fluids from them. In this sense, in these other senses or the other's senses that have become one's own, the specter itself is what's reproduced, a new life that emerges from each host body again and again.

By inhabiting Asakawa's body, Sadako not only inscribes her immaterial body onto her host's, a body constituted of electromagnetic signals, but also replaces the host's perspective with her own. The videotape begins this transition. It sees from Sadako's vantage point, inscribing her view onto the spectator's. It is not only Sadako's point of view that inhabits Asakawa but also that of a thing, an object or commodity, the videotape. At work throughout *Ringu* is the imposition of a thing's point of view, a perspective that is quasi human, from another world, outside. She is an excess second person, a perspective that subsumes the subject's ability to see the world at all, ultimately transforming you into this excess, you into her appendage, a superfluous second person. "I see," "video." "I see you, 'u' see as I." Samara is herself a camera, able to imprint psychic images onto photographic surfaces. "I see them, and then they just are," she says on a recorded video. In the novel Takayama describes the testing of clairvoyants by their ability to produce psychic images: "But there can't be too many paranormals who can actually project images onto a television tube without any equipment whatsoever. That's power of the very highest order."[19] Psychic power in the various *Ring* movies is understood as the ability to generate images automatically, without any imaging devices. The body becomes a camera and projector whose images survive the body itself. Long after Sadako and Samara have ceased to exist, their psychic energies survive them as electromagnetic signals stored in the new bodies of the VHS videotape. They live on, projected live, alive, on the TV screens that receive and display their broadcast. This is, according to Marita Sturken, the very essence of television: "Television is the image without an original," she writes, "for which the status of the copy is ultimately irrelevant."[20] Every copy, or copy of a copy—each simulacrum—is irrelevant in a world without originals. In the *Ringu* cycle the copy is less a degraded original than a deferral of it—*différance* rather than difference, postponed origins.

The piracy that *Ringu* effects, the invasion of one body through the screen of another, also appears in David Lynch's treatment of video throughout his cinema. In Lynch's films electromagnetic currency, TV, and the video image are frequently conduits from one sealed world to another. The anonymous videotapes that appear on Fred and Renee Madison's doorstep in *Lost Highway* (1997) eventually penetrate their house (VHS) and record a murder yet to occur. The perpetrator, Fred Madison, learns of the murder (of his wife, Renee) that he has committed only upon seeing it on the screen; he is absented by this videotape from his own action. Videotapes and electromagnetic signals form the world of the TV series *Twin Peaks* (1990–91) and its film prequel, *Twin Peaks: Fire Walk with Me* (1992). Killer Bob travels through the video ether, entering discrete worlds through TV screens and monitors. Everywhere in Lynch, video provides global entry and exit points.

The exemplary antecedent film on video, the one that serves perhaps as the referent for an anxiety about and fascination with video, is David Cronenberg's *Videodrome* (1983). According to Tom Mes and Jasper Sharp, "The scene in which Sadako crawls from the television screen came not from Suzuki, but was inspired by the Western horrors of David Cronenberg's *Videodrome* (1983) and Tobe Hooper's *Poltergeist* (1982)."[21] In Cronenberg's fantasy about video, illicit broadcasts, and the aporias of reality, Max Renn (James Woods), a TV producer who broadcasts pornography of various types, believes he has discovered a secret broadcast, Videodrome, that features snuff porn. In his pursuit of this explosive program, he falls victim to Videodrome, a signal that induces hallucinations and eventually tumors in its viewers. As he sinks deeper into hallucination Renn becomes increasingly unable to distinguish reality from fantasy, a condition that is transmitted to the film's viewers, who also become unable to distinguish the diegetic real from fantasy. In the process of losing this key gauge, Renn begins to imagine an organic TV apparatus made flesh, fleshly, corporeal. Videotapes pulsate; TV screens stretch elastically and protrude; and ultimately, Renn himself becomes a receptacle for the videotape transmissions, a vaginal VCR into which videotapes are inserted directly into his body, intravenously. Cronenberg's attraction to fluidity, a property that frequently unites organic and inorganic bodies in his films, seeps into *Videodrome* in the form of a lubricant that provides the quasi-sexual penetration of Renn by *the body of a fantasy*. The material properties of the video apparatus become the body of a fantasy, giving form to and embodying the viewers' desires. The video apparatus, the cameras, tapes, VCRs, and monitors become organs of a fantastic body, of a fantasy body, a body that organizes fantasy into corporeal figures.[22] During one hallucination Max Renn acts out a sadomasochistic fantasy, beating the image of a woman on a TV screen. He believes that he is beating a woman, but what he whips is the TV console rather than her body. The object has become her body, his fantasy transposed to a substitute object, a fetish. But in this moment the video body becomes what it is, an analogy, an analog body formed in the very technology that makes it possible at all.

As his body begins to mutate, to assume the dimensions of his fantasy, Renn's transformation is described as a becoming-video: "You have become the video word made flesh." Renn's metamorphosis concludes with a televised suicide (broadcast perhaps on a phantasmatic closed circuit), shouting, "Long live the new flesh!" Renn's "new flesh" consists of video images drawn from his psyche, a televisual fantasy sutured onto his body, which has become like the organic tapes that he imagines. As his body fuses to objects, forging a biotechnic synthesis or fusion, Renn becomes a complete video apparatus: VCR, camera, videotape, editing system, monitor, and program. In the end he becomes, his body and psyche become, the content of his own video broadcast.

A stream of video movies in the years leading to the turn of the millennium return to the subject of video and the anxious subjectivities it left in the wake of its withdrawal. The "squid" recordings in Kathryn Bigelow's *Strange Days* (1995) consist of virtual and viral affects recorded directly from a person's cerebral cortex, allowing viewers to feel as their own another's experience, to experience virtually another's body. Variations of this video motif appear in David

Cronenberg's own quasi sequel to *Videodrome, eXistenZ* (1999), which features a *mise-en-abîme* of virtual games, as well as Andy and Lana Wachowski's *Matrix* (1999) and its sequels, which exploit the phenomenon of experiencing another's body as one's own, or one's own body as another's, one's own body improperly, unconsciously. Similarly, Michel Gondry's *Eternal Sunshine of the Spotless Mind* (2004) and Christopher Nolan's earlier *Memento* (2000) engage the remnants of subjectivity in the wake of memory after the erasure of memories and the destruction of the architecture of memory as such. At the time of *Ringu,* numerous other films featured schizoid agency, including David Fincher's *Fight Club* (1999) and the Spike Jonze and Charlie Kaufman collaborations *Being John Malkovich* (1999), in which two or more subjectivities occupy the same body, moving freely between personae, and *Adaptation* (2002), in which multiple Charlie Kaufmans move from one diegesis to another until the lines that separate Kaufmanns and diegeses no longer hold. In each instance the video films produce a body in and from the image itself, an image of the body as an image that becomes an actual body, an audiovisual body that emerges from a body that no longer exists there in the world anywhere and yet which can, at the same time, materialize anywhere. David Lynch's *Lost Highway* (1997) and *Mulholland Drive* (2001) feature characters that switch identities with other characters, while Cameron Crowe's *Vanilla Sky* (2001), a remake of Alejandro Amenábar's Spanish *Abre les ojos* (Open your eyes, 1997), oscillates between dream and waking reality, disturbing the sense of a body in one place, in the place where it exists, that it exists anywhere at all.

A finite realization of the video body occurs in the final moments of *The Ring* when Samara passes through the TV screen, bringing her dripping world from the other side, from inside the well, into Noah's apartment. Like the liquids that leak from inside the haunted characters of *Ringu* and *The Ring,* Sadako and Samara pierce the living world as if it were a body. A video ether acts as the phantasmatic membrane, providing contours to the world's body. Sadako and Samara are the world's internal organs or, more accurately, its bodily fluids transformed into electromagnetic signals. They assume the liquid form of a video feed, an electromagnetic flow that ruptures the world conceived as an organized body. Once inside Noah's world and standing before him, Samara still flickers like a video image, the brief bursts and semitransparent figure a video image embodied, made flesh. "Samara is at her scariest," writes Benson-Allott, "when she most resembles a videocassette."[23] She has become a three-dimensional video hologram, television personified and embodied in the human world, a live broadcast, television alive. This is why the video world of *The Ring* remains in analog form: the body's pulses, even those of a body no longer alive, continue to appear on the outside world as a spectral index. Only the unfiltered signals of analog video can achieve this effect. "The ether," writes Joe Milutis, "is radically analog."[24] The video flickers or noise that infect everything in *The Ring*'s world, from the FBI warning against video piracy and the DreamWorks SKG logo that precede the film proper to the diegesis, become elemental, the liquid image of video itself, a liquefied body that enters this world from another, bringing these uncanny fluids—electromagnetic, amniotic, oceanic, ectoplasmic—into the material world. At this moment, video returns from the dead, no longer dead, undead or deadness live, alive, fully present as a lost object in this world—a world neither here nor there, *video* ether.

NOTES

1. In the register of cinema, René Bruckner argues that film appears by disappearing, that the principle of its visibility depends on an apparatus that withdraws the image to generate a moving visuality. See his dissertation, "The Art of Disappearance: Duration, Instantaneity, and the Conception of Cinema" (PhD diss., University of California–Irvine, 2007). A portion of Bruckner's thesis was published as "The Instant and the Dark: Cinema's Momentum," *Octopus* 2 (Fall 2006): 21–36. He writes of the apparatus and its images, "Cinematograph. One still image appears on the screen, a more or less faithful photographic record or reference of some past instant, but before this luminous projection has time to become visible as such, as *still,* it disappears. Masked in darkness for a brief interval, it is replaced by another instantaneous photograph, which also vanishes before being seen for what it is. Repeated for some time, this process produces the—a temporal distance, as it were—implies a continuity of movement between them, but relies on one's ability to see movement in a succession of intermittent snapshots, or as Henri Bergson famously called them, 'immobilities.' As such, the film image does not simply appear; its movement appears by disappearing into those unphotographed moments, or intervals, between successive photographic instants. The image disappears in order to appear, pushing the logic of appearance beyond its logical limits. To see movement in the film image is to *see* the failure of a certain vision's rationale: an image that gains visibility only by slipping perpetually out of sight, into the dark" (22).

2. Henri Lefebvre, *The Production of Space,* trans. Donald Nicholson-Smith (Malden, Mass.: Blackwell, 1991), 53.

3. Ibid.

4. This is the subtitle to Joe Milutis, *Ether: The Nothing that Connects Everything* (Minneapolis: University of Minnesota Press, 2006).

5. See Avital Ronell, *The Telephone Book: Technology, Schizophrenia, Electric Speech* (Lincoln: University of Nebraska Press, 1991). In her account of the telephone's invention, Ronell traces the desire to a pact between Alexander Graham Bell and his brother, an agreement to invent—should one of them die first—a device that would allow them to maintain contact between the living and the dead across the divide of life.

6. Caetlin Benson-Allott, "'Before You Die, You See *The Ring*': Notes on the Immanent Obsolescence of VHS," *Jump Cut* 49 (Spring 2007): 3. Genevieve Yue has written beautifully on *Ringu* in relation to the trope of hair that appears in Asian horror specifically and what she calls a "Medusan optics" more generally. See Genevieve Yue, "Medusan Optics: Film, Feminism, and the Forbidden Image" (PhD diss., University of Southern California, 2012).

7. Benson-Allott, "'Before You Die,'" 3 (emphasis in original). For Benson-Allot the space of the videotape is gendered and also maternal. As opposed to the DVDs that replaced them, videotapes are "uterine": "The DVD, the phallus that has no interior, that wears its images on its sleeve, exposes the videotape as uterine by contrast" (28).

8. Lucas Hildebrand writes on the spectral architecture of YouTube in "Youtube: Where Cultural Memory and Copyright Converge," *Film Quarterly* 61 (Fall 2007): 48–57.

9. The so-called Y2K scare was neither a virus nor a threat but something like an urban legend that assumed the rhetoric of a computer virus that threatened to wipe out, apocalyptically, the entire digital archive that had become, by then, a simulacrum of the world itself.

10. Benson-Allott, " 'Before You Die,' " 3. Benson-Allott notes the gendering of the videotape as feminine and monstrous in *The Ring,* a transgendering of earlier representations of the videotape—for example, in Cronenberg's *Videodrome* (1983)—as penetrating, phallic, and masculine.

11. For more on the auditory qualities of *Ringu* and J-horror more broadly, see Bill Whittington, "Acoustic Infidelities: Sounding the Exchanges between J-Horror and H-Horror Remakes," *Cinephile* 6, no. 1 (Spring 2010): 11–17. Of the particular qualities of sound in contemporary Japanese horror films, Whittington writes, "In J-horror, spiritual forces haunt the highest and lowest registers of the soundtrack's dynamic range, and, as a result, the spirit presence exists as a kind of deep structure, penetrating the entire story world and the lives of those within it" (14). For Whittington the spirit or specter exists in material form on the sound track, taking place in the registers of sound. It exists, writes Whittington, "as a kind of deep structure," pushed to "the highest and lowest registers" of the sound track, there at the extremes of the dynamic range. The spirit is audio-architecturally inscribed in the world it haunts.

12. Benson-Allot notes the erasure of DVD from *The Ring,* describing the diegesis as a "VHS world." She writes, "As opposed to *Ringu,* which premiered in 1998, just as DVD began its climb, and was written and produced even earlier, *The Ring* was conceived during the ascendency of the DVD, yet neither a single DVD nor reference to DVD technology appears anywhere in the film: it is a VHS world, and VHS is dying (or killing, as the case may be)" (28).

13. Benson-Allott, " 'Before You Die,' " 8.

14. Eric White, "Case Study: Nakata Hideo's *Ringu* and *Ringu 2,*" in *Japanese Horror Cinema,* ed. Jay McRoy (Honolulu: University of Hawai'i Press, 2005), 40.

15. White, "Case Study," 40. "We can also grasp," writes White, "the significance of the revelation that Sadako's mother had long ago spent many hours sitting by the sea, where she would address the ocean in a non-human language. We also understand why the indistinct murmuring voices heard on the videotape, when properly amplified, can be perceived as chanting 'frolic in brine, goblins be thine' (or, in another translation, 'play in the water and a monster will come for you')" (40). The water that surrounds Sadako and, especially, Samara in the remake thus not only is transported from the well in which the girls died but also may be from the oceans that constitute them.

16. Koji Suzuki, *Ring,* trans. Robert B. Rohmer and Glynne Walley (New York: Vertical, 2007), 226.

17. This scene with the fly appears to open up a line between *The Ring* and Kurt Neumann's *The Fly* (1958), in which a human's body and a fly's are mixed into two monstrous bodies when an experiment with "matter transportation" goes awry. When Rachel removes a fly from a recorded video image, she transports the fly's body across media dimensions, creating a matter teleportation that describes the movement of spectral bodies across space.

18. Suzuki, *Ring,* 146 (emphasis in original).

19. Suzuki, *Ring,* 155.

20. Marita Sturken, "The Politics of Video Memory: Electronic Erasures and Inscriptions," in *Resolutions: Contemporary Video Practices,* ed. Michael Renov and Erika Suderburg (Minneapolis: University of Minnesota Press, 1996), 2.

21. Tom Mes and Jasper Shape, "Hideo Nakata," in *The Midnight Eye Guide to New Japanese Cinema* (Berkeley, Calif.: Stone Bridge Press, 2005), 258.

22. Although video technology was not new in 1983 when Cronenberg made *Videodrome,* it was not obsolete, either. The technology was entering into the home video phase in which video was becoming part of domestic television culture. The eventual obsolescence of videotape has added a historical dimension to the film, rendering the technology now part of a fading register. The Criterion Collection's DVD of *Videodrome* comes packaged in a case designed to look like a videotape.

23. Benson-Allott, " 'Before You Die,' " 29.

24. Milutis, *Ether,* 157. "The superfine particles of the ether, which bathe everything in a telepathic atmosphere, may be recorded, though not perceived, on analog media, since analog is a direct imprint of wavelengths and radiations in which we are immersed" (157).

To Touch, Plot, and Dream the Il Ngwesi Maasai Landscape

Beverly R. Singer

The following Facebook status report was for friends who did not know I was in Africa in August 2009:

> August 8, 2009: From Nairobi . . . I found a spirit home at Il Ngwesi in north central Kenya . . . my Maasai hosts being completely welcoming are woven into their most exquisite lands living among elephants, water buffalo, giraffes, rhinos, warthogs, monkeys, eland and hundreds of other species on the savannah while herding cattle and goats for subsistence. I'll be returning to NM and Kenya soon. Photos to follow upon return to U.S.

My host and friend, Ole Shuel from Il Ngwesi, posted the following response:

> August 8, 2009: Yes, it is an amazing and such a humbling experience hosting Beverly in our space. The rains have approached since her arrival and indication of the great respect the land has for her gentle dealing with it.[1]

How We Met

In 2006 I received an invitation to share my work as an Indigenous filmmaker at a UNESCO-sponsored information and communication technologies (ICT) workshop in Spain and Andorra, where Indigenous people representing communities from Bolivia, Kenya, Peru, and Russia were taking part in a program initiative to enhance the communication capacities of Indigenous peoples.[2] The intent of the ICTs outlined by UNESCO was to foster "the creation and dissemination of local content that reflects the values, experiences and insights of the world of indigenous peoples' communities and cultures."[3] I prepared my presentation thinking about the multiple uses to be made of video production in developing Indigenous capacity for intercultural dialogue across continents and

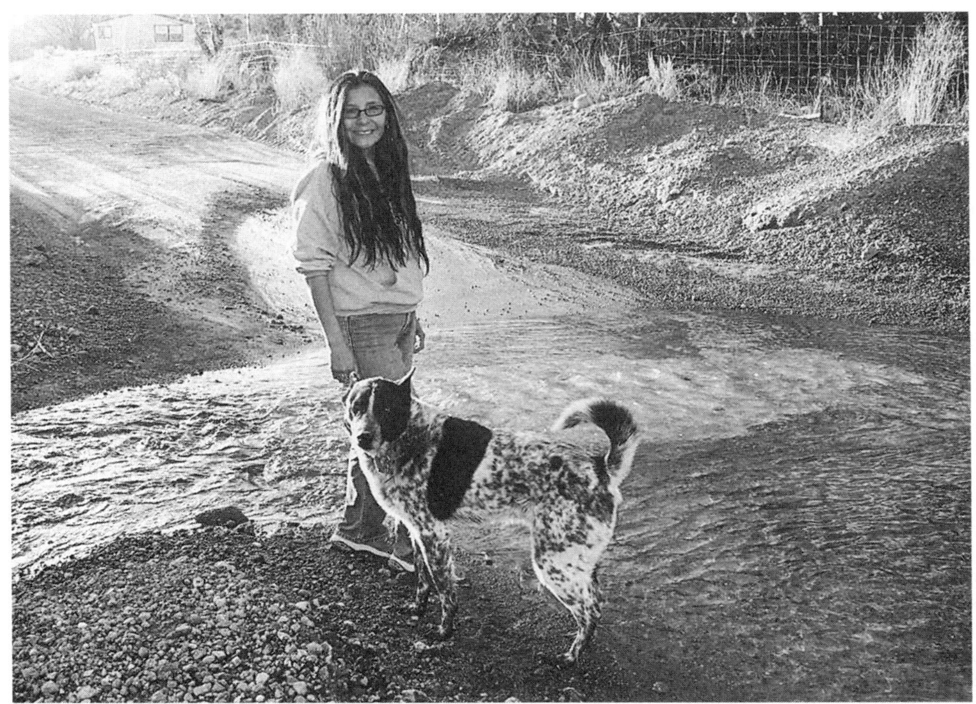

Singer and Torque. Photograph by Beverly Singer.

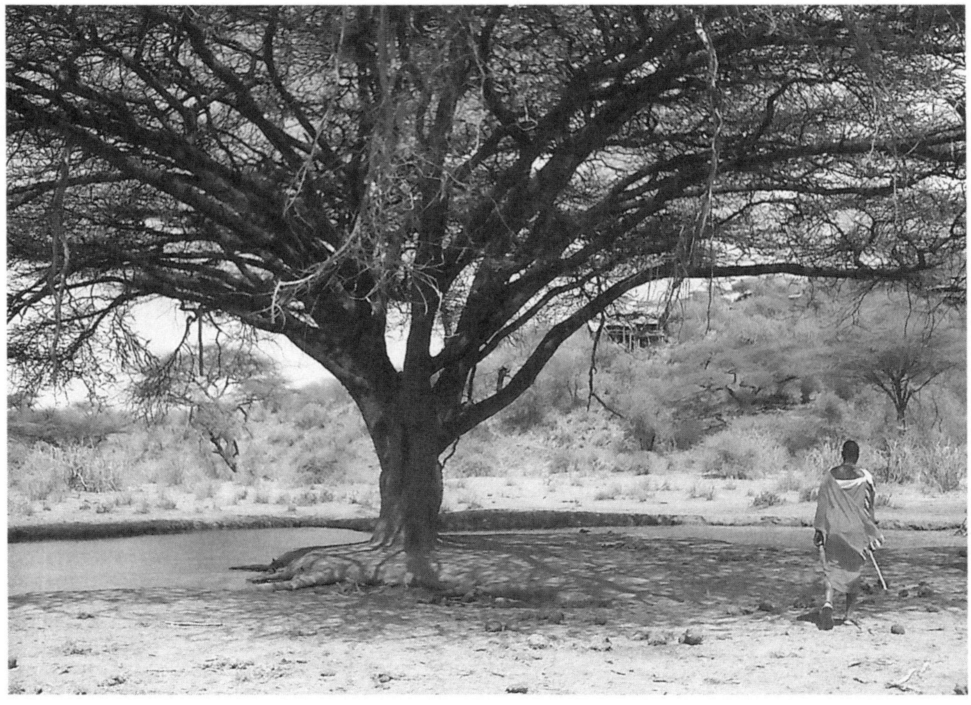

Ole Shuel of Ol Donyo Keri Safaris. Photograph by Beverly Singer.

among Indigenous communities on themes and experiences they believed to be significant. This, my first encounter with UNESCO, was formal and instructive.

At the break between sessions that followed my presentation, Yvonne Owuor, an award-winning writer from Nairobi, and Ole Joseph Shuel Nijalis, an Il Ngwesi Maasai and a former director of Il Ngwesi Lodge, introduced themselves.[4] Their enthusiasm about my presentation was energizing. As we talked about the appropriation and the perpetuation of stereotypes of Indigenous peoples in the global public mindset Yvonne said, "We want to work with you!" I said, "Yes, of course, let's talk more later." A friendship was born between myself, a Tewa woman from Khapo Owingeh (Santa Clara Pueblo) in New Mexico, and two African natives from Kenya: Shuel, from Il Ngwesi Maasai territory in north-central Kenya, and Yvonne, from Nairobi, her ancestors originally from the Lake Victoria region. Our friendship was, in part, the outcome of that fateful UNESCO-sponsored workshop.[5] The alliance established following that gathering is conveyed in this essay based on my experiences and on my reflections on the use of video as a means of connecting Indigenous lives and producing knowledge and truth-inspired communication.

Reorientation: Indigenous-to-Indigenous Thinking about Media and the Use of Video to Document Their History / My Experience

According to UNESCO, enhancing the communication capacities of Indigenous peoples is needed in the twenty-first century in order to help them present and document their stories. Such potential has implications for re-visioning Indigenous peoples as vital participants who contribute solutions to dilemmas affecting humankind. Indigenous prophecy provides lessons on how and why this friendship happened with Ole Shuel Nijalis and Yvonne Owuor (my mentor and wilderness guardian).[6] From a historical lens our relations with the earth as Indigenous Africans and as Indigenous Americans are aligned with similar thoughts concerning the big questions of survival, and our values rest with the spirit of our ancestors, who connected us in the countries of Spain and Andorra.

The sum of our communication, following three years of e-mails among Shuel, Yvonne, and myself, came to rest naturally upon cocreating voices-in-video narratives from Il Ngwesi Maasai. These narratives, being completely independent of UNESCO, were supported solely by our individual efforts. The UNESCO initiative was a demonstration of and a step toward opening Indigenous communities to participating in sharing their stories through video projects. After watching the UNESCO-sponsored ICT Kenya video *Without Boundaries: The Quest of Pastoralist People,* however, I thought it odd that the people featured did not really tell their own stories. The filmmaker assigned to train them seems to have told the story for them. For over twenty-five years, I have participated in and weighed in on film methodology and filmmaking by Indigenous peoples. Oftentimes, incorporating too many ingredients—history, politics, symbols, and/or cultural apology, all parts of documenting—can easily sidetrack the producer. The camera can be unwieldy, making it difficult to capture movement seamlessly or document a complete scene unfolding. It is something I've experienced in my own documentary work. The camera is usually not the issue; it is letting go of trying to force a story and just allowing the story to tell itself.

Shuel, Yvonne, and I moved forward with our plan to integrate a collective vision for intercultural dialogue among Indigenous peoples. The work of producing a video typically can find its significance within predictable statements about teaching and about public education as a contribution to the field. My reasons for participating in this project were more personal, however. The desire to share and spend time with Indigenous peoples was planted in me as a child by my parents—in particular, by my father, James Singer, who loved sharing Pueblo stories. He believed Indigenous people were sent out on the earth to help one another and share in each other's lives. An instinctive knowing that I was being introduced to Shuel and Yvonne by our ancestors gave power to this experience. And so what we were shouldering was rooted in the lands that we came from and in our mutual interest in each other as people from different places with similar connections and intentions for sharing our experiences and thoughts with one another, particularly about the many things possible for Shuel's community, a community that was also in transitional vulnerability.[7] For Shuel Nijalis the meeting in Andorra was important for Il Ngwesi not only in terms of contact made with other Indigenous groups grappling with survival and continuity but also in terms of Shuel recognizing and building on opportunities to utilize ICT processes and UNESCO support structures to ensure that the larger community vision, which included the creation of a globally accessible cultural knowledge and experience repository with sound, image, and narrative archives, could be developed.[8]

Video projects identified as intercultural dialogue with Indigenous peoples, such as UNESCO's ICT initiative, have appeared on the international horizon with limited critical attention or appeal. The factors for their relative anonymity intersect with the intent and the implementation of the productions, resulting in a mixed message in the videos produced. Rising to the surface are broader tensions that question what intercultural dialogue actually intends and how the deployment of video can actually facilitate communication, bridge distances, develop relationships, share perspective differences, and promote understanding of Indigenous peoples and issues. Current research among Indigenous scholars is focused on decolonizing methodologies based on the critical work by Māori educator Linda Tuhiwai Smith.[9] Her outline of a corollary relationship between colonial experiments and Western research that was used to displace, subjugate, and supplant Indigenous peoples' livelihoods and appropriate Indigenous knowledge and practices strongly advocates for change. Her essay is a full-on discussion of the impacts of research, including the need for a kind of video decolonization as Indigenous peoples remain at the forefront of global crises on all fronts, including the climate, economics, and politics. I view my participation with and observations of UNESCO and my work as a producer of Indigenous video as jumping-off points for highlighting a particular example of Indigenous video pragmatism.

My travel to Kenya and brief stay at the Il Ngwesi Lodge in August 2009 was largely due to the faculty-supported research allocations grant that I received from the University of New Mexico. My visit to Shuel's homeland began our work on the Il Ngwesi narratives featuring his people, also known as the Laikipiak Maasai, and the managing owners of the award-winning ecotourism lodge Il Ngwesi Lodge. Ole Joseph Shuel Nijalis was the first manager of the lodge and since our first meeting has become the director of their tourism company, Ol Donyo Keri Safaris, based in Nanyuki, Kenya, several hours' drive from Il Ngwesi. Shuel's confidence in my ability to relate to his people as an Indigenous person with tribal ties was immediate when I arrived at Il Ngwesi. The same energy was apparent in Nairobi, where Yvonne and her colleagues at the Aga Khan University welcomed me into their multicultural community of scholars and artists, producing effervescent conversation with regard to our visceral connections to each other, as though old friendships were being reacquainted.

The challenge we set for ourselves, to produce voice-in-video narratives from the Il Ngwesi Maasai community of 6,000 members, relied upon the tension between their pastoral lifestyle and their creatively seeking a path to a different destiny by building a lodge and providing a space for ecotourism. Prior to their building the Il Ngwesi Lodge, they had no knowledge of ecolodge management or safari tourism, living as subsistence pastoralists dependent on cattle and goats and confined to a conservation area with migrating African wildlife in the remote northern savannah of Kenya. In 1996, with the assistance of the Lewa Wildlife Conservancy, USAID, and several other grants from nonprofits, the community designed, planned, and opened the Il Ngwesi Lodge, which caters to tourists interested in efforts to protect wildlife and Maasai culture.[10] Supplanting the history of safari poaching and more recent ecotourism in Kenya, the Il Ngwesi Maasai became the first Indigenous people in Africa to open a community-owned tourism business. A cluster of Maasai villages in the Laikipia District are within the national wildlife conservation area designated by the Kenya government, and the Il Ngwesi Maasai have title to their lands, which has allowed them to pursue ecotourism.[11]

The success of the Il Ngwesi Lodge is based on their use of ecotourism principles, coupled with symbolic and ancestral forms of welcome and hospitality inherent to Maasai.[12] The lodge's staff greets guests at the entrance path, singing about the landscape and the wildlife that welcome the guests back. This practice is typical in African communities, having experienced it myself throughout southern African villages. When I arrived at Il Ngwesi and was welcomed by some fifteen staff members dressed in the red cloth worn by Maasai, I was finally home with Shuel's people. Since its opening, they have hosted thousands of international guests at the lodge, which is built on a hilly outcrop overlooking the savannah. The lodge is able to comfortably accommodate up to sixteen people in six separate *bandas*. The *bandas* are open-air cottages built with stilt-like construction and with large verandas facing an animal migration trail. Locally gathered insect-resistant hardwood and raffia from the Lewa Swamp a hundred miles away were used to build Il Ngwesi Lodge, which is aesthetically African. The *bandas* have adjoining open-air showers and a gorgeous elliptical swimming pool that is fed from a spring. In recent years the lodge has added a full-menu service to their host offerings, as well as safari walks and sunset drives to watch evening migrations.

The significance of such a venture can be seen in light of the inevitable changes in their lives, including droughts and exposure to outside influences, especially among their youth, who continue to live in the manner of their elders and ancestors as pastoralists. According to Shuel, his elders know that the upcoming generations are in need of education to help develop their livelihoods as the land base reaches maximum levels of sustainability. At the time of my visit in August 2009, a severe drought was devastating their livestock.[13] The lodge itself employs some thirty to forty Maasai as safari tour guides, wildlife conservation workers, drivers, chefs, housekeepers, wildlife guards, and lodge management, privileging wage income over subsistence pastoral living. The lodge staff employees all receive time off to return to their villages for short periods. Some if not all of these particulars about the lodge and staff were informative aspects that made for varying and constructive narratives, despite sounding like a commercial for Il Ngwesi Lodge.[14]

Africa the Continent, Kenya the Country: Context for the Maasai Voices

The vastness of the African continent became apparent to me after traveling in southern Africa some years ago and, now, in Kenya. It is obvious that Indigenous societies are imperceptible and not taking part in the major dialogues on issues directly impacting their longevity. The Il Ngwesi Group Ranch lands are located in the Laikipia District, which comprises 16,500 hectares (about 7,000 acres) and is due north of Mt. Kenya. Group ranch conservation areas were established by the Kenyan government for Indigenous populations through the Kenyan Land Act of

1968 and allow for communal land ownership, and the Il Ngwesi are one of the few Indigenous peoples in Kenya to have this arrangement. The current population of Il Ngwesi Maasai is 6,000, and they occupy 634 village households, each having an average of ten people per household. Two or more families typically occupy one homestead with their livestock. The African savannah is a dusty, almost desert-like landscape (not unlike the Southwest near Tucson, Arizona) that is home to wild herds of elephants, giraffes, baboons, monkeys, water buffalo, elands, lions, dik-diks, warthogs, zebras, and other game, along with bird species that migrate daily through Il Ngwesi territory. Huge, thorny scrub-bush trees are ubiquitous and a major water source for game, especially during droughts, and the flattop African acacia trees provide a wispy covering for the reddish soil. The Mukogodo forest, covered with Olmaroroi (the tree that grows on the mountain), is to the west of Il Ngwesi Lodge, providing contour to a feral land.

Listening to Shuel share over a meal with friends in Nairobi his passion about issues impacting Kenya at large reminded me of conversations during family dinners about the U.S. government's role in dictating policies that our community had to follow or in controlling access to creating jobs on the reservation:

> Because, in development work it means getting into the mud to do the work for ourselves, even now our government [needs to] make people feel like working using their own culture and using their ways to work things out and make the country prosper; it's not waiting for the dollar, money, sitting and saying, "OK, we're going to elect you so you can go and talk to the Zulus and bring money." . . . That is a notion we should run away from. . . . How can we make things better using our own Indigenous ways, make our country move forward, our communities move forward?[15]

Shuel was the first manager of the Il Ngwesi Lodge. He received a college education and hotel management training in Nairobi through the support of his community. He recalls at least fifteen films being made in and about his community with no benefit to them. His concern is with the primitive context in which Maasai are conveyed to the public, exclusively for commercial purposes and with little respect for them as people with unique lives. The creation of a globally accessible library of video and films produced by Indigenous peoples and that features contemporary Maasai images are relevant ideas for Shuel in helping to promote their ecotourism. One of the more complex questions to come out of our conversation was, How does ecotourism contribute to cultural preservation? When Shuel says, "We are not in control of our destiny," he is referring to countries outside of Kenya and Africa itself that have invested in corporate tourism that strips and erases Indigenous Africans' ability to share their natural ways of being with the land and the wildlife. His claim is supported in the Kenya NGO Earth Summit 2002 Forum's report on sustainable tourism, produced by Jane Kahata and Judy Imbanga, who state:

> The Government of Kenya recognized the need to involve local people in the industry and established the Kenya Tourist Development Corporation with one of its objectives being to encourage local investment in the industry. There has been some local participation but the bulk of the industry is still in the hands of non-Kenyans. The structure of the Kenyan tourism industry is that most of the visits are package tours that are organized from outside the country and most of the goods and services are also paid for out there. This is not healthy if Kenya is to have a sustainable industry and these anomalies can only be rectified if there is more participation in the industry from Kenyans.[16]

Multiple layers of memories of an integrated life system remain from my time at Il Ngwesi, where I experienced daily peace and joy emanating from the animals and the people—an extrasensorially heightened experience of reconnecting with a natural rhythm where man and fauna quietly breathe together within a land physically remote from town or city, where at nightfall there are no artificially powered lights to distract the eye or thought, only the brilliance of starlight making me aware of my own separation from the fissures of the unnatural world from which I arrived and in which I live. Kenya's abundant wildlife has only recently been protected by the Kenya Wildlife Service, the custodian of all wildlife resources in Kenya, who has direct management authority in the parks, while the local authorities manage the reserves, with the exception of those that are managed by county councils and local communities like Il Ngwesi, which is part of a protected area.

Kenya itself, which was governed by British imperialist rule until 1968, when it gained independence and began self-rule as an African country, continues to struggle with government corruption and a need for infrastructure. Poverty in Africa is identified as the greatest source of environmental degradation, especially in the developing countries, and Kenya is no exception. African scholar Ali A. Mazrui provides the following explanation:

> From Africa's point of view, the first danger of the depletion of resources is tied up with problems of dependency and underdevelopment. Africa is not in adequate control of its own resources . . . the net beneficiaries of Africa's resources lie outside of the African continent . . . many of its mineral resources help to industrialize the rest of the world without necessarily improving the African condition itself.[17]

Il Ngwesi: Land, Silence, Animals, Lodge Staff, and Meeting Oshen

To reiterate, Il Ngwesi (translated as People of Wildlife) is the name given to their award-winning ecotourism lodge, located in Laikipia East in northern Kenya. The lodge was established to enhance the livelihoods of the Il Ngwesi. From my perspective Maasai society is characterized by an imminent awareness of experience, knowledge, and belief in the lands they have inherited. A legendary people named Il Laikipiak occupied (and owned) Laikipia lands farther south, according to Il Ngwesi Lodge guide Keshine Lawrence, a young Moran who shared the story of the migration of the original peoples from present-day Sudan into Kenya and continued on to present-day land disputes, abrogated rights, and foreigners from abroad who have forced them into the confinement in which they now reside. Yvonne Owuor, mentor for myself and Shuel, offers the following view of Shuel's people: "Their sense of life—under siege—is linked to pastoralism and they have a strong and intrinsic link to the wholeness of life . . . the idea of the commodification and partitioning of existence into saleable parts is still a cause of bewilderment especially among the elders."[18]

Keshine Lawrence and I became friends in part because he was assigned to serve as my guide during my stay at the lodge. I never asked him how old he was, because it didn't matter, and even now, I hesitate to guess, since he wore his Moran braided headdress and beaded adornment. I took close notice of his gentle, quiet nature and classic Maasai stature, which I attempted to break at times with my senseless joking. He had a perfect attention to detail when he observed things on our walks, as when he pointed out the go-away-bird's nest that was constructed with two holes so that the bird could quickly escape. A bird in the turaco family, its common name derives from its loud call, which it makes when predators are near. As we stood looking up at the nest it occurred to us that our focus had been on one single nest, and we both realized that the tree we were underneath was filled with go-away-bird nests. We both smiled, recognizing our tunnel vision.

Describing a place—as in de-scribing, or taking apart to write about—is a strange way for me to think. I can tell people what I did while at the Il Ngwesi Lodge, but it has taken a longer time to realize how deeply it touched me. Actually, it took nearly a month after my visit before I told people about where I had been and what took place. Yvonne describes my feelings perfectly in an e-mailed response, titled "20 days," regarding my postvisit reminiscences:

I wondered if the soul of Il Ngwesi was sharing your dreams as it does mine for a while; peering into our illusions and where possible nudging them away. I read the wistfulness in-between the lines of your words, all those pauses of silence . . . and I smile with a twinge of the heart know-ing a little of the nostalgia for an old land that feels like home, all its fa-miliar archetypes and the certainty that there is a story about belonging here. I smile, because Kenya—the witch—has a way of summoning her children. Those she does not want she will ensure will have a most ter-rible, soul wrenching time of it. I should warn you about this land; how she will infuse herself into your soul if she wants you. How she changes you, strips you off so much, tears you down and then rebuilds you in her image and likeness after you have cried like you have never cried before, laughed from the belly of your soul and discovered that love has a tril-lion other angles. Love, Yvonne.

My original e-mail to Yvonne on September 3, 2009, titled "late evening here," is as follows:

It's been twenty some days since I was in your territory and at Il Ngwesi.

I had the most wonder filled time during my brief visit. It was so special to see you in person again. It was strange for me to see Shuel again when he and the lodge staff picked me up at the Lewa airstrip. I returned to New Mexico very very joyous and actually, the entire expe-rience of leaving the U.S. and spending the time at Il Ngwesi gave me a renewed sense of the earth and my place in it. You know all too well what Il Ngwesi does to one's senses and sensibilities, I was rocketed into a fourth dimension of timelessness with the land and I recall telling Ochen that finally being at Il Ngwesi made complete indigenous sense. What now? I ask myself.

I began the project with Shuel and Il Ngwesi and know I am commit-ted to seeing it flourish and become what the ancestors want it to be. Every day since my return home I've had a thought or two about my time in Kenya, of the people, the land, animals, and feel of the place in me. Beverly.

Stories told from lived experience are also lessons in helping one become whole, and this is what happens at Il Ngwesi. There is so much more and are so many personas to introduce, and they shall be the video-in-voice narrators. Inscribing the voice of current Il Ngwesi Lodge manager Ochen Sakita Miyani calls forth his charm, reserve, and intelligent, regal presence. He is the lodge's second manager chosen by the Il Ngwesi community following Shuel's move to the position operating Ol Donyo Keri Safaris. Ochen says he came to work for "the community as a steward who looks after his people." He started in 2002, after previously working for the Lewa Conservancy as a guard and after further training at another lodge near Mt. Kenya. He says he came back to work for his "people, to give back in a way to the community." The Kenya NGO Earth Summit 2002 Forum's report on sustainable tourism in Kenya outlines fundamental challenges for tourism to continue, suggesting:

> Conservation of tourism resources (wildlife, cultural, historical and the marine) that attract tourists to Kenya. In the absence of a comprehensive land-use policy, this may be practically impossible in the long-term especially for wildlife. Provision of an adequate and well-maintained infrastructure that will facilitate the growth and expansion of the tourism industry. The Government of Kenya views wildlife as a vehicle for rural development but this can only happen if certain amenities are provided. Increase Kenyan participation in the sector. The Kenyanization loans provided in the 1960's and 1970's by the Kenya Tourist Development Corporation have been on the decline and the high cost of borrowing credit has hampered the participation of Kenyans. A report by Sinclair (1990) indicates that approximately 78% of the major hotels in the coastal area, 67% of hotels in Nairobi and 66% of lodges in national parks have some foreign investment. The participation of local communities that live and interact with wildlife should also be increased with the aim of helping them establish economically viable and sustainable tourism enterprises.[19]

This report further encourages Kenyan government officials to recognize the wealth in the country's diverse cultural identities.

Similar ignorance in the United States exists in regard to federal Indian protections intended to support Indigenous sustainable development on federally protected Indian reservations, as get-rich development results in the devastating extraction of gas, oil, minerals, forests, and rocks for highway construction. The peculiar phenomenon among America's Indigenous tribes is the recent historical trend in economic development that has tribes competing with each other's casino-style gaming enterprises, an altered form of Indigenous tourism, but with the same issues of foreign investment, including borrowing credit with no thought as to what it does to the will of the people themselves.

Camera Work and iPhone Demonstration at Il Ngwesi: What We Imaged and How It Happened

As I unpacked my bags at Il Ngwesi Lodge, two female staff members, Benadetta and Grace, helped carry my bags to my *banda*. I briefly spoke with them, asking their names and thanking them for their help. It was a warm afternoon as the scent of difference filled my nostrils—wood, earth, and fresh air. I had with me two still digital cameras and two HD video cameras, so the day after my arrival, I awoke just before sunrise and took the still camera out to the great room at the front of the lodge. Standing there were five or six of the lodge's staff, looking east toward distant mountains, perhaps a hundred miles away, where the sun would rise. Their silhouettes were striking as I clicked the camera. James Kinyaga heard me as he held his cup of coffee, and smiling, he said, "Good morning, would you like some coffee or tea?" After the first night under the stars, having that coffee and standing at the edge of the overlook of the great room, the expectation of sunrise over the savannah was heightened by the calls made by birds and some other creatures. This was the scene I witnessed each morning during my stay at Il Ngwesi Lodge.

Getting the cameras out meant sharing and giving a camera to whomever I was with at Il Ngwesi, usually Keshine, Shuel, Henry, or Robert. I simply allowed a process to unfold within each moment, in lieu of workshopping. I'd demonstrate the buttons, adjust the viewfinder, mention things about what I was doing, and ask a few questions when they first got hold of the camera— for example, to see if what they were seeing was focused. I relied on instinct to facilitate documentation until, by themselves, they would take the camera out. As we ventured out into the land a digital audio recorder was used to collect stories told by whomever was sharing. Shuel, Ochen, and myself had more formal discussions about the documentation and set aside some time for formal interviews with staff so as not to impede upon their regular duties at the lodge. The Il Ngwesi villages were some distance away from the lodge, taking us about forty-five minutes by vehicle. My two visits to a village proved invaluable. Their homes were square in shape and made from the mud, grass, and wood poles so familiar in Indigenous construction. A tour of the village by one of the elders was provided as the lodge staff prepared a meal of barbecued goat. The village itself was not large, consisting of eight entrances that symbolically represented the eight elders who resided at that village. Several large acacia trees towered over the village plaza. The village's center space was reserved for the goat and cattle livestock pens, which were constructed of the scrub tree limbs and had large, spiked thorns for protection against predators at night. The livestock was taken daily to pasture, from sunrise to sunset. The village itself was surrounded for protection, as well, with a fence of more scrub brush.

One long and lazy afternoon, I pulled out my iPhone in the lodge's great room. Several of the staff noticed the object in my hand, and young Moran Robert inquired about it. They knew about computers and cell phones, as Ochen had one, as did Shuel. Out of character, I began demonstrating features of the iPhone, feeling afterward like I was in a commercial. Robert was intrigued with the Internet feature, though I had already tried it and could not connect with a satellite.

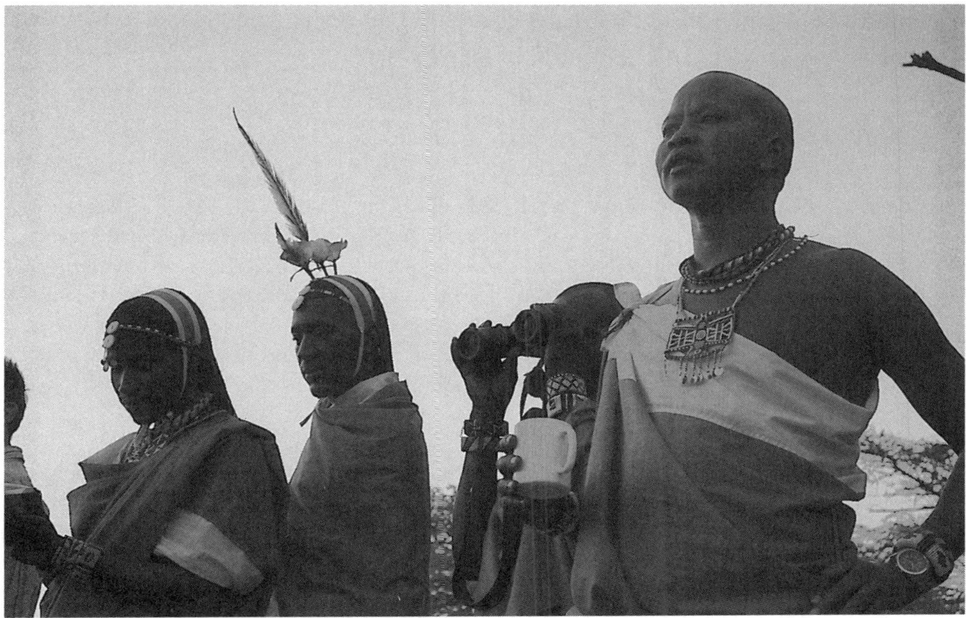

Sunrise at Il Ngwesi. Photograph by Beverly Singer.

I showed them the global clock and how to dial a call with the touch of a finger. When I began playing music, they stepped back and started moving to something I had chosen from South Africa. The spell was broken when one of them was called back to work. In hindsight the ease with which they accepted this new technological gadget produced another cultural shift from exposure to the world outside of Il Ngwesi. I asked myself about my own intervening role.

These and many other stories, alongside dense and animated images, are continuing to be collected at Il Ngwesi, as I left two cameras with them. What Shuel, Yvonne, and I share with Il Ngwesi is a lifelong bond. In order to strengthen it, Yvonne recently asked me the following:

> Is there room for a more dramatic exchange that involves experiential
> travel and discovery, a way for the young of your landscape to meet the
> rituals of the Il Ngwesi's landscape? That way you can come often, and
> I can join the journeys of discovery and meaning. A meeting of elders?
> A space of knowledge exchange?

My resolve is to host Shuel and Yvonne in my homeland of New Mexico. I will introduce them to my people, and together, we shall work on editing part one of our video-in-voices production on behalf of Il Ngwesi. Our mutual and delicate bonds with the land at Il Ngwesi reveal more than stories. For us it contains important lessons for successive generations in retrieving knowledge on how to survive and attain balance with the land and with each other.

NOTES

I dedicate this essay to my beloved aunt Catherine Amy Singer, who passed to Spirit on November 15, 2009. On August 12, 2009, our village, Khapogeh, celebrated its annual harvest feast, and for the first time in many years, I was not home to help Aunt Amy. I was in Kenya. Auntie told me, "Go, enjoy yourself, when you come back, tell us all about it." Special thanks go to Yvonne Owuor and Ole Shuel Nijalis for helping with this essay and sharing their words and to the people at Il Ngwesi for their support. Wo wa tsi (blessings). Edward Kennedy, Aunt Amy's widowed husband, deserves mention for asking after my writing and if I wanted to go out for breakfast. Yes, uncle, let's go.

1. "The early part of 2006 witnessed one of the worst droughts in recent years and it has a serious impact on Indigenous peoples. Some people lost all their livestock, although the majority were left with herds that were too few to sustain families. Pastoralists moved long distances in search of pasture and water. In the districts south of the capital, Nairobi, a lot of land is no longer in the hands of pastoralists, and private farms have put up fences all along the road. In the northern districts of Laikipia and Samburu, the government ordered pastoralists out who had sought grazing in the Mount Kenya areas following the severe drought." International Work Group for Indigenous Affairs (IWGIA), *The Indigenous World 2007* (North America: Transaction Publishers, 2007), 473.

2. The project ICTs for Intercultural Dialogue: Developing Communication Capacities of Indigenous Peoples (ICT4ID), approved by UNESCO's general conference in 2003 and extended to continue until 2007, aimed at using ICTs to preserve and regenerate Indigenous cultures and identity and to promote their dissemination locally, nationally, and internationally, thus contributing to narrowing the digital divide, a major development challenge. *UNESCO Report of Annual Meeting of Inter-Agency Support Group on Indigenous Issues,* (Rome: UNESCO, 2006), 9–10.

3. Ibid., 10

4. Yvonne Adhiambo Owuor is a fiction writer, conservationist, cultural activist, and past executive director of the Zanzibar International Film Festival who won the 2003 Caine Prize for African Writing for *Weight of Whispers.* The Caine Prize is often referred to as the African Booker.

5. Thanks go to Suzanne Schnuttgen at UNESCO, whose search on the Internet identified me as an Indigenous filmmaker and scholar.

6. Yvonne Adhiambo Owuor currently is project coordinator for academic planning at the Aga Kahn University in Nairobi.

7. "Indigenous communities in Kenya suffer from very similar problems, such as: dependency on natural resources for their livelihoods; a lack of security of tenure; a lack of infrastructure, including schools, health facilities; communication, roads, etc.; and generally a denial of their economic, social, political and cultural rights. Neither do they have the same economic strengths, organizational structures and technical capability necessary to seek protection from human rights violations." IWGIA, *The Indigenous World 2007,* 468.

8. Yvonne Owuor, e-mail message to author, May 2007, concerning completion of the ICT in Kenya.

9. Linda Tuhiwai Smith, *Decolonizing Methodologies: Research and Indigenous Peoples* (London: Zed Books, 1990).

10. The Lewa Wildlife Conservancy is a privately owned wildlife sanctuary in Kenya.

11. "There is no specific legislation governing Indigenous peoples in Kenya. Some Kenyan laws, such as the Trust Land Act Cap 288, Forest Act Cap 285 and Government Lands Act Cap 280 work against human rights of Indigenous peoples in a number of ways as, through evictions or restriction of movement, they deny Indigenous peoples access to their resources and primary sources of livelihood. The new draft land policy was published toward the end of 2006 so that the public could raise any issues they might have in this regard. . . . While some issues are sensitive towards issues relating to land and resources (issues touching directly on the livelihoods of Indigenous peoples), it falls short of recognizing collective rights . . . there is a strong move to individualize land titles and insufficient examples and precedents as to how security of tenure and development can be achieved when resources are held collectively." IWGIA, *The Indigenous World 2007*, 469–70.

12. Ecotourism emphasizes low impact on the environment and equitable distribution of benefits to the local communities. Kenya has been a mass-tourism destination for a long time, and it is slowly shifting toward embracing principles and practices associated with ecotourism.

13. In an e-mail message, Yvonne Owuor wrote, "The rains are so late Beverly and our people are hurting. The animals are dying and the Il Ngwesi people are also in anguish over the prolonged drought. It has never been so bad. If you have your rain people there, if they can, ask them to intercede for us, or if not for us, for the innocent animals at least. Shuel must be worried about his cows."

14. See www.ilngwesi.com.

15. Ole Shuel, videotaped conversation, Nairobi, Kenya, August 8, 2009.

16. Jane Kahata and Judy Imbanga, *Sustainable Tourism: A Report on the Civil Society Review of the Implementation of Agenda 21 in Kenya* (Kenya NGO Earth Summit 2002 Forum, February 2002), 7.

17. Ali A. Mazrui, *The African Condition: A Political Diagnosis* (Cambridge: Cambridge University Press, 1980), 114.

18. Yvonne Owuor, e-mail message to author, May 2007.

19. Kahata and Imbanga, *Sustainable Tourism*, 32.

14

Dante Cerano's *Dia dos*

SEX, KINSHIP, AND VIDEOTAPE

Jesse Lerner

Within the context of rural Indigenous communities in Mexico, radically altered by migration and the encroaching forces of globalization yet deeply invested in a distinctive local culture, the dramatically reduced cost and increased accessibility of digital media has made the moving image a powerful expressive tool of unforeseen proportions. Low-cost, lightweight, easy-to-use digital video cameras are in the process of transforming the face of Indigenous media production in Mexico. In this essay I briefly trace the broad outlines of this emerging body of work and then look more closely at a recent documentary by Dante Cerano, one of Mexico's outstanding Indigenous media artists.

The development of Indigenous media in Mexico has been slow. This is in spite of the fact that the Native population has been a significant presence in Mexican film since its earliest beginnings. Among the very first actualities shot in Mexico in the last years of the nineteenth century are scenes that highlight Mexico's cultural diversity—ethnographic spectacles, if you will, such as *Desayuno de indios* (1896). The national cinema of the silent era dramatizes a range of Native myths, heroes, and cultures in narrative films such as *Tiempos Mayas* (Carlos Martinez Arredono, 1914), *Tepeyac* (José Manuel Ramos, Carlos E. González, and Fernando Sáyago, 1917), *Tabaré* (Luis Lezama, 1917), *Cuauhtémoc* (Manuel de la Bandera, 1919), *De Raza Azteca* (Guillermo Calles and Miguel Contreras Torres, 1921), *El indio Yaqui* (Guillermo Calles, 1926), and others.[1] Not surprisingly, these early representations of Indigenous Mexico are, almost without exception, the work of outsiders. The first Native voices heard in the Mexican cinema were latecomers, arriving only after decades of caricatures and misrepresentations in Mexican commercial film (e.g., Pedro Infante as Tizoc, Dolores del Rio as Maria Candelaria) and assimilationist propaganda in documentaries (e.g., *Centro de educación indígena* [Gregorio Castillo, 1938]). These stereotypes proved remarkably enduring. Charles Ramirez Berg points out that in the early 1970s, when the national cinema underwent a period of upheaval and renewal provoked by crisis and representations of the relations between social classes and of gender roles went through significant revisions, the image of the Indian in commercial film remained one of rural simpletons who provide comic relief or servants who cook, clean and open doors for the light-skinned protagonists . . . recognized [by] their extremely submissive attitude, hopping, short-stepping gait, and their sing-song Spanish with mispronounced words.[2]

When Native voices initially entered the cinema, it was not as authors in control of their representations but as subjects of—collaborators with, really—well-meaning Mexican documentarians working in 16 mm, filmmakers like Nacho López (*Todos somos mexicanos,* 1958), Alfonso Muñoz (*El es dios,* 1965–66), and Paul Leduc (*Etnocidio, notas sobre el mexquital,* 1977).

A generation later, Super 8 enabled the effort sometimes called the *transferencia de medios,* or media transfer, which explored the possibility that nonprofessionals, with minimal technical training, could represent themselves and their culture "from within," with minimal aid (or interference) from media professionals, anthropologists, and bureaucrats. These professionals introduced small-gauge film equipment to Indigenous communities, offered some basic technical pointers, and then let the local community, or a few individuals from the community who expressed the most interest in the medium, create their own self-representations. The previous experiences of some of the participants in community radio projects served as an important precedent. A few outstanding documentaries emerged from the *transferencia de medios* initiative (best known is probably *La vida de una familia Ikoods* [Teofila Palafox, 1988], created as part of the Taller de Cine Indígena de San Mateo del Mar on the Isthmus of Tehuantepec in Oaxaca), but it was not until the arrival of low-cost digital video cameras and nonlinear editing systems that this promise was fully realized. Around the same time, media arts organizations, enlightened state programs, Indigenous groups, and independent activists in Australia, Brazil, Canada, and the United States were engaged in parallel efforts.[3]

In retrospect this was a transitional stage, enabling an unprecedented Indigenous control of production while being still dependent on outsiders for equipment, processing, and other indispensable resources. The hands-off approach promised in the *transferencia de medios* has come to fruition in the past decade or so. Not so long ago, high-end systems like Avid's were the exclusive domain of those with thousands (if not tens of thousands) of pesos to spend on the weekly rental of top-of-the-line equipment. Today, nonlinear editing, through software as accessible as iMovie, Adobe Premiere, and Final Cut Pro, is the point of departure for self-representation with moving images in Native communities all over Latin America, communities long marginalized by language, geography, prejudice, economics, and a host of other barriers. The massive out-migration from rural communities to both Mexican cities and to the United States has enabled and accelerated this process, both through equipment purchased and brought home to communities and the dependence on video for maintaining connections across great distances and international borders. Though media historians have linked earlier representations of the Indigenous to a colonial project of domination and extermination, perhaps most forcefully in Fatimah Tobing Rony's study *The Third Eye: Race, Cinema and Ethnographic Spectacle*, the dynamic we see here could not be more different.[4] Indigenous Mexican communities have shown themselves to be quick to capitalize on this new accessibility, creating compelling testaments to their communities, traditions, and struggles in ways that have previously eluded them. The contrast with the work of earlier representations of non-Natives who sought to document these cultures gives a clear sense of some of the terms that have changed with this transfer of control of the image, as well as other points of continuity.

Many of the concerns central to this new digital production overlap with concerns addressed by other activist- and community-based social documentary media artists working in Mexico: the destruction of natural resources by multinational corporations, political struggles in the context of nations that have persistently ignored and marginalized these communities, the transformations of cultural traditions in the face of the creeping forces of globalization, and the changes wrought by massive migration to the United States. But I propose that there is much that is new as well. I offer a closer reading of Dante Cerano's short documentary *Dia dos* (2004) and consider the ways in which it may be if not representative then at least indicative of the ways in which video production from within Indigenous communities troubles the norms of ethnographic representations and genre categories. Beverly Singer has written that "terms that identify [Native] films as 'avant-garde,' 'documentary,' or 'ethnographic' limit the understanding and information contained in Native films and videos, and they are not natural categories within our experience."[5] Although I would concur that Cerano's *Dia dos* does not sit well within any existing genre within the larger rubric of nonfiction, it is nonetheless engaged in a highly self-conscious play with recognizable genres, especially those of the ethnographic film and of the wedding video, while not remaining within either of those genre's conventions. Cerano's pastiche of genres extends beyond these two principal references. One interjection, an awkward montage of tight shots of Corona bottles being consumed at the festivities, accompanied by the music of Vivaldi, is a ham-fisted parody of an advertisement for beer. This sequence, introduced with the intertitle "la sonata de la cerveza" and a graphic of a beer bottle, suggests a kind of intertextuality closer to the spirit of *Austin Powers* than to visual anthropology. It is this play with genre that has contributed to the documentary's international success.[6] In this sense, it is different from the more familiar Indigenous features that have crossed over to reach non-Indigenous audiences (*Atanarjuat* [*The Fast Runner*] [Zacharias Kunuk, 2001], *Once Were Warriors* [Lee Tamahori,

1994], *Smoke Signals* [Chris Eyre, 1998], and others). *Dia dos* doesn't introduce the audience from outside of Cerano's P'urépecha community to another world so much as it navigates them back and forth between an unfamiliar P'urépecha world and a one of more familiar mass (and anthropological) media images.[7]

Dia dos takes on a key anthropological theme: kinship and its articulation through the marriage ritual. Given the centrality of kinship in much of anthropological theory, it's not surprising that the topic of marriage is well represented in the corpus of anthropological cinema—for example, in early romanticized narratives like *The Wedding of Palo* (Knud Rasmussen, 1937) and through staples of the anthropology classroom like *Bride Service* (Tim Asch and Napoleon Chagnon, 1975) and *Tobelo Marriage* (Dirk Nijland and Jos Platekamp, 1982). Cerano's documentary narrates how the community showers the young newlywed couple with gifts: pots, blankets, pails, pans, a *molcajete,* and kitchen utensils, which they and their relatives carry as they dance through the streets from wedding feast to wedding feast. Adopting a kind of unity that would be admired from ethnographic cinema's most conservative theorists, Cerano frames his topic around a single day, a single place, and a single sequence of events from one marriage ritual. The video represents a day in the life of a bridegroom and the continuation of a marriage ritual that began the previous day, on *dia uno,* whose highlights are summarized in a series of still images under the documentary's opening titles. Like an ethnographic film, the video is clearly directed at outsiders; it explains otherwise incomprehensible features of the ritual through a sparse and irreverent voice-over narration read by the director. A graphic summary, stylistically indebted to a 1980s-era video game, summarizes the relationships and movements over an electronic beat.

Although the electronica may be alien to the context of a traditional P'urépecha wedding, the strategy of a schematic summary—a simplified, animated diagram that explains complex social relations, movements, and exchange—is not at all an unprecedented one in ethnographic film. For much the same reasons as Cerano, the ethnographic filmmaker Timothy Asch, working in collaboration with anthropologist Napoleon Chagnon, for example, explains multifaceted and chaotic social behaviors in *The Ax Fight* (1975) by using kinship charts, offering a kind of thick description that the very participants cannot provide. Like the optical printing and superimposed arrows singling out and decoding the behaviors of key participants in Asch's canonical short, Cerano identifies key participants with superimposed titles, helping viewers navigate the social relations as they play out on-screen. And as if to underscore the ethnographer's conviction that participants themselves cannot articulate all the complexities of the social reality in which they act, the one talking head in the video is intoxicated to the point of incoherence and is ultimately censored—with the audio deleted and a text reading "censurado" on-screen—by Cerano in the editing room.

The electronic dance music is only one of multiple nondiegetic music excerpts included in the sound track, excerpts that range from hip-hop to the baroque, from kitschy neolounge to a repeated guitar riff by the 1970s stadium rock band Heart. Here, Cerano's distance from a more traditionally conceived project of ethnographic cinema, with its fly-on-the-wall, observational sensibility and positivist pretenses, is very clear. In ethnographic film the condemnation of anthropologist Karl Heider is typical of the disapproval reserved for this kind of editorial decision. As Heider writes, "Music is inevitably a distraction except when it is sound that was actually happening when the visuals were shot."[8] It's worth noting that the example Heider uses of an inappropriate music choice (Irish folk music over footage of Irish farmers harvesting their crops) is considerably less incongruous than many of the choices Cerano makes.

In the context of the wedding video, however, this sort of insertion of nondeigetic and seemingly out-of-place musical citations, often for comic effect, is not at all outside the norm. There are other indications that *Dia dos* can also be productively situated in relation to this other genre, the wedding video, one even more marginal than ethnographic film. Wedding videos are as single-mindedly directed to insiders, typically the participants and, especially, the protagonists of the event itself and their kin, as anthropological film is to the outsider. As James M. Moran points out, the wedding video is a genre that implodes the classic binaries of amateur/professional, private/public, and artisanal/industrial.[9] The text on-screen at the video's opening, from the transcendental to the banal, situates Cerano's work within the commonplaces of the wedding video genre:

Un dia especial
Dios
Amor
Confeti
Banda
Padrino
Cerveza
Vals
Pastel
Regalos
Alegria
Costumbre
Responsibilidad

A special day
God
Love

Confetti
Banda music
The best man
Beer
Waltz
Cake
Gifts
Happiness
Tradition
Responsibility

This list, mixing the clichés of the ritual with what might be items on a wedding videographer's shot list, places us firmly within the realm of the formulaic. This prescribed quality of the wedding video is precisely why it is of interest only to the participants.

Beyond the generic pastiche and irreverent humor of the video, Cerano's *Dia dos* articulates a position that is at once that of an insider and an outsider, a position that I argue is emblematic of the Indigenous media maker. The cameraman / narrator / director makes no secret that he is a participant in the celebrations. First-person point-of-view shots showing big close-ups of a chili, a red salsa ladled on a serving at the wedding banquet, and a Styrofoam cup of unidentified distilled beverage place Cerano among the revelers. A relative of the bride sweeps the documentarian onto the dance floor and introduces a split-frame sequence. Cerano places himself in the event at once as a participant, in contrast to a passing carload of gawkers, identified with the superimposed title "fueron curiosos" (they were curious), yet sufficiently distant from the event to be able to translate it all to us outsiders.

Nowhere is Cerano's position as insider / outsider more clear or more problematic than in a sequence that addresses *las bellas de fiesta*. These young P'urépecha women, dancing in slow motion, are juxtaposed with the Caucasian ideal of Marilyn Monroe and Madonna and other embodiments of female beauty, who appear floating through the image as frames within the frame. Another of Cerano's wildly incongruous musical choices—Puff Daddy (aka P. Diddy, aka Sean Combs) rapping over a sample from the 1983 hit "Every Breath You Take" by the new wave band the Police—and the camerawork both put the male gaze, his and ours, front and center. But who exactly will be watching whom? Cerano is conflating several gazes here: the male gaze at an objectified female ideal, be it Caucasian or P'urépecha; an ethnographic gaze of the outsider at the spectacle of otherness; and the P'urépecha gaze at an unattainable ideal of an imported and alien standard of beauty. Surely, we are not meant to take these all as equivalent, given the very different circumstances and power dynamics that frame these gazes. What might we read into the inclusion of P. Diddy's sometime paramour J. Lo in the sequence? That Cerano has authored this display of female beauty, albeit a restrained one, and P'urépecha ritual for us (non-P'urépecha) Spanish speakers suggests that a more familiar politically correct reading is inadequate. That Cerano is a member of one of these groups put on display (P'urépechas) but not of the other (women), that some of the representations are static (those of the Hollywood stars) while others (of the P'urépechas) are in motion, and that male dancers are not juxtaposed with some imported ideal of male beauty all suggest a politics of representation that confounds anthropological expectations and the prohibitions of political correctness.

While I have stated that I would not argue that Cerano's *Día dos* is necessarily representative or typical of recent Indigenous media arts in Mexico, I have taken it here as richly suggestive of ways in which this production strays from more documentary models and upsets the established paradigms of ethnographic film. *Día dos* is, I believe, exemplary of the way that new digital technologies and nonlinear editing software have enabled not just a new class of practitioner but new representations of Native Mexico. These representations, like Cerano's musical choices and like so much that outsiders see and experience when spending time in Indigenous communities in Mexico, are often surprising and sometimes seemingly unfathomable. What is very clear is that this Indigenous production is growing and coming of age. Though still committed to social documentary, the staple of Indigenous production, Pedro Daniel López and Mundos Inéditos's project from Chiapas have embarked on an ambitious plan for a Native film academy that also fosters fiction productions, culminating in a feature-length production recently completed (*La pequeña semilla en el asfalto,* 2009). These new initiatives and productions make connections across international borders through media art, taking the representation of Mexico's Indigenous communities far from the embarrassing impersonations of Infante's Tizoc and into an exciting new realm of self-definitions.

NOTES

1. An overview of these and other silent film productions from Mexico is provided in Gabriel Ramírez, *Crónica del cine mudo mexicano* (Mexico City: Cineteca Nacional, 1989). Surprisingly, there is no thorough historical study of representations of Indigenous cultures in Mexican film, other than the rather preliminary survey offered in Javier González Rubio I. and Hugo Lara Chávez, *Cine antropológico mexicano* (Mexico City: Instituto Nacional de Antropología e Historia, 2009).

2. Charles Ramirez Berg, *Cinema of Solitude: A Critical Study of Mexican Film, 1967–1983* (Austin: University of Texas Press, 1992), 138.

3. See, for example, the description of the Mekaron Opoi D'joi project in Monica Frota, "Taking Aim: The Video Technology of Cultural Resistance," *Resolutions: Contemporary Video*

Practices, eds. Michael Renov and Erika Suderburg (Minneapolis: University of Minnesota Press, 1996), 258–82; as well as multiple examples analyzed in Pamela Wilson and Michelle Stewart, eds., *Global Indigenous Media: Culture, Poetics, and Politics* (Durham, N.C.: Duke University Press, 2008); and Faye Ginsburg, Lila Abu-Lighod, and Brian Larkin, eds. *Media Worlds: Anthropology on New Terrain* (Berkeley: University of California Press, 2002).

4. Fatimah Tobing Rony, *The Third Eye: Race, Cinema, and Ethnographic Spectacle* (Durham, N.C.: Duke University Press, 1998).

5. Beverly Singer, *Wiping the War Paint off the Lens* (Minneapolis: University of Minnesota Press, 2001), 2–3.

6. Cerano's work was shown at the First Nations / First Features series at New York's Museum of Modern Art and the Robert Flaherty Seminar.

7. The P'urépechas, also known as the Tarascans, are an Indigenous group from the Mexican state of Michoacán.

8. Karl G. Heider, *Ethnographic Film* (Austin: University of Texas Press, 1976), 74.

9. James M. Moran, "Wedding Video and Its Generation," in *Resolutions,* eds. Michael Renov and Erika Suderburg, 360–81.

15

Tragedies without Witness

Lionel Manga

In April 2009 I was drifting through the streets of Douala with a friend of mine, enjoying a back-to-the-roots trip. Julien, a Cameroonian architect by profession, lives, works, and teaches in France, as well as performing as an artist in the local contemporary scene of Epinal, a small town in the Vosges. Absolutely dazed by the decaying state of the city in several surroundings and from many aspects, he said to me, "There is a crime going on in great need of eyewitnesses, a crucial role artists must shoulder." Bearing this in mind, we went right into a drinking place for a cold beer. The dry season was on its way, and it was sometimes hard to cope with the heat. We sat outside in order to stare at the hot bimbos wandering the edge of the warm night, who were ready to take another white round without satin until dawn unless they could snare a man and quickly satisfy his sexual need for a five-thousand-FCFA banknote—roughly ten dollars, just enough to go two or three days in the urban survival scheme. According to World Bank ratios, we on that pavement were in the waters of poverty.

Of course, the word *crime* stands here like a metaphor pointing mainly to the current postcolonial fiasco and all its collateral damage. But still, even these are not all true crimes, as there are so many tragedies going on around us without eyewitnesses reporting them—such as the February 2008 three-day uprising against the raising prices of basic commodities in a few cities in Cameroon. Among them was Douala, where history has made its entrance from the very beginning. Given the ongoing wave of independent media amid and as a feedback effect of the tsunami of smaller and smaller digital devices dedicated to pictures, sounds, and more, how is it possible that—and how can we understand why—there are still blind spots in our world that is so caught up in a digital frenzy/revolution? Is it to say that despite all the activism dedicated to the cause, we are still far from a global village and that some territories are still invisible, where seeking visibility is considered a political challenge? What truly shapes and grounds such a state of affairs ten years after entering the twenty-first century? An account of the misadventure of local visual artist Guy Wouété during February 2008 provides a glowing testimony to that information and communication asymmetry. In addition, a beam of light illuminates the status of the artist in Cameroonian society. Let's go for a brief journey close to the geographical equator.

Suspicionland

To begin, let me first introduce you to Cameroon. Known as *l'Afrique en miniature,* the country is a touristic cliché. After entering its modern history with independence, the country suffered under the fierce dictatorship of its first president, Ahmadou Ahidjo, who became prime minister on February 18, 1958, and then served as president from 1960 until resigning on November 4, 1982, airing his unlikely decision during Cameroon radio's prime-time hour and taking the whole nation, even his political supporters, by surprise. Throughout his twenty-four-year reign, he relied upon an efficient secret police (SEDOC) to infiltrate the society from top to bottom, rewarding public denouncements of his regime with treachery. He maintained a climate of deep fear, and the SEDOC, later the DIRDOC, would not have in any manner envied the evil of either the Securitate in Romania or the Stasi in the former East Germany.

Also part of the game during those dire times was a special body not unlike the Chilean and Argentinean death squads, the Brigade Mixte Mobile (BMM). It had its own thick-walled premises where men and women said to be subversive were tortured day and night and were welcomed at its entrance by the statement, written in blood, HERE GOD DOESN'T EXIST—a kind of sheer welcome to the club of suffering. In the BMM's prisons nobody heard your screams; you understood at the speed of light that this was the kind of place where one who spoke without inhibition ended up. At the time, everybody was supposed to close his or her mouth and say white when it was red, north when it was south, and east when the truth was west. This place was a no-hope venue. Suspicion was the only strategy for survival in public spaces, since no one knew who was whom. Was that man "big ears" or just a chap standing by me in a bar or sitting by me in a taxi? The number of dead and disappeared is not known exactly, but for the period from the beginning of repression to the "peace" in 1972, some reliable sources estimate close to two hundred thousand souls, or even more. The so-called Père de la Nation (nicknamed "Grand Boubou") had no difficulty exerting Julius Caesar's principle *divide imperum* while ruling this perverted multiethnic country called Suspicionland.

The Aftereffects Season

For most of the people in Cameroon, the idea of resistance came to be, in the long run, an absurdity given the violence this paranoid regime was able to exercise, often triggered by just the blink of an eye or a wrong word. Many smart men and women lost their lives in the name of freedom, and starting in 1955, brave individuals like Ouandié Ernest, Osende Afana, and others were killed and then erased from the national memory. The best and easiest way to escape responsibility was to become blind to reality and focus on daily living. For to witness, to give an account, one had to watch and take due note of what was going on and process it within one's mind. Who would have carried the burden of such a task for a peanut reward? Why would have people felt concerned about witnessing when memory was not a public issue at all? In a few words, one could not eat a memory for lunch. During that period a kind of collectively privatized mind grew, and that mind is still openly steering along the present day with fatalism and resignation, proclaiming the main goal to be money, money, money. At this point, the question of whether Cameroonian society exists as an organic, conscientious collective subject or just as a collection of individuals gathered by chance is not at all foolish but very provocative, since these alienating forces have driven the fiasco of postindependence. Like a herd of zebu taken to the abattoir, we have accepted our fate without objection. Know that the secret police headquarters in the capital city, Yaoundé, was located on the site, called La Vallée de la Mort, where Germans used to hang those sentenced to the death penalty. We are far from the idea of emancipation borne by independence.

This example alone speaks volumes about what was in the air for so many years in Cameroon. Opposite the white, stocky square building bristling with aerials is a lake dating from 1953. During French colonial times, this lake was meant for nautical leisure, a fad propagated by then–high commissioner Soucadaux. From 1960 till the present day, the lakeside residents have been the Gotha of the regime, though down the hill stands the prime minister's official mansion, also of colonial heritage. The now heavily polluted lake is no longer the *lac municipal* of yesteryear, and all demands from private initiatives to dredge it in order to revamp the site have been consistently denied. So one starts to wonder what use this cloaca could serve in the middle of a school, residential, and administrative area, besides being a free five-star hotel for mosquitoes. After asking if there has been a hidden reason behind this permanent blockage, a terrible conjecture arises and whirls like a cloud of smoke: Was it a dumping site for people who died under torture inside the secret police's headquarters? A creepy gossip is going around on the sly. After twilight only those acquainted with the vicinity dare venture through it. Fear is well known for its negative psychological effects, and it is a path toward depersonalization. Although the majority of the regulations that shaped the former regime were lifted in 1992—thanks to the Berlin Wall's falling down three years earlier and the late François Mitterrand's key speech to African leaders at La Baule—fear is still embedded in Cameroonian society and in its citizens' minds. For a very long time, the flag of apathy has been flapping in the wind, blown by helplessness, and a popular question has been uttered constantly by many in the past two lost decades: "On va alors faire comment?"(Say, how do we manage to get out of this shit?).

Eyes Wide Shut

In a context of uncertainty, anxiety, and scarcity, individuals tend to make pragmatic decisions regarding how they spend money. Buying cement, metal sheets for a roof, or a piece of land for a house are socially regarded as useful—more so than owning a camcorder. Yet if the digital device was committed to generating an earning, to making a living in one way or another, then it would be a useful purchase. Otherwise, it would be perceived as a luxury, a toy at best, a bling-bling commodity. In Cameroon not everyone can afford a camcorder, especially the high-resolution models, which are still expensive locally. Money matters here, and making a choice on what to buy can be a heartbreaking experience. As for becoming an independent information provider, that work is regarded as the duty of journalists, and taking up the position if you were not one would be considered unusual. And if you *furthermore* claimed to be independent, then how would you make a living? Who would pay for your pictures? This question is asked of artists every day in the contemporary art scene and, especially, of those working with video.

From utility to futility, there is more than a letter to go when it comes to the uses of digital devices in Cameroon. Given the low level of political and cultural activism in our country (ranked poor and heavily indebted according to World Bank standards), challenging the monopoly of dominant media is not yet a priority here. The dialectical issue of domination and resistance, for instance, is not at all a part of the local intellectual debate. A vast majority of citizens feel comfortable with CNN, FRANCE 24, BBC, and other global broadcasters—and everything is fine when one is dancing and drinking beer. The very narrow space granted to Africa in these globalized broadcasts is not challenged much, since this black land south of the Sahara is used to being invisible throughout history, as African Americans are described in Ralph Ellison's unique novel *Invisible Man*. In a country where prayer groups and charismatic churches are proliferating like locusts, Almighty God is the *only* relevant solution to the problems crippling our times—the Caretaker by Essence, the One Who Exclusively Matters. God is in fact used as the alibi for irresponsibility and more—for eyes wide shut and ears deeply closed: "I've seen and heard nothing. Please, let me go my own way." In this political, economical, social, and psychological landscape, being a witness, a watcher, a reporter is an engaging position of bravery among reluctant men and women.

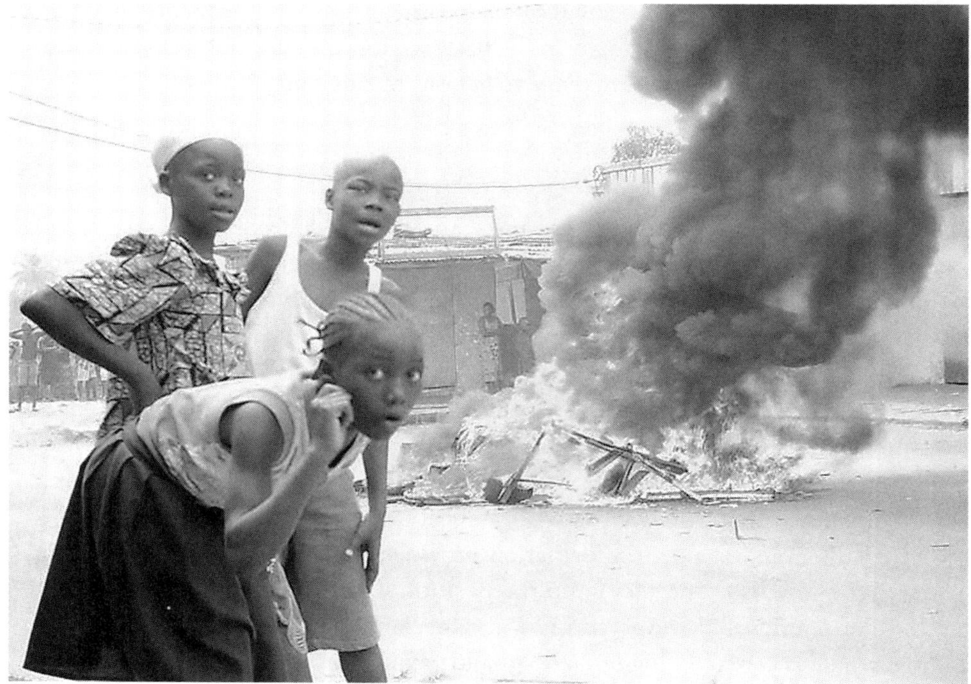

Gazing children, riots in Douala, February 28, 2008, by Patrick Wokmeni. Photograph courtesy of the artist.

No More Fear!

At daybreak on Monday, February 28, 2008, Douala's inhabitants knew that they would have to get on their feet because of the biker and taxi driver strike protesting increased fuel prices. The country was on the brink of the March Parliament session, which was mostly dedicated to the controversial modification of article 6, paragraph 1, in the fundamental law, paving the way for President Paul Biya, seventy-eight years old, to be "reelected" for the third time in a country where the average age is twenty years old. Two days earlier, a meeting on this issue organized by the Social Democratic Front, an influential political party, degenerated into a violent clash when the police tried to break it up. I was living quite far from the center of the city and had to cancel an appointment with some French artists because of the unrest. We were supposed to work together on a piece about the rebellious sixties. When birds started to sing gently at sunrise on that day, nobody imagined what would start a few hours later and last for the next two days, nor was anyone prepared for a breakthrough that would take advantage of a transportation strike.

On that fateful day my neighborhood on the right bank of the Wouri, the estuary river, unexpectedly became one of the Douala riot's hot spots. During

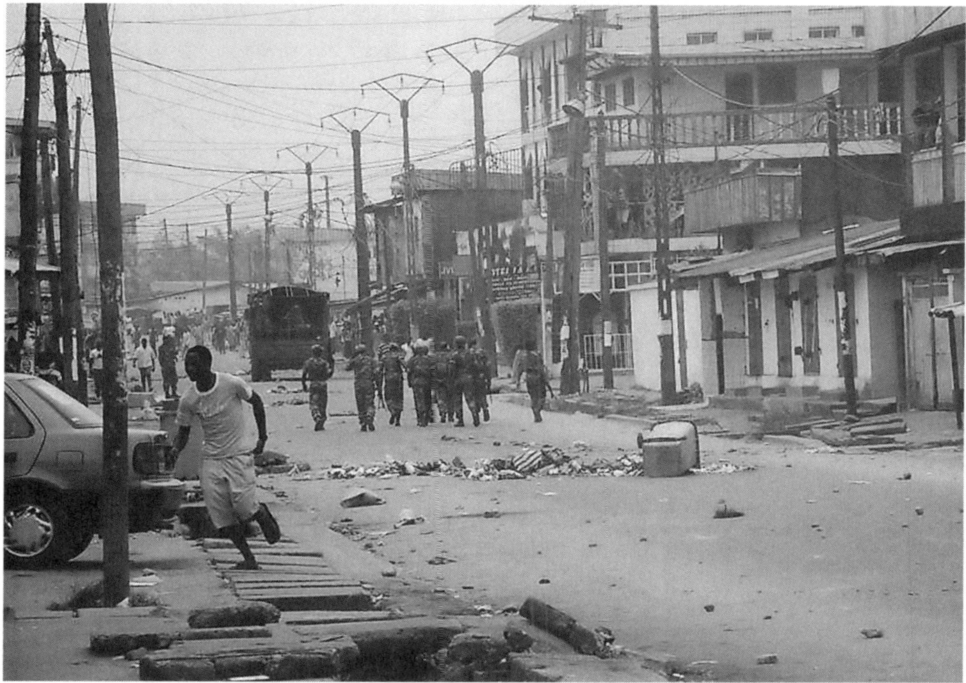

Military squad, riots in Douala, February 28, 2008, by Patrick Wokmeni. Photograph courtesy of the artist.

those two days, my eyes captured images that are now stored only in my mind. I can share them with others, but only in words. I felt so unfortunate not to have a camera! Some of these poetic and amazing images—youths of various ages facing gendarmes in the shelter of a burning barricade and brandishing placards bearing statements like "We are no longer afraid!" and "Paul Biya must go!"— deserved to be preserved, even if by just uploading them to an independent media website. The youths in my neighborhood finally took control of the street and moved from one point to another like a dangerous swarm of hornets. I saw teenagers completely upending four Total and Texaco gas stations as if they were playing some kind of pleasant game. In less than ten minutes, the shop next door was looted, and nothing was left in it. There were many more such scenes that were worth videotaping, and I've never missed a camcorder so much.

Guy's Lesson

In the same surroundings was a village named Bonendale that hosted a group of visual artists, among them Guy Wouété. Not surprisingly, he felt concerned by the events and went out to shoot footage with his digital camcorder as raw material for his future work. Since there were no other means of transportation, he had to walk some three kilometers in the blistering sun to where the riots were happening. In so doing, my young friend was 100 percent in his role as a contemporary artist living in Cameroon, ears and eyes wide open, constantly on the alert. Fees earned from residencies in Europe had allowed him to purchase the necessary equipment. By his own account, this seemingly good idea turned bad within a few minutes. Some of the hornets swept down on him instantly and relieved him of his device in a rude manner. His attempt to join the protest in solidarity was in vain. The youths were not listening to him as they busied themselves as temporary masters of the street. Guy was merely an outsider unfortunate enough to be caught in their territory, and he was fair game. Mobs and gangs—individuals in number—are not reasonable. Guy's camcorder was taken in a cycle of utilitarian appropriation in the face of hunger, riots, and more. My young friend was wise enough to laugh off his misadventure and take it as a lesson, possibly for his future work.

It doesn't take much to create a misunderstanding under such volatile circumstances. From the young rioters' perspective, nourished by envy and frustration, Guy Wouété appeared like one of the fucking happy few that morning, although truly he was not. But a camcorder was a rare commodity on that side of town and in Cameroon in general. It became an incentive to the rioting have-nots. Guy had a toy with which they could make money. Deprivation was the main engine driving their behavior and actions.

Who would report on this silent tragedy of a no-hope generation in 2010, the fiftieth anniversary of independence? Every day is a nightmare for our youth. With no money in their pockets and vain pleas for jobs, they forget about the tenderness and warmth of their families. *Chacun s'assied, et Dieu le pousse,* goes a popular adage on individualism.

Feeling more and more like detritus, these "boys" dream of Whiteland and draw plans every day to undertake a dangerous journey through the Sahara and then, if still alive, across the Mediterranean Sea in order to reach the golden Shangri-La sketched by TV sitcoms. This mythic land is also perpetuated by those who came before them, who although disillusioned by their sojourns, prefer to put on a good show and embellish a reality that is often sordid. The motherland offers nothing, and no one can say they've never tried to make it on their own. So as when a particle meets an antiparticle within the confined field of the Large Hadron Collider, this encounter took place when a team of have-nots came across an isolated have on a wild day. Although he had gathered prizes for his artwork abroad, Guy Wouété's visibility as an artist did not exceed a five-hundred-meter perimeter of his home that day. His assailants knew nothing about him; they saw him as easy prey and not as a supporter of their cause. Unfortunately, this wasn't the appropriate moment to introduce them to each other.

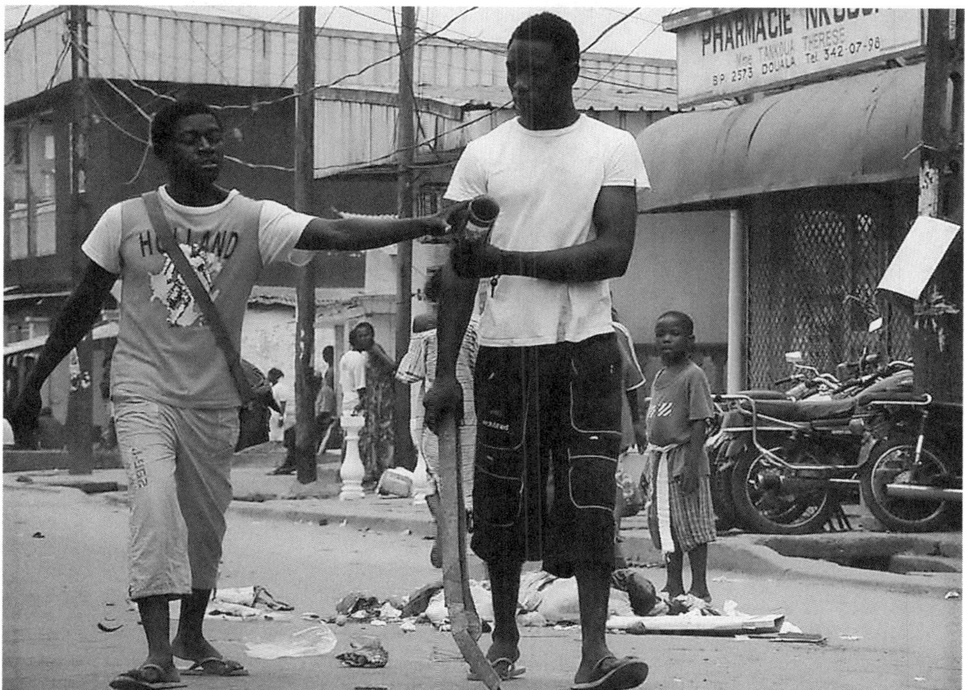

Youngsters, riots in Douala, February 28, 2008, by Patrick Wokmeni. Photograph courtesy of the artist.

Interstitial Monitoring

Visibility helps, and the world can no longer go, of course, without the independent media universe, whose activists sleep with one eye open. Eyewitnesses are needed to gives accounts and provide alternative information and viewpoints. It's a matter of interstitial monitoring supported by a smart infrastructure aimed at being reactive and, even, proactive. It is far from the paradigm of emergency and more a matter of follow-up, of keeping in touch with people and with evolving situations around the world. Local communities should be trained to use these tools within the scope and spirit of self-empowerment much more than for leisure and entertainment. As a matter of fact, before so-called progress came, each village of the Fang-Beti people had its tam-tam, and together, they constituted an efficient communication network. Thus, acquiring this savoir faire has to do with building capacity while raising the level of historical and political consciousness and with revamping the public-spirited mind. There is room for such a prospect given the *enthusiasm* among young people for digital devices such as camcorders.

When Patrick Wokmeni was twenty-three, he lived in New-Bell, a suburb of

Douala. He hung around with his peers jobless but, in 2006, caught a serious case of the photography bug. Since then, he has been shooting with his digital camera. In February 2008 he went out to make some images in his neighborhood. He was operating in his own territory, and nobody harmed him. Intruders were never welcome there; they were always persona non grata. Some of his pictures appear in my book *L'ivresse du papillon,* a transversal narrative of contemporary Cameroon published in October 2008.

Challenging the global order of information and giving the local and grassroots-based communities an ongoing opportunity for visibility is a long battle toward emancipation, and it echoes the golden jubilee commemoration of 2010 in Africa. Since going to Ghana and Mali to attend workshops and exhibit his work, Patrick has become the pride of his *kwat* (neighborhood). On the one hand, he is now part of the "travelers"—leaving the country for the first time and then again in the same year—and he has the social status that comes with it, while most people here are trapped in immobility. On the other hand, he definitely now is a part of his surroundings' décor, with his small camera gathering images night and day, building up his subjects. This young photographer of Nguangué (New-Bell) is living proof that the communication gap is not at all an unchanging condition. Challenging it will take us as human beings to the next level of global consciousness. And I say let's go far beyond bridges and borders! This was our leitmotiv in Rotterdam in September 2009, during the two weeks' itinerant residency Talking About, with Goddy Leye, Alexander Vollebregt, Emiliano Gandolfi, Lucia Babina, Zoë Gray, and other artists and curators, on the theme "I'm Public." Being public is being a witness, a watcher—it is a responsibility. In these controversial times of climate change and market chaos, we more than ever need witnesses to monitor the interstices and testify far and wide.

Contemporary Korean Video Art after Nam June Paik

Hea Jeong Lee

Translated by Doryun Chong

Videodrome versus Video Art

Fredric Jameson has suggested that cinema in the era of postcapitalism and postmodernism conveys a political unconscious, and to recognize this is the core of his film criticism. Indeed, much of his work on films such as *Jaws* (1975) and *The Godfather* (1972) demonstrates the political unconscious as an ideological apparatus in Hollywood blockbuster films, while he performs a simultaneous reading of these films in the private sphere from a Freudian perspective, as well as in the social and ideological spheres from a Marxist one. *Geopolitical Aesthetic: Cinema and Space in the World System* (1992)—a collection of essays from the 1980s and early 1990s that interpret cinema and the mass media from a combination of Marxist-Freudian theories developed in his earlier book *The Political Unconscious* (1981)—analyzes *Videodrome* (1983) and *Three Days of the Condor* (1975), contemporary films that deal with conspiracy.

Videodrome* is a work by Toronto-based director David Cronenberg and addresses a range of issues including the conflict between a petty capitalist and a multinational corporation, late capitalism via technology and media, the third world, religion, and gender.[1] In its representation of technology, *Videodrome*'s depiction of its subject matter is frighteningly similar to 1960s media theorist Marshal McLuhan's prediction that television would become an extension of the human. In its various scenes, ranging from the allegorical sexual act in which the abdomen of the porn channel owner, played by James Wood, becomes a gaping hole where a videotape is inserted to the scene of a man monstrously transforming into a television after watching a soul-corrupting snuff video, *Videodrome* poses questions to viewers from a distinctly techno-pessimist point of view. One year before *Videodrome* was released, video artist Nam June Paik, one of the early adaptors of the then-new genre, euthanized his *Robot K-456*—a quasi human with whom he had lived for twenty years. As if echoing his shocking antiestablishment performances from the past, the death of the robot was a rite of farewell, a traffic accident as an intentional death.² Focusing on these aspects, we can see both examples as tragic products of the sublimity of new technologies; Cronenberg's *Videodrome* shows the fetishization of the human in its exploration through the powerful visual apparatus of the horror film genre and of transformations in the media and the human body, whereas *Robot K-456* was the cyborg of a paradoxical destiny that received both life and death from Paik, its creator and mother.

The birth and death of Paik's *Robot K-456* is reminiscent of the artist's declaration that he used "machines to fight machines."³ Although the euthanized robot—perhaps standing in for machine technology—exhausted its life span and its existential meaning, it returns, as in the Buddhist belief in the cycle of life and death, to Paik's own work, as well as to Korean artists of younger generations, in the form of the unconscious—one that in particular affects the minds of exiles dreaming of their homeland.

Nam June Paik's Unconscious versus Nam June Paik as the Unconscious

On January 29, 2006, Nam June Paik died in Miami, Florida. Paik, as an Asian artist, left a mark in Western art history as the father of video art—a genre that emerged in the United States and Europe in the 1960s and 1970s. From his birth in Korea in 1932 until his departure in 1950, Paik was situated in the vortex of political history. He was the youngest son in the first *chaebol* (corporate) family in Korea. Marxism—a fad among intellectuals at the time—enthralled Paik in his youth, but he left Korea as the country descended into the Korean War. In a way, he decided on his own future as an adolescent in the battlefield of an extremely Confucian society and in the geopolitical location of Korea. Whether it was conscious or not, Paik's early experience of the unstable circumstances of his homeland turned him into an artistic nomad. One could say that this was a fortunate turn of events for him.

While war is the most visible manifestation of American dominance in the 1940s and 1950s, American art, beginning with abstract expressionism, similarly dominated the international art world during this period. War transforms the world and the peoples of the world. During World War I and World War II, many European artists migrated to North America and left their mark in the U.S. art world. The Korean War, which Paik experienced as a sensitive youth, must have left an indelible impression on him as a historical event. This historical situation of war in his homeland must have influenced, subconsciously, the art and ontology of Nam June Paik. The artist, who departed from the unstable Korean peninsula—to this day, the only divided country in the world—traveled beyond the traditional, quotidian medium of the canvas and headed toward the new electronic medium of television and ultimately returned to a still-divided Korea via satellite in 1984 during a period of sudden political change.

Paik's homecoming is reminiscent of an experience that caused Lu Xun, a pioneer of modern Chinese literature, to return to his country. A short time after the birth of cinema, Lu, while studying medicine in Japan, watched a film that showed Japanese soldiers beheading captured Chinese spies. The "visual shock" of this experience made Lu realize that changing the consciousness of Chinese people was far more urgent than taking care of their physical bodies.[4] In a similar move, more than thirty years after his departure from his homeland, Paik returned with video art—the cutting-edge artistic gift that impressed his oeuvre on the soil of his country. The political and cultural situation at the time, however, relegated Paik to a realm of the subconscious for the time being.

Although Paik was an internationally famous artist, his medium of video was an unfamiliar technology in the Korean art world of the 1980s. The color television was just being introduced to Korea in 1980. In addition, Korea's unstable political condition in the wake of the 1960s and 1970s military regime, coupled with conservative pedagogy at its art schools, created a situation in which there was not much freedom for artists to experiment with nontraditional media such as video and TV. Korean art in the 1980s was divided, in large part, into two camps—monochrome painting and *minjoong* (people's) art. With the exception of a small number of experimental artists such as Park Hyun-gi and Yook Tae-jin, there were not many artists in Korea consistently engaged with video in their art practice during the 1970s and 1980s.[5] The Korean art world was not in a state to welcome or accept the international avant-garde, let alone a new art form that utilized the contemporary technologies of television and satellite. In the 1980s the challenging sociopolitical and material environment established the Western-educated Paik as an object of emulation and, perhaps, envy. These feelings, subsumed in the collective subconscious of the Korean art world, has broken through and surfaced in the contemporary Korean art scene.

White Cube versus Black Box

The 1988 Summer Olympic Games in Seoul, Korea, were broadcasted throughout the world. The geopolitical position of Korea was refashioned in the 1990s as a global forerunner in information technology thanks to the democratic change of government and open-door policy instituted in the 1990s.[6] Media art began to evolve fast thanks to the emergence of a younger generation who had set the stage for a new era of computers, the Internet, mobile phones, and film culture. The increasing accessibility of technologies such as digital cameras, mobile phones, and computers provided a foundation for the output of diverse digital media art forms, including video art.

Since Nam June Paik was first introduced to Korea through his satellite-transmitted video *Good Morning Mr. Orwell* in 1984, Korean video art's lineage has included artists such as Park Hyun-gi and Yook Tae-jin in the 1980s and Yook Geun-byung, who participated in the Documenta IX exhibition in the early 1990s. Their works primarily took the form of video installations. Playing a catalytic role in this situation was the first Seoul International Media Art Biennale in 2000. From that point until the establishment of the Nam June Paik Art Center in 2008, the development of media art following Paik's transmission has grown to encompass a range of expressions including video sculpture, video installation, interactive art, Web art, mobile art, and sound art, all on a variegated topography of media cultures.[7] In reality, however, single-channel video still constitutes the mainstay of Korean media art, and screenings of these videos in movie theaters constitute the main venue for this spread of moving image.[8] In this context the term *moving image* can encompass a wide range of media practices, ranging from the existential reflections on cinema from Paik's Fluxus period to the cinematic experiences of single-channel video artists, who have been active in Korea, as well as overseas, since the 2000s.[9] This term also implies that these artists have departed from the white cube of the gallery or museum and have entered the black box of the theater and the cinema.

In early 2009 Jung Yeondoo's *Documentary Nostalgia* (2007) entered the collection of the Museum of Modern Art (MoMA) in New York. This eighty-five-minute video was only the second by a Korean artist after Nam June Paik to enter the MoMA's video collection. For most artists, to be collected by or exhibited in this museum—one of the most influential in the global contemporary art world—is a dream come true. MoMA began its life playing the roles of both a white cube and a black box. This was almost entirely thanks to its founding director, Alfred H. Barr Jr., who actively pursued the establishment of the film library in 1932. In 1935 MoMA formed its film archive.[10] Around this time the theorist Walter Benjamin was writing about the then-new medium of cinema in Germany. In the United States, Erwin Panofsky, an art historian well known for his study of iconography and an advisor in the establishment of the film department at MoMA, lectured on the "spatialization and dynamism of time-space" in cinema.[11] Furthermore, with the launch of its videotape collection in 1975, MoMA has been collecting diverse media since the 1970s.[12]

Nam June Paik was one of the first artistic warriors to break out of the gallery's white cube and into the cinematic black box. Paik first learned about Schoenberg from composer Lee Geon-wu, who studied Western avant-garde music in the 1940s. He was also fond of the work of Yi Sang, the Korean avant-garde poet. Around the time when Paik held his first solo exhibition during his Fluxus period, *Exposition of Music—Electronic Television*, in 1963,[13] he was thinking deeply about the existential form of cinema. In 1964 he made *Zen for Film*.[14]

Using a Sony Portapak, he made his first videotape, *Button Happening,* in 1965.[15] In the same year, following a meeting with Jud Yalkut, a member of the USCO media art collective and a film director, Paik collaborated with him on several film works. He also participated in New Cinema Festival (Expanded Cinema Festival) at the Film Makers' Cinematheque run by Jonas Mekas.[16] In 1970 he cotaught the history of video with Gene Youngblood, the author of *Expanded Cinema* (1970), at the California Institute of the Arts—further evidence of his engagement with avant-garde film and of his interest in cinema.

Private Memories versus Documentaries of Public Memories

The majority of contemporary Korean single-channel video artists are engaged with the exploration of both private and public memories. The reconstruction of private, everyday realities and memories constitutes a dominant concern among young artists and has become a characteristic aspect in contemporary art making in Korea. The division of Korea is a reality that in particular resonates as a repressed memory with artists of the so-called 386 Generation, who attended college in the 1980s.

Park Chan-kyong is perhaps the most prominent among contemporary artists who engage with public memories in their work. Park's *Flying* (2005), screened at the Oberhausen Short Film Festival, addresses the first summit meeting between the two Koreas in 2000—almost five decades after the Korean War. In Park's video then-president Kim Dae-joong and his team are shown flying in North Korean air space on a newly opened direct route between North and South Korea. Park's ten-minute video is edited from never-broadcast footage of the North Korean landscape shot by the reporters on the plane from Seoul to Pyongyang. Although the actual flight time to Pyongyang was an hour, the memory of the Cold War and the traumatic division of the two Koreas compressed those fifty years since the division into ten minutes of video. The video also presents a dreamlike, slow-motion image of the welcoming party of North Korean women, dressed in traditional Korean *hanbok* and waving red decorative flowers in their hands. This image may be familiar to the older generation who experienced the trauma, but for younger generations it would appear as a highly exoticized image.

The most notable element of *Flying* is its sound track, modern composer Yoon Isang's Double Concerto for Oboe, Harp, and Chamber Orchestra (1977). This composition by Yoon, who died in exile in Germany with the trauma of the divided Koreas in his heart, stirs the Korean listener's soul. This concerto is based on the mythological tale of two lovers, Gyeonu and Jiknyeo, who have been banished by a king to the opposite sides of the Milky Way but are allowed to see each other once a year on a bridge formed by birds taking pity on their sad fate;

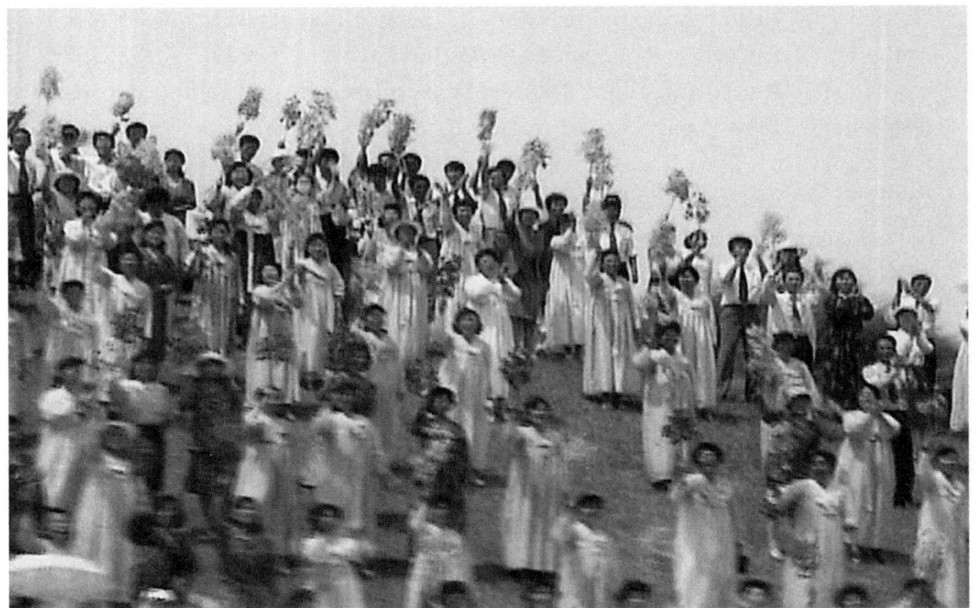

Park Chan-Kyong, *Flying,* 2005. Two-channel video, 13 minutes. Courtesy of the artist and PKM Gallery and Bartleby Bickle & Meaursault.

the story adds a sense of pathos to Park's video and its narrative of a country's division. The video gives form to a dreamlike reality—a meeting of the heads of North and South Korea—that actually took place.

Park, who studied photography with Allan Sekula at CalArts, had his first solo exhibition, *Black Box: Memory of Cold War Images,* in 1997. He works primarily in photography and video. In 2003 he published a book of photography, *Koreans Who Went to Germany: A Record of Korean Miners and Nurses,* that exhibits a strong influence from Sekula. After *Flying,* in 2008 Park completed *Sindoan,* the artist's most cinematic work to date.[17] *Sindoan,* the result of two years' research into a Korean historical site, could be interpreted as Park's move out of the gallery's white cube and into the cinematic black box. In this work Park performs a time-space travel from the time of the Korean War in the early 1950s to the Joseon dynasty, which ruled from 1392 to 1897, from the geopolitical space of Pyongyang to Sindoan, near Mt. Gyeryong, which is known as a sacred site for numerous traditional folk religions and new religions, as well.

Since Lee Seong-gye, the founder of the Joseon dynasty, originally sited his capital at Sindoan Koreans have gathered there whenever there was a crisis in the country, such as during the Japanese Invasion of the Imjin Year (1592–98), the Japanese rule of Korea (1910–45), and the Korean War (1950–53).[18] From the period of Japanese rule to the mid-1980s, hundreds of religious organizations proliferated in Sindoan. Numerous people dreaming of a new utopia settled there, relying on their faith and religious beliefs at important historical turning points. In 1984, amid the military dictatorship of Chun Doo-hwan (and when Nam June Paik returned to Korea via satellite in a video art piece that named author George Orwell in its title), Sindoan became the site of the Gyerong Joint Military Headquarters. Consequently, most of its residents and religious organizations disappeared.

Park's search of these forgotten histories begins with found footage of television interviews related to the site conducted by a broadcasting company in 1997, which are then replaced by a surreal array of imagery, including the artist's own moving image, computer graphics, and animation, resulting in a raw experimental film. *Sindoan* consists of six chapters titled, in order, "Samsindang," "Yong-ga Moo-do," "Group Photographs," "Shichun-ju," "Kubera," and "Yoencheon Hill in Gyeryong Mountain." The color images of television interviews in the beginning of the video suddenly change into black-and-white photographs. The scene in which an airplane—a symbol of modernity—suddenly appears in the sky is followed by the black-and-white image of a two-story brick building turning into a color image. Like a surgeon examining inside the patient's body, the camera carefully observes and shows the interior of this building's architecture. In a similar manner, the black-and-white images of the Sindoan of the past transform into color images of Sindoan in the present in other parts of the work, and through such processes *Sindoan* traverses the modern history of Korea.

Sindoan incorporates images of diverse religious practices, including the "superstitions" of the past and new religious symbols such as Moosang Temple, an international Zen temple for foreign devotees. Even the Sri Lankan god Kubera is included in the work. *Sindoan*'s treatment of diverse religions can be likened to the Korean dish *bibimbap*.[19] And at certain points in the video, this religious plurality overtakes the narrative. One such moment is in the sixth chapter, which shows a recording of a performance by art students that was inserted into the film to create a jarring disruption of its narrative documentary style up to that point.

What is particularly interesting in *Sindoan* is the discolored propaganda signboards of various religious organizations captured by Park's camera, which are reminiscent of the signboards of restaurants populating the streets everywhere in contemporary Korea. Viewers sense that religion, often referred to as food for the spirit, can become a refined taste; just as overeating or excessive dieting can cause our bodies to break down, religion can become the cause of our spiritual illness.[20] Even today, Korean politicians often visit fortune-tellers during an election season, and many Koreans rely on fortune-telling—a paradox of human consciousness highlighted by the film.

Another example of how contemporary Korean video artists explore the relationship between Korean history and its geopolitical sites can be seen in the group exhibition *Dongducheon: A Walk to Remember, a Walk to Envision.*[21] The exhibition was about Dongducheon, a small city located between Seoul and the Korean Demilitarized Zone, and it set out to reclaim some of the histories and memories of the city's population of 88,000, half of whom have lived under occupation by a foreign military power since the end of Japanese rule. The artists in the exhibition—Go Seung-wook, Kim Sang-don, Noh Jae-oon, and siren eun young jung—made single-channel documentary videos based on interviews with local citizens.

The method of reclaiming public memory through interviews in these artists' videos has been a part of the expansion of public art in Korea, one of the diverse changes that has occurred in the Korean art world during the twenty-first century. During this time participatory public art projects involving local citizens have commonly utilized the documentary format. Siren eun young jung, the only female artist in *Dongducheon,* has long addressed women and gender issues in her work. The global character of Dongducheon has long been a subject of intellectual exploration among Korean women artists. As an American military camp town, the existence of the town has been a taboo subject in Korean society. In particular, the lives of women who work in Dongducheon have been misrepresented for a long time. For this exhibition siren eun young jung presented a single-channel video, *The Narrow Sorrow* (2008), in which she recorded different location sounds and voices, such as the chatter of migrant night club workers on the street and their seductive singing, and added them to the sound track of the work.

Cho Hye-jeong has also been making works about female immigrants and migrant workers as mothers and grandmothers. In 2005 she made a documentary film titled *Little Chicago, Dongducheon* about Ha Seon-ae, a woman who lived and worked in the camp town for almost thirty years.[22] In 2008 Cho studied her own hometown, Naegok-Ri, for a year and made a documentary, *From Dust to Dust: Chronicles of Women in Naegok-Ri, Kyungsang Province,* about a group of old women who had the same last name as herself. Her film *What They Remember from the Lost* (2009) addresses deeply rooted political and social problems through exploring her personal pain of losing her friends and the unprecedented historical incident of ex-president Roh Moo-hyun's suicide. *What They Remember from the Lost* combines handmade 16 mm and 8 mm films through a digital process. Her process includes intentional scratching of the film that produces an effect reminiscent of 1920s European avant-garde film, which together with black-and-white images of *What They Remember from the Lost* adds a material formalism to her representation of the past.

Whereas Cho's work integrates private and public memories, enclosing private stories within historical spaces, Jung Yeondoo's work addresses everyday landscapes and stories about communication among ordinary people. Beginning with *Hero* in 1998, Jung made the *Hope* series of projects, which includes

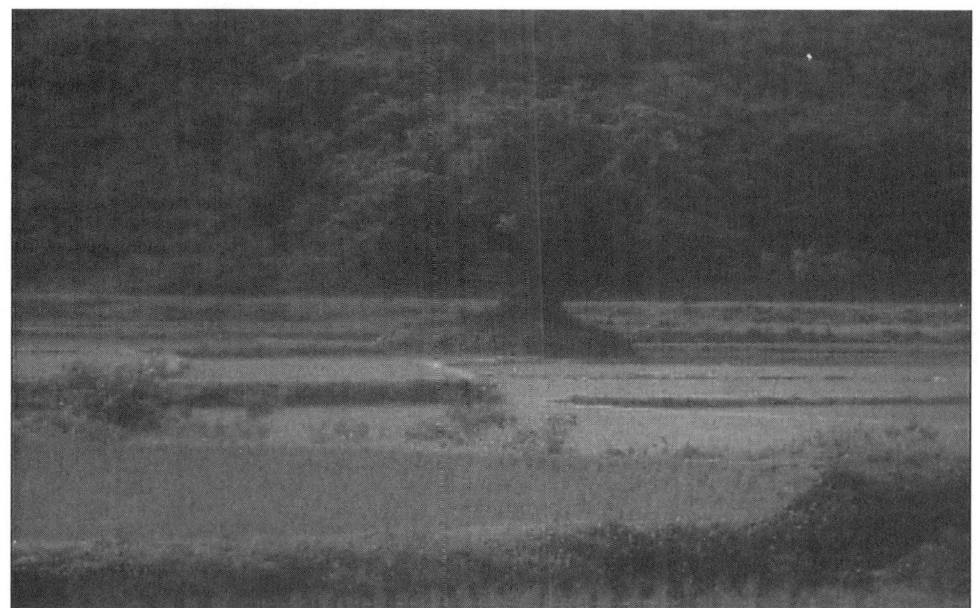

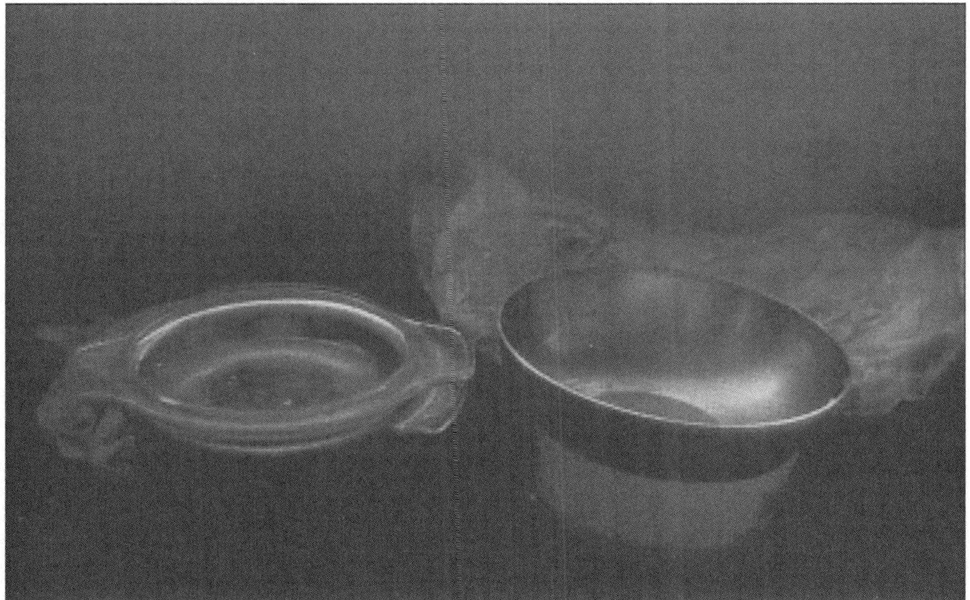

Still from *From Dust to Dust: Chronicles of Women in Naegok-Ri, Kyungsang Province,* 2008, video by Cho Hye-jeong. Photographs courtesy of the artist.

Borame Dance Hall (2001), *Bewitched* (2003), and *Wonderland* (2005). In these works Jung realizes individuals' unrealizable dreams through photography. His 2007 photographic series *Locations,* which presents foregrounded figures against scenery that is used in stage plays, TV dramas, and films, is an appropriation of the cinematic apparatus, suggested also by the series' title. His work *Documentary Nostalgia,* presented as a part of MoMA's Modern Mondays program, is an eighty-four-minute video in one continuous shot. Consisting of six scenes of everyday landscapes, such as the inside of a room, a country road, an alleyway, and mountains, the video records all the action that takes place at these locations, including scene changes, manipulating the camera only for exposure and focus adjustments.

In Jung's *Hanging Garden* (2008), a newscaster familiar to the Korean public narrates a fictional scenario. Borrowing from the format of the Korean television show *History Special,* this work takes the form of a fictional history program. In the video the Gyeongbok Palace is shot from the rooftop of the former Defense Security Command Complex while the history of the palace garden is recounted.[23] Jung's most recent work, *Cinemagician* (2009), was staged at the Asia Society in New York. This live event, with the participation of Lee Eun-gyeol—a new-generation magician popular among many Koreans—combined magic and performance with an interactive video projected onto a big screen above the stage where the magician performed. What is especially interesting is that Jung's *Cinemagician* is reminiscent of Georges Méliès's famous film *A Trip to the Moon* (1902). Méliès was a magician before he started making film, and Jung got the idea for the title of his performance from a film in which Méliès is called a "cinema magician."[24] In a similarly synergistic manner, Jung directed and staged the performance in *Cinemagician* as a media maker.

The crux of *Cinemagician* is that the narrative of Jung's story unfolds on a stage set, and he shows all that takes place on the set, whereas in most cinematic narratives the production processes are concealed to make the image appear realistic. In *Cinemagician* Jung utilizes the façade of the stage to let the audience enjoy the magic tricks while they simultaneously experience the actual mise-en-scène as a live, moving image. Jung studied sculpture in Korea and at Goldsmith College in London. Even though he never formally studied photography and film, his appropriation of cinematic apparatuses in his work warrants particular attention.

Animation as Moving Image

In 1997, in a gesture toward restoring the relationship between Korea and Japan, the Korean government lifted a long-standing ban on Japanese cultural products, including anime.[25] Furthermore, as the Korean government's policy of

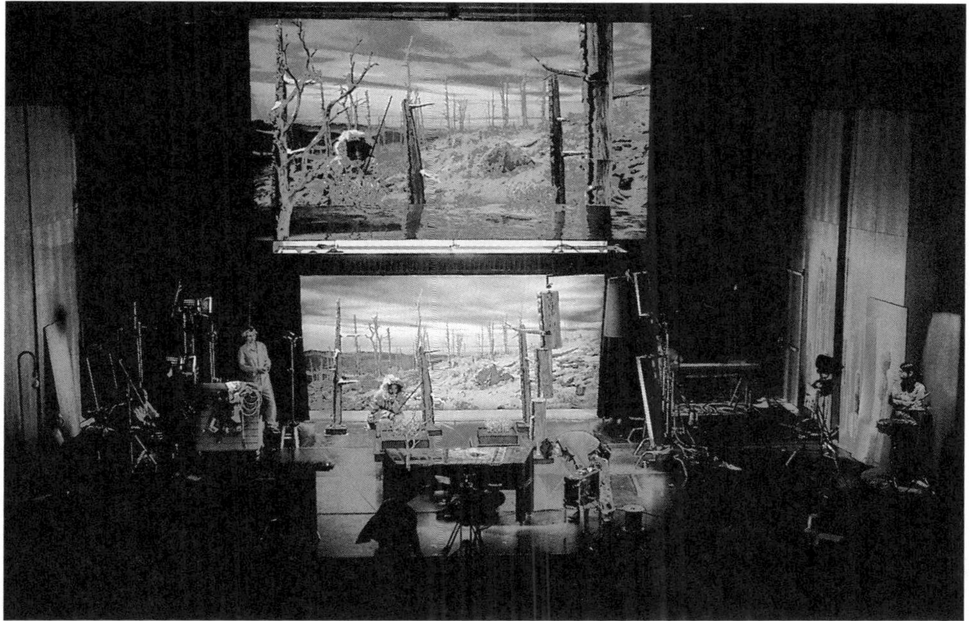

Still from Jung Yeondoo, *CineMagician,* 2010. Digital video, 55 minutes. Performance at Marry Hall in Seoul as a part of Festival Bom. Photograph courtesy of the artist.

promoting moving image cultures critically contributed to the development of domestic film and animation industries, artistic expressions by the new generation of moving image makers have extended into the field of animation and have produced diverse works and exhibitions.

Around this time, the surge of Japanese pop art led by Takashi Murakami, itself a reference to anime, also influenced the art of animation itself.[26] In 2007 Murakami created a short animation, *Planting the Seeds,* and a music video for Kanye West, *Good Morning,* which blended live action and animation, and he included them in his solo exhibition at the Museum of Contemporary Art in Los Angeles. Murakami also made other short animation works that crossed between art and popular culture, such as *Superflat First Love* for Louis Vuitton in 2009.

Drawing experimental cartoon images since his university days in the late 1980s, artist Lee Donggi fused the animation character Astro Boy from 1993 with Mickey Mouse, creating his own character, Atomaus.[27] Regarded as the progenitor of pop art in Korea, Lee created a short animation about the adventures of Atomaus in 1999. Born in a generation who spent their childhood and adolescent years in the 1970s and 1980s and grew up watching American Mickey Mouse and Japanese Astro Boy cartoons, Lee fuses the everyday culture of his childhood into his art. As such, the everyday life of a Korean youth from this period has become, in an organic way, Lee's inspiration. The Korean government's interest in visual media starting in 1997 and the twenty-first-century worldwide anime trend, led by artists like Murakami, have also contributed to the popularity of contemporary animation works.

Kim Hye-ran, who has been active in making animation since her college years in the mid-1990s—before animation became popular in Korea—has made works such as *A Certain Fear* (1998) and *Cabbage Heads* (2007). Shon Kim, who studied experimental animation at the California Institute of the Arts, lives and works in Los Angeles.[28] He has won many awards at film festivals, and his practice involves diverse forms of animation. His animated drawing *Latent Sorrow* (2005), which explores an encounter between abstraction and figuration, is part of his *Moving Painting* series. Recently, Kim's *Hemorrhage* (2009) won Best Video Art and Computer Art Film at the 2009 Asolo Art Film Festival in Italy. Kim's animation notably emphasizes sound as it combines with image. *Hemorrhage* features the voice of Spanish singer Araki, effectively conveying ambiguity as well as intensity. Araki's vocal performance creates strange, unfamiliar sounds that complement the fluid transformation process of abstract images in Shon Kim's work, functioning to strengthen its visual impact.

Lee Lee-nam, a beneficiary of the mentioned governmental policy, initially studied sculpture but moved into making claymation and then ran a commercial animation company. Thanks to the booming domestic art market and the popularity of Korean artists at international art fairs, Lee has been concentrating on making single-channel works. His representative work, *The Conversation between Monet and Sochi* (2009), is a series of encounters between traditional Chinese ink painting and classical Western painting. These works from the distinct time-spaces of East and West meet one another not on the canvas but on the screen. Just as *animation,* in the etymological sense, means endowing a still image with life, Monet's *Sunrise* and Sochi's *Autumn Landscape* are reborn as a new work on the digital monitor screen. In a collaborative project with Samsung Electronics, Lee inserted semiconductor chips into 5,000 LED television monitors so that ordinary television viewers could enjoy media art at home. This project, another example of expanded thinking about public art in Korea, utilizes the possibilities of media art to communicate with the public.

Beyond Nam June Paik

The Media City Seoul Biennale, an influential force in Korea's media art culture since the introduction of Nam June Paik, is now a decade old. This cultural event, a product of the encounter between the local (Seoul) and the global (international art world), has emphasized communication with the public and has highlighted the presentation of interactive artworks. With their focus on exhibiting interactive works in which the audience must stand in front of the artwork to activate the sensor or move the mouse and touch the keyboard to complete the artwork, the biennial is often criticized for placing public interaction over artistic factors.

Nonetheless, from relatively accessible single-channel videos to interactive artworks that require sophisticated technology and engineering, Korean media art continues to develop and evolve. Since the introduction of Paik's video art in 1984, there has been no other moment like the present, when so many diverse artists are expressing themselves and their artistic sensibilities through technology and media. We could characterize this as the result of a zeitgeist ushered in by the fusion of art and technology in the digital age. If we presume that this zeitgeist forms one axis of the consciousness that has materialized in contemporary Korean media art, then the other is Nam June Paik, who was repressed by the political and historical realities of Korea's past. We are now witnessing a return of the repressed in which Paik, as the artistic subconscious, breaks through our digital age consciousness and emerges as a part of this zeitgeist. If the younger generation, exemplified by Lee Lee-nam, transcended analog image making—exemplified by Paik's magnetized television sets—through their embracing of the twenty-first-century technologies of digital video and animation, then Paik, the pioneer of video, becomes an inalienable historical existence, a giant on whose shoulders younger artists are standing. This imparts a particular significance to the opening of the Nam June Paik Art Center, the main venue for research on the pioneering spirit and free philosophical thinking of an artistic nomad who, for a large part of his life, longed for his homeland and is now longed for by it.[29]

NOTES

1. Fredric Jameson, *Geopolitical Aesthetic: Cinema and Space in the World System* (Indianapolis: Indiana University Press, 1992), 22–35.

2. Examples of Paik's performances include *Exposition of Music—Electronic Television* (1963), in which he hung a dead cow head, an object featured in some Korean traditional religious rituals, at the entrance to a gallery, and *Etude for Pianoforte* (1960), in which he destroyed a piano.

3. Judson Rosebush, ed., *Video 'n' Videology 1959–73*, exhibition catalog (New York: Everson Museum of Art, 1974), 12.

4. In her book *Primitive Passions: Visuality, Sexuality, Ethnography, and Contemporary Chinese Cinema* (New York: Columbia University Press, 1995), Rey Chow discusses this visual experience of Lu Xun before delving into her analysis of contemporary Chinese cinema. Her discussion resonates with Walter Benjamin's "The Work of Art in the Age of Mechanical Reproduction." In the essay Benjamin argues that the rapid change of scenes in cinema stimulates the human visual unconscious to cause a "visual shock," and by way of this argument, he foregrounds the problem of visuality in modernity. Jole Snyder, "Benjamin on

Reproducibility and Aura: A Reading of 'The Work of Art in the Age of Its Technical Reproducibility,'" in *Benjamin: Philosophy, History, Aesthetics,* ed. Gary Smith. (Chicago: University of Chicago Press, 1989), 158–74.

5. Park Hyun-gi (b. 1942) began making video art in the 1970s and was the first artist in Korea to use the medium. He died in 2000, and his first retrospective exhibition was held at the Gallery Hyundai in Seoul from March 9 to 28, 2010. See www.eyeball.or.kr. Yook Tae-jin (1961–2008) began making video art in the 1980s.

6. As mentioned, since the fall of the Berlin Wall in 1989 and the formal reunification of Germany in 1990, Korea has remained the only divided country in the world.

7. Nam June Paik Art Center is located in Yong-In, in the province of Gyeonggi, near Seoul.

8. I feel it is necessary to discuss Nam June Paik's and many others' video art in the larger context of the moving image. According to its definition in the United Kingdom, moving image studies is a vast field that can encompass Paik's magnet-distorted TV sets and synthesizer-generated images, as well as videos shot with camcorders and produced via digital media, commercial films, and even YouTube videos. Notable publications on the topic include Tanya Leighton, ed., *Art and the Moving Image: A Critical Reader* (London: Tate Publishing, 2009); and Stuart Comer, ed., *Film and Video Art* (London: Tate Publishing, 2008).

9. The first artist's film in Korea was *A Meaning of 1/24 Second* (16 mm film, 1969) by the avant-garde pioneer Kim Gu-rim. The film is a highly personal, documentary-style recording of everyday stories from the artist's surroundings at the time.

10. Thomas Y. Levin, "Iconology at the Movies: Panofsky's Film Theory," in *The Visual Turn: Classic Film Theory and Art History,* ed. Angela Dalle Vacch (New Brunswick, N.J.: Rutgers University Press, 2003): 85.

11. Ibid., 85–86. Levin argues that Panofsky's lecture "On Movies," presented in Princeton University in 1934 and the Metropolitan Museum of Art in 1936, entered the realm of public debate when it was reported on in the *New York Herald Tribune* (November 16, 1936) in the article "Films Are Treated as Real Art by Lecturer at Metropolitan" and that this marked the occasion in which film was endowed with its placement in the New York art world.

12. Barbara London, "Video: A Selected Chronology, 1963–1983," *Art Journal* 45 (Fall 1985): 257.

13. Before going to New York, Nam June Paik had a solo exhibition of magnetized TV sets at Parnas Gallery, Germany, March 11–20, 1963. This is regarded as the first video art exhibition in history. Wolf Vostel, another member of Fluxus, viewed Paik's exhibition before he opened his exhibition, titled *Television Decollage,* on May 23, 1963, in New York.

14. *Zen for Film* (1962–64, 8 min.) consists of unexposed 16 mm film leader being run through a projector. It is a reflection of the philosophy of Zen Buddhism, which emphasizes meditation. The work can be seen as an element in Paik's existential exploration of cinema.

15. *Button Happening* (1965, 2 min.) was recently restored and screened at the Nam June Paik Art Center.

16. Howard Junker, "The Underground Renaissance," *Nation,* December 27, 1965, http://www.brockman.com/press/text/1965.12.27.Nation.pdf. The festival also included artists such as Andy Warhol and Robert Rauschenberg.

17. *Sindoan* was shot in HD film, and its running time is forty-five minutes. Park, the younger brother of director Park Chan-wook, made the work with support from Hermès Korea after receiving the 2004 Hermès Korea Art Prize, which was included in his solo exhibition at the Atelier Hermès in Seoul. The Park brothers recently made the short film *Night Fishing* and won the 2011 Berlin International Film Festival. This film was shot using an iPhone.

18. The capital was ultimately established in Seoul.

19. *Bibimbap* is a Korean dish of rice mixed with different kinds of vegetables and meat.

20. In *Gyerong Mountain* (1969), a feature film by Lee Gang-cheon made at the same location during the regime of the military dictator Park Chung-hee, a male character tells the female protagonist that she should go to Gyerong Mountain in order to cure her adultery. This is another example of how religion perceives women only through sexuality and supposed primitivity—which makes it the cause of human spiritual illness.

21. This exhibition of Korean artists opened in May 2008 at the New Museum of Contemporary Art in New York.

22. See the artist's web page, http://hyejeongcho.com.

23. The Defense Security Command Complex (Gimusa, in Korean)—recently designated as a modern cultural heritage site—has been the center of heated debates. The National Museum of Contemporary Art, which has long been criticized for its distance from Seoul and limited accessibility, is planning to open a branch at the site of Gimusa in 2013. The opening of the new branch is expected to have a significant impact on the contemporary Korean art scene.

24. The documentary DVD on Méliès's film, *Landmarks of Early Film, Volume 2: The Magic of Méliès* (Image Entertainment), includes a section titled "Cinema Magician."

25. The popularity of anime has produced anime *otaku* (fan) cultures around the world. Many of the Korean artists in their thirties and forties belong to the generation that was exposed to anime during their youth. For instance, the internationally active Korean artist Lee Bul's *Cyborg* series, which was exhibited at the 1997 Venice Biennale, was inspired in part by images of disassemblage and deconstruction of bodies seen in anime, such as Oshii Mamoru's *Ghost in the Shell* (1995). Hea-Jeong Lee, *Contemporary Art and Japanese Animation: Analysis of Cyborg of Lee Bul, Mori Mariko, and Takashi Murakami* (Seoul: Art in Culture, 2002), 78–89.

26. Murakami is also an anime fan himself and had wanted to be an animator. Instead, he is realizing his anime dreams in his artwork. See Amada Cruz, Dana Friis Hansen, and Midori Matsui, *Takashi Murakami: The Meaning of the Nonsense of the Meaning* (New York: Center for Curatorial Studies Museum, Bard College, in association with H. N. Abrams, 1999).

27. See his website, www.atomaus.com, and his exhibition catalog, *Crash* (Seoul: Ilmin Museum, 2003).

28. See the artist's web page, www.shonkim.com.

29. The Nam June Paik Art Center opened in October 2008 and announced the recipients of the first Nam June Paik Art Center Prize in November 2009. We need in-depth research on how Nam June Paik opened up a new world of video art based on an Eastern mentality and philosophy in the West. The Nam June Paik Art Center, founded to establish Paik's "eternal home," is expected to publish a research volume based on Paik's notes from his student days in Germany and other documents from the 1950s and 1960s. See http://www.njpartcenter.kr.

17

Transitland

VIDEO ART IN CENTRAL AND EASTERN EUROPE

Kathy Rae Huffman

A unique selection of video work by Central and Eastern European artists is presented in the archive Transitland.[1] An international jury of experts with extensive experience with Central and Eastern European video selected ninety-five video works from several hundred nominated by fifty curators, artists, and critics representing the twenty-five countries in the four main subregions of the former Eastern Bloc: the Balkans, the Baltic states, the former Soviet Union, and Central Europe. The final selection shows a representative body of work created since 1989 and produced by artists who have freely reacted to the political and social changes influenced by the political upheaval they experienced.[2] The works reflect the various and specific personal, social, and political issues of these artists' homelands during the transition to capitalist culture. They collectively contribute to our understanding of the reality of the twenty years of evolution since the fall of the Berlin Wall.

Before these political changes, to avoid attention contemporary artists living behind the Iron Curtain, especially those exploring political topics, worked clandestinely. They performed or exhibited their avant-garde works among trusted friends. Without imported art supplies, artists resorted to using common materials, found objects, and their bodies for artistic expression. The oppositional character of the underground art created in this environment resulted in a strongly developed tradition of conceptual work and a deep discourse over ideas. Performance art and the numerous public interventions in the 1990s have these essential beginnings.

Because media was carefully controlled throughout the Eastern Bloc, cameras, recording devices (especially video), and other technologies were regarded as highly suspicious and required some secrecy or an official permit to import or possess. The most active and earliest use of video in Eastern Europe is generally acknowledged to be in the 1970s. The first experiments were believed to have been in Slovenia and the former Yugoslavia, and video artworks by the duo Nusa and Sreco Dragan were created in 1968.[3] In Hungary in 1976, artists and filmmakers could experiment with video at the Béla Balázs Studio (which acquired black-and-white open-reel tape and half-inch Sony or Akai recorders).[4] Early video production also took place in Poland and was adopted by filmmakers when they could no longer obtain film stock and by performance artists, who found in video a new way to explore their actions and a way to send their works abroad (when they could not travel personally). Although video was practiced in Eastern Europe in the 1970s, it was rare and located in the more active capitals of artistic activity. In general, video arrived in the 1980s, when access to equipment and contact with video artists in neighboring countries or the West provided the conditions.

In the early 1980s, international video festivals became popular gathering places for artists from around the world, namely the World Wide Video Festival in Den Haag, which was convened by Tom van Vliet,[5] and the European Media Art Festival in Osnabruck, Germany, which began as a cross-platform film and video festival in 1981.[6] There were other unique events in the 1980s where Eastern Europe–based artists could see video works created in the West and, also, participate. These programs were often organized with the cooperation and support of foreign embassies and sometimes in association with international film festivals. In 1982 the first edition of *Infermental* was published, a video magazine that featured works from Eastern Europe and was organized by Gábor Bódy in Budapest.[7] For many in the West, it was an exciting discovery, and it established new artists for the European media community. The Alternative Film and Video Festival in Belgrade began in 1982 as a forum for Yugoslav alternative productions (from 1991 until 2003, the festival ceased operation and acknowledged that it was the victim of a "decade with very few possibilities for alternative").[8]

In Ljubljana, Slovenia, in 1983, the International Biennial Video CD was initiated by Miha Vipotnik and Marie-Claude Vogric, which established video in a public forum of presentations, performances, and discussions.[9] Starting in 1986, Belgrade's Student Culture Center hosted the annual Spring Video Week, which I had the pleasure of attending in 1987.[10] In the 1980s artists throughout the former Yugoslavia were given access to professional video by national television, which provided camera operators, editors, and crews for sound and technical assistance. These works were nationally broadcast on the program *TV Gallery*, produced by Dunja Blaževic.[11] Early video productions made with VHS in Yugoslavia were considered amateur and not competitive with more professional productions, but in reality these experimental half-inch works made with low-quality consumer home video equipment were highly provocative and exciting.

In Russia in 1986, Parallel Cinema was founded with an underground publication, and then in 1987, the first Cine Fantom Festival was established in Moscow.[12] In 1989 the WRO Sound Basis Visual Art Festival, featuring various audiovisual art forms, was founded in Wrocław, Poland.[13] Now the WRO International Media Art Biennale, it celebrated its twentieth anniversary in May 2009.

In November 1989 security at the restricted border crossings between East and West Berlin collapsed after massive public demonstrations. This was part of a domino effect of demonstrations taking place throughout Eastern Europe. The Hungarian border had already allowed the passage of East Germans into Austria earlier in the year, and this somewhat relaxed border created a public awareness that contributed to the eventual dissolution of the restrictive Iron Curtain and Soviet dominance. Berlin, traditionally a portal to the West throughout the Cold War, was a destination for artists from the Eastern countries. Once the borders opened, the environment for these artists changed drastically. Collectors and curators flooded into not only Berlin but also the formerly closed countries, which were not often visited because of restrictive import/export regulations. The possibility for travel allowed for a coming out for contemporary and experimental art, and new contacts brought instant success for many artists. Mostly, it was an opportunity to bring extraordinary creative activity—still of a largely conceptual nature—into the public realm. The Budapest Art Expo 1991 introduced several Hungarian video artists to the world, including Media Research, an active association of media artists who had planned and hosted the April 1990 international symposium The Media Art with Us, whose topic was the role of television in the Romanian revolution.[14]

All of the video and media events throughout Eastern Europe were produced under extremely limited financial circumstances and were the result of a few dedicated and passionate individuals who persevered, a critical mass of new work, and a growing alternative audience (locally and internationally). Already in the 1980s, video equipment was regularly taken into countries where it was formerly forbidden. It was shared and used by artists, who worked collectively and individually. By the end of the 1980s, artists could access higher levels of portable equipment, and through their unique style, intensity, and content, they gained international interest in their work. In 1989 *Deconstruction, Quotation & Subversion: Video from Yugoslavia,* a curated program of video art, was presented in New York at Artists Space and at the Institute of Contemporary Art/Boston, a result of several visits made to Yugoslavia to research and meet artists.[15]

The 1990s witnessed a huge new expansion of possibilities for using video and media throughout the East. In 1991 *SVB VOCE,* a large-scale exhibition of contemporary Hungarian video installations, was the first comprehensive exhibition of its kind in the East.[16] Presented in Budapest at the Mücsarnok and curated by Suzanne Mészöly, it was organized by the Soros Foundation Fine Art Documentation Center. This successful public presentation of video art was closely linked to the birth of the Soros Center of Contemporary Art (SCCA) Network, which was established in Budapest in 1992 with the mandate to establish centers of contemporary art around the most-populated Eastern European cities. They were intended to serve a new, informed international audience and become the entry point for the young, nonofficial generation of artists. In general, SCCA centers had an open-door policy to expand knowledge about local cultural histories, and they supported artists interested in video and new technologies, as well. Western curators traveled to the East, and Eastern artists traveled to the West, all under the support of the SCCA. Through the SCAA, many artists received their first travel grants and support with catalog production. Likewise, many video works were funded, exhibited, and archived by the regional SCCA organizations.

Video became widely used by artists, and alongside film festivals that presented video art, like Berlin, Oberhausen, and Rotterdam, dedicated video art festivals continued to emerge to present the work of Eastern European artists. In the 1990s festivals were created in the many new countries of the former Eastern Europe. In 1993 the OSTrananie Festival was organized by Stephan Kovats, primarily to profile video from Eastern Europe.[17] It was held in Dessau at the famous Bauhaus in the former German Democratic Republic. It was a biennial with two additional gatherings, one in 1995 and the other in 1997. Another significant event for Eastern European artists was The Next Five Minutes, first held in Amsterdam in 1993.[18] It focused on tactical television and included contributions dealing with the sometimes violent changes in the Eastern European political landscape, especially the broadcast medium. In 1994 Meta Forum was launched in Budapest, organized by Geert Lovink, Diana McCarty, and Janos Sugar.[19] This festival took place at the very beginning of Internet activity, and it focused on community, interactive media, and cultural politics. Other lively topics were also addressed and discussed. In 1996 the Dutch Electronic Arts Festival at V2 in Rotterdam presented the program Media Art in Eastern Europe, where curators, producers, and artists contributed their histories and presented selected screenings.[20] At this event the Syndicate was created, a mailing list that brought together artists from around Eastern Europe in an e-mail dialogue.[21]

In 1991 the countries of the former Yugoslavia entered a long period of bitter war and national self-interest. Croatia and Slovenia were the first in the struggle for independence from Serbian jurisdiction of Yugoslavia, but Macedonia and Bosnia and Herzegovina soon followed. The long-standing prejudices among the ethnicities and nationalities were the rationales for well-documented military incidents that resulted in embattled communities. Small digital camcorders, introduced in 1989 as new tools for activists, had revolutionized video in the West and were used by artists, journalists, and ordinary people. They allowed activist and opposition positions to be distributed abroad and sometimes even broadcast. The small-format tapes could be hand carried by travelers and were sent out of conflict zones, telling stories from very personal perspectives. Video became the primary method of telling the stories of the war and gave voice to the people caught in the crossfire.

Videomedeja began in Novi Sad in 1996 as an annual international festival of video art.[22] Its first festival was held during the demonstration marches between Novi Sad and Belgrade against the war and ethnic cleansing and during the early days of sanctions. Diana McCarty and I (the only foreign guests brave enough to travel to the festival) cheered the arriving demonstrators when they arrived in Novi Sad and, with about three thousand people gathered in the town square, collectively watched a single monitor that screened video footage of antiwar demonstrations just filmed in Belgrade. The Alternative Film and Video Festival in Belgrade restarted in 2003 and continues today.[23] An important media communications agency from Belgrade was the alternative voice of radio B92.[24] Active throughout the 1990s, it broadcast under the radar of the authorities until 1999, when the station was (temporarily) closed down. B92 was a community of media activists who transmitting internationally via the Internet, regularly gave updates on antiwar demonstrations alongside news of the desperate living conditions during UN sanctions. Today, it is an online information portal about Serbia in English. Nearby, SEAFair, or Skopje Electronic Arts Fair, was held annually from 1997 to 2002 in the capital city of Macedonia.[25] It focused on topics of geography, science, and technology and was organized by SCCA director Melentie Pandilovski. Artists from around Eastern Europe were invited for technical workshops and discussions, performances, and demonstrations.

At the millennium, discussions around issues concerning nationalism, ethnic identity, military war crimes, privatization, retribution, and legal compliance to qualify for membership in the European Union dominated the news in Western Europe and throughout Central and Eastern Europe. The complexity of the economic, political, and social status for individuals, along with specific national issues, is portrayed in many of the videotapes in the Transitland selection. Video, a powerful tool for communication, allows for alternative and individual viewpoints. It is also a medium of contention. The specific issues concerning the various conflicts around the emergence of political independence in Eastern Europe are vast and beyond the scope of this essay, but they have left a mark on the individual lives of artists. To even attempt to describe the scope of video activity and give a brief history in such a short space would be both an unfair and an impossible-to-complete task.

Therefore, to overview and select one hundred works from diverse countries with different political histories, languages, geographies, and ethnic backgrounds was a daunting challenge for the jury. Before starting the selection, there were no categories set up, no quotas to meet, and no predetermined views on how the works would become a cohesive program. The guidelines clearly stated that those countries established by the European Union as Central and Eastern Europe had to be represented, that the dates of production must be observed, that only single-channel video would be considered, and that artists from not only the larger, more sophisticated centers of video production but also the newly emerging countries, whose artists' voices were rarely heard, had to be included.

Content was the key issue for selection, and the jury agreed to look favorably on works that reflected social and cultural events, ideas, and responses to the specific period of transition (1989–2009). Many excellent works were nominated and reviewed that fell outside the content guidelines for transitional reference and were therefore not included. Nevertheless, all works were reviewed and discussed, making the selection process an active and rewarding experience. Only after the final selection was made could an analysis and overview of the Transitland juried selection be attempted. This overview emerged as a response to the works themselves (not from a preset curatorial position) and was a personal response, but one based on the discussions and opinions of the jury members. What each of the works shares is a strong, individual voice expressing a message different from that of its country's political machine and the ability to portray specific aspects of the transition toward European (capitalist) culture within a contemporary, artistic framework. There is humor that can be recognized cross-culturally in many of the works, and there is also sorrow and loss. There is an overall willingness, even an eagerness, to observe and create new narratives.

The works selected fall into four main categories: performance, conceptual, documentary, and what might be called artistic license (including animation, music, theater, and poetry). Many of the works fit into more than one category and are structurally complex. The performance works are an excellent starting point for further discussion. Performance, a traditional form of the avant-garde, is understood throughout Eastern Europe. It is rich in irony. Performance can be as simple as the artist standing before the camera (her audience) and facing up to a personal issue. It can also manifest as the organization of people who then become actors who perform or react to instructions within certain parameters set by the artist.

What is important about the performance works included in Transitland is the variety of styles, the scale of artistic activity, and the numerous political interventions created by artists. Performance works that challenge the political or cultural power structure are created in many ways, and individual performances are the most intimate. In *Mantra* Gordana Andjelic-Galic (Bosnia and Herzegovina) marches in isolation on a deserted road and fumbles with an armful of large flags, each one representing a past ruling government of her country. There is no audience to applaud her struggle. In *Traffic Control* Ivan Moudov (Bulgaria) performs in public dressed as a Bulgarian policeman and conducts traffic in a busy Austrian intersection. The unknown uniform causes some confusion before he is carried off. In *Red Daddy* Martin Zet (Czech Republic) directly performs for the camera, slowly evolving into a clown while relating a telephone conversation he had about living on Marxova Ulice (Marx Street).

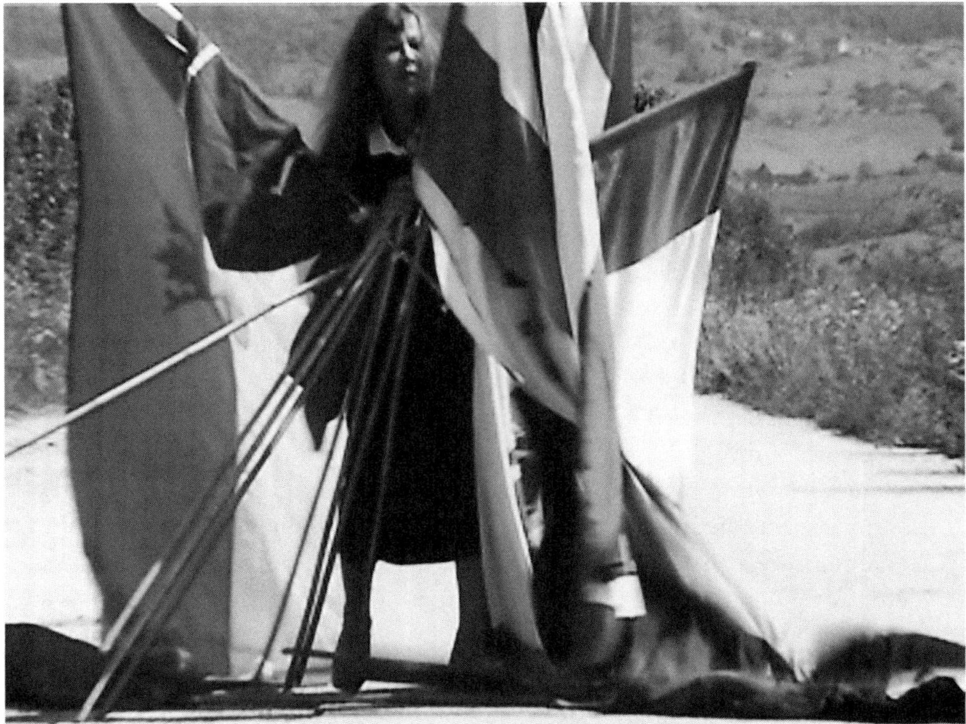

Gordana Andjelic-Galic, *Mantra,* 2006. Image courtesy of the artist.

Facing the camera to reveal strong female identity is the concern of many female artists. Elena Kovylina (Russia) exemplifies the strength of Russian women in *Waltz.* Her performance is an endurance test of her capacity to drink shots of vodka. Initially, she appeals to the audience to applaud her, but when her ability to remain standing falters, she becomes pathetic and hopeless. Vodka, which at times has been more available than clean water in Russia, is a social reality that signifies camaraderie. In *Striptease or Not?* Hajnal Nemeth (Hungary) places her performer on the highway, confidently and in very public view. The stretch of highway leading into Budapest from Vienna is also known as an active pickup spot for truck drivers looking to find women for sex. The evolving role of women in transitional society is questioned by the artist. Kai Kaljo (Estonia) explores her position as artist within the changed conditions of predatory capitalism in *Loser.* It is a test of her integrity to continue to announce her attributes. Natalija Vujoševic (Montenegro) tells the video camera her secrets and reveals her private passions in the performance *Pink Confession.* Each of these video works is an honest attempt to communicate a social truth and daily reality and the conditions that inform artistic expression.

Milica Tomic (Serbia) discloses the pain of identity in her performance *I Am*

Milica Tomic. The work exemplifies the essence of political ethnic cleansing, as one's identity is ultimately why someone is persecuted and why another is in power. Boryana Rossa (Bulgaria) conducts a discourse on pain, love, and suffering in *The Moon and the Sunshine.* An insight into her deeper feelings, the performance tests her thresholds of pain and pleasure. Mavromatti Oleg (Russia) has created a performance video as a work of art in its own right with *The Last Valve,* a piece that demonstrates Boryana Rossa's most intimate performance. The investigation of the environment and a keen personal reference concerns Calin Dan (Romania) in *Sample City.* This staged endurance performance brings to life the traditional folk character Pacala, the simpleton and deceiver. The performer, who carries a door on his back while walking around in the various quarters of Bucharest (and meanwhile giving the viewer a tour), represents this folk legend as a modern-day hero—the door being a symbol for closing the door behind you or minding one's own business (good advice in a repressive social context). Mare Tralla (Estonia) reenacts her childhood curiosity. Her Cold War concept about Westerners and how they perceive Russians is acted out in *Feltboots.* Wearing these traditional soft boots, she explores the Western city streets as the clichéd image of a peasant. Instead of attracting attention, she is invisible, no longer a threat as a political enemy. Mariana Vassileva (Bulgaria) also explores her environment in her ongoing video work *Journal.* This episode reveals her physical exploration of small details in the city with her hands. It is a sensual, personal method of observation.

The interaction between performers provides an additional level of discourse and creates a less personal relationship with the viewer, who is positioned to consider the activity being witnessed. In *Untitled* Sona Abgaryan (Republic of Armenia) presents two performers who interact with each other in an infantile manner. Their baby-like movements bring up issues including naïveté and the social awkwardness of dealing with new cultural practices. In *Essential Current Affairs* Dan Acostioaiei, with Ann Wodinski (Romania), presents a male and a female, framed in a close-up image, embracing through the balaclavas they wear. No dialogue is necessary to understand it as a commentary on violence. Azorro (Poland) hires actors to perform the work *Everything Has Been Done,* a humorous response to artistic practice today. Yael Bartana, an Israeli artist working in Poland, stages the performance *Mary Koszmary* in an empty Warsaw stadium. She mobilizes youth and an actor to deliver a speech by Sławomir Sierakowski inviting three million Jews to return to Poland. Pavel Braila (Republic of Moldova) invites his mother to cook a traditional dish and send it across the border to his exhibition opening in *Eurolines Catering of Homesick Cuisine,* pointing out the common practice of using coaches to transport food and goods between families. One of the most elaborate performance works is *Crossing Over* by Tanja Ostojic (Serbia). It is a marriage to Klemens Golf (Germany) and part of the bigger project *Looking for a Husband*

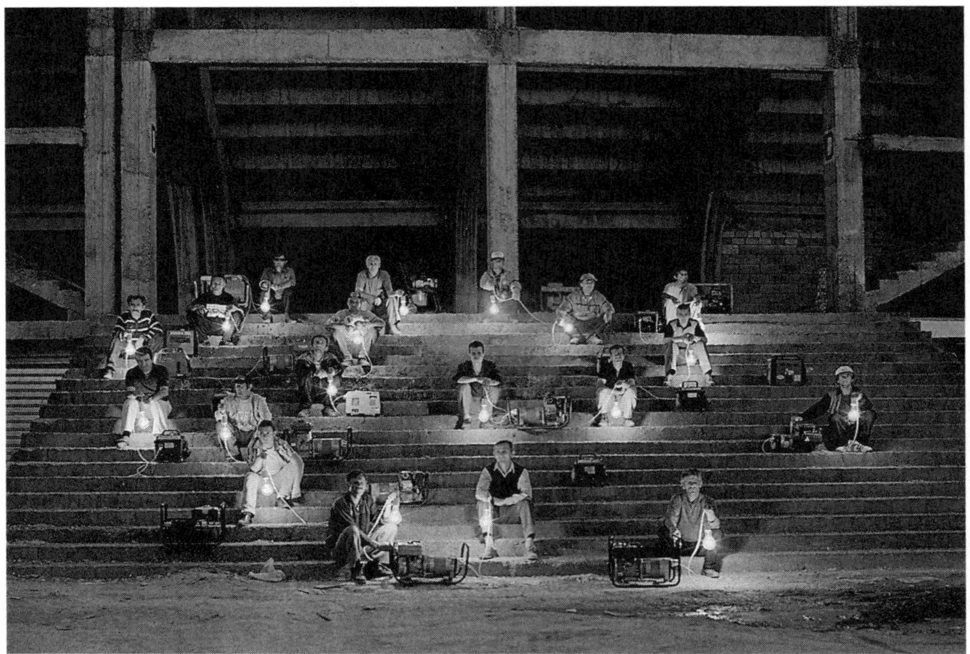

Adrian Paci, *Turn On*, 2004. Image courtesy of the artist.

with EU Passport. In this work Tanja meets Klemens for the first time in Belgrade. He has answered her Internet ad regarding finding a husband in the European Union for the purpose of obtaining a passport. It is a personal yet public event that ends up with her eventual move to Germany.

Performance as a public event is a powerful intrusion in the normal daily routines that take place everywhere around the world. In Eastern Europe these actions usually refer to political issues. They may be a happening like *In the City* by Anna Janczyszyn-Jaros (Poland), a group intervention like *Demonstration* by the RADEK Group and Dmitri Gutov (Russia), or an action like *Georgian National Anthem* by Nadia Tsulukidze (Georgia), a humorous performance of Georgia's national anthem performed in the busy roundabout Europe Square. The orchestration of performers to present the position of social groups and their conditions are clear in several of the videotapes. In *Rhythm* Vladimir Nikolic (Bulgaria) manipulates a small group who contradict the Orthodox Christian signing of the cross in time to a techno beat. Adrian Paci (Albania) orchestrates a group of men who represent the scores of unemployed and reveals the harmony of social action in *Turn On,* a symbolic act of unity. Rudina Xhaferi (Kosova) gathers a group of men who sit in the middle of a busy intersection and discuss the political situation in *O How Good Is to Be an Albanian.* Artur Żmijewski (Poland) assembles four groups with different beliefs, all known to be uncompromising, and asks them to a workshop in *Them*. This social experiment performance work evolves and fails to negotiate agreement among the differing perspectives, proving the division and gaps in post-Socialist society. These performance actions reveal the interactions between people and accentuate the frustrations and complex references in countries that formerly were extremely restrictive.

The many symbolic, representational, impressionistic, journalistic, subjective, narrative, informative, humorous, and mainly political video works in Transitland communicate a diverse message of transition and change. Today, these works can be shown in Eastern European art galleries, festivals, and museums, not only abroad. But they would have been considered subversive and unacceptable during Soviet censorship and control of art and the media. Now, we consider these video works not only a window into the reality of the new Europe but also a view into the lives and histories of people and places who have been all too often forgotten or ignored.

NOTES

1. See http://www.transitland.eu. Transitland is funded with support from the European Commission, and the project coorganizers are the Agency for Contemporary Art Exchange (Budapest), the transmediale festival for art and digital culture (Berlin), and the InterSpace Association (Sofia).

2. Together with five commissions, the complete archive contains one hundred video works.

3. Valerie Smith and Kathy Rae Huffman, eds., *Metaphysical Visions: Middle Europe: Deconstruction, Quotation & Subversion: Video from Yugoslavia*, exhibition catalog (New York, Artists Space, 1989), 26.

4. Miklós Peternák, "Cross-Chronology: A History of Hungarian Video Art," in *SVB Voce: Contemporary Hungarian Video Installation*, exhibition catalog (Mücsarnok, Hungary: Soros Foundation, 1991), 21.

5. See http://www.wwvf.nl/oindex.html.

6. See http://emaf.de/_emaf/index.php.

7. See http://www.infermental.de.

8. Smith and Huffman, eds., *Metaphysical Visions*, 26.

9. Ibid., 28.

10. Ibid.

11. See http://kuda.org/eng/tv-galerija.

12. Igor Aleinikov, "Parallel Cinema in the USSR," in *Red Fish in America: New Independent Film and Video from the Soviet Union*, eds. Marie Ciere and Igor Aleinikov (Cambridge, Mass.: Arts Company, 1990), 7–11.

13. WRO Art Center, ed., *Expanded City*, festival catalog, 13th Media Art Biennale WRO 09 (Wrocław, Poland: WRO Art Center, 2009).

14. *Budapest Art Expo 1991*, festival catalog (Budapest, Hungary: Budapest Art Expo Foundation, 1991), 122–23.

15. Kathy Rae Huffman, curator, *Deconstruction, Quotation & Subversion: Video from Yugoslavia,* Artists Space, New York, May 25 to July 1, 1989.

16. Suzanne Mészöly, curator, *SVB VOCE: Contemporary Hungarian Video Installation,* Mücsarnok/Kunsthalle, Budapest, 1991.

17. See the OSTrananie 93 announcement archived at http://www.projects.v2.nl/~arns/Archiv/Ost93/prmt1093.htm.

18. Geert Lovink, "Tactical Media, the Second Decade: Preface to the Brazilian Submidialogia Publication," October 2005, http://laudanum.net/geert/files/1129724590.

19. See http://www.mrf.hu/mf94.html.

20. See http://www.v2.nl/events/media-art-in-eastern-europe.

21. Geert Lovink, "Deep Europe: A History of the Syndicate Network," in *New Media, Old Media: A History and Theory Reader,* eds. Wendy Hui Kyong Chun and Thomas Keenan (New York: Routledge, 2006), 287.

22. See http://videomedeja.org/en/archive.

23. See http://www.alternativefilmvideo.org.

24. "B92," *Wikipedia,* last modified May 30, 2012, http://en.wikipedia.org/wiki/B92.

25. See http://seafair.scca.org.mk/99.

18 Native Makers/New Media

Kathleen Ash-Milby

It should surprise no one that Native American art practice uses video to represent and explore identity, sexuality, representation, language, and a host of contemporary issues. Native artists have used video to control their image and engage in postcolonial discourse in a manner and mode similar to but distinct from the work of Native photographers. It may be a "messy dialogue," as curator Steve Loft writes, but recent work has demonstrated that these artists use video to capture potent expressions of anger and humor and, most of all, to offer a unique interpretation of the complexities of the Native experience as it is both perceived and lived.[1]

Recent Native video art has its most direct roots in multiple sources, including photography, performance art, and narrative film. Although video does not carry the same metaphoric weight as photography in its historical representation of Native Americans, there is a history of misrepresentation and parody to be considered. To wit, the "wild" Indians from popular mid-twentieth-century Westerns, the eternally stoic Tonto from *The Lone Ranger* TV series of the 1950s, the ignorant and primitive Indians of Disney's *Peter Pan,* the bumbling braves of *F Troop* in the 1960s, the single tear of Iron Eyes Cody and the Indian adventures of *The Brady Bunch* in the 1970s, and even the more recent representations of Native culture in science fiction like *The X-Files* and *Star Trek: Voyager.* There are seemingly inevitable "Indian" storylines in most long-running American television series, from *The Incredible Hulk* and *The Simpsons* to *Seinfeld,* some more memorable than others. Whether they reify or parody stereotypes of Native people, they continue to reinforce them and introduce them to new generations.

As an art form, video is an equally potent antidote that several Native artists have used to engage these stereotypes and perceptions, often through humor. Kent Monkman (Cree), whose work as a visual and performance artist deconstructs stereotypes and parodies the historically reductionist representations of Native people in Western art, has created several video works that play with romantic and fetishistic ideas about Indians. In *Group of Seven Inches* (2005), a "titillating Taxonomy of the customs and manners of the European Male," the roles are reversed as Monkman's performative cross-dressing alter ego, Miss Chief

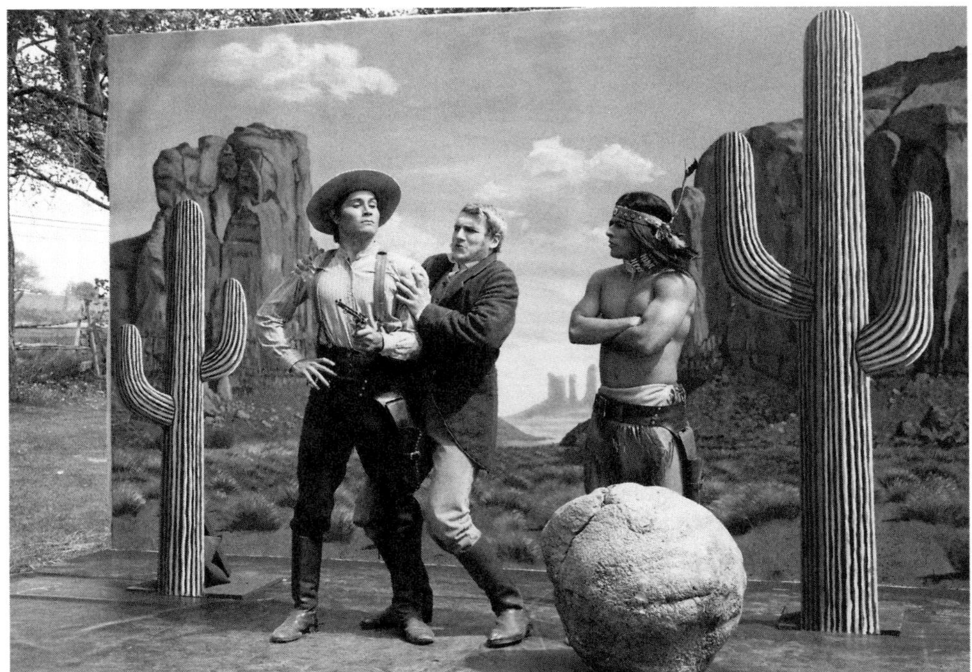

Shooting Geronimo, 2007. Written, directed, and produced by Kent Monkman. Super 8, black-and-white, 11:11. *From left to right:* Anthony Collins, Dustin Peters, and Quetzal Guerrero. Courtesy of the artist.

Eagle Testickle, approaches the European male with the same demeaning and objectifying gaze as early Western "frontier" artists George Catlin (1796–1872) and Paul Kane (1810–71). The short work is presented in silent film format, and intertitles with excerpts from Catlin's and Kane's actual journals alternate with scenes of two European boys who are found in the woods and lured into the artist's studio, where they are taken advantage of, seduced with liquor, and eventually dressed in stereotypical European dress (powdered faces, wigs)—after which they pose for the artist. *Shooting Geronimo* (2007) takes a similar approach, slipping behind the camera in the silent film era to create a minidrama that mocks early filmmakers' (and photographers') manipulation of the Native story to fit stereotypes about Indian nobility and exoticness. Each of these works playfully draws the audience in with humor and exaggeration but also skillfully skewers not only the objectifying but the sexualizing gaze of the European.

Metrosexual Indian (2007) by Terrance Houle also uses humor and plays with common stereotypes to deconstruct and question what it means to be a contemporary Indian. In this vignette the aforementioned metrosexual Indian is a pretty typical urban young man, filmed in slightly shaky and fuzzy Super 8 as he makes his daily rounds in an anonymous cityscape that could be Toronto or

Brooklyn. He stops for an espresso drink, checks his wristwatch, walks about the neighborhood, and looks at the shops while a jaunty sound track underscores his happy-go-lucky demeanor. Unfortunately, some shady reservation boys, wearing cartoonish tourist-trinket war bonnets, violently confront him, his wristwatch, and everything progressive his urbanity represents.

Houle and Monkman both use a narrative approach in these works to tease out issues with visual commentary, whether they are stereotypes outside or within Native communities. The majority of work by Native artists over the past twenty years in media has been in the format of narrative film with a traditional dramatic arc or storyline. For example, *Honey Moccasin* (1998), a lauded work by Shelley Niro (Mohawk), is a short, comedic melodrama with an all-Indian cast set in a reservation community. Known since the early 1990s for her work in film, she retains a narrative structure that often incorporates Haudenosaunee cultural stories as subjects and integrates Mohawk artistic traditions—for instance, the lush curvilinear Iroquois beadwork whimsically repurposed to depict the opening titles in *Honey Moccasin* and *It Starts with a Whisper* (1992). Her later work has become less literal and more symbolic and abstract in nature, such as *Tree* (2006), in which a woman, representing the spirit of mother earth, appears and sadly confronts the severe and desolate environment of the city before transforming into a tree.

In recent years several artists have been engaged in work, sometimes labeled as experimental, that disengages from the standard approaches to film and storytelling and, instead, fragments and mixes images and sound. Another approach to unpacking the kitschy imaginary Indian, *The Story of Apanatschi and Her Red-headed Wrestler* (2008), by Bear Witness (Cayuga), is from a suite of work commissioned for the 2008 imagineNATIVE project *Culture Shock* curated by Loft. As a response both to the reductionist imagery of Native people in German *Indianerfilmes* and to cartoonish portrayals in video games, Bear Witness skillfully remixes excerpts from the film *Winnetou und das halbblut Apanatschi* (Winnetou and the half-blood Apanatschi) (1966) and an arena battle from the game *Virtua 5*, featuring the First Nations character Wolf Hawkfield. A recurring Native character since the original game was released in 1992, Hawkfield is customized by the artist/player to wear an eagle feather war bonnet, "dream catcher" necklace, and sunglasses. In this work the stuttering, repetitious replay of scenes of Apanatschi walking in her Apache costume is contrasted with Hawkfield engaging in acrobatic battle moves, repeated and manipulated to appear as a dance against an energetic dance track. It is hard to ascertain which invented Indian is more false or constructed.

Red Man (2005), a more confrontational work by Erica Lord and Noelle Mason, takes us deep into the internalized anger of Native people through the singing of a racist song about Indians.[2] Lord, who is Athabaskan and Inupiat, has examined race and conflict through photography, installation, and performance.

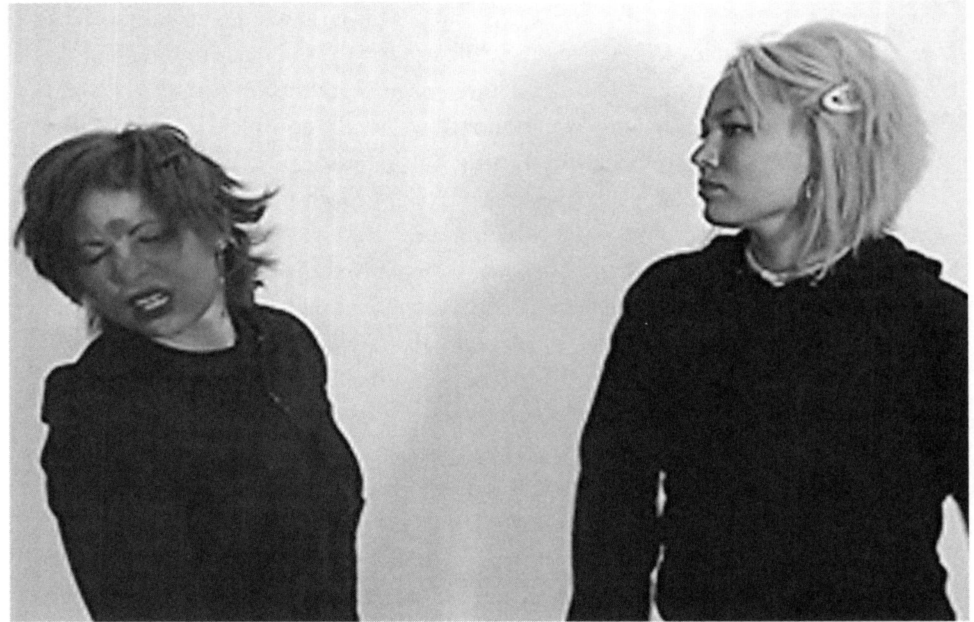

Erica Lord and Noelle Mason, *Redman*, 2005. Courtesy of the artists.

She has used video in the past as documentation of her performative work, such as *Nanook of the North Side* (2004–5), which follows Lord as she explores the Native Alaskan collections of the Field Museum in Chicago dressed in traditional Athabaskan clothing with faux chin tattoos, questioning how her experience living as a contemporary Indian could relate to museum displays of her culture. *Red Man* is a collaboration with Mason, a non-Native fellow student at the School of the Art Institute of Chicago. In this powerful work the camera alternates between each of their faces staring directly and silently at the viewer until Mason begins singing the first verse of the campfire song "We Are the Red Men," including crude gestures that mimic Indian sign language to animate the action in the lyrics.

> We are the Redmen, feathers in our headband, down among the deadmen.
> Pow wow.
> We can fight with sticks and stones, bows and arrows, bricks and bones.

Lord continues to listen silently until Mason begins singing it again; the perspective suddenly shifts to a long view of Lord violently striking Mason across the face between lines of the song. Again, the two face the camera silently, this time

with Mason's face bloodied. After several uncomfortable seconds, the white protagonist, undeterred and defiant, angrily sings the song again and again.

Whereas *Red Man* confronts the seeming futility in fighting stubborn, entrenched stereotypes, Thomas Isaac (Navajo) attacks another taboo in *How I Froze
to Death in the Cold Night or Red or Green* (2005).[3] In this work Isaac creates an almost silent, hypnotic mirrored tableau of himself standing in a pristine, white environment. He drinks heavily from a green bottle, jumps about playfully, smashes
the empty bottle on the floor, and then vomits excessively, exposing a visceral,
alcohol-laced underbelly to this neutral scene. Like Lord, Isaac pulls the viewer
into a calm narrative that is suddenly and violently interrupted. The sound track,
which is largely silent, is jarred by the mistimed and unpredictable sound of the
glass breaking and then deep, guttural heaving and splashing. Our somnolence
is broken, and we are confronted with raw, ugly issues that we do not want to
think about, such as alcoholism, violence, and racism. As a child of an alcoholic,
Isaac's purge may be an exorcism of his own personal demons or a furious expul-
sion of the colonial stew that has disempowered Native people for generations.
Whichever it is, he carefully tiptoes around and around the mess before the video
finally ends.

The use of the artist's body as symbolic of greater struggles often stems from
performance art. Rebecca Belmore (Anishinaabe), for instance, is critically renowned for her conceptual work in both live performance and video installation.
Seeking to draw attention to the high number of young, Indigenous women
who disappeared each year off the city streets of Vancouver, Belmore created
the *The Named and Unnamed* (2002). This poignant work features a video of Belmore's performance of her *Vigil* on a Vancouver street corner in which she calls
out the name of each missing woman and writes her name on her body.[4] In the
installation the video is projected over a wall of lights. She also is the protagonist
in the multimedia work *Fountain* (2005), a video designed to project over a huge
screen of cascading water in the Canadian Pavilion at the 2005 Venice Biennale.
This intense work layers ritualistic images of Belmore emerging from a lake,
throwing a bucket of blood over the screen, and burning materials on the shore.
Although Belmore does not appear in her more recent work *March 5, 1819* (2008),
a two-channel video, the work has a performative quality, as two individuals,
dressed in contemporary clothing, reenact the attempted escape of Demasduit
(renamed Mary March by her colonist captors) and her husband. The only image
of Demasduit, at the time one of the last surviving members of the Beothuck in
Newfoundland, is a serene portrait by Henrietta Hamilton, a dramatic counterpoint to the desperation and sorrow captured in Belmore's interpretation.

Many Native artists choose to challenge colonial histories as well as conventional understandings, even daring their audiences to reconsider their ideas
about culture and tradition. In the two intriguing, complementary works *Tsu*

héidei shugaxtutaan I and *Tsu héidei shugaxtutaan II* (2006), Nicholas Galanin (Tlingit) mixes a Tlingit raven dance and contemporary popping to create a simple but sophisticated commentary on the intersections of the modern world and Tlingit cultural expression. The title, which translates as "we will again open this container of wisdom that has been left in our care," challenges conservative interpretations of tradition by combining a traditional Tlingit raven dance with electronic music in one video and a robot dance with raven dance music in the other. Mixing seemingly disparate audio and video tracks is not terribly innovative (on YouTube, see "Inappropriate Soundtracks" for numerous examples utilizing mainstream film or, even, the painful scene "Dancin'" from the movie *Xanadu* [1980]), and the mixing of Indigenous dance with completely different music has been done, as well. For instance, in 2008 Jason Lujan (Apache) staged *Fancy Dance Good Luck Lion,* a performance that combined the music of a drum and singers with several Plains fancy dancers and Chinese lion dancers and musicians. Each group danced with their traditional music first and then traded dancers and musicians. Although their movements and music eventually combined to a limited degree—and it was interesting to see the similarities in their bright regalia and movements—each group maintained its own separate integrity.[5]

The dancers in *Tsu héidei shugaxtutaan I* and *Tsu héidei shugaxtutaan II* achieve a remarkable synergy with the unexpected music they perform to.[6] The raven dancer Dan Littlefield improvises his performance in Sitka, Alaska. David "Elsewhere" Bernal improvises with his unique pastiche of illusory dance to a recorded track in an art studio in Brooklyn. The musical track was not substituted for another in the mixing studio, and there were neither rehearsals nor choreography. Even the use of a black-and-white format further distills the work to its essence: dancers and music. Yet despite the simplicity of its composition, it still offends some conservative voices in the Native community who consider it to be a corruption of tradition.[7]

Language is inextricably tied to culture and has thus played a prominent role in Native video, as well. Mohawk artist Greg Staats has created several video works that incorporate language, including *What Remains* (2007), which utilizes excerpts from old letters to evoke emotions and memories that are personal, cultural, and universal ("I still have no pain," "Rake purchased for leaves," "He waved everybody goodbye"). These excerpts, gleaned from family journals and letters, appear sequentially above a row of swaying tree branches, the sometimes shaky cursive or print belying the age or infirmity of the writer. Several of the artist's other video works use the Mohawk language throughout, both spoken and sung, with no translation for non-Mohawk-speaking viewers, suggesting that the memories they are meant to elicit are personally or culturally private.

Kevin Lee Burton (Swampy Cree) selectively includes subtitles in *Nikamowin (Song)* (2007), an experimental work that examines the interstices between the

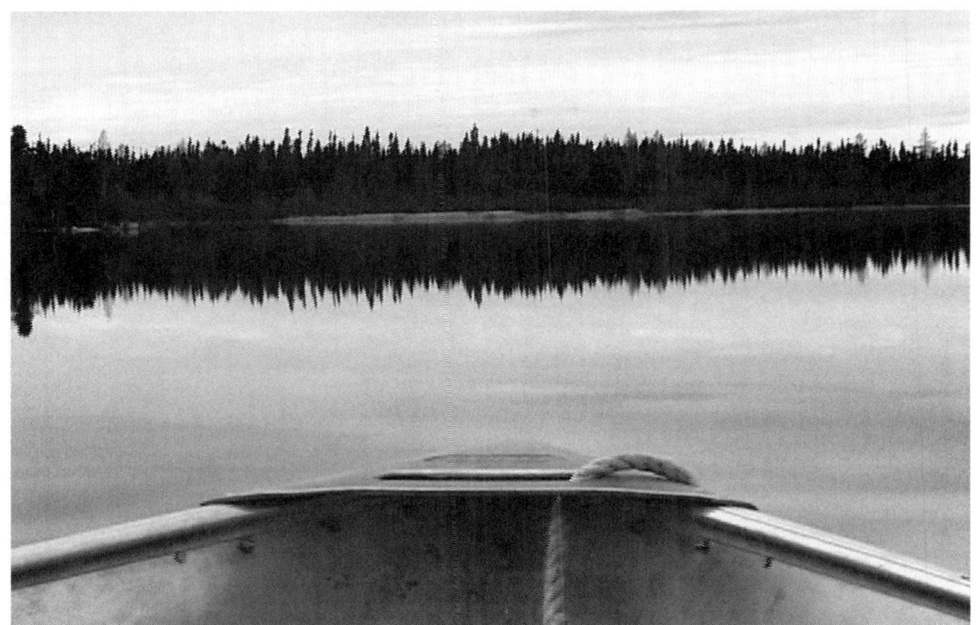

Kevin Lee Burton, *Nikamowin (Song)*, 2007. Courtesy of the artist.

Cree language and culture.[8] The title is apt for a work that starts with a conversation in English about how one Cree man can speak his language and the other cannot. Framed within a peaceful scene in a small boat on the water, it quickly becomes a sometimes visually and aurally frenetic deconstruction of the Cree language, the natural environment, a reservation community, and an anonymous city. Words are broken, repeated, and reconstructed to create a hypnotic and lyrical soundscape of language that may be foreign to the ears of most viewers but is clearly an homage to the essential beauty of the Cree language. As alluring as the imagery is—recalling visually chaotic scenes in *Koyaanisqatsi* (1982), though Burton creates a harmonious unity between language and the city as a living environment—the dialogue elicits a deep concern over the reality of language loss and its ability to frame the world in new and surprising ways.

The diversity and depth of Native video art is impossible to summarize in an essay of this length, but it is clear that video is a medium that has allowed Native artists to delve deeper into subjects and ideas that have long been expressed in more traditional forms, such as painting, photography, and sculpture. With the ability to combine sound and image and the freedom to use these tools with multifarious approaches, one could argue that recent Native art is reaching even greater depths of emotion and sophistication than are narrative and documentary formats. There certainly is room for both types of expression, and it is refreshing to observe the proliferation of work that challenges viewers on multiple levels, whether the artists choose to utilize the format's linear, narrative possibilities or to create more expressive, experimental forms.

NOTES

1. Steven Loft, *Culture Shock* (Toronto: Vtape, 2008), 12.

2. To see this video, go to http://www.thenaica.org/edition_three/index.html and click "Erica Lord" and then "Audio + Videos."

3. See Thomas Isaac, "How I Froze to Death in the Cold Night or Red and Green," YouTube video, 10:02, posted by "tjonisaac," November 12, 2008, http://www.youtube.com/watch?v=45olk8e7oIo.

4. For a more complete discussion and illustration of this work, see Charlotte Townsend-Gault and James Luna, *Rebecca Belmore: The Named and the Unnamed* (Vancouver: Morris and Helen Belkin Art Gallery, University of British Columbia, 2003).

5. A related photographic series based on *Fancy Dance Good Luck Lion* is a much more successful remix, with the dancers exchanging items such as masks to dramatic effect.

6. See Nicholas Galanin, "Tsu Heidei Shugaxtutaan Pt. 1," YouTube video, 4:36, posted by "ngalanin," November 20, 2006, http://www.youtube.com/watch?v=Ue30aKV1LF8; and Nicholas Galanin, "Tsu Heidei Shugaxtutaan 2," YouTube video, 4:06, posted by "ngalanin," November 20, 2006, http://www.youtube.com/watch?v=Vg2c1jtm590&feature=related.

7. The artist has been quite severely chastised online in the videos' YouTube comments.

8. See "Kevin Lee Burton: Bio," Beat Nation website, http://www.beatnation.org/kevin-lee-burton.html.

19
You Dropped a Bomb on Me

Jessica Lawless

I'm looking for the new video revolution. Where is the video camera mediating radical social change? It's hard to find it in the video-saturated consumer cultural landscape of the early twenty-first century, but not impossible. In fact, if the frame is shifted 45 degrees so that it is slightly askew, what comes into focus is quite queer. Through two different experiences, one from behind the camera and one as a viewer, I found something new when the camera intersected with real-time gender queering. More visually stealthy than gender transgressions that operate across 180 degrees, 45 degrees is a deceptively quieter upheaval. It is also a more difficult shift to identify than some other, more explosive moments in the ongoing video revolution.

At the turn of the century, the revolution was easier to spot. Signs were visible, such as the shot of the sticker that read "Resistance is Fertile" in *Showdown in Seattle,* the Deep Dish video compilation of the 1999 protests against the World Trade Organization. Something revolutionary was in the air during those heady days of protest on the cusp between the twentieth and the twenty-first centuries. A lasting legacy of those protests has been the Indy Media Centers (IMCs), a decentralized transnational network of local DIY media outlets. As Ana Nogueira writes in her essay "The Birth and Promise of the Indymedia Revolution":

> From Seattle to Sydney, Chiapas to the Congo, the Indymedia phenomena has indeed spread like wildfire, recklessly endangering the corporate media's monopoly on expression and intellectual property . . . [evolving] into a hopeful vision that a new media landscape is on the horizon.[1]

The IMCs' contribution to a new media landscape is vast, with more than 150 sites around the world reporting on grassroots protests and local issues that rarely make it into mainstream news. The IMCs model fiercely democratic production methods and editorial policies. It can be even argued that these methods model a radical form of democracy. Unfortunately, though the IMCs represent a deep scratch on the surface of corporate media's monopoly, they have not endangered corporate media's dominance. Nogueira's hopefulness in the potential

IMCs represented is indicative of activist thinking in the late 1990s, which saw the Internet as a great equalizer, a radically democratizing force that "empowered citizens to reclaim and redefine the public sphere."[2] That view is a contemporary extension of Walter Benjamin's early twentieth-century essay arguing that the age of mechanical reproduction would democratize the arts by dismantling uniqueness as the determining factor in cultural and monetary value.[3] For both Nogueira and Benjamin, the public sphere becomes a place for the cacophony of the multitudes, where each opinion is of equal value to the next.

Yeah, right. The marketplace of ideas in the early twenty-first century, even as we are sifting through the ruins of a recession, is still a marketplace. In this late stage of the game, producers are, equally and always, still consumers—like my eleven-year-old niece Paulie and her friend Frankie. Paulie and Frankie recently asked me to help them make a video. "We want to be on YouTube," they told me. Paulie and Frankie's desire for their ten minutes of fame (it's been reduced since Warhol's time) and ability to make it happen can be read as a positive result of the vast changes in video production and distribution over the past decade or so. These two young people have access to cameras, computers, software, and video hosting platforms on the Internet that facilitate putting their voices into the public sphere in a way that was not conceivable for my friends and myself a generation earlier. Paulie and Frankie choreographed a dance sequence, crafted a homemade clapper to mark scenes, and ran through take after take until their rendition of the song "You're the One that I Want" from the musical *Grease* was caught on tape, edited, uploaded, and ready for an opening-night celebration. A marker of technological and cultural shifts, Paulie and Frankie's video was not a Molotov cocktail lobbed at the stranglehold of corporate media. YouTube is owned by Google and has partnerships with CBS, BBC, Sony, and Warner Music groups, among others, and, of course, has an iPhone app.[4] Paulie and Frankie's desire to be on YouTube was, through one frame, a desire to be at the center of corporate consumer culture. But if I shift the focus, if I reframe how I look at Paulie and Frankie's video, I can see it much less cynically. More than an example of the inescapable confines of corporate media, Paulie and Frankie's video can be read in the context of 1980s- and 1990s-style identity politics.

Ensuring their own visibility as young girls, as mixed-race mestiza kids born and raised in Los Angeles, and as self-described "not girly-girls," Paulie and Frankie re-created a classically heteronormative musical number to fit their vision of selves. They created that moment of emergence, as Pratibha Parmar calls it, inserting their minoritized voices into a very dominant public sphere.[5] Here, I can find the politicized narrative through which to read their version of "You're the One That I Want": young girls of color using video to have a voice, queering a musical number into their own vision. At eleven, however, Paulie and Frankie are not (yet?) expressing a queer sexual orientation. Even if that were the case, even if the video were a we're-here-and-we're-queer moment, the singular goal of putting it up on YouTube diminishes the possibility of the camera mediating a radical politic. It is melding into rather than speaking against that corporate-controlled sphere. The significance of putting the means of production in the hands of marginalized and minoritized peoples is not what's diminished. This remains an important and radical practice as evidenced by, for one example, the Chiapas Media Project, a significant part of the Zapatista movement, which shares a genealogy with and has influenced the IMCs. But in the context of twenty-first-century consumerist capitalism, the politics of visibility is often reduced to simply being seen by as many as possible, a less-than-radical proposition when facilitated by corporate-owned platforms such as YouTube.

As Rosemary Hennessy points out in her essay *Queer Visibility in Commodity Culture,* "Politically, the aim of queer visibility actions is not to include queers in the cultural dominant but to continually pressure and disclose the heteronormative."[6] Once a video is uploaded to YouTube, it enters a literal marketplace of images where viewers consume a little of this and a little of that. Videos become commodities assigned worth by how many hits, or views, they get—the higher the number, the higher the value, a decidedly capitalist concept. When the larger context or community for making meaning is gone, the image or video is easily fetishized, an exotic, ahistorical artifact. The potential for oppositional meaning, to disrupt business as usual, is lost. Yet it is difficult not to impose a queer read on Paulie and Frankie's video. The quintessential summer romance between Danny and Sandy in *Grease* has been transformed into something different, something potentially queer. This point of transformation is generally where we look for oppositional strategies, whether they are intentional or excavated from the text. Hennessey suggests that "as a political practice, critique acknowledges the importance of 'reading' to political activism. . . . Although they often go unacknowledged, modes of reading are necessary to political activism. . . ."[7] Moving from critique to radical change occurs, according to Hennessey, not just when the commodified object changes form but when there is a demand to make the invisible social relations that produce the object visible. What makes Paulie and Frankie's video new, something to contend with in the here and now, is not the potential for 1990s-style identity politics to be read into it but, instead, the moments where the invisible becomes visible.

Frankie, who performs the role of Danny, looks like she could be Danny. Frankie wears only boys' clothing and is often misrecognized as a boy. While we were taping, two teenage girls watching the action asked if Paulie and Frankie were brother and sister. Paulie laughed and "corrected" the older girls, saying Frankie was a she. Talking about this later, Frankie expressed frustration at such moments. Frankie would rather Paulie let others think she was a boy. Frankie doesn't use male pronouns but does prefer to use a gender-neutral nickname.

When Paulie and Frankie decided to make a video to put on YouTube, it was Frankie who stayed up for days choreographing the dance sequence that allowed Frankie to be Danny. Again, these two young people, at eleven, are not actively expressing queer identities. In fact, they often giggle about crushes on boys. But assuming these crushes are an expression of heterosexuality makes no more sense than assuming their insistence on not being girly-girls means they are lesbians. Either interpretation is premature and simplistic. Paulie and Frankie's video may have caught two young people on the cusp of puberty who will develop into a bisexual tomboy and a gay transman or a femme dyke and an androgynous soccer mom or many other configurations of gender and sexuality that are not simply straight or gay. In his essay *Queering the Binaries: Transituated Identities, Bodies, and Sexualities,* Jason Cromwell writes:

> Transituated discourses are produced by transpeople whose identities, bodies and sexual desires fall outside of the dominant discourses and even outside of the available lesbian and gay discourses. . . . Transituated discourses reverse ontological premises . . . [and] begin the process of reordering the order of things (Foucault 1970). . . . The possibilities open in unexpected and multiple ways. For many within the mainstream of society, the reordering of things and the expression of that reordering in transituated discourses are threatening and subversive.[8]

Paulie and Frankie's video is not an attack on the corporate stranglehold of dominant media practices or an intentional queering of *Grease.* Rather, Paulie and Frankie's video is a production by two young people who transgress their assigned gender roles by simply being themselves. Their simply being reorders a viewer's assumptions of what they are seeing. It is a transituated discourse through visual means and a fundamentally profound shift in how video mediates marginalized and underrepresented voices.

To be clear, simply being is not an essentializing move. I am not suggesting that the profound use of the camera is that it captures an essential core of these two young people. It captures something that is seen but not yet named. Whether this is nature or nurture, something one is born with or something one becomes, is not the point. As José Esteban Muñoz in his book *Disidentifications* notes, "The use-value of any narrative of identity that reduces subjectivity to either a social constructionist model or what has been called an essentialist understanding of the self is especially exhausted."[9] What is exciting here is that the video camera moves from being a tool that gives voice to those excluded from mainstream media productions to also being a tool that captures the changing landscape of gender and sexuality *as it is shifting.* In Paulie and Frankie's video, the camera makes visible the conditions of possibility for configurations of gender and sexual identity outside of hetero- and homonormative playing fields. Reviewing the tape after the shoot, the camera was paused on a frame of Frankie wearing dark sunglasses, leaning jauntily against a jungle gym with arms folded. Frankie looked at the shot and laughed giddily. Frankie asked to rewind to that frame several times, looking and grinning at a self that was both familiar and unknown. The misrecognition of Frankie as a boy that frequently happens is also a recognition of a part of Frankie's gender that does indeed exist. There is a twist in this transituated discourse that shifts the threatening and subversive into a low-flying stealth bomber. There is no transition going on. Frankie is not crossing boundaries or borders. Frankie just is, as is Paulie for that matter. They transgress and traverse multiple identities, including multiple femininities and masculinities. But this transgression cannot be seen, or recognized, until it is misrecognized for something else. It's a tricky proposition. How can we recognize something different if it isn't evidently different? It's something like gaydar, but more finely tuned. As Robbin VanNewkirk points out in her essay "'Gee, I Didn't Get That Vibe from You': Articulating My Own Version of a Femme Lesbian Existence," gaydar is less than accurate. VanNewkirk writes, "If I do not register on the gaydar then the technology is broken by its very rigidness and inability to register complexity."[10]

The technology needed to misrecognize something we actually know is not a technology to serve the machinations of passing—i.e., LGBTQI folks who intentionally pass for straight, as well as assimilationist LGBTQI folks. The technology is closer to the knowledge one in the know employs with trans folks who live stealth, undetected as transgender in dominant hetero- and homonormative cultures. One in the know may not always identify as a stealth FTM or MTF; the misrecognition of a trans person as cisgendered is likely even if in the know. But being in the know allows for the possibility of the interplay between misrecognition and recognition, exactly what the video camera mediates for Frankie. This interplay is the technology that not only changes the form of what we are seeing (straight to gay, cisgendered to transgendered) but also makes visible the social relations that produce the subject. The point is to blow up the shield of invisibility, not hide behind it. The technology, or the camera, is not meant to detect what is stealth; it is meant to detect the stealth bomber—in this case, the queer identity that does not invert. In Kami Chisholm and Elizabeth Stark's documentary *FtF: Female to Femme,* Cornell English professor Masha Raskolnikov explains:

> The fact that femme is so hard to read, the fact that femme in the culture is almost always invisible, except to countercultural insiders somewhat means that the criteria that [Judith] Butler talks about . . . you have to iterate to be real, you perform and in the performance reality is what happens to you, femme is almost that that is not real. . . . In the wider

> culture we get female wrong enough that the thing we really are is not
> even visible, it is not actually real. Our femaleness is, we're playing the
> game right enough that we are not some abjected thing outside the
> magic circle of the real, but our specific thing, the thing we intend, is
> not . . . seen . . . so my colleagues can't see what thing I'm doing even if
> you [the directors] can. And so the fact that I am only real to [you] is an
> effect of a kind of failed iteration.[11]

Moving away from the potentially troubling location of preadolescents, queer
femme identity allows for a deeper exploration of the interplay between misrecognition and recognition. VanNewkirk writes, "I have had my sexuality challenged because I don't think I was *born gay* and I didn't *come out* through some mo-
mentous definitive move. In many ways, the challenge of my version of sexuality
and gender requires (re)identification and *coming out* every day"(emphasis hers).[12]

Elizabeth Stark, the director of *FtF*, suggests there is a social misunderstanding
of the queer femme body similar to ways trans bodies are misunderstood. For
Stark, transitioning is a relational process where "gender as a transition is going
to have to transition society, it's going to have to be a revolution."[13] As writer and
activist Jewelle Gomez declares in the documentary, "To be a femme is to be a
guerrilla in the warfare for a feminist world."[14] These calls to arms can be heard
as a demand for recognition and representation and to be seen. But because queer
femme is that which cannot be seen, either in or out of queer space, recognizing
her is not always possible. At times there is a relational context where she can be
seen by those not in the know: if she is with a butch, a masculine female, or a non-
passing transman. But this relation is insufficient since she is who she is regardless
of proximate masculinity. Chole Brushwood Rose and Anna Camillieri write in
the introduction to the anthology *Brazen Femme,* "What cannot be seen, what
cannot be held or pinned down, is where femme is."[15] Through this frame Stark
and Gomez's demands are not a call to be seen but a call to become conscious of
the power of being both misrecognized and recognized. Here, we can employ the
technology of the frame—literally and as a methodology of critique.

This moment occurred when Frankie looked at the video frame and saw
what others misrecognized. It also happened when I saw a banner hanging over
Olympic boulevard in Los Angeles advertising a video exhibition at the Getty
Museum. The image on the banner was of a pretty white woman with long
flowing hair wearing sunglasses and a sundress and looking out over the LA
landscape in a pose to be looked at. At least that's what I thought the first several
times I saw it. I passed the banners often, glancing out of the corner of my eye
as I drove by. Each time I thought, with frustration, Why is the Getty using the
same tired cliché to sell the video exhibit, the same sexist use of an image of a
woman floating over the streets of LA that sells beer, cars, jeans, you name it?

But there was something about this particular image, and every time I saw it I had an internal dialog about beauty standards, hegemonic definitions of "woman," and the visual reinscription of beauty standards in Los Angeles—white/light skin, thin, long hair, normative femininity. Though I often have this inner dialogue while driving the billboard-laden streets of LA, this particular banner got under my skin. It was the woman in the image. She iterated certain hegemonic tropes of femininity, and she also did not. Her hair was thick, curly, and unruly. There was a tattoo just above the crook of her arm, a place one gets a tattoo for the symbol or because the tattoo artist is a friend, not because they are enhancing a particularly feminine curve. Her dress and sunglasses looked like they could have come from a thrift store rather than a Beverly Hills boutique. She had a slight smirk on her face, like she knew something the one looking at her could never know. She didn't look "available." She looked occupied with her own task, her gaze focused just beyond the viewer, making it clear they weren't a part of her world or a factor in her being seen, her being real.

Rebecca Ann Rugg in her essay "How Does She Look?" describes the picture of queer femme performer Lois Weaver on the cover of the book *How Do I Look? Queer Film and Video*:

> She looks straight . . . but she doesn't look like lesbian chic as seen on
> the cover of *Newsweek* . . . she doesn't have the shiny gloss of the rich.
> That she is beautiful even without that gloss pushes at the conventions
> of beauty. She looks at the unseen screen rather than at the viewer
> who sees her . . . she does not look (like a lesbian, rich, directly at the
> camera). . . . In order not to read her as straight, one must know of her,
> so her status as femme dyke depends on extratextual knowledge.[16]

After visiting the Getty exhibition, I realized I knew the woman on the banner, and I was in the know that she, at least in some contexts, identified as a queer femme.[17] The image was a video still from *Whacker* by Stanya Kahn and Harry Dodge, and the woman was Kahn. That an aspect of Kahn's identity was queer femme wasn't information on the didactic panel accompanying the video in the exhibition. It was a piece of knowledge I had from being in similar communities and art circles with Kahn for several years. Realizing that piece of knowledge gave the banners a completely new meaning. They no longer simply reproduced modes of consumption where art images and exhibitions are devoured as glibly as other products in LA's vast consumer landscape. The banners became another example of how the video camera mediates the interplay between misrecognition and recognition, helping to recklessly endanger (to borrow Noguira's term about the IMCs) hetero- and homonormative iterations of gender.

What was interesting was that I became "one in the know," able to read the image through a queer counterveillance, even though I already was "one in the know." Though I didn't recognize Kahn on the banner, I knew her in another context. In context, I also identify as queer femme. I was in the know without knowing, that strange proposition I suggest of not being able to recognize transgression until it is misrecognized. I return to José Esteban Muñoz's *Disidentifications* to make sense of this. Muñoz borrows the term "identity in difference" from radical Chicana feminist writers Gloria Anzaldúa and Cherríe Moraga and the idea of "differential consciousness" from Chela Sandoval. Muñoz argues that there are ideological restrictions in place that prevent queers of color from completely fulfilling the identification process at a particular site of emergence. He writes, "Identities in difference emerge from a failed interpellation within the dominant public sphere. Their emergence is predicated on their ability to disidentify with the mass public and instead, through this disidentification, contribute to the function of a counter public sphere."[18]

The movement from not recognizing and then recognizing a larger-than-life image of a queer femme was an interrupted moment of emergence. I needed to literally return to the site over and over, a continual failed interpellation of both Kahn and myself, until the extratextual knowledge filtered through and allowed for the streets of LA to shift into a counterpublic sphere that encompassed us both. The examples of disidentification in Muñoz's book are literal staged performances for an audience. Some include a camera; some don't. In the video stills of Frankie in *You're the One that I Want* and Kahn in *Whacker,* these are performances intentionally mediated by a camera for an audience. In these cases the camera captures invisible social relations and mediates a subversive action through a pact that occurs between the performer and the viewer—once the viewer realizes they are in the know.

How can this radical use of the camera translate into concrete political activism that effects social change? Especially when neither of these stills are from videos that are explicitly political? Paulie and Frankie's video is a fun summer project for two young people who want their ten YouTube minutes of fame. Kahn and Dodge's videos engage with social and political issues but are not "political art." They have been described as being too surreal to be overtly political[19] and as having oblique politics "responding to a sociopolitical situation without holding a protest sign."[20] Filmmaker Barbara Hammer writes in her essay "The Politics of Abstraction," "Radical content deserves radical form," and abstract images present "a more amorphous work which allows the maker and the viewer the *pleasure of discovery*" (her emphasis).[21] I agree. I want art to be expansive and have space for the pleasures *and* discomforts of discovery. To visually express the process of misrecognition/recognition, abstract and conceptual language is necessary. At the same time, I want to place the video practice involved in mediating this process in a genealogy that includes the IMCs and all the fantastic and empowering videos that give voice to marginalized and minoritized peoples. These are the roots of the misrecognition/recognition practice.

A way to do this is to stop confining the definition of political art to protest art and, conversely, to recognize the sublime in openly political artworks. It is also necessary to shift the concept of *oblique* to *stealth*. Oblique is a cop-out; stealth is intentional. Oblique can be likened to passing, whereas stealth, if one is being conscious and strategic, can contribute to the dismantling of normative gender and sexuality in explosive ways. This isn't just a rhetorical move. It's queering an approach to video making, queering how one looks through the camera, and queering how one sees what is captured. To be queer, one must become conscious of one's location. Queering one's approach to making video is not to become queer in one's sexual practices but to become conscious of looking 45 degrees off center, askew and somewhat bent.

Similarly, from a queer perspective nuances in naming carry concrete significance. Queer naming is a mode for making invisible social relations not only visible but also productive. This is the other side of the coin to Hennessey's modes of reading and equally important to political activism. Sitting in a bar, lesbian or straight, I may not be read as queer in either. If I consciously name myself a tranny-chasing queer femme, all sorts of invisible social relations become visible, ensuring passing is not the operative mode. Naming myself something other than lesbian queers my location in both hetero- and homonormative spaces. What is significant is that the radical action is more than just naming and visibility: it is the intent to blow up normative social relations. Certainly, this happened when I realized the woman on the banner was Kahn. The frame shifted, halting my ruminations on sexist advertising practices. My engagement with gender, in theory and embodied, became more nuanced and more tangible. I was standing on shifting grounds, in movement, rather than entrenched in an old battle. I was standing in the center of the bull's-eye, *and* I was the stealth bomber. The camera, from either side, was the weapon. I found the revolution, and without realizing it, I was already signed up for the battle.

NOTES

1. Ana Nogueira, "The Birth and Promise of the Indymedia Revolution," in *From ACT UP to the WTO: Urban Protest and Community Building in the Era of Globalization,* eds. Benjamin Shepard and Ronald Hayduk (London: Verso, 2002), 294.

2. Ibid., 291.

3. See Walter Benjamin, "The Work of Art in the Age of Mechanical Reproduction," Marxists Internet Archive, marxists.org, http://www.marxists.org/reference/subject/philosophy/works/ge/benjamin.htm.

4. "YouTube," CrunchBase website, http://www.crunchbase.com/company/YouTube.

5. Pratibha Parmar, "That Moment of Emergence," in *Queer Looks: Perspectives on Lesbian*

and Gay Film and Video, eds. Martha Gever, John Greyson, and Pratibha Parmar (New York: Routledge, 1993), 3.

6. Rosemary Hennessy, "Queer Visibility in Commodity Culture," *Cultural Critique,* no. 29 (Winter 1994–95): 36, http://www.jstor.org/stable/1354421.

7. Ibid., 70–71.

8. Jason Cromwell, "Queering the Binaries: Transituated Identities, Bodies, and Sexualities," in *The Transgender Studies Reader,* eds. Susan Stryker and Stephen Whittle (New York: Routledge, 2006), 519.

9. José Esteban Muñoz, *Disidentifications: Queers of Color and the Performance of Politics* (Minneapolis: University of Minnesota Press, 1999), 5.

10. Robbin VanNewkirk, "'Gee, I Didn't Get That Vibe from You': Articulating My Own Version of a Femme Lesbian Existence," *Journal of Lesbian Studies* 10, nos. 1–2 (2006): 81.

11. Kami Chisholm and Elizabeth Stark, *FtF: Female to Femme* (San Francisco: Frameline, 2006), DVD.

12. VanNewkirk, "'Gee, I Didn't Get That Vibe from You,'" 76.

13. Chisholm and Stark, *FtF: Female to Femme.*

14. Ibid.

15. Chloe Brushwood Rose and Anna Camillieri, *Brazen Femme: Queering Femininity* (Vancouver: Arsenal Pulp Press, 2002), 11.

16. Rebecca Ann Rugg, "How Does She Look?," in *Femme: Feminists, Lesbians, and Bad Girls,* eds. Laura Harris and Elizabeth Crocker (New York: Routledge, 1997), 177–78.

17. I first learned of Kahn from her role in *By Hook or by Crook* (2001), directed by Harry Dodge and Silas Howard. Kahn wrote the dialogue for her character, Billie, a queer femme. I was at a screening of the film shortly after it was released where Dodge and Howard spoke. They described the main characters (which included Billie) as being who they are, "butches who love femmes." Howard and I have also had private conversations about the character of Billie, Kahn's portrayal and dialogue, and queer femme representation. Ironically, it was from Howard and Dodge, two butches, that I first gained insight into Kahn's identifying as a femme.

18. Muñoz, *Disidentifications,* 7.

19. Howard Halle, "An Artist Duo Puts the Id in Idiocy," *Time Out New York,* July 17, 2008, http://newyork.timeout.com/articles/art/39161/harry-dodge-and-stanya-kahn.

20. Jori Finkle, "Unsettling, in a Funny Sort of Way," *New York Times,* March 2, 2008, http://www.nytimes.com/2008/03/02/arts/design/02fink.html.

21. Barbara Hammer, "The Politics of Abstraction," in *Queer Looks,* eds. Gever, Greyson, and Parmar, 70–73.

Representing Uncertainty/ Claiming Indeterminacy

ALIZA SHVARTS'S UNSEEN YALE ART PROJECT

Jennifer Friedlander

In April 2008 Yale senior Aliza Shvarts made international headlines when reports circulated that her senior year art project involved documenting a nine-month cycle in which she repeatedly inseminated herself while taking herbs to induce a miscarriage. Her project, which was cut from the university's senior show amid controversy, consisted of projecting video footage documenting her bleeding in her bathroom onto a cube draped in blood-stained sheets. Although the media dubbed her piece "abortion art," Shvarts maintained that the crux of the piece lay in rendering ambiguous, for both herself and her viewers, whether she had become pregnant and miscarried or whether the blood was the result of menstruation.

In Yale University's official response to the controversy, spokesperson Helaine Klasky described Shvarts's project as a piece of "performance art"—a "creative fiction"—designations that from Klasky's point of view implied that Shvarts's acts were not "real." Klasky also reported that Shvarts had admitted to several Yale administrators that "she neither impregnated herself nor induced any miscarriages"—a statement rendered by media reports as an acknowledgement of a hoax. When asked to comment on this revelation, Shvarts characterized Klasky's testimony as "ultimately inaccurate," maintaining that she did indeed carry out the procedures that the piece documents, although she left the outcome of the acts uncertain.[1]

Customarily, an institution's admission that a documentary art piece under its auspices was a hoax would be an embarrassing if not credibility-breaching disclosure. Yet in the Shvarts case such a declaration was made to augment rather than impeach the institution's integrity. To further complicate matters, Shvarts bristled at the allegations of a hoax, asserting, "I'm not going to absolve them by saying it was some sort of hoax when it wasn't. . . . I started out with the University on board with what I was doing, and because of the media frenzy they've been trying to dissociate with me." In another twist, Klasky responded to Shvarts's reply by announcing that Shvarts had "vowed that if the University revealed her admission," she would deny it. Her denial was part of her performance: "We are disappointed that she would deliberately lie to the press in the name of art."[2]

At first blush such rhetorical gymnastics appear to invoke the logic of a "double deception," in which a subject lies "by telling the truth."[3] According to Jacques Lacan, such double deception distinguishes humans from animals. Animals are unable to "pretend to pretend. . . . [An animal] does not make tracks whose deception lies in the fact that they will be taken as false, while in fact being true ones, ones, that is, that indicate his true trail."[4] In double deception we expect that what we are told or shown is a lie, so if it turns out that we have been given the truth, we feel lied to—doubly deceived. This is what Slavoj Žižek refers to as telling the "truth in the guise of a lie."[5] Žižek, following Lacan, argues that such acts, which "imitate the dissimulation of reality," are "the properly human way to deceive a man."[6] They carry disruptive potential by facilitating an unexpected confrontation with the truth when one is confidently expecting fiction.

At first sight it might appear that Shvarts did indeed "deceive by pretending to deceive," in the sense that her statements were framed as a lie (part of her performance), so that her arguably truthful claim that the events she documented did indeed take place might be taken as further evidence of a hoax.[7] But in order to qualify as a double deception she would have had to claim that it was all just a performance when it really *was* all just a performance. Instead, I suggest, rather than telling the truth in the guise of a lie, Shvarts merely lied in the guise of the truth. When she announced that her piece was not a hoax, she may have been "technically" telling the truth. Nonetheless, she "lied" in the sense that a denial of a hoax was likely to be interpreted as an admission that the accusations that she became pregnant and induced miscarriages were true. In contrast with the truth that emerges in the guise of a lie, I argue, the lie that emerges in the guise of the truth has potentially conservative effects in that it works to confirm the existing social order.

More generally, this essay uses Shvarts's case as an opportunity to assess the political implications of artistic forms in which modes and/or claims of deception play a central role. Specifically, the Shvarts controversy enables us to focus on the respective difficulties encountered in both dissimulation and simulation as strategies for upsetting the social order. Ultimately, I argue that by falling short of creating a double deception and by bungling an attempt at staging a simulation, her piece not only fails to act as a socially disruptive force but also provides institutions geared toward upholding order with an opportunity to strengthen their grip.

The controversy surrounding Shvarts's project differs from more familiar controversies surrounding video documentary, which tend to center on the truth claims of documentary forms of representation. We commonly encounter accusations that a video "lies" by representing fiction in the form of fact—a form of deception that follows the straightforward logic of the fake. But in Shvarts's case, no one questions whether the events displayed in the video—Shvarts's bleeding in her bathroom—really occurred. Rather than trying to fool us into mistaking fiction for fact, Shvarts encourages us to experience facts as if they are no more than fictions. Such a strategy, Žižek suggests, carries subversive potential if it succeeds in upsetting the fantasy framework upon which reality depends. Shvarts's case reveals, however, the way in which this strategy can also be deployed in the service of a conservative form of postmodern thought. In such cases a mere epistemological uncertainty, such as our inability to know whether Shvarts became pregnant and miscarried, gets mistaken for an ontological certainty that there is no real event to be known and, as such, reduces reality retrospectively to a discursive artifact.

We can see this mistake at work in Shvarts's rhetoric. She boasts that "no one can say with 100% certainty that anything in the piece did or did not happen."[8] But she then confuses epistemology with ontology by adopting Jean Baudrillard's language of the simulacrum (or as he sometimes calls it, simulation, as opposed to dissimulation). For example, she explains in the *Yale Daily News* that "the piece only exists in the telling. This telling can take textual, visual, spatial, temporal and performative forms—copies of copies of which there are no originals." Here, she jumps explicitly from the inability to know to the claim that nothing exists to know. Her confusion points to a key tension within the political potential of the simulacrum as a transgressive form. Simulation is a form of deception that in its proper form presents us with the ontological puzzle of indeterminacy. By disrupting the symbolic order—or in Baudrillard's terms, the "principles of reality"—such a form has transgressive political potential. As a result of its potentially disruptive nature, such revelations of indeterminacy are often met by efforts on behalf of the symbolic order to reframe them as examples of mere uncertainty.[9]

Rather than actually accomplishing a simulacral piece, however, Shvarts merely fakes it. She engages in a dissimulation rather than a simulation. Thus, I argue that her claim to have created a simulation is itself a dissimulation—a contention that reveals the implicitly and inherently reactionary nature of the project, despite the subversive political potential suggested by her rhetoric. I further argue that in faking or dissimulating a simulation, Shvarts not only falls short of undermining the principles of reality but also provides institutions of power and order with opportunities to more firmly stake their claims.

For Baudrillard a proper simulation—or what he also calls a simulacrum—carries the subversive possibility of eroding the reality principle upon which law and order thrive. But insurmountable difficulties arise in any attempt to stage a simulacrum. If it were successful, then it would be mistaken for reality. Consider, for example, Baudrillard's question of what the police would make of a simulated holdup. Even with harmless weapons and a hostage who was in the know, one would nonetheless find oneself mixed up with reality. As he suggests, the victim would really give over their money, someone would have a heart attack, a police officer would fire a gun, and so forth. The pragmatic difficulties of staging a successful simulacrum are further complicated by the efforts of those in power to deny that a simulation has occurred. As Baudrillard contends, "The repressive apparatus would . . . react MORE violently to a simulated hold up than a real one."[10] A "real hold up," he argues, "only upsets the order of things . . . whereas a simulated hold up interferes with the very principle of reality."[11] Thus, for Baudrillard a simulated crime poses a much greater disturbance to law and order than does a real crime. A real crime emerges as an aberration that reinforces existing law and order, whereas a simulated crime "suggests . . . that law and order themselves might really be nothing more than a simulation."[12] As a result, when faced with a simulacrum holders of power "always opt for the real." They work to "reinject realness and referentiality everywhere, in order to convince us of the reality of the social."[13]

Baudrillard carefully distinguishes simulation (in which notions of true and false are rendered inoperative) from the more common category of dissimulation (in which the false is presented as true). Dissimulation involves pretending or feigning: one can dissimulate being ill by going to bed and surrounding oneself with crumpled-up tissues and cups of tea. If one wishes to simulate illness in Baudrillard's sense, however, then one must "produce 'true' symptoms" of the illness, which would raise doubt over whether that person was not indeed ill.[14] Thus, a simulation makes indeterminate the health status of the person simulating an illness. Such indeterminacy escapes the confines of reality and confronts us with glimpses of what Lacan calls the Real, the dimension in which the symbolic order fails.

This connection between Baudrillard's concept of simulation and Lacan's notion of the Real helps to foreground why a true simulation is both so potentially subversive and so difficult to achieve. For Lacan the Real refers to points of limitation within the sociosymbolic order that violate the consistency of what we think of as reality. Such anomalies must be covered over by the symbolic system in order for what we perceive as reality to make sense. Since it defies symbolization, the Real can never be fully apprehended, only glimpsed through unsettling missed encounters. Eruptions of the Real disturb our sense of reality by confronting us with phenomena that more than uncertain are indeterminate. Their disruptive potential lies in such indeterminacy that defies systems of classification. In the words of Paul Verhaeghe, these disturbances "can no longer be put into words. . . . This dimension beyond the signifier is the Lacanian real."[15]

True simulations can exist, as is my contention, only within this realm of the Lacanian Real. In the other two registers posited by Lacan, the imaginary (which facilitates identifications through appearance) and the symbolic (which structures the world through systems of signification), simulation is impossible. In these realms we can ever only dissimulate. I learned this all too well while in college when for a period I was preoccupied with trying to look taller than I really was. My first attempt at faking a tall appearance was a disaster. I wore pants that were a bit too short, applying the logic that if I really was a tall person, then it would be difficult to find pants long enough to suit my limbs. Therefore, I reasoned, even if I did not *appear* tall, any thinking person would deduce that I must nonetheless actually *be* tall. The visual effect was, of course, that I actually looked shorter, since the foreshortened pant legs created the appearance of even squatter legs. Because it relied upon cultural knowledge and inference, this was an attempt at dissimulation at the level of the symbolic.

After catching sight of myself in a full-length mirror, I soon realized the ineffectuality of this strategy of symbolic deception and took my dissimulation to the level of the imaginary. This involved the more obvious but opposite approach of wearing pants that were a bit too long, creating the illusion of longer legs. Yet this approach also failed, because anyone who really thought about it would know that pants appear too long only on people who are too short. In sum, it seemed the only option was the impossible prospect of creating indeterminacy about my height that would throw into crisis the very categories of short and tall. Such a radical undermining could take place only through simulation in the realm of the Real, the difficulty of which I was unable to negotiate.[16]

Despite its attempt to enter the transgressive realm of simulation, Shvarts's piece, like my own misguided dissimulation of height, fails to move beyond the status of a dissimulation. Yale University's insistence that Shvarts had confirmed that her piece was a "creative fiction" (or in the mass media's terminology, a hoax) and that she therefore had not become pregnant precisely enacts the move that instruments of power would be expected to make when faced with a threat to the existing order—namely, attempting to diffuse the threat by assimilating it into the symbolic order, thereby reinstituting the binary logic of true and false that is characteristic of dissimulation. By substituting uncertainty for indeterminacy, Shvarts herself unintentionally appropriates this tactic in which conservative forces defuse simulations. To be specific, she ambiguates the question of the piece's truth or falsity by stating that "no one can say with 100% certainty that anything in the piece did or did not happen."[17] She thus creates mere epistemological uncertainty rather than the full-blooded indeterminacy required for simulation to occur. Despite her implicit invocation of Baudrillard, Shvarts misses the mark in creating a simulation. Instead, as I did with my strategy of wearing pants that were too short in order to fake a taller stature, she does no better than achieve a dissimulation in the symbolic realm.

But against expectation, the move by Yale University to pull the piece from the senior show does at least open up the piece to transgressive possibilities associated with the simulacrum. To be specific, by remaining absent and unseen—a gap in the symbolic—Shvarts's piece threatens to become not merely uncertain but rather truly indeterminate, thus injecting it with the spirit of the Lacanian Real. Ultimately, it therefore seems that the only sure success Shvarts's piece achieves is as evidence of the overwhelming difficulties of undertaking politically transgressive work in the realm of artistic production.

NOTES

1. Zachary Abrahamson, Thomas Kaplan, and Martine Powers, "Shvarts, Yale Clash over Project," *Yale Daily News,* April 18, 2008, http://www.yaledailynews.com/news/university-news/2008/04/18/shvarts-yale-clash-over-project.

2. Ibid.

3. Henry Krips, *Fetish: An Erotics of Culture* (Ithaca, N.Y.: Cornell University Press, 1999), 17.

4. Jacques Lacan, *Ecrits: A Selection,* trans. Alan Sheridan (New York: Tavistock, 1977), 305.

5. Slavoj Žižek, "Desire: Drive = Truth: Knowledge," lacan.com, http://lacan.com/zizek-desire.htm.

6. Slavoj Žižek, *The Sublime Object of Ideology* (London: Verso, 1989), 196.

7. Ibid., 197.

8. Abrahamson, Kaplan, and Powers, "Shvarts."

9. Jean Baudrillard, "Simulacra and Simulations" in *Jean Baudrillard, Selected Writings,* ed. Mark Poster. (Palo Alto, Calif.: Stanford University Press, 1988), 8.

10. Ibid., 7.

11. Ibid., 7.

12. Ibid., 7.

13. Ibid., 9.

14. Ibid., 2.

15. Paul Verhaeghe, *Beyond Gender: From Subject to Drive* (New York: Other Press, 2001), 39.

16. These distinctions also illuminate a key limitation within mediated attempts at creating realist images. The strategy of aesthetic realism deploys the logic of the symbolic: conventional codes of filmic realism, for instance, such as black-and-white footage and shaky camera work, conspire to create a realist illusion. We recognize them as indicators of realism even though in actuality they work to distance the image from its real-world appearance. The strategies employed by transparent realism operate, by contrast, within the logic of the imaginary. They involve efforts to create the illusion that one is witnessing a real world unfolding before one's eyes. The appearance of reality is thus maximized only when one suspends one's cultural knowledge.

17. Abrahamson, Kaplan, and Powers, "Shvarts."

21 I Got This Way from Eating Rice

GAY ASIAN DOCUMENTARY AND THE REEDUCATION OF DESIRE

Nguyen Tan Hoang

In Ming-Yuen S. Ma's experimental documentary *Slanted Vision* (1995), film scholar Laura Marks describes her pleasure in watching hard-core gay male pornography in a sequence entitled "Confession of a Porn Viewer, Part 2." She proposes her "fag hag gaze" as part of her theory of an S/M model of looking. In place of the phallic gaze's fixed opposition between the male subject of the look and the female object-to-be-looked-at, an S/M model of erotic looking offers a "fluidity of movement" between subject and object, domination and submission and produces pleasure through the negotiation and exchange of power.[1] In this sequence a female hand scans a small video monitor over the body of an Asian man; on the video monitor plays a porn clip of an Asian man getting fucked by a white man. As the sequence juxtaposes two views of eroticized Asian male bodies, characterized by Marks as "haptic and optical" looking, we hear Marks's narration:

> Looking at gay porn, I borrow a gay man's look at another man. If a man has a desiring gaze at another man, I could sort of drop in on it. I can take it for a ride. It feels especially liberating for me in gay porn because it's two men, so they're at least potentially equals. There's this feeling of playfulness I so long for between two people who can take turns looking and being looked at, touching and being touched, fucking and being fucked, being the top, being the bottom. There's this feeling that they can always switch. And also, the image of a man being vanquished, a man giving in to pleasure, and to being *done* to, is exciting for me because it's so rare in hetero images. I hate these theories that say we must disarm the objectifying, phallic, powerful gaze upon other people's bodies. I think that these theories give too much power to this kind of look. . . . I don't want everybody to be disarmed, equal, touchy-feely, always treating each other like full, autonomous subjects. I think this is a tedious democracy of looking. I think it's a bore. Sexuality is not

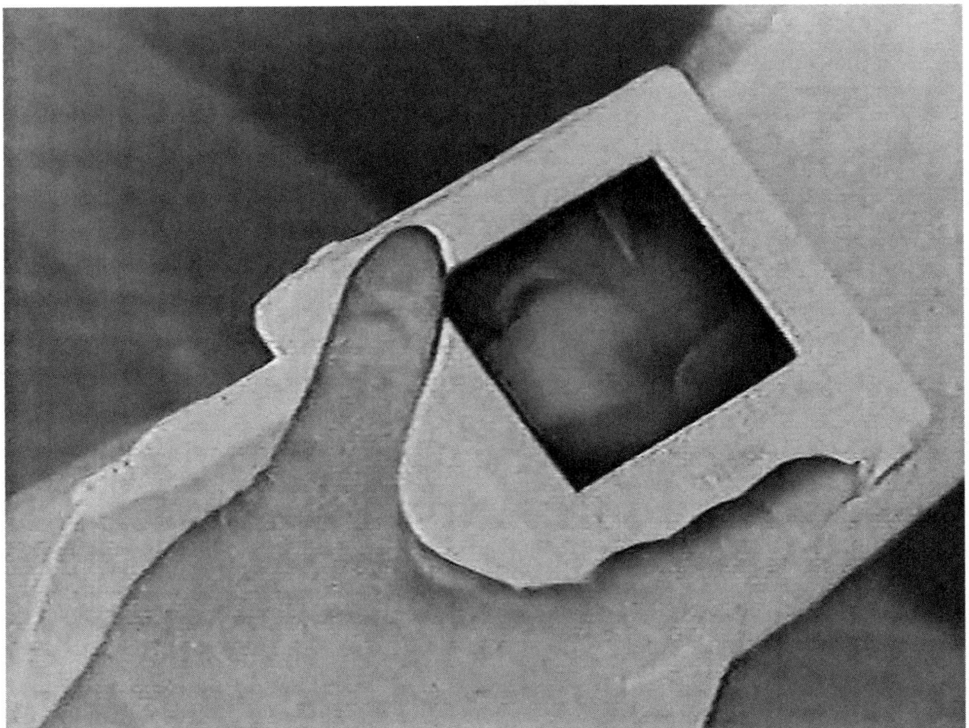

Still from *Slanted Vision (1995),* by Ming-Yuen S. Ma. Courtesy of the artist.

about equality; it's about an exchange of power. What I want is for that power to flow around more.

Watching two gay men fucking allows Marks to adopt a dominant position by borrowing "a gay man's look at other men" and to witness a liberating reversibility of the gaze. Her frank rejection of a "disarmed, equal, touchy-feely, . . . tedious democracy of looking" rings true. I must register, however, my reservation with the ways in which Marks glosses over the specific relations of power in gay male porn that remain resistant to the kind of mobility and play that she champions. As numerous gay Asian North American cultural critics and artists have noted, the playfulness and negotiation between "looking and being looked at," "fucking and being fucked," and "being the top, being the bottom" continue to be inaccessible to gay Asian men, who are relegated to only one side of the equation, that of bottomhood, when they figure in the equation at all.

In spite of its problems, her argument resonates with me because it echoes the claims of a group of documentaries produced by gay Asian men in the United States, Canada, and Australia in the mid- to late 1990s. These experimental documentaries include the aforementioned *Slanted Vision* by Ming-Yuen S. Ma (USA,

1995), my own video *7 Steps to Sticky Heaven* (USA, 1995), Tony Ayres's *China Dolls* (Australia, 1997), and Wayne Yung's *The Queen's Cantonese* (Canada, 1998).[2] These experimental documentaries construct an erotics of looking that mobilizes the charge of interracial sexual representation only to cast it out—that is, to replace this politically troubling depiction with a more equal, touchy-feely, and politically palatable imagery.[3] They seek to contest the feminization and desexualization of Asian men in gay visual culture by presenting self-consciously performative, sexually explicit material, which acts as an urgent *counterpornography*. A central component of the reeducation of desire for these films' intended gay Asian male audience is the goal of replacing the so-called wrong, misguided desire for white men with a supposedly more empowering desire for other Asian men—i.e., the conversion of potato queens into sticky rice.[4] Such a shift ostensibly signals a concomitant shift in masculine agency from passive sexual object (the Asian boy toy) to active sexual subject (the politicized agent). I contend, however, that this politically correct lesson fails to account for desires and identifications that cannot be so easily disciplined, especially those desires that embrace bottom-hood and femininity. In other words, such a reeducation ends up arresting the play of desire and marginalizing a gay Asian male subject's desire for submission and domination—in effect, a move that curtails a gay Asian subject's choice and sexual possibilities.

By describing these videos' ideological project in this way, my defense of the gay Asian male desire for bottomhood and femininity circles back to Marks's championing of an S/M erotics of looking. Instead of viewing these competing claims as irreconcilable (my critique of both Marks *and* the gay Asian documentaries' prescriptive reeducation of desire), a more illuminating perspective would be to consider Marks's position as demarcating the social and political context in which the gay Asian documentaries provide a fundamental critique. More specifically, the documentaries contest Marks's subsuming of race under sexuality and gender. As Richard Fung notes, though "'the spectator's positions in relation to . . . [gay male pornographic] representations are open and in flux,' this observation applies only when all the participants are white. Race introduces another dimension that may serve to close down some of this mobility."[5] The fact that the gay Asian videos also end up closing down some of this mobility in their highlighting of same-race desire does not undermine their important and necessary intervention into the discourse of gay Asian sexual representation at the specific historical juncture of mid-1990s sexual-racial politics. Rather, my interrogation of Marks's S/M model of looking and of the gay Asian documentaries' sticky rice lesson seeks to challenge both projects' relegation of bottomhood to a low status. Instead of advocating for an equal-time, reversible S/M scopic and sexual play or to legislate meaningful sex acts with partners of the right race, a more radical lesson would be to endorse a politics that enables a multiplicity of desires and identifications, including those that insist on fixity rather than mobility. For certain subjects, dwelling in the abject space of bottomhood and femininity can be a mode of critical resistance.

In his landmark study on gay and lesbian cinema *Now You See It,* film scholar Richard Dyer identifies three central goals of gay and lesbian affirmative documentary (his corpus are all pre-1980). To combat negative portrayals of queers in dominant culture, gay affirmative documentary advocates positive representation, which entails "thereness, insisting on the fact of our existence; goodness, asserting our worth and that of our life-styles; and realness, showing what we were in fact like."[6] Significantly, Dyer points out that a conflict exists between the first two goals, thereness and goodness, and the third, realness. Consequently, gay documentaries from the early years of gay liberation frequently sideline "conflict, contradiction and difficulty" within gay communities in order to project a united public face.[7]

In addition to the pre-1980 corpus analyzed by Dyer, the gay Asian documentaries owe their aesthetic and political debts to the work produced by queer of color filmmakers coming out of the United States, Canada, and the United Kingdom in the 1980s such as Marlon Riggs, Isaac Julien, Pratibha Parmar, Cheryl Dunye, and most important, Richard Fung.[8] These pioneering works—which mostly are experimental documentaries—pose a critical challenge to the hip "homo pomo" narrative films of the early 1990s hyped as the New Queer Cinema, which did not explicitly concern itself with questions of racial politics. As Eve Oishi notes, the works of Riggs, Parma, and others are "ostensibly and explicitly *about* queer black, Latino, or Asian identity . . . [and represent] a certain committed identity politics necessitated by the state of queer cinema and activism, the politics of communities of color, and the alternative invisibility or demonization of queers and people of color within conservative political climates."[9] In addition to these filmic lineages, another significant enabling context for the production of these works was the new queer Asian visibility that emerged in the 1990s as a result of political organizing around gay and Asian identity issues, as well as HIV/AIDS activism.

As these different, overlapping filmic and political genealogies make clear, the work of queer of color filmmakers constitutes a dramatic intervention in independent gay and lesbian film and video making with its attention to racial matters and expands the concerns of ethnic-based film and video productions with its analysis of sexuality. In their anthology *Q & A: Queer in Asian America,* which effectively launches the field of queer Asian American studies, David Eng and Alice Hom posit that "one does not become queer merely through sex or sexuality" and that "one may also become queer in opposition to other queers."[10] In that same volume, Jasbir Puar's analysis of "queer diaspora" offers an incisive critique of the trendy celebration of "transnational sexualities."

She cautions against the careless importation of "visibility politics," couched in terms of "coming out or being out," across cultural and national borders: "This privileging of being out sets forth sexual identity as separable from other identities, or at least as primary and uninflected by other subject positionings. This narrative posits a domestic perspective as a diasporic perspective that becomes a globalizing tendency."[11] It is precisely these vexed intersections of domestic and transnational, queer and diaspora that the gay Asian documentaries thematize.

In constructing a queer diasporic space that allows for the enactment of sticky rice desire, these gay Asian videotapes critically rework the project of gay affirmative documentaries in two essential ways: the first is the displacement of the centrality of the voice; the second is the role of sexual performance. The videos consistently interrogate the privileging of the voice as a source of knowledge, truth, and authenticity. A key issue here is the fact that for the majority of these interview subjects, English constitutes a second language. Again and again, these videotapes cogently thematize the difficulty of speaking about sex and sexuality on camera in a foreign tongue. *Slanted Vision* foregrounds processes of translation and mistranslation by offering awkward literal translations from Chinese to English of sex parts, such as *broccoli, jade flute,* and *chicken's ass,* and sex acts, such as *shooting airplanes, flying a kite, sitting on a candle,* and *squeezing black beans.* Wayne Yung's tape, *The Queen's Cantonese,* most compellingly examines the role of language and the dominance of the speaking voice with its investigation of gay Asian North American identity and sexual politics in the framework of a conversational language course. In place of heteronormative roles and rituals presented in conventional language tapes, the exercises and dramatizations in Yung's language lessons include gay-sensitive scenarios such as cruising men in the park, bargaining at the bathhouse, and politely asking your trick to leave after sex. The language student learns to speak Cantonese through being interpellated as a gay Asian subject. At the beginning of "Lesson I," the "Occupations" dramatization introduces us to the three protagonists who will accompany us in our Cantonese-language excursions. The first is a bleached-blond young Asian man who announces, in Cantonese, "I am a potato queen, which is someone who likes to do it with white men." The second, a dark-haired white French Canadian, states, "I am a rice queen, which is someone who likes to do it with Asian men." The third, another young Asian man, tells us, "I mostly do it with white guys, so that makes me a potato queen; but now I like Asians too, so maybe I'm sticky rice." As the lessons in the rest of the video reveal, a central aim of the conversational course is to teach the student to learn to appreciate and adopt the position of sticky rice.

Though most explicit in *The Queen's Cantonese,* a pedagogical project pervades the other videos, as well. A key pedagogical strategy utilized in these works is the use of sexual imagery. All four videotapes contain material of differing

Stills from
*The Queen's
Cantonese* (1998),
by Wayne Yung.
Courtesy of
the artist.

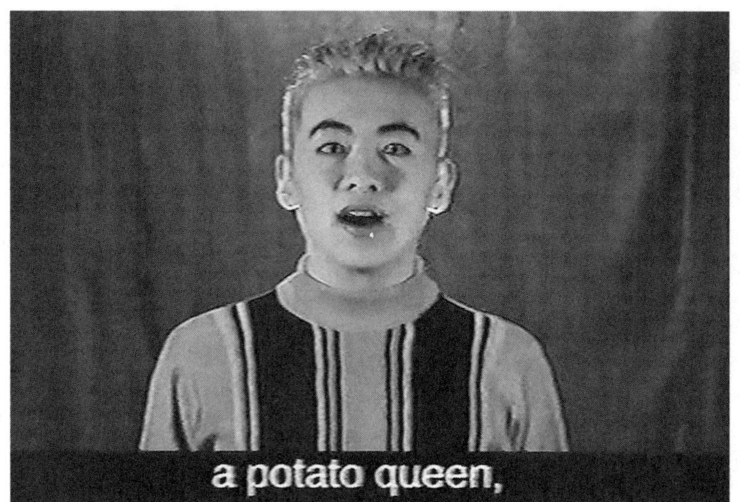
a potato queen,

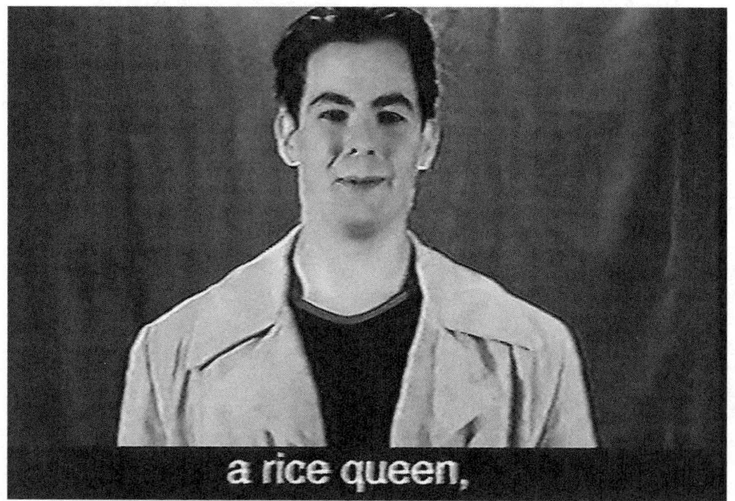
a rice queen,

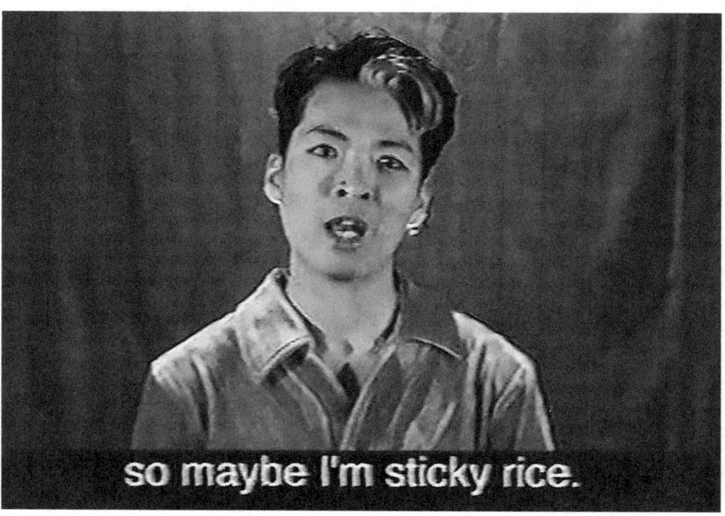
so maybe I'm sticky rice.

levels of sexual explicitness, from lyrical soft core to raunchy hard core, images that could be said to function as a counterpornography, combating the ways that Asian men have been typecast in gay pornography as passive, submissive bottoms. As numerous gay critics have pointed out, pornography occupies a central place in gay male culture: it is the *one* arena where gay men get to see their sexuality imaged and affirmed. As Dyer has famously observed, however, although pornography gives us experiential knowledge of our bodies, porn as it exists teaches us the wrong kind of knowledge. Gay pornography, like its straight counterpart, privileges the experience of the fucker and his relentless drive toward visible coming. Dyer writes, "At the level of public representation gay men may be thought of as deviant and disruptive of masculine norms because we assert the pleasures of being fucked and the eroticism of the anus, in our pornography this takes a back seat."[12] In his essay "Looking for My Penis," Richard Fung fleshes out Dyer's critical observations by exposing the racial coding of North American gay porn, which as he persuasively argues, persistently relegates Asian men to the back seat, where they automatically lift their legs in the air and are taken for a ride by white tops.

We witness such an exercise of the gay racial hierarchy of desire operating in a sexually explicit sequence from *7 Steps to Sticky Heaven*. In "Step 3: XXX," characterized as a "commercial interruption" to the video's presentation of "sticky rice boys," a gay Asian informant testifies in voice-over that "everyone falls for . . . images of white men with tight bodies, six packs, and bulging biceps" and that the speaker himself wants to have "some white gay man . . . take me [and] dominate me." Another man confesses that he likes to have rough sex with Caucasian men but pretends that there is more meaning to the sex he has with Asians. On the image track, we see the "dominant trip" and "rough sex" enacted by the Asian video maker himself: he gets spanked, fucked, and dominated by his white ex-boyfriend. Following up on the insight offered by Dyer and Fung, we can identify this sexually explicit sequence as the "bad knowledge" that porn offers—the fantasies of domination and submission responsible for what Fung posits as the conflation of Asian and anus. And yet the fact that I include such a sequence in a video that is supposed to extol the joys of Asian men getting together betrays the irresistible attraction to this allegedly bad knowledge based on racial objectification and abjection.

If these gay Asian videos are invested in a pedagogical project, what is the lesson being taught? A lesson in sticky rice eroticism. The rehearsal of various subject positions in these tapes—namely potato queens, rice queens, and sticky rice—sets up a crucial appendix to the coming out narrative found in conventional gay affirmative documentaries. In addition to realizing one's gay feelings and making them audible and public, these works complement the coming out narrative with the *coming into consciousness* as sticky rice. Interview subjects begin by confessing their desire for white men in embarrassed tones and nervous giggles and end with giddy, celebratory proclamations about discovering the novel *and* familiar sexiness of Asian men. My own video instructs the intended gay Asian viewer how to reach sticky heaven in seven easy steps. Interestingly, the video not only defines but also *justifies* sticky rice desire. My voice-off interview questions include "What's sticky rice all about?" and "What kind of rice do you like?," as well as "Why did you turn sticky?" and "How is sex different with Asian men?" For all of its sexual explicitness, the affective tone of the video corresponds more to an antiporn feminist definition of erotica, which views sexuality as "a way of bonding, of giving and receiving pleasure, bridging differentness, discovering sameness, and communicating emotion."[13]

Up to this point, my discussions of *The Queen's Cantonese* and *7 Steps to Sticky Heaven* have highlighted the ways in which the construction of a sticky rice field, as an in-between queer Asian diasporic space, rests on the maintenance of a sexy, productive tension between the homoscape and the ethnoscape.[14] I now turn to an example that encourages us to interrogate the assumption that queer diasporic discourse is necessarily always oppositional. Exploiting food analogies, the sequence titles in *China Dolls* tracks a similar trajectory as *The Queen's Cantonese* and *7 Steps* with its shifts from "Potato Queen" to "Sticky Rice" to "Fruit Salad." In the "Sticky Rice" segment, Ayres describes a formative sexual encounter with another Chinese man when he traveled to China for the first time on a work assignment. While the image track shows Ayres snapping pictures and the images of his trip projected on-screen, we hear his narration, "I was looking for my roots, a sense of my Chineseness. Unfortunately though, most people on the mainland mistook me for a Japanese tourist." Ayres's narration continues:

> But one significant thing happened. I met a man called Robert, and we spent the night together. I had never slept with a Chinese man before. But it was as familiar as touching myself. Chinese skin. Hard and smooth and polished. Perhaps for the first time, I felt desire which had nothing to do with race. He didn't want me because I was Chinese. I didn't not want him because he was Chinese. We were simply attracted to each other. It was the most liberating experience of my life.

In contrast to the raunchy and thrilling rough sex between an Asian man and a white man in *7 Steps*, the erotic charge of sticky rice coupling in *China Dolls* results not from difference and power imbalance but from familiarity and symmetry. As Ayres narrates his desire for another Chinese man, a desire that "had nothing to do with race," we see two young, muscular Asian men kissing and caressing each other's "hard and smooth and polished" skin. Moody lighting, dramatic close-ups, a chroma-keyed background of fuzzy yellow swirls, and a

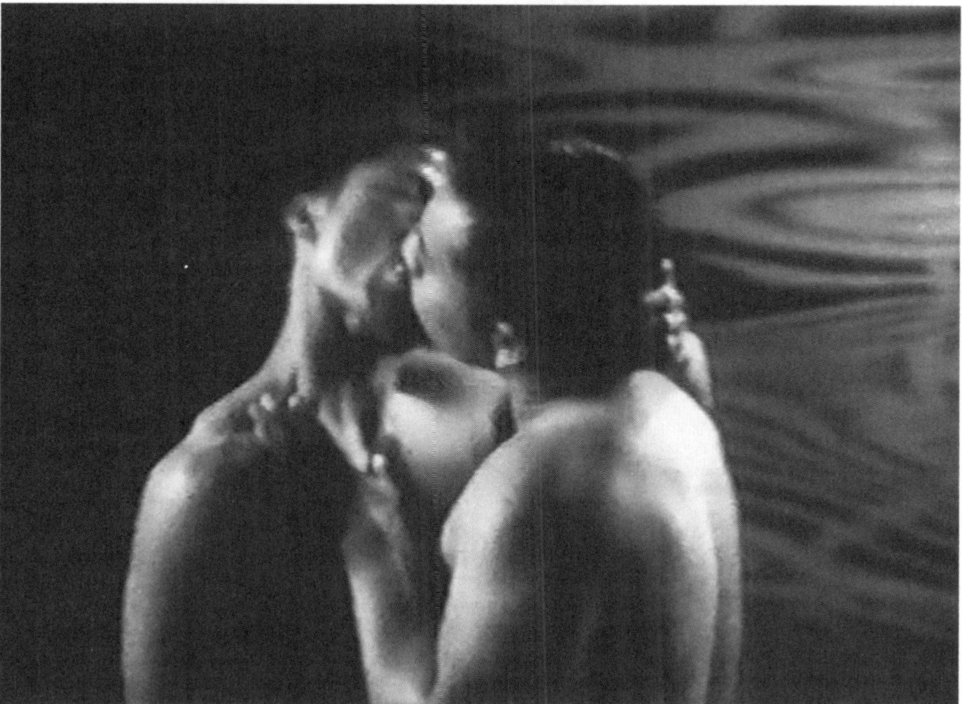

Still from *China Dolls* (1997). Written and directed by Tony Ayres. Produced by Helen Bowden. Courtesy of the artist.

slow-motion frame rate work together to blur physical differences between the two men. In watching the "most liberating experience" of the filmmaker's life unfold, we witness how both partners partake in an "equal, touchy-feely" mode of relating, how they treat "each other like full, autonomous subjects," to recall Marks's apt description. It is noteworthy that this "democracy" of looking and being looked at, touching and being touched, is made possible only by Ayres's return to his roots. Like the affirmative documentaries Dyer discusses, conflict and contradiction are smoothed over in the liberation afforded by Asian/Asian eroticism; national, class, and linguistic antagonisms become subsumed under the banner of race and ethnicity. Never mind the fact that the Chinese locals mistook him for a Japanese tourist, in the end what mattered was, as Ayres eloquently pronounces about his first Chinese lover, that "he didn't want me because I *was* Chinese. I didn't *not* want him because he was Chinese. We were simply attracted to each other." Although such a claim might simply be read as a description of a desire unadulterated by race (*and* racism)—an attraction exceeding history, space, and time—the use of a double negative suggests another potential claim: "I wanted him *because* he was Chinese."

Of the four videos discussed here, *Slanted Vision* concerns itself most explicitly with the subject of gay Asian men and pornographic representation; hence, it deals directly with the question of how to reenvision such representation. Early on in this visually and theoretically dense video, Ma confesses his inability to enjoy porn videos featuring Asian men, because these videos often cast Asians in offensive, stereotypical roles, such as waiters, houseboys, masseurs, and exchange students. Consequently, Ma's own video progresses from a dry, intellectual analysis of the pornographic depictions of Asian men in such badly dubbed titles as *Shanghai Meat Company, Eggroll for Two,* and *Pacific Fever* to a sequence later in the tape titled "Non-Gratuitous Sex Scene," in which Ma engages in sex with another Asian man. This sequence cogently demonstrates the function of sexual performance in the gay Asian works I have been discussing.

Self-reflexively pointing to the conditions of its making, the sequence cuts between two views of the sexual action. One is composed of medium shots in blue, grainy Super 8 film stock from the perspective of an "outside" cameraperson (Quentin Lee); the other view, shot with a video camera, resulting in red-hot hues, and set in slow motion, is from the perspectives of the participants in the scene (Ma and Napoleon Lustre) as they hand the camera back and forth. The sequence is backed by the hypnotic West Javanese popular song "Tongeret," by Idjah Hadidjah, along with a whispery recitation of a poem by Lustre. Toward the conclusion of the sequence, the aural lyricism is interrupted by an interview voice-over in which the HIV-positive narrator relates an incident where he had to stop his sexual partner from swallowing his cum.

What is interesting for our discussion at hand is the manner in which the scene of sticky rice sexual coupling is culturally, politically, and aesthetically situated—that is, the scene's multilayered self-reflexivity calls attention to this sticky rice space neither as a field of dreams waiting to be found nor as a fantasy of origins to be discovered but as one that is self-consciously constructed in a specific time and place. As a queer Asian diasporic invention, this sticky rice field is made up of heterogeneous, impure, inauthentic, and competing elements: shaky cameras, underexposed Super 8 film footage, electric video colors that bleed, an exotic- and traditional-sounding (because it's untranslated) Indonesian song, a poem being recited in accented English so hushed that the viewer can barely make it out, a Chinese American man performing sex with a Filipino American man expressedly *for* this video (that is, there is no romantic justification for the sex here), and most remarkably, the "intrusion" of disease into a scene that is supposed to signify a new and improved, sexy and pleasurable vision of Asian/Asian homoeroticism. Lustre's poetic allusion to a pilgrimage to Lourdes to find an AIDS cure and the unnamed narrator's mention of HIV-infected semen constitute two crucial moments in the scene that announce the unavoidable framework of HIV/AIDS as the broader context for *any* project of reeducating desire in the 1990s.[15] Instead of seeing sticky rice desire as a natural manifestation of an essential gay Asian sexuality that has somehow been perverted and co-opted by a white gay racial economy of desire, *Slanted Vision* acknowledges sticky rice as a politically inflected and culturally specific intervention in Western gay male sexual politics and the politics of sexual representation.

Though *Slanted Vision* historicizes sticky rice desire much more effectively than the other three documentaries, I maintain that all four works participate in a similar political project. Taken together, they critique the placement of Asian men on the bottom of the gay sexual hierarchy; sexual performance in the documentaries seeks to make up for the paucity of sexy images of Asian men and to engage the spectator "politically . . . [and] also physiologically."[16] Producing spectatorship as sexual exchange, these videos seek to *move* the spectator by producing Asian men as desiring subjects *and* desired objects. A sticky rice eroticism based on familiarity, symmetry, and sameness but also strangeness, imbalance, and novelty triumphs over a rice queenliness based on domination, objectification, and rough sex.

Unfortunately, for some gay Asian men this lesson is hard to swallow. The road from object status, Oriental boy toy, to subject status, liberated sticky rice man, is riddled with potholes: the persistent desires and identifications of Asian bottomhood return with a vengeance. For instance, in *Slanted Vision* Quentin Lee, reflecting on his star turn in the porn video *Shanghai Meat Company*, claims that being objectified in an Orientalist manner actually made him feel desirable. In the same documentary another interviewee confesses his intense pleasure from being tied up, humiliated, and fucked by a white man, simply because he was showering him with so much attention. Even the usage of rice as the preferred metaphor runs into complications. As Song Cho points out in the introduction to his edited collection *Rice: Explorations into Gay Asian Culture and Politics*, rice constitutes a "life-sustaining staple of Asian cultures" but also represents a dominant "metaphor for gay Asians *and* how we are consumed by white gay culture as exotic 'tricks.'"[17]

In the same vein, in *7 Steps to Sticky Heaven* Asian gay boys list the same traits that rice queens often mention to account for why they find other Asians attractive: slanted eyes, smooth skin, hairless body, little brown nipples, and cute dick. A sense of ambivalence about rice as sexual metaphor is registered in the video itself, specifically in the transitional segments that show the video maker eating from a bowl of rice. One particular moment late in the video displays a dramatic cut between a high-angle medium close-up of the maker sucking another Asian man's cock to another shot from a similar perspective of him ravenously shoveling rice into his mouth. While the graphic match of sucking rice dick to shoveling rice bowl makes literal the link between cultural sustenance and sexual empowerment, the voraciousness of the sucking and shoveling also

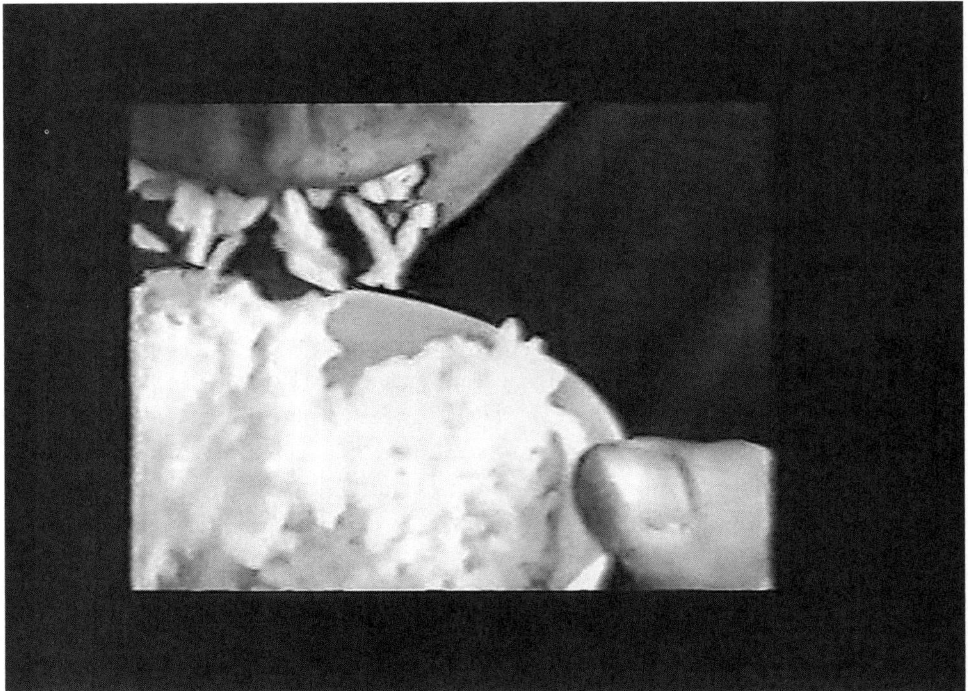

Still from *7 Steps to Sticky Heaven* (1995), by Nguyen Tan Hoang. Courtesy of the artist.

bespeak a certain ambivalence: do these actions signify insatiable hunger or a force-feeding? Earlier in the same video, one sticky rice convert cheerily explains that dating Asian men is "kind of a hot thing right now. Ethnicity is in!" Another points out that Asian men whose partners are white must remain in the closet about their relationships: it's a "shame thing," he admits.

By way of concluding, I offer a forceful challenge to such a shaming and disciplining of desire by turning to the work of Asian American lesbian artist Erica Cho. Along with the practices of her cohorts Lynne Chan, Lala / Felix Endara, and Yvette Choi, Cho's work reflects an extremely exciting, smart, and sexy tendency in Asian American lesbian artistic productions that irreverently resignifies Asian masculinity, a project that is decidedly not invested in the (straight *and* gay) Asian American male recuperation of masculinity. Refreshingly, Cho consistently poses her resignified masculinity in relation with femininity, rather than as an exclusion of it. Instead of the gay Asian male context, Asian American lesbian makers like Cho draw inspiration for their reconfigurations of masculinity from queer, feminist, dyke, and FTM (female to male) transgender sexual communities. These communities adopt a more multivalent and capacious view of gender, allowing for more flexibility, subversion, and the production of alternative masculinities.[18]

The Asian American lesbian productions are insistently marked by identifications across race, ethnicity, gender, generation, and national contexts.

Cho's reformulation of masculinity is not necessarily linked to what is (already) "real," but it points to possibilities and permutations available through artistic imagination and erotic fantasy. The powerful work of fantasy is exemplified in her passionate representation of the vulnerable ethnic male body in the videotape *We Got Moves You Ain't Even Heard Of (Part One)* (1999).[19] In it Cho reenacts specific scenes from *The Karate Kid* (John G. Avildsen, 1984) in which Daniel (Ralph Macchio), the Italian American transplant from New Jersey, gets beaten up and humiliated by his buffed, blond-haired Southern California high school classmates. Instead of zooming in on the climax, when Daniel the underdog triumphs over his opponent, Cho finds the moments when Daniel suffers most spectacularly at the hands of the macho bullies most generative for Asian dyke erotic inspiration. For example, a scene in which Daniel gets attacked and made to eat sand is reenacted by Cho (in character as Daniel with a big black eye) repeatedly taking stunt dives into the sand at a deserted beach. In another reenactment, a particularly painful scene in which Daniel gets a plate of spaghetti dumped in the crotch of his white pants in a public restaurant with his female love interest watching nearby is transformed by the video maker into a masturbation session. Rejecting facile notions of ethnic male empowerment through knee-jerk reclamations of subordinated masculinities, Cho harnesses affects such as shame and humiliation for their productive potential—mined in this case by the rerouting of shame and humiliation into sexual pleasure. Turning an emasculated and brutalized ethnic teenage boy, perennially youthful teen idol Macchio, into a dyke icon, Cho also activates the homoerotic potential in the student-teacher relationship between Daniel and Mr. Miyagi (Pat Morita).

In a more recent video, Cho brings to the fore the homoerotic tension in the male pedagogical situation hinted at in *We Got Moves*. *School Boy Art* (2004) tells the story of Franz, a protoqueer Latino teenager who dreams of going to art school. He attends portfolio day and meets the old, inscrutable Asian art professor (played by Cho herself in male drag), who is so impressed with Franz's talent that he offers him a one-on-one tutorial. The climatic scene takes place when the bow-tie-wearing professor comes to the aspiring art student's apartment for a private lesson on dynamic hand drawing. A lesson in rendering male anatomy doubles here as a lesson in queer sexual seduction of said anatomy.

Instead of a model of homosexuality based on gender equality, like the one Marks and the sticky rice documentaries espouse, Cho revitalizes a prominent form of homosexual relations buried in queer cultural history: the older/younger, mentor/mentee, professor/student, intergenerational relationship that has become tabooed in the contemporary assimilationist gay scene. Playing the role of

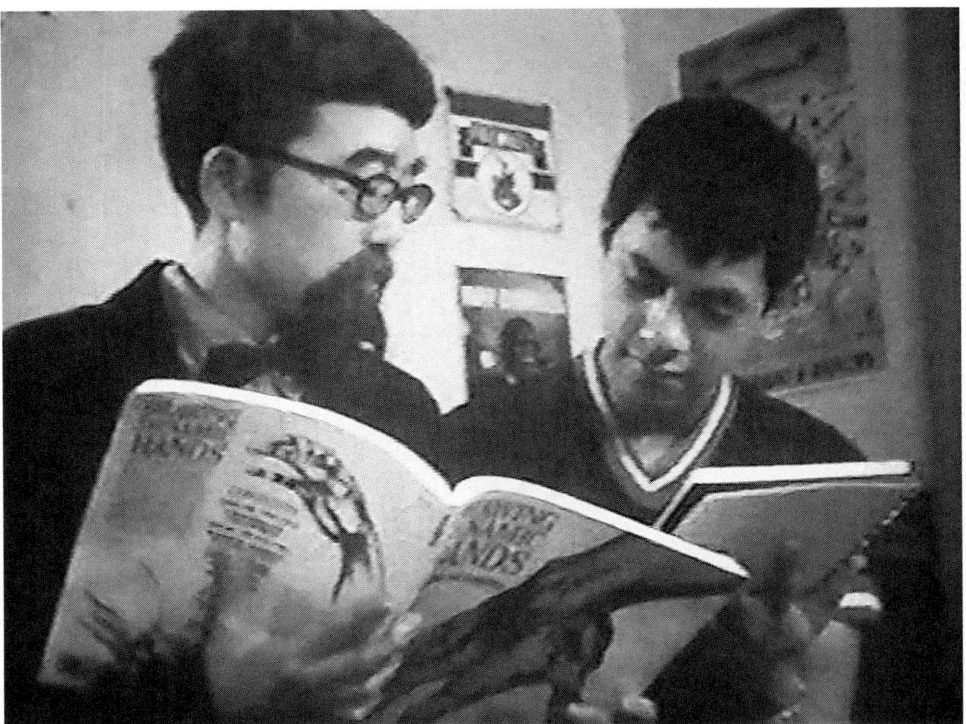

Still from *School Boy Art* (2004), by Erica Cho. Courtesy of the artist.

the lecherous Asian professor who gives his young protégé a helping hand, in art and in life, Cho's perverted sex act offers a bridge across generational, racial, ethnic, and aesthetic opportunities and openings. Unlike the sticky rice videos, Cho's performance as a very hirsute Asian queer subject is not bent on repairing Asian masculinity wounded by emasculation and feminization but represents a critical reworking of the pathologizing discourses around homosexuality, as well as "deviant" Asian male sexuality.

The seduction scene with its sexually explicit jack-off action garnered the most attention from audiences regarding the open-ended aims of its reeducation of desire. In contrast to the gay Asian videos' substitution of objectionable potato for enticing sticky rice, Cho's Korean dyke in Mr. Miyagi drag's manhandling of a swishy Latino teenager's hard, erect cock destabilizes any coherent queer position and properly aligned sexual identity and desire. As Cho riffs on this sex scene "designed to arouse" viewers:

When people see [the cum scene in] *School Boy Art,* their second major reaction after laughter is often a delighted arousal. They will exclaim out loud, "But is that real, or is it a dildo?" or "Is she/he really doing that?" or "How could they?" The performativity of a sexual act brings up all these questions that reveal another level of playfulness. . . . Are they relating as a fag and a dyke, a fag and a transfag, two friends leaving their gender behind, a man and a woman, "opposite-sex" virgins? . . . Both fags and dykes are intrigued by their own delight as well, because it challenges what they usually find arousing, not just in terms of intergenerational sex, or old Asian man sex, but gendered sex. . . . It's a more corrective model of masculinity because I invite people's open curiosity, fascination, or unintentional bleeding between the character and the actor, or the actor and the director. It doesn't threaten the masculinity or attractiveness of the two characters, and it doesn't threaten my own sexuality. (Actually, it enhances it).[20]

Cho's provocative questions bring us back to Laura Marks's fluid model of S/M spectatorship with which I begin this essay. However, instead of Marks's deployment of a sex scene with two (racially unmarked) gay men as an example of an effortless and sexy reversibility of looking and being looked at, fucking and being fucked, I would offer Cho's sexual scene of queer pedagogy, in its mobilization of competing social antagonisms, as an extremely valuable and rich terrain for what Marks herself describes as a "process of struggle, negotiation, or pleasurable play" that produces a "coalition audience for erotic identification."[21] In sum, Cho's queer dyke of color project perversely enacts and performs the destabilizing *and loving* cross-gender, cross-sex gaze fantasized by the straight feminist critic.

NOTES

For originally commissioning this essay, Petrus Liu deserves a special shout out. I express my gratitude to Petrus and Lisa Rofel for their incisive feedback and enthusiastic encouragement on an earlier draft. Any misstep in this final version is, of course, my own.

1. Laura Marks, "Love the One You're With: Straight Women, Gay Porn, and the Scene of Erotic Looking," in *Touch: Sensuous Theory and Multisensory Media* (Minneapolis: University of Minnesota Press), 77.

2. I want to note that in including Wayne Yung's video in this grouping, I am employing a broad understanding of what constitutes documentary practice, since one can make the case that *The Queen's Cantonese* might be better characterized as an experimental videotape. However, I feel justified in my expanded categorization of Yung's work due to the blurring of these formal distinctions in the realm of queer film and video. As Chris Holmlund and Cynthia Fuchs acknowledge in the introduction to their anthology on gay, lesbian, and queer documentary, "Firm distinctions among documentary, fiction, and avant-garde films and videos

are increasingly untenable"; see Chris Holmlund and Cynthia Fuchs, eds., *Between the Sheets, in the Streets: Queer, Lesbian, Gay Documentary* (Minneapolis: University of Minnesota Press, 1997).

3. Admitting that "no 'straight' lines can be drawn around documentary," they go on to argue that "the force of these films, television shows, and videos stems from the fact that they remain *narratives grounded in some version of actuality and experience, involving social actors, as opposed to characters*" (11; emphasis mine).

4. *Potato queen* refers to an Asian man who primarily dates white men; *sticky rice* describes Asian men who date other Asian men; and the third term in this triangle, *rice queen*, refers to a white man who primarily dates Asians. The political project of the gay Asian documentaries I discuss operates from the assumption that gay Asian men living in the West do not consider other Asian men as desirable sexual partners. The "natural" coupling comprises a younger Asian and an older white man (although white/Asian pairings of similar age and economic status are becoming the norm, à la *The Wedding Banquet*). Until recent years, it was rare to find visible Asian/Asian gay couples in gay communities in the West.

5. Richard Fung, "Looking for My Penis: The Eroticized Asian in Gay Video Porn," in *Asian American Sexualities: Dimensions of the Gay and Lesbian Experience,* ed. Russell Leong (New York: Routledge, 1996), 187.

6. Richard Dyer, *Now You See It: Studies in Lesbian and Gay Film* (New York: Routledge, 1990), 274.

7. Ibid., 246.

8. In addition to his influential video work, including *Orientations* (1984), *Chinese Characters* (1986), *Steam Clean* (1990), and *Dirty Laundry* (1996), Fung's critical writing, especially the article "Looking for My Penis," has been immensely generative for experimental queer Asian American male film and video making. For a critical assessment of (and celebratory tribute to) Fung's work, see Helen Lee and Kerri Sakamoto, eds., *Like Mangoes in July: The Work of Richard Fung* (Toronto: Insomniac Press, 2002).

9. Eve Oishi, "Bad Asians: New Film and Video by Queer Asian American Artists," in *Countervisions: Asian American Film Criticism,* eds. Darrell Hamamoto and Sandra Liu (Philadelphia: Temple University Press, 2000), 226.

10. David L. Eng and Alice Hom, eds., *Q & A: Queer in Asian America* (Philadelphia: Temple University Press, 1998), 12.

11. Jasbir K. Puar, "Transnational Sexualities: South Asian (Trans)nation(alism)s and Queer Diaspora," in *Q & A,* eds. Eng and Hom, 405.

12. Richard Dyer, "Coming to Terms: Gay Pornography," in *Only Entertainment* (New York: Routledge, 1992), 128.

13. Gloria Steinem as quoted in John Champagne, *The Ethics of Marginality: A New Approach to Gay Studies* (Minneapolis: University of Minnesota Press, 1995), 43.

14. Thomas Waugh offers a cogent theorization of "the clash of homoscape with ethnoscape" in his essay "Fung: Home and Homoscape," in *Like Mangoes in July,* eds. Lee and Kerri Sakamoto, 66–77.

15. Indeed, one of the central concerns of *Slanted Vision* is the impact of HIV/AIDS on the sexual practices of Asian Pacific Islander gay men. The third and final chapter of the video is titled "Culinary: The Cooking Show," which is a spoof of *Yan Can Cook*. In the place of Yan, we have Martina, a Filipino drag queen, and her trusty Asian nerd assistant demonstrating a recipe for "Chicken Fuk Yew"—that is, safe-sex practices utilizing dildos, zucchinis, dental dams, and a willing chicken, among other latex and organic ingredients.

16. Thomas Waugh, "Walking on Tippy Toes: Lesbian and Gay Liberation Documentary of the Post-Stonewall Period 1969–1984," in *The Fruit Machine: Twenty Years of Writing on Queer Cinema* (Durham, N.C.: Duke University Press, 2000), 267.

17. Song Cho, *Rice: Explorations into Gay Asian Culture and Politics* (Toronto: Queer Press, 1998), 1.

18. Judith Halberstam's theorization of female masculinity constitutes an important and enabling contribution in this sense. Yet I suggest that Cho's work expands such projects as Halberstam's due to its attention to other masculinities beyond white and black models. See Judith Halberstam, *Female Masculinity* (Durham, N.C.: Duke University Press, 1998).

19. Cho made the tape under the pseudonym Clover Paek.

20. Erica Cho, e-mail message to author, December 1, 2005.

21. Marks, "Love the One You're With," 87.

Screen Eroticisms

EXPLORING FEMALE DESIRE IN FEMINIST FILM AND VIDEO

Amelia Jones

Feminist art practice in Euro-America has since the 1960s been a site of radical questioning of media in how it conveys, constructs, and positions sexed subjects in its representational field. In order to explore the limit cases of how film and video can be exploited to examine the production of sexed subjectivity, it is strategic, then, to focus on key feminist practices. To this end, this essay addresses a profound technological and ideological shift in the feminist visualization and conceptualization of eroticism (and the sexed subject in general) in screen-based culture, from experimental cinema in its heyday of the 1960s to experimental video in the 1990s.

In order to ground this exploration of the differing ways in which these two media have been exploited toward a critical enactment of sexed subjectivity, I perform an extended comparative analysis of two major feminist screen-based projects, both of which are now viewed as classics within these media: Carolee Schneemann's experimental film *Fuses* (1964–67) and Pipilotti Rist's video *Pickelporno* (*Pimple Porno*, 1992). By focusing on these two pieces, each produced by a key feminist artist at different periods in the history of contemporary art and in different locations, I seek to explore the shifting articulation of a female eroticism through specific screen-based media (16 mm film and video, respectively), each having its own potential to render and position the human subject differently. Ultimately, by showing how each artist pushes the technological capacities of each medium (film and video) to render different modes of female sexual agency through the spatial, temporal, and narrative capacities of each medium, this essay points to broad transformations in beliefs about sexual identity and embodiment in the contemporary period.

The screen (cinematic versus televisual) is the operative pivot in both a literal and a metaphorical sense for the visual culture works at hand and a locus for understanding how Schneemann and Rist produce contrasting possibilities of erotic subjectivity in *Fuses* and *Pimple Porno*. As film theorists have argued since the 1970s, particularly feminists such as Laura Mulvey, Mary Ann Doane, and Kaja Silverman, dominant versions of subjectivity or ways of being in

Euro-American culture have been partly projected via the screen cultures of the mass media. These screens (cinematic, televisual, and now computer) position us most often, still, through binary codes relying on oppositional conceptions of identification—gender (male/female), sexuality (heterosexual/homosexual), race (white/not white), ethnicity (European/otherwise), class, nationality, and so on. These screens also position us literally as spectators in front of perspectivally constructed spaces: Albertian windows onto worlds, themselves presented as truth. As such, we are encouraged to believe that when we watch screens, we are in some way witnessing the truth. At the very least, we tend to absorb screen images as driven by bodies we engage with through reiterated codes of identification that in turn structure our ways of being in the world.

In contrast, although they both nominally narrate erotic encounters between two people who appear to be male and female (and, thus, to convey what on the surface appear to be heteroerotic relations), both *Fuses* and *Pimple Porno* are experimental projects that as such push the boundaries of each medium in terms of content, narrative, and spatial/temporal structure. In so doing, they explore and produce embodied erotic possibilities for viewers that counter these conventional binary structures via screen-projected imagery. In the case of *Fuses,* this imagery is produced through the pellucid, glowing transparencies of 16 mm film (although the film is often, today, viewed in a compromised VHS version marketed by Mystic Fire Video). In its original version *Fuses* is a dense twenty-three-minute collage of abstracted images of a woman and a man making love (Schneemann herself and her lover of ten years, James Tenney), as viewed by her cat.[1] In the case of *Pimple Porno,* a twelve-minute PAL format video, the erotic bodies are conveyed via the even, bright tones of digital video projection (originally produced as an analog videotape to be viewed on a monitor, the work is most often today transferred to digital video and projected for public display).[2]

Working through the specificity of how the erotic screen bodies in each piece are conveyed and can be engaged by artists working in different parts of the world (Schneemann in New York and Rist in Zurich) and from different generations of feminist practice (Schneemann was born in 1939; Rist, in 1962), this essay concludes with thoughts on what these two projects tell us in the most embodied of ways about different modes of envisioning and enfleshing the erotic (gendered, sexed) screen subject in 1967 versus 1992. These thoughts are, of course, provisional. Part of my point is that screens make available visual fields (in this case, those of eroticized bodies) that open out to the other who views them; the appearance of the bodies and their particular relationship to the screens suggest identificatory responses but do not legislate how these bodies come to mean in a final way. Screens are hinges between self and other, both literally and figuratively, not final sites where a body solidifies into a subjectivity. Screens are passageways allowing us entry into eroticisms that might unhinge our usual static relation to the other(s) before us. And of course, the screen of cinematic projection functions to this end quite differently from the screen of the video monitor, or even the modified gallery screen of video projection.

Experiencing Screen Eroticisms: Watching *Fuses*

I have shown the twenty-three-minute VHS version of the original film *Fuses* numerous times to classes of young and eager students, who to this day tend to find its erotic textures quite radical. I have also recently shown the newly reedited and remastered twenty-nine-minute version on DVD, with original footage added by Schneemann.[3] The cinematic version of *Fuses* is powerful in a way singular to the liquid spectacle of projected film—Schneemann knows how to make use of celluloid in a haptic way that draws one into the film as material: a glowing rectangle of flame on the wall sutures the viewer into its larger-than-life acts of heterosexual encounter (bodies sliding and mingling with one another, hands rubbing, gleaming, taut muscles and wet folds of skin). Even when watching the twenty-three-minute video version of the piece (which among other things is cropped to fit the televisual monitor), one becomes enfolded in the erotic logic of the video screen, which pulls one into its depths with its flesh encounters.

As Schneemann notes about *Fuses,* "I wanted the bodies to be turning into tactile sensations of flickers. . . . [The film is] a painterly, tactile translation edited as a music of frames. . . . That's why it is collaged, and cut and baked."[4] This tactile manipulation of the film stock, which turned it into skin, makes the film itself *embodied.* As I view the film I encounter the bodies making love there—the rhythmic thrusting of one into the other beautifully rendered, if in fragmented form, with the scratched and scumbled surface of the film mitigating my full access to the bodies. I thus experience the screen itself as enfleshed, as having its own logic and depth—the screen like a kind of skin, the rippling contours of which signal a body (bodies?) writhing within it.

Schneemann unfurls herself like a wave both powerful and receiving. Her cunt is wet and red (the whole film is colored in saturated rubies, tangerines, and at some points, cool blues), deliciously stroked by her lover. His penis—we see the male organ without its explosive eruption and detumescence being the sole point of the narrative (as in hard-core porn)—appears again and again, lovingly rendered both as an object of desire (certainly female and potentially otherwise) and as a fleshy but vulnerable rod, slick with bodily juices, that works as a visual counterpart to her invaginated receiving body. Wet is the operative feeling: wet and pulsating, alive, electric, sexed (the bodies but also the body, the flesh, of the screen itself).

But *Fuses* hardly is simply a personal exploration in eroticism unattached to

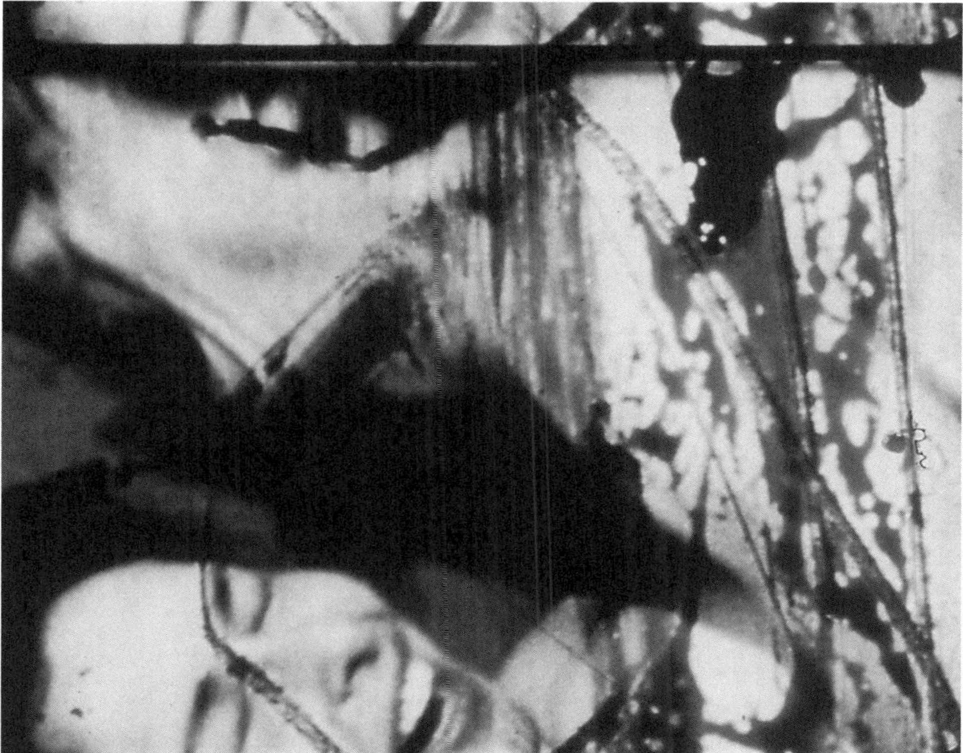

Still from Carolee Schneemann, *Fuses*, 1967. Photograph courtesy of the artist.

the vicissitudes of political history. By the early to mid-1960s, Schneemann was an artist and simultaneously an activist working against the U.S. government's actions in Vietnam. Training male friends how to avoid the draft and others how to deal with police brutality (which was common at antiwar protests in the United States during this period), she was also creatively driven by a sense of outrage to produce two projects directly linked to the war: the 1967 kinetic theater event *Snows,* an environment in which her 1965 film *Viet-Flakes* was projected. Along with projected atrocity images from the Vietnam war as collaged in *Viet-Flakes,* she used film in the *Snows* event, projected through dual projectors (making live and filmed bodies collide in space), "as integral to [live] performance . . . handled as tactile, palpable material."[5]

The sound track to the *Snows* project, by James Tenney, included the noise of trains punctuated with "sounds of orgasm." This accompanied the live performances, in which performers were "aggressor and victim, torturer and tortured, lover and beloved."[6] So too in *Fuses,* the body of the film (enacted through the erotic bodies of lovers), scratched and made into "flesh," symbolizes the manipulated flesh of bodies elsewhere. Though *Fuses* is in no way a direct commentary on Vietnam, its visceral approach to embodiment clearly parallels Schneemann's strategic attempt in her other projects to unveil the political and military violence perpetrated by U.S. troops abroad. *Fuses* does not convey a political critique in the manner of *Snows* or a political documentary; it *activates* the political as integral to the articulation of sexed subjectivity via the materiality of the film itself. *Fuses* functions in part as an attempt to redeem the flesh through an eroticism that seeks to transcend the violence of nations through the personal euphoria of the orgasm.

This approach of activating live and film bodies as flesh across Schneemann's work during this period is very "1960s." While harrowing and visceral, it is also very uplifting if one takes this attempt at transcendence—undoubtedly utopian and willfully essentializing (what other way, after all, did there seem to be to call Americans back to their bodies in an era of imperialist invasion on the part of the United States?)—within its brutal historical context, a context in which activating the body erotically via the seductive medium of cinema could be aimed at reclaiming its capacity for positive union over its tendency to wreak bloody havoc.

Experiencing Screen Eroticisms: Watching *Pimple Porno*

A high-heeled woman (thin, glamorously dressed, and apparently white) walks over an urban grating, approaching a man who looks to be from an East Asian background and who is dressed in a blue suit. Her eye in close-up *sees him,* establishing a female gaze of desire—difficult in its potentially racially fetishizing dimension. Their hands clasp, are solarized into a glowing meshing of skin and bone; he hands her a rather excessive pink flower; her body falls onto an artificially bright-blue surface. As in *Fuses,* human eroticism is paralleled by the carnality of animals and the burgeoning of nature—in this case, freewheeling animal locomotion. We see birds flying across the virtual sky of the televisual screen, landscapes (technicolor, with the hyped hues of a vacation brochure), and flowers layered over, under, or within the contours of the two bodies, which in turn mesh, caress each other, and twirl in the strange gravityless space of the televisual box. Rist turns her camera around, refusing its authority as a stationary eye and opening its purview onto an intergalactic space in which landscapes turn upside down and bodies float, rotate, and spin in the dimensionless space of the monitor.

The eye of the woman becomes the vertiginous eye of the video camera / screen itself. In a subversion of the classical cinematic structure of the gaze (where the screen is a visualized window onto the world produced and absorbed by a centralized camera / viewer), we are swallowed into vision *as* representation.

Bodies float in space, a space textured through glorious skeins of technicolor, ripples of skin, landscape, water. Countering the potential racial fetishism of the

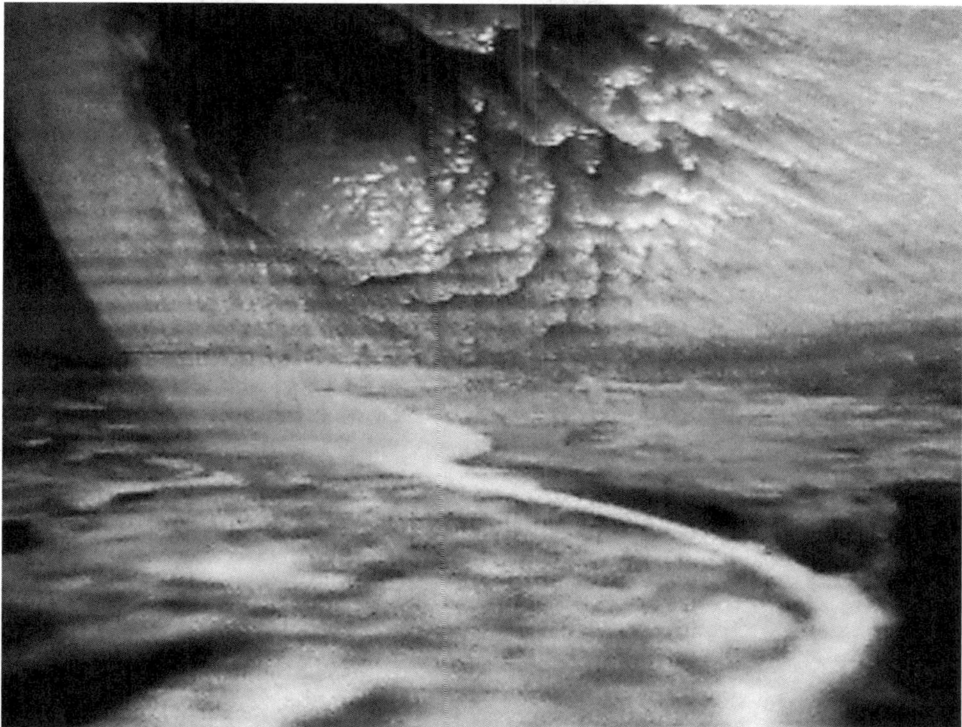

Still from *Pickelporno (Pimple Porno)*, 1992 by Pipilotti Rist. Courtesy of the artist and Hauser and Wirth.

apparently white woman's gaze, the infinitesimal line where one body begins and another ends is effaced; there are no borders. There is no binary separating "man" from "woman," "black" from "white." His apparently Asian body and her apparently white body look equally luminous and sensual, in some cases distorted through a fish-eye lens, in others eaten into by the billowing layers of color. A hand strokes a thigh (whose hand? whose thigh?); globes of fruit (tangerine vibrant) against the downy-haired, pitted skin of legs (whose legs?) mark human skin as infinitely soft when compared with the rude, rubbery, and pock-marked skin of the citrus fruit. The screen itself dissolves (at one point shimmering away into an orange/yellow interference pattern, a televisual grain that's like technologized skin).[7]

Rist's project is specific to video: originally displayed on a monitor, it is profoundly televisual. *Pimple Porno* is made like television, and I argue it is to some degree *about* television (not so much network television as its attenuated, more creative televisual forms such as MTV, the music television station founded in 1981, or to some extent artists' videos). The melting together of the bodies is the melting of experience into the screen, the flesh into the televisual, that people born after 1960, like myself (1961) and Rist (1962), have learned (in our bodies) to accept as the way things are—call this the real or call it simulation. Either way, it is how we know the world around us.

As much as we allow ourselves to be lured into the world of the televisual, we know (we feel in our bodies) that the televisual is artifice about artifice: the smell of fire rarely accompanies the image of a fire visible on the screen. In *Pimple Porno* the orgasm between the man and the woman is signaled by an increasingly frenetically paced visual and aural extravaganza, a feast of images of lava, fire, meshing bodies, a hard cock floating through a flower-filled field, a cunt opening itself into/as the screen. Synaesthetically, fire, simulacrally rendered via televisual representation, both symbolizes and is signaled (through the saturated reds and the images of flames and exploding volcanoes) as hot, with *hot* linked (parodically—this is a very funny moment) to the heat of consummated desire. One experiences the images of fire—the explosive, hot effects of which are exacerbated by the heated, rapid cadences of the music and the overlaid sounds of people moaning in pleasure—as having a (metaphoric) temperature. Through these visually coded means, we can feel the texture and friction of the sex between the man and the woman.

Perceived racial, gendered, and sexual identifications condition how we experience (synaesthetically view and apprehend) bodies in the world, in "real" time/space, or in representations. *Pimple Porno,* with its seemingly white female and Asian male bodies, mixes up our (Euro-American) expectations about how such bodies would interact sexually (the woman is at least as aggressive in her desire-driven touch; the man is both sculpted in his physique [masculine] and ephemerally sensual, desiring; the white person is an object of desire, as well as a "colonizing" subject, and the Asian person, his penis shown hard in its active pursuit of his object of desire, full with agency).

At the same time, the seeming visible differences of the two bodies beg the very question of the binaries through which we give bodies (and other kinds of interactions) meaning. If in most societies these binaries function to contain and control especially when they are perceived to be entwined in an erotic relation, to police what kinds of bodies are allowed to couple, then in *Pimple Porno* these boundaries are pleasurably and humorously melted into fields of luscious videographic color. Thinking we know a body is that of an "Asian man" or a "white woman" is already a fraught enterprise of categorization based on presumed identifications connected with visible codes. *Pimple Porno,* I argue, creatively participates in the growing interrogation of beliefs about identity and of the role of identity politics in conceptions about what visual images (and bodies in general) mean. *Pimple Porno* is a visual examination and refutation of the dominant Euro-American idea that we can know what or who we see based on our interpretation of visual cues.

What Rist, like the other most interesting artists and visual theorists of our time, makes clear is that visibility is never enough to determine how bodies/subjects identify themselves and how they in turn relate to others. Characterized by billowing fields of videographic color, interwoven images of bodies and a hyperbolic "nature," strange seminarratives that loop repetitively and eschew linearity, and confusing spatial effects that penetrate, saturate, or dissolve spaces (even, as in this case, the video monitor or gallery screen), Rist's works in general continually exacerbate the constructedness of the visual field and thus foreground the contingency of our interpretation of what we see on multisensory input siphoned through impossibly intricate webs of identification and desire. *Pimple Porno* explores the unfixable complexity of these webs and projections, exploring the interconnectedness between bodies *on* the screen with bodies *engaging* the screen through its confusion of boundaries between bodies and identifications and its solicitation of an array of sensory responses all through the audiovisual medium of video.

Thus, in *Pimple Porno,* as in all of Rist's work, the interconnection of image and sound is crucial, as is the way in which she narratively depicts touch across these multiply identified bodies (much of *Pimple Porno* is devoted to images of bodies touching, rubbing, caressing). The touch of skin and the touch of sound mesh bodies, blurring their boundaries. Rist's eerie sound track conditions our experience of the bodies on the screen: it includes Rist singing in German with Les Reines Prochaines (the feminist punk group for which she was lead singer from 1988 to 1994), her voice filled with longing, the sounds of moaning and chanting, noises from a hyped-up version of nature (birds twittering, water rushing), and various techno-sounding versions of acoustic instruments.[8]

As I hope my descriptions enact, *Pimple Porno* exemplifies the way in which Rist's work evokes what Laura Marks calls a "haptic visuality," a "feminine" (rather than penetratory and perspectival, as is typical in Western visual culture) visual relation wherein the viewer is encouraged to engage with the surface of the image as having substance (as if it could be touched, haptically). Haptic visuality encourages an "intersubjective eroticism" not only (in the case of *Pimple Porno*) between figures or characters *within* the work but *between* these bodies and ours. Marks notes, "What is erotic about haptic visuality, then, may be described as a respect of difference, and concomitant loss of self, in the presence of the other. . . . [It is a] giving-over to the other."[9]

Elsewhere, Marks notes, "We cannot help but change in the process of interacting."[10] Giving over to the other (Rist's lovers, Rist, perhaps even the other in ourselves or our imagined/actual lover) through synaesthetic visual encounters can open up a process of change. This is the radical potential opened up by *Pimple Porno*'s erotic televisual scene. And it is a radical potential signaled in an early, nascent state by *Fuses*.

The Screen 1967 and the Screen 1992: Two Feminist Eroticisms

Schneemann's and Rist's two projects are profoundly complementary in effect and in apparent motivation but mark two different feminist eroticisms—themselves linked to two different relationships to visuality and to two different technologies of imaging (producing as well as engaging) the self from the two different periods and locations in which they were produced. To some extent they can be viewed as informed by two different generational approaches to the erotic body. As noted, Schneemann was born in 1939 and Rist in 1962. Their approaches are profoundly informed by the very technologies that end up conveying them (film versus analog video and then digital video projection). They are also informed by feminist views about how various representational media function to reinforce particular gender and sexual identifications and about allowing for women's agency in relation to the visual field—attitudes that are critical but also celebratory of ways of articulating women's sexual pleasure.

Both artists respond critically to the Western history of positing or assuming a mythical centered subject of vision in relation to the visual field—one who is implicitly white, male, and heterosexual and "outside" the image, in command of its purview. In this Renaissance to modernist model, meaning and value are phantasmagorically viewed as existing inherently in objects, to be excavated by the centered subject of interpretation situated in a position of perspectively determined total knowledge outside the picture. The increasingly common location of vision in the subjectivity of the viewer in Euro-American visual culture after 1960 ultimately led to a new regime of knowledge in which it could be constituted only in reciprocal relation between the perceiving subject and the object—knowledge then would always be partial and contingent and the subject of knowledge thus never fully centered or determinable. This shift away from the idea of the meaning of the text as generated from an originating author to the visual agency of the viewer (linked to the insights of poststructuralism) marks the difference between most visual works made before the 1960s and many works made afterwards.[11]

Schneemann's *Fuses* straddles the two belief systems: as my analysis makes clear, she is central to our apprehension of the work—both as we see her within the text and as we imagine her authorial agency producing the text—and yet *Fuses* is clearly not giving us a sense that we know (entirely) what we think we see. Binaries are gorgeously evoked only to be confused in the roiling layers of flesh and color. Rist's *Pimple Porno,* in contrast, relinquishes authorial coherence to a greater degree, locating the meaning of the eroticism in our embrace of the bodies on the screen, bodies that we may associate with her but that do not seem to "be" her (or even to stand in for her). To different degrees and in different ways, Schneemann's and Rist's works are thus exemplary of the kinds of visual works produced out of this new understanding—they mine the capacity of film and video to open out the reciprocity between seer and seen. The remainder of this essay teases out technologically and ideologically driven differences between Schneemann's and Rist's projects.

Fuses and the "Skin of the Film"

Though *Fuses* straddles older and newer modes of screen culture, it still clearly occupies the tail end of a modernist trajectory in the overlapping history of experimental art and film, one that originally took shape in the historical avant-gardes of the 1910s and the 1920s in Europe (particularly surrealism) and resurfaced in the post–World War II period especially strongly in the context of North American cinema with the work of filmmakers such as Maya Deren and Stan Brakhage (not incidentally, Schneemann worked with Brakhage for a period before making *Fuses*). This kind of avant-garde work seeks to disrupt the visual field via strategies of montage and disjunction in order to distance the viewer, ultimately aiming to shift and contest dominant beliefs. In the case of Schneemann's film, the key belief system addressed is that relating to the positioning of women as objects of heterosexual male desire but not as agents of their own sexual experience and identification.

At the same time, one of the most important things about Schneemann's work and *Fuses* in particular is that it crosses over this kind of avant-garde strategy with a feminist strategy of exploiting what Marks calls the "skin of the film" (the film's capacity to engage viewers in a circuit of identification that is embodied and, as such, potentially highly politicized).[12] This strategy in its feminist variant produces bodies in such a way as to preclude the simple fetishization of the woman's (and in this case the man's) body. In Schneemann's *Fuses* both the male and the female body, not always differentiable in the skin of the film, offer potential sites of identification, motivating the viewer to position herself differently in relation to heterosexual difference and thus perhaps to challenge the structures of fetishization that are foundational to conventional Hollywood cinema.

Schneemann was one of the artists who developed this strategy in the most dramatic and successful way. *Fuses* thus moves us toward what comes to be defined as a postmodern kind of cultural production, one that is not avant-gardist in any simple fashion (not oppositional or distancing) but that still attempts to intervene in or create friction in relation to the structures of capital and subject formation in such a way that as we engage the film, we feel our own participation in its structures of desire. By manipulating the flesh of the celluloid itself, "burning, baking, cutting, and painting it, dipping . . . footage in acid, and building dense layers of collage . . . held together with paper clips," Schneemann made the conventional film text into a "skin," enacting her own agency as a making (and active sexual) subject and encouraging us to remember the materiality of bodies (and of film itself).[13] This strategy counters both fetishization (the turning of usually female bodies into detachable objects of [heterosexual male] desire) and spectacle (the way in which conventional cinema veils its structures of production in order to seduce the viewer into its world as if this world is real). The enfleshed movie deobjectifies the lovers' bodies, turning them into limpid surfaces that are also depths, and yet there is a tension between this effect and our identification of Schneemann as the author of the film. *Fuses* enacts itself as a made thing, as well as a screen of desire.

It is crucial to stress as well that Schneemann's relationship to the binary of gender identification is never clear-cut. Unlike many feminists working in the 1960s and 1970s, she does not simply seek to reverse the poles of subject (male) and object (female) to empower women as subjects; rather, in this early work she confuses the binary altogether while keeping "male" and "female" as intact entities, involved as they are in a clearly heterosexual romance. Schneemann's activation of herself as a subject (rather than only object) of the visual field in *Fuses* thus is not at the cost of the other with whom she makes love. Of *Fuses,* she emphasizes that she worked in complete collaboration with Tenney, situating his participation "as both object and subject." Her goal was pointed: "I really wanted to see what 'the fuck' is [from a woman's point of view] and locate it in terms of a lived sense of equity . . . we have to remind ourselves that throughout the sixties, only men maintained creative authority: women were muses, partners."[14]

Schneemann's project thus complicates dominant models of interrogating structures of sexual difference in feminist film theory from the 1970s and 1980s. Film, as many feminist theorists from Laura Mulvey onward have pointed out, is a modernist medium and as such is predicated on the binary logic of heteronormative sexual relations and identifications. But in *Fuses,* as film theorist David James argues, "a new copulation between the filmic and the erotic is traced, in which female sexuality is enacted in a practice of mutuality."[15] *Fuses* blurs the boundaries of the binary and thus interrogates the cinematic itself, as well as (to some degree) heterosexual gender conventions. It does this partly through its character as a deeply painterly (rather than seemingly strictly photographic and indexical) film. As noted, like Brakhage, Schneemann manipulates the film stock itself, treating it like flesh; the scratched and rubbed celluloid, through which light is projected onto the screen, moves and gyrates and pulsates like erotically charged patches of flesh (paralleling, for example, the pulsating skin of

Tenney's scrotum, visible at one point in the film, or the moist labia and opening of Schneemann's cunt, stroked by Tenney at another point).

Though it is materially and sensually resolutely cinematic, through this meshing of flesh and screen image *Fuses* refuses to simply render the bodies indexically as somehow representatives of clearly demarcated bodies in the "real." In this way, although *Fuses* is cinema, it radically moves toward while not fully embracing what I call a televisual sensibility, one newly available to American artists coming of age in the 1950s and 1960s, just as televisions became ubiquitous in American households. *Fuses* includes some cinematic landscape views (notably of Schneemann running across a beach), but it is primarily structured through close-ups that interweave and layer the bodies of Schneemann and Tenney into and as their environment, pressing them into the screen (and thus into *our* space). The film thus merges certain cinematic structures and qualities with what at the time was a relatively new televisual approach to representing the body (often in close-up with camera angles that render the body as if pressed into the screen).

Fuses marks one of the earliest and most successful instances of the enactment of what Marks calls "haptic visuality." The screen in *Fuses* becomes a site of exchange (both within the film's internal narrative and between the images on the screen and the viewers).

Pimple Porno and the Shift to Televisuality

As noted, Marks argues there is an erotics in haptic visuality, which indicates a "respect of difference, and concomitant loss of self, in the presence of the other. . . . [It is a] giving-over to the other."[16] Expanding on the potential opened up by *Fuses,* Rist's *Pimple Porno* is a further exploration of the potential of televisual screen space to enact multiply identified bodies that mesh and intertwine, that merge both with the surface of the televisual monitor and with the paradoxical space "behind" it (which seems both infinite and contained by the box).

But *Pimple Porno* pushes the dissolution of the binary logic of screen identification and heterosexual gender relations even further than does *Fuses*. In *Pimple Porno* the embodied (three-dimensional) space of the monitor parallels the embodied yet simulacrally rendered (dissolved, solarized, twirling in space) bodies of the lovers. Rist's piece draws on the erotic content and visual and editing strategies of *Fuses* but pushes this content and these strategies further in the direction of a radically disorienting televisual screen texture in which we are encouraged to give over to the other, to recognize (via a haptic visuality) the impossibility of remaining "outside" the image, as one is to some extent forced to do in viewing a projected cinematic text.

This giving over takes place technologically via the specific spectatorial mechanisms made possible through video art, as well as ideologically and psychically in terms of identification. Although we give over to otherness in *Fuses,* the otherness is still marked in terms of conventional and heterosexual white middle-class versions of sexual difference as articulated through the fundamentally modernist medium of cinema (albeit radically opened out into the skin of the film). In *Pimple Porno* the otherness is metaphorically marked in terms of a sexual difference that is understood *as determined in relation to the highly marked terms of racial difference.* The meshing of flesh is marked in terms of a web of interrelated identifications in Rist's piece where the woman, while apparently white, is also marked as racially/ethnically identified rather than neutral or, as Peggy Phelan would put it in her 1993 book of this title, "unmarked." Rist articulates bodies that are *identified* but not knowable, as if in answer to Phelan's argument about identity: "Identity cannot, then, reside in the name you can say or the body you can see. . . . Identity emerges in the failure of the body to express being fully and the failure of the signifier to convey meaning exactly."[17]

It has been rightly noted by writers such as bell hooks that feminism was dominated by an assumption of whiteness from the 1960s through the 1980s and that this whiteness was largely invisible to most (white) feminist artists, critics, and art historians.[18] Feminist film theorist Mary Ann Doane puts this critical point in a way that resonates with Schneemann's work and that of many white feminists from the 1960s into the 1990s, including my own early publications on feminism: "What can a white woman know about racial difference or oppression when her social regime is constituted as the denial or evacuation of racial identity . . . ?"[19] While the majority of feminists working in North America and Europe in the 1960s and 1980s were white middle-class women who thus did not (or could not) see beyond their/our whiteness to explore the structures hooks and Doane identify as coarticulating sexual and racial difference, by the 1990s Rist's video articulated a feminist screen eroticism that foregrounded (without overemphasizing) racial/ethnic identifications as constitutive of gendered and sexual identifications—with these identifications (as Phelan suggests) never fully knowable through visual cues.

The dissolving of binaries into complex multiple networks of interrelated identifications is related to the specific representational mode through which *Pimple Porno* was made and is displayed. Technologically, *Pimple Porno* offers a related but ultimately different experience from that of *Fuses.* Rist grew up with the ubiquity of television, handheld video cameras, and by the mid-1970s into the 1990s, VHS players and MTV. As noted, she was herself the member of a female punk band from 1988 until 1994, and her work is deeply informed by the aesthetic of the MTV generation, as well as by the history of artists' video. Drawing on visual tropes from these histories, Rist manipulates the video image using various strategies of solarization, fades, and other distorting techniques that render the bodies both more visible as central tropes and less stable as material entities (at many moments we are even made unsure which body we are seeing).

Although it is now often digitally projected onto a large screen, *Pimple Porno* was made for a monitor and remains resolutely "of the box": the bodies take on dimensionality as they twirl in a televisual (monitor) space, not as they mesh into a projected film image (as occurs with the bodies in *Fuses*). Video viewed on a monitor encourages a particular viewing relation. There is at least a perceived intimacy with televisual screens that prompts those who make television shows, or those who made art videos in the days when they were confined to monitors, to produce different narratives (which tend toward fragmented stories that adapt to commercial breaks and the vicissitudes of everyday life as it interrupts television viewing in the home) but also to structure the narratives through much more intimate kinds of images, which are often close-up—a composition more amenable to the visual format of the televisual screen.[20] In a monitor-based piece such as *Pimple Porno,* too, the bodies are perceptually contained in what is experienced as a piece of furniture (at least until the advent of the flat screen).

Placed in the box of the monitor, the video screen is a container. As Rist notes, the video monitor swallows up the viewer:

> At first you look at the box, at the screen or projection, but when you concentrate on the sequences you feel as if you're inside the box, behind the glass, within the wall. You forget everything around you and concentrate completely on the box: you're swallowed. . . . *Reconquering the space inside the TV set: that's one of my aims.*[21]

If classical Hollywood film labors to position the viewer so as to purvey a traditional binary structure of subject and object, with the filmic body *over there,* then television as produced in the centers of the entertainment industry seeks to suture the viewer, but in a different way, via positioning itself not only as "furniture" but also as conveying stories that swallow up the viewer, bringing her into the televisual world as a space of everyday "truth." If Schneemann's project purveys the body of the film as flesh in order to extend but also disrupt avantgardist strategies of rupture, opening the door to a meshing of bodies and screen space, then Rist's project pushes this further. "Reconquering the space inside the TV set," using tools from rock video and from earlier experimental film projects such as Brakhage's and Schneemann's, Rist produces liquid bodies the texture of whose flesh is reciprocally defined in relation to the grained texture and box structure of the traditional televisual screen.[22]

Conclusion

Both *Fuses* and *Pimple Porno* enact the sexed subjects through the materiality and structure specific to their medium. The media employed and the particular bodies depicted indicate a broad and deep shift in experiences and representations of sexed subjectivity from the late 1960s to the 1990s in Euro-American culture. Schneemann (as had to be the case in the 1960s) strategically retains to some degree the gender binary and articulates her own agency clearly within the film, whereas Rist, partly due to being empowered through earlier works such as *Fuses,* is freed to interrogate the very oppositional terms of this binary. The potential of the immersive imagery in the video to "swallow up" viewers provides a different viewing experience and, thus, a mode of subjectification different from that of cinema.

Schneemann's *Fuses* works through the self/other dialectic of dominant (white middle-class) heterosexual relations, enacting on a personal (turned political) level the way in which such lovers can trouble the easy binary structuring both sexual difference and photographic and cinematic imaging technologies. Rist's *Pimple Porno* gives over more completely to the other—the viewer and, metaphorically, the potentially nonwhite, nonheterosexual other left out of dominant Euro-American models of sexual difference (even, until recently, feminist ones). If as Marks notes, "we cannot help but change in the process of interacting," then both projects offer ideal openings for such change in the cutting-edge versions of the technologically and ideologically inflected languages of their time.[23]

NOTES

1. In this way, Schneemann arguably "animalizes" the gaze; although given her role as filmmaker, the film can also be viewed, as it most often is, as portraying heterosexual sex from the woman's point of view. Schneemann has noted of the film, "*Fuses* was made as an homage to a relationship of ten years—to a man with whom I lived and worked as an equal. We are perceived through the eyes of our cat. By visualizing the cat's point of view I was able to present our coupled images in the contexts of the rectangles and the seasons surrounding us." "Notes on *Fuses* (1971)," in *Imaging Her Erotics: Essays, Interviews, Projects* (Cambridge: MIT Press, 2001), 45.

2. For full credits on *Pimple Porno,* see "Pipilotti Rist: *Pickelporno,*" videoart.ch, accessed June 5, 2012, http://www.videoart.ch/shop/index.php?page=shop.product_details&flypage=flypage.tpl&product_id=1109&category_id=25&option=com_virtuemart&Itemid=26.

3. The new version, available through Anthology Film Archives, has additional explicitly sexual footage. I am deeply grateful to Schneemann for making a study copy of the film available to me while I was finishing this essay.

4. Carolee Schneemann, "Interview with Katie Haug," in *Imaging Her Erotics,* 43.

5. Carolee Schneemann, "Snows," in *More than Meat Joy: Performance Works and Selected Writings,* ed. Bruce McPherson (1979; Kingston, N.Y.: Documentext, 1997), 129.

6. Ibid., 131–32.

7. I expand on these issues in my book *Self/Image: Technology, Representation and the Contemporary Subject* (New York: Routledge, 2006), esp. chs. 4 and 6.

8. Les Reines Prochaines is a shifting group of women who straddle the music, visual art, and performance worlds. Rist was active in the group as a founding member from 1988 into the 1990s. I am grateful to Sus, current member of Les Reines Prochaines, for providing dates on Rist's activities with the group. E-mail to author, October 31, 2007.

9. Laura U. Marks, *The Skin of the Film: Intercultural Cinema, Embodiment, and the Senses* (Durham, N.C.: Duke University Press, 2000), 7, 183, 192–93.

10. Laura U. Marks, *Touch: Sensuous Theory and Multisensory Media* (Minneapolis: University of Minnesota Press, 2002), xvi.

11. See Roland Barthes's distinction in his later work between readerly and writerly texts, noting the shift to the reader as writer (or maker of meaning) in contemporary literature.

12. See Marks, *Skin of the Film*, 1–20.

13. Schneemann, "Notes on *Fuses*," 45. She notes that she shot the film over three years, belying the sense one gets of a single, intense erotic encounter. As Schneemann observes, she was motivated to make *Fuses* by her long experience of being positioned as an object in men's work, including in Brakhage's films and in the now famous 1964 performance work *Site,* which has been attributed to Robert Morris but was initially collaboratively designed by Schneemann and Morris. Carolee Schneemann, conversations with author, 1996.

14. Schneemann, "Interview with Katie Haug," 26, 23.

15. David James, *Allegories of Cinema: American Film in the Sixties* (Princeton, N.J.: Princeton University Press, 1989), 317–18.

16. Marks, *The Skin of the Film*, 192–93.

17. Peggy Phelan, *Unmarked: The Politics of Performance* (New York: Routledge, 1993), 13.

18. See bell hooks, "Black Women Shaping Feminist Theory," in *Feminist Theory: From Margin to Center,* ed. Manning Marable (London: Pluto Press, 2000), 1–17.

19. Mary Ann Doane, "Dark Continents: Epistemologies of Racial and Sexual Difference in Psychoanalysis and the Cinema," in *Femmes Fatales: Feminism, Film Theory, Psychoanalysis* (New York: Routledge, 1991), 247.

20. See Tania Modleski on soap operas and this kind of fragmented, repetitive narrative time as specifically female in her classic book *Loving with a Vengeance: Mass-Produced Fantasies for Women* (Hamden, Conn.: Archon Press, 1982).

21. Pipilotti Rist quoted in Hans Ulrich Obrist, "Interview," in *Pipilotti Rist* (London: Phaidon, 2001), 15 (emphasis mine).

22. Of course with the advent of flat-screen televisions in the past few years, this structure has shifted somewhat. Now televisions are often hung like pictures on the wall—a configuration that makes them into artworks rather than furniture and affects our relationship to screen images.

23. Marks, *Touch*, xvi.

23
Media and Desire in the Sport Spectacle

Jennifer Doyle

Soccer (2004) is an atypical sports text. The video installation features Wu Ingrid Tsang and Math Bass performing as the queer collaborative couple Marriage. Dressed in purple satin bodysuits with pads slipped over their knees and elbows, Tsang and Bass run in place while they rehearse the basic gestures that define soccer training. In this short video (the first of their Fortunate Living trilogy), the two look like aliens belonging to a third or forth sex. Should we see them as boyish girls? Girlish boys? They have the ungainly and inchoate sexual presence peculiar to the teenage: an inherently queer failure to aspire to "adult" sexualities. They run in place and sweep the ground to their left and to their right as they shout, "Touch left!" and "Touch right!" They jump in the air and jerk their heads as they shout, "Head left!" and "Head right!" They each awkwardly juggle a ball with their feet, knees, and shoulders. They kick the balls against the wall. Sometimes they just sit. Or stretch. Or catch their breath. One seems slightly more competent than the other, but both seem unsure. They are clumsy, goofy, and shy in relation to each other—ill at ease, too, in and of themselves. They are sweet, and weird.

This weakly choreographed, lo-fi, and oddball work gestures toward the specifically queer nature of the girls sports team—and toward what Judith Halberstam describes as the "utopian vision of a world of subcultural possibilities" associated with transgender experiments in gender ambiguity.[1] That utopian impulse registers on the screen, though, in a gesture—in a shy look, a stolen glance, and a slight discomfort with being caught in this setting, in which the two are both perpetually together and not. An odd tenderness develops between the two "players" as they rehearse these routines together, moving in parallel lines toward some form of unspoken intimacy. If I describe this work as queer, it is neither because it depicts girls wanting to be boys (they are far too gender ambiguous to be that for the viewer) nor because it shows two girls together (they are "together," but they do not exactly interact with each other—they are not quite a romantic couple). It is more nearly because it playfully draws out the erotics specific to queer fantasies about what it means to play together—and what it means to play together as boys.

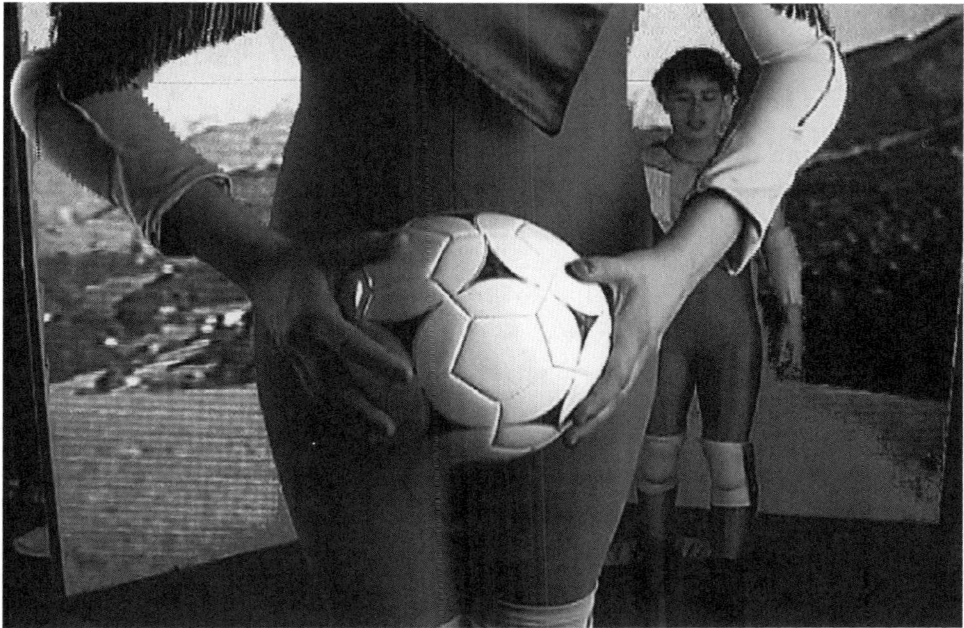

Wu Tsang, *Marriage, Soccer* (from *Fortunate Living* trilogy), 2004. Courtesy of the artist.

Soccer is a half-baked dream, an incomplete sentence, a desire not quite formed but nevertheless strewn across the field of vision. This is what makes it feel "queer"—if as José Muñoz writes, "queerness is essentially a rejection of a here and now and an insistence on potentiality or concrete possibility in another world," then that queerness registers as a gesture, as "that thing that lets us feel that this world is not enough, that indeed something is missing."[2] *Soccer* refuses to offer the basic elements demanded of the sports text: there is no virtuosity; there is no competition; there is no game; there is no audience.

This essay considers the intersection of gender, mediation, and sport in a handful of works by contemporary artists. It was written to address a negative space. When asked to speak at an exhibit centering on masculinity and sport in contemporary art, I found myself disturbed by the absence of images of female athletes from the exhibit (which did, however, include work *by* female artists).[3] Surveying contemporary art overly engaged with sport, I found a dramatic difference in both the amount and the formal character of work featuring images of women engaged in sport—this essay represents the beginning of an attempt to figure out why this is so.

On one level the answer is simple: many of the most high-profile works engaged with sports are less interested in sport, or the athlete, than they are in the spectacle of sport. Harun Farocki's *Deep Play* (2007) and Douglas Gordon and

Phillipe Parreno's *Zidane: A 21st Century Portrait* (2006), for example, center on our romance with the technology of the sport broadcast. The media spectacle of men's sports is overwhelming in both its volume and its complexity. In especially the televised sports spectacle, media itself becomes the platform through which the spectator experiences his passion for the sport. Glossy production, rapid edits, dynamic graphics, and elaborate sound effects theatricalize spectatorship in terms of technology and, implicitly, gender. Statistical forms of analysis turn bodies into arrows, diagrams, and numbers. The distance between the visual experience of watching an NFL broadcast and the visual geometry of a game like *Madden NFL* decreases with each revolution in product development (moving now toward 3-D). Such technological rituals organize an enormous amount of attention and desire around the male athlete's body for the pleasures of the presumed male spectator/consumer.[4] Technology itself operates as an alibi for the homosociality of men's sports by making subjective pleasure look and feel like objective facts, by rendering a desire for proximity into a need for accuracy. Farocki's twelve-channel installation *Deep Play* submerges the spectator in a room full of visual data—all culled from the 2006 FIFA World Cup final. Lines move across one screen, tracking the offside position; another channel tracks each player's movement across the field; one screen camera is trained on the French national team's bench, another only on that of their Italian opponents. We have an external shot of the stadium over the duration of the match and even a security camera's view of the parking garage. The work teases out the neurosis embedded in the sport spectacle—a paranoid demand for more information, for more detailed tracking of the body, for more accurate forms of measurement.

Elaborate protocols of reading and viewing manage how we see and experience these scenes of intimacy and belonging. Gordon and Perrano's *Zidane: A 21st Century Portrait* is perhaps the most perfect expression of the collision of intimacy and publicity in the sport spectacle. Multiple cameras reproduce for us the experience of keeping company with the athlete in the middle of the arena. The film exploits what Eve Sedgwick calls the "privilege of unknowing," which allows us all to luxuriate in the spectacle of Zidane's athleticism without, however, considering what it is that we are doing as our eyes linger over the crook of Zidane's neck, as we admire the sweaty sheen of his skin, or as we contemplate the sublimity of the athlete's weathered face.[5] Take art historian Michael Fried's remarkable appreciation of Zidane's total absorption in the game:

> Indeed, Zidane's dazzling and unerring footwork, his astonishing control of the ball, his instantaneous decision making—all exemplify his seemingly unremitting focus on the game even as they combine to keep the viewer perceptually on edge, as does the sheer violence of his high-speed

physical encounters with rival players as they try to strip him of the ball and vice versa. . . . Another factor in all this is Zidane's physiognomy, not just its leanness and toughness, emblematized by his balding, graying, closely cropped skull, but its basic impassiveness . . . which adds to the impression of an inner ferocity that, not at all paradoxically—think of the great stars of classic Westerns—could scarcely be more photogenic. (To say that the seventeen cameras "love" Zidane is an understatement.)[6]

Gordon and Parreno's film is an intricately choreographed ballet of admiration and disavowal. This beautiful portrait reaches toward something like the experience of keeping company with Zidane while he plays this match, but it is also a deep mediation on how Zidane is visibly "produced" as a spectacle by cameras, by radio, and by television broadcasts. It is marked by a nearly painful awareness of the fact that it is hard to see through the spectacle of the game (the moodiness of the film is amplified by Mogwai's deeply melancholic sound track). As we watch Zidane move around the field in the early minutes of the film (and the game) his thoughts stretch across the screen. The player recalls his boyhood attraction to evening football telecasts:

> As a child, I had running commentary in my head when I was playing. It wasn't really my own voice. It was the voice of Pierre Cangion, a television anchor from the 1970s. Every time I heard his voice, I would run towards the TV as close as I could get, for as long as I could. It wasn't that his words were so important. But the tone, the accent, the atmosphere, was everything.

Even Zidane's primal scene, in other words, is not the sensual immediacy of the action on field but the intimacy of the television broadcast. *Zidane* takes not desire as its subject but the mediation of desire—not our desire for the man but our desire for the image of the man. Zidane explains, "I love the idea of transmitting the image of the player, of this guy on the field that brings happiness to those looking at him."[7] When he plays now for the cameras, he knows he is on that screen, pulling another little boy toward him. In fact, that little boy is us.

Although *Zidane* clearly cites *Fussball wie noch nie* (1971), Hellmuth Costard's real-time portrait of George Best as he played a Manchester United match against Coventry (a nearly Warholian film in both its simplicity and its erotics), *Zidane's* closest contemporary cousin actually is the YouTube football homage. Hundreds (if not thousands) of homemade compositions set the highlights and lowlights of a player's career to pop songs. *Zidane: The Emotional Movie,* for example, created by rapidwands/zizou312 and posted by multiple users on YouTube in 2007, scores clips of Zidane on and off the pitch (many of these are pulled from Gordon's film) to the Timbaland/One Republic pop song "Apologize," which then fades into the Sick Puppies song "All the Same." The opening lyrics of *that* painfully sincere rock ballad are, "I don't mind where you come from, as long as you come to me." Other Zidane homages draw their music from Coldplay ("Beautiful World"), Madonna ("Love Tried to Welcome Me"), and even the Spice Girls ("Viva Forever"). At last check the videos set to Madonna and the Spice Girls had recorded well over 100,000 views each. There seems to be no irony in the use of pop ballads to score these montages. If anything, these songs (culled from European pop radio playlists) are perfect vehicles for communicating the powerful longings that undergird world soccer culture.[8] These texts—*Zidane: A 21st Century Portrait* and *Zidane: The Emotional Movie*—are formally linked by their explicit deployment of what James Tobias describes as "the musicality of time based media" and by the movement of sentiment along the currents of popular music.[9] But Gordon and Parreno's film is a big-budget and highbrow translation of a popular, wildly sentimental, and decidedly lowbrow hobby in which the "art" is produced by the disavowal of the popular.[10] *Zidane* elaborates on the spectacle that substitutes for the person to allow for a viewing pleasure that might otherwise be too visibly queer. In doing so, the film raises the homosocial intensity of football culture by another factor. It repeats it, aestheticizes it, washes it clean, and makes it respectable. *Zidane* is a successful spectacle (an image in which we are interested, an image for which there is an audience, an image that we feel permission to look at and enjoy)—it is in fact a hyperspectacle in which the thrill of the enjoyment on offer is derived from the awareness that we, as audience, are part of a global spectacle. We are happy spectators to our own spectatorship. *Zidane* turns homosocial desire into a glowing spectacle.

Women's team sports live in the abject shadow of that world. Women's sports are framed by mainstream media as making a bad spectacle, either via sensationalist stories of female monstrosity or via the reproduction of the notion that women's sports are boring. Broadcasts of women's team sports use fewer cameras and little to no graphics, and they are scheduled at less desirable broadcast times, often on floating cable channels that do not appear on digital menus. Audiences are smaller—watching your team from your living room can be doubly isolating when you can see very few people watching them in the stadium. The circulation of what broadcast footage exists is tightly regulated—with so little material out there, the illegal distribution of Olympic soccer matches on YouTube, for example, is easier to police.[11]

Viral videos about women's sports are less likely to feature the prowess of athletes than they are to luxuriate in overt misogyny. This was the case for a 2008 viral video mocking the idea of a "WNBA Live" video game (*NBA Live* is the most popular basketball game series). In the video parody a man in lesbian drag

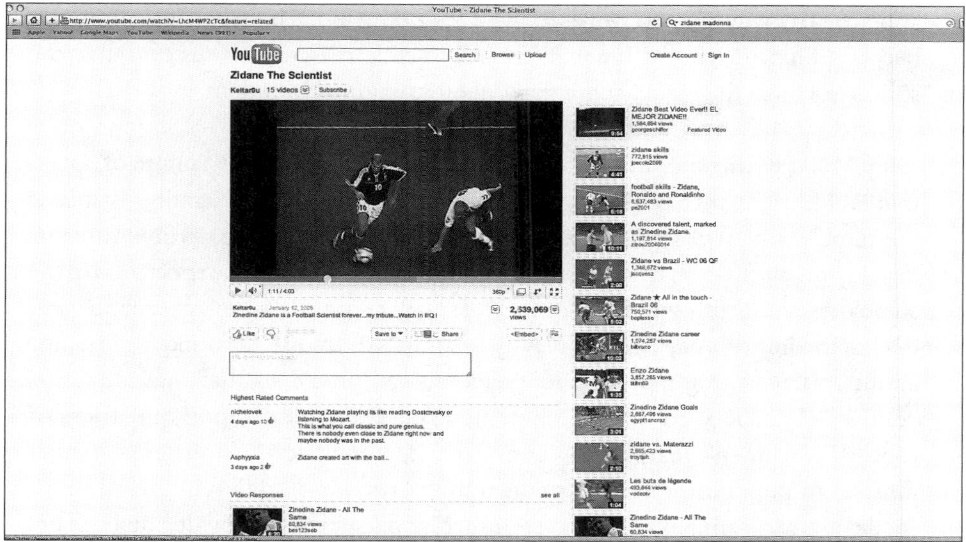

KeitarOu, *Zidane the Scientist,* 2006. Scored to Coldplay's "The Scientist," the video had received 5,443,472 views on YouTube as cf June 1, 2012.

plays at being a WNBA star introducing his bored friends to the new game—an abject, outdated, and comically slow-moving "virtual" basketball game in which a lone female stick figure limps across the scene and makes a bad shot. The player then falls over "injured" when she gets a "yeast infection."

There is, it turns out, a whole subgenre of YouTube videos mocking the WNBA—not because the authors of these videos have a problem with the organization but because they can't get over the idea that women play basketball and that there are people who want to watch them. The "WNBA Live" parody has a home on *Sports Illustrated*'s website, where it is posted in their "Hot Clicks" section without critical comment.[12]

More problematic, in the fall of 2009 ESPN broadcast a story about a "catfight" on a soccer field (a series of unpunished hard fouls in a regional college match, broadcast on a local television channel). ESPN's video went viral and international. Multiple posts of clips from the ESPN story on YouTube have been viewed well over one million times each. Elizabeth Lambert, the college student who was the center of the footage, became an international headline. The story became a media phenomenon and was, by far, the most exposure given to women's soccer in 2009. The referee who failed to discipline her in the game (as was his job) was never named in the media, nor was he sanctioned for letting the game get out of control. It is hard to imagine video footage of a regional men's game in any sport becoming this newsworthy, even if such a game involved clearly violent behavior (soccer players of both sexes sometimes throw punches and are normally ejected from the field for doing so). The story was attractive because it fed into the notion that female athletes are female monsters—that the sports in which they participate make them unnaturally violent.

Toby Miller points out that the entry of women into the visual sphere of sports media is fraught with "cosmic gender ambivalence."[13] The becoming visible of the female athlete raises gender and sexuality immediately as problems to be visually managed—on the field, in the visual presentation of the sport, and in the stands.[14] Pat Griffith writes, "Women's presence in sport as serious participants dilutes the importance and exclusivity of sport as a training ground for learning about and accepting male gender roles and the privileges that their adoption confers."[15] Anxiety about the inherent, structural, and defining queerness of especially women's team sports constrain the circulation of images of female athletes in popular media. That constraint plays out on different levels: sports media is always already uninterested in women's sports (having decided it is not appealing to male spectators and consumers), and women athletes themselves have a lot to lose. Marriage plays with this in *Soccer*; the low-fi, DIY aesthetics, their oddity, and their isolation speak to the abjection of female athleticism. But it also suggests that the homosocial space of women's sports is a more generous and more elementally *queer* one for its "failure" to produce a good media spectacle. Bass and Tsang play, but they aren't playing along.

Artists like Gordon and Farocki collaborate with the sport spectacle. Their works in fact require the full cooperation of the institutions that produced the matches they choose as their respective subjects.[16] Gordon and Parreno worked with La Liga, Spain's professional league, and Zidane's club, Real Madrid. They had the athlete's full cooperation, as well as that of his teammates. Farocki's project required the cooperation of FIFA (which controls the use of World Cup broadcasts) and the numerous television networks whose feeds he appropriated. These works and others like them extend the sport spectacle into the museum. Work like this can't be made about women's sports. Queer feminist work that takes mainstream sports spectacles as its subject won't be made with the cooperation of sports media.[17] The character and quality of the image, the geometries of desire that connect athlete and spectator, are qualitatively different.

The ideological limits that organize and contain mainstream representations of the female athletic body aggressively and ambivalently surface in *Stand Your Ground* (2008), Moira Lovell's photographic installation of claustrophobic portraits of the women who play for the Doncaster Rover Belles. The Belles are one of the older women's soccer teams in England. Women working the stands selling programs for the local professional men's team, the Doncaster Rovers, founded the Belles in 1969.[18] In Lovell's portraits the contemporary Belles do not meet the camera with the obligatory disarming smile asked of women athletes on those anomalous days when the media takes interest. Nor are these traditional team photos presenting the united front arranged in tidy rows on the pitch, bodying forth the team's identity en masse. Lovell's images are anxious. Each portrait couples a player with the team's coach. Taken as a series, the work seems to manifest the pressure to "straighten" the female athlete out, to reassure the spectator by forcing us to read these women via the mediating presence of the manager. This framing isolates each from the other, triangulating "us and them" through the male managerial body. Lovell edges the game, too, out of the frame. The athletes are off the field, still in their training outfits, caught in the semiprivate, transitional space of the locker room. They are defensive portraits and overtly refuse the traditional heroic, action-oriented approach to the athlete. Lovell shows us that within this setting and with these subjects, the conditions of possibility for representing pleasure and identity are fraught. The installation draws attention to the biggest threat to mainstream visual culture especially posed by women's football: you can't not see lesbians everywhere. The entire composition seems designed to ward off this possibility.

As much as the game is marked in England as a working-class sport, it is even more deeply coded as masculine thanks largely to the English Football Association's fifty-year ban on women from its fields, an act explicitly intended to kill off the popular women's game in the 1920s not only because the women who played it were unseemly—cigarette smoking, swearing, and hard playing (and plainly gay)—but because those women had politically organized to support striking workers.[19] Because of this history and the sports culture that it created, in those countries where women's soccer was in essence outlawed (England, Germany, Spain, and Brazil, for example), one's *kit* feels like a black leather motorcycle jacket. Even as it signifies membership in a team, a collective identity, it also signals a form of rebellion.[20] Furthermore, when the English FA banned women from its pitches, it also banned male FA members from supporting the women's game as referees, linesmen, etc. The ban was not just an attempt to regulate women footballers out of existence but an attempt to ban the rewiring of men's and women's relationships to each other that women's athletics invariably brings about. It was an attempt to undo the queering effects of the women's game on gender and sexuality. The manager's presence in *Stand Your Ground* is contradictory—on the surface he seems to ward off the queer reading, but in fact his is not a traditional masculine presence. Take one of these portraits, and perhaps you see a couple. Look at the installation series, however, and the male body becomes a superfluous and awkward presence. He is not a heterosexual chaperone but a queer collaborator.

The mediatedness of the spectacle of the men's game seems to provide the artist and the fan with a distance that gives him permission to adore his subject. Without that visual archive, without the spectacle of the spectacle filtering us from them, the task of representing the female athlete is more charged and more

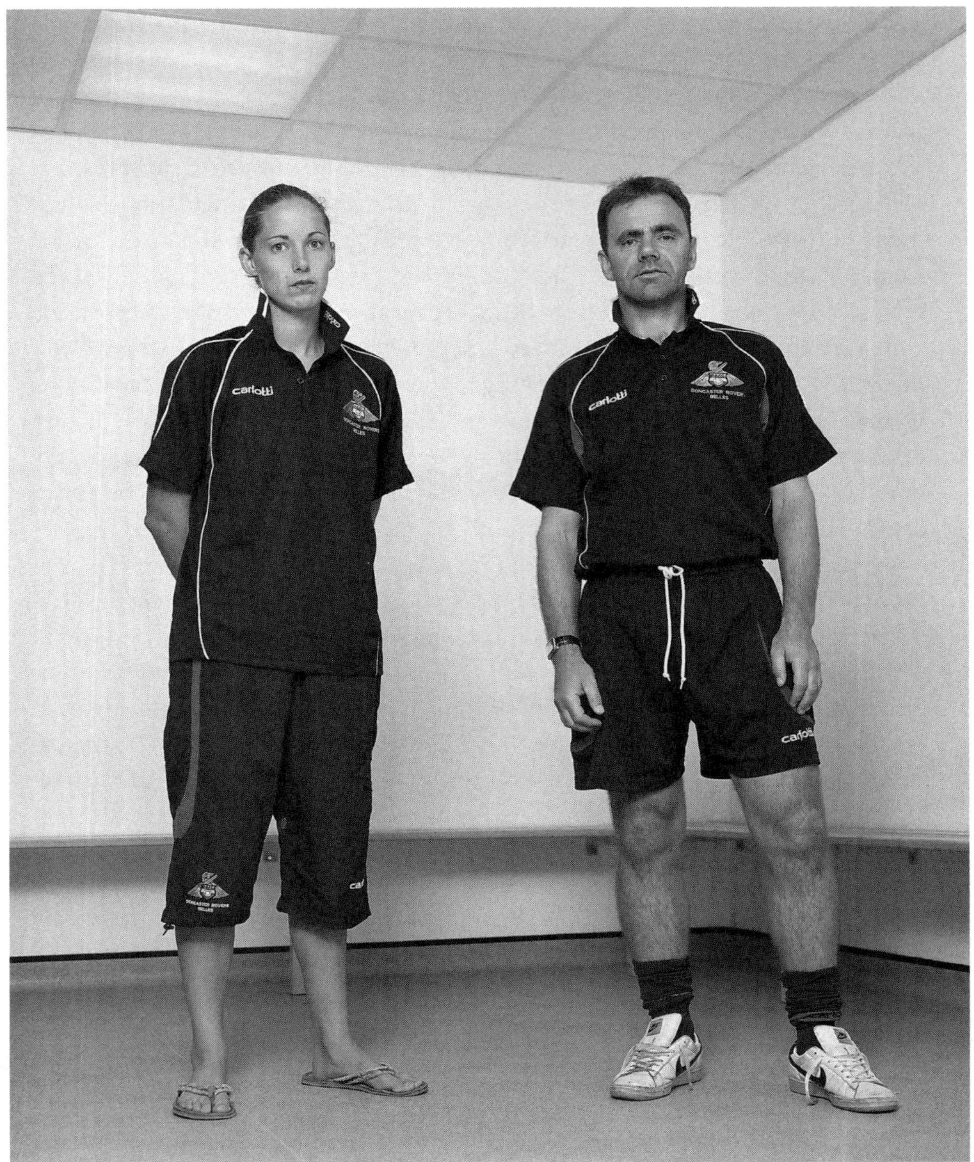

Moira Lovell, *John and Precious,* 2008. Precious Hamilton, 21, center midfield, was with the Doncaster Rover Belles one year at the time of the photograph. C-print; 70 × 60 cm. Commissioned by Pavilion. Courtesy of the artist.

overdetermined. Zidane can act like the cameras aren't there—his absorption in himself, in himself as athletic spectacle, lets him get on with his work and lets you look at him without the particular discomfort of fearing that somehow he might look back, as if he knew what you wanted. In the world captured by Lovell's camera, when the lens is trained on her the female athlete doesn't move. The spectator is an unwelcome presence in this space, in much the same way that these women are unwelcome within the deeply patriarchal and homophobic spaces of English football. The artist refuses to give us either a moving image or an image of motion. These women do not have the luxury of disavowing the camera's presence and all that it implies. We are intruders, and the Belles stand in formation *against* us. It is as if these women are defending their space of play from the intrusive presence of the camera. These players are not on television, not in the newspapers, and not in the movie theaters. And in a way, they are not here, either, in these photographs of an antiseptic locker room.

The defensiveness of their stance in relation to the camera and the spectator is not incidental to Lovell's subjects: On January 3, 1995, BBC1 broadcast a documentary featuring the team. Paul Pierrot's The BELLES was, in the words of sports journalist Pete Davies, "a romp; it showed them playing, training, working, clubbing, going ten-pin bowling, winning the FA cup, drinking and dancing with the trophy, getting back to the business in the league the next Sunday and winning that, too."[21] The women were shown to be rowdy, working class, and certainly in terms of their relationship to femininity, queer.[22] This was too much for the English Football Association, which sent a strongly worded letter of rebuke to the club. Players who had been on the national team were dropped, and star forward Gil Coutaurd was stripped of her captaincy of the national squad. Davies followed the team for a season and saw first hand the impact of the broadcast of this documentary on the team. After that broadcast the club avoided all contact with the media—Davies described the team as suffering from a "dread of publicity."[23]

In representations of men at play, intensely homoerotic scenes flourish under our noses, but only with the promise that we not "see" them. The "obviousness" of the queerness of women playing together means that we are barely allowed to see them play at all—and given the threat of homophobic retaliation, women do not necessarily look to the visual field for affirmation. The queer feminist artist who ventures into this territory must generate a space from which media has been exiled. Math Bass and Wu Ingrid Tsang give us access to that imaginary space and call it "soccer." Moira Lovell gives us individual players but tells us that the team's field of play is beyond the camera's reach.

NOTES

1. Judith Halberstam, *In a Queer Time and Place: Transgender Bodies, Subcultural Lives* (New York: New York University Press, 2005), 96.

2. José Esteban Muñoz, *Cruising Utopia: The Then and There of Queer Futurity* (New York: New York University Press, 2009), 1.

3. *Hard Targets: Masculinity and Sport,* at the Los Angeles County Museum of Art, October 2008–January 2009.

4. That presumption is at odds with market research, as women constitute an increasingly significant percentage of the audience for nearly every major spectator sport.

5. Eve Kosofsky Sedgwick, "The Privilege of Unknowing," in *Tendencies* (Durham, N.C.: Duke University Press, 1993), 23–51.

6. Michael Fried, "Absorbed in the Action," *Artforum* 45 (September 2006): 333–35.

7. Zinédine Zidane and Frédéric Hermel, "L'impression d'être Zidane sur le terrain," in *Zinédine Zidane: Un portrait du 21e siècle* (Paris: Hors Collections, 2006).

8. The use of "feminine" genres of music to score homosocial celebrations of masculine prowess becomes less surprising when one learns that women comprise at least 38 percent of fans worldwide. See the overview of the SPORT+MARKT study in "Female Fans Can Boost Sponsorship during Crisis," *International Herald Tribune,* January 27, 2009.

9. James Tobias, "Cinema, Scored: Toward a Comparative Methodology for Music in Media," *Film Quarterly* 57, no. 2 (Winter 2003–4): 26–36.

10. Taha Belal, in contrast, openly mines popular visual culture in his looped compilation *Renaldo Remix* (2008). Belal directly appropriates clips from a series of viral homages to Cristiano Ronaldo's foot skills. The result is a mind-numbing repetition of Ronaldo's flicks and stopovers scored by alternating strands of rock, techno, pop, rap, and disco.

11. YouTube videos of the FIFA Women's World Cup and the Olympics are rare. These international tournaments are the only events in women's soccer that are broadcast on mainstream network channels and that attract media attention. FIFA and the networks that contract with the Olympics aggressively restrict the circulation of match footage.

12. See "WNBA Video of the Day," SI.com, May 23, 2008, http://sportsillustrated.cnn.com/2008/extramustard/05/23/hotclicks.0523/index.html.

13. Toby Miller, *Sportsex* (Philadelphia: Temple University Press, 2001), 130.

14. In the summer of 2009, the WNBA's Washington Mystics banned "kissing cams." Kissing cams scan crowds at baseball and basketball games to broadcast images of kissing couples in the stands. The audiences at WNBA games include many lesbian couples, so such a camera would probably catch a kiss between women fans who are there to root on a team that most likely includes lesbian players. In their statement explaining the ban, the Mystics explained that they didn't consider such displays of lesbian affection appropriate. Sheila Johnson, managing partner for the Mystics, quoted by Mike Wise in "Mystics Give Big Issue the Kiss-Off," *Washington Post,* July 27, 2009.

15. Pat Griffin, *Strong Women, Deep Closets: Lesbians and Homophobia in Sport* (Champaign, Ill.: Human Kinetics, 1998), 17.

16. In contrast, Fred Poulet and French national team player Vikash Dohrasoo documented the latter's experience in the 2006 World Cup without permission from FIFA or France's football federation. Although he had featured in the team's qualifying matches, he was not fielded in the World Cup itself—thus, the resultant film's title, *Substitute.* Unable to use footage of training or matches, the film shows Dohrasoo in his hotel room only, struggling with his disappointment at being benched. Many suspect Dohrasoo's participation in this documentary led to his being benched throughout the competition.

17. The English Football Association launched a campaign against homophobia in 2010 with a video that featured not a single player nor match footage. The video shows a typical English fan (white, male) moving through his day, pouring homophobic abuse on the people around him (a newspaper salesman, fellow passengers on the train, coworkers). The advertisement's message is, homophobic abuse is not tolerated outside the stadium, so it should not be tolerated inside it. This ad does nothing, however, to raise awareness of the almost genetic association of English football with homophobia on a cultural and institutional level—it apparently never occurred to the Football Association's committee that gay

and lesbian sports fans might by offended by the ad or that it might actually represent gay and lesbian athletes in such an advertisement. See Owen Gibson, "Gay Rights Groups Attack FA Delay over Anti-homophobia film," *Guardian,* February 8, 2010.

18. Women fans of the men's clubs who wanted to play started nearly all of the most prominent women's teams in the United Kingdom.

19. See Barbara Jacobs, *The Dick, Kerr's Ladies: The Factory Girls Who Took on the World* (London: Robinson, 2004), for a history of women's soccer in England at the end of World War I and for her insights into the relationship between the English Football Association's ban against women's soccer and the support women's teams were then offering to striking factory workers.

20. For more on the history of women's soccer in England, see Jean Williams, *A Game for Rough Girls: The History of Women's Football in Britain* (London: Routledge, 2003).

21. Pete Davies, *I Lost My Heart to the Belles* (London: Mandarin Press, 1996), 99.

22. For scholarship on gender, sexuality, and women's football in England, see Jayne Caudwell, "Women's Football in the United Kingdom: Theorizing Gender and Unpacking the Butch Lesbian Image," *Journal of Sport and Social Issues* 23, no. 4, 390–402; "Femme-Fatale: Rethinking the Femme-inine," in *Sport, Sexualities and Queer/Theory,* ed. Jayne Caudwell (London: Routledge, 2006), 145–58. Pete Davies's writing about the Belles does not directly address the sexuality of the players—that the team included a number of lesbian players is legible via the occasional use of the term *partner* and the pronoun *her,* as well as his accounts of postmatch outings to local gay pubs. Significantly, his book opens with an anecdote about the team's links to the Hackney Women's Football Club, a historically important out lesbian, feminist soccer club that fought a number of battles in support of women's football and against homophobic behavior on the part of players, referees, and the Football Association itself. See Jayne Caudwell, "Women Playing Football at Clubs in England with Socio-Political Associations," *Soccer and Society* 7, no. 4, 423–38.

23. Pete Davies, "Belles Left Running to Stand Still," *Independent,* March 11, 1996.

24

Everything Is Possible, but Nothing Is Real

Derek A. Burrill

I borrow the title of this essay from the song "This Is the Life" from the album *Time's Up* (CBS Records, 1990) by the heavy metal/funk band Living Color, a group who made a particular mark in the late 1980s and early 1990s for their unique sound, aesthetic, and mash-up sensibility. What was perhaps most remarkable about Living Color was that they ostensibly were the first all-black band who used the heavy metal aesthetic and style as central to their sound. Of course, they incorporated other styles and genres (funk, African folk, punk, sound collage), but at their core they were a heavy metal band. What makes them remarkable was not just the fact that they were all black[1] but that they co-opted a (formerly) exclusively white musical genre for their forceful, black-populist imagination.[2] And as critics at the time pointed out regularly, Living Color used white metal musical technique and vocabulary as well as or better than their white counterparts. A great deal of hoopla surrounded them, in fact, because they simply outplayed the previous owners of the genre, freewaying a very particular racial tension in the time of rap groups such as Public Enemy and NWA, the seemingly never-ending battles between the Crips and the Bloods in South Central Los Angeles, and shortly after, the Rodney King incident and riots. Clearly, a great deal of the trauma of this moment came from the radical racial ideology and identity politics of African and Caribbean Americans and the "truth" of the white fear and frustration over black permeation of all forms of media. Living Color, in essence, inversely co-opted from the white entertainment establishment and did it masterfully. Yet at this particular moment in U.S. history, white America was clearly uncomfortable with this co-optation. After all, it's the white culture that has traditionally done the co-opting.

I begin with this sociohistorical snapshot to make a larger point about media, particularly about digital media. "Everything is possible, but nothing is real." For Living Color the fight was not only in the street but also articulated/enunciated more according to Gramsci—know the hegemonic monolith, and rewrite the language, the embodied code. The idea in this lyrical twist, it seems, is to wonder why we ever valued the real if value is based upon a scale called "everything."

Baudrillard has waxed and waned about this for decades—sometimes signaling the end in the beginning and sometimes the reverse:

> It is culture that clones us, and mental cloning anticipates biological cloning. It is the matrix of acquired traits that, today, clones us culturally under the sign of monothought—and it is all the innate differences that are annulled, inexorably, by ideas, by ways of life, by the cultural context. Through school systems, media, culture, and mass information, singular beings become identical copies of one another.[3]

Baudrillard is particularly valuable here in that his thinking demands reflection, comment, and more reflection based on a self-replicating epistemology. He upends our sense of the world and our surroundings (as well as our passion for individuation) through a slinky cloak-and-dagger of teetering digital abyss versus a dis(re)membered 1968 political street fight. This births the logic of the tweaker, those who remake and refashion using the manufacture and materials of previous forms. In contemporary pop culture, tweaking across media and disciplines shows us that focusing on image value or the image-essential acknowledges the political efficacy of mixing, mash-ups, and montage. Fredric Jameson calls this "pastiche," a kind of blank parody. Whereas Jameson saw this as a postmodern marker of depthlessness (it seems obvious that he got lost in the Westin Bonaventure Hotel), the tweaker (or the modder, in the digital generation) implicitly understands value as mixture. Authenticity hasn't lost its cultural capital; it's just that it can be a roadblock to the articulation of choice. Since the popular embrace (and technological availability and complexity) of digital technology across various media forms, a slow but steady ideation of the possibilities of digital code has flipped. It is my argument that the old model of pure reproduction, copying, and sharing has been replaced with tweaking—the impulse (in many ways the necessity) to physically alter the source code to align with the user's desires. In this sense, Living Color's admonition that "everything is possible, but nothing is real" hails us deeply and articulately. Additionally, their musical (and political) act of inverse co-optation (assuming a certain hegemonic, albeit waning, position of whiteness in the media at that historical moment) signals that at the outset of the viral spread of digital popular technologies, an inherent disruption was always already in place. But what does tweaking mean for artists, users, gamers, and YouTubers? What are its politics?

I want to better articulate this situation and impulse by focusing on a particular type of tweaking: video game modifications, or mods, which are changes and alterations (in some cases entirely new stories, spaces, and games in themselves) in the original design code often made by the players themselves. Mods enable the designer/creator/gamer to extend and reimagine the products built by design houses and then share them with other gamers. Often, these mods are intertextual and parodic versions of the original, but at root they are attempts to build or remake worlds. As McKenzie Wark writes, "Games are not representations of this world. They are more like allegories of a world made over as gamespace."[4] Additionally, the mass availability of these world-making tools (computer languages, HTML, open-source code) also serves as its own reminder of the very alterability of the code. Pop culture swims in this desire. Think here of the Tyler Perry sitcoms based on the traditions solidified in the white television comedy genre and formula or of the Detroit rapper Eminem and his white, angst-ridden, carnivalesque hip-hop formula. As Jon McKenzie writes, "The model of creativity often associated with digital media is not that of originality or uniqueness but recombination and multiplicity, a model hardwired to the computer's uncanny ability to copy and combine images, sounds, texts, and other materials from an endless array of sources."[5]

Press Start

Mods are part of a general technological impulse that finds its home in tinkering, hacking, the DIY movement, and the longing to personalize mass-produced objects and experiences (the "My" in MySpace). Typically, the term *mod* refers to changes or innovations in the software code, but occasionally, it can refer to the system hardware. For the purposes of this study, I focus on software and code mods, but a large community exists that focuses on the game system modification, or case mod. This impulse and practice also finds its roots in tweaking but emphasizes the reconstruction and modification of the hardware, akin to the bad-boy aesthetics and mechanics of the performance collective Survival Research Laboratories. "The overall visual aesthetic of the modded gaming systems has a number of subcultural reference points: car culture, raves and techno club culture, industrial chic, science fiction films, and computer games themselves. Yet despite the development of case modding as a form of folk art, it remains intimately tied to machine performance."[6] With software mods (hereafter referred to as *s-mods*), modders concentrate on specific games or genres. Most often, modifications are made to first-person shooters (FPS) or real-time strategy games. This is likely because of the strong community bonds that these games foster but also because coding elements for these games are more straightforward and systematic, as these games rely on a strong mapping element in gameplay (requiring spatial reasoning and tactical knowledge of war/ battle strategies). This mapping element (as far as gameplay is concerned) is highly transferable between games in each of these genres, as is basic coding skill (particularly since these games are played overwhelmingly on PCs; there are, however, what are called modchips for video game consoles such as the PlayStation or Xbox). In order to construct a mod, the gamer/modder must have the original source code in the form of the original game's code. Interestingly, the original game is almost always designated, if for instance, we are referring to the first-person shooter *Counter-Strike* (Vivendi, 1999), as *vCounter-Strike* or VCS—the *v* or *V* signifying "vanilla." I return to this term later. Largest are the entire-level s-mods (in what sometimes seems like a whole expansion pack for a particular game), but smaller s-mods are more the norm—for example, weapons, characters, objects, and music and sound.[7] Larger mods are often constructed by mod teams. Official patches are designer or publisher based, whereas unofficial patches are often used to fix bugs and come from the modder community. Overhauls are complete redesigns of gameplay, strategy, or style that leave the original game concept, story, or world, and mod spin-offs result in s-mods that function effectively as new games. Again, as in the game *Counter-Strike,* an s-mod might have a completely separate player/modder community from an entirely different source game, in this case *Half-Life* (Sierra Studios/EA, 1998). Thus, s-mods can function as versions of spin-offs of source games ad infinitum.

A guiding concept behind all s-mods is that the design aesthetic of the original is mimicked (or at least closely followed) so that there is a level of familiarity for the player. If it is set in a particular world—a futuristic alien planet, for instance—the most intricate and detailed elements of the original world are often copied or rendered in greater detail. Artistic choices are, however, intrinsically limited to the parameters of the game engine (the processor that the game is built out of and runs through) and/or how complex the s-mod is meant to be. Additionally, game genre has a large role in aesthetic constraints—*Dungeons & Dragons*–style fantasy games tend to feature more organic, curvilinear objects and character lines, whereas a science fiction–based FPS would more likely reference the cold, mechanistic feel solidified by sci-fi cinema design (such as the iterative patterns depicted in the *Alien* series or the noir-esque moodiness of *Blade Runner* replicated in the genesis film *Prometheus*). Most important, though mods are constructed out of the same 1s and 0s as all digital code, the overwhelming pleasure of their construction, sharing, and utility lies in the level of graphic sophistication (and how this can function as a source of designer ingenuity, community commentary, and game loyalty), usually in comparison with the source game's graphics.

Again, these reconfigurations are based on a shared outcome—a particular person or team's vision of what the game *could* and *should* be. It is, at its most basic structure, an expansion of the gameplay and game space where the modder's creation is negotiated between the original design, the limits of the game engine and hardware, his or her individual vision of each game's inherent, unlocked possibilities, and a desire to share this negotiated invention with other insiders who can revel equally in its novelty, elegance, and purpose. Again, deeply embedded in tweaking and modding is an assumption that digital code is always already meant to be tweaked, a challenge that constantly hails the hacker geek, the console cowboy, and the digital boy populating films such as *WarGames, Tron,* and *Hackers.*[8] Typically offering their work over the Internet as shareware, modders are often adamant about supporting the open-source movement and the expansion of Linux. This has spawned, of course, numerous lawsuits filed by game companies over intellectual property, but most corporate developers and publishers realize the substantial street cred their company can gain by either ignoring or supporting s-mods. Though authorship has not developed as an identity in the business and art of game design as it has in relation to, say, film and film direction (except for a few lead designers who have clearly articulated, personal styles and aesthetics), when a new s-mod is released for public play a distinct back-and-forth is witnessed in which its authors clearly enjoy the notoriety but are at the same time punished by the gaming community for too much hubris or self-promotion. Authorship and textuality are, of course, issues that have been well covered in literary criticism, critical theory, and other segments of the humanities. In his compelling article "New Media Theory: Electronic Games, Democracy and Reconfiguring the Author-Audience Relationship," Rob Cover argues that digital media at its core challenges the author/text/audience debates developed through earlier media studies discourse not simply as an extension of the older media but as a sharp break from presentation/reception media. He writes:

> It is possible to suggest that one way in which we can view both the popularity of electronic gaming and the historical development of digital interactive media technologies is from a perspective that understands their emergence as driven by a cultural—that is, popular—demand or desire for interactive engagement and a democratization of control over the text. This is a demand to take the narrative text out of the sole hands of authors; a demand to participate both imaginatively and in line with given structures of form in the co-creation of a narrative, of a text that has an always *unfinished* form that is played with.[9]

Here, Cover is describing a reordering and shifting of hierarchy within the author/text relationship. I argue, however, that in the case of modding (and tweaking in general), reconfiguring or challenging the designer/game/player (or author/text/audience) relationship isn't the essence of the matter. It is the modification itself, the s-mod, that stands as a shared prosthetic for gamer, modder, designer, and community. Again, everything is possible, but nothing is real when the modder uses pirated design and communal use-values to crack open assumptions about text, structure, representation, ownership, and property.

Coffee Break

Much has been written about *Grand Theft Auto: San Andreas* (Rockstar, 2004). It has an Entertainment Software Rating Board (ESRB) rating of AO (Adults Only). Many criticisms have been leveled against the game: it promotes violence against women; it uses negative stereotypes of urban black men as a narrative and gameplay imperative; it teaches our children how to carjack; it is one of the greatest games ever. Regardless, for a video game its popular shelf life and position in the media spotlight has been considerably longer and larger than most other games. As a game, structurally, it is usually classified as an action-adventure sandbox game, so that the player (like a child in a sandbox) is offered a number of toys (vehicles, weapons, avatars) and is left to her own devices to create the world and narrative of the game. So instead of a series of metaphorical cones (as if a player begins at the widest conic section and proceeds toward the narrow end point), the player proceeds through the game world in order to move forward, or level up. Instead of a steady stream of tasks, hurdles, or battles the player must complete, *San Andreas* offers an open-ended series of choices set in vast, scalar locales modeled very closely after cities in California and Nevada. Thus, the kid in the sandbox is expected to formulate an individual narrative (or not) and gameplay style and structure. Ben DeVance and Kurt D. Squire in "The Meaning of Race and Violence in *Grand Theft Auto*" write that "the player makes meaning in concert with the ideological world of the game through play, and play entails some form of acceptance of the semiotics of the gamespace, if only temporarily. Even though the game is a designed space, meaning is plural, multiple, and situated because it is a possibility space—an open work that allows the player many potential actions and thus styles of play."[10] The authors of this essay argue for a locally situated study of play (i.e., the game space itself) in order to tease out how players make meaning of race and violence within an urban, threatening, and complex space. I bring this up to tie a specific s-mod within *San Andreas* to the larger questions of tweaking and the ideological, racial, and subcultural work of a group like Living Color: an s-mod called "Hot Coffee." The "Hot Coffee" minigame (in that it fit into the larger ideation of *San Andreas* but was not central to any of the narrative strings) was originally a segment of code that remained locked in the official design code of the game but was unlocked through an s-mod released in 2005 for Windows-based computers. It was also later unlocked for the PlayStation 2 and the Xbox, but in all of the more recent copies of the game (post-2005), the s-mod has been completely disabled. The beginning of "Hot Coffee" features an exterior establishing shot of CJ's (the central avatar/character) girlfriend's house. CJ may date up to six different women.[11] In the original game the gamer hears muffled sounds of sex emanating from the house; in "Hot Coffee" the player/CJ is allowed to go into the house and have intercourse with that particular girlfriend. The sex is rough and demeaning but ostensibly consensual.

Shortly after its release, recalls, legislative action in the United States, Europe, and Australia, and lawsuits and civil suits followed. Originally rated M (Mature) by the ESRB, it was then changed to AO (Adults Only) and then changed back to M. As an s-mod, "Hot Coffee" still retains much of its infamy, so much so that series spin-offs and sequels have not garnered much critical or player praise, even while Rockstar Games continually attempts to up the offensive ante with games like *Grand Theft Auto: Chinatown Wars* (Rockstar, 2009) and *Grand Theft Auto: The Ballad of Gay Tony* (Rockstar, 2009).[12]

Although many games exist that contain explicitly violent, misogynistic, or racist content—particularly games specifically designed to offend—what was particular to the controversy surrounding "Hot Coffee" was CJ's ethnicity (African American) and the ethnicity of his, in game terms, most useful girlfriend (a nurse that enabled better medical care when CJ was injured), who is white. The idea of a black man engaging in sex with a white girl is a social and cultural trope that has been widely theorized but still carries with it a degree of anxious transgression for conservative Middle America. And to boot, anxieties about interactivity and player effects (particularly in regard to malicious yet impressionable white boys *impersonating* a black guy screwing a white girl) inevitably played themselves out in the media, parent group meetings, and legislative committees. The public uproar was further inflamed by the fact that a designer at Rockstar had written this s-mod into the game and that the company itself most likely enabled the clandestine release of the s-mod.

This brings us back to the term *vanilla,* used for an original game sans modifications. The term *vanilla* has a recognizable history in popular culture—it refers to a person, body, or object that is racially white, sexually conservative, or repressed in general—such that the term itself can exist only in relation to the racial, cultural, and social term *black.* Thus, both stereotypes follow the problematic binary of the exotic, nonwhite other and, conversely, the transfixed white subject longing to be "real," to escape his unmodified body. So the "Hot Coffee" controversy and the use of the term *vanilla* are interwoven signifiers for which popular culture and its co-opting, intertextual, stereotyping, and ravenous excesses function as a type of digital code. Here, the mod and modder serve to illustrate the efficacy of digital code as popular culture engine and, therefore, ideology machine. Everything is

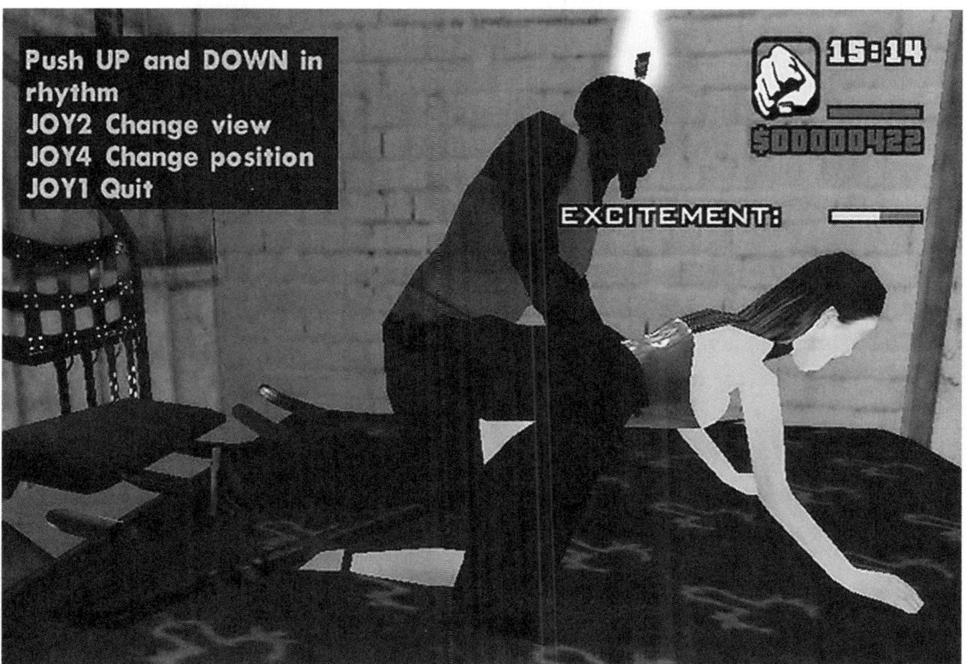

A screenshot from the "Hot Coffee" mod, *Grand Theft Auto: San Andreas,* Rockstar, 2004. Courtesy of Rockstar.

possible, but nothing is real. In this case we see traces and symptoms that signal the complexity of race relations in the "postrace" United States, an issue that forms, in many ways, the core of pop culture and, therefore, the production of codes and signification—real, imagined, or digital.

Tweakology

It seems obvious when playing through mods that the ghost in the machine is the gamer sensibility, a method and mode where fun is serious business, competition is an ontological extension of survival, and the creation of novel forms of pleasure skates the space between necessity and art. Why do gamers/modders bother with this much effort? For when we speak about gamers, many committed players don't mod, but it is still implied that a knowledge of user-fabricated code is as important as any of the shared information the community circulates on bulletin boards, chat rooms, and game networking sites. And why bother considering the vast choices available to the player/consumer? Imagine expanding an already realized digital space at will. This space is not real and might never be, but it is still constructed to signify and function the same way as real space, defined by physics, hemmed in by ownership and territory, full of noise, and always contested. At the epistemological root of video game space is a contract between designer and user in which movement serves as a function of power. So to construct a mod is to learn a space; memorize and map it; and then create a facsimile that contains not just things but the function of those things as experience. A modder is then an architect of constructedness. These are not parodies or pastiche, nor are they odes or sources cited. Baudrillard writes, "The territory no longer precedes the map, nor survives it. Henceforth, it is the map that precedes the territory. . . . The real is produced from miniaturized units, from matrices, memory banks and command modules—and with these it can be reproduced an indefinite number of times."[13] Writing in 1983, Baudrillard understood the coming storm but miscalculated the direction. Tweaking, as practice and impulse, uses the source code to redefine and reconstruct objects and space according to the inverse co-optation principle. Modders aren't so worried about the production of space as they are the construction of spaces to be in, and through this being in, a natural elision occurs.

Like Living Color, the modder is fully cognizant of the utility of the master's tools and the possible mess that can come out of co-optation (political, ethical, ideological), but the space itself allows disavowal of responsibility. It is, after all, still about *play*. And play always denies its culpability. Mods aren't radical politics, nor are they revolutionary art, but they are lucid evidence of how digital code enables and encourages the tweaking impulse and, therefore, the self-generating nature of the human game. Again, Baudrillard writes:

> It is culture that clones us, and mental cloning anticipates biological cloning. It is the matrix of acquired traits that, today, clones us culturally under the sign of monothought—and it is all the innate differences that are annulled, inexorably, by ideas, by ways of life, by the cultural context. Through school systems, media, culture, and mass information, singular beings become identical copies of one another. It is this kind of cloning—social cloning, the industrial reproduction of things and people—that makes possible the biological conception of the genome and of genetic cloning, which only further sanctions the cloning of human conduct and human cognition.[14]

There has never been a material so malleable as digital code, a vision machine and world-building architecture that implies its own tweaking, its self-same reproduction and genesis. Everything is possible, but nothing is real. Walter Benjamin's provocative reading of Klee's painting *Angelus Novus* is useful here. Where history is caught up in—and catching—the wings of the angel, it is the expression of terror on his face we must attend to, his witness to the piles of bodies and fog of souls ground down by the boots of men and the machines of war. It is historical materialism that Benjamin reminds us of, pleading with us to look now at what will have become. He is hailing us to ruminate on what progress means and, particularly relevant to the time of his comments, the progression toward ideological traps like fascism.[15] "The finished work is the deathmask of its conception."[16] As well, I draw attention to Benjamin's comments in that where he focuses on the angel as subject, we should also consider the shrouded implication of the body as signifier itself and the materiality that surrounds it. So then, digital code is a kind of breeze that is nagging at our bodies, reminding us that like genetics, codes are not just another form of materiality. Codes are seductive ubiquities that generate their own temperature, air, direction, and pressure. Tweaking is then a pleasurable and unofficial celebration of an authorship that knows its words are impermanent, stolen, and shared yet still worth writing.

NOTES

1. I use the past tense to refer to the historical moment; Living Color released a new album, however, in 2009 after a long absence.

2. Each of their first two albums feature cover art consisting of hyperchromatic pastiches of pop culture icons, context tweaked and politically upended—an African mask with missile-bound fighter jet wings—and their physical appearance is an over-the-top mélange of hipster 1980s fluorescent bagginess alongside dreadlocks on three of the members and a fade cut on the fourth. The mood is upbeat but snide, committed but distrusting, detached yet silently enraged.

3. Jean Baudrillard, *The Vital Illusion*, ed. Julie Witwer (New York: Columbia University Press, 2000), 25.

4. McKenzie Wark, *Gamer Theory* (Cambridge: Harvard University Press, 2007), section 020 (no page number).

5. Jon McKenzie, "Response by Jon McKenzie," in *First Person: New Media as Story, Performance, and Game*, eds. Noah Wardrip-Fruin and Pat Harrigan (Cambridge: MIT Press, 2004), 118.

6. Bart Simpson, "Geek Chic: Machine Aesthetic, Digital Gaming, and the Cultural Politics of the Case Mod," *Games and Culture* 2, no. 3 (July 2007): 190.

7. Occasionally, as is the case of *Counter-Strike*, modders will use not only the source code but the actual game engine, the software system consisting of various parts that deal with graphics rendering, physics in the game, memory, sound, AI, sharing and networking, etc. Using a game engine repeatedly saves a design team or a modder a great deal of time and effort when creating a mod or a new game. Many sequels, such as in the *Tomb Raider* series, are clones of the previous game with adjusted graphics, spaces, and outcomes.

8. I extensively write about this subjectivity in the form of boyhood in the digital imaginary in *Die Tryin': Videogames, Masculinity, Culture* (New York: Peter Lang, 2008).

9. Rob Cover, "New Media Theory: Electronic Games, Democracy and the Reconfiguring of the Author-Audience Relationship," *Social Semiotics* 14, no. 2 (August 2004): 176.

10. Ben DeVane and Kurt D. Squire, "The Meaning of Race and Violence in *Grand Theft Auto,*" *Games and Culture* 3, nos. 3–4 (July 2008): 281.

11. In *San Andreas* CJ is rewarded with additional weapons and vehicles if he successfully dates any of these women. At the end of a successful date, CJ is invited back to her house for "coffee."

12. See rockstargames.com, gamefly.com, or gamestop.com for a full summary of the series, its history, fan sites, fan fiction, fan art, merchandise, bulletin boards, and of course, downloadable s-mods.

13. Jean Baudrillard, *Simulations* (New York: Semiotexte, 1983), 3.

14. Jean Baudrillard, "The Final Solution: Cloning beyond the Human and Inhuman," in *The Vital Illusion,* ed. Julia Witwer (New York: Columbia, 2000), 25.

15. Walter Benjamin, *Gesammelte schriften,* trans. Harry Zohn, vol. I (Frankfurt am Main: Suhrkamp Verlag, 1972), 691–704.

16. Ibid., 107.

25 Vector, Space, and Time

Sean Cubitt

Vector in the Database Economy

Our key media of the twenty-first century are fundamentally spatial. The truly dominant media of the early twenty-first century are geographical information systems (GIS), spreadsheets, and databases. These workplace media operate by spatializing time. Where once voyagers recorded their journeys as narratives, the early imperial navigations turned to the grid of longitude and latitude. With the introduction of ZIP codes in 1963, mapping could be associated not only with physical but with sociological information. This basic zoning tool could then be associated with such other datasets as census returns, and the move to geographical information systems commenced. The history of the spreadsheet migrated from the double-entry ledger to electronic spreadsheets, which no longer carried the residual chronological ordering pairing accountancy with narrative. That move had been achieved rather earlier in bureaucratic record keeping with Edwin Seibels's invention of the vertical filing cabinet in 1898 (and the slightly earlier innovation of horizontal filing systems). Again, the ledger retained some aspects of temporal ordering, especially in terms of how searches were to be conducted. The filing cabinet spatialized these searches, allowing alphabetical and numerical searches and metadata such as labeled drawers. The database completed this spatialization of data, separating, for example, biographical from geographical, financial from medical records but allowing for cross-referencing. These three instruments—GIS, spreadsheets, and databases—express and enable the managerialization of society. These spatializing tendencies correspond with the arithmetic drive in digital media. The grids and the arithmetical nomenclature for color distinctions identify points rather than continua, ideally replicable entities excluding both semantic reference and temporal change. Yet a key component of the grid retained and retains a strange autonomy from the timeless grid—the line.

The province of as yet undeveloped life sciences and only reintroduced to physics around 1850 by Clausius as the second law of thermodynamics, time was irrelevant to the abstract world of mathematics or the theological world of a creator god. Introduced by Bolzano, Poncelet, Chasles, and Möbius between 1804 and 1827, one of the earliest statements of vector geometries, that of Bellavitis in 1832, was that the line segments AB and BA are not identical, a thesis that proposes that the direction—and therefore the time—of travel along a line is a component of it. As early as 1827, Möbius had constructed a plane from whose apices were suspended weights, which gave mathematical expression to irregularly curved surfaces. It was this property of vectors that was central to the development of vector graphics for computers, specifically for the design of complex curves in industrial CADCAM (computer-aided design and manufacture) software.

Such surfaces can be calculated in a three-dimensional grid, but the synthetic geometries developed during the first half of the nineteenth century allowed swifter and more direct methods of calculation, efficiencies that were not lost on early computer engineers. To define a complex surface in coordinate space requires an address for every single point on the plane. Vector geometry allows the whole plane to be expressed in a single algorithm, which then generates the plane as an expression of the algorithm. Equally valuable was the ability to scale: the algebraic expression of a vector remains the same whether the resulting output is the size of a postage stamp or of a billboard, without the jagged edges and blocky color of similarly scaled bitmaps. This quality found a home among animators, whose work can appear on anything from a mobile phone to a cinema screen. Efficiency and scalability made vector graphics central to manufacturing, design, and motion pictures. But at the same time, the importance of time to vector graphics opens up a contradiction within the apparently seamless, managed space of protocological government[1] and information capitalism of the database economy.[2]

This contradiction is not however without risk. The H.261 codec (compression/decompression file system) that forms the basis of Adobe's Flash Web animation software uses vectors to predict future frames from the state of keyframes nominated by the animator or automatically ascribed when files in other codecs are uploaded to services like YouTube.[3] This predictive mechanism has all the virtues of efficiency: it squeezes files into much smaller packages for network transmission. It also diminishes the information content of the file, discarding anything the program does not see as relevant and providing protocological constraints on the kinds of image that will work best in the format. This is, however, less significant to this discussion than the use of vectors to secure predictive control over the future. This should alert us to the ominous truth that there is nothing intrinsic about time in the abstract that makes it a force for or, indeed, an expression of change. Other models see time as risk and the task of systems to minimize risk, change, and difference. In H.261 the unfolding of a line into unforeseen directions is constrained by the algorithms governing the passage from keyframe to keyframe, a return to the Cartesian principle that a line is determined by its end points—that is, spatially—rather than by its temporal unfolding. The problem for the arts is then to grasp the hidden qualities of the vector. Vector prediction as risk management *processes* time: it produces time not in the raw, as the experience and actuality of difference and change, but as a passage between two states of affairs that are already known or planned. The task of the media arts in the immediate future is to challenge processed time with a renewal of the thesis, not at all unknown in the early years of cinema, that time is a raw material for the moving image.

It is ironic that the earliest computer graphics program was written as vector and shown on a vector screen. Ivan Sutherland's *Sketchpad* (1963) is widely regarded as the first graphics application for a computer. Sutherland's program had a number of key innovations, among them treating a collection of lines as an object, such as a square, so that transformations performed on one part of the object (displacement, rotation, scaling) would apply to the others. The interface was a light pen, so linked to the gesture of drawing, and the output was to a plotter and a cathode ray tube (CRT) monitor. The plotter may have been a point plotter rather than a vector plotter, the former based on Cartesian addressing, the latter based on algorithmic instructions to move in a certain direction. The monitor was not, however, a standard line-scanning television monitor but an oscilloscope, a screen that like radar screens is not illuminated by a cathode ray gun scanning horizontally across the whole screen. Instead, these vector screens instruct the electron beam to perform movements across the plane of the screen in order to illuminate only those points that fall on the vector.[4]

Such vector screens dominated early arcade games. The first U.S. patent for a cathode ray tube amusement device (no. 2,455,992), filed in 1947, used vector graphics on an oscilloscope, whereas the breakthrough *Spacewar* used the vector display of the DEC PDP-1, and Atari's influential *Asteroids* of 1979 used a proprietary vector display. By this stage, however, home gaming had already migrated to the domestic television screen's raster format, and the economics of mass production drove the specialized vector screens from the commercial arena. Atari's major competitor, Taito Corporation's *Space Invaders,* an arcade game, already used raster graphics at its launch in 1978.[5] Video games standardized around the scanning CRT, and the vector display was left as a backwater in specialist applications in scientific instruments and air traffic control. True, early game vector displays were exclusively wire frame, but it appears that the high cost of screens rather than issues concerning color and shading seemed to have dominated this decision. As a result, even when vectors are used to generate images, they are transformed into bitmaps for display, a process that gives rise to the common artifact of judder, when the raster screen cannot match the transformative power of the vector instruction set.

Vector Theory

The vector is not a point but a trajectory, one that may well be unforeseeable and that has consequences. Such consequences can be understood as information—in the definition given by Gregory Bateson, "a difference that makes a difference *in some later state of affairs.*"[6] Bateson's emphasis on the temporal dimension of information is often lost, not least in a turbo-charged digital economy where information is treated as a commodity. As a commodity, information is exchanged in a market where any piece of information—say, the value of the yen at a certain moment in time—can be exchanged as equivalent to any other piece of information, the arrest of a Kurdish leader, for example. Thus treated, information is stripped of its semantic dimension, its use value, in favor of its exchange value, and in the end everything is exchangeable for our most ubiquitous form of information, money. Information may want to be free, but it is everywhere in a market where it is bought and sold. That market is itself a spatial system rather than a temporal one. Data exchanged in news services, for example, is primarily a good to be exchanged and only secondarily a good to be used. Temporality only enters when specialist professions put a premium on real-time information, as in the finance sector, where privileged access to real-time news comes at a premium price, whereas nonprofessionals can have the same data for the mere cost of attending to a few advertisements once it is no longer urgent—that is, useful for trading. The question concerning time is then also a question of political economy. But to the extent that the goal of financial traders is to make money and that of financial markets is to ensure that money circulates, neither acts to create a difference *in some later state of affairs.* Moving money from here to there or from you to me makes no difference to either the total amount of money or the systems through which it circulates. The temporal question posed by Bateson's theorem and very differently by the life sciences' use of the term *vector* points instead toward a future that is neither planned nor foreseen. It suggests an embrace of risk rather than its management. It suggests that time as change and danger, as loss indeed, is integral to our experience and the only dimension in which we can now discover an alternative to an increasingly global regime of power and wealth whose design principles are also expressed in its core technologies, from accounting media to the design of screens and camera chips.

Art is a space where experiments occur, where the making of something new is a daily challenge and where wrestling with and at times against the affordances of inherited media constitutes a core technical competence. Art exists in the contradictions of society, is itself a contradictory form, and generates novelty as it does critique out of the materials that it finds at hand—human, technological, and natural. Vector graphics are just such contradictory factors: media of change and of prediction, digital entities that are overwhelmingly presented on nonvector devices. We therefore ought to be able to inquire of art made using vector graphics whether it is able to create unforeseen, unforeseeable, risky differences in the world.

At the same time, we must recognize the political economy of vector graphics. Now dominant in 3-D graphics, AutoDesk is best known for its CADCAM applications, industry leaders in industrial design and architectural markets. Its aggressive expansion by purchases since 2005 has brought it a series of industry-standard 3-D graphics applications—Alias, 3ds Max (previously Studio Max), Maya, and SoftImage, purchased for $35 million in October 2008. AutoDesk also owns the Discreet family of effects, compositing, grading, and intermediary and workflow tools. Like Apple's Final Cut suite and Adobe, whose 2006 amalgamation with Macromedia consolidated the dominant packages in 2-D design, the firm's dominance is in part a result of its powerful workflow management and the standardized set of controls across the entire suite, significantly reducing learning curves. At the same time, it can be argued that these software families have standardized norms of working practice and, to a degree, of end products for all aspects of 2-D and 3-D design, despite competition from other commercial and open-source programs. Such tools are characteristic of the feature animation business and the coherent, scripted, and predictable worlds they construct. Where then can artists find an entry into creative spaces in vector graphics?

The composition of space in layers is a characteristic of digital media, fundamentally different from the projective geometry of perspective. In motion graphics, compositing space depends on scale and the parallax effect: small equals far away, and things closer to the eye seem to move more swiftly than do distant things. The only remnant of traditional constructions of pictorial space is fog, the use of diffusion to dim the light reaching the perceiver from more distant objects, a variant on the painterly technique of chiaroscuro. Instead of painterly perspective, digital space draws on the history of stage design, especially the use of flats to produce illusions of recession on shallow stages. This theatricality is apparent in *The Tale of How* (The Blackheart Gang, 2006),[7] an interesting phase in the remediation of theater by the moving image.[8] Particularly interesting in *The Tale of How* is the interplay between the layered space of Photoshop and the vector space of AfterEffects (both Adobe products), creating an incoherent spatial orientation that neatly expresses the surreal world of the Piranhas. Such clashing spaces undo the numerical cartography of layers. But more important still, the lines, which compose the vast majority of the vectors in this work, are unforeseeable, taking on shapes that not only create a diegetic universe but also constitute the events, which it exists to give birth to. These events are not key-framed, a process that defines action by its start and end points, but autonomous within the plane of the screen and through the incoherent construction of space in the depth of the screen, as well. The effect of the disruption of space is to

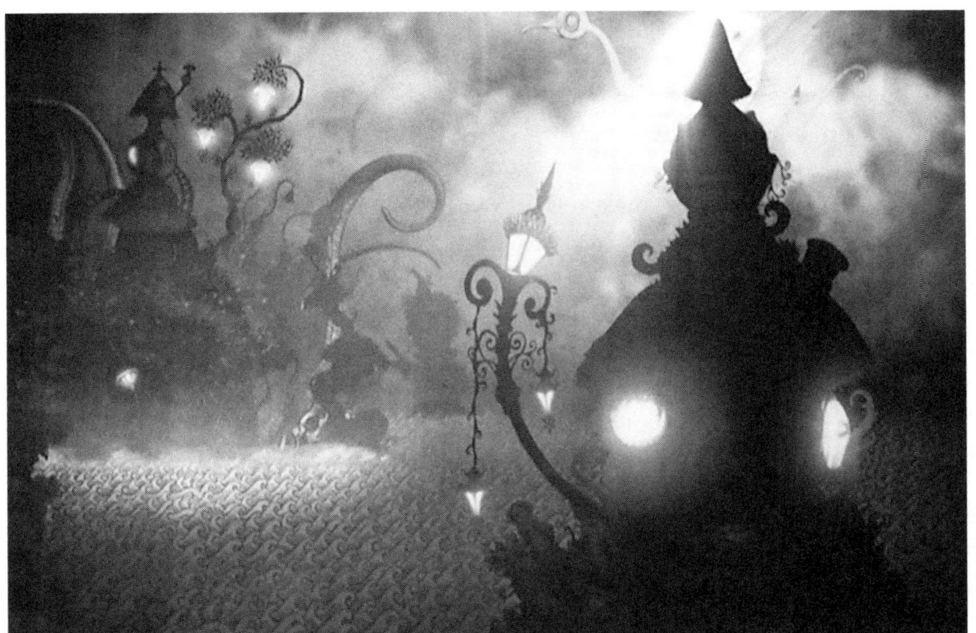

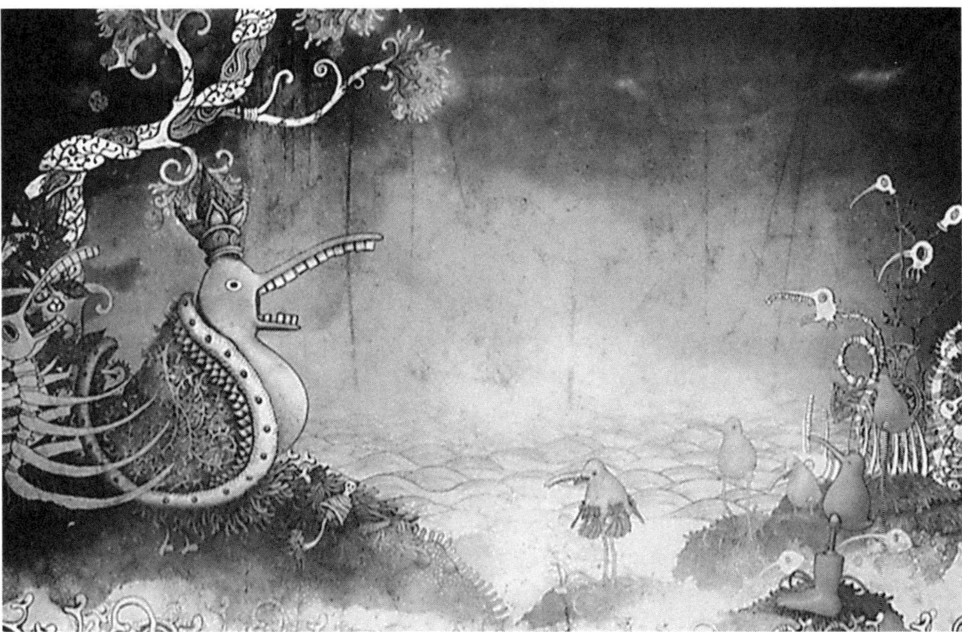

The Blackheart Gang, *The Tale of How*, 2006.

make possible a work on time that is, free of conclusion, operating without the determinations of the map, the grid—an aesthetic presentation of an alternative to the dominance of the database economy.

Vector Practice

These uses of vectors to contest the structuration of space and the denial of time are not exclusive to works produced using vector graphics programs. They also provide a way of understanding works that undertake fundamental reorganizations of video time that don't fall under any usual description of animation. Yet in some ways, the pieces to be discussed are animations: they do not take the camera's normative record of time as a given but work either in the camera itself or in postproduction to traduce that chronometric time, unpacking it to reveal other temporalities subsisting within and beyond it. Thus, for example, in a series of landscape works produced over a period starting in 2004, Susan Collins developed a practice in which the presentation of a landscape over a set period—twenty-fours hours for *Fenlandia* (2004–6) and *Glenlandia* (2005–7) and the period between tides in *Seascape* (2009)—is achieved by programming one or several high-resolution color security cameras to expose one pixel at a time.[9] The result is a screen image (in *Seascape,* a suite of five) gradually filing with momentary samples of light from a fixed position, shown live in a gallery at a high resolution and streamed online at a low resolution.

Collins deploys an array of Axis 2120 cameras that use high-resolution CMOS (complementary metal-oxide semiconductor) chips, distinct from the CCD (charge-coupled device) chips commonly used in digital-still and video cameras. Each pixel has a light-sensitive JFET (junction gate field-effect transistor) whose activation by incoming photons pinches the current flowing through the transistor from source to drain. Each JFET is attached to three other transistors in the commonest 4T cell design. Less noisy than CCD because the JFET is completely drained of charge after each shot and because of the different architecture of the pixel array, webcams, like mobile phone cameras, use an active-pixel sensor (APS) architecture in which the charge moves from the JFET's light-sensitive element directly to a buffer transistor that acts as an amplifier before passing it on to a third row-select transistor (which allows whole rows of pixels to be transferred to the read-out electronics), where it is stored in memory as a digital array. This triggers the fourth transistor, a reset gate, which drains residual charge from the pixel prior to the next exposure. This combination of the movement of the charge within the pixel itself and the inclusion of an amplifier in every individual pixel was produced by Eric Fossum and his collaborators on the back of the mass-manufactured CMOS chip. Far more widespread and, thus, more cheaply manufactured than CCDs, CMOS chips are characteristically not power hungry

Susan Collins, *Seascape,* 2009.

and, therefore, very useful in battery-powered devices and have a low signal-to-noise ratio. CMOS chips use both positive and negative (p-type and n-type) semi-conductors in pairs, which reduces the waste heat produced by other types of logic chips. In effect, each pixel operates as if it were a whole CCD chip, but with less noise and less of the blooming and smear effects associated with the quantum effects and transfer of charge across CCD chips. Perhaps equally significant is that CMOS APS webcams deliver digital output, which requires only buffering before being delivered to its output, and the output is external to the chip itself rather than integrated, as it is in CCDs. But it remains the case that the size of pixels—currently well above the diffraction limit of visible wavelengths—means that they must sample the light across their surface area and over the duration of exposure, that like CCDs they are manufactured in discrete unit arrays, and that under low-light conditions they will produce artifacts of virtual light through their built-in amplification of incoming photon signals.

Most Internet video (a low-resolution webcam, for example) restricts its color palette to 256 colors and uses vector-prediction technology to average out the likelihood of new colors appearing (and therefore new motions) in any area of the screen. The JPEG compression Collins uses (more recent models use motion JPEG, which gives a subtly different compression) is unusual among the available technologies in retaining the millions-of-colors standard and in maximizing the ability to capture movement. Her LCD projections remain true to this by deploying the 32-bit XGA true color standard where each pixel on-screen is composed from red, green, and blue beams. The camera outputs are transmitted via DVI (digital video interface) connectors, affording a one-to-one relation between the camera output and the pixels of the display and so avoiding both the analog compression associated with older VGA (video graphics array) connections and the vector prediction used in compressed video signals. The elegance of Collins's solution lies not just in her minimizing dependence on compression and display formats that rely on averaging movement and light and enforcing crude numerical reductions. She also builds into the work the specificity of her devices, how they become part of the image growth, and their role in its elaborated history of formation, deformation, and transmission. The machines take their part in a narrative and a temporality embedded in the evolving surface of the seas she depicts.

Writing a pixel approximately every 0.25 seconds, the *Seascape* cameras scan the sea, building an image over a period of around eight hours. Admiring the steady build of the pixels in *Seascape,* you have the sense of the image being grown like a crystal lattice seeded by what it views and that the image has the orientation and structure of the world in front of it even though the process is such that it never resembles a snapshot and that however slow, it is perpetually in motion. This compares with a curious design feature of CCD chips. To make the orientation and structure of the crystal lattice identical to that of the underlying chip, the crystals are grown on the chip itself. This is the reason why their production is called *fabrication* rather than *manufacture*: the scales are far, far smaller than human hands or tools. Collins's imitation of crystalline seeding is a game with the very fabric of the world.

Taking an average of the illumination in front of it during exposure, each pixel is as if considered yet entirely dependent on the sensing of the camera. This is a gradual revelation of a quality of the world that we could not have foreseen. Each square pixel adds its own slice through time, abstracted from the normalized time of screen refresh rates, reanchored in the changing climate outside the system. This interchange between climate, technical apparatus, and human perceivers, framed in both scientific instrumentation and the cultural traditions of painting and postcards, unearths a new order to time as it displays a new order to the endless changing of the sea, a new relation between permanence and ephemerality.

Projection

Uncovering lost time, the time between frames, and the time of interlaced or progressive scanning, Robert Cahen's brief projection piece *L'étreinte* (The embrace,

8:50) of 2004 is designed to screen on the now dominant DLP (digital light processing) projectors developed by Texas Instruments. At its heart lies the DMD (digital micromirror device). Containing up to 1.3 million digitally controlled mirrors (in 1280 × 1024–resolution machines) each of them sixteen micrometers square, or about a fifth of the diameter of a human hair. The micromirrors, which fit on a DMD chip the size of a postage stamp, tilt ten degrees, with sixteen-millisecond response times, to reflect optically programmed light toward or away from the projector lens. Black is equivalent to a turn away from the lens; gray is produced by flickering at a higher rate than the basic sixteen milliseconds as appropriate to the shade desired. High-end projectors use one DMD chip each for red, green, and blue signals, using additive color to make white and absence to make black. The proximity of DMD cells to one another is far greater than in LCD screens, giving a far greater apparent density, required given the difference between light source and reflected light.

By introducing delay into the image track in postproduction, Cahen and his technical assistant, Bernard Bats, create emphatic zones of different luminance, a technique that forces the edge-finding action of DLP devices to produce extremes of contrast but also a rich palette of grays and near blacks with a surprisingly haptic surface, even as the objects—landscape, bird, couple—diffuse into clouds of pixilation, fields, and frames. Significant here is the way that both contrast within a given frame and contrasts between successive frames produce perhaps the most lustrous black that I have seen in a digital production. Here, the black is consciously produced as effect, first by tricking the projection apparatus and, then, by stimulating the viewer's eyes toward an optical experience in which the tonalities of unilluminated screen generate a spectral opposition between black and the fierce illumination of the brightest areas.

As Schöenberg democratized the notes in the twelve-tone row, removing the dominant, Cahen's work democratizes not only shots but also the very grain of the image in all-over compositions in which illumination and its absence are of equal significance. The sheer mass of detail is a fundamental challenge to composition. At the same time that it atomizes its elements, *L'étreinte* composes them into fields whose succession gestures toward a limit of possibility. The construction of objects was the great modernist strategy of defense against the autonomous elements of signification: in the era of the DMD chip, that objectality is breaking down and, with it, the autonomy of the screen as a universal manager of space and time. The massing of differences in *L'étreinte* disrupts the smoothing over of time and makes time the engine of flux and dynamism. It makes of screen space itself a vector toward an unknowable goal.

These three video works contradict Wittgenstein: they are not reduplications of what is the case but statements of the nonidenticality of the present from which all possibility of future change must spring. In the works of such artists,

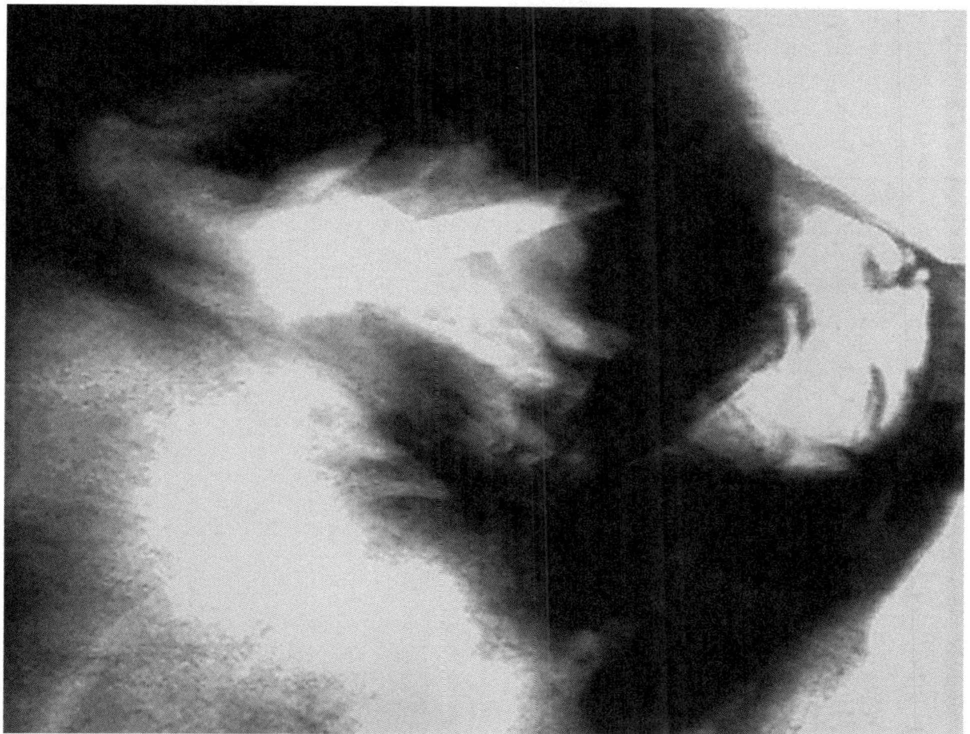

Robert Cahen, *L'étreinte* (The embrace), 2004.

the thesis that space has engulfed time is contested even in the forms of the media that most richly enshrine the doctrine of space's domination of the contemporary world. More than contradictions, these enactments of the power of the vector as nonteleological orientation into an unmapped future suggest that the work of remaking media need not be constrained to the remaking of technologies but can be opened to exploding the forewarned and forearmed managerialist commodification of the grid and pointing with whatever trepidation, whatever uncertainty, toward a dim and distant shore where things are no longer as they are.

NOTES

1. See Alexander R. Galloway, *Protocol: How Control Exists after Decentralization* (Cambridge: MIT Press, 2004).

2. See Christian Fuchs, "A Contribution to the Critique of the Political Economy of Transnational Informational Capitalism," *Rethinking Marxism* 21, no. 3 (July 2009): 387–402.

3. See Sean Cubitt, "Codecs and Capability," in *Video Vortex,* ed. Geert Lovink (Amsterdam: Institute of Network Cultures, 2008), 45–52.

4. Ivan Edward Sutherland, *Sketchpad: A Man-Machine Graphical Communication System,* with a new preface by Alan Blackwell and Kerry Rodden (Cambridge: University of Cambridge Computer Laboratory, 2003), http://www.cl.cam.ac.uk/TechReports.

5. See Mark J. P. Wolf, ed., *The Video Game Explosion: A History from PONG to PlayStation and Beyond* (New York: Greenwood Press, 2007).

6. Gregory Bateson, *Steps to an Ecology of Mind: Collected Essays in Anthropology, Psychiatry, Evolution and Epistemology* (London: Paladin, 1973).

7. The Blackheart Gang, *The Tale of How,* Vimeo video, 4:29, South Africa, 2006, http://theblackheartgang.com/the-household/the-tale-of-how.

8. See Jay David Bolter and Richard Grusin, *Remediation: Understanding New Media.* (Cambridge: MIT Press, 1999).

9. See *Seascape* website, http://www.susan-collins.net/seascape.

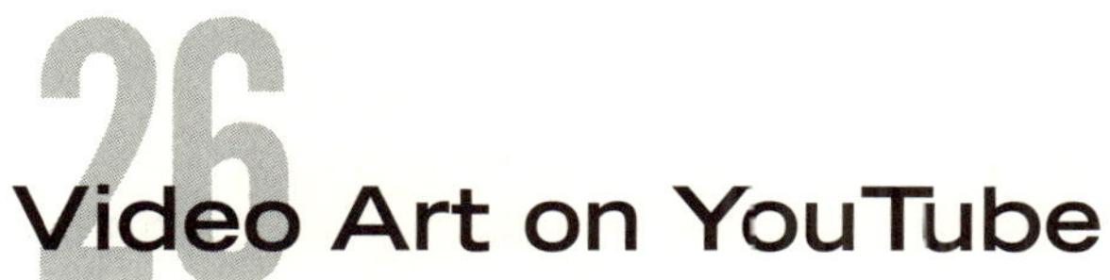

Video Art on YouTube

Alexandra Juhasz

Video Art (Writing) on YouTube via the Book and the Web

In this essay I draw several distinctions between old and nouveau art video given the fact of YouTube and how it alters the production, distribution, and consumption of video (art) via Web 2.0 technologies and a corporate architecture. But not only video has been changed; our new technologies affect our writing about video in equal measure. Just so, this essay was first posted as short but inter-related blog posts about video art on YouTube, always also anticipating their place in an essay in this edited volume. And this essay pales and fails in all the ways old technologies now must: there is no place for video here; it is not interactive; it is slow and outdated. I hope you will excuse this clunky exercise in translation from new to old media because it so concisely demonstrates my analyses about video's new forms through form. Without its original links (to videos), there are places you just can't go, so I've signified the place of video (a major part of the writing in my blog) through the addition of frozen and un-yielding frame grabs. Of course, this paper version also evidences the particular strengths of our quickly vanishing and outdated forms: how a book, such as this one, can create context, breadth, focus, and the build of intertextuality allowed by the collected efforts of experts authorized by elite institutions like an academic press. Even so, whenever possible I prefer to publish my YouTube writing on the Internet (see my video book about YouTube, published online in 2011 by the MIT Press), where it points to (if not yet achieves) promises that had similarly compelled (old) video artists: of people-made, networked, multimodal, community-produced, and community-producing media culture.[1]

Video Art on YouTube: A Matter of Vetting and Consumption
October 26, 2009

I have been commissioned to write an article about video art on YouTube for the forthcoming scholarly anthology *Resolutions 3* (in the next few months I'll be testing fragments of the article on my blog). The third in a trilogy, this anthology will embark on an "analysis of the third decade of video as marked within and outside the margins of art production, broadcast interventions, festival codification, projected spectacle, museum entombment, digital tracing, 24/7 streaming, activist tool, essay and camcorder document."[2]

As you can see, *Resolutions 3* engages the common usage of the term *video art*—one used rather unselfcritically across the art world, community media, and academia since the late 1960s—to refer broadly to two of the major strands of nonindustrial uses of the medium that quickly emerged after the invention of the Portapak: video that speaks to and against the art world and/or to activist communities and goals. In this rather rarified usage, *video art* carries assumptions about method, form, and audience. The term refers to varied uses of the medium that nevertheless succeed at demonstrating (1) some self-awareness of previous forms (of art, media, or evidence) and an attendant attention to craft and (2) some manner of nonindustrial funding, production, and distribution often in clear defiance to those models that organize industrial television, advertising, or film. Those (already) aware of this tradition understand how it loosely includes a wide variety of work that receives its authorization not within the text itself but via display or consumption: installations and single-channel work that circulate and are sold within museums, galleries, and other venues of the art world; another body of video that is sold or at least marketed by distributors so as to be bought/rented and screened primarily within institutions like libraries, universities, and nonprofit organizations; work that circulates in festivals and other nonindustrial exhibition settings; and work that the artist self-circulates as art to these audiences.

> Video art has been given a bad name, and rightly so, by the sort of chi-chi experimentation that goes well with brie and white wine and mauve-walled art galleries and designer hair dos. Video is cheap enough to produce, by feature film standards, and yet its very cheapness and accessibility has created a contradiction: video-making is within the financial reach of many, and yet, like most modern art, it's surrounded by a noxious aura of elitism.[3]

In Peter Rainer's 1986 essay for the first Resolution(s) book, video becomes art only when it is vetted, circulated, or consumed as such. Thus, it is not immediately evident what this term might mean when applied to the millions of videos that circulate for free "outside the margins of art production" on YouTube, neither made nor seen as video art even if they are about "art."

> The project's focus is not, therefore, on "video art," as that term is commonly understood, or on video as an autonomous medium

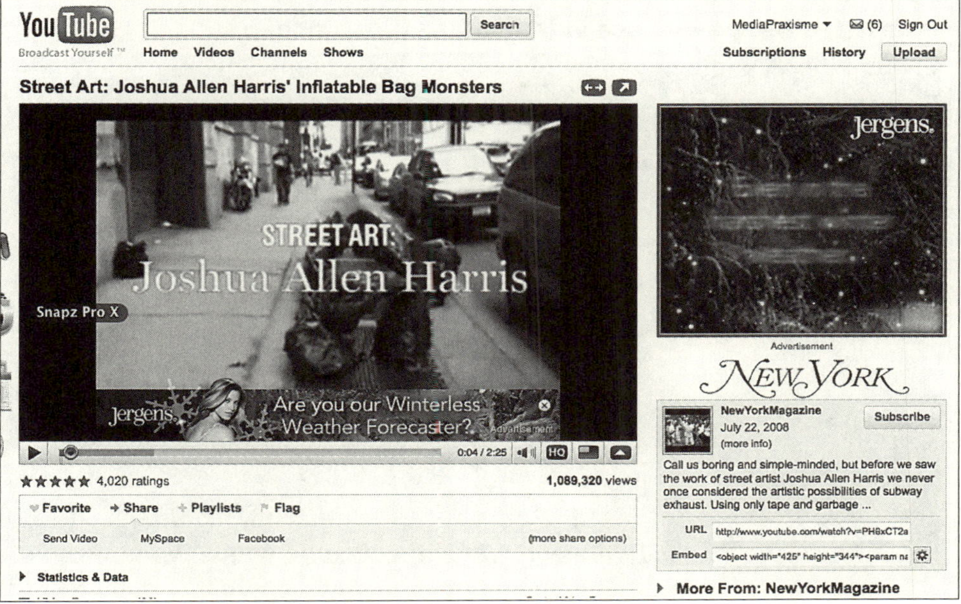

Street Art: Joshua Allen Harris' Inflatable Bag Monsters, 1,089,320 views, by *NewYork* magazine, July 22, 2008, sponsored by Jergens. Accessed June 5, 2012. This video had been seen 1,089,320 times when I submitted this article in 2009.

possessing essential features, but on video in relation to ongoing cultural, aesthetic, and political agendas and activities—video as a source and as a medium for contemporary expression that is allied with and paralleled by myriad cultural and critical discourses in specific and sometimes surprising ways.[4]

Much of the video on YouTube (I speak of that made by people and not corporations) is home video, the third major strand of common non-industrial uses of the medium. This tradition has been only sporadically understood to be within video art (most typically when it is used as a formal strategy by an already known video artist) because it by definition must fail the vetting and the circulation standards of the art/political strands of video art—that is, until YouTube began to change that. Home video is by definition made by one who is not formally trained and speaks neither to histories or theories of meaning making (outside the very real conventions of home video and YouTube itself) nor to larger communities but rather quite literally to oneself (and family and friends and all of YouTube).

Circulation without vetting. Access without training. Video without funding. Image outside traditional tradition. Video art on YouTube? Pole Art.

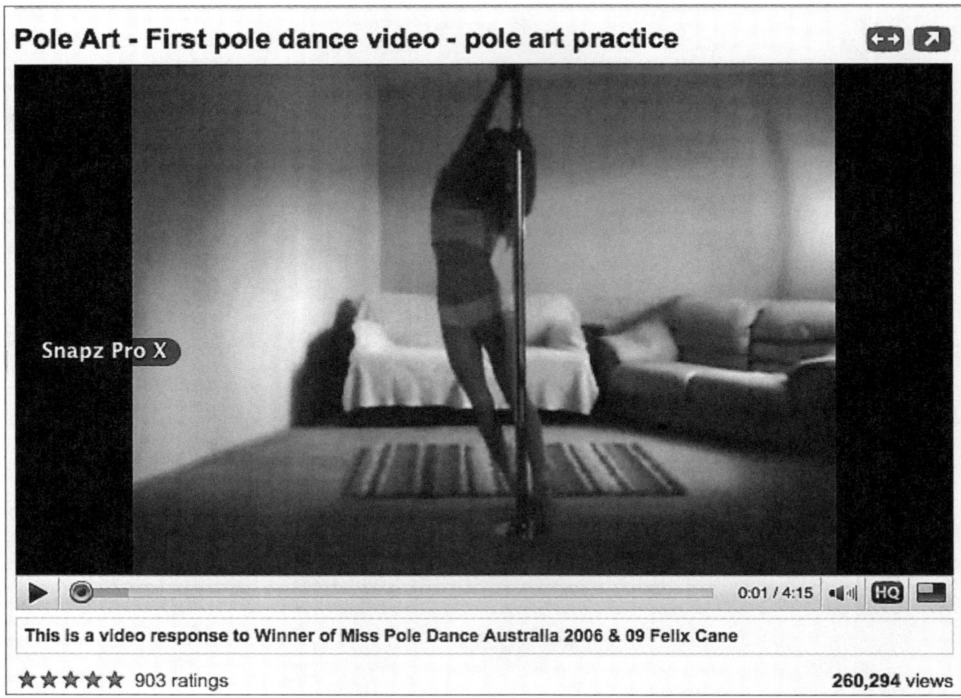

Pole Art–First Pole Dance Video–Pole Art Practice (This Is a Video Response to Winner of Miss Pole Dance Australia 2006 & 9 Felix Cane), 1,285,166 views. Accessed June 5, 2012.

Video Art on YouTube: The Name Is Equivocal
October 27, 2009

> VIDEO ART. The name is equivocal. A good name. It leaves open all the questions and asks them anyway. Is this an art form, a new genre? An anthology of valued activity conducted in a particular arena defined by display on a cathode ray tube? The kind of video made by a special class of people—artists—whose works are exhibited primarily in what is called "the art world."
>
> —David Antin, "Video: The Distinctive Features of the Medium"

Have you tried to find an equivocal name like *video art* on YouTube? Searching for anything is never the best way to find it (random, happy surprise loosely calculating the flow all the while inventing terms by channeling the zany, half-baked logic of a teenager is the only method I know that gets you anything near like what you want). I'll attest that you can't find much video

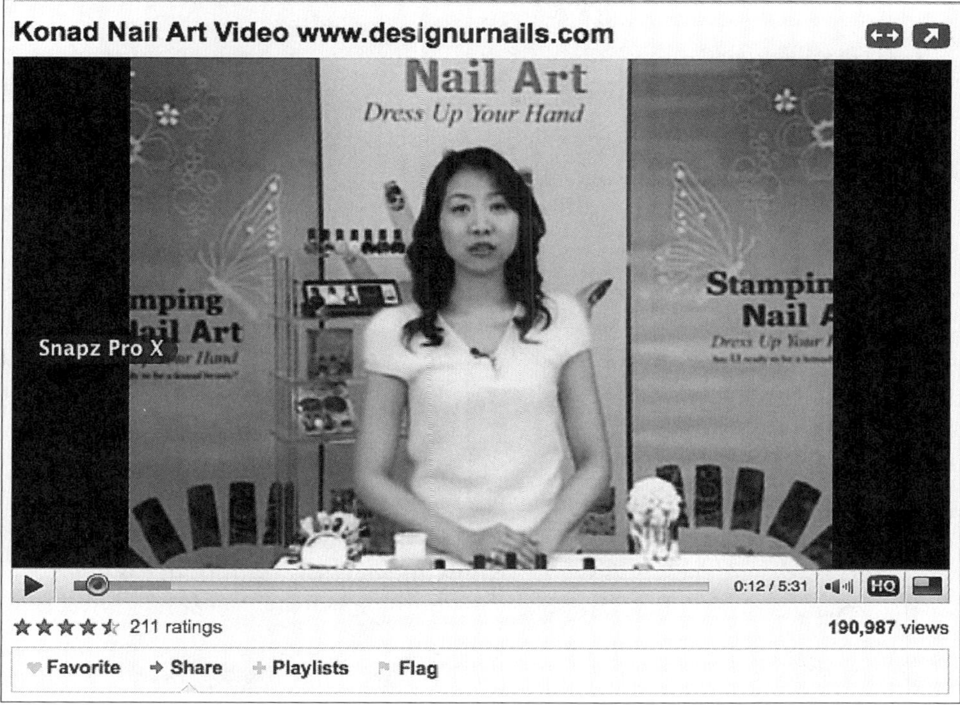

Konad Nail Art Video www.designurnails.com, 701,347 views. Accessed June 5, 2012.

art there by using that or any other term, like the other common one, *art video*—that is, if one is looking for the practices already heralded as such by the authorities of the art world, academia, or independent media.

As proves typical of the site, what you *do* find gives some indication of regular people's understanding of both things and the words that define them, signifier and signified all mixed up, of course, with corporate and individual's shenanigans as terms are gamed hoping to achieve higher hits.

A search under *video art* finds videos about art—little of it high, most very low—as well as things with the word *art* in their titles: whether that be the man's name, the antiquated use of *to be,* or industrial crafts repackaged in hopes of better sales.

As ever, the populist ways of YouTube dominate. The everyday practices (and crafts) of everyday people—making coffee and doing nails, skateboarding and pole dancing, painting with sand or trash bags—snatch the term from its home in the realm and things of experts, professionals, and artists, reattaching it to products and activities understood and loved because they are easy to make and ready to buy and consume.

Ad Hoc, Piecemeal Video Art
October 30, 2009

> Towards the end of the middle decade of the twentieth century, a perplexing and complex form emerged in Europe and the United States. Variously called video art, artists' video, experimental video, artists' television, "the new television," even "Guerrilla TV," the genre drew on a diverse range of art movements, theoretical ideas, and technological advances, as well as political and social activism. In this period of dynamic social, economical and cultural change, much new art was formally and politically radical.
>
> —Chris Meigh-Andrews, *A History of Video Art*

(Traditional) video art on YouTube is (1) hard to find, (2) ad hoc in its inclusion, (3) made more accessible because it's there, and (4) not made for that place and, thus, is ill suited. (Nouveau) video art on YouTube is made for (and probably therefore about) online, people-made, corporate-hosted media.

Everything on YouTube Is Video Art . . . Nah
September 10, 2009

Again, I am moved to respond to Virginia Heffernan's intelligent analyses of YouTube. She made some provocative claims about YouTube and the avant-garde this weekend in the *New York Times*—"It's a place for art"—scooping me in the process, at least in regard to the claim by which I am starting an essay about video art on YouTube (to be published in the scholarly anthology *Resolutions 3*), currently in draft form. There, I make the claim, "Let's imagine that everything on YouTube is video art."

In my draft writing, I had decided that although all the people-made stuff *could* be considered art—in the sense that it had been carefully crafted by somebody and then consciously distributed with the intention of the public communication of self-expression—I didn't want to consider the volumes of clearly unconsidered work on YouTube to be art after all. In its self-aware isolation (I made this in my room or in my backyard using my butt and with my wrestling buddies), it doesn't consciously connect to other bodies or theories of video or to other artists; it doesn't show enough care or community. I suppose there could be a scene of butt catchers, as Heffernan suggests, but toward what project, with what beliefs, and in the name of what end, other than another derivative video? You need a shared

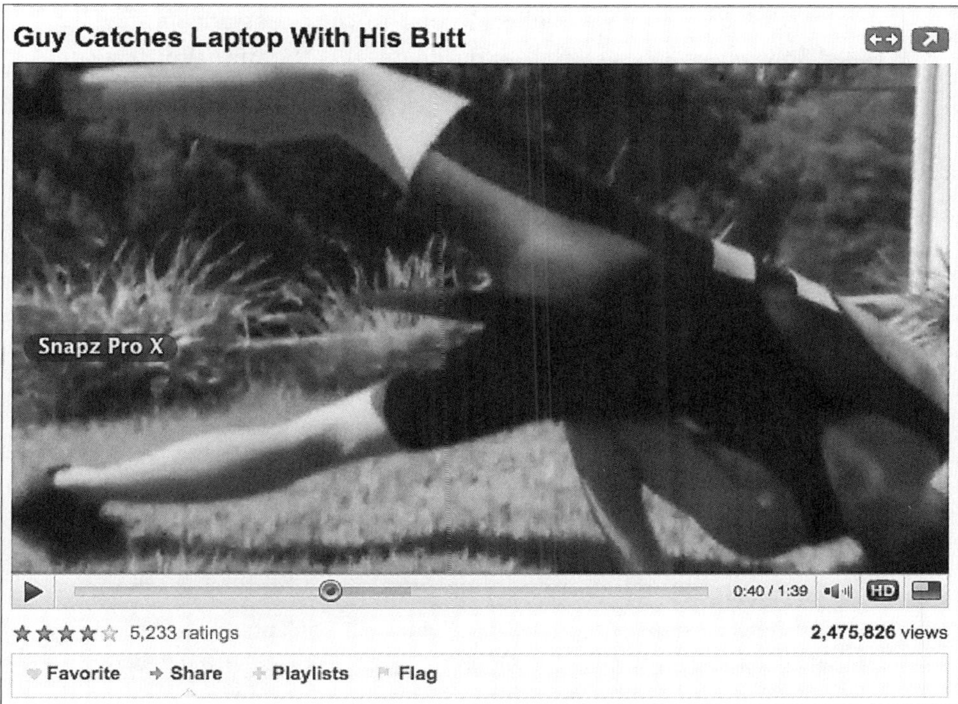

Guy Catches Laptop with His Butt, 2,475,826 views. Accessed November 30, 2009.

vocabulary, agenda, history, and set of goals to make an art scene or an art video.

Of course, as I often suggest, art video can be found on YouTube (like every other marginal form or desire) sitting precariously on the edge of NicheTube, and I believe that Heffernan is right to characterize Manhattan Bridge Piers in this way.[5] I remain unconvinced, however (even as I'd like to dream), that this presents the possibilities of an art vernacular; most of what people are making on YouTube can not be so easily traced back to the aesthetic or poetic preoccupations of art traditions or even alternative culture—in fact, quite the opposite.

Heffernan begins with the beginning and suggests that the first You-Tube video, "Me at the Zoo," sets a standard for YouTube: "visually surprising, narratively opaque, forthrightly poetic." I find, however, that most of the videos on YouTube are neither surprising nor poetic, falling as they so easily do into the quickly consolidating vernaculars of either "good" corporate production or "bad" people-made videos (a case I have made in regard to her previously published euphoric read of Susan Boyle). While DIY video may provide us with the lovely surprises she goes on to convincingly detail in the *haul-fail* genres (linked, I think, to what my students and I have called flow videos), these are all, at the end of the day, quite similar spectacles highlighting the outrageous talent or odd behaviors of regular people made to be mocked, adored, or both. Of course, dominant television is already dominated by reality media that mocks and rewards the talent and aspirations of regular people. I would suggest that professional media looks more and more like the (worst) of people-made media and that this is at least too bad, if not surprising.

Everything *off* YouTube is Video Art
October 31, 2009

I recently wrote on this blog (October 26, 2009) that for video art "authorization needs to occur via display or consumption. Video becomes art when it is vetted, circulated or consumed as such." So what happens to real video art found on YouTube, hidden among the mayhem? If it can't be vetted, can it be video art?

Like classic video art, people-made video on YouTube speaks to the traditions of video (on YouTube), which mostly speak to conventions of dominant media. And whether the video is good or bad, people construct YouTube work using the craft at their disposal. Furthermore, such video, like its old-school precursor, is made outside (but eerily congruent to) dominant modes (including video art).

But sitting as it does on YouTube and, thus, only authorized by numbers (of hits)—itself a mark of populist mediocrity—and never understood as art in the first place but construed through a logic of everyday practice, home production, and consumer fun, it can really be art only if it moves *off* YouTube.

Video Art(ists) of the YouTube Archive
November 2, 2009

> The many types of video art have been made with a variety of intentions, ideas, working styles, and structures. Some address pure aesthetic concerns, where others prioritize content in less formal but still original and more deeply personal ways.
> —Kate Horsfield, "Introduction to the Video Data Bank Collections"

(Here, you should see Kate Horsfield interviewed in the 1970s about video, but Google video won't let me embed to this blog. You can also see my interview with Horsfield for the 1990s *Women of Vision* here.)

If everything on YouTube is video art (at least the stuff made by individuals and not corporations) but very little of this art can ever truly be understood as such because it wasn't really made to be art and cannot be recognized as such, either (and even if it were, it wouldn't gain sanction, context, or community unless it went off YouTube), then it is the archivist (the curator, the choreographer, the tour guide) who becomes the final, visible, verifiable YouTube video artist herself by making visible the links (to other forms, communities, ideas) that the artist alone might once have made (offline, in a place, on a box, for an audience). See the YouTube work of Natalie Bookchin, for example. In *Me Dancing* (2009) she composes the solo programs of hundreds of YouTubers into a pageant of lonely, high-kicking, routine-repeating hoofers, making meaning (about YouTube) from a sea of found, undifferentiated, repetitive, pop culture rip-offs.

Looking for Video Artists
November 3, 2009

The easiest way to find (established) video art on YouTube is to search the site using the name of an already famous video artist. What you will find, then, is one of three possibilities: (1) their work is not on YouTube, (2) an interview with the artist is on YouTube, or (3) their work has been (badly) scanned and anonymously and probably illegally posted, in fragments, probably without the artist's permission. These three truisms have some associated corollaries: most established video artists do not put their art on YouTube, because it undermines the already highly tentative (and quickly collapsing) underpinnings of the (dying) form; it is (was) at least partially financed by sales; it is (was) confirmed through institutional sanction; it needs to be viewed in and through controlled contexts and formats (in a white room with a specified duration on a black box without ads and surrounding text).

Though the interview of the artist does contribute some sort of sanctioning function, its appearance on YouTube (as is true of everything there) follows much the same distorted logic of authorization already in place in the dominant culture that is recorded on YouTube: the more famous you are, the better chance that you have actually already been interviewed, that your interview can be found, or that a viewer would think that she might want to watch it.

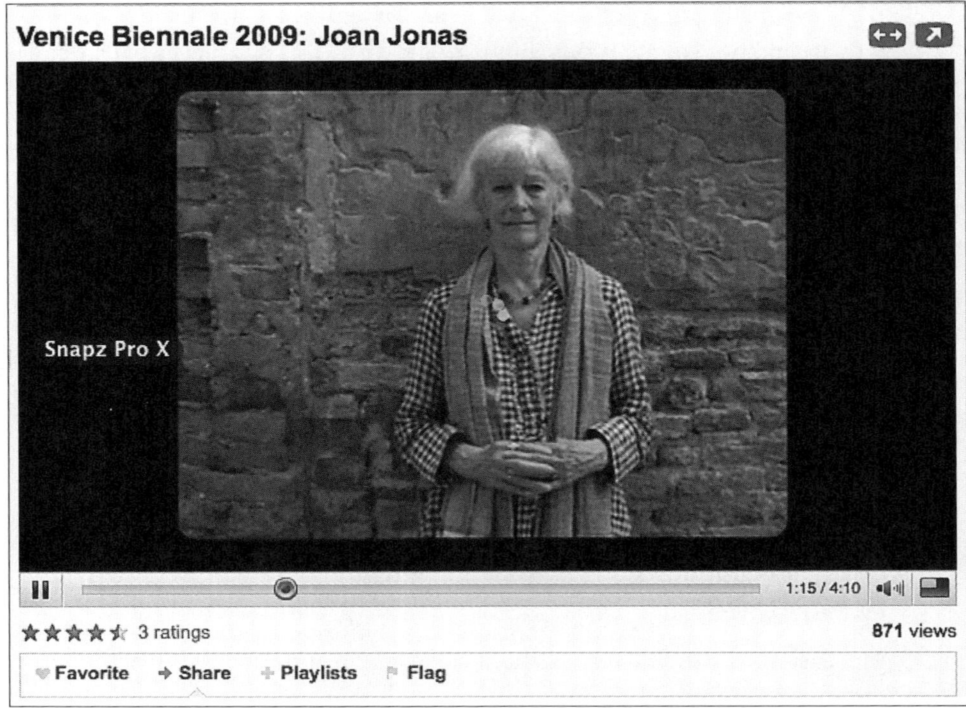

Venice Biennale 2009: Joan Jonas, 6,364 views. Accessed June 5, 2012.

Video Art: Does Access Matter?
November 4, 2009

> The promise held by video, that it could create "personal media," that normal people could control the production of video imagery and bypass the tightly controlled corporate structure of commercial media, seemed like a revolutionary and democratic advance. Video was seen as a potentially radical political tool that could subvert the relationship between dominant media structures and audience, eventually allowing artists and anyone else to directly address the public without the need of a support structure of broadcast television, museums, galleries, or other forms of distribution.
>
> —Glenn Phillips, introduction to *California Videos, Artists and Histories*

Though a certain strand of video art was made with the distinct purpose of reaching an audience so as to express opinions, ideas, analyses, images, or ways of being usually left unexpressed through dominant media, it seems important to note that only a small portion of this has since been posted

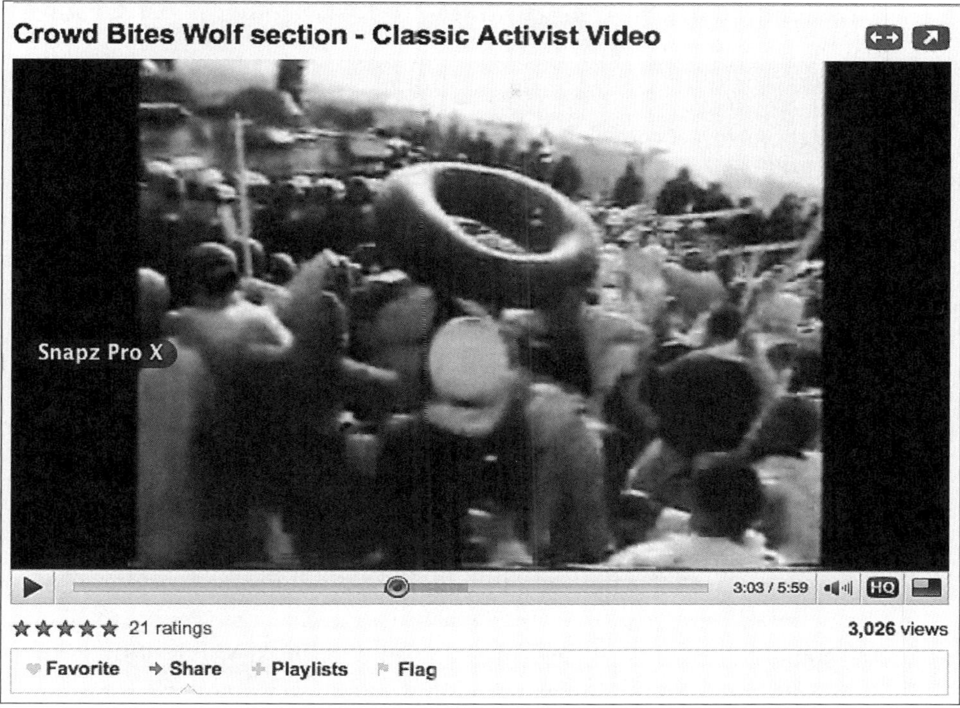

Crowd Bites Wolf Section—Classic Activist Video, 5,327 views. Accessed June 5, 2012.

onto YouTube, making good use of this newly available tool to expand audience, using video and YouTube as a "radically political tool . . . to directly address the public" by using this (new) tool to allow for expanded exposure to these (old) radical ideas and images.

Why? As a "video artist" myself who has often used the medium to expand the reach of my voice—or my community's (see my work on AIDS activist video for example)—in the name of a cause, I've only chosen to put one of my videos on YouTube (RELEASED: *5 Short Videos about Women and Prison*); while SCALE, about my sister Antonia, was loaded onto YouTube by the corporation that distributes it [snagfilms] against my better wishes.

The reason(s) are clear: activist videos are made to be shown within organized settings where context, dialogue, community, and continuing actions (see my sister Antonia Juhasz's recent protest "Marching on Chevron," organized along with the screening of the Yes Men's new film) need to be as carefully engineered or constructed as is the video text itself. In fact, radical contexts for screenings are often understood to be as much a part of activist video (art) as is the videos themselves. Since this is impossible on YouTube, the lack of context and community trumps the power of access, and old-school video activists choose to stay home (or march without the help of YouTube).

Loving the Archive, Controlling the Archive
November 5, 2009

The archivist brings work to visibility by seeing it, knowing it in her way, and connecting it to other video and viewers that will frame and hold it: giving context, making friends, building arguments, forming associations. Unruly archives need curators. Their holdings are nothing but inconsequential detritus until they are loved and repurposed by someone.

I have been criticizing YouTube for a few years, which is easy enough to do given its perplexing gaps in capability and coherence—all the things it won't let you do like find things, surround them with meaningful stuff and people—not to mention all the crap videos on it. Could I repurpose the site to succeed at functions I require for video art? To better prepare for this nouveau art video project, I first considered what comprises YouTube's strengths and unique powers: the capability to update and version; to allow the audience (or users) to participate and even for the subjects (of traditional documentary) to become producers of their own stories; to create communities within media who can speak for themselves and to each other. Then, I thought about what I don't like about YouTube: how strong feelings, voices, and ideas remain siloed, individuated, unlinked, going nowhere and powerfully alone. I wanted to construct a YouTube page, instead, as a collaborative, interactive, communal work with a singular and defined set of purposes, a commitment to hard ideas, and a sense of safety and intimacy that is definitive of community and allows for the kind of video art that matters to me: personal, intellectual, political, and artistic.

I have proposed a feminist video archive love fest. I want to take the dead work of the LA Woman's Building (recently archived at the Getty's Research Institute) and repurpose it online. Bring it back to life. Make it relevant. Make it visible and reusable. Put it on YouTube.

A proposed (pending funding) continuation of my work with the Getty's Pacific Standard Time Project, I hope to move old tapes online— linking this inspiring (and too invisible) retro-video vision to the hyper-mediated now. I am eager to repurpose YouTube as a productive archive of video art that addresses some of the contradictions engendered by this unique "process archive." Women's Building video was made and saved by countless (often anonymous) women who were mutually developing and enjoying a uniquely feminist theory and practice of video fundamentally informed by a consciousness raising that was itself conversant with contemporary art and primarily engaged with video at its inception. Throughout feminist art education at the Building, (video) process was valued and itself documented, as well as being document, and all of this was meant to be made public (often through video) and then saved for history (as video) even counterintuitively as it was also, most critically, marking something entirely internal and ephemeral.

In videos from the Building, there is a consistent and self-aware project that evocatively links video across this archive to both feminist process and preservation. I would continue their past project on YouTube by selecting videos from the archive and with the artists' permissions putting them online and producing prompts, frameworks, and tools for their contemporary reuse. In so doing, I would be attempting to make this archive newly usable for present-day digital (video) processes, thus unmooring it from its obscure, frozen, and misunderstood place as feminist history and encouraging it to better engage with our feminist present (which was once its undertheorized future) and in the meantime allowing past work to remain relevant, become active, and embark in dialogue with the present.

[Author's note (June 2012): Like so many activist video projects, this never came to pass, although my feminist efforts online continue to develop on my blog, www.aljean.wordpress.com, on my website, www.feministonlinespaces.com, and in my Massively Distributed Collective Learning Experiment, Dialogues in Feminism and Technology, www.fembotcollective.org.]

Video Dada
February 1, 2010

> From the start I realized that dealing with YouTube videos called for an approach different from the ground usually covered in art criticism: artist's oeuvre, aesthetic strategies, links to current tendencies in exhibition, comparisons with other artists' work.
>
> —Martha Gever, *Video Dada*

I drove out to UC–Irvine with the kids to catch the *Video Dada* show ("dealing with intersections of video, art, and the internet," according to the exhibition catalog).[6] Martha Gever, the show's curator, was kind enough to also drive out and chat with me afterward. The show puts into action and onto the wall many of the concerns I have been expressing here about video art on YouTube by transforming curating into the real video art practice and allowing YouTube work to become art by surrounding its three hundred unruly videos with to-be-expected, large-screen, flat, chic monitors. Gever also provides thrift store couches and big, scrawled, messy handwritten quotations from media / cultural theorists as varied as Marcel Proust, Geert Lovink, and the *New York Times*'s Virginia Heffernan on the gallery's walls. Without their raucous, ugly YouTube pages to frame them (ads, other videos, comments, tags), the projected videos looked pretty, like nothing other than honest-to-goodness video art in all its varied polyphony: cut up, hand painted, home video–like, music video inflected, found ads, and so on. It was that frame that did it, making art out of madness—slick screen, black box, curator's stamp of approval. The wall demands respect, as does the hushed room with the guard. And unlike YouTube, the quotes create context.

Gever formally enacts many of the contradictions of video art on You-Tube through the fitting design of her show. The Dada reference marks the play between art production and popular / capitalist consumption as definitive of YouTube video as it was of Duchamp's urinal. Furthermore, Dada suitably organizes the cacophony and distraction of undifferentiated material—"All the objects in the [YouTube] archive have equal weight. . . . They are de-contextualized and flattened," proclaims Robert Gehl, written on the wall—that defines both YouTube and the show (there are three hundred videos playing, almost randomly, on something like ten monitors, with nothing but typed lists of titles and authors to anchor them; you never really know or care what you are seeing). Gever notes in her catalog that although the order of the videos is not important, she carefully and rigorously selected all of them (as "artful: carefully constructed, inventive, mindful of technique, and infused by sophisticated cultural intelligence") through a painstaking, multiyear process of looking for video art in the sea of crap that included the additional looking labor of several TAs, as well as Gever putting the names of hundreds of contemporary artists into You-Tube to see if anything might come up (it did . . .).[7] Refreshingly and tellingly, I recognized only a few names from the video art pantheon. When I went to find things to review on YouTube, however, I couldn't (like LaToya Ruby Frazier's *A Mother to Hold,* which I watched all the way through its grueling home movie–like interaction with the artist's crack whore mother or Guthrie Lonergan's *Office Party* or *Kids*). While I couldn't refind them on YouTube, Gever had located both of these YouTubers through searching from the New Museum's *Younger than Jesus* show.)

It seemed important for me when I noted that I didn't really want to watch most of the videos. Unlike on YouTube, I couldn't fast-forward them, cut them off when bored, or jump to something else vaguely related.

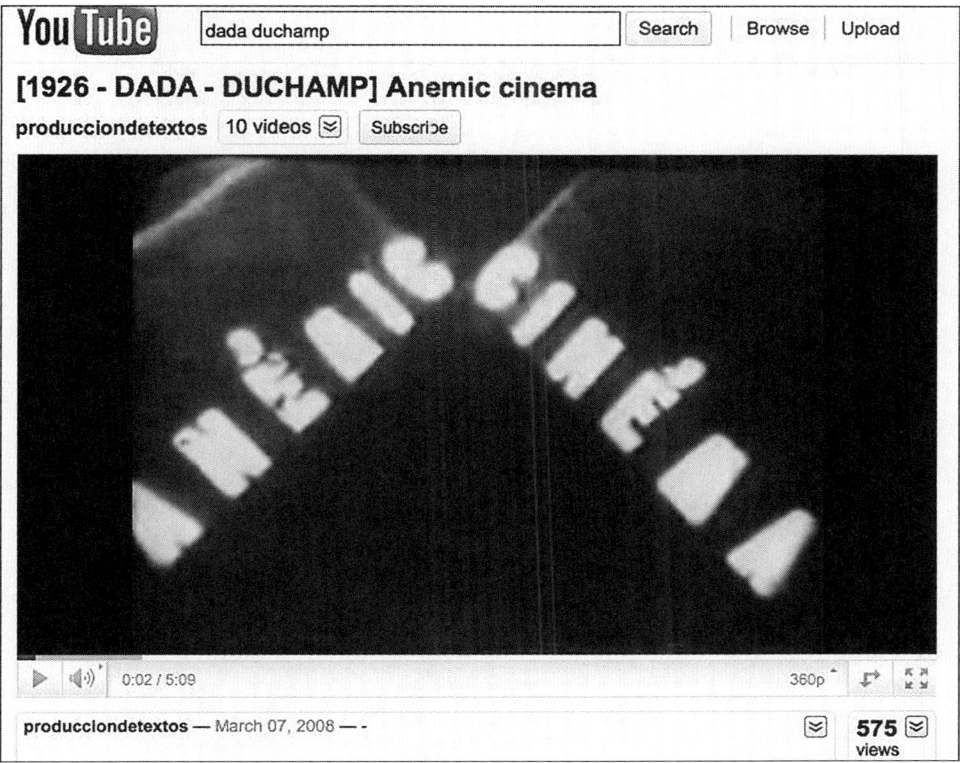

[1926—DADA—Duchamp] Anemic Cinema, 13,007 views. Accessed June 5, 2012.

The myth of audience participation is completely denied here, and the work suffers from it, proving an affront to another definitive quality of YouTube video, but not in the best Dada sort of way. Gever writes, "The non-hierarchical, uncurated organization of YouTube provides a fitting venue for videos that are fleeting, provisional, rowdy, rude, epigrammatic, overtly political, or otherwise unruly in the themes that govern more disciplined precincts of art."[8] With this I agree, which allows me to see how YouTube can't be as radical as Dada hoped to be. Upon leaving, my twelve-year-old daughter remarked that the show wasn't really Dada enough in that it didn't feel like much of an affront, nor did it inspire strong feelings, since a lot of the video was simply fun or funny, and more so, in the end, the sheer undifferentiated totality of it quieted one, as YouTube always seems most wont to do.

NOTES

1. Alexandra Juhasz, *Learning from YouTube* (Cambridge: MIT Press, 2011), http://mitpress.mit.edu/catalog/item/default.asp?ttype=2&tid=12596.

2. Ming-Yuen Ma and Erika Suderburg, "Resolutions 3: Video Praxis in Global Spaces," prospectus, September 16, 2008, http://pzacad.pitzer.edu/~mma/teaching/MS71/reading/res_3.pdf.

3. Peter Rainer, "Captain Video," in *Resolution: A Critique of Video Art,* ed. Patti Podesta (Los Angeles: Los Angeles Contemporary Exhibitions, 1986), 105.

4. Michael Renov and Erika Suderburg, introduction to *Resolutions: Contemporary Video Practices* (Minneapolis: University of Minnesota Press, 1996), xvi.

5. See Alexandra Juhasz, "Learning the 5 Lessons of YouTube: After Trying to Teach There, I Don't Believe the Hype," *International Journal of Learning and Media* 1, no. 1 (Winter 2009), http://ijlm.net/knowinganddoing/10.1162/ijlm.2009.00002.

6. Martha Gever, *Video Dada,* exhibition catalog (Irvine: University of California, 2010), 1.

7. Ibid.

8. Ibid.

27. African Video Art

WAR, DREAMS, AND FREEDOM

Myriam-Odile Blin

The Remarkable History of African Video Art

Only since 1998 have more and more artists in Francophone Africa, including Cameroon, Senegal, and the African diaspora, been using video and new media. There, such mediums do not have the same meaning that they have in Europe and the United States, where the members of Fluxus and other artists began multimedia experimentation in the late 1950s and early 1960s. For some African artists today, video is a primary medium, but for most it is only one choice among a diverse set of tools. The means and attention allotted to video art in countries such as Cameroon and Senegal cannot be compared with the resources available to Western research centers such as MIT, ZKM, CICV, and CITU. But African video art has the privilege of a lightness of means.[1]

In the 1998 Dak'art Biennale, Goddy Leye (Cameroon/Netherlands) and Mansour Ciss Kanakassy (Senegal/Germany) showed experimental videos for the first time. Afterward, many artists began to use this media. This practice is linked to the possibility of receiving video training and of traveling abroad to Europe, where these technologies are more common and accessible. After this exposure Goddy Leye, Achille K, Guy Wouété, and Luc Forster Diop made short works in Cameroon. In Senegal—following the pioneering Fatou Kandé Senghor and Mansour Ciss Kanakassy—Art Fang Saar, Kan S (Kane Sy), Samba Fall, Douts, Piniang, and Solly Cissé have been using video in their work. Whereas African cinema has already been well studied, African Francophone video art is a recent practice that has not yet been analyzed to see what issues are at stake. For video art in Anglophone Africa, the scenery is quite different, of which Kimani Njogu has written an overview in *African Video Art Today*.[2] In Francophone texts scholars often debate the place of digital art in African art, but the practice of video art itself remains unexplored by researchers.[3]

Messages and/or Medias

In Europe and the United States, video as an experimental art form has been claiming since its inception, as Nam June Paik states, that "the medium is the medium." Up until now, European video art has been foremost concerned with a deconstruction and exploration of the medium itself.[4] But in our approach to video art in Africa, the political context and the content of art itself are seeing a strong resurgence as subjects with a marked urgency. Artists are facing situations where violence, lack of freedom, and poverty are so intensely present that it seems impossible not to engage them. African video art is a witness to quotidian social situations. Some video artists in Africa use the distance of humor, poetry, or experimental forms, and these choices of genre serve their feelings and opinions about the political situation through vital international exchanges among African countries and beyond. These feelings could lead to despair, since these situations obviously are extreme and difficult, but it is in this context that many powerful works emerge.

Describing a selection of African films in 2005, Jean-Pierre Chrétien explains that all the films show a great sadness that comes out of the contrast between a present time without a future and a past time that should have been better.[5] This pessimistic vision is often described as Afro-pessimism, a view engendered by poverty, crisis, injustice, and a failure of policies in Africa to aid homegrown development. In this essay, I analyze select video works and the contexts in which they are situated in order to understand the feelings expressed by their authors and how these viewpoints contribute to a contemporary cultural milieu. In the geography of human affects is there only sadness, anger, and violence in Africa?[6] Is this continent the only place in which violence can be found?[7] Sadness will not be the only affect explored here. On the contrary, strength of affirmation, humor, freedom, and hope are created by art and often replace the usual litany of complaints of disinherited populations. A few years ago, Hassan Musa, an African artist, was painting Osama Bin Laden.[8] But today, Ndary Lo is painting Barack Obama. Hope against despair!

Goddy Leye, Achille K, Bonendale, and the Global Village

Cameroon is a country where contemporary artists, especially video artists, are exploring certain topics in a specific way. Goddy Leye is the starting point for showing how art can take on political color and make it possible to express what other disciplines, such as journalism or politics, cannot. Leye, Achille K, and other Cameroonian artists have been working together in an artists' residence called Art Bakery, created by Leye and located in Bonendale, a suburb of Cameroon's second city, Douala.[9] They constitute a group called Dreamers Rêveurs,

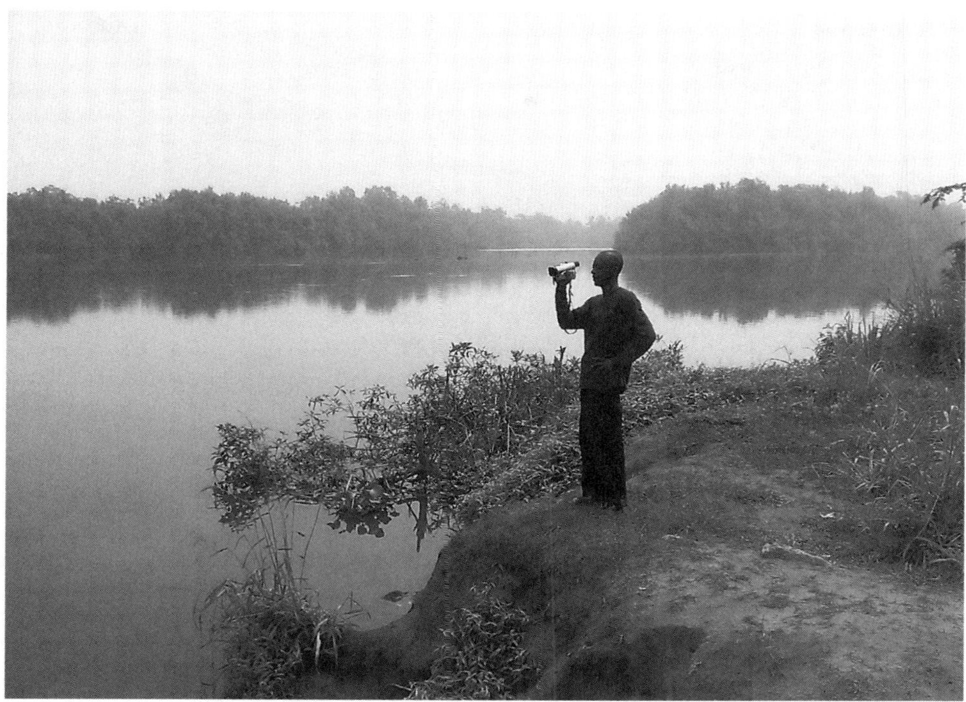

Goddy Leye. Photograph courtesy of the artist.

a reference to Dr. Martin Luther King Jr. Let us try to imagine what Bonendale is like: no Internet connections, unless one walks for miles toward the city, but nevertheless a wonderful laboratory for experimental video; no three-star hotels but old colonial houses with the bourgeois charm of the German, French, and English colonial expatriate communities that disappeared some time ago; no running water but many local traditions, such as Ngondo, a ritual of the Sawa, the people of the river. And in the center is the huge river the Wouri, like a strong, warm, and infinite love stream.

Leye, Achille K, Luc Forster Diop, and Guy Wouété are children of the TV age. These artists have a common aim: to fight the desperation, the poverty, and the melancholy that is this common gift of the country to its youth—the same youth whose summary of the situation is, "No future!" Leye and his friends aim their actions at children and young people. In Bonendale there is a library, an artists' residence where people can learn how to shoot and edit digital video, and daily living resources that help the village inhabitants with everyday life's struggles. Bonendale is a place where artists, writers, and museum curators meet, a site that is out of time and beyond the reach of the World Wide Web but at the center of a new modernity that has emerged since the end of colonialism and a tragic period of repression in Cameroon. Goddy Leye and other artists have created this oasis of peace and art where people come to visit from the four corners of the world.

We Are the World

Leye named his video *We Are the World* after the famous hit song by USA for Africa, recorded in 1985 while famine was decimating Ethiopia. He showed it at a private party in Bonendale in 2005.[10] In this humorous work he demonstrates the link between being hungry and being angry. The phrase "we are the world" also means that one can find the entire world in a small village of Africa—*le tout dans la partie et la partie dans le tout* (the whole in the element and the element in the whole). In the video we can see Leye himself lying on the ground and either singing "We Are the World" or eating bananas—not both at the same time but one after the other, turning his head first to the right and then to the left. The memory of a beggar in the street singing this song and eating fruit in the coldness of a northern city gave Leye the seed idea for this work. Everybody knows that poverty often means eating every day is not so easy, especially in Africa and in Cameroon, where poverty consumes a large part of the population. Cholera, yellow fever, HIV/AIDS, and many other epidemics in Douala and in other places in Cameroon kill hundreds of people a day. Leye says that it is necessary to have enough to eat to be able to speak. He is, as an artist, like the voice of those who cannot eat, go to school, or have access to modernity. He asks, How can man be free when he cannot eat? What is freedom? Let us dream about this world. Are universal human rights equal for everyone? Is comfort in everyday life equal for everyone? Some of these questions cannot even be written, because the nightmare of lack begins the moment the questions are asked. So Leye uses humor, with a mise-en-scène of himself eating bananas. Nevertheless, the title of the video has a specific resonance in Bonendale, as the world is Bonendale. The village receives people from all around the world via its website. Bonendale can be reached from everywhere, as the Art Bakery and the residence situate the village in a specific place and space in the international art world.[11]

The Voice of the Moon

Leye's *The Voice of the Moon* uses the televised images of man's first walk on the moon in which the U.S. astronauts plant a flag on the moon.[12] These famous images belong to global visual culture. Leye appropriates them and imagines that the American flag slowly disappears and is replaced by that of the United Chiefdom of Africa, a concept and a flag of his creation. The idea of the place of Africa in the world and in the conquest of space is made ironically apparent. The hierarchies of the world are changed via humor. To change the hierarchies of domination, of hegemony, is the legitimate wish of man: "Aucun argument n'a jamais convaincu une population placée en situation d'infériorité de rester à la place des vaincus."[13]

In his video *Postcard* a young girl carries a pot on her head in the traditional way as she guides the viewer down the streets of a small village where Leye used to spend his holidays, the village of his father. But Leye explains that today people of the village look at him both as a stranger and as someone from the family. The artist becomes more and more distant from the traditional rural society at the same rhythm and speed with which he becomes more and more of an international artist. Despite the geographical distance, the symbolic distance between the rural village and Bonendale perhaps is more important than the one between Bonendale and new modernity. For Leye, Bonendale remains the central place the world can be appropriated from and the place where he can work for his people. Between local and global, the video art of Leye explains that Africa is not on the margins of the world but can become the center of consciousness, just like Bonendale can become the destination of the contemporary art world. The power differentials between the fringe and the center of contemporary society—thanks to video art, the Internet, websites, and the wishes of a few people—can be reversed. This fact meets the vision outlined by historian Joseph Ki-Zebo:

> We should not define ourselves too much in relation to others nor conceive marginalization as a function of the center. The center is first in ourselves. Who are we? Where do we want to go? Since our independence, haven't we answered these questions? Starting from these questions, we have to establish a strike force able to gain its place in international exchanges.[14]

Achille K in the installation *Précarité* shows the streets of Cameroon, where traffic is insane, so obviously overcrowded and overwhelming.[15] Everything is over, but one thing is not, the dream of a future city. Now, the conditions for freedom of expression in the arts and media are rare, however, and many artists continue to make paintings that are not linked to the social reality. Ironically, it is often easier for foreigners to speak about this situation, who can then return home and sleep quietly without dreaming and without nightmares.

Leye and Achille K often travel to Europe and to other countries in Africa. They are a voice for the people of Cameroon, and they give back—thanks to the exposure their art receives—a kind of consolation and witness, a special taste of freedom. Video is a fast and facile media that can be easily sent, broadcast on the Web, passed from hand to hand, and distributed to large or small groups. Their art and its message are well known inside and outside the country. They

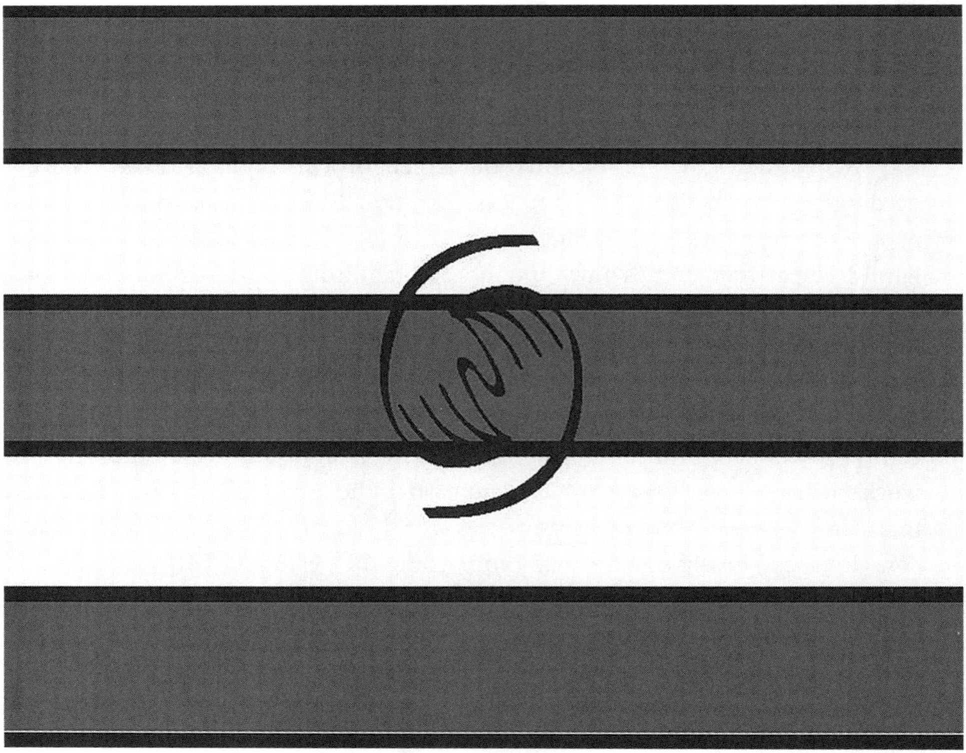

Goddy Leye, flag for *United Chiefdom of Africa.* Photograph courtesy of the artist.

benefit from a kind of freedom thanks to their status as international artists. Is African video only a militant and political activity? Of course not, but having the access to make video is already the result of a political fight. The Cameroonian institutions for the arts do not help artists enough or at all, and people look for subsidies from abroad. Leye could have received training at the Rijks Academy in Amsterdam—and he shows his work in many international exhibitions—but he has decided that for him his priority and the center are Bonendale, where he always returns.

Guy Wouété: The Strength of Crying

From Edvard Munch to Guy Wouété, nothing has been lost from the power of a scream. His work *Volcano* (2008) shows us a static shot of a prone young body. But this body is a volcano body, and the mouth is a crater from which lava spews. In Roberto Rossellini's *Stromboli, terra di dio* (1950), the volcano is controlling the life of the inhabitants of the island, their rhythms, and their madness. The face of the actress Ingrid Bergman is inscribed in the frame of the film like a spark of fire disturbing the loneliness of the world. In Wouété's work the volcano is becoming a man because to speak means to spit and, perhaps, die in the process. Many dark pages of Cameroonian history have been neither written nor spoken; there are too many dead, and there is too much horror. That is the meaning of *Volcano*. It is like a mountain that would speak when people cannot, their faces mute, their voices dumb in the face of horror—to speak but to stay alive, to take risks without falling down, the precise point where silence and words, surviving and death, can meet and combine, no more, no less. The score is written, but the musicians are no longer playing. Today, old Europe is colonized by its old colonies; now, suburbs are slowly and gradually gnawing from the inner earth and in its core. We can speak about human rights, but what are they and for whom? Which world tomorrow and which citizens today? The volcano is now silent. The volcano man speaks no longer. The poison has worked, Gall Moon, late silence—lies where once was truth, now disappeared with the volcano man in his last convulsive jolt of lava. In the first part of the video, which is a long, static shot, nothing happens, but in the second part, lava comes out of the man's mouth; the body is finally slowly consumed by fire. In the last shot one can see only fire.

Cameroon's dark years, years of blood and torture, of violent repression, are over, but many remnants still exist: insufficient technological equipment, disorganized art schools, lags in economic developments, limited freedom of expression, self-censorship. All the ingredients for a latent explosive situation are in place. For the time being, however, all is quiet. The strength of pacifism and collective conciliation are at work, and new solidarities, linkages, and intercultural dialogues give a hopeful counterpoint to African postmodern disenchantment.

We can appreciate *Volcano* for its aesthetic dimension, but Sami Tchak, a contemporary African writer and sociologist who describes poverty, child prostitution, and murders in Colombia in his novel *Le paradis des chiots,* asks the question, If poverty becomes a spectacle, an aesthetic regard, do the languages of art and literature have any chance of contributing to the evolution of the world?

Patrice Nganang's introductory chapter to *Cameroun: La culture sacrifiée* describes the dark situation of culture and of free expression in Cameroon:

> The Cameroonian imagination is written in the deepest conflicts of the country. These conflicts are even deeper than the actual, tangible misery resounding through the words of the people of this culture. It is important to consider as prolegomena of interpretation (of art in Cameroon) the facts that in this country, since the period of German colonization, the legitimacy and even the legacy of political power have always been contested, that power has always been usurped, and that, most important, the political conflicts that have resulted from this situation have always been treated with violence and exclusion.[16]

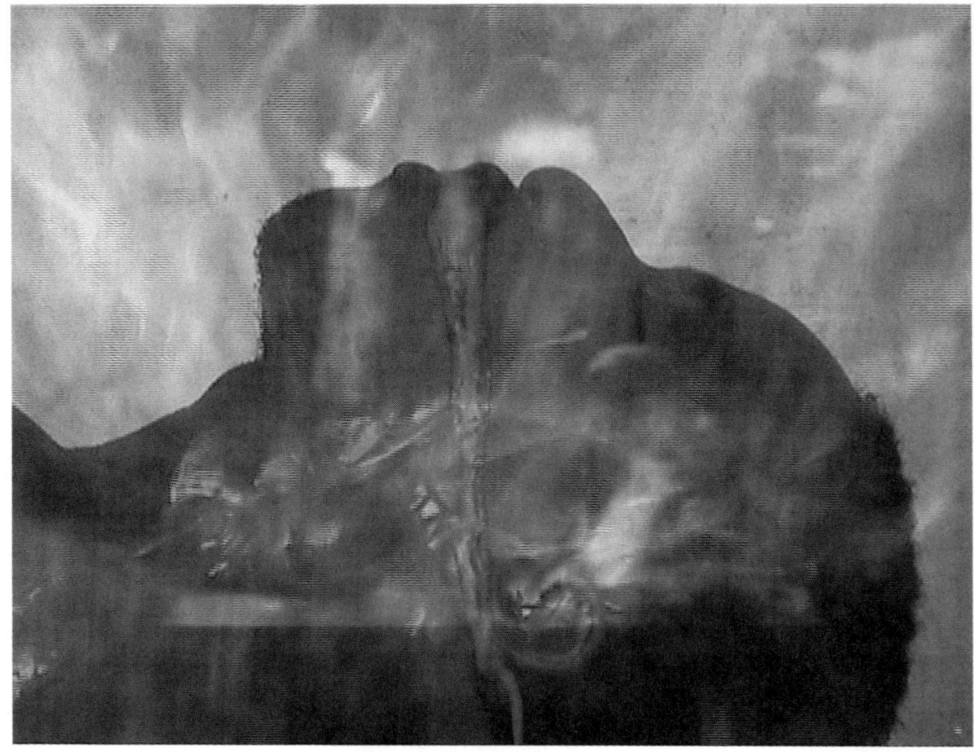

Guy Wouété, *Volcano,* 2008. Photograph courtesy of the artist.

Therefore, we can understand the particular energy to which Wouété's work testifies. It is not the energy of despair but shout energy, scream energy. Other pieces by Guy Wouété, such as *Codes noirs,* evoke contradictions between black codes and human rights and show the Ouidah beaches in Benin from which boats of black slaves originally left Africa. He denounces global capitalism and its impact on poverty in Africa, a poverty that author Manuel Castells describes as a consequence of the new order of the information world.[17] But *Volcano* can metaphorically explain in an expressive and powerful way the feelings of black people silenced in their own countries, where freedom of art and speech is not always possible.

Fatou Kandé Senghor: The Dialectic of Tradition and Modernity

Fatou Kandé Senghor is a multimedia artist who created the production studio Waru Studio in Senegal. She worked with Wim Wenders and teaches film and photography to young artists and students. Fatou Kandé Senghor travels all over Africa as a TV and radio reporter, and she is one of her country's most famous artists. Her compassion and concern compelled her to do work about child soldiers in Africa. She has filmed many of them in different countries during her travels and can tell the stories of children enrolled in war, not school, losing humanity and setting off-balance the psychic structure of a whole people. She examines a permanent African situation: war. Postcolonial interethnic or economic wars are going on in many places on the continent. How does one show it? What does one show? And where and for which audience? Fatou Kandé Senghor is sometimes called to speak in her own country, but she has no specific political status. She uses different mediums (radio, TV, and the Web) to distribute her work. Today, Senegal is a liberal democracy and a Muslim society. Animism, Islam, and occidental influences intermingle. One can often see in the suburbs, on t-shirts and on walls, paintings of Osama Bin Laden, whose discourse, for some African people, is considered the only answer to an unequal world shared by the World Trade Organization and the World Bank. Street children have no shoes while embassies use so much electricity for cocktail parties that the night sky often looks like a fairy tale. The city of Dakar combines these two worlds as best as it is able as ever-growing poverty and street children, the *talibés,* tenuously coexist with mosques and high-rise business centers.

African modernity in Senegal is a Muslim modernity, similar to Middle Eastern cities like Istanbul or Cairo, where behind the chador, young, educated women dream of modernity and freedom. Fatou Kandé Senghor has created artwork about the chador, which was somewhat recently adopted in Senegal. Young girls wear it as a political message, whereas their mothers wear the traditional Senegalese hair coverings. The connection between African and Muslim identity is very complex in Senegal, and Fatou Kandé Senghor embodies different identities, including African animism. Her artwork shows the multiplicity of African identities in Senegal. She directed *Diola Tigi* (2008), about an ancestral ritual, the *bukut,* that takes place every thirty or forty years in the south of Senegal in Diola country to preserve the memory of traditions in a world where standardization is always an easier option. This standardization can be seen in many young girls' adoption of Western clothes and hairstyles. Clothes are just a part of identity, and Fatou Kandé Senghor stresses the dominant occidental feminine beauty stereotypes in Africa. Muslim clothes remain in the minority, and to be thin and dressed in torn trousers is becoming fashionable. The question remains, what is beauty? As Aminata Traoré explains:

> Our historical, cultural, and touristic heritage is a rich one. There is no such thing as two Djenne or two Tambouctou. They are ours, but they are for humanity, as well. They are testimony to our intangible yet long-lasting connections with the world. The same could be said of Gorea Island in the context of Senegal, and it could be remarked, then, that

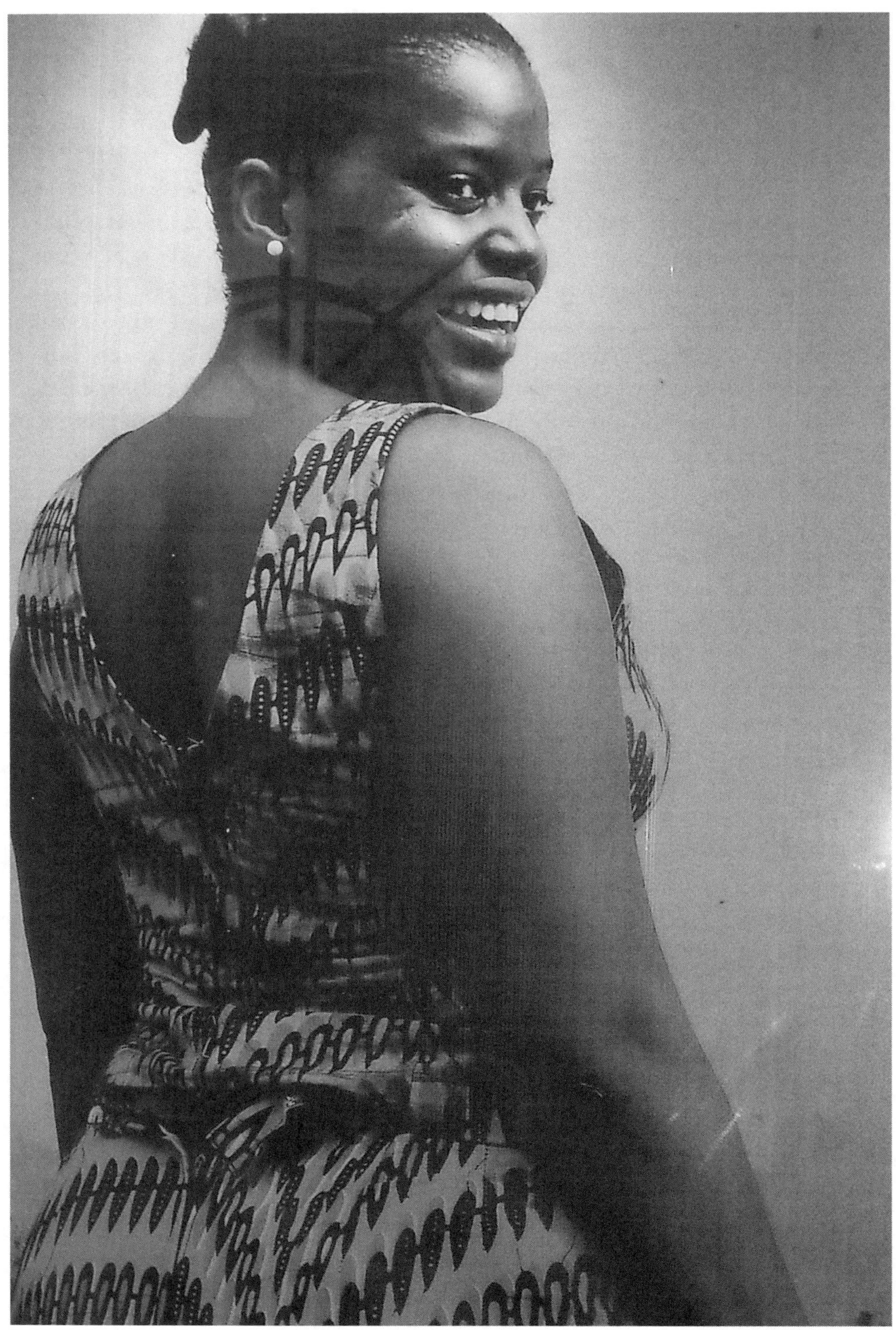

Fatou Kandé Senghor, *Pas touche,* 2008. Photograph courtesy of the artist.

black people's contributions to world capital circulate today on a planetary scale while we cannot dismiss our part of it.[18]

Art Fang Saar and Mansour Ciss Kanakassy use video in a traditional way: they don't use metaphors. They make films that are critically grounded in reality. Art Fang Saar gives a satirical point of view of ONG in *La boutique aux ONG* (2005). It was presented as a video installation for the exhibition *Refflexif, Dakar*. In *Les cent papiers* (2005), Mansour Ciss Kanakassy explains the difficulties that illegal migrants meet when entering and staying in European countries and the nostalgia they use to cope. Many other young Senegalese artists, including Samba Fall, Piniang, and Douts, make video animation. Its purpose is to explore the artistic possibilities of the medium and to translate an aesthetic language from painting to animation. Samba Fall, who lives in Oslo, gives an interesting critic of consumption society via his installation *Consommania* (2008).

Michèle Magema: Abduction of Black History

In her works Michèle Magema recalls a history erased from daily life and from official history. Her *Au bord de la Loire* is inspired by the French city of Nantes, a big harbor with international traffic that in prior centuries participated in the slave trade. French provincial cities are full of massive monuments to the glory of the republic but are silent about some less glorious events of the past. Looking for traces of this aspect of history during her stay in Nantes, Magema found merely a sober commemoration: flowers were thrown in the river exactly in front of the place where black slaves were kept before leaving for America. Some warehouses are still there as silent tracks of a forgotten legacy. Magema creates a personal, quiet ritual: she films herself slowly and silently walking along the Loire, one time dressed in white and another in black. As she walks we can hear a deep voice coming from nowhere that simply says, "Thank you." The light is soft, the walk cool, the atmosphere calm—but for the whisper of water and the beauty of the evening light enfolding the artist's slow journey. Her subtle art consists of evoking violence without performing violence. Smooth and quiet, the image nevertheless expresses the memory of violence, a paradox of art and metamorphosis: beauty against the loss of memory.

A second video, *Fleur de Lys* (2008), also deals with the history of slavery with purified pictures. Two hands are digging in the ground to excavate chains, and then the hands lay on the disturbed earth a beautiful bouquet of lilies in their sumptuous whiteness. For those who know the history of African slavery in France, this flower is a symbol of devastating cruelty. It is the brand that slaves who tried to escape had seared into their flesh as punishment and by which they could be forever identified as property. The fleur-de-lys was, as a symbol of royal

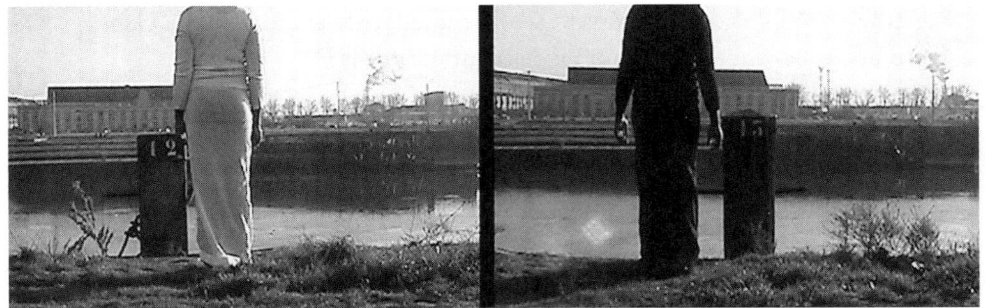

Michèle Magema, *Au bord de la Loire,* 2006. Photograph courtesy of the artist.

power, the symbol of their subjugation. The brand was inscribed onto the legs of runaway slaves, who then could no longer run or even walk. The cruel stamp of the king erased any possibility of freedom. In history's maelstrom some events appear or disappear because they glorify people and places or they don't. The memory of African history in France finds a similar destiny as the memory of European Jewish history. Parts of these two histories have remained hidden even until the present day. Exclusion, xenophobia, slavery, and anti-Semitism historically cloud the face of France. Sometimes, horror and shame bring elements of this past silently to light, as if back to memory. But Magema neither judges nor makes a political plea. She only makes it possible to see the forgotten story of her ancestors through video art, through beautiful images that offer these erased people a witness, a moving image ancestor altar of memory. By utilizing beauty, Magema can speak about and show what has been taboo in France up until the present day. *Fleur de Lys* is part of a collective exhibition that took place in Jerusalem in 2009–10. This work about profound memory acquired a particular meaning in this city among those who fought for the recognition of their own history. *La parole n'a de sens que dans la mesure du silence qu'elle couvre, qu'elle rompt ou alors qu'elle instaure* (Words have meaning only in the context of the silence they cover, they interrupt, or they create).

Conclusion: David versus Goliath

The position of African artists' video work in the contemporary art world is one of resistance that step by step is fighting the last fight, one of marginal cultures working against the giant Moloch: the globalized market of media cultural industries. African artists are not marginalized in this battle of David versus Goliath. From one international biennial to another, they show more and more work. Their videos are filled with strong, poetic, and political accents that work in relationship to larger global contexts. Some even become nomadic artists,

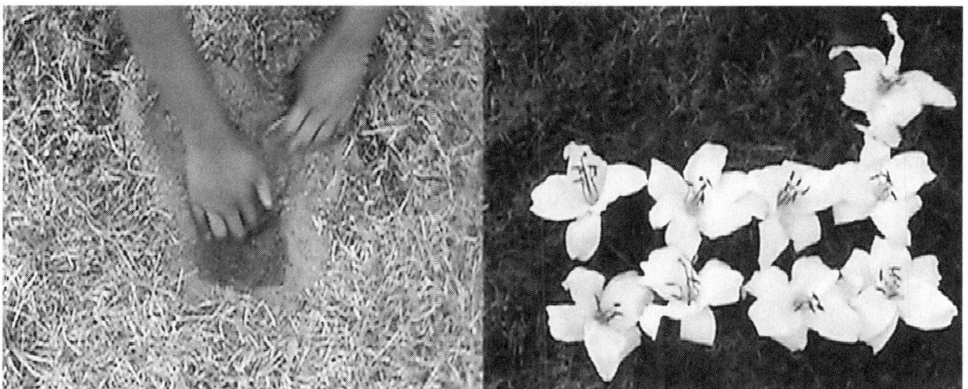

Michèle Magema, *Fleur de lys,* 2007. Photograph courtesy of the artist.

travelers across continents. Thus, for example, our art resistance fighters walked from Douala to Dakar for the 2006 biennial under the banner of the collective project Exit Tour. This was a pacifist and nonviolent fight through action in which walking, patience, peaceful action, and humor replaced terrorism, criminality, and the thirst for blood. But how long can art replace violence? Between the technological access available to a blockbuster like *Avatar* and that available to these artists, any comparison would be displaced and meaningless for at least two reasons: (1) the criteria for the aesthetic quality of an artistic message is not dependent on technical means, and (2) the gap is gigantic.

While the products of the United States flood the screens of the world with elaborate special effects, Luc Forster Diop, a Cameroonian artist, is using the Bafia dance to present his self-portrait in an intimate one-minute movie starting from a simple but powerful frontal static shot. The incredible simplicity of Diop's means of production strongly and appropriately translates the artist's conceptual voice. A black aperture that reminds us of a camera aperture encircles his figure. His dancing body calls another body to meet him, a woman's body now between his thighs. For the poor and the rich, the joy of sex is accessible and supplies outbursts of joy and pleasure, the core of life. The artist is dancing the Bafia and is slowly slipping into a vertigo created by rhythm. The only music is the sound of his shoes on the ground. This particular sound reminds us of communication codes in song and rhythm exchanged amid African workers in the mines of South Africa or in American cotton fields, and the movement of the dancer echoes the first black tap dancers in the United States. The traditional Bafia dance, or snake dance, is usually executed in Cameroon by a group of men, but Luc Forster Diop is dancing alone because man is alone, alone at birth and alone when dying. Between these two moments exists companionship—loves, friends, and the fusion of minds, memories, and bodies. But this basic loneliness is his first and last story. Diop represents this loneliness in many short works to remind the world of the comforting truth that when facing death, man is naked, man is alone, and all the injustices of the world, between north and south, east and west, the humble and the powerful, are abolished with the last breath—that is the universal truth.

The artists mentioned in this essay advocate a new hybrid race, the weaving of all races and all talents. The cross-cultural identity ground becomes the wellspring of the culture of the future. Contemporary artists such as Goddy Leye and Achille K explain that they no longer recognize boundaries, borders, ethnocentrist points of view, or community isolation. The art miracle is that such artists, whether they come from Africa or elsewhere, are the last of the Mohicans and moreover, through a hard-won solidarity, are the first because they remain human beings in spite of the growing inhumanity and violence surrounding them in today's world. Their new pacifist universalism, advocated from the heart of an Africa of the future, will hopefully become the *vade mecum* for all the marginalized, as well as the mainstream.[19]

NOTES

1. Myriam-Odile Blin, "L'insoutenable légèreté des arts numériques," *Réro international spécial Afrique,* no. 20 (2006): 15–18.

2. Kimani Njogu, *African Video Art Today* (Swaziland: African Books Collective, 2007), 45.

3. Amadou Gueye Ngom critiques them in the article "Les arts numériques," *Ethiopiques,* no. 80 (1er semestre 2008): 208.

4. In France artists such as Maurice Benayoun or Miguel Chevalier are currently in such a position.

5. Jean-Pierre Chrétien, "Regards africains au cinéma," *Esprit: Vues d'Afrique,* no. 317 (August–September 2005): 19.

6. Arjun Appadurai, *Fear of Small Numbers: An Essay on the Geography of Anger* (Durham, N.C.: Duke University Press, 2006), 36.

7. In the book *Au delà de "Blade Runner": Los Angeles et l'imagination du désastre* (Paris: Allia Petite Collection, 2006), Mike Davis explains how violence is expanding and mutating in Los Angeles. Yvonne Mignot-Lefebvre and Michel Lefebvre point out the same process in many parts of the world in *Les patrimoines du futur: Les sociétés aux prises avec la mondialisation* (Paris: Éditions L'Harmattan, 2000).

8. Hassan Musa is living between France and Soudan; see the painting *Great America Nude* (2002).

9. The name Art Bakery was given to the residence in reference to Andy Warhol's Art Factory.

10. An article about this party is in Marie Amilhon, "Video crêpes à Bonendale," *Ishango revue internationale des arts et des technologies,* no.1, http://www.africartec.com/uploads/revuepdf/1226248921.pdf.

11. See goddyleye.lecktronix.net.

12. Goddy Leye's *The Voice of the Moon* installation (Yaoundé, 2005) was first exhibited at Chiasma in Berlin.

13. "No argument has ever convinced a population placed in the situation of inferiority to stay in the place of the defeated." See Mignot-Lefebvre and Lefebvre, *Les patrimoines du futur,* 32.

14. "Il ne faut pas trop nous déterminer par rapport aux autres et concevoir la marginalisation en fonction d'un centre. Le centre est d'abord en nous-mêmes . . . qui sommes nous? Où voulons nous aller? Depuis que nous sommes indépendants, n'avons nous pas répondu à ces questions? . . . A partir de cette plate forme d'ensemble, il faudrait mettre sur pied une force de frappe qui puisse se tailler une place dans le rapport des forces mondiales." Joseph Ki-Zerbo, *A quand l'Afrique?,* in collaboration with René Holenstein (La Tour-d'Aigues, France: Éditions de l'Aube, 2003), 24.

15. Achille K, or Achille Komguen Kamsu, created the magazine *Diartgonale* and made many art videos, including *Sentier ridé* (2004) and *Introspection* (2009), a video installation. Achille K also participated in the *World One Minutes* exhibition in Bejing in 2009 and is the recipient of many international prizes.

16. "L'imagination camerounaise est inscrite dans les conflits les plus profonds du pays . . . ces conflits sont même beaucoup plus profonds que la palpable misère matérielle qui résonne dans les propos de maintes personnes de culture. . . . Il est important de prendre comme prolégomènes de lecture . . . le fait que dans ce pays, depuis la période de la colonisation allemande, la légitimité et même la légalité du pouvoir politique auront toujours été contestées, bref, que le pouvoir aura toujours été regardé comme usurpé, et, beaucoup plus important, que les conflits politiques qui plusieurs fois en auront découlé auront toujours été traités dans la violence et l'exclusion." Patrice Nganang, "Le Cameroun qui se réinvente," in *Cameroun: La culture sacrifiée,* Africultures 60 (Paris: Éditions L'Harmattan, 2004), 42. Patrice Nganang is a writer and university teacher in the United States and comes from Cameroon. He is the recipient of many important literary prizes.

17. Manuel Castells, *End of Millennium* (Oxford: Blackwell Publishers, 1998), 61.

18. "Nous sommes riches de notre patrimoine historique culturel et touristique. Il n'y a pas deux Djenne ni deux Tambouctou. Ils sont nôtres mais aussi pour l'humanité. Ils témoignent de l'intangibilité et de l'ancienneté des liens qui nous unissent au monde. On pourrait en dire de même de l'Île de Gorée quand il s'agit du Sénégal et rappeler alors le rôle du peuple noir dans la formation du capital mondial qui circule aujourd'hui à l'échelle de la planète sans que nous puissions disposer du nôtre." Aminata D. Traoré, *L'étau: L'Afrique dans un monde sans frontières* (Arles, France: Actes Sud, 1999), 23.

19. Tjade Eone explains that thanks to new media, a new culture of peace can appear and flourish. See Michel Tjade Eone, "De la culture de la haine à l'émergence d'une nouvelle conscience planétaire par les médias," *Présence africaine: Revue culturelle du monde noir,* no. 167–68 (2003): 12–15.

28 Images Ungoverned

A DIALOGUE

Faisal Devji and David Joselit

I have long felt frustrated with how politics is implicitly or explicitly defined among too many art historians and art critics as the illustration of social crises and contradictions. In writing my book *Feedback: Television Against Democracy* (2007), I sought something different—a political economy of a particular image substrate—video, encompassing commercial television, media activism, and works of art. In trying to sort out analogous questions in contemporary video art, I began to read the work of Faisal Devji on the modernity of the current jihad, whose evocation of a global network is accomplished in great part through the production and distribution of videotapes meant to be broadcast on world media (including Arab media networks like Al-Jazeera) and the Internet. I found in Devji's writing something I wanted: a theory of the *ethics* of images. Devji explicitly argues that it is in its visualization that the local actions of jihad, disseminated worldwide through media, become influential events.

Martyrdom, he argues, is founded in a shared witnessing on both the part of the martyr's partisans and coreligionists *and* her or his victims and opponents. He writes:

> Because martyrdom in Islam is thus connected to seeing in a much
> more general as well as much more specific sense than in Christianity, it
> is capable of cohabiting in productive ways with the global practice of
> news reportage. . . . Only in mass media does the collective witnessing
> that defines martyrdom achieve its full effect, as the various attempts by
> would-be martyrs to film their deaths or at least to leave behind video-
> taped testaments, illustrates so clearly.[1]

The crux of Devji's argument is that under conditions of globalization, where visible and invisible vectors of financial and political influence have made the nation-state absolutely porous and increasingly incoherent, the platform for action has shifted from specific political demands to general ethical demonstrations that are, it hardly needs to be said, rooted in questions of life and death—in the limits of the individual human organism. He declares, "The jihad is a global movement in this sense, a perverse call to ethics in an arena where old-fashioned politics can no longer operate—because it can no longer control."[2] The crucial insight here, which is indeed as relevant to the actions of jihad as to other forms of contemporary protest, including most recently the Occupy Wall Street movement, and which holds true regardless of one's position on the morality of jihad, is that as fewer and fewer citizens of the world exercise political power or even choice in the policies that determine their everyday lives the playing field for dissent shifts from politics to ethics and the ground of such actions is delineated by life itself—the living organism. As Devji suggests, a spectacular visual event that may be widely disseminated is an action appropriate to transnational networks that are neither restricted nor controlled by a single state, despite the real impediments and regulations information confronts as it crosses national borders. It is in this regard that Devji convincingly diagnoses the current jihad as an artifact of modernity, since it is absolutely dependent upon the spectacular infrastructure of contemporary media. For this reason I have sought to engage him in a series of reflections on the nature of images and, more specifically, of video as forms of political speech.

DAVID JOSELIT. In both of your books, *Landscapes of the Jihad: Militancy, Morality, Modernity* (Cornell University Press, 2005) and *The Terrorist in Search of Humanity: Militant Islam and Global Politics* (Columbia University Press, 2008), you identify terrorist actions as an effort to address a truly global public that reaches far beyond any particular state. Indeed, the global public sphere to which acts of terrorism have redress is founded in a transnational (largely commercial) media that is predominantly situated in the West, leading you to argue for both the modernity of al-Qaeda and its imbrication in the very machinery of its enemy. You have discussed such media events as being ethical rather than political in part because they induce and require witnessing on the part of both sides. Can you discuss the role you feel images have in this new (as yet unformed) model of politics?

FAISAL DEVJI. Even when they give rise to contestation and debate, images are often held to supplement a politics dependent on words. But in a global arena, images, like acts, have been freed from being mere instruments of the political word. Indeed, no instrument can be controlled in this arena, which transforms them all into gestures and gambles that are more speculative than tactical. This is especially true for terrorists, who are not constituted to take much advantage even of their own spectacles once performed. And of this they appear to be fully conscious, which is what makes them into the pioneers of media practice. The intention that results in the production of militant videotape, for example, destroys itself once these images have been broadcast, so that there is no longer anything "behind" them but a history. After all, video attributed to that invisible outfit called al-Qaeda cannot distinguish an audience of friends from one of enemies, both being served by the same images, thus rendering impossible any differentiation between messages for us and them, unless one is willing to read secret signals into such narratives as though in a detective story.

DAVID JOSELIT. I find your diagnosis of a "floating" or rootless narrative very suggestive with regard to how narrative has been treated in contemporary video art practice—which might be thought of as a compendium of models that concentrate or crystallize forms of distribution (what might be called *dispositifs*) in the broader media. I think, for example, of the repetitive film loop used by artists ranging from Stan Douglas to Isaac Julian in which scenes are configured as units of media DNA that through repetition show small variations but ultimately circle back endlessly in a diagram of global image circulation (i.e., small variation, constant repetition). There has also been a strong interest in what seems almost unedited documentary footage among artists, as though what one needs to do is to capture a slice of life and send it on the road of international exhibitions and biennials. These, too, seem to be ethical challenges thrown out to an imagined world—the art world. But how does one create a dialogue with a detached media fragment?

FAISAL DEVJI. Well, for instance, given al-Qaeda's invisibility, there can be no dialogue with it outside the realm of media images, which therefore constitute the core of terrorism's practice rather than its supplement. And in fact, we can go further and say that neither global militancy nor the Muslim community to which it refers exists outside media, both having become subjects that in the absence of representative institutions at a planetary level can recognize themselves only through its images. But if there is nothing "behind" the image to make an instrument of it, then these media products may partake of aesthetics but not politics, or at least not yet. This is in essence the problem such globally disseminated images pose our traditional politics—that they are not yet amenable to its dictates.

DAVID JOSELIT. Again, I see an analogy with art practice. You seem to be posing a fascinating conundrum. How can images converse with other images? I have thought a lot about this with regard to the work of the artist Catherine Sullivan, whose video scores in works such as *The*

Chittendens (2005) create a series of human images (stereotypes) that interact with one another only by adjacency or superimposition. In other words, rational conversation cannot occur between images, but rather, they can create accumulations, aggregations, almost like media tumors. In other words, instead of speech there is what we might call fluidity and viscosity of circulation. How can one speed up or slow down images?

But to return to jihad, it is one thing to say, as you do, that global militancy exists entirely within the media—but you take it even further to encompass the Muslim community. What happens to religious doctrine under such conditions (after all, this form of Islam is often termed *fundamentalist,* which would situate it as a strict response to the Koran)? Do you feel there are new forms of image- or media-based religiosity that have affected local expressions of faith?

FAISAL DEVJI. The rise of mediatized religion is an important phenomenon, lifting television clerics, for example, out of their local and institutional contexts to make global celebrities of them. And while it is often not the most serious of such scholars in the eyes of their peers who attain fame, important divines like Khomeini, who was in fact Islam's first global icon, have also managed to occupy this arena from time to time. Despite their traditional backgrounds and learning, however, these men end up destroying the institutional integrity of the scholarly class itself, as happened in postrevolutionary Iran, where the most radical and indeed apocalyptic religious language is now deployed by a layman president who has no claim to religious authority. In this sense, even Khomeini's global reputation was derived not from his clerical authority so much as from its absence. For we should not forget that as a Shiite the ayatollah was a nonrepresentative and indeed minority figure in the Muslim world as a whole and that rather than becoming a media icon despite this sectarian background, he might well have done so because of it. I would like to suggest, in other words, that the popularity of such figures is more often premised on their nonrepresentative character than otherwise, as indeed is probably the case with most media personalities. We should not mistake popularity for representation in any of its political or aesthetic senses. In this global arena religion tends to be divorced from local histories to become "universal" precisely because it is seen as lacking "culture," a word that for many believers has come to stand for historical particularity alone. In other words, the increasingly generic practices of those named Islamists or fundamentalists can become universal only once they are dead or detached from any living tradition to be derived from texts alone. As a rejection of particularity and so interest, it is not clear if this attitude serves merely as a criticism of representative politics or looks toward another political future. In either case, it is entirely congruent with the fact that global icons like Osama bin Laden were, like this politics that either has ended or is yet to come, unreachable, unknowable, and indeed invisible, even as he is forever on display. And the fact that Bin Laden's body was made to disappear immediately after his killing inadvertently played into this logic of militant practice, even as it illustrated the American desire to deny him the status of a martyr whose grave could become the site of veneration. But also important for the United States might have been the desire to vanish evidence in a way that has become the norm in the war on terror, for which the principle of habeas corpus has been rendered a dead letter. Does this ubiquitous invisibility represent that of politics itself in the global arena?

DAVID JOSELIT. I am very interested in the question of whether and how images might be governed. In your discussion of the notorious Danish caricature published in *Jyllands-posten,* you state, "The materiality of the images themselves had nothing to do with the protests they inspired, only the apparent injury done to Muslim feeling by the report of their circulation, which made the experience of hurt one of hearing rather than sight."[3] I would argue, however, that certain images lend themselves to such explosive media mobility and that one of the great political questions right now is how to govern such unruly images when they erupt and, conversely, how to make one's own image as a politician or dissident equally virulent. Do you agree with this? Do we need to develop a political science of the image?

FAISAL DEVJI. Disputes over objects like books, films, or pictures are routinely governed by invoking freedom of expression as a principle of civic life, whether to point out its contradictions or define its limits. The public sphere and its freedoms, we are told, provide the space where all such contestation is neutralized by words exchanged between the parties concerned. If today words cannot contain such disputes, this has little to do with unruly passions on one side and misguided tolerance on the other but, instead, with the fact that such images no longer belong to the public sphere and do not partake of its freedoms. This is true not only because the great controversies over some Danish cartoons, papal remarks, or a novel called *The Satanic Verses* that kicked off this history of protest happened to occupy a global arena in which such freedoms had no institutional presence. Also important is the fact that unlike controversial texts and images in the past, these possessed no content, for it was not anything about their materiality that offended the Muslims, who for the most part did not see them. The visibility of these objects was constituted simply by the rumor of their circulation, possessing in this respect the same effect that was achieved in the West by the equally unseen videotapes of beheadings that used to be released by militants in Iraq.

DAVID JOSELIT. I can't help but remark on your fascinating model of a visibility function that has nothing to do with literally seeing an image for oneself. It is interesting that such strategies of rumor, reputation, and second- or thirdhand documentation are also widespread strategies among conceptual and postconceptual artists from the 1960s to the present. Obviously, this relationship isn't causal, but it says something about the status and sovereignty of images today.

FAISAL DEVJI. Of course, it is true that certain images appear to be more conducive to popular mobilization than others. Among many in the Muslim world, for example, such controversies have to do with relatively small and even obscure depictions said to be insulting to the Prophet or with news of some fairly limited desecrations of the Koran. Among many in the West, however, it is the spectacular and widely broadcast destruction of infrastructure that seems to generate the most offense, whatever the death count involved, which is often quite limited. For these are insults to one's outward power and prestige, compared with the offenses against one's inner convictions that agitate so many Muslims. Whatever their ostensible subject, nevertheless, such images are in fact "empty," the unintended vehicles for self-representation globally. This is indicated by the apparently random elevation of some images and not others to the status of global causes, something that illustrates not the success or failure of those who would arouse controversy so much as the image's lack of instrumentality. Why should the Dutch politician Geert Wilders's film on the evils of Islam cause no real ruckus despite his best efforts to publicize it but a phrase from an obscure speech made by the Pope create an avalanche? Because whatever political use is made of an image or statement once it has become controversial, the unpredictability of its career suggests that the problem posed by such entities has to do precisely with their distance from politics, which has little institutional purchase in the global arena where they circulate. To govern or produce an entity of this kind, then, is an aesthetic task more than anything else, though one whose affect can only be achieved in an arena that politics has not yet occupied. The politics of global protest is, in other words, one bereft of institutional foundations and so highly unpredictable. It is if anything a politics in search of itself and for the moment ungovernable.

DAVID JOSELIT. It is significant, as you say, that the creation of what you call an empty image requires an affirmative effort—an aesthetic act. It is actually quite difficult to produce such screen images that allow for projection on a broad scale, and it's hard to anticipate what sort of images will produce this effect. However, do you think that on the one hand al-Qaeda is attempting to craft such images in their communications? And on the other, have you noted more localized forms of popular culture that may in fact function differently to consolidate local communities of Muslim militants or even simply Muslim faithful? To be more specific, does local news matter?

FAISAL DEVJI. The militant image needn't be expressly oppositional to be what it is. Indeed, I would hazard a guess that most such images are reversible, like American or British portrayals of terrorism, which are valued by militants, though they are meant to turn people against them. Thus, it seems clear that even the most antiterrorist and in fact anti-Muslim websites that put up al-Qaeda communiqués to criticize them receive many of their hits from those who support holy war. Sometimes, this reversion is very subtle. For instance, I remember images of Bin Laden and texts by him that were culled from official U.S. sources and posted on the Internet in the aftermath of 9/11. Only a sound track of joyous Arabic music made it clear that these were "terrorist" paraphernalia. Such incidents give the lie to the hackneyed narratives of media manipulation and indoctrination that abound on either side of the militant divide. Of course, images of this kind are not necessarily global in scope, and there are frequent attempts to create and sustain local repertoires—for instance, among the Indian Mujahideen, who in communiqués released during their short-lived terror campaign of 2008 insisted on emphasizing their domestic character. But this insistence is telling and suggests that such outfits find it difficult not to be drawn by either their friends or their enemies into a planetary arena. The great media problem of our time, then, is not how to achieve global notoriety, for however difficult that might be, more difficult still is the effort to evade the desire if not the possibility of such celebrity. In political terms this means forsaking the universal for the particular without becoming irrelevant.

DAVID JOSELIT. Do images have more power in a global political sphere than they did in a politics rooted in individual states?

FAISAL DEVJI. Images in global circulation are more powerful than their local or national counterparts not by reason of a more expansive terrain but because they lack a political–institutional base and are so ungovernable. Their power derives from the fact that they invoke a politics either dead or yet to come—thus, the curiously confessional nature of the images of prisoner abuse that emerged from Abu Ghraib or the videotapes of beheadings and martyrdom that were also produced by informal groups for global distribution in the early years of the U.S.-led war in Iraq. Rather than being seen instrumentally, either as public or as clandestine statements of responsibility, such images might be described as risk-taking displays of vulnerability that exit the realm of politics by inviting the destruction of their makers for no particular reason. The Abu Ghraib images, as well as those martyrdom videotapes that are made before the attacks they depict (and as we know from recent arrests in Europe and the United States, even before such attacks are planned), can easily be cited as examples of this process. What is interesting about such displays is that they all gesture toward an instrumental notion of politics in a situation where it seems to have vanished—thus, the American soldiers at Abu Ghraib who not only attributed their abusive acts to vague claims of authorization given them by superiors but also explained their photographing of such acts as an equally vague effort to record the abuses that the U.S. army permitted its personnel. Similarly, the forced confessions of prisoners in beheading and other militant videotapes can be read as attempts to personify some political agency that otherwise remains abstract. In either case, the instrumentality on display is not one's own but that of the enemy, which is alone capable of rationalizing one's actions. If torture, for instance, were a properly political procedure, it would function like other disciplinary forms and become invisible, not because it wasn't known but because it could only be seen as an open secret. This is indeed the traditional form of torture practiced by states, known but unacknowledged and therefore all the more fearful. Even more political would be the attempt to regularize torture as a sad necessity, as certain American and Canadian intellectuals have done, thus transforming it into a form of punishment, like jailing or execution, that is invisible precisely because it is acknowledged. How different in this respect are the images from Abu Ghraib and militant videotapes, the sheer visibility of whose excessive and "irrational" cruelty seems directed away from institutional politics? And so again we come back to images in the global arena as indications of political absence as much as of a desire for a new global politics.

DAVID JOSELIT. Do you think that in addition to creating a global image of vulnerability, the production of images for ostensibly private consumption (e.g., the soldiers involved in the Abu Ghraib photos) or for distribution (e.g., al-Qaeda) have anything to do with a personal assertion of power or sovereignty through the *capture* of a photograph or video? I agree completely that the images you mention are speculations on a global community yet to come, but they may simultaneously function as a form of self-assertion not unlike those of social networks such as Facebook. And this combination of ungovernable speculation and attempts at asserting self-sovereignty each simultaneously circulate around image technologies.

FAISAL DEVJI. Self-assertion and even sovereignty are certainly claimed through media practices, though very often in negative form. For instance, those militants who fall under the rubric of al-Qaeda are well known to claim as their own only acts of sacrifice or martyrdom, everything else being deemed merely a response to infidel provocation. In this sense, such practices of sovereignty are able to manifest themselves only posthumously—after suicide attacks and in martyrdom videotapes—or in gestures of risk and vulnerability like that which made Osama bin Laden renounce a life of wealth and comfort for a most dangerous existence. The negative form taken by self-assertion is, I think, a commentary not on the eclipse of individual agency and politics in a global arena so much as on its generalization, something that has ended up emptying out both categories of any content. This was evident to thinkers like Carl Schmitt in the wake of the First World War when it became clear that politics could no longer be confined to some juridical or institutional category like the state but had been set free in notions like class struggle as a global civil war.[4] Schmitt famously tried to ground politics in the friend–enemy distinction, which served both as its most minimal and excessive definition, since death and killing was always implicit in it. Might we say that in resorting to death and killing for their own part, militants today are also attempting to reinstate the political relation in a world from which it seems to have vanished?

NOTES

1. Faisal Devji, *Landscapes of the Jihad: Militancy, Morality, Modernity* (Ithaca, N.Y.: Cornell University Press, 2005), 95.

2. Ibid., 156.

3. Faisal Devji, *The Terrorist in Search of Humanity: Militant Islam and Global Politics* (New York: Columbia University Press, 2008), 178.

4. Carl Schmitt, *The Concept of the Political,* trans. George Schwab (Chicago: University of Chicago Press, 1996).

Contributors

Kathleen Ash-Milby is associate curator of contemporary art at the Smithsonian National Museum of the American Indian. She is the editor of *HIDE: Skin as Material and Metaphor* (2010) and *Off the Map: Landscape in the Native Imagination* (2007) and the coeditor of *Most Serene Republics: Edgar Heap of Birds* (2007).

Myriam-Odile Blin is a freelance art critic and curator, as well as a researcher and teacher at Rouen University, France.

Nancy Buchanan was a founding member of F Space, Grandview I & II Galleries at the Los Angeles Woman's Building, and Double X, a feminist art collective. Her own work includes video, installation, performance, and mixed media. She was faculty at the School of Film / Video at the California Institute of the Arts from 1988 to 2012.

Derek A. Burrill is associate professor of media and cultural studies at the University of California–Riverside. He is the author of *Die Tryin': Videogames, Masculinity, Culture.*

Sean Cubitt is professor of film and TV at Goldsmiths, University of London, professorial fellow at the University of Melbourne, and honorary professor at the University of Dundee. His publications include *EcoMedia, The Cinema Effect, Simulation and Social Theory, Digital Aesthetics, Videography: Video Media as Art and Culture,* and *Timeshift: On Video Culture.*

Faisal Devji is university reader in history and fellow of St. Antony's College, Oxford. He is the author of *Landscapes of the Jihad: Militancy, Morality, Modernity* and *The Terrorist in Search of Humanity· Militant Islam and Global Politics.*

Jennifer Doyle is professor of English at the University of California–Riverside. She is the author of *Sex Objects: Art and the Dialectics of Desire* and coeditor of *Pop Out: Queer Warhol.*

Jennifer Friedlander is the Edgar E. and Elizabeth S. Pankey Professor of Media Studies and associate professor of media studies at Pomona College. She is the author of *Feminine Look: Spectatorship, Sexuation, Subversion* (2008) and *Moving Images: Where the Police, the Press, and the Art Image Meet* (1998).

Kathy High is associate professor of video and new media at Rensselaer Polytechnic Institute. She was awarded a Guggenheim Fellowship in 2010. Her works have been shown in festivals, galleries, and museums nationally and abroad, including the Guggenheim Museum, MoMA, and MASS MoCA.

Lucas Hilderbrand is associate professor of film and media studies at the University of California–Irvine and the author of *Inherent Vice: Bootleg Histories of Videotape and Copyright*.

Nguyen Tan Hoang is assistant professor of English and film studies at Bryn Mawr College. He is also an experimental video maker whose work has screened at the Musée National d'Art Moderne at the Centre Georges Pompidou and the Museum of Modern Art in New York.

Kathy Rae Huffman is a freelance curator based in Manchester and Berlin. She has held curatorial posts at the Long Beach Museum of Art, the ICA Boston, and Cornerhouse, Manchester. Huffman cofounded, with Diana McCarty and Valie Djordjevic, FACES, the international online community for women media artists.

Amelia Jones is professor and Grierson Chair in Visual Culture at McGill University. Her recent publications include essays on performance art histories, feminist art, and curating. In 2012 she published *Seeing Differently: A History and Theory of Identification and the Visual Arts* and *Perform, Repeat, Record: Live Art in History*, coedited with Adrian Heathfield.

David Joselit is Carnegie Professor of History of Art at Yale University. He is the author of *Infinite Regress: Marcel Duchamp 1910–1941*, *American Art since 1945*, *Feedback: Television against Democracy*, and *After Art*.

Alexandra Juhasz is professor of media studies at Pitzer College. She has directed several documentary features, including *SCALE: Measuring Might in the Media Age*, *Video Remains*, *Dear Gabe*, and *Women of Vision*, and produced the narrative films *The Owls* and *The Watermelon Woman*. Her publications include *Learning from YouTube*, *AIDS TV*, *Women of Vision*, and *F Is for Phony* (with Jesse Lerner) (Minnesota, 2006). She blogs about YouTube, video art, and Internet culture at www .aljean.wordpress.com.

Jessica Lawless is an educator, writer, and artist living in Santa Fe, New Mexico, where she teaches gender and media studies at the Santa Fe Community College. Her work has been widely exhibited in film festivals, art galleries, and community spaces, alike, and she is a regular contributor to *Make/Shift Magazine: Feminisms in Motion.*

Hea Jeong Lee (aka Ian) is a Seoul-based art critic, curator, and director of the media arts webzine EYEBALL.

Jesse Lerner is professor of media studies at Pitzer College and a documentary media artist. He is the author of *F Is for Phony* (with Alex Juhasz) (Minnesota, 2006) and *The Shock of Modernity.* His short films *Natives* (with Scott Sterling), *T.S.H.,* and *Magnavoz* and feature-length documentaries *Frontierland/Fronterilandia* (with Rubén Ortiz-Torres), *Ruins,* and *The American Egypt* have won numerous prizes at film festivals in the United States, Latin America, and Japan.

Akira Mizuta Lippit is professor of cinematic arts, comparative literature, and East Asian languages and cultures at the University of Southern California. He is the author of *Ex-Cinema: From a Theory of Experimental Film and Video* (2012), *Atomic Light (Shadow Optics)* (Minnesota, 2005), and *Electric Animal: Toward a Rhetoric of Wildlife* (Minnesota, 2000).

Ming-Yuen S. Ma is a Los Angeles–based media artist and professor in media studies at Pitzer College. His experimental videos and installations have been exhibited internationally. He is the coeditor of Moving Image Review in *GLQ: A Journal of Lesbian and Gay Studies* and codirector of the Resolution 3: Global Video Praxis project.

Lionel Manga is a cultural activist and writes a daily column for *Le messager.* He is the author of *L'ivresse du papillon.*

Laurence A. Rickels is professor of art and theory at the Academy of Fine Arts, Karlsruhe, Germany, and Sigmund Freud Professor of Media and Philosophy at the European Graduate School. His most recent books are *The Devil Notebooks* (Minnesota, 2008), *Ulrike Ottinger: The Autobiography of Art Cinema* (Minnesota, 2008), and *I Think I Am: Philip K. Dick* (Minnesota, 2010).

Kenneth Rogers is assistant professor of digital media in the Department of Film at York University. He is the author of *The Attention Complex: Media Technology and Biopolitics* and president of the board of Los Angeles–based media arts organization Freewaves.

Michael Rush is director of the Eli and Edythe Broad Art Museum at Michigan State University, an award-winning curator, and a widely published author and critic. He was director of the Rose Art Museum at Brandeis University from 2005 to 2009. Among his numerous books are *Video Art*, *New Media in Art*, *New Media in Late 20th-Century Art*, *Marjetica Potrč: Urgent Architecture*, and *Hans Hofmann: Circa 1950*.

Freya Schiwy is associate professor of media and cultural studies at the University of California–Riverside. She is the author of *Indianizing Film: Decolonization, the Andes, and the Question of Technology* and the coeditor of *Digital Media, Cultural Production, and Speculative Capitalism* and of *Indisciplinar las ciencias sociales*.

Beverly R. Singer is associate professor of anthropology and Native American studies at the University of New Mexico and director of the Institute for American Indian Research. She is the author of *Wiping the War Paint off the Lens: Native American Film and Video* (Minnesota, 2001).

Yvonne Spielmann is research professor and chair of new media at the University of the West of Scotland. Her books include *Video: The Reflexive Medium* (2008) and *Hybrid Culture* (2012).

Erika Suderburg is a filmmaker and writer. She is the coeditor with Michael Renov of *Resolutions: Contemporary Video Practices* (Minnesota, 1995) and the editor of *Space Site Intervention: Situating Installation Art* (Minnesota, 2000). She is currently on the faculty of the University of California–Riverside.

Catherine Taft is project specialist and curatorial associate in the Department of Architecture and Contemporary Art at the Getty Research Institute, where she helped organize the 2008 exhibition *California Video* and the 2011 initiative Pacific Standard Time. She is a regular contributor to *Artforum*, *Art Review*, *Modern Painters*, and exhibition catalogs in the United States and abroad.

Holly Willis is assistant professor of cinematic arts and director of academic programs for the Institute for Multimedia Literacy at the University of Southern California. She is the author of *New Digital Cinema: Reinventing the Moving Image*.

Index

Page numbers in italics refer to figures.